25/-
ps/rc.

POPULATION

POLICIES AND MOVEMENTS IN EUROPE

POPULATION
POLICIES AND MOVEMENTS IN EUROPE

BY

D. V. GLASS

25/-

OXFORD
AT THE CLARENDON PRESS
1940

OXFORD UNIVERSITY PRESS
AMEN HOUSE, E.C. 4
London Edinburgh Glasgow New York
Toronto Melbourne Capetown Bombay
Calcutta Madras
HUMPHREY MILFORD
PUBLISHER TO THE UNIVERSITY

PRINTED IN GREAT BRITAIN

PREFACE

SOMETIME in the future, we shall, I hope, look about us and take stock of the various social and economic problems which need solution. Among such problems it is probable that the population trend will be one of the more important. We may be faced with a population considerably reduced by war casualties. We shall almost certainly be faced with one which is at least on the verge of decline. Some writers have already made up their minds that a declining population is undesirable; others believe that, at least for some years, a decline may bring, or may be used to bring, considerable advantages. But many writers agree that to adjust ourselves to population changes of the kind most likely to occur, or to adjust the population to our aims, will need much forethought and planning. In this book I do not deal with the question of planning. Instead I have tried, by summarizing the work I have done in recent years as Research Secretary of the Population Investigation Committee, to give a general background which may be helpful when we come to consider which way we ought to go, and what we should do to go there.

To many readers the book will appear over-long. Yet it can scarcely do more than describe the broad structure of the subject, for it attempts to cover, in five hundred pages, problems which would need many large volumes for satisfactory discussion. Because of this inevitable superficiality I have included a fairly wide documentation, so that readers who are interested enough to go further into the problems may at least find their introductory bibliographies here. The text of the book is not very technical. But I felt it would be rather unfair to make use of statistical methods without including somewhere in the book an outline of the methods actually applied. Consequently, the Appendix is devoted to a résumé of some of the most important techniques of measuring reproductive trends, and I hope that this résumé may be of help to readers as an introduction to demographic analysis.

Many experts have generously helped me with information

and friendly criticism. I owe a special debt to Mr. A. M. Carr-Saunders and Dr. R. R. Kuczynski for their unfailing interest and advice. I should like to thank Monsieur F. Boverat of the Alliance Nationale; Professor N. E. Himes of Colgate University; Mr. E. von Hofsten of the Stockholm Statistical Office; Dr. A. J. Lotka, Assistant Statistician of the Metropolitan Life Insurance Company; Mr. A. Skaug of the Norwegian Central Statistical Office; Mr. R. Sterner of the Swedish Population Commission; and Monsieur R. Storms of the Belgian Caisse Nationale de Compensation. I should also like to thank Miss D. Frost and Miss P. Symmons for their assistance in the statistical work. The indexes were compiled by Miss Symmons.

D. V. G.

LONDON,

March 1940

CONTENTS

I. POPULATION MOVEMENTS IN ENGLAND AND WALES 1

II. INTRODUCTION TO STATE INTERVENTION . 86

III. FRANCE AND BELGIUM. I. FAMILY ALLOWANCES 99

IV. FRANCE AND BELGIUM. II. POPULATION POLICIES AND THEIR RESULTS . . . 145

V. THE ITALIAN STRUGGLE FOR POPULATION . 219

VI. GERMAN POLICY AND THE BIRTH-RATE . 269

VII. SCANDINAVIA AND THE POPULATION QUESTION 314

VIII. NATURE AND CONSEQUENCES OF POPULATION TRENDS 344

APPENDIX 374

NOTES 416

SELECTED LIST OF ARTICLES AND BOOKS containing Estimates of Future Populations or Discussions of such Estimates 468

INDEX OF SUBJECTS 473

INDEX OF AUTHORS, PERSONS, AND ORGANIZATIONS 481

INTRODUCTORY NOTE

THIS study has not, in general, attempted to discuss changes in legislation occurring since the middle of 1939. For the various Acts and decrees passed since the beginning of the present war it is advisable to consult the journals which specialize in publishing current legislation. It is, however, worth noting here that, with a few modifications, the French *Code de la Famille* is actually being applied, most sections coming into force by 1 April 1940. As yet no date has been set for introducing the marriage loans for the rural population. But the other forms of economic assistance to the family come into effect without any fundamental change.

To assist the reader in translating foreign currencies into sterling equivalents, the following data are given, taken from the *Statistical Year-Book of the League of Nations, 1938/9*, p. 12.

Country	*Unit of currency*	*Value in £ sterling (average for 1938)*
France	franc	0·0059
Belgium	belga (5 francs)	0·035
Italy	lira	0·011
Germany	mark	0·08
Norway	krone	0·05
Sweden	krona	0·05
Denmark	krone	0·045

I

POPULATION MOVEMENTS IN ENGLAND AND WALES

BIRTHS, deaths, and migration make up the balance-sheet of a country's population movements, and this balance-sheet may be analysed in a number of ways. The simplest way is to look at the extent to which the total population is growing from year to year, or between the successive censuses which, in this country, have been taken every ten years since 1801. The earliest censuses were defective, and it is not possible to make accurate allowances for the deficiencies. If we suspected that the census of 1831 was incomplete, but regarded that of 1841 as reasonably complete, we could estimate with fair reliability the actual population in 1831 provided that two kinds of data were available. First, we should need accurate statistics of births and deaths for the intervening period. Secondly, we should need no less accurate statistics of the numbers of emigrants from and immigrants into this country in the ten-year span. But such statistics are not available. Compulsory national registration and co-ordination of births and deaths did not begin in this country until 1837, and the registration of births was not fully effective until 1875.[1] Thus even after 1837 there were deficiencies in birth registration and probably also—though on a smaller scale—in death registration. For migration we have never at any period had fully adequate direct information, particularly as migration between England and Scotland (including migration from Ireland through Scotland) cannot be measured directly. In sum, therefore, we have for the earlier periods deficient birth, death, and migration statistics with which to correct deficient census enumerations. This does not mean that the earlier censuses are useless. On the contrary, they are mines—to some extent still unexploited—of highly valuable material for the economic historian and the sociologist, and the total populations which they record are sufficiently accurate to

[1] See Note I*a*, p. 416.

provide a good indication of the numbers of people living in England and Wales at various periods. But they are not satisfactory for the analysis of short period changes, and for this reason they are omitted from the present study.

If we begin with 1851, from which date the censuses may be accepted as reasonably accurate, and the registration statistics as not very far from complete, we may obtain a table on the following lines:

TABLE 1. *England and Wales—Population Growth**

Date of census	*Total population*	*Intercensal increase*	*Percentage intercensal increase*	*Excess of births over deaths (1,000's)*	*Outward balance of migration (1,000's)*	*Percentage natural increase*	*Percentage outward migration*
1851 March 30/31	17,927,609	..	..	..	..	..	..
1861 April 7/8	20,066,224	2,138,615	11·93	2,267	128	12·65	0·71
1871 April 2/3	22,712,266	2,646,042	13·19	2,721	75	13·56	0·37
1881 April 3/4	25,974,439	3,262,173	14·36	3,426	164	15·08	0·72
1891 April 5/6	29,002,525	3,028,086	11·66	3,629	601	13·97	2·31
1901 March 31–April 1	32,527,843	3,525,318	12·16	3,594	69	12·39	0·24
1911 April 2/3	36,070,492	3,542,649	10·89	4,044	501	12·43	1·54
1921 June 19/20	37,886,699	1,816,207	5·04	2,436	620	6·75	1·72
1931 April 26/27	39,952,377	2,065,678	5·45	2,238	172	5·91	0·45

* The total populations are from the *Census of England and Wales, 1931, General Tables*, London, 1935, p. 149. The other data are derived from the 1931 Census, *Preliminary Report*, London, 1931, pp. xi & 1, except for the excess of births over deaths for the periods 1851–61 and 1861–71, which were calculated directly from the relevant *Statistical Reviews* of the Registrar General, allowance being made for the census dates. The percentage data for outward migration having been calculated directly, they are not always exactly equal to the percentage natural increase minus the percentage total increase. War deaths occurring outside England and Wales have been imputed to natural decrease instead of, as in the 1931 *Preliminary Report*, to migration.

It will be seen that the relative intercensal increase reached its maximum in 1871–81 and has been declining fairly consistently since that time. But this total increase is made up of a number of factors, and in order to show the separate contributions of natural increase—the excess of births over deaths—and migration columns giving information on these points are included in the table. These columns show that the rate of growth of the population by natural increase has been even greater than is shown by net intercensal increase. That is, in every intercensal period included in the table we have lost a certain number of persons by outward migration. We do not know exactly how many, for there may well have been Scottish migrants and Irish migrants coming through Scotland, who entered England in, say, 1901, but left the country for some other destination before the 1911 census was taken. Since we have only the 1901 census figures, giving the population before these migrants came in, and the 1911 figures, giving the population after they had left, we have no record of any intercensal movements which may have taken place. Similarly, we do not know how many immigrants have entered and how many emigrants have left during a period, but only the net balance, inward or outward, resulting from these opposed movements. There are some separate statistics for these two different movements,[1] but they are not complete. However, for the purpose of analysing general trends the data given in Table 1 are sufficient. Since 1930 the net movement of migration seems to have changed. Each year the Registrar-General makes an allowance for net migration in estimating the mid-year population,[2] and if we calculate this allowance we find that in 1931–2 there was a net immigration of about 71,000 persons, and that the approximate inward balance was 43,000, 16,000, 50,000, 88,000, and 88,000 for the separate years from 1932–3 to 1936–7. Part of this change has been due, in the most recent years, to the immigration of political and religious refugees. These, however, form a very small total—there were probably not more than about 11,000 of such persons settled in England and Wales at the

[1] See Carrothers, W. A., *Emigration from the British Isles*, London, 1929, pp. 305–14; Johnson, S. C., *A History of Emigration from the United Kingdom to North America, 1763–1912*, London, 1913, pp. 344–55.

[2] The allowance is not published but may be derived by subtracting natural increase in, say, the period from mid-1932 to mid-1933, from the total population growth in the same period. Quarterly births and deaths used for this purpose are given in the *Registrar-General's Statistical Review of England and Wales*. Incidentally, it should be noted that in this country, as in a number of other countries, the published statistics relate to births and deaths registered though not necessarily having occurred in a specified period. This introduces an error which is probably small but which may not be constant.

end of 1938[1]—and the greater part of the change has been due to the onset of depression in other parts of the world. In many countries, since the last War, immigration has been fairly rigidly controlled by some form of quota system,[2] and this has certainly cut down the outward flow from Britain. But emigrants tend to go to countries which show signs of relative prosperity,[3] and the depression which spread over the world after 1929 not only made emigration less attractive, but also caused many people who had emigrated to return to their original countries. At the same time it has caused some diversion of the remaining flow of migrants. Thus, whereas the United States used to be the main destination of Irish emigrants, in recent years they appear to have chosen England instead. A statement made by Mr. Malcolm MacDonald, Secretary of State for Dominion Affairs and Colonies, in 1937, suggested that about 11,000 persons migrated from the Irish Free State to the United Kingdom in 1934, about 14,000 in 1935, and about 24,000 in 1936.[4] But except in this most recent period migration has not shown a net inward balance,[5] and we must return to natural increase to discuss the causes of population growth since 1851.

Between 1851 and 1931 the population of England and

[1] Sir S. Hoare, Home Secretary, said in Parliament, 'The Prime Minister said only a week or two ago that 11,000 refugees had been settled in this country, and I added the information that, as a result of that, as far as I could gather, about 15,000 British workers had been employed who would not otherwise have been employed' (*Parliamentary Debates*, H. of C., 1 Dec. 1938, Vol. 342, col. 579). Speaking in the House of Commons on 26 June 1939, Sir Samuel Hoare said that the number of German, Austrian, and Czech refugees in the United Kingdom on 20 May 1939 was 34,909—15,548 men, 12,760 women, and 6,601 children under 18. Presumably many of these are here only temporarily, but in any case the increase is considerable (*Parliamentary Debates*, H. of C., 26 June 1939, vol. 349, col. 42).

[2] For a general account of restrictions on migration see Carr-Saunders, A. M., *World Population*, Oxford, 1936, ch. xiv.

[3] For a study of the causes of emigration from one specific country, see Skaug, A., *Memorandum on Fluctuations in Migration from Norway since 1900*, ch. v (International Studies Conference, Paris, 1937—mimeographed).

[4] *Parliamentary Debates*, H. of C., 3 Dec. 1937, vol. 329, cols. 2411–13. A more recent statement (30 June 1939) made in the House of Commons by Mr. Cross, in reply to a question by Mr. Amery, said that the annual net immigration into Great Britain from Eire was estimated at between 18,000 and 19,000 in the period 1934–8 inclusive (*Parliamentary Debates*, H. of C., 30 June 1939, vol. 349, col. 799).

[5] See Note I*b*, p. 416.

Wales increased by more than 120 per cent., and Table 1 has shown that this growth was due to natural increase. If we split up the increase into its components, births, and deaths, we can construct rates for the annual averages of the three years centred on each census, as in Table 2.

TABLE 2. *Birth, Death, and Fertility Rates, England and Wales*[1]

Period	*No. of live births per 1,000 of the total population*		*No. of deaths per 1,000 of the total population*		*No. of live births per 1,000 women aged 15–49 years*		*No. of legitimate live births per 1,000 married women aged 15–44 years*	
	Rate	*Index 1870–2 =100*	*Rate*	*Index 1870–2 =100*	*Rate*	*Index 1870–2 =100*	*Rate*	*Index 1870–2 =100*
1850–2	34·1	96	21·8	98	131·7	95	284·2	97
1860–2	34·8	98	21·5	96	134·2	96	281·7	96
1870–2	35·5	100	22·3	100	139·2	100	292·5	100
1880–2	34·1	96	19·7	88	134·2	96	286·0	98
1890–2	30·8	87	19·7	88	117·9	85	263·8	90
1900–2	28·7	81	17·2	77	104·4	75	235·5	81
1910–12	24·5	69	13·8	62	88·5	64	197·4	67
1920–2	22·8	64	12·4	56	80·5	58	179·1	61
1930–2	15·8	45	11·9	53	56·4	41	122·7	42

It will be seen that the birth-rate per thousand of the total population has fallen since 1870–2 and did not rise a great deal before that date. Even the small rise shown by the rates between 1850–2 and 1870–2 is dubious, because, as has been mentioned, birth registration was not really compulsory until 1875. It is therefore not unlikely that the birth-rate for the three periods up to and including 1870–2 was actually constant.[2] Since the birth-rate fell after 1870–2, an important factor in maintaining a high rate of increase in

[1] See Note Ic, p. 416.

[2] William Farr, the distinguished vital statistician, gave two estimates of the deficiency of birth registration. In the first he believed that in 1841–50 the annual deficiency was 38,036; in 1851–60, 19,323; and in 1861–70, 13,614; or 65, 29, and 18 per 1,000 births occurring in the three decades (*Thirty-Fifth Annual Report*, for 1872, p. v). In the second he suggested a deficiency of 1,441,603 births between 1837 and 1876, or 5 per 100 of the births (*Thirty-Ninth Annual Report*, for 1876, p. v). For a criticism of these corrections see Kuczynski, R. R., *The Measurement of Population Growth*, London, 1935, pp. 12–13.

population in the subsequent period was the fall in the death-rate. But before we discuss the relative importance of the birth and death factors in any more detail, we must consider the meaning and validity of the various rates which are used to measure trends in these components. The rate most commonly used to measure birth trends is the crude birth-rate—the number of live births per thousand of the total population. But this rate is inappropriate for two reasons. First, it compares incomparables. That is, births occur only to a small section of the population—generally defined as women in the reproductive ages of 15 to 49 years—while the birth-rate is based on the total population. In extreme cases this may lead to quite ludicrous results. Thus in the State of Colorado, in 1860, women in the reproductive ages constituted only 3·2 per cent. of the total population, so that even if half of the potential mothers had actually borne children in 1860—a frequency higher than has ever been observed in the world—the crude birth-rate would still have been only 16 per thousand,[1] about the same as in England and Wales in 1930–2. Secondly, the potential child-bearing section of the population varies in size and age over periods of time. If we are comparing two successive years, it is unlikely that the change in the proportion of potential mothers in the total population will be great enough to invalidate the comparison. But over a long period of time the change may easily be considerable. In 1881, for example, women aged 15 to 49 years formed 25·38 per cent. of the total population of England and Wales, while in 1921 they formed 28·27 per cent. The crude birth-rate would thus need to be adjusted for these differences. Even within the reproductive age group there may be significant changes over a period of time. In 1891 in England and Wales women aged 15 to 19 years formed 19.59 per cent. of women aged 15 to 49 years, but only 15·41 per cent. in 1931, while women aged 45 to 49 years, forming 8·75 per cent. in 1851, constituted 12·22 per cent. in 1931. This change also means that some adjustment needs to be made to the birth-rates before they can be comparable over time. Similarly, the crude death-rates relate the annual total of deaths to a population which may be

[1] Kuczynski, R. R., *Fertility and Reproduction*, New York, 1932, p. 4.

changing very significantly in age. Our population to-day is a good deal older than it was sixty or seventy years ago, and if the chances of dying at any given age were identical in 1871 and 1931 the crude death-rate for 1931 would be considerably higher than that for 1871. This may be seen by taking the total male population at each date as 100,000, distributing it into age groups equivalent to the age grouping at the two dates, and applying the specific death-rates—in five- and ten-year age groups—of 1926–30 to the two populations. The 1931 age distribution would yield 13·4 per cent. more deaths than the age distribution in 1871. At the same time the present age distribution is still a relatively young one in relation to the current chances of dying at the various periods of life. In 1930–2 the crude death-rate was 11·9 per thousand of the total population. If this were an accurate indication of mortality in that period it would mean that out of 1,000 persons only 11·9 would die each year and that it would take about 84 years for the whole thousand to be 'killed off'. In other words, each person could expect to live about 84 years. But an accurate analysis of the mortality of 1930–2 shows that, according to the life table, each person could expect to live only 60·76 years, so it is evident that the relative youthfulness of the population depresses the crude death-rate. With an expectation of life of 60·76 years, this would be the period required to 'kill off' a thousand persons, and each year 16·46 of the thousand would die. This latter figure would thus represent the life table death-rate according to the mortality of 1930–2.

The difficulties caused by changes in the age and sex composition of a population can to some extent be allowed for in computing birth- and death-rates. But the allowances are not really satisfactory from the point of view of accuracy, nor are the resultant rates in any way explicit. By the last term is meant simply that if we used what are known as 'standardized' birth- and death-rates we should be no nearer answering the basic question—what is the future trend of the population likely to be? In fact, of course, this question cannot be answered. We do not know the trend that fertility —the frequency with which women bear children—or mortality will follow in the future. Physiological discoveries may eliminate cancer and tuberculosis, postpone the onset of senility, and greatly increase the number of years people may expect to live. People may return to an older form of family pattern and raise larger families or they may do so on new terms, or they may, in the face of the continuous threat of world war, refuse to bear any children at all. War itself may destroy large sections of the populations of the belligerent countries and thus affect not only the immediate but also the future size of the populations. It is nevertheless permissible to ask—what will be the future trend of the population supposing that fertility and mortality remain at their present level and that neither war nor migration take place? This question cannot be answered by using crude or 'standardized' birth- and death-rates. Nor can it be answered by computing annual rates of growth. We might find that in the twenty years ending with 1931 the annual rate of growth was about 0·5 per cent. compound interest, and that at this rate the population would double in about 139 and quadruple in about 278 years. But this would simply be an extrapolation of the crude rates of growth of the past without any relation to the basic components of migration, fertility and mortality, and the distortions caused by the current age and sex composition of the population. To answer the question we must use a different approach; we must attempt to estimate the number of children each woman bears in her lifetime.

If we were to divide the population of potentially fertile women—those aged 15 to 49 years—into single years of age, and if we had the ages of the women who actually bore children in a given year, we could calculate fertility rates for each year of age. We might find that 1,000 women aged 15 years had given birth to 2 children, that 1,000 aged 16 years had borne 7, that 1,000 aged 17 years had borne 19, and so forth throughout the reproductive period. The number of children per 1,000 women would probably tend to be highest between 25 and 30 years of age, and would then tail off until at the age of 49 years the rate would be very small. If we added these separate fertility rates, the resultant total fertility rate would give us the total number of children who would be born to 1,000 girls who having been born alive, passed through the child-bearing ages without any of them dying, assuming that at each year of age they exhibited the fertility observed in the particular year for which the rates were calculated. We might find that, in these circumstances, they would bear about 1,904 children, of which the majority would be boys. In 1930–2, 512 out of every 1,000 live births were boys and 488 were girls. Assuming that this sex ratio at birth applies to our case, we can say that in the specified circumstances 1,000 girls passing through the child-bearing period without any loss by death would replace themselves by 929 girls, or that each girl would replace herself by 0·929 girl children in the next generation. This latter figure is called the 'gross reproduction rate'. First used by R. R. Kuczynski,[1] it is the best index of pure fertility, unaffected by mortality, and it will be employed a great deal in subsequent discussions.

But there is a further question—how many of the original group of girls will pass through the child-bearing period? According to the mortality in this country in 1930–2, out of 1,000 newly born girls only 904 would reach their fifteenth and only 790 would reach their fiftieth birthday. If, then, we begin with 1,000 newly born girls, 96 will have died before reaching the reproductive period of life, and another 114 before the reproductive period is completed. These girls will therefore replace themselves with rather less than 929 girls in the next generation. In fact they will bear only 805 girls. That is, assuming the specified fertility and mortality, each newly born girl will replace herself by only 0·805 of a girl in the next generation. This figure is called the 'net reproduction rate'.[2] When it is exactly 1·0, it means that each newly-born girl will just replace herself, assuming that the given conditions of fertility and mortality remain unchanged, and that ultimately the population will become stationary. A net reproduction rate of less than 1·0 means that the population will ultimately fall, while a rate above one means that the population will grow, and the rapidity of decline or growth is shown by the extent to which the rate

[1] See Kuczynski, R. R., *Fertility and Reproduction*, p. 7; same author, *The Balance of Births and Deaths*, vol. i, New York, 1928, pp. 21–3.

[2] It was apparently first used by R. Boeckh in 1884. Boeckh did not, however, use the gross reproduction rate, though it is the first stage in calculating the net reproduction rate. See *Fertility and Reproduction*, op. cit., p. 15.

differs from 1·0. A rate of 1·5 means that the population will ultimately grow by 50 per cent. every generation, while one of 0·75 means an eventual fall of 25 per cent. every generation.

In the net reproduction rate we have, therefore, a simple and adequate measure of the prospects of growth of a given population, assuming that there is no migration and that fertility and mortality remain unchanged. This rate will also be used a great deal in subsequent discussion and it is advisable to mention at this stage a number of points which should be borne in mind when interpreting it. First, the rate of growth indicated refers to the percentage increase or decrease which will occur in a 'generation'. There is no really simple explanation of this term, which in its exact meaning is a statistical concept. But as a first approximation we may define it as the mean age of mothers (at the birth of their children) in the life table population used for calculating the net reproduction rate. If we take this figure, which in most Western countries is now not very far from 30 years, we can calculate an approximate version of the annual rate of growth from the net reproduction rate by using the compound interest formulae $A = P(1+r)^n$ or $A = P.e^{rn}$. In the second formula A is the net reproduction rate, P is unity, e is the base of Naperian logarithms, n is 30 years, and r, the annual rate of growth, will be $(1/30) . \log_e A$. The resultant rate, known as 'the true rate of natural increase,' or 'the true rate of annual growth,' is due, in its conception and analysis, to A. J. Lotka. It is used in later sections of the present book and for certain calculations it is essential. But for general comparisons of reproductive trends the net reproduction rate is adequate and will be more frequently used.[1]

The second point is that the generation rate of growth indicated by the net reproduction rate, or the annual rate indicated by the true rate of natural increase, is not necessarily taking place at the point of time for which these rates have been calculated. The rates will apply only when the population has attained what is known as a 'stable age com-

[1] For a more detailed discussion of the meaning, significance, and calculation of the true rate of natural increase and its derivatives, see Appendix of the present study, section 5.

position'. For example, the population of England and Wales at the present time is the product of many factors—high fertility and mortality and emigration in the past and low fertility and mortality and immigration in the present. If there were no migration in the future, and mortality and fertility remained constantly at their present level, the age and sex composition of the population would change, and after a period of time would become fixed. That is, although numbers would continue to change, the percentage distribution of the population among the various age groups and between the two sexes would become stabilized. From that point on, the present net reproduction rate would indicate the actual rate of growth, but before that point the rate of increase or decrease would be quite different. Thus, if we have a net reproduction rate of 0·8 at the present time, it does not mean that our population, in 30 years' time, will be 20 per cent. smaller than at present. It may only be 5 per cent. smaller. The population would not begin to fall at the rate of 20 per cent. per generation until about 60 to 100 years from now, assuming that fertility and mortality remained unchanged, and that there were no migration in the future.

Thirdly, to say that a constant net reproduction rate of 1·0 would eventually mean a stationary population, does not necessarily mean that it will be stationary at the size obtaining in the year for which the rate was calculated. It has already been noted that our present population contains an abnormally large proportion of women in the fertile age groups—abnormal, that is, in relation to present mortality. If we were to have a stationary population containing the same number of women aged 15 to 49 years as were alive in 1935, the total population would be considerably larger than that of 1935. In 1935 there were 11·215 million women aged 15 to 49 years in England and Wales, constituting 27·59 per cent. of the total population. But in a stationary population based on 1935 mortality these women would form only 23·82 per cent., and a stationary population containing 11·215 million potential mothers would have a total of about 47·082 millions instead of the 40·645 millions of 1935. Similarly, if we constantly maintained, with 1935 mortality and the estimated age distribution of fertility of that year, a net reproduction rate of unity, we should arrive at a stationary population not of 40·645 but of about 44·857 millions. These different points are not criticisms of the net reproduction rate as a measuring rod, but qualifications of its precise meaning. They do not in any way invalidate its use as an index of replacement, but they should be remembered in interpreting the rate.[1]

To obtain a picture of replacement trends in England and Wales a number of rates have been computed and are given in Table 3. These rates have not been constructed in the normal way, for, until the application of the Population (Statistics) Act in July 1938, births in this country were not tabulated by the age of the mothers. There is, however, a method—discussed in some detail in the Appendix to the present book—which, by applying specific fertility rates obtained for other countries, yields estimated gross and net reproduction rates not very different from the results which would be obtained if all the necessary basic data were available. It has been found that in practice the margin of error is not more than 6 per cent., and that in most cases it is less than 3 per cent. This method has been used for compiling Table 3, and data for Scotland, obtained in the same manner, have been included for comparison.[2]

An examination of these rates[3] brings out a number of significant points. First, the rise in fertility—as shown by gross reproduction rates—in England and Wales between 1850–2 and 1870–2 was small, being about 7 per cent. Allowing for the margin of error in the estimated rates,[4] and remembering that registration was incomplete in the period but approaching completeness towards the end of it, it seems

[1] See Note I*d*, p. 417. [2] See Note I*e*, p. 417. [3] See Note I*i*, p. 418.

[4] The discussion in the Appendix, pp. 387–93, shows that the age composition of the female population is the vital factor influencing the margin of error. The ratio between the (numerically) largest and the smallest age group of potentially fertile women was higher in 1851 to 1871 than in 1931, and the margin of error was thus larger in the earlier period. A general discussion of trends in the period prior to 1871 is given in Marshall, T. H., 'The population problem during the industrial revolution', *Economic Journal* (*Economic History Series, No.* 4) January 1929, which contains, *inter alia*, a commentary on Griffith, G. T., *Population Problems of the Age of Malthus*, Cambridge, 1926, and Buer, M. C., *Health, Wealth and Population*, London, 1926.

TABLE 3. *Estimated Reproduction Rates, England and Wales and Scotland*

	England and Wales								Scotland	
		Gross reproduction rate (per woman)		Net reproduction rate (per woman)						
Period	Total fertility rate (per 1,000 women)	Rate	Index 1870–2 = 100	Rate	Index 1870–2 = 100	No. of years lived by a woman in the childbearing period, according to the life table	Minimum gross reproduction rate required to yield a net rate of 1·0	Minimum no. of children per woman necessary to yield a net rate of 1·0	Gross reproduction rate (per woman)	Net reproduction rate (per woman)
1850–2	4489	2·195	93	1·328	91	20·97	1·653	3·38	..	..
1860–2	4614	2·256	96	1·410	97	21·65	1·600	3·27	2·271	1·398
1870–2	4794	2·349	100	1·461	100	21·50	1·608	3·28	2·288	1·389
1880–2	4642	2·279	97	1·525	104	23·12	1·494	3·04	2·260	1·480
1890–2	4157	2·041	87	1·388	95	23·63	1·470	2·99	2·005	1·344
1900–2	3514	1·725	73	1·241	85	24·84	1·390	2·83	1·856	1·312
1910–2	2947	1·444	61	1·129	77	27·07	1·279	2·61	1·567	1·191
1920–2	2757	1·345[1]	57	1·111	76	28·60	1·211	2·48	1·545	1·233
1930–2	1904	0·929[2]	40	0·805	55	29·99	1·154	2·37	1·163[2]	0·971
1932	1843	0·899	38	0·779	53	30·00	1·154	2·37	1·108[3]	0·923
1933	1739	0·850	36	0·738	51	30·03	1·152	2·36	1·038	0·881
1934	1787	0·870	37	0·758	52	30·19	1·148	2·36	1·074	0·911
1935	1781	0·866	37	0·764	52	30·57	1·134	2·33	1·057	0·909
1936	1796	0·875	37	0·773	53	30·61	1·132	2·32	1·069	0·914
1937	1816	0·883	38	0·782	54	30·67	1·129	2·32	1·051	0·901

[1] See Note I*f*, p. 418.   [2] See Note Ig, p. 418.   [3] See Note I*h*, p. 418.

doubtful if any appreciable rise actually occurred. Secondly, after 1870–2[1] the fall was unmistakable, amounting to about 60 per cent. by 1930–2. And whereas by 1900–2 the fall was only about 27 per cent., in the next thirty years—that is, 1930–2 in relation to 1900–2—it amounted to about 46 per cent. Thirdly, the net reproduction rate fell by only about 45 per cent. between 1870–2 and 1930–2 as compared with the 60 per cent. of the gross rate, and this is due to the decline in mortality in the period. In studying reproductive trends we are concerned only with female mortality in the first fifty years of life, and the change in this mortality may be seen, approximately,[2] by examining the minimum gross reproduction rates necessary, at different periods, to yield a net reproduction rate of unity. These minimum rates show a fall of about 30 per cent. between 1850–2 and 1930–2. Alternatively, and more accurately, we may look at the number of years lived in the child-bearing period by the average woman, according to the relevant life tables, and we find a rise of about 43 per cent. by 1930–2.

In view of the importance often attached to reductions in mortality as a counterpoise for falling fertility, it is interesting to consider the trend of mortality in the past and the possibility of altering replacement trends by further reductions of mortality in the future. As regards past trends, it is clear that mortality has fallen very considerably in the last hundred years. In 1841, according to the official life tables, the expectation of life at birth in England and Wales was 40·19 years for males and 42·18 years for females.[3] By 1891–1900 this had risen to 44·13 and 47·77 years for males and females

[1] The precise date when the fall began cannot be known exactly, for incomplete registration, absence of reliable intercensal estimates of population by age and sex in the period, and lack of basic data on the distribution of births by maternal age make accurate calculation impossible. Thus we cannot say that it immediately followed the Bradlaugh-Besant trial (see subsequent discussion). Innes, J. W., *Class Fertility Trends in England and Wales, 1876–1934*, Princeton, 1938, p. 14, gives estimated legitimate birth-rates per 1,000 married women aged 15–44 years, which decline after 1876, but the factors mentioned prevent these rates from being regarded as completely accurate (in addition to any errors involved in estimating intercensal populations of *married* women).

[2] Approximately, because these rates are also influenced by changes in the age distribution of fertility over time. Thus the minimum gross reproduction rate would change if the distribution of fertility changed, even if mortality remained constant.

[3] See Note I*j*, p. 419.

respectively, no doubt influenced by the development of public health and sanitation measures in the intervening period, from 1848 onwards, though neo-Malthusians regarded the decline in mortality as primarily dependent upon the decline in the birth-rate.[1] By 1930–2 the expectation of life had risen to 58·74 years for males and 62·88 years for females, and in 1935, as a result of the continued fall in mortality, it was 60·47 and 64·50 years for males and females respectively.[2] No doubt mortality will fall appreciably in the future, excluding, of course, the influence of war.

But, in considering the influence of further changes on population trends, two points should be noted. First, reductions of mortality beyond the child-bearing ages cannot affect reproductive capacity, although they would influence the size and age-structure of the population. That is, reductions in mortality after the first 50 years of life will not raise the net reproduction rate—unless, of course, they result in an extension of the effective child-bearing period—but will increase the size of the population resulting from any given annual supply of births. An expectation of life of 50 years means that, with an annual supply of 100,000 live births, the total population would be 5 millions, while with an expectation of life of 70 years the resultant population would be 7 millions. At the same time such reductions in mortality would increase the proportion of old persons in the population, a fact which we shall have to discuss in more detail at a later stage. The second point is that the influence of reductions in mortality within the first 50 years of life depends upon how far fertility has already fallen. The net reproduction rate for England and Wales is now considerably below unity—falling below that level between 1922 and

[1] Thus Drysdale, C. V., *The Malthusian Doctrine and its Modern Aspects*, London, n.d. (but it is a collection of articles which appeared in *The Malthusian* in 1916 and 1917), pp. 34–50. See the instructive cross-examination of Drysdale by Professor Major Greenwood in *The Declining Birth Rate* (First Report of the National Birth Rate Commission), London, 1916, pp. 104–8, 130–2.

[2] These 1937 figures are 60·18 and 64·40 years, but the difference between these figures and the figures for 1935 are too small—in view of the fact that intercensal estimates of population have necessarily been used as the basis of the life tables—to be significant. Comparative figures for expectations of life are given in Dublin, L. I., and Lotka, A. J., *Length of Life*, New York, 1936, pp. 346–9, 354–7, 362, 364–74, and *Statistical Year-Book of the League of Nations, 1938–39*, Geneva, 1939, pp. 52–4.

1925, as far as can be judged from estimated rates—in spite of the rise since 1933. If none of the newly born girl children died before reaching their fiftieth birthdays, they would each exactly replace themselves by bearing one girl child or—taking into account the sex-ratio of live births in 1937—about 2·06 children. But according to the fertility of 1937, each woman would bear only 1·82 children or 0·88 of a girl child, so that no reduction in mortality—short of immortality—would prevent the population from falling eventually. This is no argument against attempts to reduce mortality. The expectation of life in England and Wales is still well below that in New Zealand—65·04 and 67·88 years for males and females respectively in 1931—and Australia—63·48 and 67·14 years for males and females in 1932–4—and a glance at the mortality rates in the 'depressed areas' or among the economically poorer sections of the community is enough to show the marked and needless waste of life that still occurs to-day.[1] But efforts to reduce mortality are not generally inspired by a desire to raise the net reproduction rate and can, in fact, have little effect upon it. At present, according to the life table for 1937, a newly born girl can expect to live 30·67 years between her fifteenth and fiftieth birthdays, out of the 35 years she would live if there were no chance of dying before the age of 50. If the actual number of years lived were raised to 34—and that would require an enormous reduction in mortality, and is not very likely—the net reproduction rate, with the fertility of 1937, would still be only about 0·87, well below replacement level.

We have seen that fertility, which is now the major factor influencing replacement trends, has undergone a very marked fall in the last sixty years. The question which now arises is —why has this fall taken place? There are two parts to this question. First, what are the means by which it has come about, and, secondly, what are the underlying factors in this change? The first part is concerned with what may be called 'mechanical causation'. Is fertility so much lower to-day than in 1871 because there is less marriage, or because of a diminution of physiological fecundity, or because of a deliberate restriction of family size by the use of various methods

[1] See Note I*k*, p. 419.

of birth prevention? The second part of the main question is concerned with fundamental problems of social change. If birth restriction is practised on a large scale to-day, why is this the case? Has the position and function of the family so changed that children are no longer regarded as the necessary accompaniment of marriage, or was this attitude always present but not previously capable of overt expression? Many of these questions of mechanical as well as of social causation are practically impossible to answer at the present time, and some may never be satisfactorily answered. All that the present writer can do is to pick out some aspects of the general problem and discuss the information which is so far available.

TABLE 4. *England and Wales. Proportion of Married Women (excluding Widows and Divorcees) in each Age Group, recorded at the Censuses from* 1851 *to* 1931[1]

Census date	*Percentage married in each age group*				
	15–19	20–24	25–34	35–44	15–44
1851 . . .	2·52	30·77	64·26	75·72	47·33
1861 . . .	3·05	33·14	66·68	76·27	49·13
1871 . . .	3·16	34·32	67·57	76·24	49·64
1881 . . .	2·53	33·06	68·15	76·50	49·14
1891 . . .	1·94	29·62	65·26	76·07	47·07
1901 . . .	1·55	27·17	64·30	75·08	46·84
1911 . . .	1·20	24·15	63·16	75·31	47·70
1921 . . .	1·75	27·00	63·08	74·54	48·54
1931 . . .	1·80	25·68	65·77	75·22	50·05

The first question is thus—how far have changes in marriage frequency influenced replacement trends? This is answered fairly easily. At the present time the proportion of potentially fertile women who are actually married does not differ significantly from the proportion in earlier periods when the gross reproduction rate was very much higher. In Table 4 census data on this question have been summarized, and show no serious change except in the youngest age groups where the proportion of married women is so small that large percentage changes would have small absolute results. To test in a more precise way the effect of the various changes shown in Table 4 upon the reproduction rate, we

1 From 1931 Census, *General Tables*, Table 21, p. 150.

may use the fertility data derived from the 1931 census, adjusted to the annual average of births in 1930–2,[1] as shown in Table 5.

TABLE 5. *England and Wales, Legitimate, Illegitimate, and Total Specific Fertility Rates*, 1930–2

	No. of legitimate live births per 1,000 married women		*No. of illegitimate live births per 1,000 single, widowed, and divorced women*		*No. of live births per 1,000 all women*
Age group	*Registrar-General's rates*	*Adjusted rates*	*Registrar-General's rates*	*Adjusted rates*	*Adjusted rates*
15–19	372	371·91	5·46	5·47	12·07
20–24	267	266·93	10·80	10·82	76·58
25–29	187	186·95	6·04	6·05	112·23
30–34	127	126·97	0·55	0·55	93·22
35–39	81	80·98	..	..	61·13
40–44	33	29·99	..	..	22·47
45–49	..	3·00	..	..	2·20

Using these adjusted rates we obtain a gross reproduction-rate of 0·927 and a net rate of 0·803 for 1930–2. Let us now assume that the 1931 population of women in each 5-year age group from 15–19 to 45–9 years showed the same proportionate marital condition as in 1911,[2] and distribute the 1931 population accordingly. Applying the legitimate and illegitimate specific fertility rates of 1930–2 to this population would yield a total of 607,102 births instead of the actual average of 631,621, and relating the total births in each age group to the total women in the same age groups, we should obtain a gross reproduction rate of 0·892 and a net rate of 0·773. That is, the marital condition of the 1931 population was more favourable to fertility than the 1911 population, yet in 1911 the gross reproduction rate was about 1·444 and the net rate about 1·129. Similarly, we may apply the marital proportions of the 1871 population,[3] when the proportion of married women in each age group

[1] See Note I*l*, p. 419.

[2] That is, 1·196; 24·151; 55·840; 71·069; 75·186; 75·458; and 72·867 per cent. married in the seven quinquennial age groups. (1911 Census, vol. vii, Tables, p. 1.)

[3] That is, 3·155; 34·318; 62·385; 73·536; 76·598; 75·848; and 74·007 per cent. married in the seven quinquennial age groups. (1871 Census, vol iii, Summary Tables, Table V, p. xxiv).

was larger than in 1931, and we should then obtain a gross reproduction rate of 1·013 and a net rate of 0·879. That is, the marital condition of the 1931 population was less favourable to fertility than the 1871 population. But the difference made to the gross and net reproduction rates by this factor is very small and does not by any means account for the decline in fertility in the last sixty years.

Census data on marital condition do not describe current trends. The fact that, in 1931, 75·22 per cent. of the women aged 35 to 44 years were actually married is the result of past marriage frequency, mortality, and migration and not by any means an expression of marriage habits in 1931. By using this data we may therefore be missing importan changes in marriage habits, and we need to approach the question in a different way. In analysing mortality the best method of summarizing current conditions is to use a life table. The best method of analysing current marriage frequency is to apply the life table method to marriage data and construct a nuptiality table, substituting spinster marriages for deaths and spinsters for all females. If we exclude mortality[1] we can then calculate the probability of being married at least once before the end of the reproductive period. In England and Wales, 1850–2,[2] this was 858·71 out of 1,000, or 0·859. That is, according to marriage frequency in 1850–2, out of 1,000 girls who were unmarried at the age of 15, 859 could expect to have married at least once by the time they reached their fiftieth birthdays. In 1860–2 the probability was 0·848, and in 1870–2 it was 0·866. For 1881 to 1901 inclusive the census data are not detailed enough to allow reasonably accurate computations to be made, but for 1910–12, 1920–2, and 1930–2[3] the likelihood

[1] Spinster deaths are actually used in constructing gross nuptiality tables, but only for the purpose of excluding the influence of mortality. That is, if we have the number of spinsters (f) aged x to $x+1$, and the number of spinster marriages (m) and deaths (d) in the same age group, the number remaining spinsters at age $x+1$ out of 1,000 at age x, excluding mortality, will be $1{,}000 \times (f+\frac{1}{2}d-\frac{1}{2}m)/(f+\frac{1}{2}d+\frac{1}{2}m)$. See Appendix to the present study, pp. 399–405, and Kuczynski, R. R., 'The analysis of vital statistics', I, *Economica*, May 1938.

[2] Marriage ages were not given in 1850, but the distribution of spinster marriages by age was assumed to be the same as in 1851 and 1852.

[3] From 1920–2 onwards spinster deaths have been taken into account in calculating gross nuptiality.

that a spinster would be married by her fiftieth birthday was 0·818, 0·860, and 0·826. The results, therefore, are similar to those obtained from the census analyses—that marriage frequency has not changed fundamentally during the period, and that between 1910–12 and 1930–2 it actually rose while fertility fell rapidly. Since 1930–2, the probability of marriage appears to have risen considerably—0·836 in 1933, 0·863 in 1934, and 0·875 in 1935—and this may be the explanation of the rise in the reproduction rate after 1933. It is, however, impossible in this country to construct accurate intercensal population estimates by marital condition, and although it is certain that the probability of marriage has risen since 1933, it would be unwise to accept the above figures as precisely describing that rise. Nevertheless, it is likely that in 1934–5 the probability of marriage was higher than it had been in any relatively normal period in the previous sixty years.

This does not mean that changes in marriage frequency would not make any difference to replacement trends. If, for example, we take the fertility data of 1930–2, we can make use of a nuptiality table to calculate the extent to which married women were replacing themselves, given the fertility, mortality, and marriage frequency of the period. For the purpose of this investigation we are concerned only with first marriages, because the important distinction is between women who never marry and those who marry at least once before they reach the end of the reproductive period. For this reason we construct a nuptiality table for spinsters and combine this with the mortality data for the period,[1] and at the same time we readjust the specific fertility rates, relating illegitimate births to women who have never married and legitimate births to married, widowed, and divorced women. In this way we obtain the data summarized in Table 6. For our purpose the important rates are the net fertility rates given in the last two columns. Summing these, and multiplying by the appropriate sex ratios at birth (the proportion of female to all live births being 48·8 per cent. for legitimate

[1] That is, $(f-\frac{1}{2}d-\frac{1}{2}m)/(f+\frac{1}{2}d+\frac{1}{2}m)$ for each year of age. The single year l_x's are used for computing the number of years lived in the state of spinsterhood, and are then summarized in 5-year age groups.

TABLE 6. *England and Wales, Marital Reproductivity*, 1930–2

Age	*No. of spinsters surviving at the beginning of each age group*		*Specific fertility rates*		*Years lived by 1,000 females, mortality accounted for*			*Net fertility rates live births per 1,000 females, mortality accounted for*	
	Mortality excluded	*Mortality from birth included*	*Illegitimate*	*Legitimate*	*Total*	*In the single state*	*After first marriage*	*Illegitimate*	*Legitimate*
15–19	1,000	904	5·47	370·92	4,495·075	4,414·875	80·200	24·15	29·75
20–24	919	822	10·84	265·59	4,437·900	3,256·685	1,181·215	35·30	313·72
25–29	533	469	6·15	184·83	4,373·125	1,729·915	2,643·210	10·64	488·54
30–34	297	258	0·59	123·87	4,303·625	1,094·660	3,208·965	0·65	397·49
35–39	225	191	..	76·98	4,226·075	880·590	3,345·485	..	257·54
40–44	197	164	..	27·45	4,133·750	777·080	3,356·670	..	92·14
45–49	183	148	..	2·64	4,015·450	709·495	3,305·955	..	8.73
50	174	136	..	..	..	..	..	..	..
					29,985·000	12,863·300	17,121·700	70·74	1,587·91

and for illegitimate births in 1930–2), we obtain a legitimate net reproduction rate of 0·775 and an illegitimate rate of 0·035, giving a total net rate of 0·810,[1] as compared with the net rate of 0·803 obtained in the ordinary way. The rate of 0·775 indicates the number of girl children born to a woman in that part of the child-bearing period which occurs after the first marriage, mortality being taken into account. But not every woman marries before reaching her fiftieth birthday, and the chances of marriage by this age were 0·826 in 1930–2.[2] If we take only those women who were married before passing out of the child-bearing period, then the replacement per woman was (0·775)/(0·826), or 0·938, so that even married women were not replacing themselves adequately. The figure of 0·938 is known as the marital or nuptial net reproduction rate, and its interpretation in the present discussion is that if every woman had married at the same ages as was shown in the nuptiality table for 1930–2—the only difference being that all women are assumed to have married at least once by their fiftieth birthdays—and if mortality and marital fertility had remained unchanged, the total net reproduction rate would still have been below unity, that is, 0·938.[3] This was the case in 1930–2, when fertility was fairly high and the probability of marriage somewhat low. By 1935 the probability of a spinster marrying by her fiftieth birthday had increased to about 0·875, while the total net reproduction rate had fallen to about 0·764, so that the effect of universal marriage—assuming that no rise in marital fertility accompanied this change in the probability of marriage—would be still less. Data for 1935 are naturally more precarious, but using the method described above we can estimate that in 1935 the net reproduction rate of women who marry at least once was about 0·9.

1 The increase in the net reproduction rate produced by splitting fertility into legitimate and illegitimate sections and weighting each section by appropriate mortality and nuptiality coefficients is small in this case. This is because there had been no sudden change in marriage frequency in preceding years. But when there is a sudden change in marriage frequency, and births have not had sufficient time to show the effect of this change, splitting up fertility in the way described may yield a total net reproduction rate considerably higher than the rate obtained in the ordinary way.

2 That is, (1,000 − 174)/1,000.

3 See Note I*m*, p. 420.

In Table 3 we gave a column of figures showing the number of children per woman necessary, at various times, to produce a net reproduction rate of unity. In 1930–2 this was about 2·37. In the same way we can calculate the number per married woman necessary in different circumstances. Keeping to the period 1930–2, for which the data are more reliable, we find that accounting for fertility and marriage frequency, but excluding mortality, each woman who married would bear 2·22 children. But the total net reproduction rate obtained from the data in Table 6 was only 0·810, so that assuming illegitimacy to continue at the 1930–2 level, each married woman would have to bear 2·74 children to maintain a net reproduction rate of unity for all potential mothers. If the average were 2·37, married women would be replacing themselves, but would not be covering the deficit due to women who would not marry. If at the present time 20 per cent. of marriages are childless,[1] then each married woman actually bearing children would have to bear 3·43 children to maintain a net reproduction rate of unity for all women. We can also estimate the distributions of families of different sizes necessary to maintain exact replacement, the reliability of the estimates depending, of course, upon the accuracy of the basic data. Thus, for example, if we had the requisite data we might perhaps find that about 30 per cent. of present-day fertile marriages would produce only one child each.[2] It should be emphasized that this percentage is simply a guess and that there are no data for England and Wales which could be used for arriving at a reasonable estimate. But if, for the sake of illustration, we make the assumption mentioned above, the remaining fertile marriages would need to produce an average of 4·47 children per marriage to ensure the adequate replacement of the total population of potential mothers. If, on the other hand, only 10 per cent. of marriages are childless, then the estimates just mentioned would be lower. They would be: 3·04 children per fertile married woman, and 3·91 children per marriage for each marriage yielding more than one child. The differences between the estimates show the urgent need for comprehensive statistics on

[1] See subsequent discussion, pp. 25–7.

[2] See Note I*n*, p. 420.

childlessness and birth order. Since 1930–2 mortality has fallen and marriage frequency has increased, so that the number of children per married woman needed to ensure adequate replacement of all potential mothers is now less. In 1935 it was about 2·6 instead of the 2·74 of 1930–2, and the other figures given above would be correspondingly reduced.

Since the discussion of the relation between marriage and reproductivity has been somewhat complicated, it may be useful to summarize the general conclusions. They are: First, the decline in fertility since 1870–2 has not been linked in any significant way with changes in the marriage frequency, and has been in the main due to a decline of fertility within marriage. Secondly, marital fertility is now so low that married women are not replacing themselves. Consequently if all women married at least once—assuming that marriages would take place at the same ages as they do at present—this would not by itself ensure a total net reproduction rate of unity. This is especially the case for the most recent years when marriage frequency has been higher, but the net reproduction rate lower, than in 1930–2. Primarily, therefore, the provision of a net reproduction rate of unity depends upon raising marital fertility. Nevertheless, an increase in marriage frequency would raise the reproduction rate, other things being equal, and the rise might be greater if this increase in marriage were accompanied by a lowering of the average age at which marriages take place, because mortality wastage would then be less. But lowering the marriage age would tend to decrease the length of the generation, and with a net reproduction rate below unity this might merely accelerate the rate of decline of the population. Suppose with a net reproduction rate of 0·70 the generation was 30 years. This would mean an eventual decline in the population of 30 per cent. every 30 years. If the net reproduction rate remained unchanged but the generation were suddenly reduced to 20 years, the new rate of decline in the population would be 30 per cent. every 20 years. How far lowered mortality wastage is counterbalanced by a shorter generation depends upon the circumstances of each specific case.[1]

[1] See Note I*o*, p. 421.

It has been shown that the decline in fertility must have been produced very largely within marriage. Some writers have suggested that this has been due mainly to physiological factors, and that natural fecundity—the ability to conceive and bear children as distinct from the frequency with which they are actually borne—is now lower than in former times.[1] Recent research on vitamins has introduced, as a possible explanation, lowered reproductive capacity due to changes in the manufacture of food, as in flour milling, and in the kinds of foods eaten to-day. But it is extraordinarily difficult to appraise the importance of these factors. It is true that roller-milling was introduced about the time when fertility began to fall, yet fertility has fallen very greatly in countries—such as Germany—where the consumption of white bread has spread far less than in England or the United States. Moreover, so far as physiological factors are concerned, there have been no investigations into the frequency of absolute or relative physiological sterility in this country, so that it is impossible to say what changes have occurred in the past sixty years. The records of gynaecologists are obviously not suitable as indications. First, involuntary sterility is a good reason for visiting a gynaecologist, so that the patients seen are unlikely to be a random physiological sample of the population. Secondly, people are less willing to-day to 'accept their lot', and it is likely that a larger proportion of the involuntarily sterile now seek medical advice than would have been the case 50 or 60 years ago.

It is important to distinguish between involuntary sterility, on which we have practically no frequency data, and total childlessness, for which some estimates are available. Thus, we find commonly quoted the estimates which Matthews Duncan summarized at the end of the nineteenth century,[2] ranging from 1 marriage in 7 to 1 in 12. Duncan concluded that we might 'have considerable confidence in laying down 1 in 10 as very nearly the true amount of sterility of marriage in Great Britain', in addition to a certain amount of what he called 'only-child fertility or one-child relative

[1] See Note I*p*, p. 421.

[2] Duncan, J. Matthews, *On Sterility in Woman*, London, 1884, esp. pp. 8–15.

sterility'.[1] But the sources used by Duncan were of very unequal value and even the best was not completely satisfactory as regards accurate and relevant statistics, so that it is difficult to regard Duncan's estimate as more than a speculation deriving from some but not fully dependable material.

The largest collection of data relating to the frequency of childlessness in England and Wales derives from the 1911 census. It was found that of all the wives for whom information was available,[2] 16·6 per cent. were recorded as being childless. Excluding those who did not marry until they were 45 years of age, childlessness was recorded among 15·5 per cent. of the wives. If we further restrict the analysis to women whose marriages had lasted 10 or more years by the time of the census, the frequency of childlessness falls to 9·5 per cent., similar to the estimate given by Duncan. But it should be noted that these statistics almost certainly exaggerate the frequency of childlessness, because the question asked at the census related to the number of children born alive to the current marriage. So children born to previous marriages, as well as any illegitimate children born outside of marriage, were presumably omitted. The data relating to women who might perhaps have been married more than once, or who might have had illegitimate children before their current marriage, cannot, consequently, be accepted as accurate evidence of the degree of childlessness. We can, however, use the data relating to women who contracted their current marriage between their fifteenth and twentieth birthdays, for it is very unlikely that they were married more than once, or that they bore illegitimate children not included in the census statistics. If, taking these women, we restrict the analysis to those whose marriages, at the date of the census, had lasted 10 or more years, we find that the frequency of childlessness was only 3·2 per cent.

[1] Duncan was careful to say, p. 12: 'I know no estimate of those who are absolutely sterile—that is, who do not conceive, or who, if they do conceive, give birth to not even an abortion. But there is a large number in the better classes, for within the last five years there have consulted me at my house, mostly on account of sterility, 504 absolutely sterile women, married between the ages of fifteen and forty-five, and of these, 337 were more than three years married. Though this shows a large number in existence, it gives no ground for an estimate of frequency among the married.'

[2] See Note I*q*, p. 421.

Women who were married between the ages of 20 and 24 years—the possibility of exaggeration of the degree of childlessness will be greater here—and whose marriages had lasted 10 or more years, showed only 5·8 per cent. of childlessness. It seems, therefore, that popular estimates of sterility in marriage are much too high, since the *total* amount of childlessness—voluntary and involuntary—in the marriages for which the chances of error are least is relatively small. But these data related to marriages enumerated in 1911. No fertility census was taken in 1921 or 1931, and we therefore have no idea at all of the way in which the frequency of childlessness may have developed in the last 20 years.[1] We can only say of the position in England and Wales that so far as can be judged from the 1911 census, complete infertility is less common than is often believed, and that we do not know how far it is caused by involuntary factors. It is not unlikely that the bulk of childlessness is unwanted, and that most married couples wish to have one child even if they are not attracted by a larger family. But it is impossible, so far as this country is concerned, to assign a proportion to physiological causes. Nor do we have any data on the causation of one- or two-child infertility—that is, we do not know how far families of one or two children are the result of deliberate restriction or of involuntary infertility after the birth of the last child. It seems unlikely that physiological factors are the main forces responsible for the small families of the present time, and that these factors should have developed so rapidly as to produce a 36 per cent. fall in the gross reproduction rate between 1910–12 and 1930–2. Some writers have suggested, as a partial cause, semi-physiological factors. Thus, Hogben has mentioned the possible effect of changes in personal hygiene. The more frequent and thorough washing and bathing, the more widespread use of soap, which has spermicidal properties, are suggested influences,[2] and there may have been significant changes in the customary frequency of coitus between husband and

[1] See Note I*r*, p. 422.

[2] *Genetic Principles*, op. cit., pp. 187–9. Also Charles, E., *The Practice of Birth Control*, London, 1932, pp. 85–6, and Charles, E., *The Twilight of Parenthood* (now called *The Menace of Underpopulation*), London, 1934, pp. 182–3.

wife. These factors are mentioned for they throw some light on special aspects of the question. But we know even less about them than about the more strictly physiological aspects.

Although we cannot tell, from data available at the present time, how far changes in reproductivity have been affected by physiological factors, we can approach the question from the other side and attempt to estimate, in general terms, the growth of deliberate family limitation or birth prevention in the past 60 years. The term 'birth prevention' is used advisedly because it covers abortion as well as those practices —which range at the present time from *coitus interruptus* and the restriction of sexual intercourse to the 'safe period', to the use of chemical and mechanical pessaries and the condom —which are generally called 'birth control', though they would be more accurately described by the term 'contraception'.[1] The actual techniques have changed, especially in the last 20 years, but the general practice of birth prevention has been known and applied since the earliest days of society. A Chinese recipe for abortion is said to date back, in writing, to about 2737–2696 B.C.,[2] and was almost certainly known long before that. Various Egyptian papyri—the Petri or Kahun Papyrus (1850 B.C.), the Ebers Papyrus (1550 B.C.), and the Berlin Papyrus (1300 B.C.)—contain recipes for contraception and abortion. That the latter practice was known in ancient Babylon is shown by the provision of fines, in the *Code of Hammurabi* (about 2080 B.C.), for blows resulting in the miscarriage of a pregnant woman.[3] Throughout the literature of Greece and Rome there are references to abortion and some of the recipes for contraception—as those given by Soranos—are as rational as can be found up to quite

[1] Himes, N. E., 'Note on the origin of the terms contraception, birth control, neo-malthusianism, &c.', *Medical Journal and Record*, 18 May 1932, pp. 495–6, says that the term 'contraception' seems to have been used first by Edward Bliss Foote (1829–1906), an American author of popular medical works and a pioneer birth controller, and that 'birth control' was first used by Margaret Sanger in Apr. 1914, in an article in a radical journal, *The Woman Rebel*, of which she was editor.

[2] Himes, N. E., *Medical History of Contraception*, London (printed in U.S.A.), 1936, pp. 111–12 and p. 112 *n.* 14. This is, of course, the standard work on the subject and is drawn upon considerably for the subsequent discussion, especially for the general perspective. See also Taussig, F. J., *Abortion, Spontaneous and Induced*, London, 1936, pp. 31–45.

[3] See Note I*s*, p. 422.

recent times.[1] Official attitudes towards abortion varied at different periods and in different countries, but it should be noted that the ranking of abortion with infanticide was an innovation due to Christianity. Nevertheless, the practice of abortion continued, and the Jesuits were at one period accused of using this method to terminate illegitimate pregnancies. Nor was the practice of contraception abandoned, though such evidence as exists points to a relatively low level of knowledge on the subject, and away from a widespread desire seriously to restrict the size of families. The conditions specifically favouring small families were lacking in Europe until the nineteenth century, though individuals, especially in wealthy and fashionable circles, refused to be burdened with large families. Among primitive tribes the need for family limitation generally appears to have been more urgent and a wide range of methods—with concentration upon abortion and infanticide—is known to have been and still to be applied to this end.[2]

This brief, general discussion has been included to show that the *idea* of controlling or preventing birth is not a product of modern times. It is now necessary to analyse more recent developments in England and Wales and to see how far the use of methods of family limitation has increased in the period during which fertility has fallen. Theoretically, considerable attention should be paid to the question of recent improvements in contraceptive technique, for this will clearly have an important bearing upon birth-rate trends. Unfortunately this question is largely outside the competence of the present writer. It may, however, be noted that the condom, one of the most reliable methods, first became available to the general public after the process of vulcanizing rubber had been discovered in the mid-nineteenth century, and that the industry has undergone another

[1] Himes, op. cit., pp. 98–101. A general account is also given by Monpin, R., *L'Avortement provoqué dans l'antiquité*, Paris, 1918, esp. pp. 133–4, and Klotz-Forest, Dr., *De l'Avortement. Est-ce un crime?*, Paris, n.d. (*B.N. Catalogue* gives 1919), ch. i, pp. 15–42. The rest of the chapter carries the account up to the *Code Pénal* of 1810, which is then dealt with separately in ch. iv.

[2] Himes, op. cit., pp. 53–6; Aptekar, H., *Anjea*, New York, 1931, chs. v–vii; Carr-Saunders, A. M., *The Population Problem*, Oxford, 1922, chs. vii, viii, and ix. In general the purely contraceptive methods do not seem to be effective.

revolution in the last 10 years with the use of liquid latex instead of crêpe rubber.[1] Mechanical pessaries have long been known, but here, too, the manufacture of relatively cheap and reliable forms dates from the end of the nineteenth century, while reasonably dependable chemical (soluble) pessaries are even more recent.

While, therefore, both the idea of birth control and various birth-control practices are very old, the development of reliable techniques and apparatus is recent, accompanying modern progress in physiology and chemistry. It should be emphasized, however, that at the present time, in spite of the progress made since the last War, contraception is far from being completely reliable, if only because even the least uncertain method requires a degree of care in use which apparently is not always forthcoming. Consequently, there must still be a high frequency of 'unwanted births'[2] every year, due either to ignorance or fear of the use of birth control on the part of some sections of the community, and to 'accidents' or unskilled use of available methods on the part of other sections. But this does not mean that birth control has been or is ineffective. It means only that it has not the certainty attributed to it by many people.[3]

The case for birth restriction was first communicated to the literate public in England through the medium of T. R.

[1] See Himes, op. cit., pp. 186–206. The first published record of the condom—the origin of this name is not known—is in Fallopius, G., *De Morbo Gallico*, 1564, where it was recommended as a protection against syphilis (Notice that in those European countries which have specific laws against birth-control propaganda and/or the sale of contraceptives, the condom is still defined as a protection against venereal disease and not as a contraceptive, in spite of the fact that its use ranks with *coitus interruptus* and douching as the most popular methods of contraception) and it was advertised in England at the end of the eighteenth century. Himes cites an estimate that about 317 million condoms per year are manufactured in the United States alone.

[2] The term 'unwanted birth' is used only in the sense that the birth was not hoped for. By the time the child has been born it may be very welcome.

[3] Among the various inquiries into the extent to which the use of contraceptives reduces overt fertility, two of the most interesting are: Stix, R. K., and Notestein, F. W., 'Effectiveness of birth control', *Milbank Memorial Fund Quarterly*, Jan. 1934, and same authors, same journal, Apr. 1935. These two studies refer to a sample of women in New York, and both show a marked reduction in pregnancy rates when contraceptives are used. The second study indicates that the condom seems to be the most effective method in practice. See also Pearl, R., *The Natural History of Population*, pp. 206–24, for indications derived from a much larger sample.

Malthus's *Essay on the Principle of Population as It Affects the Future Improvement of Society*, originally published in London in 1798, and the spread of the doctrine was helped no less by the attacks of Shelley, Godwin, Cobbett, and Hazlitt than by the support received from the economists, led by Ricardo.[1] But the method advocated by Malthus was the postponement of marriage.[2] The case for birth control was first fully presented to the public, and the use of simple and relatively active techniques to be applied within marriage, were first reasonably urged and described, by Francis Place, founder of the English birth-control movement. The word public is not used here in a literary or metaphorical sense, but as a precise description of the contribution which Place made, especially by means of the 'diabolical handbills' of 1823 which, recommending and briefly describing the use of *coitus interruptus* and the sponge,[3] were rather widely distributed in the eighteen-twenties among the working-class population of London and the north. Place was aided in his aim by Richard Carlile, editor of *The Republican*, whose 'What is love?', published in that journal in 1825,[4] was reprinted in pamphlet form the next year, and, though obtaining a large circulation, did not result in any prosecution of its author. T. J. Wooler, editor of *The Black Dwarf*, though not agreeing with Place's views, helped the movement by reprinting one of the handbills in his journal in 1823, and threw open its columns to discussion of the question.[5] Two other supporters of Place, Hassell and Campion, discussed and supported his ideas in their journal, *The*

[1] 'Malthusian' views were expressed before (see Stangeland, C. E., *Pre-Malthusian Doctrines of Population*, New York, 1904, pp. 341–6, 355–6), but Malthus was the first to elaborate and document them, and the first to have any real influence on public opinion. For the Malthusian controversy see *Essays on Population and Other Papers by James Alfred Field*, ed. Hohman, H. F., Chicago, 1931, pp. 1–86, 'The Malthusian controversy in England'.

[2] Malthus was antagonistic to the idea of birth restriction within marriage, regarding population pressure as a necessary incentive to social progress. The ability to restrict births within marriage would lead to idleness and the pursuit of luxury. See 7th ed., 'Everyman' reprint, vol. ii, London, 1928, pp. 157–8.

[3] See Note I*t*, p. 423.

[4] See Note I*u*, p. 423.

[5] A long discussion began with an article, 'Inquiry into the principles of population', signed A. Z., in the issue of 12 Nov. 1823, pp. 661–78, which supported Place. According to Himes, A. Z. was Francis Place and A. M. was J. S. Mill.

Newgate Monthly Magazine.[1] Further ammunition also came from abroad in two publications: Robert Dale Owen's *Moral Physiology*, first published in New York in 1831, and in London in 1832, selling about 75,000 copies in America and England by 1877, and Charles Knowlton's *Fruits of Philosophy*, published in New York in 1832, and in London in 1833 or 1834, which sold about 10,000 copies in the United States up to 1839. In England its sales, in the editions issued by various publishers, are estimated to have been between 700 and 1,000 copies per year in the period 1834 to 1876–7.[2] Yet in spite of the publications and the propaganda—further aided by Dr. George Drysdale in the 'fifties—little effect was produced. Certainly the trend of fertility in England and Wales showed no signs of falling in the 'fifties or 'sixties. The most that can be said is that the ground was being prepared during the period. Some special influence was, however, necessary before real growth could take place. That influence was the Bradlaugh-Besant trial of 1877.

The Knowlton pamphlet, recommending douching as the most satisfactory method of contraception, had been sold in England for over 40 years without interference from the authorities. But in 1876, Henry Cook, a Bristol bookseller, was sentenced to two years' hard labour for issuing an edition of Knowlton interleaved, it is alleged, with obscene pictures.[3] Charles Watts, the London publisher, was also prosecuted but was let off with the payment of costs. Charles Bradlaugh, who had long been a supporter of birth control, and Mrs. Annie Besant, decided to create a test case, and republished the pamphlet, informing the police where and when it would be sold, 'so as to put no technical difficulties in the way of prosecution'.[4] The trial, in 1877, was first conducted at the Guildhall, but removed to the Court of Queen's Bench 'on the writ of the Lord Chief Justice, who, after reading the pamphlet, decided that it was a scientific

[1] See Note I*v*, p. 423. [2] See Note I*w*, p. 424.

[3] Cook himself appears to have denied this. In *The Malthusian*, July 1879, p. 45, the following item appears in the report of the Council meeting of the League: 'A letter was read by Mr. Parris from Mr. Cook, bookseller, of Bristol, who alleged that he had never been a circulator of loose literature.'

[4] Besant, Mrs. A., 'Theosophy and the law of population', *Lucifer*, July 1891, pp. 394–9 at p. 396.

work, not an "obscene" one, in the ordinary sense of the word. To use his own phrase, it was a "dry physiological treatise".'[1] In spite of a very favourable summing up by Lord Chief Justice Cockburn, the verdict went against the defendants—though the jury exonerated them while finding the book obscene—largely, according to Mrs. Besant, because of the religious and political hatred against them and because of the fact that the jury contained men like Mr. Walter, of *The Times*.[2] Judgement was reserved, and the defendants allowed to go on their own recognizances. But when coming up for judgement later,[3] they refused to surrender the pamphlet and insisted that they would continue to sell it, and, in consequence, were each sentenced to six months' imprisonment, a fine of £200, and recognizances of £500 for two years. They gave notice of appeal and were again allowed to go on their own recognizances, having promised not to sell the pamphlet until the appeal was decided. The case came up for appeal in February 1878, and on purely technical grounds—that the words alleged by the prosecution to be obscene had not been set out—the judgement of the Queen's Bench division was reversed. It should be emphasized that this was not the victory or vindication of a principle, and that one of the appeal judges, Bramwell, L.J., said: 'I wish it to be understood that we express no opinion whether this is a filthy and obscene, or an innocent book. We have not the materials before us for coming to a decision upon that point. We are deciding a dry point of law, which has nothing to do with the actual merits of the case.'[4] Brett, L.J. added: 'Although on a point of law the judgment in this case must be reversed, yet if the book complained of is published again, and the plaintiffs in error are convicted upon a properly framed indictment, the reiteration of the offence must be met by greater punishment.'[5] But the confiscated copies of the pamphlet were recovered from the police and *Fruits of Philosophy* continued to be sold by Bradlaugh and Mrs. Besant until it was evident that no

[1] Ibid. The trial before Cockburn, C.J. was on 18 June 1877.

[2] *Annie Besant. An Autobiography*, London, 1893, p. 210.

[3] See Note I*x*, p. 424.

[4] 1878 L.R., 3 Q.B., 607 at 625.

[5] Ibid., at 639.

further legal action would be taken. The sale was then discontinued and Mrs. Besant issued, instead, her own small book, *The Law of Population*, first published in 1878–9. By October 1880 this sixpenny pamphlet was in its fortieth thousand in England.[1]

But the case for freedom of the press, so far as birth-control literature was concerned, was not yet vindicated. In 1877 Edward Truelove, a Freethought publisher, was brought up to Bow Street for issuing two pamphlets—Robert Dale Owen's *Moral Physiology*, and J. H. Palmer's *Individual, Family, and National Poverty*. The case was postponed to await the decision in the Bradlaugh-Besant trial, and in February 1878 was tried before the Queen's Bench and, as the jury could not agree, retried, three months later, at the Old Bailey. Truelove was found guilty and sentenced to four months' imprisonment and a fine of £50. He was at that time in his sixty-eighth year. Appeals and protests were useless and the sentence was served. But from the point of view of the birth-control movement, this was probably better than a successful appeal, for the propaganda resulting from the trial and the sentence was remarkable. Truelove was greeted as a hero on his release and presented, on behalf of the National Secular Society and the Malthusian League, with a testimonial and a purse containing £200.[2]

This was not the last birth-control prosecution. In 1891 H. S. Young was fined £20 and costs at Bow Street, for sending through the post a leaflet advocating birth control,[3] while in 1892 Henry Loader, a Newcastle-on-Tyne phrenologist,[4] went to prison for a month for procuring for sale the *Fruits of Philosophy* and selling a publication by Dr. H. A.

[1] See Note I*y*, p. 424.

[2] Anon. [but really G. Standring], *The Malthusian Handbook*, 4th ed., London, 1898, pp. 28–9; *The Queen* v. *Edward Truelove*, London, 1878 (stenographic report of the first trial).

[3] *The Malthusian Handbook*, pp. 32–3.

[4] See *The Malthusian*, Feb. 1892, pp. 9–11, and May 1892, pp. 35, 36. There were two trials, the jury having disagreed on the first occasion. Loader was found guilty but recommended to mercy, and the judgement was that he enter into his own recognizances with one surety of £50 and himself in £100. He refused to find the surety and was sent to prison for a month 'with such hard labour as you can do'. It is not clear whether Loader actually sold the *Fruits of Philosophy*, though copies were found on his premises, and he was charged with procuring them for sale, as well as for selling the Allbutt publication.

Allbutt, *The Wife's Handbook*, for issuing which the author had had his name removed from the Medical Register in 1887.[1] There were also prosecutions in the twentieth century. But the Truelove prosecution was the last important one, and the birth-control movement in England was not afterwards seriously hindered by legal interference.

The immediate result of the Bradlaugh-Besant trial was the creation of the Malthusian League, which held its first meeting in the Minor Hall of the Hall of Science, Old Street, London, on 17 July 1877,[2] and its first Council meeting on 2 August of the same year in the rooms of Dr. Charles R. Drysdale,[3] who had been elected President in July. In February 1879 a monthly journal, *The Malthusian*—the subtitle *A Crusade Against Poverty* was added in January 1880[4]—was published, and the first issue was sold out in a week and reprinted with some new matter.[5] This journal was published without a break until the end of 1921—December 1921, saw its last appearance—after which it was replaced by *The New Generation*, which has continued up to the present day. Anxious to spread the ideas which were later known generally as 'neo-Malthusian'—a term first used in English, as far as the present writer can tell, early in 1879[6]—the Malthusian League published pamphlets and leaflets, held conferences and gave lectures throughout the country. It was the promoter of the birth-control movement of the present day, and though originally concerned to spread the gospel of family limitation and not itself publishing any account of the techniques of contraception until September 1913,[7] it was the main inspiration of what system of birth-control clinics we now have in England.

To gauge the influence of the neo-Malthusian movement we need to consider, first, the propaganda undertaken and

1 See letter by Dr. Allbutt in *The Malthusian*, Jan. 1888, p. 5.

2 See Note I*z*, p. 424.

3 Standring, G., 'Malthusian memories', *The Malthusian*, 15 Aug. 1909, pp. 57–8 at 57.

4 Added at the suggestion of Standring, though the actual phrase was one of two possibilities mentioned by the editor of the journal. Ibid., Dec. 1879, pp. 85–6.

5 See page 4 of the second edition of the first number, Feb. 1879.

6 See Note I*aa*, p. 425.

7 *Thirty-seventh Annual Report of the Malthusian League* [for 1914–15], pp. 3–4.

publications issued and, secondly, the economic and social background of the period in which the movement was taking place. We can then discuss the present situation in relation to the existing birth-control movement and attempt to estimate how far the total influence reached the adult population of the country. The first point is probably best illuminated by analysing the work of the Malthusian League in its early years from the columns of its journal. Taking 1879 alone, we find that Mr. Page (an original member of the Council of the League) lectured at the Commonwealth Club in January, with the Reverend Stewart Headlam in the chair, and that Mrs. Besant had been invited to lecture in the agricultural areas of Lincolnshire 'under the auspices of a large Agricultural Labourers' Union'. Dr. Drysdale was to speak in Chelsea at the Eleusis Club, and also at the London Dialectical Society, in February.[1] In the May issue of the journal Mr. Parris reported the success of his lectures in Paisley, Edinburgh, and Hartlepool and Dr. Drysdale announced that he was to speak at the Working Men's Club at Hammersmith.[2] In the July issue there was a report of a discussion, opened by Dr. Drysdale, at the Phoenix Temperance Hall, in the East End of London,[3] and an announcement that two lectures—by Dr. Drysdale and Mr. Parris—had also been given at the same hall. Mr. Parris had arranged to lecture twice a month and Mr. Haines, of the Phoenix Hall, had urged that population lectures should be given monthly at his place.[4] Mr. Parris lectured in Manchester on 20 July, in London on 3 and 18 August,[5] in Liverpool on 31 August, and in West Hartlepool on 14 September,[6] while Mrs. Besant lectured at Lockwood, near Huddersfield, on 20 September.[7] In October Dr. Drysdale gave two lectures in Edinburgh,[8] and read a paper on differential mortality to the Medical Society of London,[9]

[1] *The Malthusian*, Feb. 1879, p. 7.

[2] Ibid., May 1879, p. 28.

[3] Ibid., July 1879, p. 42.

[4] Ibid., July 1879, p. 45. It is probable that Dr. Drysdale's lecture was in fact the 'discussion' which he opened, so that he spoke once only at the Phoenix Hall that month. But *The Malthusian* is not explicit on this point.

[5] Ibid., Sept. 1879, p. 62.

[6] Ibid., Oct. 1879, p. 71.

[7] Ibid., Nov. 1879, p. 80.

[8] Ibid., Nov. 1879, p. 77.

[9] Ibid., Dec. 1879, p. 81.

while Mr. Parris spoke at the Tower Hamlets Radical Club and in Manchester.[1] At about the same time Mrs. Besant spoke in Bradford, Chester-le-Street (Durham), and Nelson (Lancashire), Mr. Parris gave further lectures at Woolwich and in Halifax,[2] while a Manchester branch of the Malthusian League was set up.[3]

Nor was lecturing the only method of publicizing the principles of the League. In 1879 there was already some house-to-house 'canvassing', and in the journal of July 1879 G. A. Gaskell wrote that he and a fellow worker

> 'have set ourselves the task of distributing Malthusian tracts and leaflets throughout the poorer parts of Bradford. We are doing it systematically, street by street, and giving advice as we go. I may say we have been very well received, and the poor mothers have practically felt so strongly the evils of large families that they listen eagerly to what we have to say. Sometimes we find the knowledge has gone before us, but we see the great good which may be done by *encouraging* the practice of conjugal prudence. . .'.[4]

George Standring, in his 'Malthusian Memories,' reports two further examples of this 'personal propaganda'. T. O. Bonser, who gave much financial help to the League, used to go on walking tours through the country in the Summer, 'talking to the peasantry and distributing Malthusian leaflets *en route*', while an itinerant musician named Williamson, 'travelled through the country playing a violin, addressing wayside audiences on the population question, distributing leaflets and selling copies of "The Wife's Handbook" and other publications of a similar nature'.[5] The leaflets mentioned in these quotations were issued by the Malthusian League. The February 1879 number of *The Malthusian* contains notices of six pamphlets—priced at a halfpenny and a penny—and four free leaflets,[6] and these were added to in subsequent years.

No thorough study has as yet been made of the influence

[1] Ibid., Dec. 1879, p. 86.
[2] Ibid., Dec. 1879, p. 86.
[3] Ibid., Dec. 1879, p. 87.
[4] Ibid., July 1879, p. 44.
[5] Ibid., 15 Aug. 1909, p. 57.
[6] Ibid., Feb. 1879, p. 4. The present writer has traced 26 of the pamphlets, tracts and leaflets (excluding membership forms and annual reports) issued by the Malthusian League, but this must be a small proportion of the total. By the end of 1880 there were at least 15.

on the Press of the Malthusian League and its propaganda. But citations in *The Malthusian* from various newspapers show sympathy and approval in many outlying parts of the country from 1879. Places as unlike as the Isle of Wight, Merthyr, and Aberdare, and Staffordshire gave evidence of Press approval, this approval ranging from whole-hearted adherence to the Malthusian League principles to the publication of 'Malthusian' poetry.[1] Nor was the influence of the League confined to England. In the June 1879 issue it is noted that subscriptions to the League had been received from six persons (ladies) of Wanganui, New Zealand.[2] Paul Robin had written, promising to produce a pamphlet for the Working Man's Association meeting to be held in Marseilles in August 1879,[3] and Dr. Drysdale and Dr. Allbutt were to read papers at the Amsterdam meeting of the International Medical Association in 1879.[4] By the end of 1880 the Malthusian League had, in accordance with the proposal described by Dr. Allbutt,[5] set up a Medical Branch,[6] and when the International Medical Association held its London meeting in 1881, the League convened a special meeting of its Medical Branch to discuss family limitation.[7] The beginnings of an effective neo-Malthusian movement on the

[1] *The Malthusian*, April 1879, p. 24, cites from the *Isle of Wight Chronicle*, a poem 'The Song of the Land', by Bill Hood, containing the following verse:

'Oh, married men, and boys!
If your wages you would raise,
Just start a laugh at brother Hodge
When the parson gives him praise
For rearing children ten,
That he finds it hard to keep;
For when there 's many to work, you know—
You must sell your labour cheap.'

[2] Ibid., June 1879, p. 36.

[3] Ibid., July 1879, p. 45. The meeting was actually held in Sept. The pamphlet was a single-page translation of an address specially written by Dr. Drysdale, dated from London, 10 July 1879, entitled *Adresse de la Ligue Néo-Malthusienne de Londres aux membres du Congrès Ouvrier de Marseille, Septembre, 1879.*

[4] Ibid., July 1879, p. 45. The meeting was held in Sept.—Ibid., Oct. 1879, pp. 66–71.

[5] Ibid., Nov. 1879, p. 77.

[6] Ibid., Nov. 1880, p. 176, contains the first notice of the existence of this Branch, though later issues refer to it as having been founded in Aug. 1881.

[7] Ibid., Sept. 1881, pp. 249–51.

Continent may probably be dated from these events of 1879 and 1881.[1]

In subsequent chapters some account is given of the neo-Malthusian movements in a number of countries, and for the present it is not necessary to make more than a brief reference to them. The Dutch Nieuw-Malthusiaansche Bond was founded in 1881[2], the German Sozial-Harmonische Verein in 1889,[3] and the French Ligue de la Régénération Humaine in 1896.[4] The first International Neo-Malthusian Conference was held in Paris in August 1900, and it was unanimously resolved to set up an International Federation of Neo-Malthusian Leagues, to be known as the Fédération Universelle de la Régénération Humaine.[5] The second international congress was held in Liége in 1905,[6] the third at The Hague in 1910,[7] and the fourth at Dresden in 1911.[8] In the interval Dr. C. R. Drysdale had died—on 2 December 1907[9]—but the work of the League was continued under his widow, Dr. Alice Vickery, who succeeded him as President,

[1] Though not the actual origins—e.g. in Holland the origins date from 1876, in which years articles by Dr. Van Houten and Professor Greven appeared (ibid., 15 Aug. 1910, p. 65), while shortly afterwards (in 1882) Dr. Aletta Jacobs was giving free birth-control advice to poor mothers. (The dates given for this vary. Dr. B. Dunlop, ibid., 15 April 1921, p. 28, says 1881, while How-Martyn, Mrs. E., and Breed, M., *The Birth Control Movement in England*, London, 1930, p. 13, give 1878.) The 1882 date was given by Madame Rutgers-Hoitsema, President of the Dutch League in 1910.

[2] *The Malthusian*, 15 Aug. 1910, p. 64 (address by Mme Rutgers-Hoitsema, President). The dates given on the cover of the issues of *The Malthusian* are often incorrect—this is so for Holland—but they are cited when other, more circumstantial accounts are not available.

[3] But birth-control support and information was given earlier—e.g. Hellmann, R., *Ueber Geschlechtsfreiheit*, Berlin, 1878, pp. 204–6, gives an account of various techniques of contraception. So, according to Stopes and Himes, did Wilde, F. A., *Das weibliche Gebär-Unvermögen*, Berlin, 1838.

[4] Giroud, G., *Paul Robin*, Paris, 1937, p. 217. This gives the best history of the French movement.

[5] *The Malthusian*, Sept. 1900, pp. 67–9.

[6] Ibid., Oct. 1905, p. 73.

[7] The report extended to a number of issues of *The Malthusian*, beginning in that of 15 Aug. 1910, p. 59.

[8] Ibid., 15 Sept. 1911, p. 65.

[9] Ibid., Jan. 1908, pp. 1–2, for obituary notice by Mrs. Bessie Drysdale. This contains the best short biography known to the present writer. McCabe, J., *A Biographical Dictionary of Modern Rationalists*, London, 1920, col. 223, gives very little. It is surprising that there should be no full-length biography of a man who had such a profound influence on modern society.

and his son, Dr. C. V. Drysdale. By the time that the fourth international conference met, there were constituent bodies of the Fédération Universelle in France, Holland, Germany, Spain, Belgium, Switzerland, Bohemia, Portugal, Brazil, Cuba, and North Africa, with Sweden joining a little later, while activity was also being carried on in the United States. At the third conference an International Neo-Malthusian Bureau of Correspondence and Defence had been created. The League carried on during the War, though with somewhat diminished activity, and after the War there was a fifth international conference in London in 1922[1] and a sixth in New York in 1925,[2] while the World Population Conference, held in Geneva in 1927, was also organized by Margaret Sanger.[3]

To continue the discussion to the second stage, we need to estimate the circulation of neo-Malthusian publications in England and Wales. This cannot be done with any real accuracy, and any total figure quoted must be regarded as a very rough approximation. If we take a few of the best-known publications, we can obtain an estimate for their circulation by various dates. Thus George Drysdale's *Elements of Social Science*, first published in 1854,[4] was in its thirty-seventh thousand by 1880,[5] its fifty-third thousand in 1885,[6] its sixty-first early in 1887,[7] and its sixty-fifth by the end of 1887,[8] while by 1908–9 the total sales in England had amounted to about 88,000, and it was still selling steadily.[9] The total sales by 1914 cannot, therefore, be placed at much less than 100,000 copies, of which perhaps 80,000 had been sold after the Bradlaugh-Besant trial.

[1] Pierpoint, R., ed., *Report of the Fifth International Neo-Malthusian and Birth Control Conference*, London, 1922.

[2] Sanger, M., ed., *The Sixth International Neo-Malthusian and Birth Control Conference*, 4 vols., New York, vol. i, 1925, vols. ii, iii, and iv, 1926.

[3] Sanger, M., ed. *Proceedings of the World Population Conference*, London, 1927.

[4] Himes, *Medical History*, p. 233, n. 74. It was originally published under the title *Physical, Sexual and Natural Religion*. The title was changed for the second edition in 1857. See letter from N. E. Himes in *The New Generation*, May, 1928, pp. 59–60.

[5] *The Malthusian*, Nov. 1880, p. 176.

[6] Ibid., Jan. 1885, p. 575.

[7] Ibid., Feb. 1887, p. 16.

[8] Himes, *Medical History*, Bibliography, p. 445.

[9] *Annual Report for 1908–9 of the Malthusian League*, London, 1909, p. 8. It had been translated into many languages: French, German, Dutch, Italian, and Portuguese, and probably others too.

Of Knowlton's *Fruits of Philosophy* there were many different issues—some published by Watts, others by the Freethought Publishing Company (Bradlaugh and Besant), and several by less well-known London firms and by provincial printers. Taking only the Freethought Company editions, there were issued probably not less than 200,000. It is unlikely that all other issues amounted to much less than 100,000 from 1870 onwards,[1] making a total of about 300,000, the sale of which was probably concentrated largely in the years 1870–90. Robert Dale Owen's *Moral Physiology* was still being sold in the 'seventies, though the editions give no note of total sales.[2] It will be remembered that after the Bradlaugh-Besant trial Mrs. Besant produced her own *Law of Population* in 1878–9, and that this was in its fortieth thousand in 1880. By 1888 the hundred and tenth thousand was in print,[3] while Professor Himes gives a bibliographic reference to an 1889 issue stated to be in the hundred and fifty-fifth thousand, and to an 1891 issue making the hundred and seventy-fifth thousand.[4] In 1891 Mrs. Besant, having become a follower of Madame Blavatsky, found theosophy irreconcilable with the advocacy of neo-Malthusianism, and she ceased to publish her book and refused to sell or give away the copyright.[5] Unless, therefore, there were pirated editions, *The Law of Population* stopped at under the 200,000 mark in England. We have also to include among the most popular publications Dr. H. A. Allbutt's *The Wife's Handbook*, probably first published in 1884–5. This was in a second revised edition in 1886, and a third in the same year, reaching the eleventh edition in 1889, the twenty-third in 1894, and the forty-fifth in 1913.[6] By about 1929 it was in its five hundred and fourth thousand, and, although very dated, was probably still selling quite steadily at the time.[7] Dr. Allbutt also published *Artificial Checks to Population* in 1889, and this was in its fourteenth edition in 1909.[8] Another

[1] See references to various issues in Himes, *Medical History*, pp. 460–63.

[2] The present writer's copy is the ordinary Truelove edition, published in the early 'seventies (n.d.).

[3] *The Malthusian*, June 1888, p. 47.

[4] *Medical History*, p. 437.

[5] See Note I*bb*, p. 426.

[6] *British Museum Catalogue*.

[7] See advertisement in *The New Generation*, April 1929, p. ii.

[8] *B.M. Catalogue*.

popular work was Dr. R. T. Trall's *Sexual Physiology and Hygiene*, first published in 1866,[1] in its ninety-fifth thousand in 1917,[2] and still being published in 1937. These are just a few of the more popular works giving information on birth control. There were many other publications giving similar information and a host of pamphlets supporting birth control though not actually giving details of techniques. In particular we should take into account the pamphlets, tracts, and leaflets actually published by the Malthusian League itself. The present writer has not been able to find a full statement of the number of these publications or of their individual circulations, but a very rough estimate may be obtained of the total circulation. Thus in 1885 the secretary of the League said: 'During the last five months we have sent out no less than sixty-one thousand copies, and we are still receiving many applications for them every day.'[3] If we turn to the twentieth century, we find similar figures. The 1908–9 report of the League gives a circulation of about 1,200 copies per month for *The Malthusian*, plus about 50,000 leaflets sent out by the General Secretary, and also 'several thousands' distributed by the Corresponding Secretaries and others.[4]

When the League published its practical pamphlet, *Hygienic Methods of Family Limitation*, in September 1913, a further impetus was given to publicity. Taking this pamphlet alone, by 31 March 1915, 3,740 copies had been distributed in response to applications,[5] and the additional circulation was 5,580 in the next year,[6] 3,947 in the next,[7] and 8,147 in the next.[8] The last edition seen by the present writer—it must have been published after 1927—was in the hundred and third thousand. It would be reasonable to conclude that, excluding *The Malthusian*, the League itself issued about three million pamphlets and leaflets between

[1] On Trall see Stopes, M. C., *Early Days of Birth Control*, 3rd ed., London, 1923, pp. 9-11 and 16–18.

[2] *B.M. Catalogue*.

[3] *The Malthusian*, Nov. 1885, p. 655.

[4] *Annual Report for 1908–9*, p. 8.

[5] *Thirty-Seventh Annual Report* (for 1914–15), n.d., p. 4.

[6] *Thirty-Eighth Annual Report* (for 1915–16), n.d., p. 3.

[7] *Thirty-Ninth Annual Report* (for 1916–17), n.d., p. 3.

[8] *Fortieth Annual Report* (for 1917–18), n.d., p. 1.

1879 and the end of 1921, after which date the original journal was replaced by *The New Generation*.[1] The League publications, though urging family limitation, did not, except for the 1913 pamphlet, actually describe methods of limitation. So far as the total for publications giving information on contraception is concerned, Professor Himes estimated that in 1876–91 not less than a million, and more probably about two million, represents the circulation,[2] and hoped later to substantiate an estimate of not less than fifteen millions in England between November 1918 and the latter part of 1928.[3]

Until the end of the War of 1914–18 the birth-control movement in England concentrated almost exclusively on spreading the *idea* of and reasons for family limitation. It would be quite incorrect to assume that neo-Malthusians aimed at a ceaseless fall in the birth-rate: they merely wished to reduce poverty by encouraging a satisfactory equilibrium between available resources and family size. They wanted to obtain what is known as the 'optimum population', and their argument was almost entirely economic. As was stated in *The Malthusian* of August 1915:

'Because we still advocate a reduction of the birth-rate in this country, there seem to be very many people who think we are out for a universal 'two-child system'. Nothing is further from our thoughts . . . The only real difference between us and the majority of eugenists lies in our belief that some degree of limitation is necessary even among the most fit, in order to relieve the general pressure of population upon the means of subsistence. Hence we took the view before the war that the maximum family should be four children, and that couples should have no more children than they can do full justice to.

1 Dr. C. V. Drysdale kindly commented on this estimate, and on the method of estimation. He said (in a letter, dated 9 June 1939) that on second thoughts—he was originally of the opinion that the total figure was lower—the estimate of 3 million by the end of 1921 did not seem excessive. The present writer has made no estimate of the circulation of pamphlets since 1921. Note, however, that in 1925 alone, in furtherance of a campaign to arouse public opinion to the need for giving birth-control advice at Government Welfare Centres, a million leaflets were printed. See *The New Generation*, Aug. 1925, p. 85. An article by Mrs. Bessie Drysdale in the same issue, pp. 90–91, states that about 150,000 had already been distributed.

2 Himes, N. E., *New England Journal of Medicine*, 6 Sept. 1928, op. cit., p. 465.

3 Himes, N. E., 'British birth control clinics: some results and eugenic aspects of their work', *The Eugenics Review*, Oct. 1928, pp. 157–165 at 163.

As regards the wage-earners, Dr. Dunlop's rough rule of one child for each pound of wages may be regarded as very reasonable.'[1]

But for Dr. Drysdale the *idea* underlying family limitation was of primary importance, while, as George Standring pointed out in his short-lived journal, *Birth Control*, 'the advocacy and extension of birth control is a secondary and less important object'.[2] Standring's own view was that 'birth control is a principle so beneficial *in itself* that its general recognition and adoption is desirable in the public interest, without regard to any qualifications whatever'. Since the last War this, largely, has been the attitude of supporters of the birth-control movement.

The movement has therefore changed somewhat, laying more emphasis upon individual liberty and needs, and upon the desirability of spacing births. At the same time it has extended its field of action by creating a system of birth-control advice centres. As early as 1913 the Malthusian League had begun the dissemination of contraceptive information through its pamphlet, *Hygienic Methods of Family Limitation*. In March 1921 Marie Stopes, who had already published *Married Love*,[3] *Wise Parenthood*,[4] and her *Letter to Working Mothers*,[5] started the first birth-control clinic in this country.[6] She also founded the Society for Constructive

[1] *The Malthusian*, 15 Aug. 1915, p. 64. See also the editorial reply to a correspondent, *The New Generation*, Jan. 1931, pp. 3–4: 'During the next fifty years the birth-rate can fall as low as it likes, for anything we care. Eventually, however, there will have to be a stand, as we do not desire to see the human race disappear. We merely desire an optimum population, or as near an approach to it as we can get.'

[2] February, 1919. (This publication was a separate venture, and appears to have seen only two issues—February and September, 1919—the first issue consisting of a single sheet.) Dr. Drysdale argued that the reduction in the birth-rate had in some ways worked harmfully—by masking the struggle for existence, bolstering up inefficiency and weakness, allowing the exaltation of a 'slave morality'. See Drysdale, 'Practice v. theory', *The Malthusian*, 15 Oct. 1918, pp. 73–5.

[3] Stopes, M. C., *Married Love: a New Contribution to the Solution of Sex Difficulties, &c.*, London, 1918.

[4] *Wise Parenthood: a Sequel to 'Married Love', &c.*, London, 1918.

[5] *A Letter to Working Mothers on How to Have Healthy Children and Avoid Weakening Pregnancies*, Leatherhead, 1919. See also her *Early Days of Birth Control*, 3rd ed., London, 1923. *Mother England* (letters to Dr. Stopes), London, 1929; *Contraception (Birth Control): Its Theory, History and Practice, &c.*, London, 3rd ed., 1931. See also the issues of *Birth Control News*, the monthly journal of the Society for Constructive Birth Control, first published in May 1922 in newspaper format. It changed its format in May 1929 and is still published.

[6] See account by Dr. B. Dunlop in *The Malthusian*, 15 April 1921, p. 28.

Birth Control (August 1921),[1] and gained considerable publicity both for herself and for the birth-control movement in general by emphasizing the need for birth control as an element in marital adjustment.[2] By separating birth control from the original bases of neo-Malthusianism, and making its relevance much more personal, Dr. Stopes was undoubtedly responsible for a considerable increase in the interest taken in the question by the ordinary person. In 1921 the Malthusian League was also particularly active. It undertook a six weeks' propaganda campaign among the working classes of South London,[3] and at the end of the year opened the Walworth Clinic,[4] control of which was transferred in 1923 to the Society for the Provision of Birth Control Clinics. In subsequent years the Workers' Birth Control Group, the Birth Control Investigation Committee, and the Birth Control International Information Centre were founded, all of them later amalgamating with the National Birth Control Association, Mrs. Bessie Drysdale initiated and carried out a motor campaign-tour to rouse public opinion in favour of the provision of birth-control advice at Government Welfare Centres,[5] and Marie Stopes began her scheme of Birth Control Caravans.[6] At the end of 1927 the Council of the Malthusian League decided to cease its activities and remain merely as an advisory body, ready to revive activity if any emergency required it.[7] But *The New Generation* continued its activities, and in March 1929 helped to carry out a birth-control 'mission' to the Welsh

[1] Stopes, *Early Days of Birth Control*, p. 31.

[2] Her statement, in *Early Days, &c.*, p. 28, is that 'Constructive Birth Control implies definite *control* in the placing and spacing of children: it is concerned just as much to ensure conception in a woman longing for motherhood as to secure a proper spacing of the children born to a prolific mother or the absolute bar to parenthood on the part of those racially tainted.'

[3] See *The Malthusian*, 15 July 1921, p. 53.

[4] The actual existence of this clinic (the East Street Welfare Centre for Pre-Maternity, Maternity and Child Welfare) is first mentioned in *The Malthusian* of 15 Nov. 1921, p. 94. The clinic should have been opened earlier, but there was some unavoidable delay.

[5] *The New Generation*, July 1925, p. 75.

[6] How-Martyn and Breed, op. cit., p. 15.

[7] *The New Generation*, Dec. 1927, pp. 138–40. In Aug. 1922 it had changed its name to the New Generation League, but the annual meeting on 26 May 1925 voted to return to the old name, which appeared again in *The New Generation* in June 1925.

coal-fields, giving free contraceptives—condoms—to about 150 unemployed applicants and making small charges to others, and distributing copies of various pamphlets.[1]

There has been a steady growth in the number of voluntary birth-control clinics created by various associations, all of which—with the exception of those affiliated to the Society for Constructive Birth Control—are now members of the Family Planning Association, formerly called the National Birth Control Association, founded in 1930 to co-ordinate the birth-control work which was being undertaken in this country. In June 1939 this Association had 65 branches in the United Kingdom, running 66 voluntary birth-control clinics.[2] (Two more clinics at Warrington and Perth were shortly to open.) There were also 5 clinics affiliated to the Society for Constructive Birth Control. In addition, by June 1939, 247 Local Authorities in England and Wales and 6 in Scotland had taken action in one way or another, under the terms of the various Ministry of Health Circulars,[3] to provide facilities for birth-control advice for those married women for whom further pregnancy would be detrimental to health.

We cannot tell, however, how far the modern birth-control movement is reaching the adult population. It is estimated that in 1937 only about 19,000 new patients received instruction at the voluntary and municipal clinics,[4]

[1] *The New Generation*, May 1929, p. 53 and a special pamphlet—*A Masculine Birth Control Commission to South Wales*, London, n.d.—which though reprinted from that issue also contains some additional information.

[2] Information kindly supplied by the Secretary of the Family Planning Association. The change of name, which was voted in May 1939, is indicative of changes in public opinion and in the motives inspiring the birth-control movement. Prominent among the objects of the Association is the advocacy and promotion of Health centres where women may, in addition to advice on scientific contraception, also receive advice on involuntary sterility, minor gynaecological ailments, and difficulties connected with the marriage relationship.

[3] *Memorandum 153/M. C. W.* (March 1931); *Circular 1208* (July 1931); *Circular 1408* (May 1934); *Circular 1622* (May 1937). Information concerning the number of Local Authorities acting under the terms of these circulars was obtained from the Family Planning Association, which keeps up-to-date records of developments in this field.

[4] Jenkins, Mrs. A., *Conscript Parenthood?*, London [1938], p. 27, estimates 14,000, but a memorandum (mimeographed) dated Dec. 1937, submitted to the Inter-Departmental Committee on Abortion by the National Birth Control Association, estimates (p. 3) 16,000 new patients at voluntary clinics in England

but it must be remembered that these women may give some information to their friends and relatives, though since most clinic patients are fitted with a cap, and since the need for individual fitting is impressed upon them, it is unlikely that very much useful information can now be passed on. Other women may be persuaded to attend the clinics, but this would be included in the figure for new patients. In addition there is now an enormous range of publications giving contraceptive information, including many pamphlets given away freely by manufacturers or distributors of contraceptives. To obtain an adequate picture of the impact of all of this we need really to undertake a large sample inquiry among the adult population, similar to that directed by Professor Pearl in the United States.[1] But up to the time of writing there have been no extensive investigations, and very few investigations of any kind. There are some analyses of the contraceptive histories of women before they attended the clinics at which they later received advice.[2] Thus for the Cambridge clinic an investigation reports that of 265 patients for whom the information was available, 76 had never tried any form of contraception.[3] A more recent investigation, concerning the new patients attending the Sheffield voluntary clinic in 1937–8, shows that of the 396 new patients, only 20 had not practised any form of limitation before.[4]

and Wales, and about 3,000 at clinics set up by Local Authorities. Subsequent information (16 June 1939) from the Secretary of the Association suggested that the figure had probably increased to 20,000.

[1] Professor Pearl gives a summary of his results in *The Natural History of Population*, chs. iv and v. (See also same author, 'Contraception and fertility in 2,000 women', *Human Biology*, Sept. 1932; 'Contraception and fertility in 4,945 married women. A second report on a study of family limitation', Ibid., May 1934.) The term 'similar' has been used because although the investigation was both extensive —yielding usable data concerning 25,316 white and 5,633 negro women—and very careful, it related only to women who had already borne at least one child

[2] e.g. Stopes, M. C., *The First Five Thousand*, London, 1925; Himes, N. E., 'British birth control clinics: some results and eugenic aspects of their work', *Eugenics Review*, Oct. 1928, pp. 157–165; Stopes, M. C., *Preliminary Notes on Various Technical Aspects of the Control of Conception*, London, 1930 (analysis of 10,000 cases); Robinson, C. H., *Seventy Birth Control Clinics*, Baltimore, 1930 (includes some English data); Florence, L. S., *Birth Control on Trial*, London, 1930 (experience of Cambridge Women's Welfare Association).

[3] Florence, L. S., op. cit., p. 91. The data relates to the first 300 patients registered at the clinic in 1925–7. Information was not available for all of them.

[4] Sheffield Women's Welfare Clinic, *Fifth Annual Report, 1937–8*, p. 6.

But as regards the methods of limitation, 2 of the patients stated that abstinence was their practice, while 293 stated that *coitus interruptus* was the method employed. The writer is at present undertaking an investigation into the contraceptive histories of women who attended the voluntary birth-control clinics in the United Kingdom for the first time in 1937 and 1938. Up to the present, histories have been obtained for 2,608 women who attended the clinics for the first time in 1937, and 3,260 who attended in 1938. Of the 1937 patients 390 did not state whether or not they have previously used any form of contraception, but of the remainder 214, or 9·6 per cent. who gave the required information, stated that they had never practised any form of deliberate family limitation. Of the 1938 patients, 318 did not give the required information, but of the remainder, 11·7 per cent. (345) stated that they had never deliberately restricted the size of their family. Of the 2,608 women in 1937, those practising contraception before attending the clinics used one or more methods, and the forms show a total of 2,824 cases of contraception. Of these, *coitus interruptus* was used in 1,244 cases—that is, 44·1 per cent.—either as the sole method of contraception, or in conjunction with some other method. As is to be expected it was generally the sole method. For the 1938 patients the comparable figures are 3,583 cases, among which *coitus interruptus* was used either alone or in combination with other methods in 1,495, or 41·7 per cent. of the cases. The importance of *coitus interruptus* was still greater in cases where only one form of contraception was used, amounting to 57·2 per cent. in 1937 and 50 per cent. in 1938. This is a clear indication of the importance of this method, and shows how incorrect an idea of the practice of contraception would be obtained by an inquiry which did not specifically explain to women that withdrawal is in fact a method of contraception.

But these analyses relate to groups of women selected for one or other of two opposite reasons. They may be more fertile than the average married woman—using fertile in the physiological sense in this case—and thus have a greater need to practise contraception. They may therefore contain a higher proportion of women who actually practise or have practised contraception than would be found in the general adult female population. On the other hand, they may be specially selected for ignorance, since if they had known how to practise contraception reasonably effectively they would not have needed clinical advice.[1] Moreover, it is clear that the women who attend birth-control clinics are not those burdened by religious scruples. Investigations of this kind will, therefore, omit devout Catholics and adherents of other religions if they (the adherents) regard the practice of family limitation as immoral.[2]

The one attempt at a fairly representative inquiry made in recent years was that undertaken by the Birth Control Investigation Committee and analysed by Dr. Enid Charles.[3] But even this inquiry is very far from being truly representative, for the questionnaires were sent out by post after a preliminary card had shown that the intended recipient would be willing to give information on the practice of contraception. Consequently, the investigation must have very largely excluded those women who object to birth control for religious or ethical reasons, and it is not surprising to find that among the 432 usable questionnaires, only 12 stated that contraception had *not* been practised. Moreover, even within the selected group further selection is evident. First, the questionnaire could not have been absolutely easy to fill up, so the replies—925 women asked for questionnaires but only 487 returned completed forms, of which only 432 could be used—were probably from the more intelligent proportion of the women to whom the forms were originally sent. Secondly, there was an overwhelming preponderance of middle-class women among those who sent usable replies—over 83 per cent. We are, then, still largely unaware of the extent to which contraception is actually practised in this country.[4] Professor Pearl found that among his sample of

[1] Pearl, R., 'Statistical report on the fourth year's operations of the Bureau for Contraceptive Advice', *Fourth Report of the Bureau for Contraceptive Advice*, Baltimore, 1932, pp. 3–15, found higher actual fertility among the women sent to the clinic. The data for England are too sparse for any comparable analysis.

[2] See Note I*cc*, p. 426.

[3] Charles, E., *The Practice of Birth Control*, London, 1932, pp. 21–5. See also the analysis and commentary by Dr. C. P. Blacker in *International Medical Group for the Investigation of Contraception*, Fifth Issue, London, 1934, pp. 41–51.

[4] See Note I*dd*, p. 426.

25,316 white women in the United States of America, all of whom had given birth to at least one child, 54 per cent. had definitely *not* practised any form of contraception at any time in their lives, and estimates that, allowing for under-representation owing to the way in which the investigation was made, probably not more than 55 to 60 per cent. of the white women exposed to the risk of pregnancy in the general population—of the 15 States dealt with—were practising or had practised some form of contraception.[1] In England, where the population is more compact and urbanized; where organized publicity about or in favour of birth control has been carried on for a longer period; and where there are much fewer first-generation immigrants from eastern European States, it seems probable that a considerably higher proportion of married women practise or have practised some form of contraception. But, as in so many other branches of demography, there are no satisfactory data from which to draw conclusions.

Before undertaking a general discussion of the part played by deliberate family limitation in reducing fertility in England and Wales, attention should also be drawn to induced abortion as a factor of some importance. Exactly how important, no one can possibly tell. In almost all Western countries non-therapeutic abortion[2] is a punishable offence. This being so, inquiries into the frequency of abortion are not likely to yield reliable results. Moreover, if a promise of secrecy is given and accepted, a woman asked to estimate the number of abortions induced during her lifetime may well be unable to remember all of them, especially as they are events which she would not be over-anxious to remember. Consequently, even detailed investigations—such as the inquiry conducted by Professor Pearl—can yield only minimum figures, and there is no way of telling how far the minimum differs from the reality. When investigations

[1] There is some difficulty in obtaining a correct figure for the frequency of *coitus interruptus*, which many women do not realize is a form of birth control. Unless great care is taken in approaching the subject, a woman may well say that neither she nor her husband has ever practised contraception, although further inquiry would show that *coitus interruptus* was regularly used.

[2] The term 'therapeutic' has a fairly wide meaning in some of the Scandinavian countries. See present study, Ch. VII.

are less detailed, the resultant estimates will be still less reliable, and may greatly exaggerate the incidence of abortion[1] or unduly minimize it.[2] In this and in subsequent chapters of the present study many estimates of abortion frequency are given, and they have been chosen to show the considered opinions of persons who are relatively well-informed on the subject. In interpreting their significance it should be emphasized that they are at best estimates, and at worst guesses. But, bearing this qualification in mind, such data may be used as very rough indications of the part played by abortion in restricting the annual supply of births or the size of the family.

The first study to give extensive references to the prevalence of abortion in England was Dr. E. M. Elderton's detailed investigation of the decline of the birth-rate in northern England.[3] The references are not quantitative, but they represent the opinions of local correspondents whose judgements, according to Dr. Elderton, 'were based on considerable medical, economic or charitable experience'. For most areas in the north these correspondents emphasized not only the importance of contraception, but also of abortion. Newspaper advertisements of reputed abortifacients were common, and there were many cases of poisoning due to the use of diachylon.[4] Reports from York showed that the practice of taking drugs to procure abortion was extremely common, while throughout the region the use of crude instruments—including knitting needles—was by no means infrequent. Although, therefore, no attempt was made by Dr. Elderton to estimate the amount of pregnancy wastage

[1] Consider, for example, the statement of Toësca, L., *Les Crimes d'alcôve*, Auxerre, 1911, p. 27: 'Je lis dans un numéro récent du *Journal des Médecins* des chiffres stupéfiants. Il y a, paraît-il, sans exagération, actuellement, en France, deux fois plus d'avortements que de naissances.'

[2] For example, the German sickness Funds show, since 1933, a considerable fall in the ratio of abortions to normally terminated pregnancies. But since there is now compulsory notification of abortions in Germany, it is possible that women who would formerly have gone to the clinics after having had abortions, in order to receive any medical attention which might be desirable, now avoid being attended by doctors as far as possible. If this is so, it would cause a fictitious decline in the abortion rate. See discussion in Ch. V.

[3] Elderton, E. M., *Report on the English Birthrate: Part I, England, North of the Humber* (Eugenics Laboratory Memoirs, xix and xx), London, 1914.

[4] See Note I*ee*, p. 427.

attributed to induced abortions, the general impression given by the report is that abortion was both a well-known and a frequently attempted method of birth prevention in the early part of the twentieth century,[1] and the fear of legal proceedings was not mentioned as a deterrent.[2]

More recently there have been various hospital studies, analysing the reproductive histories of series of women patients and providing data on the extent to which abortion is a factor in pregnancy wastage. Thus, for example, Professor Beckwith Whitehouse analysed the records of 3,009 patients who had attended the Gynaecological Clinic of the Birmingham General Hospital or who had been treated privately.[3] Taking the whole group of patients, with a total of 11,430 admitted pregnancies, 1,972, or 17·25 per cent., of these pregnancies had resulted in abortion. For the private patients 16·1 per cent. of the pregnancies had resulted in abortions. Of the remaining patients, those who had attended the clinic during the period 1909–13 had admitted 17·7 per cent. of their pregnancies resulting in abortions, while those who had attended between 1924 and 1928 admitted only 16·9 per cent. On the other hand, a much lower figure is given by analysis of the histories of 17,931 women whose confinements took place in London County Council general hospitals in 1936. Of a total of 22,559 previous pregnancies, only 1,536, or 6·8 per cent., were recorded as having ended in abortions. But these patients excluded all women who had had abortions but no full-term births or whose last pregnancies had ended in abortions, and may thus underestimate the real frequency. A sample analysis of the histories of 635 of the 3,870 women treated for abortion in the Council's general hospitals in 1937 showed that 20·8 per cent. of their previous pregnancies had ended in

[1] See especially the following pages in Dr. Elderton's report: 38, 43, 50–1, 53, 54, 64, 67, 77, 79–80, 96–7, 98, 110, 116, 124, 126, 135–40, 199–202. There are also copious references to the use of various contraceptive practices. The propagandist campaigns of Charles Bradlaugh and Mrs. Besant seem, in many areas, to have focused attention on the possibilities of family limitation.

[2] See Note I*ff*, p. 427.

[3] Whitehouse, B. (in joint discussion on causes of early abortion and sterility—section of obstetrics and gynaecology and section of comparative medicine), *Proceedings of the Royal Society of Medicine*, vol. 23, 18 Oct. 1929, pp. 241–50, esp. pp. 241 and 248.

abortions.[1] Some additional data, collected by Dr. D. Pindar, of the Jessop Hospital for Women, Sheffield, are given by the Inter-Departmental Committee on Abortion.[2] The histories of 6,444 patients attending the hospital in 1925–9 showed that out of 20,260 pregnancies 3,518, or 17·4 per cent., were recorded as having ended in abortions. But lower figures are given in an analysis, by the Society for the Provision of Birth Control Clinics, of a random sample of 10,000 of the patients attending these clinics. Of 34,959 recorded pregnancies, 3,379, or 9·7 per cent., were stated to have been aborted. Here again, however, there is some question of underestimation, as the patients are never pressed to answer the questions concerning abortion.[3]

There is, then, a range of variation in the abortion frequencies estimated by various authorities and individual workers. In addition, there is the question of how far the abortions recorded are spontaneous or induced. The Society for the Provision of Birth Control Clinics record that 27 per cent. of the stated abortions were admitted to have been criminally induced, but believes that a large proportion of the remainder were also criminal. Dr. R. G. Cooke, Medical Superintendent of the Derby City Hospital, concluded that of the 350 abortion cases admitted to hospital in 1930–7 about 40 per cent. had been induced.[4] Dr. T. N. Parish, investigating 1,000 cases of abortion treated in St. Giles's Hospital, Camberwell, in 1930–4, noted that in 48·5 per cent. of the cases illegal interference was admitted, in 24·6 per cent. the abortions were regarded as spontaneous, while in the remaining 26·9 per cent. causation was unknown, though the high sepsis-rate suggested that some of these cases had been induced.[5] On the other hand, an inquiry by the Joint Council of Midwifery (about 3,000 cases, mostly hospital cases) found that, on the basis of the information supplied by the medical officers co-operating in the investiga-

[1] *Annual Report of the Council, 1937*, vol iii, part i, London, 1938, pp. 18–19, and *Report of Inter-Departmental Committee*, pp. 8–9.

[2] Ibid., p. 8.

[3] Ibid., p. 8.

[4] Cooke, R. G., 'An analysis of 350 cases of abortion', *British Medical Journal*, 14 May 1938, pp. 1045–7.

[5] Parish, T. N., 'A thousand cases of abortion', *Journal of Obstetrics and Gynaecology of the British Empire*, Dec. 1935, pp. 1107–1121.

tion, only 23 per cent. of the abortions could be classed as criminal, while 49 per cent. were stated to be spontaneous, and the remaining 28 per cent. were classed as doubtful, though probably most of them were spontaneous.[1]

The British Medical Association committee which discussed the problem of abortion in its medical aspects stated that 'It is generally reckoned that in this country from 16 to 20 per cent. of all pregnancies end in abortion',[2] and concluded, on the basis of some German material, that abortions were largely induced and not spontaneous.[3] It is doubtful if there is really general agreement on the first point, while it is certain that on the second there is very considerable disagreement. Nevertheless it should be remembered that by the very nature of the subject, the recorded investigations almost certainly underestimate the total frequency of abortion, and it is unlikely that the lower figure given by the committee—16 per cent.—is an exaggeration. The data cited on spontaneous abortion give rather higher proportions than the British Medical Association report, and the discrepancies do not allow an average to be chosen. The present writer therefore assumes, following the Inter-Departmental Committee, that spontaneous abortions are more frequent than induced, and arbitrarily allocates the 16 per cent. total in the proportion of 9 to 7 (56 to 44 per cent.). Using these arbitrary estimates, we should find a very considerable pregnancy wastage. Thus, in England and Wales there were registered, in 1935, 598,756 live births and 25,435 stillbirths, and these would be the product, according to the lower B.M.A. figure, of only about 84 per cent. of the original pregnancies from which they derive. Of the estimated total of 743,100 embryos originally conceived, 67,000 would have ended in spontaneous abortions, and 52,000 in deliberate abortions. If we use the upper B.M.A. figure of 20 per cent., there would be 780,200 embryos from which the 1935 births derived, 88,000 ending in spontaneous and 68,000 in induced abortions.[4] But whether the role played

[1] *Report of the Inter-Departmental Committee*, p. 11. The exact number of cases is not given. On p. 5 it is referred to as 'about 3,000 cases' and on p. 11 as 'rather less than 3,000 cases'. Irish cases are excluded from this estimate.

[2] *Report of Committee on Medical Aspects of Abortion*, London, 1936, p. 5.

[3] See Note I*gg*, p. 428.

[4] See Note I*hh*, p. 428.

by abortion is now more important than formerly, and how much more important, it is impossible to say. Dr. Elderton's material cannot be evaluated quantitatively. Professor Whitehouse's data suggest a decrease in the post-War period. But some additional data cited by the *Interim Report of Departmental Committee on Maternal Mortality and Morbidity*[1] suggest a rise in the proportion of pregnancies ending in abortion since the middle of the nineteenth century. Parry says 'there can be no doubt that the illegal induction of abortion is very considerably on the increase',[2] and a similar opinion was expressed in a Ministry of Health investigation into maternal mortality,[3] and in the *Report of the Inter-Departmental Committee on Abortion*.[4] In view of the tenuous nature of the available material, it would be unjustifiable to draw more definite conclusions.[5]

Summarizing and interpreting the discussion on contraception and abortion, the following points may be made. First, the desire to control reproduction has probably always been present in society, even when it did not imply a serious restriction of births,[6] and at almost all times and among

[1] See Note I*ii*, p. 429. [2] Parry, L. A., *Criminal Abortion*, preface.

[3] *Report of an Investigation into Maternal Mortality* (Ministry of Health), Cmd. 5422, London, 1937, p. 221—'There does not appear to be any reliable means of estimating the incidence of abortion. It is difficult and often impossible to differentiate in clinical practice between an abortion occurring spontaneously and one induced by artificial means. From statements made in the areas visited, however, the impression has been gained that the practice of artificially-induced abortion (*a*) is frequent and appears to be increasing; (*b*) is more prevalent in some districts than in others; (*c*) is not restricted to any one class.'

[4] Pp. 11–16. The Committee does not believe that total abortion frequency (spontaneous and induced) has increased, but considers that the proportion which criminal abortions form to all abortions has increased, accompanied by a decrease in the frequency of spontaneous abortion. The number of cases of criminal abortion known to the police has not been very great. The Committee reports (p. 45) that the numbers of offences known were 98, 98, 78, 55, 73, 116, 141, and 197 in the separate years from 1930 to 1937 inclusive. In the same years the numbers of persons convicted were 44, 36, 35, 33, 33, 54, 50, and 57. (Offences and convictions under sections 58 and 59 of the Offences Against the Person Act, 1861.)

[5] A brief but very well-balanced and useful discussion of the part played by contraception, abortion, and physiological factors in the decline of fertility in England is given by Young, J., 'The part played by contraception and abortion', *Medical Press and Circular*, 28 July 1937, pp. 72–5.

[6] It is found, in the family limitation investigation mentioned on p. 426, n. *dd*, that in some of the pre-War marriages birth control appeared to be used primarily for spacing births, serious family restriction not really being considered in these cases. Circumstances of this kind may account for the fact that a 1920 investigation into

most peoples some knowledge of methods of birth prevention has been available. So far as England is concerned, a birth-control propaganda movement was begun in the early part of the nineteenth century, but did not have any visible effect upon national fertility. From the eighteen-seventies, however, the reborn and much extended propagandist movement was accompanied by a marked decline in fertility. In interpreting this 'coincidence' it should be remembered that the methods of birth control had not greatly improved in the immediate past, and that until 1913 the Malthusian League did not itself issue any publications describing contraceptive techniques. Contraceptive information, of a kind already recommended in the early nineteenth century, was given in a number of books and pamphlets, the sale of which was enormously stimulated by the Bradlaugh-Besant and Truelove trials, and by the propaganda of the Malthusian League. The effect of trials and propaganda was thus to focus public attention on information which had long been available, and to make it evident that many educated and distinguished people believed family limitation to be not merely permissible but, indeed, socially desirable. The leaders of the neo-Malthusian movement may have been shunned by large sections of the English middle class, but other large sections of the public gave them their support. As Mrs. Besant wrote:

'No one save myself will ever know what that trial [the Bradlaugh-Besant trial] cost me in pain: loss of children (though the judge said that my atheism alone justified their removal), loss of friends, social ostracism, with all the agony felt by a woman of pure life at being the butt of the vilest accusations. On the other hand there was the passionate gratitude evidenced by letters from thousands of poor married women —many from the wives of country clergymen and poor curates—thanking and blessing me for shewing them how to escape from the veritable hell in which they had lived.'[1]

the reproductive histories of 634 middle-class married women found no appreciable difference in family size between those restricting births and those denying such a practice. On the other hand some of those who denied deliberate restriction may have practised *coitus interruptus* or abstention. (See Brown, J. W., Greenwood, Major, and Wood, F., 'The fertility of the English middle classes', *Eugenics Review*, Oct. 1920, pp. 158–211, esp. pp. 200–3.)

[1] *Lucifer*, July 1891, p. 397.

And although birth control may not have become a subject for polite drawing-room discussion, the practice of family limitation gradually became accepted as part of the pattern of family and social life.[1] The reports collected by Dr. Elderton testify to the influence of the propaganda in this period upon the population of large parts of northern England, and there is no reason to believe that the situation was very different in the south.

Propaganda by itself might not have been very effective. But it was launched at a time when circumstances increased the likelihood of its reception. First, the 'seventies saw the onset of the 'Great Depression'. The period 1874–9 was probably the worst part of the slump in prices, profits, and employment, and some upward movement occurred after this. But further depression was encountered in the 'eighties, with demonstrations and rioting in London, Manchester, and other parts of the country, and the industrial situation was again disturbed by the Baring crisis in 1890. It was not until after this latter event that prosperity really began to return.[2] Secondly, legislation was seriously changing the economic structure of the family. Factory Acts were limiting the range and conditions of child labour. In the early nineteenth century the fourteen-hour day for children seems to have been fairly common. But from 1833 onwards—the 1833 Act was the first really to be enforced—the number of hours worked was reduced, the minimum age for beginning work raised, and the range of permissible employment for children narrowed. In time, regulations covered the bulk of industry.[3] Proceeding from the other side, the creation of a national system of education had even more appreciable results. The 1870 Act made the provision of elementary education compulsory, and the 1876 Act obliged parents to see that their children received elementary education between the ages of 5 and 14 years, and prohibited the employment

[1] See Note I*jj*, p. 429.

[2] Clapham, J. H., *An Economic History of Modern Britain*, vol. ii, Cambridge, 1932, pp. 453–6, vol. iii, Cambridge, 1938, pp. 6–8; Ensor, R. C. K., *England: 1870–1914*, Oxford, 1936, pp. 100–1, 111–12.

[3] Hutchins, B. L., and Harrison, A., *A History of Factory Legislation*, 3rd ed., London, 1926, *passim*; Woodward, E. L., *The Age of Reform: 1815–1870*, Oxford, 1938, pp. 11–12, 142–9, 589–90.

of children under 10 years of age. The 1880 Act compelled full-time attendance at school until the age of 10, and this minimum was raised to 11 years in 1893, and to 12 in 1899, while the 1900 Act gave school-boards the power to make by-laws raising the age in their regions to 14 years, and the 1918 Act made the minimum school-leaving age 14 years and abolished all exemptions. At the same time the 1902 Act began the creation of a national system of secondary schools.[1] The double process of limitation still continues. The 1920 Act which raised the minimum age for entering industry to 14 years, with higher minimum ages for special occupations, the 1932 Act which prohibited boys and girls under 16 years from being employed in street trading—save in so far as local authorities allow them to be so employed by their parents—and the Shops Act of 1934 are all extensions of the movement initiated by the Factory Acts of the early nineteenth century,[2] while the 1936 Education Act, under which, from 1 September 1939, the general school-leaving age was to be raised to 15 years—subject to certain exemptions[3]—is a continuation of the movement which was first effectively begun in 1870. All this legislation has reduced the extent of parental control over children and made children increasingly an economic burden. On the other side, we should note the social changes which have reduced the

[1] Lowndes, G. A. N., *The Silent Social Revolution*, Oxford, 1937, pp. 29–30, 76; Ward, H., *The Educational System of England and Wales and Its Recent History*, Cambridge, 1935, chs. v, vi, and vii, and pp. 243–4. The relationship between education and the family in England is discussed in detail in a forthcoming study by Dr. G. G. Leybourne.

[2] See Gollan, J., *Youth in British Industry*, London, 1937, ch. i. The movement is still far from complete. Towards the end of 1931 it was found that 79,545 children aged 12 to 14 years were being employed out of school hours in England and Wales and Scotland, in addition to 2,300 children employed in Scotland during the holidays in potato lifting and harvesting. These figures probably considerably underestimate the extent of present-day child employment, since in England and Wales 9 counties and 11 boroughs and urban districts failed to give returns in the Home Office inquiry from which these figures are derived. See Hallsworth, J., *Protective Legislation for Shop and Office Employees*, rev. ed., London, 1935, p. 146.

[3] See Tawney, R. H., *What is Beneficial Employment?* (pamphlet issued by Workers' Educational Association), London, n.d., and *London Regional Advisory Council for Juvenile Employment: Fourth Annual Report: 1938* (Ministry of Labour), London, 1939, pp. 2–4. The raising of the school-leaving age has been postponed on account of the war.

burden of individual provision against the contingencies of sickness, unemployment, and old age—the National Insurance Act of 1911, covering both sickness and unemployment, the various Unemployment Acts from 1920 to 1936, the non-contributory Old Age Pensions Acts of 1908 to 1924, and the Widows', Orphans', and Old Age Contributory Pensions Acts of 1925 and 1929.[1] Nor should we forget the change in the status of women. Part of this change has occurred without legal interference—as in the opening to women of occupations formerly reserved largely for men—but much of the change has been given definite legal expression. Within the latter category are the various Acts relating to married women's property, to mothers' rights of guardianship, to sex equality in the grounds necessary for obtaining a divorce, and so forth[2]—points which can only be referred to very briefly here, since to present a detailed study of the social and economic background would require a separate and very large volume.

It is not suggested that the legal and extra-legal changes described are the basic causes of the decline in fertility. Parents do not generally regard the bringing up of children as an economic enterprise. Women have not, on account of the various changes, turned from home to industry, and, in fact, there has been no significant change since 1871 in the proportion of women engaged in gainful employment, although it is popularly believed that the feminist movement resulted in the greatly increased employment of women.[3] But the changes mentioned have reduced the incentive to parenthood. 'Necessity', as *The Malthusian* put it, 'is the mother of prevention'.[4] Being offered a range of methods for obtaining the advantages of marriage without the increasing disadvantages of a large family, it is not unreasonable to suppose, especially in view of the indirect evidence

[1] See P.E.P. *Report on the British Social Services*, London, 1937, chs. v, vi, and vii; *Public Social Services* (National Council of Social Service), 6th ed., London, 1935, chs. ii, iii, and vi; Pipkin, C. W., *Social Politics and Modern Democracies*, vol. i, New York, 1931, chs. v and ix.

[2] For a general discussion see Goodsell, W., *A History of Marriage and the Family*, rev. ed., New York, 1935, pp. 433–55.

[3] See Note I*kk*, p. 430.

[4] *The Malthusian*, 15 Sept. 1910, p. 73. The dictum is signed 'E. B.', presumably Major-General E. Begbie, a Vice-President of the Malthusian League.

already described, that married couples made use of these methods. The cumulative fall in fertility would support this explanation, for it is reasonable to believe that fundamental changes in social habits do not occur at once. The spreading of what really amounts to a new cultural pattern requires a fairly long period of time, especially when it is initiated in a community which—as was the case in England in the 'seventies—under the influence of state intervention, is gradually becoming literate. Once the pattern has become accepted by an important section of the community, it spreads by example, and because other circumstances conspire to mould the community into the specific form. A decrease in the size of families may cause a change in the type of house building, and this, when carried on, may in turn affect the size of families.[1]

Professor F. A. E. Crew, addressing a meeting of the British Medical Association in 1928, suggested that

> 'it is very doubtful indeed if birth control has affected the population growth-cycle—the crude birth rate. The fall in the birth rate has been too gentle; it has proceeded with evolutionary steadiness, and it has been universal. It would seem, therefore, that the fall must be the expression of some biological factors, and not due directly to some local disturbance which produced repercussions throughout the world. Birth control, like migration, does not put waves into the curve of growth of a population already of a certain absolute size; it merely alters a population by altering the proportions of the different sections.'[2]

The present writer does not agree with this conclusion. So far as England and Wales is concerned, the decline in fertility has not been gentle, for the gross reproduction rate fell by 62 per cent. between 1870–2 and 1937. Moreover the decline became steeper after 1900, since which date the gross reproduction rate has fallen by 49 per cent. Nor does the universal nature of the decline need to be explained in biological terms, since in all Western nations legal, economic, and social changes have increased the disadvantages of

[1] It is likely that the change in tenor of the birth-control movement after the last War increased its acceptability by the public, since it was no longer basically associated with Malthusian economic doctrines which, to many people, were unpalatable.

[2] Crew, F. A. E., 'The falling birth rate. I. The biological aspect', *British Medical Journal*, 15 Sept. 1928, pp. 477–9 at 479.

raising families without, except in a few countries in recent years, providing any counterbalancing material advantages. And in all Western nations there have been birth-control movements, though of very different intensities, and some access to the various means of birth prevention. So far as mechanical causation is concerned, the present writer believes that the decline in fertility since the eighteen-seventies can be explained largely, though probably not completely, in terms of the increased practice of deliberate family limitation. This view is not by any means original, and the object of the preceding discussion has been merely to see how far it can be substantiated by direct and indirect evidence.[1]

Two further questions relating to the decline in fertility have some interest for students of social change. First, how has the decline varied in the different parts of the country? Secondly, how has it affected the reproductivity of the separate social or economic classes? On the first question a considerable amount of information is available, and some of it is summarized in Table 7, which shows that the degree of regionalization in fertility has varied very greatly from census to census. The most clear-cut divisions appear to be shown in 1870–2, when a line drawn north-west across England and Wales from the Kent-Sussex border to the Cardigan-Montgomery boundary would leave most of the high fertility areas to the north, with the exception of the high fertility area of South Wales. Differences are more marked in 1890–2, but regional divisions less definite. The four regions of highest fertility—Durham, Glamorgan-Monmouth, Stafford-Derby, and Essex—have secondary high zones attached to them, while the rest of the country has gross reproduction rates mainly below 2·1. By 1930–2 only two areas of high fertility remain—Monmouth and the Durham-North Riding area. There are secondary high zones along the east coast, and to the north-west and north-east of Monmouth, and a band of relatively high fertility stretching across Cumberland and Northumberland, but the central and southern areas of the country show gross reproduction rates below 1·0. It will be seen that the county with the highest fertility in 1930–2—Durham, with a gross

[1] See Note I*ll*, p. 431.

TABLE 7. *England and Wales—Registration Counties (County Boroughs included) Estimated Gross and Net Reproduction Rates*

	Gross reproduction rates							*Net reproduction rates*
	1850–2	*1860–2*	*1870–2*	*1880–2*	*1890–2*	*1910–12*	*1930–2*	*1930–2*
1. Surrey	1·996	2·018	2·062	1·945	1·526	1·119	0·767	0·697
2. Kent	2·292	2·246	2·304	2·248	1·894	1·258	0·919	0·826
3. Sussex	2·096	2·016	2·142	1·991	1·493	1·006	0·772	0·702
4. Hampshire	2·139	2·166	2·157	2·158	1·742	1·300	0·976	0·864
5. Berkshire	2·260	2·240	2·268	2·307	1·866	1·332	0·916	0·828
6. Middlesex	1·910	1·915	2·103	2·171	1·796	1·286	0·806	0·724
7. Hertfordshire	2·323	2·214	2·223	2·304	1·893	1·143	0·829	0·754
8. Buckinghamshire	2·389	2·456	2·429	2·368	2·130	1·251	0·898	0·804
9. Oxfordshire	2·314	2·338	2·346	2·278	1·941	1·297	0·935	0·845
10. Northamptonshire	2·419	2·433	2·558	2·525	2·238	1·323	0·787	0·702
11. Huntingdonshire	2·517	2·422	2·588	2·191	2·023	1·456	1·089	0·975[1]
12. Bedfordshire	2·410	2·193	2·326	2·184	1·774	1·174	0·863	0·772
13. Cambridgeshire	2·364	2·338	2·447	2·296	2·020	1·487	0·931	0·843
14. Essex	2·262	2·379	2·450	2·537	2·306	1·471	0·917	0·814
15. Suffolk	2·308	2·348	2·408	2·397	2·136	1·447	1·030	0·921
16. Norfolk	2·169	2·178	2·283	2·324	2·056	1·458	1·005	0·895
17. Wiltshire	2·295	2·337	2·361	2·362	2·109	1·424	0·994	0·888
18. Dorsetshire	2·190	2·265	2·222	2·204	1·830	1·249	0·939	0·835
19. Devonshire	2·004	2·097	2·096	2·073	1·691	1·133	0·847	0·753
20. Cornwall	2·335	2·370	2·178	2·059	1·800	1·209	0·875	0·777
21. Somersetshire	2·046	2·166	2·188	2·189	1·893	1·186	0·837	0·755
22. Gloucestershire	1·985	2·048	2·172	2·136	1·837	1·183	0·898	0·795
23. Herefordshire	2·090	2·268	2·238	2·207	1·987	1·363	1·027	0·907[1]
24. Shropshire	2·094	2·346	2·425	2·259	1·990	1·541	1·034	0·917
25. Staffordshire	2·661	2·663	2·853	2·672	2·480	1·807	1·074	0·924
26. Worcestershire	2·214	2·273	2·316	2·233	1·942	1·071	0·971	0·844
27. Warwickshire	2·293	2·325	2·386	2·370	2·153	1·593	0·924	0·809

28. Leicestershire	2·304	2·324	2·485	2·495	2·155	1·399	0·907	0·794
29. Rutlandshire	2·175	2·318	2·247	2·187	1·857	1·433	1·040	0·923[1]
30. Lincolnshire	2·359	2·349	2·399	2·437	2·086	1·567	1·096	0·961
31. Nottinghamshire	2·243	2·340	2·402	2·452	2·203	1·645	1·000	0·857
32. Derbyshire	2·283	2·327	2·540	2·532	2·330	1·553	0·995	0·864
33. Cheshire	2·163	2·244	2·299	2·218	1·987	1·236	0·836	0·733
34. Lancashire	2·281	2·202	2·369	2·286	1·996	1·363	0·898	0·757
35. Yorkshire, West Riding	2·530	2·356	2·469	2·245	2·003	1·450	0·903	0·772
36. Yorkshire, East Riding	2·067	2·290	2·371	2·358	2·181	1·523	1·083	0·920
37. Yorkshire, North Riding	2·315	2·373	2·497	2·514	2·212	1·644	1·137	0·967
38. Durham	2·580	2·731	2·975	2·754	2·566	2·080	1·275	1·047
39. Northumberland	2·268	2·359	2·473	2·393	2·285	1·652	1·031	0·875
40. Cumberland	2·263	2·312	2·383	2·438	2·141	1·513	1·073	0·915
41. Westmorland	2·121	2·328	2·255	2·317	1·896	1·113	0·847	0·750[1]
42. Monmouthshire	2·316	2·501	2·702	2·552	2·533	2·066	1·140	0·959
43. Glamorganshire	2·352	2·564	2·689	2·614	2·565	2·078	1·029	0·868
44. Carmarthenshire	2·355	2·298	2·337	2·321	2·143	1·674	0·916	0·777
45. Pembrokeshire	2·070	2·336	2·262	2·276	1·980	1·513	1·021	0·869[1]
46. Cardiganshire	1·908	1·976	1·862	1·825	1·569	1·211	0·759	0·655[1]
47. Brecknockshire	2·228	2·349	2·387	2·364	2·272	1·699	1·029	0·871[1]
48. Radnorshire	2·307	2·407	2·532	2·477	2·034	1·340	1·028	0·908[1]
49. Montgomeryshire	2·153	2·371	2·392	2·367	1·976	1·486	1·086	0·955[1]
50. Flintshire	2·285	2·279	2·542	2·389	2·248	1·552	1·002	0·876[1]
51. Denbighshire	2·076	2·197	2·435	2·298	2·114	1·552	0·993	0·841
52. Merionethshire	2·029	2·146	2·457	2·285	1·861	1·416	0·964	0·828[1]
53. Carnarvonshire	2·232	2·049	2·115	2·045	1·567	1·248	0·860	0·746
54. Anglesey	1·992	1·847	2·004	1·949	1·624	1·209	1·044	0·887[1]
55. London	1·762	1·918	2·022	2·023	1·774	1·304	0·780	0·680

[1] For these counties deaths were few and varied considerably. A five-year average of deaths was therefore used in constructing life tables. In other cases a three-year average was used.

reproduction rate of about 1·275—was nevertheless well below the lowest rate observed for counties in 1870–2—Cardigan, with a gross reproduction rate of about 1·862. By comparing the gross reproduction rates with the estimated minimum gross reproduction rates necessary, at the different periods, to produce a net reproduction rate of unity (Table 3, p. 13), a rough idea may be obtained of the extent to which adequate replacement was being achieved in these periods, assuming that the life tables for the whole country apply fairly appropriately to the separate regions. For 1930–2 separate life tables have been constructed for each county and used in the computation of estimated net reproduction rates, and the results for this period are therefore more reliable. From this comparison it appears that fertility in all the counties was adequate or more than adequate until 1910–12, for which years fertility was below adequacy in 17 counties.[1] In 1930–2 the rates in Table 7 show that replacement was inadequate for population maintenance in all the counties except Durham.[2] Such an analysis does not, of course, tell us anything about the extent to which women are replacing themselves *within* each area. The reproduction rate measures only the average fertility of women in a given region. If we wish to know—and it is an important question—the numbers of women who are bearing or have borne the numbers of children necessary for their replacement, we must use statistics relating to order of birth and to the total issue in completed families, and such statistics are not available for England and Wales.[3]

Looking more closely at the fall in fertility in the separate counties, we may note a number of points of interest. First,

[1] These counties were: Surrey, Kent, Sussex, Hertford, Bucks., Bedford, Dorset, Devon, Cornwall, Somerset, Gloucester, Worcester, Cheshire, Westmorland, Cardigan, Carnarvon, and Anglesey. Note that the counties referred to are total registration counties, including administrative counties and county boroughs.

[2] A more detailed study, for 1911, 1921, and 1931, is given by Charles, E., and Moshinsky, P., 'Differential fertility in England and Wales during the past two decades', *Political Arithmetic*, pp. 106–60. For Scotland a detailed analysis for 1911 and 1931 is given by Charles, E., 'Differential fertility in Scotland, 1911–31', *Transactions of the Royal Society of Edinburgh*, 1937–8, vol. lix, part ii, pp. 371–83, and 1938–9, vol. lix, part iii, pp. 673–86.

[3] As was mentioned on p. 26, the fertility data in the 1911 census relate only to the live births of current marriages.

in each successive twenty-year period between 1870–2 and 1930–2 the average percentage decline in the counties increased. In 1870–2 to 1890–2, the average percentage decline was 14·6, while it was 29·6 between 1890–2 and 1910–12, and 31·6 between 1910–12 and 1930–2. Secondly, there was a considerable variation, within each period, in the fall in the separate counties, the coefficients of variation being 37·3, 20·5, and 23·2 per cent. respectively in the three periods.[1] But for the whole period 1870–2 to 1930–2, in which the average percentage fall in the counties was 59·3 per cent., the coefficient of variation is only 6·0 per cent., so that in one of the periods the trends of decline shown in previous periods must have been reversed. This is found to be the case in the period 1910–12 to 1930–2. Between 1870–2 and 1890–2 counties which, initially, had the highest gross reproduction rates experienced the smallest percentage falls in fertility, while in the period 1910–12 to 1930–2 the trend was exactly the opposite.[2] Thus, while in the former period the way in which the decline made itself felt intensified the differences in the fertility of the separate counties, in the latter period these differences tended to become smaller, and the coefficient of variation of the county gross reproduction rates is 8·52 per cent. in 1870–2, rising to 12·37 in 1890–2 and to 16·65 in 1910–12, but falling to 11·29 per cent. in 1930–2. It seems, therefore, that regional differentials in fertility are marked only when industrial expansion has not gone far enough to urbanize the whole country. With the creation of a dense network of local communications by means of road transport, the development of national newspapers, and the introduction of the cinema and the radio, a common cultural pattern appears to have been produced and, as a result, a marked diminution in geographical fertility differentials.

[1] The coefficient of variation is $\frac{100 \times \text{standard deviation}}{\text{arithmetic mean}}$.

[2] The correlation between initial fertility (G.R.R.) and percentage fall in the subsequent 20 years yields coefficients of $-0{\cdot}374 \pm 0{\cdot}116$ for 1870–2 to 1890–2 and $+0{\cdot}703 \pm 0{\cdot}068$ for 1910–12 to 1930–2. In the present study correlation coefficients are given with their standard deviations, $\pm(1-r^2)/\sqrt{n}$. Where the number of items in the series is less than 30, the standard error, $\pm 1/\sqrt{(n-1)}$, is a better test of significance, and is given where necessary.

There is, of course, still a differential, and it is associated with a number of measurable factors. Thus we find a significant inverse correlation between the gross reproduction rates and the proportions of unmarried women in the age group 20–44 years, though the correlation has been diminishing since 1890–2.[1] That is, in 1890–2 marriage was generally productive of a fairly large family, but by 1930–2 not only were there fewer children per marriage, but also the likelihood of any children being produced in a marriage had diminished. There is also a close association between low fertility and high employment of women at the successive censuses after but not including 1851, though when the employment percentages are standardized to take into account changes in the age composition of the female population the association appears to decline between 1910–12 and 1930–2.[2] Additional analysis shows that in 1851 marriage and employment were not competing occupations for women, or at least that employment did not generally interfere with marriage. Since that period, however, the employment of women seems to reduce the amount of marriage—that is, in areas where there is a considerable amount of female employment, relatively large proportions of women in the marriageable ages remain unmarried.[3] We find, too, that in both 1870–2 and 1930–2 relatively high fertility is shown in the mining areas and, though to a much smaller extent, in the agricultural areas, while in 1930–2, in counties in which more

[1] The coefficients of correlation between the percentages of women who have never been married and the county gross reproduction rates are: 1870–2, $-0{\cdot}841 \pm 0{\cdot}04$; 1890–2, $-0{\cdot}849 \pm 0{\cdot}038$; 1910–12, $-0{\cdot}724 \pm 0{\cdot}064$; 1930–2, $-0{\cdot}433 \pm 0{\cdot}110$. For 1911 and 1931 higher coefficients are obtained if the counties are split into county boroughs, aggregate urban districts and aggregate rural districts and correlated with marital proportions in the specific age groups of 20–4 and 30–4 years (see Charles and Moshinsky, op. cit., pp. 152–4). But trend between 1911 and 1931 is the same as that mentioned above.

[2] Standardized for the proportion which women aged 20–44 years constitute in the total female population aged 15 years and over. The correlation coefficients (fertility and female employment) are: 1850–2, $-0{\cdot}156 \pm 0{\cdot}149$; 1870–2, $-0{\cdot}422 \pm 0{\cdot}125$; 1910–12, $-0{\cdot}708 \pm 0{\cdot}067$; 1930–2, $-0{\cdot}622 \pm 0{\cdot}083$.

[3] Charles and Moshinsky, op. cit., pp. 154–6, find that low marriage proportions are also associated with above average ratios of females to males. It should be noted that all the estimated rates given by Charles and Moshinksy are calculated on the births of single years—i.e. 1911, 1921, and 1931. The rates given by the present writer are, on the other hand, based on a three-year average of births centring on each census.

than the average proportion of occupied males was engaged in commerce, fertility tended to be particularly low. Probably separate explanations are needed for each of these peculiarities. The high fertility of the mining areas is associated with low female employment, while the moderately high fertility of the agricultural districts may be due to stability of the family pattern in these districts. That is, agricultural families may not be very large, because the question of splitting-up inherited property is a consideration. On the other hand, it is easier to bring up children in rural areas, and they can give some help on the farm or in the vegetable allotment at a relatively early age. Consequently, in periods of rapid industrial expansion, when fertility appears to be generally high, agricultural districts may not exhibit a particularly high fertility as compared with the areas of mining and heavy metal industries. But when there has been a general fall in fertility, those agricultural districts may project as islands of relatively high fertility. The relatively low fertility of commercial areas may be associated with the class composition of the areas—that is, they might contain a more than average proportion of middle-class persons—and with the greater degree of urbanism. It should be noted, however, that the large towns do not necessarily have the lowest fertility. London, for example, is not by any means the least fertile area in England. Charles and Moshinsky found, in their study, that both in 1911 and in 1931 the aggregate of rural districts showed the highest gross reproduction rate, with the aggregate of county boroughs next. The lowest aggregate rate was shown by the urban districts.

The regional analysis summarized[1] in the preceding paragraphs has been based on estimated gross reproduction rates. If legitimate fertility rates—the number of legitimate live births per 1,000 married women aged 15 to 44 years—were used, as in three very interesting and suggestive studies by Mr. W. J. Martin,[2] substantially the same results would

[1] The brief analysis in the three preceding paragraphs is from the present author's study 'Changes in fertility, &c.', already cited, except where otherwise specified.

[2] Martin, W. J., 'Studies in the declining birth-rate, Wales and South England', *Journal of Hygiene*, Aug. 1936, pp. 402–37; 'Studies in the declining birth-rate, the Midlands and London', ibid., April 1937, pp. 188–224; 'Studies in the declining birth-rate, England and Wales: 1. The Northern counties. 2. Summary of

be found. But whatever the particular type of vital index chosen, regional analysis does not—or, at least, has not done so up to the present—throw much light upon the fundamental causes of the decline in fertility in England and Wales. It has been pointed out that there is an association between low fertility and low marriage proportions at various points of time. But we have also seen that over periods of time the association is not significant. All we can say, for example, of the twenty years after 1910–12 is that where marriage increased most, fertility fell least. But in spite of a general increase in marriage during the period, there was a very large decrease in fertility. And for the sixty years between 1870–2 and 1930–2 the changes in the extent of marriage are insignificant compared with the fall in fertility. Similarly, the analysis has shown that at the various points of time, with the exception of 1850–2, low fertility appears to have been associated with high employment of women. Yet over the period 1870–2 to 1930–2 changes in the extent of female employment have also been extremely small, and do not explain the fall in fertility. Nor can we discern specific factors each of which is responsible for the decline in a different part of the country. The decline over the sixty-year period after 1870–2 has been general and similar in extent in the different counties, and could only be explained by factors common to all parts of the country. So far there has been no conclusive analysis along such lines.

Regional variations in fertility form one aspect of the general question of differential fertility. Another aspect to which much attention has been drawn is fertility variations between the different social or economic classes, and there is a vast literature dealing with this subject. Concentrating, in this chapter, only on England and Wales, we may note some of the attempts which have been made to ascertain how far the social classes have different rates of replacement, and whether the differences are growing or tending to disappear under the double influence of birth control and the spread of a common cultural pattern. On the first part of the

results for all areas', ibid., Oct. 1937, pp. 489–511. These three studies cover the whole country and analyse the situation not only by counties but also by groups of registration districts and urban and rural districts within the counties.

question the largest collection of data is that derived from the fertility inquiry undertaken in connexion with the 1911 census.[1] Space is too limited to give the results in any detail, and they have already been considered with great care by Dr. J. W. Innes.[2] We may, however, note that the total number of live born children per 100 families—that is, of children *ever* born in the current marriage to women alive at the time the census was taken—was 249, 311, 350, 356, 399, 308, 423, and 433 for social classes I to VIII. These classes, based upon an occupational analysis,[3] are I, upper and middle class (including the professional class); II, intermediate (including farmers); III to V, skilled, semi-skilled, and unskilled workers respectively; VI, VII, and VIII, textile workers, miners, and agricultural labourers respectively (excluded from the previous classes). Standardizing the rates for age of wife at, and duration of marriage, they become 277, 321, 353, 359, 392, 319, 433, and 399 live children ever born per 100 current marriages in each class for classes I to VIII respectively, showing the part played by marriage in reducing the fertility of textile workers and increasing that of agricultural labourers. This type of fertility inquiry was not repeated at subsequent censuses, but both for 1911 and 1921 an attempt was made to calculate *current* fertility rates for the social classes by using the census data relating to the distribution of children under one year of age, and correcting on the basis of legitimate births registered in the census years. From this material were computed fertility rates—the number of legitimate live births per 1,000 married men under 55 years of age in each social class, and comparisons may be obtained for 1911 and 1921. Using the same social classes as those already mentioned, the rates were 119, 132, 153, 158, 213, 125, 230, and 161 legitimate live births per 1,000 in 1911 for classes I to VIII respectively,[4] while in 1921 the rates were 98, 105, 134, 153, 178,

[1] See *Census of England and Wales, 1911*, vol. xiii; *Fertility of Marriage*, part ii, London 1923, esp. Tables 28, pp. 24–6; and Stevenson, T. H. C., 'The fertility of various social classes in England and Wales from the middle of the nineteenth century to 1911'; and discussion, *J.R.S.S.*, May 1920, pp. 401–44.

[2] Innes, J. W., *Class Fertility Trends in England and Wales, 1876–1934*, Princeton 1938, pp. 37–69.

[3] See Note I*mm*, p. 431.

[4] *Annual Report of the Registrar-General* (for 1912), Tables XV–XVIII, p. xxiii–xxx.

110, 202, and 155 per 1,000.[1] But there is no real comparability here, for allowances for age differences have not been made either for husbands or for wives. So far no similar rates for 1931 have been published.[2]

In addition to the static class comparisons—that is, comparisons relating to a given point of time or to a short period—based upon official data, some mention should also be made of studies undertaken by individuals. One of the earliest is that of Ansell,[3] based upon questionnaires circulated among members of the upper and middle classes in 1871, and providing data relating to the informant, to his brothers and sisters, and to his parents, and therefore covering two generations. Taking only the marriages of bachelors with spinsters, and where both partners in the marriage could be assumed to have survived the child-bearing period, Ansell found an average of 5·28 live-born children per marriage. Analysing the marriages by occupational class, Ansell found averages of 5·39 live-born children per marriage for 'general occupations'—that is, members of the aristocracy, merchants, bankers, manufacturers, and others not included in the subsequent classes—5·25 for clergymen, 5·18 for the legal, and 4·82 for the medical professions.[4] In 1910 E. V. Birchall published a study based upon 4,000 cases of applicants for help from the City of Birmingham Aid Society in 1908–9. Excluding all childless applicants, he appeared to find a positive association between income and size of family. When the wage of the father was 30*s.* per week or more, the average number of children per father was 3·83, while it was only 3·27 when the wage was under 20*s.* per week.[5]

[1] The 1921 rates are from Carr-Saunders, A. M., and Jones, D. C., *A Survey of the Social Structure of England and Wales*, 2nd ed., Oxford, 1937, p. 219, specially supplied by the Registrar-General. The rates for 1921 given in *The Registrar-General's Decennial Supplement: England and Wales: 1921*, part ii, London, 1927, p. xcvi, are not strictly comparable with the 1911 rates for they (the 1921 rates) merge classes VI to VIII with the earlier classes.

[2] In any case the social class allocation of occupations at the 1931 census was rather different from that in 1911 or 1921, so that the 1931 rates, when they are published, will not really be comparable with earlier rates.

[3] Ansell, C., Jun., *On the Rate of Mortality at Early Periods of Life, the Age at Marriage, the Number of Children to a Marriage*, &c., London, 1874.

[4] Ibid., pp. 10 and 50–2.

[5] Birchall, E. V., 'The conditions of distress. An investigation of 4,000 Birmingham cases', *Economic Review*, Jan. 1910, pp. 25–40.

But the results are probably not a record of differential fertility, but simply a demonstration that poverty depends upon the number of children in the family as well as upon the earnings of the head of the family.[1] In more recent years an interesting static analysis was carried out in connexion with the social survey of Merseyside, the data being collected in 1929–30. Taking mothers aged 40 to 49 years, but not allowing for differences in the duration of marriage, there is a steady rise in the average total number of children born per family as the occupational grade of the family falls, the figures ranging from 2·35 children per family in the top three grades to 5·42 in the lowest grade, and a similar, though not so consistent trend is visible for mothers aged 50 years and over.[2] There are also other studies which give some account of fertility differentials at various points of time, but since they are concerned primarily with changes in these differentials over periods of time, they may be mentioned more conveniently in the next paragraph.

For the second part of the question—how far have fertility differentials changed over periods of time—attention should again be drawn to the official data of the 1911 census. Stevenson, in analysing these data, found a very marked increase in the differential during the nineteenth century, attaining a maximum about 1891–6, and then apparently decreasing slightly. Marriages contracted in the period 1851–61 did not appear to show very significant class fertility differences, and Stevenson believed that had it been possible to carry the material twenty years further back, substantial equality between all classes might have been found. The substantial equality is, however, very dubious, for there is nothing to show that the differences found for the earliest marriages were not stable ones. Moreover, the material relating to the earliest period has been criticized on the ground that it relates to persons living exceptionally long lives, and that longevity may be positively correlated with

[1] See, for example, Booker, H. S., 'Parenthood and poverty', *Economica*, Nov. 1937, pp. 448–54, and Tout, H., *The Standard of Living in Bristol*, Bristol, 1938, esp. pp. 37–46.

[2] *The Social Survey of Merseyside*, ed. Jones, D. C., vol. iii, Liverpool and London, 1934, ch. 21, esp. p. 541, and Carr-Saunders, A. M., and Jones, D. C., *A Survey of the Social Structure of England and Wales*, 2nd ed., Oxford, 1937, p. 224.

fertility.[1] Stevenson himself thought that the apparent decrease in the differentials after 1891–6 might be largely a function of the statistical material, since the results for the most recent period would be strongly influenced by marriages of relatively short duration, in which the full differential had not had time to show itself. Bearing in mind all the difficulties of interpretation and valuation of the basic material, one cannot say more than that the differentials increased after the middle of the nineteenth century. The position at the middle itself, and at the end, remains statistically unverifiable, and since the inquiry has not been repeated at subsequent censuses, we have no further census data to give support to the analysis. The 'current fertility' analyses undertaken in connexion with the 1911 and 1921 censuses are too much subject to the warpings of age composition to yield reliable conclusions. We should notice, however, that Stevenson's hypothesis of substantial equality in the first half of the nineteenth century, and his record of insignificant differentials of marriages contracted in the middle of the century, are not supported by Heron's analysis of differential fertility in London.[2] Correlating current legitimate fertility rates with various indices of economic and social status, Heron found a strong negative correlation between fertility and status in the different districts of London in 1851 and a considerable increase in this negative correlation between 1851 and 1901. Subsequent continuations of this study by Lorimer and Osborn,[3] Mitra,[4] and W. J. Martin,[5] do not show any fundamental decrease in the correlation in the twentieth century. It is likely, too, that Heron underestimated the association by using legitimate fertility rates,

[1] See Note I*nn*, p. 432.

[2] Heron, D., *On the Relation of Fertility in Man to Social Status, and on the Changes in this Relation that have taken place during the Last Fifty Years* (Drapers' Company Research Memoirs), London, 1906.

[3] Op. cit., pp. 79–80, giving data for 1921 and 1929.

[4] Mitra, K., 'Fertility and its relation to social conditions', *Journal of Hygiene*, Jan. 1937, pp. 108–123, giving data for 1930–2.

[5] Op. cit., *Journal of Hygiene*, April 1937, pp. 219–23, giving data primarily for 1920–2 but also for 1911–13 and 1930–2. This study is particularly interesting because it measures differential social status by placing the Registrar-General's class divisions for 1921 on a normal scale, and thus obtains a composite index instead of a series of separate indexes.

since illegitimate births would be largely attributable to the poorer classes. This underestimation would apply particularly to 1851, when illegitimacy was higher.[1] Apart from the Heron type of analysis, to which more attention will be paid in the following paragraph, we may also note two studies of the fertility of specific social sections of the community. The first was undertaken by a sub-committee of the Fabian Society,[2] on the basis of the records of two Friendly Societies which gave 'lying-in benefits' for each confinement of the wife of a member. The Hearts of Oak Friendly Society, covering 272,000 adult male members from all parts of the United Kingdom, showed a rise in the number of claims for 'lying-in benefit' between 1866 and 1880, from 217·6 to 247·2 per 1,000 members, but a decline to 116·5 per 1,000 by 1904, and similar results were shown by the smaller Royal Standard Benefit Society. The larger society—and presumably the smaller, too—had, as members, mainly the artisan and skilled mechanic class, together with some small shopkeepers. The second study, by W. C. D. and C. D. Whetham,[3] dealt with more exalted sections of the population. Taking from *Burke's Peerage* the data relating to families who had held their title to nobility for at least two previous generations, and choosing 100 consecutive fertile marriages for each decade from 1830 to 1890, the authors found 7·1 births per fertile couple for 1831–40, 6·1 for 1841–60, 4·36 for 1871–80, and 3·13 for 1881–90. Using *Who's Who* as a source—probably less

[1] Remember, too, that birth registration was incomplete at this period, and probably especially so for illegitimate births. But the 1851 analysis is in any case lowered in validity because it was not until 1911 that births were transferred and imputed back to the place of usual residence. The presence of hospitals, nursing homes, and women renting accommodation in London in order to have the benefit of London doctors during their confinement, would reduce the accuracy of the legitimate birth-rates and perhaps unduly raise those in the areas of relatively high status.

[2] See Note I*oo*, p. 432.

[3] Whetham, W. C. D. and C. D., 'The extinction of the upper classes', *Nineteenth Century*, July 1909, pp. 97–108. The authors concluded that 'This systematic depletion of the best blood of the country is a new phenomenon in the history of England. Nothing like it has been seen in all the thousand years since she became a nation'. See also same authors, *The Family and the Nation*, London, 1909, and Whetham, W. C. D., 'Heredity and destitution', *Eugenics Review*, July 1911, pp. 131–42. Incidentally the Whethams mention that 1909 was the first time in England that income-tax rebates for children were introduced.

reliable than *Burke's Peerage*—marriages contracted before 1870 were found to yield 4·99 children on the average for clergy and 5·2 for lay families, while for marriages contracted after 1870 the averages were 4·2 and 3·08.

In recent years[1] the 'dysgenic' aspect of differential fertility has received much attention, especially since various studies have shown a negative correlation between fertility and measured intelligence.[2] It has thus been asserted that the population is recruited not only from the economically poorer sections of the community, but also that these poorer sections, with their higher fertility, have a lower native intelligence than the wealthier sections. One writer has gone so far as to predict, other things being equal, a fall in the national intelligence of one point of I.Q. for every ten years,[3] which would place most of the population in mental homes in two hundred years' time.[4] How far these results are valid the present writer is unable to judge, though it seems to him that since the maximum correlation found, in large sample inquiries, between fertility and intelligence, is not more than −0·30, and since, too, that even by a conservative estimate, the part played by nurture in affecting

[1] Attention should be drawn to Pearson, K., *The Chances of Death and Other Studies in Evolution*, vol. i, London and New York, 1897, ch. 3, Reproductive Selection, pp. 63–102, and to Elderton, E. M., Barrington, A., Jones, H. G., Lamotte, E. M. M. de G., Laski, H. J., and Pearson, K., *On the Correlation of Fertility with Social Value. A Cooperative Study* (Eugenics Laboratory Memoirs, XVIII), London, 1913. The underlying causes of differential fertility are discussed in Galton, F., *Hereditary Genius*, London, 1869, pp. 131 ff.; Cobb, J. A., 'Human fertility', *Eugenics Review*, Jan. 1913, pp. 379–82; Fisher, R. A., op. cit., ch. xi; Charles, E., *The Twilight of Parenthood*, ch. iv.

[2] See *inter alia*, Sutherland, H. E. G., 'The relationship between I.Q. and size of family', *Journal of Educational Psychology*, 1929, pp. 81–90; Fraser Roberts, J. A., Norman, R. M., and Griffiths, R., 'Studies on a child population. III. Intelligence and family size', *Annals of Eugenics*, 1938, part ii, pp. 178–215; Moshinsky, P., 'The correlation between fertility and intelligence within social classes', *Sociological Review*, Apr. 1939, pp. 144–65.

[3] Cattell, R. B., 'Is national intelligence declining?', *Eugenics Review*, Oct. 1936, pp. 181–203; 'Some further relations between intelligence, fertility and socio-economic factors', *Eugenics Review*, Oct. 1937, pp. 171–9; *The Fight for Our National Intelligence*, London, 1937.

[4] On the other hand, some journalists insist that, in view of current fertility trends, there will be almost no population left in 200 years, while the extent to which the population is, according to advertisements, already disease-ridden, makes the present writer feel that, to adapt a religious 'slogan', thousands now living are really dead.

I.Q. is between 18 and 33 per cent. as compared with 67 to 82 per cent. for nature,[1] there is a considerable range within which the disadvantageous aspects of present fertility and inheritance patterns may be counterbalanced by environmental changes. But whatever the true position may be, it is clear that a considerable amount of importance attaches to trends in differential fertility. Unfortunately, the material described is subject to so many qualifications and internal warpings that it is impossible to deduce from it what precisely has been happening in the last twenty years or so, and whether the differentials visible in the nineteenth century still obtain. Two points in particular should be noted. First, correlation technique by itself merely summarizes a relationship and—quite apart from any causal connexion—the correlation coefficient does not indicate any change in the plane upon which the relationship is taking place. Secondly, legitimate fertility rates, whether current or cumulative, still leave untouched the central problem of differential fertility—whether the social groups exhibit significant differences in their total replacement. Two sets of similar legitimate fertility rates may mean quite different replacement rates, if there are differences in marriage frequency and marriage ages between the groups to which the rates refer, while, for similar reasons, different legitimate fertility rates may hide equivalent total replacement rates. Theoretically it would be best to begin with gross and net reproduction rates. Marital fertility rates and nuptiality tables could then be used to elucidate the causes of any visible differences in total replacement.[2]

To solve the correlation problem Dr. J. W. Innes has recently undertaken a study of differential fertility trends in London,[3] using a compound index of socio-economic status

[1] See Note I*pp*, p. 432.

[2] So far as the present writer is aware, the only studies in England of marriage by social class are: *Forty-Ninth Annual Report of the Registrar-General* (for 1886), p. viii, which gives the average ages at marriage of bachelors and spinsters in occupational groups, 1884–5 (bachelors: miners, 24·06 years; textile hands, 24·38; shoemakers and tailors, 24·92; artisans, 25·35; labourers, 25·56; commercial clerks, 26·25; shopkeepers and shopmen, 26·67; farmers and sons, 29·23; professional and independent class, 31·22. Spinsters, same class orders, 22·46, 23·43, 24·31, 23·70, 23·66, 24·43, 24·22, 26·91, and 26·40 years); 1911 census, vol. xiii, part ii, pp. xiv–xix; and Stevenson, T. H. C., op. cit., p. 426.

[3] Op. cit., pp. 70–126.

—domestic servants, professional occupations, and financial and commercial occupations being covered by the index—and applying not only the correlation technique, but also grouping the districts chosen into a series of classes and obtaining average class legitimate fertility rates—average annual legitimate live births per 1,000 married women aged 15 to 49 years—for 1909–11, 1922–4, 1931–3, and 1934. The correlation coefficients show a steady high level during the period, but the class analyses show a practically complete obliteration of differentials in the top three groups by 1934, with the fourth group not very much higher, and only the fifth—lowest—social class still projecting as an area of markedly higher fertility. Taking the five class divisions, the legitimate fertility rates for 1934, adjusted to the weighted average of wives 15 to 49 years, are 80·85, 81·31, 82·44, 85·51, and 101·75 per 1,000 in descending order of socio-economic status.[1] If only the top four classes are taken, the adjusted rates for 1934 are 79·23, 80·01, 79·95, and 82·80 per 1,000.[2] To attempt to solve the double problem of correlation and the measurement of total replacement,[3] the present writer undertook a brief study, also for London, based upon estimated gross and net reproduction rates.[4] This study, which yielded results substantially similar to those obtained by Dr. Innes, was, however, confined to the districts within London proper, whereas Dr. Innes's study extended to the outer fringe. Agreeing with Dr. Innes that the Metropolitan Boroughs of London cannot be cut off from the outside world, the present writer has therefore reconstructed his study to include those immediately contiguous urban areas for which the requisite basic material is available, and the results are summarized below.[5]

[1] Innes, J. W., op. cit., p. 99, 50 districts.

[2] Ibid., p. 111, 40 districts.

[3] Estimated *male* replacement rates for the main social classes of England and Wales, 1911, are given by Tietze, C., 'The measurement of differential reproduction by paternity rates', *Eugenics Review*, July 1938, pp. 101–7. For a discussion of paternal reproduction rates, see also Kuczynski, R. R., *Fertility and Reproduction*, ch. v.

[4] Glass, D. V., 'Fertility and economic status in London', *Eugenics Review*, July 1938, pp. 117–24.

[5] Only summarized because the writer hopes in the near future to discuss in a separate study the general problems involved in measuring differential fertility.

This study, which clearly derives from Heron's work, is based on the Metropolitan Boroughs of London (28, excluding the City) together with 11 other districts on the outskirts of London, for which the requisite information is available. For each of the 39 areas estimated gross reproduction rates have been computed for various years since 1911. Table 8 shows the rates for 1911–12[1] and 1930–2, the two periods which hold most interest. To construct an index of the economic status of the separate areas four factors have been chosen, for each of which the censuses of 1911 and 1931 provide the necessary data. These factors are (*a*) the number of males aged 14 years and over engaged in professional and subordinate professional occupations per 100 of all occupied males aged 14 years and over; (*b*) the number of males in all occupations per 100 males employed in occupations indicative of areas of low economic status;[2] (*c*) the number of female domestic servants per 100 of the total population excluding domestic servants;[3] and (*d*) the percentage of the total population in private families living less than two in a room. These factors have been arranged so that they all suggest height of economic status rather than the reverse, and since they are economic indices they avoid, to some extent, begging the question of what constitutes 'social class'. Changes in the census groupings of occupations prevent complete comparability over time, but the data are reasonably comparable as between 1911 and 1931. The factors were combined on the lines of an unweighted price index. For each factor the separate proportions for the individual areas were turned into indices by using the corresponding proportion for the whole region—London and the outer

[1] Not for 1910–12 because 1911 was the first year in which births and deaths were imputed back to the usual place of residence. Note that the estimated rates differ somewhat from those given by Charles and Moshinsky, op. cit., pp. 122–3. But the latter use only a single year of births whereas the present writer uses a two-year and a three-year average.

[2] These are: 1911, general shopkeepers and dealers, pawnbrokers, costermongers, hawkers, street sellers, newsboys, vendors (street and undefined), and general labourers; 1931, pawnbrokers and moneylenders, costermongers, hawkers, newspaper sellers, rag, bone, and bottle, &c., sorters, and general and other undefined labourers.

[3] Servants in inns, hotels, and institutions were excluded in 1911, but could not be excluded in 1931 as any expedient adopted for the purpose would introduce an unknown margin of error.

TABLE 8. *County of London and parts of Greater London*

	Estimated G.R.R. 1911–12	Estimated G.R.R. 1930–32	G.R.R. percentage fall 1911–31	Four-factor index of economic status	
				1911	1931
London:					
Battersea	1·511	0·888	41	90	79
Bermondsey	2·097	1·006	52	54	55
Bethnal Green	2·014	0·928	54	51	57
Camberwell	1·456	0·813	44	92	86
Chelsea	0·778*	0·589*	24	173	204
Deptford	1·576	0·920	42	77	68
Finsbury	1·890	1·044	45	61	63
Fulham	1·483	0·817	45	105	99
Greenwich	1·542	0·894	42	85	78
Hackney	1·239	0·749	40	97	95
Hammersmith	1·280	0·852	33	99	91
Hampstead	0·527*	0·434*	18	249	266
Holborn	0·909*	0·437*	52	117	171
Islington	1·351	0·928	31	92	90
Kensington	0·713*	0·605*	15	203	203
Lambeth	1·300	0·822	37	106	101
Lewisham	1·067	0·758	29	135	113
Paddington	0·925*	0·649*	30	176	165
Poplar	1·975	1·073	46	53	51
St. Marylebone	0·758*	0·478*	37	170	218
St. Pancras	1·365	0·770	44	100	108
Shoreditch	2·148	1·076	50	51	53
Southwark	1·847	1·031	44	58	64
Stepney	2·021	1·026	49	53	65
Stoke Newington	1·005	0·721	28	146	140
Wandsworth	1·084	0·650	40	133	128
Westminster	0·576*	0·422*	27	171	232
Woolwich	1·440	0·854	41	74	78
Essex:					
East Ham	1·549	0·831	46	82	77
West Ham	1·927	1·039	46	64	56
Leyton	1·346	0·733	46	107	93
Walthamstow	1·569	0·766	51	91	83
Middlesex:					
Acton	1·282	0·800	38	113	104
Ealing	0·953*	0·729	24	173	137
Hornsey	0·728*	0·591	19	212	196
Tottenham	1·601	0·821	49	90	81
Willesden	1·386	0·841	39	114	102
Surrey:					
Croydon	1·197	0·810	32	114	115
Wimbledon	0·995	0·596*	40	159	161

For notes to table see opposite.

areas—as the base, and the indices were then added and a simple average taken. The results are shown in Table 8, and, although suffering from a number of defects, appear to be fairly reasonable as an indication of the relative economic status of the areas at each census.[1] Correlating fertility and status we obtain a coefficient of $-0{\cdot}932 \pm 0{\cdot}021$ for 1911–12 and $-0{\cdot}922 \pm 0{\cdot}024$ for 1930–2, for the 39 areas, showing very little change in the period.[2] But it is difficult to know whether we can justifiably use the data relating to all the districts. In the first place, some of the districts—such as Holborn and Paddington—contain large transient hotel and boarding-house populations, and the birth statistics of these boroughs may not be a real indication of the fertility of the resident population. Secondly, since gross reproduction rates are computed on the basis of all women in the fertile age groups, they will be depressed considerably for areas with large populations of domestic servants. If these domestic servants are so influenced by their occupation as not to marry or, if they marry, not to have children, then the low reproduction rates will be a genuine index of their fertility. But if domestic service is only a temporary occupation, to be given up on marriage, then the low reproduction rates are a false indication. The present writer therefore decided to exclude certain areas and used as the basis for exclusion the existence of abnormally high proportions of women aged 20 to 44 years who had never been married. The arbitrary division is at the 50 per cent. line—all those areas in which the proportion of unmarried women in the age groups of 20 to 44 years is 50 per cent. or more being excluded. These areas are starred in Table 8, and their exclusion leaves 30 areas in 1911 and 31 in 1931. In order to obtain comparability, three further correlation coefficients are therefore

[1] It also appears to be a fairly sensitive index. See the coefficients of variation of the status index, Table 9.

[2] The coefficient for 1920–2 is $-0{\cdot}906 \pm 0{\cdot}029$ (39 areas).

---

* Indicates areas excluded from the analysis of selected areas.

In 1911 Stoke Newington had just *under* 50 per cent. of the female population aged 20–44 years unmarried, and Ealing had just *over* 50 per cent. of the female population aged 20–44 years unmarried.

In 1931 Wimbledon had just *over* 50 per cent. of the female population aged 20–44 years unmarried.

required: 1911 and 1931 for the districts selected on the basis of 1911 conditions, and 1931 for the districts selected on the basis of 1931 conditions. The first two are $-0{\cdot}940 \pm 0{\cdot}021$ for 1911–12 and $-0{\cdot}884 \pm 0{\cdot}040$ for 1930–2, while the third is $-0{\cdot}864 \pm 0{\cdot}046$ for 1930–2. Thus, using the selected districts, there appears to be a slight fall in the inverse association between fertility and economic status. But it is too small to be accepted as conclusive evidence, especially as the data for the two periods are not completely comparable.[1]

But it has already been suggested that the correlation coefficient is a faulty measure of changes in differential fertility, for it is possible to maintain the same intensity in the relationship between status and fertility while the range covered by fertility falls considerably. The correlation would be perfect if, for every rise of 10 points in status, fertility fell by 25 points, but it would also be perfect if, for a 10-point rise in status, fertility fell by only 5 points. What is important, therefore, is not so much the correlation coefficient, but the range in which fertility is moving in relation to a given change in status. Data on this point are given in Table 9, and show that, while there has been no significant change in the coefficient of variation of the index of economic status—in fact, that the average level and the range of deviations from it have remained fundamentally unaltered—there has, on the other hand, been a very marked fall both in the average gross reproduction rates and in their coefficients of variation.[2] That is, in 1931 differences in economic status appeared to be very similar in magnitude to those in 1911, but fertility

[1] Scatter diagrams showed signs of curvilinearity in the relationship between the two factors, and log./log. correlations seemed most suitable for dealing with this. The coefficients are: (*a*) all districts, 1911, $-0{\cdot}951 \pm 0{\cdot}015$; 1931, $-0{\cdot}936 \pm 0{\cdot}020$: (*b*) selected districts (1911 basis), 1911, $-0{\cdot}962 \pm 0{\cdot}014$; 1931, $-0{\cdot}907 \pm 0{\cdot}032$: (*c*) selected districts (1931 basis), 1931, $-0{\cdot}914 \pm 0{\cdot}030$. The trends exhibited are thus similar to those noted for the ordinary correlations.

[2] In the present writer's earlier study on the same subject, op. cit., *Eugenics Review*, July 1938, pp. 117–24, similar results were found when using estimated net reproduction rates (for selected districts only). For most of the additional areas included in the present study the basic material required for constructing life tables (deaths by age and sex) were not obtainable, so the net reproduction rate section of the study has not been extended. For the 21 selected districts in the earlier study the coefficients of variation of the estimated net reproduction rates fell from 17·4 per cent. in 1911–12 to 12·0 per cent. in 1930–2.

TABLE 9. *Fertility and Status in London*

		Estimated gross reproduction rates				Indices of economic status			
		Mean	*Standard deviation*	*Coefficient* of variation %*	*Index*	*Mean*	*Standard deviation*	*Coefficient* of variation %*	*Index*
All districts (39)	1911	1·344	0·4348	32·35	100	112·6	48·7099	43·26	100
	1931	0·790	0·1777	22·49	70	113·5	55·0160	48·47	112
Selected districts 1911 basis (30) .	1911	1·518	0·3290	21·67	100	91·5	28·5899	31·25	100
	1931	0·862	0·1230	14·27	66	87·8	26·1361	29·77	95
Selected districts 1931 basis (31) .	1931	0·857	0·1236	14·43	..	90·5	30·6035	33·82	..

* The coefficients of variation have been calculated on the basis of a larger number of decimals than are here given for the means and standard deviations.

had attained a much greater uniformity than in 1911, because the areas which, being low in economic status, showed the highest fertility in 1911–12, experienced the largest percentage falls in fertility in the next twenty years.[1] This analysis is not, of course, conclusive. The methods used are crude and the basic data unsatisfactory, and we shall have to wait until more detailed census and registration data make it possible to construct accurate class reproduction rates. But the results of the present makeshift analysis are both suggestive and plausible—in keeping with the view that deliberate family limitation has been spreading downwards in the last twenty years.[2] The decrease in the fertility differentials between counties suggests that a similar movement may have been occurring throughout England and Wales. If this is the case, then the trend of the latter half of the nineteenth century has been reversed, and the incidence of the decline in fertility is now bearing more heavily upon the lower than upon the higher economic groups.

The preceding discussion will have shown that a considerable amount of interest has been taken in the past—and is still taken at the present time—in the differential aspect of the population question. In recent years much attention has also been paid to the purely numerical aspect—that is, to the problem of whether, and if so, at what rate, the total population is going to decline. No one has made a study for England and Wales of the changes in public opinion in this field, and short of a detailed analysis of newspaper and periodical literature for the past hundred years it would be impossible to say with any accuracy if and how attitudes have changed. However, it is not within the province of the present study to produce a survey of such detail, and it will be sufficient to suggest a number of points. First, although there was an active neo-Malthusian movement in England in the late nineteenth century, it is probably true to say that

[1] Correlation between the gross reproduction rates in 1911–12 and the percentage fall by 1930–2 (all districts) yields a coefficient of $+0{\cdot}797 \pm 0{\cdot}058$. Note that in 1930–2 none of the London districts given in Table 8 had net reproduction rates of 1·0 or more. Net reproduction rates for 21 London boroughs are given in the present writer's earlier study of the same topic, and comparison will show that the remaining districts must also have been below unity in 1930–2.

[2] See Note I*qq*, p. 433.

there was still a widespread view that population and prosperity were positively correlated. The fact that many parents might have, regarded from their own point of view, valid reasons for limiting the number of their children would not prevent them from deciding that it was 'good' for the community to have a large and growing population. Issues of *The Malthusian* contain references to newspaper articles expressing disapproval of the continuous decline in the birth-rate.[1] One such article inspired J. M. Robertson to a magnificent burst of invective.[2] It should also be remembered that Socialist doctrine did not agree with the Malthusian theory of the ever-present pressure of population upon the means of subsistence. For Socialists—as distinct from mere members of the Labour Party—the remedy for poverty was not primarily a restriction of births but a change in the basis of society.[3] Eugenists were not concerned with total numbers, but almost exclusively with the rates of replacement of the 'biologically valuable' strata of society.[4] Concern at the rapid growth of population seems to have developed suddenly after the Great War, influenced by the mass of post-War unemployment.[5] This is interesting because, first, the birth-control movement was at that time beginning to sever itself from Malthusianism, and secondly, because it was in the post-War period that the net reproduction rate fell below unity. Yet at the same time the National Birth Rate Commission, in its second report[6]—which, according to Dr. Dunlop, 'diagnosed an earthquake and prescribed a few pills

[1] See, for example, the issues of 1887, Feb., pp. 9–11; 1899, Dec., pp. 93–4; 1901, Aug., pp. 57–60; 1903, Nov., pp. 81–2; 1904, May, pp. 36–7; 1905, Dec., pp. 89–90; 1906, Apr., pp. 28–9; 1908, July, p. 55; 1910, 15 July, pp. 50–1.

[2] See Note I*rr*, p. 433.

[3] Webb, S., op. cit., lamented the decline in the birth-rate. He wrote, p. 17: 'Twenty-five per cent. of our parents, as Professor Karl Pearson keeps warning us, is producing 50 per cent. of the next generation. This can hardly result in anything but national deterioration; or, as an alternative, in this country gradually falling to the Irish and the Jews. Finally, there are signs that even these races are becoming influenced. The ultimate future of these islands may be to the Chinese!'

[4] See Note I*ss*, p. 433.

[5] See the controversy between Sir W. H. Beveridge and J. M. Keynes, *Economic Journal*, Dec. 1923, pp. 447–75 and 476–86, and *Economica*, Feb. 1924, pp. 1–20. See also Dalton, H., 'Two more books on population', *Economica*, Nov. 1923, pp. 224–8.

[6] See Note I*tt*, p. 434.

for it'[1]—lamented the falling birth-rate, while the League of National Life was founded as an association explicitly antagonistic to birth control and in favour of raising the birth-rate.[2] In recent years interest has been stimulated by various estimates showing that, with a continued fall in fertility, or even with its maintenance at the current level, the population of England and Wales would fall very considerably within the next century.[3] Attention was particularly drawn to the estimates of Dr. G. G. Leybourne[4] and Dr. Enid Charles.[5] The former calculated that, with a decline of fertility until 1944, the population of England and Wales would fall to 28·657 millions by 1976. The latter calculated that, assuming a continued decline of fertility until 1985 and of mortality until 1965 (these are the assumptions of Dr. Charles's most publicized estimate), the population of England and Wales would fall to 31·452 millions by 1975, to 17·685 millions by 2000, and to 4·426 millions by 2035.[6] It is not surprising that a good deal of publicity was given to these estimates. Further stimulus was given by the initiation of a comprehensive pro-natalist policy in Germany, and this also drew attention to the policies—already in existence for some

[1] *The Malthusian*, 15 June 1920, p. 44.

[2] It publishes *National Life*, first issued in Feb. 1929, and holds frequent meetings. See also Vaughan, B., *The Menace of the Empty Cradle*, London, 1917 and Marchant, J., *Cradles or Coffins? Our Greatest National Need*, London, 1916, (both in the 'National Life' series. Marchant was Secretary of the National Birth Rate Commission and also wrote *Birth Rate and Empire*, London, 1917). The League of National Life has produced a series of pamphlets dealing with various aspects of contraception and with the population question. See also Newsholme, A., *The Declining Birth-Rate: Its National and International Significance*, London, 1911.

[3] Professor E. Cannan was the first to suggest, on a reasonable basis, a decline of the population of England and Wales. See 'The probability of a cessation of the growth of population in England and Wales during the next century', *Economic Journal*, Dec. 1895, pp. 505–15. Professor A. L. Bowley also published some estimates—see 'Births and population in Great Britain', *Economic Journal*, June 1924, pp. 188–92, and *Estimates of the Working Population of Certain Countries in 1931 and 1941*, Geneva, 1926—and so did Professor Major Greenwood—see 'The growth of population in England and Wales', *Metron*, 1 Sept. 1925, pp. 66–85. But since these estimates were not long-distance projections, showing a marked decline in numbers, comparatively little publicity was given to them.

[4] 'An estimate of the future population of Great Britain', *Sociological Review*, Apr. 1934, pp. 130–8.

[5] 'The effect of present trends in fertility and mortality, &c.', *London and Cambridge Economic Service*, Special Memorandum No. 40, 1935.

[6] A general discussion of the validity and implications of these and other estimates is given in the present study, ch. viii.

years—of France, Belgium, and Italy. In 1937 there were suggestions that a Royal Commission should be set up to investigate the whole problem, and at the same time the parliamentary machine was set in motion to make the most important revision of the system of vital statistics undertaken since the 1836 Act. The Population (Statistics) Act, the provisions of which came into force in July 1938,[1] will make it possible, for the first time in England and Wales, to calculate fully accurate reproduction rates and to analyse in detail current changes in fertility. The passage of the Act is indicative of the heightened interest in population trends. Public opinion has not, however, undergone any crystallization. Population now has 'news value', and there have been many individual suggestions for positive policies, especially for family allowance schemes,[2] but Parliament has not so far shown a great deal of interest. In other countries—France, Belgium, Italy, Germany, Sweden, and Denmark—there are, on the other hand, pro-natalist policies designed to check the falling birth-rate and to encourage an upward movement. The next six chapters of the present study are concerned with such policies, and attempt to outline their main provisions and estimate their success. But before proceeding to a study of the individual countries, it may be useful to include a short discussion of the history of population policies, and this is given in the following chapter.

[1] See Population (Statistics) Act, 1938, 1 & 2 Geo. VI, ch. 12. For debates during the passage of the Act see *Parliamentary Debates*, H. of C., 29 Nov. 1937, vol. 329, cols. 1717–1850; 1 Feb. 1938, vol. 331, cols. 105–41; H. of Lords, 1 March 1938, vol. 107, cols. 959–68. For other recent parliamentary discussions of population problems see *Parliamentary Debates*, H. of C., 10 Feb. 1937, vol. 320, cols. 482–537; 18 June 1937, vol. 325, cols. 774–5 and 795–6; H. of Lords, 21 June 1939, vol. 113, cols. 600–48.

[2] See Note I*uu*, p. 434.

II

INTRODUCTION TO STATE INTERVENTION

GAETANO FILANGIERI, an Italian jurist writing towards the end of the eighteenth century, said:

'Let us turn over the dusty and numberless volumes in which the Chaos of European Legislation is comprised, and we shall find no one government that has not reserved some prerogatives for the fathers of families, that has not granted some privileges and exemptions to those citizens who have given a certain number of children to the State; that has not provided some express laws to increase the number of marriages.'[1]

The aim of the present chapter is to give some idea of the truth of Filangieri's statement—not to show the continuity of population policy, for that would need a separate and very large volume, but to indicate by examples the extent to which governments have in the past been concerned to promote population growth. In that way we shall obtain a basis for comparison with the policies which have been adopted by so many countries since the War.

Leaving aside the pro-natalist clauses in the Babylonian *Code of Hammurabi*[2] and the various attempts made by the Greeks to encourage marriage and the raising of children—accompanied, in this case, by a desire to prevent over-population—let us begin with the legislation of Augustus,[3] the three laws—*Lex Julia de adulteriis coercendis; Lex Julia de maritandis ordinibus; Lex Papia et Poppaea*—probably passed between 18 B.C. and A.D. 9. Apart from the difficulty of knowing what precisely were the clauses of these laws, there is the further question of estimating how far they were intended purely as population measures. It is true that they aimed at raising or restoring the prestige of the family by suppressing behaviour which might lead to family disintegration—that is, by attacking adultery on the part of wives and

[1] *Analysis of the Science of Legislation, from the Italian of the Chevalier Filangieri*, translated by W. Kendall, London [1791, acc. to *B.M. Catalogue*], p. 28.

[2] See Korherr, R., 'Die Bevölkerungspolitik der alten Kulturvölker', *Congrès International de la Population, Paris, 1937*, vol. ii, Paris, 1938, pp. 2–3.

[3] Stangeland, C. E., *Pre-Malthusian Doctrines of Population*, New York, 1904, ch. i; Last, H., 'The social policy of Augustus', *Cambridge Ancient History*, vol. x.

various sexual offences on the part of husbands. At the same time marriage was encouraged by the removal of hindrances and the provision of positive inducements. Thus, in the first category, fathers were prevented from placing unnecessary obstacles in the way of their children's marriages, and clauses in wills were declared invalid if they involved some general restraint on marriage. Within the second category fell the basic assumption that marriage was a duty for men between the ages of 25 and 60 and for women between the ages of 20 and 50. Attached to this assumption were various supporting clauses reducing the ability of unmarried persons to inherit, except from their nearest relatives, and to take part in public life, and widows and widowers were subject to similar disabilities unless they remarried within specified periods. To increase the chances of fertile unions the laws discouraged marriages in which one partner had already passed beyond the reproductive period while the other was still in the fertile age groups. Further, the raising of children—described as a duty in the *Lex Papia et Poppaea*—was encouraged by giving the fathers preferential treatment in the allocation of public office (generally in accordance with the number of children in the family) and relieving them of the restrictions attaching to inheritance. Matrons—probably the mothers of three or more children—were given the right to wear distinctive clothes and ornaments and exempted from the limitations of guardianship and inability to benefit from wills generally imposed upon women.

In the course of time the effectiveness of the laws was markedly reduced by a vast series of exceptions under which the privileges originally designed for the parents of large families were extended to persons who did not fulfil this requirement. That is, there were 'honorary parents' in Rome just as there are 'honorary Aryans' in Germany. But even the original laws were much more severe in appearance than in reality. For example, the term 'nearest relatives' meant blood relations up to the sixth or seventh degree, and was extended, under the *Lex Papia et Poppaea*, to include relatives by marriage. There could not, consequently, have been much interference with normal family inheritance.

Even outside the defined family circle the bars to inheritance were smaller than might be imagined from the general tone of the laws and from Dion Cassius' comments upon the reasons for their introduction. Men who refused to marry were not, for example, fully debarred from benefiting under wills unless they already possessed more than 100,000 sesterces, and childless married couples were allowed to benefit to half the extent to which they would have been entitled if their marriages had not been barren. This latter clause, introduced under the *Lex Papia et Poppaea*, was apparently a recognition that in some marriages sterility might be involuntary. Moreover, the laws seem to have been far more concerned with the biological replacement of a special class of people than to promote the growth of the population as a whole. Thus, although marriages between freeborn and freed persons were recognized, members of the senatorial class—descendants of senators down to the third generation in the male line—were not allowed to marry freed men or freed women, actors or actresses (or their children), while it was generally made illegal for a freeborn citizen to marry any woman whose mode of life had brought her into disrepute. The class bias of the legislation is also clearly shown by the kind of privileges given to the parents of large families and in the disabilities placed upon the unmarried or married but childless. Preferment in public office and the right to inherit property from persons other than near relatives could only have applied to a very small section of the population. Tacitus described the Julian laws as designed to punish celibacy and enrich the exchequer. It is likely that the second motive was not less important than the first. Or, as Ciccotti suggests in an extremely interesting study,[1] the whole system of Augustinian marital legislation had the threefold aim of moral reform, the maintenance of the senatorial class, and the provision of additional revenue for the State at a time when the expenses of government were increasing.

However, subsequent laws, introduced by Nerva and Trajan and extended by their successors, were not speci-

[1] Ciccotti, E., 'Considerazioni sulle leggi matrimoniali di Augusto', *Congrès International de la Population, Paris, 1937*, vol. ii, Paris, 1938, pp. 23–37.

fically concerned with the senatorial class. Thus Trajan provided from the treasury a series of loans to agriculturists and used the interest paid on the loans (apparently at a maximum rate of 5 per cent.) to set up a fund for giving allowances for children. This seems to have been the earliest example of a family allowance fund, and the system was adopted in many parts of Italy and supplemented by private endowments. In the provinces, too, similar funds were created, though in this case they derived entirely from private gifts. Nevertheless, they appear to have become very widespread by the latter half of the second century, for Septimius Severus and Caracalla had to issue special regulations for their administration, and placed them under the permanent supervision of the provincial governors.[1]

Whether the Augustinian laws and the later family allowance funds had any effect upon population trends in the Empire, it is, of course, quite impossible to tell. Different historians have different views on this question, though many of them do not seem to realize that detailed and accurate census and vital statistics are necessary if opinions upon such questions are to be reasonably near the truth. Even to-day, in spite of the regular censuses and the practically complete systems of vital registration, it is extremely difficult to gauge the extent to which present population policies have influenced reproductive trends. For the Roman Empire the data are quite inadequate to allow such analyses to be made. We know only that the Augustinian measures remained in force for a long period, though they were subjected to numerous modifications. In fact, they continued as part of the general system of law until the acceptance of Christianity as the official imperial religion. Under the new religion a different view was taken of celibacy and of population policies in general. It was not that the religion was antagonistic to large families; on the contrary, it viewed them with favour. But it regarded celibacy from a different point of view, and it was less sanguine about the influence of man-made laws. The attitude may be seen very clearly from the account given by

[1] Homo, L., *L'Empire Romain*, Paris, 2nd impression, 1930, pp. 62–3, 336–7. See also Orestano, F., 'L'assistance sociale dans l'Empire romain', *Supplément de la Revue les Assurances Sociales*, Nov.–Dec. 1938, pp. 574–81.

Sozomenus, the ecclesiastical historian, of the new laws introduced by Constantine. Sozomenus wrote:

'There was an ancient Roman law, by which those who were unmarried at the age of twenty-five were not admitted to the same privileges as the married; . . . The object of this ancient Roman law was to increase the population of Rome and the subject people, which had been much reduced in numbers by the civil wars, not a long while before this law. The emperor, perceiving that this enactment militated against the interests of those who continued in a state of celibacy and remained childless for the sake of God, and deeming it absurd to attempt the multiplication of the human species by the care and zeal of man (since nature always receiving increase or decrease according to the fiat from on high), made a law enjoining that the unmarried and childless should have the same advantages as the married. He even bestowed peculiar privileges on those who embraced a life of continence and virginity. . . .'[1]

At the same time, the State had found other means of obtaining revenue. So the laws were chipped away under Honorius and Theodosius, and the remaining clauses were repealed by Justinian.[2]

But although the Augustinian measures were repealed, some memory of their pattern remained. At the next large scale efflorescence of population policy, during the Mercantilist period, the old pattern was again largely adopted, not this time to ensure the maintenance of a senatorial class, but more usually to promote that general growth of population with which the statesmen of the day associated a corresponding growth of manufactures and exports. This view had, of course, been expressed much earlier. In its most typical form it had induced Louis XI to quote Proverbs xiv. 28, 'in multitudine populi, dignitas regis est, et in paucitate plebis, ignominia principis' ('in the multitude of people is the king's honour; but in the want of people is the destruction of the prince'), and to encourage immigration and trade and

[1] *The Ecclesiastical History of Sozomen, Comprising a History of the Church, from A.D. 323 to A.D. 425.* Revised by C. D. Hartranft, in A Select Library of Nicene and Post-Nicene Fathers of the Christian Church, 2nd series, vol. ii, Oxford and New York, 1891, pp. 245–6.

[2] For an analysis of general concepts see Sauvy, A., 'La politique de la population dans l'histoire et la notion moderne de population dirigée', *Congrès des Sciences Historiques, Warsaw, 1933.* M. Sauvy was kind enough to send the present writer a typescript copy of his paper.

lower the taxes levied upon the urban population.[1] But the formulation of definite policies by statesmen was left largely until the seventeenth century. During that century we find a large series of laws specifically designed to discourage celibacy and encourage marriage and the raising of families, to promote immigration and prohibit emigration, except to the colonial possessions of the mother country. As the two main examples we may mention the Spanish Edict of 1623 and the French Edict of 1666. The Spanish Edict was designed by Philip IV primarily to make up for the loss of population in the sixteenth and seventeenth centuries. According to Elster the population of Madrid, which had been about 400,000 at the beginning of the seventeenth century, was only 150,000 by the end of the century, while Seville had in 1662 only about a quarter of the number of inhabitants living there a hundred years before. There seem to be at least four versions of the Act, and the following account is taken from a Spanish compilation. To men who married before the age of eighteen the Edict offered exemption from certain taxes, billeting, and certain official duties for the first four years after marriage, and exemption from royal and local taxes for the first two years. As a counterpart, men who remained unmarried at the age of 25 would not be entitled to any kind of exemption. To encourage the raising of children, parents with six or more male children were offered exemption for life from taxes. To encourage foreigners to settle in Spain, all immigrants who took up agricultural or industrial pursuits were to be exempted from the various taxes, while on the other hand emigration was forbidden. But there is some doubt as to whether these measures were ever really put into practice on any significant scale. However, the law itself still seemed to be in existence at the end of the eighteenth century, for in 1782 an Edict was issued to settle a question of interpretation as regards the way in which the 1623 Edict should be applied in Catalonia. As for results, we have no accurate data; but Joseph Townsend, an Englishman who travelled in Spain at the end of the eighteenth century and produced a three-volume record of his journey, gave an account of the clauses

[1] Schöne, L., *Histoire de la Population Française*, Paris, 1893, p. 106.

of the Edict, and prefaced each clause with the words 'in vain'.[1]

A considerable amount of work seems to have gone to the making of the French Edict of 1666. Colbert himself wanted the Edict to have a twofold result—to encourage the growth of the population and to restrict the numbers of priests and nuns. He made the first draft of the Edict and handed it to two councillors, Auzanet and de Gomont, instructing them to examine and complete it and to see what previous attempts had been made to encourage population growth. The Edict contained four main provisions. Persons liable to taxation and who married before their twentieth year were exempt from all taxes and other public charges until the completion of their twenty-fifth year of age, and those who married in their twenty-first year received similar exemptions up to the completion of their twenty-fourth year. Every father who had ten living legitimate children—those who had died fighting for France to be counted as living—provided that none of them were priests or nuns, was exempted for life from all taxes and public charges, including the billeting of soldiers in his house. The third provision covered the nobility, described as the 'strongest support of the crown, and in whose maintenance lies the main power of the State'. All who had ten living legitimate children[2] were to receive annual pensions of 1,000 livres per year, while those with twelve children were to receive 2,000 livres per year. The fourth provision granted half these annual allowances to persons who, not being members of the nobility, were bourgeois inhabitants of the free cities[3] and who fulfilled the requirements as regards the numbers of living children. They were also exempted from the duty of acting as watchmen or from any other public duties associated with town life. But here, again, the laws broke down in practice. It should have been clear from the outset that members of the nobility would not generally have found an annual grant of 1,000 or 2,000 livres large enough to outweigh the disad-

[1] See Note II*a*, p. 435.

[2] The other conditions being the same as in the second clause.

[3] '. . . les habitants des villes franches, bourgeois non taillables ni nobles . . .', cited in Schöne, op. cit., p. 148.

vantages of large families. In fact, so few of them applied for the pensions that in 1667 a second edict extended the pensions to all subjects without distinction of class. In 1669 similar pensions were also granted to the French population in Canada. Moreover, religious distinctions were made in applying the law. Colbert, who had hoped to encourage marriage, was compelled to approve the prohibition of marriages between Catholics and Protestants, and in writing to the Intendant at Tours, he had to say, 'when you send me the accounts of the nobles who have the requisite number of children, do not omit to tell me if they are Catholics, for His Majesty does not wish to grant the same privilege (*grâce*) to those who profess the so-called reformed religion'. These distinctions were, of course, the early signs of the policy which culminated in the revocation of the Edict of Nantes in 1685. In the granting of the family allowances there was much disagreement as to the precise meaning of the law, and a number of cases in which the grants were given to parents who had fewer than the stipulated number of children. The difficulties might perhaps have been overcome in time, but the opportunity was not available, for the Edict was revoked in 1683, and in the period during which the law was in force it is doubtful if many grants or exemptions were actually given. Certainly neither in theory nor in practice did the law live up to its flowery and ambitious preamble, with its reference to Roman population policies and its expressed aim of encouraging marriage.[1] Nor was Colbert much more successful in his desire to limit the number of ecclesiastics, estimated by a seventeenth-century observer to amount to some 267,000. The most he was able to obtain was the obligation to receive the royal authorization of any religious institution established less than thirty years, or to be established in the future. It was not until 1768 that the State limited the number of monasteries and raised the

[1] See Isambert, Decrusy, Taillandier, *Recueil Général des Anciennes Lois Françaises, Depuis l'An 420, Jusqu'à la Révolution de 1789*, vol. xviii (Aug. 1661–31 Dec. 1671), Paris, 1829, pp. 90–3. The preamble begins: 'Bien que les mariages soient les sources fécondes d'où dérivent la force et la grandeur des états, et que les lois saintes et profanes aient également concouru pour en honorer la fertilité et la favoriser de leurs grâces; néanmoins nous avons trouvé que par la licence des temps, ces priviléges étoient anéantis, et la dignité des mariages déprimée.'

age for taking the final vows of celibacy to 25 years for men and 18 years for women.[1] On the other hand Colbert succeeded in tightening the laws against emigration. From 1669 onwards the penalties for emigration—except to the colonies—were made increasingly severe, until finally the death penalty was prescribed for persons who furthered this emigration, while informers were offered half the property of those persons who attempted to leave the country and against whom they laid information.[2] These laws, coupled with the revocation of the Edict of Nantes, created a situation somewhat similar to the present position in Germany. But large numbers of believers in the 'reformed religion' managed to escape—many contemporary writers estimated the emigrants at between 400,000 and 500,000, and some at as high a figure as two millions[3]—and since other countries also had mercantilist policies, the emigrants received a warmer welcome than do most modern refugees. In some countries the beginnings of religious toleration may almost be dated from the time when, in order to attract these foreigners, special laws were passed to give Protestants the same rights as normal Catholic citizens. Thus in Austria there was the famous Patent of Tolerance of 1781, which gave non-Catholic immigrants the right to buy houses and land, to become citizens and master-craftsmen, to be given academic degrees, and to be employed in the civil service. In most countries the immigrants were at least helped to settle and take up occupations by being granted exemption from taxation for varying lengths of time, or free building

[1] See Mathorez, J., *Les Étrangers en France sous l'Ancien Régime*, vol. i, Paris, 1919, pp. 46–8.

[2] See Schöne, op. cit., pp. 142 et seq.; Levasseur, E., *La Population française*, Paris, 1889–92, vol. iii, ch. v; Bertillon, J., *La Dépopulation de la France*, Paris, 1911, pp. 259–61; Roscher, W., *Principles of Political Economy*, New York, 1878, vol. ii, pp. 347–54; Hecht, G. H., *Colbert's politische und volkswirtschaftliche Grundanschauungen*, Freiburg i. B., Leipzig and Tübingen, 1898, pp. 37–42.

[3] The Abbé Pierre Jaubert, the reputed author of *Des Causes de la Dépopulation et des Moyens d'Y Remédier*, London and Paris, 1767, says, p. 59, of the 'fameuse émigration que causa en France la révocation de l'Édit de Nantes', 'Combien de familles ne passèrent pas chez l'étranger! quelles richesses! quels arts! quelle population n'y ont elles pas apporté! quel contraste de la solitude de plusieurs de nos villes & de l'abandon de nos villages, avec celles qu'ils ont repeuplées chez nos voisins, ou dont ils ont étendu le territoire . . .', and on p. 60, 'Depuis que ce terrible Édit a été donné, ses suites ont été plus funestes à la France que ne le fut son exécution.'

materials or sums of money, free transport or a legally obligatory warm welcome from the local population. It should of course be noted that any measure which resulted in emigration ran counter to Colbert's policy. For him every person who left France for religious reasons was one asset less in the national balance sheet.

Attention has been concentrated on France and Spain because in those two countries the population policies were most explicitly enunciated. But many other countries had measures designed for the same purposes. Thus in some countries certain public offices were reserved for married men, and the entry to certain trades was allowed to bachelors only if special permission had been given, and upon payment of special charges. There were examples of this kind in England, during the reign of Elizabeth. In a number of German States the property of unmarried persons who died without leaving surviving parents, brothers, or unmarried sisters, was seized by the Treasury. Such laws continued in some cases practically to the end of the eighteenth century. The Empress Maria Theresa in 1767 issued an edict allowing soldiers to marry, and in the following year attempted to encourage their marriage by granting 3 *kreutzers* a day to privates, corporals, and sergeants for each legitimate child. And Frederick the Great had the same motive when, in 1747, he reduced the prescribed period of mourning and allowed widows to remarry nine months after the death of their husbands, and widowers three months after the death of their wives.[1] Within marriage, fertility was encouraged by laws similar to those of France and Spain. Thus edicts along the same lines were issued in Savoy in 1648 and in Lorraine and Barrois in 1729. Moral codes were relaxed in order not to discourage too strongly the bearing of illegitimate children. The aim here was not to encourage illegitimacy, but, since an illegitimate child was regarded as better than no child at all, to reduce the disgrace attaching to

[1] Frederick William I was also concerned with such policies. See his marginal comment on an inquiry sent to him in 1721—'in alle Provinzien, das ich will lieber ein Premium setzen, das sie heirahten als sie weill sie heirahten geldt gehben lassen.' Stadelmann, R., *Friedrich Wilhelm I. in seiner Thätigkeit für die Landescultur Preussens*, Leipzig, 1878, pp. 243–4. [*Publicationen aus den K. Preussischen Staatsarchiven, Zweiter Band.*]

unmarried mothers and their children. This was particularly the case in Germany after the Thirty Years War, in eighteenth-century Iceland, and in Prussia under Frederick the Great. Foundling institutes were established to take care of illegitimate children and orphans. Similar reasons prompted the regulation, issued in Lorraine in 1711, compelling unmarried women to notify their pregnancies. This, it was hoped, would reduce the probability of abortion and infanticide. Most countries, including England and Wales, also attempted to encourage immigration and suppress emigration. In the same year as the revocation of the Edict of Nantes a Patent issued in Prussia invited the French refugees to settle there, and Patents in 1688, 1721, 1726, and 1736 extended the invitation to refugees from the Palatinate, Salzburg, and Bohemia. Frederick the Great is reported to have spent some five million *talers* in establishing colonists, though some of them seem to have proved a bad investment. Peter the Great and Catherine adopted similar means of attracting emigrants to Russia, and this policy was still being continued by Alexander in 1803. As a counterpart there were, in Prussia and Austria for example, severe penalties—death in Prussia under the 1721 law—for any one helping attempts to emigrate.[1]

On the other side of the world, in Japan, there were also measures for encouraging population growth. It is often assumed that in China and Japan large families are, for religious reasons, traditional. But in Japan, at least, this was not true of the Tokugawa period, during which the population appears to have been practically stationary. Abortion and infanticide were commonly practised, and a report to the authorities of the Sendai clan, in 1754, said that whereas 'up to fifty or sixty years ago a couple on the farm used to bring up five or six or even seven or eight children . . . it has become the custom in recent years among the farmers for each married couple to rear no more than one or two children. As soon as a baby is born, its parents put it to

[1] For information on population policies in Italy see Casanova, E., 'Dodicesima prole', *Genus*, May 1938, pp. 169–86. A detailed study of the population policy and measures of Maria Theresa is given by Schünemann, K., *Österreichs Bevölkerungspolitik unter Maria Theresia*, vol. i, Berlin, n.d. (but not earlier than 1935).

death. . . . Even rich families follow this evil custom, and deliberately restrict the number of their children.' Among the Samurai, friends were not congratulated upon the birth of a child until it was clear that the child was going to be allowed to live. Attempts were made to combat these trends by prohibiting abortion and infanticide, subsidizing poor families, and making moral appeals. The attempts seem to have been intensified after the Meiji Reformation of 1867–8. Thus the 1873 Code prescribed a hundred days' imprisonment for abortion and ranked infanticide with murder, offering rewards for information which would lead to the capture of offenders. Contributions, voluntary and obligatory, were obtained from relatively wealthy people, and used for establishing a kind of family allowance fund for subsidizing the birth of children, and a number of societies was set up with the object of arousing interest in, and providing funds for, bringing up children.[1]

Speculations about the effects of these population measures are not very valuable. For most of the countries concerned we have no data on fertility changes and very poor information about changes in total populations. In those countries in which there appears to have been an increase in population during the period explanations other than in terms of pro-natalist policies seem appropriate. It should be remembered, moreover, that the policies were seldom completely consistent. That is, while attempting to prohibit emigration they often introduced measures which practically compelled groups of people to leave the country. This applies to France, to the Palatinate, and to Bohemia. On the other hand, there were half-hearted policies of expulsion of certain classes of people. Thus, for example, the Jews in France were threatened with expulsion but apparently managed to remain by paying 200,000 livres as 'blood-money'. A similar situation existed in Lorraine, though in this case the date of expulsion was continually postponed. Further, some aspects of the marriage laws were inconsistent with a desire to promote general population growth. Thus in France,

[1] See Ishii, R., *Population Pressure and Economic Life in Japan*, London, 1937, pp. 14–16 and 31–7; Skene Smith, N., (ed.) *Tokugawa Japan*, vol. i, London, 1937, pp. 27–31.

shortly after the death of Colbert, common soldiers and sergeants were discouraged from marrying by a regulation which deprived them of their seniority if they married. In Württemberg, in 1633, the authorities were enjoined to discourage people from making 'untimely' marriages, and in 1712 the consent of the authorities to a marriage was made conditional upon evidence of a religious education and the ability to support a family.[1]

Lack of space forbids any further account, in the present chapter, of historical population policies, though they are referred to again in Chapter IV. But the examples given certainly lend support to Filangieri's thesis, and it would seem that at most periods there have been governments concerned not merely to maintain but also to increase the populations of their territories. This should be borne in mind when weighing up the 'novelty' of the population policies discussed in subsequent chapters. As to the influence of early policies, it has been pointed out that the data are too scanty and undependable to warrant any conclusion. Filangieri himself was very doubtful, and wrote: 'I do not deny that the means hitherto adopted by Legislators for the encouragement of population, have had some degree of utility, but they can be considered only as so many slight impulses which might perhaps have assisted the motion of the machine, had no obstacles opposed; but the resistance of the one infinitely exceeds the influence of the other.'[2] That is a philosophic judgement. Unfortunately we do not possess the means of deciding whether or not it is objectively correct.

[1] See Roscher, op. cit., pp. 356–61.
[2] Op. cit., p. 29.

III

FRANCE AND BELGIUM

I. FAMILY ALLOWANCES

WE have seen that policies to encourage population growth are to be found at almost every stage of history. What distinguishes present policies from those of the past is not so much the kind of measure adopted as the intensity with which it is applied. From this point of view France and Belgium are particularly interesting because, in these two countries, at least one measure—family allowances—is applied to almost every section of the population. It is worth while, therefore, to consider family allowances in some detail—the more so because other countries have since followed the example set by France and Belgium, and because in recent months the question of family allowances has been seriously discussed by statesmen in many other countries.

By the term 'family allowance', as used in this book,[1] we mean a cash grant, quite separate from and in addition to a man's wage or salary, given to help cover the costs of raising a family. The grant, therefore, generally varies in amount with the number of children, and is given only while the children are dependent—that is, until they begin to earn their own living. This kind of assistance may be aimed directly at stimulating the birth-rate, by making it easier to bring up families. But in France and Belgium family allowances were not originally given with the intention of promoting population growth. Consequently they may not, even now, be in a form or of an amount best suited to such a purpose. Nevertheless, they may have some effect upon fertility even if not intended primarily for that purpose, and an examination of existing systems of allowances may suggest ways of modifying them in order to produce a more direct influence upon fertility, if that is desired.

In France both the theory and practice of family allow-

[1] Family allowances may also of course be given in kind and, as will be seen later, there are cases of such allowances. But the term 'family allowance' is used in this book to indicate money grants, and allowances in kind are referred to separately.

ances are much older than is commonly realized.[1] Some early instances were mentioned in the previous chapter, but leaving aside such cases, the idea was introduced again in 1840 by an industrialist, Harmel,[2] and in 1860 by the Ministre de la Marine, who granted 10 centimes per day and per child to the lower ratings in the French Navy who had served more than five years. But these schemes were not followed elsewhere until more than twenty years later. Then, in 1884, family allowances were introduced by the firm of Klein at Vizille, by Léon Harmel (son of the previous Harmel) in his factory at Val-des-Bois in 1891, and by a group of industrialists at Lille, Roubaix, and Tourcoing, also in 1891. It should be remembered that in 1891 Pope Leo XIII issued his Encyclical, *De Rerum Novarum*, which lent support to the idea of a family wage. This could not be expected to have a very pronounced influence at a time when the struggle between Church and State was still at its height in France—though it appears, along with the work of Le Play, to have influenced Léon Harmel—but it subsequently helped to reinforce the other currents of social feeling which were becoming noticeable towards the end of the nineteenth and the beginning of the twentieth centuries. By 1914 some thirty or more additional firms had adopted some form of family allowances,[3] in addition to the grants given to certain grades of persons employed by the Treasury, the Post Office, and the Colonial Office, as well as to school-teachers and to officers (lower ranks) and men in the army.[4]

[1] Family allowances are discussed historically by Vibart, H. H. R., *Family Allowances in Practice*, London, 1926, ch. iv; Douglas, P. H., *Wages and the Family*, Chicago, 1925, chs. v and vii; Bonvoisin, G., and Maignan, G., *Allocations Familiales et Caisses de Compensation*, Paris, 1930, pp. 1–20; Pinte, J., *Les Allocations Familiales*, Paris, 1935, Part II, chs. i, ii, and iii; Helleu, Y., *Les Caisses de Compensation d'Allocations Familiales*, Paris, 1937, ch. i. References to specific aspects and to other countries than France are given subsequently.

[2] Pinte, op. cit., p. 70, says that this early form of allowance was really in the nature of a 'liberality' given only to allow the employer to know his workers more intimately and to be able to help them in periods of difficulties. The family fund introduced by Léon Harmel is stated by French authorities to have begun in 1891, while Vibart gives the date as 1854. The latter date probably refers to Harmel's father.

[3] Twenty-six between 1900 and 1910, and 14 between 1910 and 1916 are the figures given by Pinte, op. cit., p. 72.

[4] Monsieur F. Boverat, in a letter (dated 6 April 1939) to the present writer, says that the first important decision in France was in 1913, giving family allowances to commissioned and non-commissioned officers. This decision passed by Parlia-

But the beginnings of the real movement took place during the Great War, and from the point of view of modern developments the first important scheme was that introduced by E. Romanet, manager of the firm of Joya, engineers, at Grenoble. The actual introduction occurred in November 1916, at a time when rising prices were making it increasingly difficult for workers with dependent children to maintain their standard of life. Civil servants were, of course, also feeling the effects of the rise in prices, and the existence of isolated State allowances made for a great deal of inequality. In 1917, therefore, an Act was passed to grant a new set of allowances to cover the rise in the cost of living—120 francs per year for bachelors, 180 francs for married men, and 100 francs for each child legally dependent upon the employee concerned, and either under sixteen years of age or, through some infirmity, incapable of working. This Act, however, applied only to those civil servants whose incomes were not more than 3,600 francs per year, if they had two or fewer children, and not more than 4,500 francs per year if they had more than two children. In the following year further Acts extended the principle of allowances to other branches of governmental employment, while the Act of 14 November 1918 repealed all income limits and generalized the application of allowances to all servants in the employment of the Central Government. The Acts of 1917 and 1918 also influenced the sphere of local administration, and under this influence comparable schemes were set up for local government employees. Similar progress was made with allowance schemes for railway workers and miners. The railways had been in the field fairly early, allowances being introduced in 1890 by the Nord and Paris-Orléans companies, by the Grande Ceinture in 1891, and by the P.L.M. in 1892. They were generalized by an agreement in 1916, and the system was codified—with the upper income limit removed—under the Act of 1918. Allowances to miners were generalized by an agreement in 1917—apparently inspired by the Minister of Munitions—though no unity was imposed as regards rates or conditions of payment.

ment in 1913 at the instance of the Alliance Nationale, subsequently led the Government to extend family allowances to all civil servants.

In industry the Romanet scheme spread to other engineering and metal firms in the Grenoble district, but, as it did, there was the danger that some employers might avoid the new charge on industry by refusing to take on married men with families. To meet this difficulty equalization funds were created. Two were set up at practically the same time —at Lorient in April 1918, grouping the main firms in the district, and at Grenoble in May 1918, covering the engineering firms of the Isère region. The idea underlying the fund was quite simple. Instead of giving allowances directly to his workers and thus having to bear a heavier charge if the bulk of his workers were married men with children, the employer made a regular contribution to the equalization fund, which distributed the allowance itself. The employer's contribution varied directly with the total number of workers employed,[1] and not simply with the number of married workers, and there was thus no incentive to discriminate against married men. It is this equalization fund principle which has been adopted in practically all subsequent developments in France and Belgium, and it is safe to say that without this principle the spread of family allowances would have been greatly hindered. Later growth saw the formation of two kinds of funds—the professional, embracing workers in the same occupation, and in some cases covering the whole country, and the regional or multiprofessional, covering many kinds of occupations in a specified region. The second type is probably the more satisfactory, for it prevents industries which employ a large proportion of juvenile or unmarried female labour from reaping a costs advantage over those industries in which married men with dependent children constitute the bulk of the labour supply. At the same time multiprofessional funds could be more easily attuned to the circumstances of a particular locality, and would experience less difficulty in adjusting their rates of

[1] Broadly speaking the equalization fund estimated the annual cost of family allowances and divided this cost by the total number of employees in the firms embraced by the fund. This cost per head was then used as the basis for calculating the charges to be borne by the separate employers. The equalization funds sometimes used the total number of days worked as a basis and, in the case of agriculture, the area under cultivation. In addition the employers also had to bear the cost of administering the scheme. No contributions were made by the employees.

allowance to regional differences in the cost of living. It is therefore natural that the development of the family allowance system should have been to a large extent in the direction of regional funds.

We must not forget that up to 1932 the family allowance system in French industry and commerce was almost exclusively voluntary, supported by contributions obtained only from employers. That so extensive a development[1] should take place is, consequently, rather remarkable, and it is worth while looking at the main factors which helped this growth. In the first place, there were the demands made by the workers themselves. For most of the period prices were rising and conditions were thus made particularly difficult for married men with dependent children. The workers saw in family allowances a means of raising their standard of life, and supported them in spite of initial trade union antagonism. Secondly, rising prices increased the employers' willingness to extend the system, since the additional charge was not great. Also, as Vibart points out, where cost of living bonuses were given, 'there was no doubt a desire on the part of employers to economize: the [cost of living] allowances appeared to be increasing with extreme rapidity and employers naturally desired to limit their commitments and to give the big advances demanded only to those whom they considered specially needed them'.[2] It would be untrue to say that rising prices were the only cause influencing employers, since, in the period from the end of 1920 to the end of 1922, when prices fell, the number of workers covered by industrial and commercial schemes increased by about 60 per cent. But in the main the development of the system took place under a rising price level, and by the time prices began to fall again, in 1930 to 1932, the State intervened and made the institution compulsory. Among the other factors which may have influenced employers is one given by the Director of the fund for the Stéphanoise Region,[3] who says that the payment of allowances has prevented trade unions from making use of family men for helping in their 'revolutionary' aims, and that the

[1] See Note III*a*, p. 435.
[2] Vibart, op. cit., p. 6.
[3] In a letter to the present writer, 4 Mar. 1935.

majority of family men among the workers have remained outside the 'class-struggle'. If this is true, the employers had very strong grounds for extending the system. There was also, of course, the point that allowances probably tended to stabilize the labour supply and reduce the rapidity of labour-turnover. So far as raising the birth-rate is concerned, it is difficult to say how significant this motive was originally. Bonvoisin and Maignan deny that the employers had any population motive, and say that the small size of the early allowances should be enough to convince any one that it would have been impossible to expect a result sufficient to counteract the desire to restrict the number of births.[1] Initially, therefore, it is probable that the family allowance movement was connected almost exclusively with the problem of rising prices. But once the movement had begun it received strong support from groups of public opinion with pro-natalist views—such as the Alliance Nationale, the various Congresses held to discuss problems of fertility, the Ligue pour la Vie, and so forth.[2] A statement made by a committee appointed by one of the chief equalization funds shows that by 1919 some consideration was being given to the population aspect of allowances,[3] while war-time losses of man-power and the post-war labour shortage must have helped to strengthen this emphasis. By 1924 the Central Committee[4] of the family allowance system decided to include in the proceedings of the annual congress on family allowances a survey of the effects of allowances on the birth and infant death-rates, and since that time the population motive has assumed a rapidly growing importance. In particular it should be noted that the allowances are so graded that, up

[1] Bonvoisin and Maignan, op. cit., pp. 172–3.

[2] Family allowances were supported, for this reason, by the Congrès de la Natalité as early as 1919. (Pinte, op. cit., p. 92.) For more detailed references to these bodies, see next chapter.

[3] The 1919 Report of the *Commission d'étude du règlement de la Caisse de la Région Parisienne*. See Bonvoisin and Maignan, op. cit., p. 174.

[4] Founded in 1921, primarily to co-ordinate the work of the individual funds. It has also undertaken a great deal of propaganda in favour of family allowances, produces a number of periodicals, and organizes the national conferences which have been held each year from 1921 onwards. There was also a survey, contained in the *Compte Rendu, IIIe Congrès National des Allocations Familiales, 1923*, of demographic data for 1920–3, undertaken by Dr. Peret. (See Douglas, op. cit., pp. 93–4.)

to a point, each successive child receives a larger grant. This clearly puts a premium on large families.

Confronted with a rapidly growing movement, the State could scarcely avoid taking an active interest in the system. From 1917 onwards governmental action was gradually extended in scope to cover public utility companies and other public bodies. The law of 1922 and the decrees of 1923 obliged the central government, and authorized the Départements, Communes, and public bodies to insert a family allowance clause in the public works contracts they gave to private firms, so that any firm undertaking public works for these bodies might be compelled to grant family allowances to their employees.[1] In December 1928 the government introduced a Bill for applying the family allowance system to all public works contracts. But at the same time there was considerable pressure for the generalization of the system—that is, for applying it to all occupations and throughout France. As early as 1920 Monsieur Bokanowski and a number of his colleagues had urged Parliament to pass an Act for this purpose. But although an investigation had been made by the Commission d'Assurance et de Prévoyance Sociales, the government was not anxious to enter a field of which it had little real knowledge, and in which a good deal was being done by private initiative. In 1929, however, two motions were introduced by individuals and the Poincaré government introduced a Bill, all these proposals aiming at the generalization of family allowances. The three proposals were handed to the Commission d'Assurance and to the Commission du Travail, and these bodies recommended a modified version of the governmental proposal. This text was then submitted to a newly established committee—Commission Supérieure des Allocations Familiales—and to the various committees of the Chambre concerned with the different sections. Finally, a complete scheme was produced, and was passed by the Chambre des Députés in March 1931, and by the Sénat in

[1] Firms receiving contracts for public works from the central government were compelled to affiliate to an equalization fund recognized by the Minister of Labour. (*Manuel Pratique des Allocations Familiales*, p. 2. (Throughout this chapter references to the *Manuel Pratique* are to the edition brought up to date for the position in Dec. 1938.)

January 1932. The Act came into force on 11 March 1932, but could not be applied until the appropriate administrative orders had been issued. This meant that the actual implementation of the law did not take place until October 1933.[1]

Briefly, the Act gave legal recognition to the system of family allowances already in existence, and extended it to cover all industries and occupations, though, partly to prevent a sudden increase in the costs of industry, the application of the law was made gradual.[2] But ultimately all employers (except public bodies,[3] railway companies and mines, which pay allowances directly to their employees) were to affiliate to equalization funds in their region or industry, and all employees, wage-earning and salaried, no matter how large the income they already received, were to be given allowances for their dependent children. The term 'dependent child' applied primarily to children who were under the legal school-leaving age, which was originally 13 years but is now 14 years,[4] but might be extended to 16 years if the child were a student or apprentice or physically or mentally incapable of earning his own living.[5] The question of nationality did not arise,[6] and so long as the employee was working in France he was entitled to an allowance for each dependent child living in the country. The allowances were also paid for the dependent children of an employee who was injured at, or who contracted an illness from, his work, whether he were temporarily or permanently incapacitated, or if he died.[7]

[1] Helleu, op. cit., p. 26, says that the procedure of applying the 1932 Act is reminiscent of the 1919 law concerning the 8-hour day, which had not yet been applied to all professional categories by the time that the 1936 Act instituted the 40-hour week.

[2] Between Aug. 1933 and July 1937 inclusive there were 26 decrees applying the law to various occupations and regions in France. [3] See Note III*b*, p. 435.

[4] The present minimum of 14 years is the result of the law of 9 Aug. 1936, and the decree of 6 Oct. 1936, modified by the decree of 21 Dec. 1937. *Manuel Pratique*, pp. 10 & 10 [1].

[5] The 1932 Act (Art. 74*b*) stipulates that allowances are due for every child or descendant (apparently of whatever degree of relationship—Pinte, op. cit., p. 167), legitimate or illegitimate (if paternity has been recognized), adopted or being a ward, living in France and dependent upon a wage-earner or salaried employee. *Manuel Pratique*, p. I.

[6] See Rhein, R., *Les Allocations Familiales Obligatoires*, Paris, 1932, p. 76.

[7] A fairly large number of funds pay allowances to the widows and children of workers whose deaths have not been caused by industrial accidents. See Helleu, op. cit., pp. 166–7.

There were no provisions for payment during unemployment, for the Act states that allowances are to be given for effective working days, but the bodies which apply the law are at liberty to give a full monthly allowance, without any deduction for days not worked when the absence from work is not voluntary on the part of the attributary.[1] In some cases the allowance is made during a period of three months' unemployment, while where there is 'short time' it may be continued indefinitely. This was the case in the Rouen Fund for the cotton and artificial silk industry, although in the second part of 1934, 27 per cent. of the workers were on short time.[2]

There were no binding regulations concerning the method of payment of allowances. Legally the father is in most cases entitled to receive the allowance, but in practice it is the mother who most often is paid directly,[3] and this is probably a more satisfactory method of ensuring that the money is actually spent on the children. The allowances are paid either monthly or three-monthly, and payment may be made by the employers or the funds. A common method is to send a postal order directly to the mother of each family entitled to allowances. The 1932 Act also defined the position and membership of regional and professional equalization funds[4] and provided official inspectors to ensure the efficient working of the system. Finally, a permanent Family Allowance Committee was set up to advise the Minister of Labour, after consultation with the committees for the Départements, on general questions of administration, minimum rates of pay, and on cases where allowances may be given directly by employers without affiliation to an

[1] An extract from *L'Usine* of 2 July 1936 (cited in *Bulletin Mensuel des Allocations Familiales*, Aug.–Sept. 1936) says that although the law makes no provision for allowances except in proportion to effective working days, certain funds had decided to give full allowances for the month of June, making no deductions for strikes. This was not, however, to be regarded as anything but a humanitarian gesture, and did not create a precedent. In a circular of 9 April 1938 the Minister of Labour suggested that allowances be paid for days of unemployment which might be regarded as the counterpart of the hours worked in excess of the 40-hour week during periods of great activity. (*Manuel Pratique*, p. 12 [4].)

[2] In a letter to the present writer, dated 27 Feb. 1935, from the Director of the Caisse Patronale d'Allocations Familiales du Textile.

[3] See Note III*c*, p. 436.

[4] See Note III*d*, p. 436.

equalization fund. This permanent committee consists of representatives of the Chambre and Sénat, of the funds, and of workers and employers, &c.

As the law was intended to be applied gradually, it did not even by the summer of 1939 cover the whole employed population. For one thing, domestic servants were excluded[1] and agricultural workers have only recently been brought into the obligatory scheme.[2] For another, large numbers of employers—generally the small employers—are still evading their legal obligations. Leaving aside agriculture, by the beginning of 1938 the family allowance system actually embraced 228 funds in which were enrolled the 5,315,000 employees of 390,000 industrialists and other private employers.[3] If we add to these employees in private establishments about one million employees in special enterprises (railways, mines, &c.) and about 800,000 central and local government employees,[4] we have an employed population of approximately 7,115,000 actually coming within the family allowance system. To these employees about 3,300 million francs were given in allowances in the year ending 1 January 1938. This does not include the cost of other services provided by the funds, and no total figures are apparently available. But, although these figures are very

[1] Helleu, op. cit., p. 132, says that a domestic servant could not claim a family allowance except in so far as his work was entirely related to the professional life of his employer. (The *Manuel Pratique*, p. 12 [2] substitutes 'mainly' for 'entirely'.) A maid whose duty was to receive the patients who came to attend a doctor would therefore, apparently, be entitled to a family allowance, but a parlour-maid would not. Incidentally, it should be mentioned that, save in one instance, the fact that both husband and wife may be included in a family allowance scheme does not entitle them to two allowances. The one exception is where one of the couple works in private and the other in public employment. But the Minister of Labour intends to dispose of this exception (*Manuel Pratique*, p. 4 [6]).

[2] See subsequent discussion.

[3] These figures are from Bonvoisin, G., in *XVIIIe Congrès National des Allocations Familiales*, Nancy, 25 May 1938, p. 92. They relate to 1 Jan. 1938, but they do not agree exactly with data for the same period received by the present writer from the Comité Central des Allocations Familiales. The latter figures show a total of 225 recognized funds embracing 409,400 employers and 5,378,879 employees, plus 847,882 employees in special enterprises, thus making a total (excluding public servants) of 6,226,761. The figures given above would show a corresponding total of 6,315,000 employees.

[4] No figures for public servants and employees in special enterprises were given at the 1938 Congrès. They have been taken from the latest available data and relate to 1 Jan. 1936. (Bonvoisin, G., in *XVIe Congrès National*, p. 105.)

impressive, it should be realized that the total employed population in France (excluding the agricultural population, domestic servants, and all employers and independent workers) was 9·53 millions according to the 1931 Census.[1] A considerable proportion of the industrial, commercial, and professional population was thus still excluded.[2]

We have said that agricultural workers were still excluded from the obligatory system until recently. This anomaly needs some further discussion. During the period of private initiative the development of a family allowance system grew much more slowly in agriculture than in industry. A number of factors were responsible for this difference, and we may mention such points as the large part played in French agriculture by small farmers employing no hired labour, or hired labour to only a very small extent—according to the 1931 Census, there are over a million agricultural undertakings employing from 1 to 5 workers, with an average of 1·7 workers per undertaking;[3] the markedly varied conditions as between different branches of agriculture and even within each branch; and the individualism on the part of the agricultural employers. By 1932 there were less than 40 agricultural equalization funds, and many of them were very small—that for the Commune of Glos-sur-Lisieux giving allowances to only 24 children, that of Malroy to 36 children, while even the largest, for the Soissons area, distributed allowances to only 1,980 children.[4] By 1934 the whole allowance system in agriculture was distributing only about 2 million francs per year.[5] Consequently, officials of the family allowance system as well as pro-natalist associations constantly urged the application of the 1932 Act to agriculture.

After a number of years of hesitation a statutory order of

[1] 1931 Census, vol. i, part 3, p. 94. Including, however, those *isolés* classed by the 1931 Census, vol. i, part 3, p. 65, as being employees in irregular employment. It is impossible to distinguish home workers (in the employed sense) from independent workers and *petits patrons*. Excluding all *isolés*, the total would be 9·28 millions. Unemployed wage earners and employees would amount to a further 407,000.

[2] See Note III*e*, p. 436.

[3] Cf. Ferté, J., 'Les allocations familiales en agriculture' in *XVIe Congrès National des Allocations Familiales*, p. 97.

[4] Pinte, op. cit., pp. 103–10.

[5] Information in a statement from the Comité Central des Allocations Familiales to the present writer.

5 August 1936 suddenly applied the obligatory system to the whole of France, this order to take effect in short stages between 16 November 1936 and 1 July 1937.[1] The result was to create almost as great an outcry against the extension of the Act as there had been for it. However, there appears to have been a good deal of justification for this new outcry, for the system introduced in agriculture suffered from a number of disabilities. For one thing, the new super equalization, a practice similar to that used in Belgium, which it was intended to apply on a national scale, and which would therefore make the regions with low costs pay for those with high costs, might not work out in practice. In view of the extent to which small employers in the existing system have succeeded in evading their obligations, Bonvoisin is justified in believing that the new agricultural scheme would mean that the 'honest' areas would have to pay for the evasions of those regions in which evasion was the rule.[2] Actually it is doubtful if national equalization is practicable without state monetary assistance, for the difference in charges between the various Départements will be very great. An inquiry made by the Minister of Agriculture in 1932[3] showed that a uniform rate of allowance would result in a cost to employers varying from practically nothing to about 4 per cent. of the total wages bill, and showing a range of about 70 to 1. This is because in some regions hired labour is almost non-existent and what there is of it consists largely of unmarried workers, while in others large numbers of family men are employed.

[1] The statutory order was applied under the decrees of 7 Nov., 8 Nov., and 31 Dec. 1936, and of 30 Jan. 1937. See *Manuel Pratique des Allocations Familiales en Agriculture*, 2nd ed. (n.d., but presumably the beginning of 1937), Appendix. Subsequent decrees determined the ways in which the various sections of the system should work. Three main divisions may be noticed: (*a*) Funds with a départemental competence—at least 100 employers and 3,000 workers, or not less than 50 per cent. of the number of agricultural workers in the Département. (*b*) Funds not limited to a Département—at least 100 employers and 3,000 workers, or not less than 50 per cent. of the workers in their region. (*c*) Funds attached to associations functioning under the law of 4 July 1900—at least 100 employers but no minimum number of workers. These funds had to affiliate to a super-equalization fund, to which they had to give at least 25 per cent. of their levies for the payment of allowances.

[2] Bonvoisin, G., 'Rapport moral', in *La Journée Agricole du XVIIe Congrès des Allocations Familiales*, Toulon, 4 May 1937, p. 56.

[3] *Manuel Pratique des Allocations Familiales en Agriculture*, p. 5.

The new scheme did not envisage a uniform rate of allowance, but the range of variation was apparently not great enough to discount variations in the type of agricultural economy, and super-equalization would be a difficult task. The agricultural funds themselves, in 1937 and 1938, passed various resolutions bearing on these questions, the most important being: that within each Département there should be a uniform rate of equalization arrived at on a basis of the average rate of contribution by employers to the funds in the Département; that the scheme should be applied effectively;[1] that the smaller agriculturists should be brought into the system, not merely those who employed workers for at least 75 days per year; and that an obligatory allowance scheme should be applied to all persons engaged in agriculture—employers as well as employed—not as an extension of the 1932 Act, but as a new social reform, and to be bound up with and conditional upon a revalorization of agricultural products.[2] Some of these proposals were implemented by the decree-laws of 31 May and 14 June 1938. Under the first, the small farmers were brought into the scheme—that is, those employing workers for less than 75 days per year. Under the second, the system of obligatory allowances was to be extended (originally as from 1 January 1939, but postponed) to the employers themselves.[3] The new scheme applied only to the class of small farmers—those who do not pay income-tax and who are often far worse off than the urban wage-earners—and the allowances were to be given for the *second* and subsequent children.[4] At the same time, it should be noted that, unlike the scheme for industry, commerce, and the professions, the agricultural

[1] Bonvoisin, G., 'La progression des allocations familiales', in *XVIIIe Congrès des Allocations Familiales*, Nancy, 25 May 1938, p. 103.

[2] Resolutions passed at the *Journée Agricole*, and included in the report thereof, pp. 59–60.

[3] *Métayers* were to have been included earlier, but had not been brought into an obligatory system by mid-1939.

[4] For those *exploitants* whose taxable income for the agricultural profits tax was less than 500 francs, affiliation to the scheme was to be optional; for the rest, it was obligatory. For the category of occupations coming under the decree of 14 June 1938, the choice was between family allowances and *encouragement national*. Accepting the one automatically deprived the family of the ability to receive the other. A discussion of the *encouragement national* is given in the next chapter.

system was to have a State subsidy, in addition to the contribution made by the agriculturists for their own allowances.[1]

So far as the numerical growth of the agricultural family allowances system is concerned, there are relatively few statistics. Nor are these statistics comparable with census data or with the estimates given for the family allowance system in industry, commerce, and the professions, as in agriculture the basis of contribution is generally the area of land, so that the number of employed persons is not known. But some idea of the recent growth may be obtained from the following figures. In 1930 there were 35 agricultural funds and by 1939 this number had risen to 115. For the year 1930 it is estimated that 4,370 families were in receipt of allowances in respect of 11,250 dependent children, the total allowances amounting to just over 2 million francs for the year. In 1938, 170,000 families were receiving grants for 378,000 children, the total allowances paid during the year amounting to about 150 million francs.[2]

In spite of the detailed complexities introduced by recent legislation, the 1932 Act and its derivatives did not radically change the system which grew up through private initiative. As has been pointed out, there were some very important modifications, especially in connexion with agriculture. But on the whole it may be said that the work of the legislator—and probably very wisely[3]—had been largely to consolidate and extend the previous system. The allowances which—apart from the case of the State subsidy to agriculture—are still obtained by contributions from the employers, are calculated, raised, and to a considerable extent distributed[4] by the equalization funds. As a whole these allowances probably amounted in 1938 to about 3½ per cent. of the total wages bill of the employers concerned, varying between under 2

[1] See 'Les allocations familiales en agriculture', *Bulletin Mensuel*, Nov. 1938, pp. 184–6.

[2] See Note III*f*, p. 437.

[3] It is likely, however, that if decrees relating to details are issued with the rapidity shown in recent years, that there will soon be a need for a new codification of the entire system. Administrative requirements are already assuming a vast complexity. Part of this complexity is indicated in the subsequent discussion of rates of allowance.

[4] An analysis of the information given in the *Annuaire* for 1938 shows that about 43 per cent. of the funds either pay the allowances themselves, or jointly with the employers, while almost 47 per cent. arrange for the allowance to be paid by the employers. One fund pays through a savings bank.

and over 8 per cent. in different regions and occupations.[1] The method of calculating the employers' contributions remains unchanged. It is similar to the system of local rating in this country, in that a rate is struck after calculating the total sum needed, and is based, in industry and commerce, upon the average number of employees, the number of days worked (with complications introduced by the 40-hour week), or the total value of wages or salaries paid.[2] In agriculture the basis is usually the area cultivated, having due regard to the different types of cultivation. This basis having been chosen, the total expenses of the fund are then estimated, administrative costs included, and the contribution of the individual employer calculated. The employer may thus pay more or less than the total amount his workers actually receive in allowances.

The question of the actual money allowances is, historically at least, very confused. A large number of changes has occurred in recent years, and it is probably best to summarize these in order to provide the background for the present situation. In the first place, the 1932 Act provided for the computation of legal minimum rates of allowance for each Département. These rates were largely based upon the rates of allowance which were already being given. But the various funds have complete liberty to pay higher rates or to provide additional services, and are, in fact, encouraged to do so. So that while there is a minimum rate of allowance which is the lowest any fund in a given Département is allowed to pay, there are no upper limits. Up to the end of 1936, however, very few funds paid rates which were higher than the minima, and of the 201 commercial and industrial funds in operation in March 1935, and for which the requisite data were available, only 15 were paying higher rates. The tendency was to use surplus money, after the minimum allowances had been paid, to provide non-

[1] Bonvoisin, G., 'La progression des allocations familiales,' op. cit., p. 93. This figure apparently relates to all funds affiliated to the Comité Central as well as to the special undertakings and the public services. The figure is naturally very rough, and relates to the period before the new decrees came into force.

[2] Monsieur F. Boverat, in a letter (dated 6 April 1939) to the present writer, indicates that most of the funds, or nearly all the important ones, levy contributions based on the total wages bill of the employers covered by them.

monetary services, especially medical attendance. Moreover, there was probably some fall, after the enforcement of the 1932 Act, in the rates of allowance actually given, and this may be demonstrated by an analysis of the position in 1935, as compared with that in January 1933, when the new system had not yet been introduced. In 1935 in only 4 Départements were the legal minimum rates of allowance[1] higher than those actually given in 1933, and since only 15 of the funds in 1935 gave allowances above the legal minima, it is fairly evident that the 1932 Act was followed by a fall in the amount of money paid in respect of dependent children. This is also true of agriculture, where the voluntary system had not yet come under the clauses of the 1932 Act.[2] In both cases the worsening of economic conditions in France was important in depressing the rates of allowance, but an additional factor was also important in the industrial, commercial, and professional funds. It was said that the legal minimum rates were based upon the existing rates given by the various funds. A number of these funds reduced their rates at the end of 1931, when it was clear that the family allowances Bill was going to be passed, in order that they should not be put at the disadvantage of having to maintain their rates during the economic crisis through which the

[1] The following table shows the range of the legal minimum rates established as from Oct. 1933.

	Rates per month in francs			*Total allowances per month in francs*			
	Lowest	*High*	*Highest*	*No. of children*	*Lowest*	*High*	*Highest*
1st child .	15	30	25	1	15	30	25
2nd " .	15	40	60	2	30	70	85
3rd " .	15	50	115	3	45	120	200
4th " .	20	80	120	4	65	200	320
5th " .	20	80	120	5	85	280	440
6th " .	20	80	120	6	105	360	560

The lowest rate applies to Corsica, while rates scarcely higher were given in four other Départements. The high rates apply to the Départements of Seine, Seine-et-Marne, and Seine-et-Oise, and the highest to Aube. These Départemental minima also apply to agricultural rates since the extension of the 1932 Act. (*Manuel Pratique*, 1935 ed., Appendix.)

[2] In agriculture the average rates for 1 to 5 children were: 1930—11, 33, 62, 95, and 134 francs per month; 1935—10, 30, 55, 85, and 120 francs per month (from information supplied by the Comité Central des Allocations Familiales, and Bonvoisin and Maignan, op. cit., p. 279).

country was passing.[1] The legal minima were therefore in some cases based on rates lower than those currently applied a year before the 1932 Act was passed.

But in the last two years the position has changed very markedly. October 1936 saw the beginning of a movement, among the funds, to increase the rates of allowance, particularly to the third and subsequent children.[2] In the early stages this was not connected with any legal pressure, though it was encouraged by exhortation from the Comité Central and the Assemblée Générale of the family allowance system,[3] and by the Alliance Nationale. The movement was associated with the wage increases, which first began on a relatively large scale in June 1936, and which, by raising the cost of living, placed special burdens on the workers with dependent children, for whom the old rates of allowances were still being given. Following the rise in the allowance given by the fund for the Paris Region,[4] announced in the October 1936 issue of the *Bulletin Mensuel*, almost every subsequent issue of this journal contained notices of increases in the allowances given by the various funds. Other factors then came into play. From February 1937 onwards changes in family allowance rates were included in many of the collective agreements and arbitrations under which wages were increased, and this trend was viewed favourably by the Minister of Labour. Since the 1932 Act prescribes that the legal minimum rates may be revised when changes have occurred in the rates actually in force among the various funds in a Département or an industry, it is only natural that the spontaneous raises in the monetary value of the allowances should have been followed by increases in the minimum rates for the Départements. At the end of 1938, therefore, the absolute monetary value of the family allowances was generally considerably higher than in 1935 or 1932.[5]

But a much more important question—both as regards the relative value of family allowances and their possible effect

[1] Pinte, op. cit., pp. 126–8.

[2] *Les Allocations Familiales et leurs Services Sociaux* (published by the Comité Central, in 1937), p. 21.

[3] Bonvoisin, G., 'La progression des allocations familiales', in *XVIIIe Congrès National des Allocations Familiales*, pp. 94–8.

[4] See Note IIIg, p. 437.

[5] Bonvoisin, G. 'La progression des allocations familiales', op. cit., pp. 95–6.

upon fertility—is the relation between the allowances and the basic wages or salaries received by the employed population. It is estimated that in 1932–3 the average family allowance gave a 15 to 20 per cent. increase in income to an unskilled worker with four dependent children—that is, between 4 and 5 per cent. for each child.[1] No general averages have been computed for more recent periods, but a number of calculations show that in the period 1934–5 the range was between about 12 and 37 per cent. in industry, commerce, and the professions, and between about 14 and 16 per cent. in agriculture, these percentages indicating the increase, due to family allowances, in the income of a family with four dependent children.[2] The average increase per child in these circumstances was between 3 and 9 per cent. in industry and commerce, and between 3½ and 4 per cent. in agriculture.[3] During recent years, as was noted earlier in the discussion, the various funds have increased the rates of allowance given for dependent children, and although in some cases the legal minima had also been increased, yet in general the funds, in 1938, were giving higher allowances than were legally obligatory.[4] However, it should be

[1] Green, M. E., 'The theory and practice of family allowances', *Le Assicurazioni Sociali*, Sept.–Oct. 1933. Bonvoisin, at the VIIe Congrès National des Allocations Familiales (1927) said that in a group of funds for the metallurgical and affiliated industries the average wage would be raised by about 4 per cent. by the family allowance for 1 child, 10 per cent. for 2 children, and 40 per cent. for 5 children. In Bonvoisin, G., and Maignan, G., op. cit., pp. 195–6, it is estimated that the average wage would be raised 50 per cent. by the average allowance for 6 children given by the industrial funds—i.e. about 8 per cent. per child at this level.

[2] The percentages are calculated on the basis of (*a*) the minimum legal rates in the various Départements and (*b*) the average monthly earnings of workers in industry, commerce, and, separately—these relating to Oct. 1934, in almost all cases (*Bulletin Trimestriel de Statistique*, Jan.–March 1935) and being computed on the assumption of an 8-hour day (or 48-hour week) and a 25-day month for workers. It is probable that the percentages should be higher, since, according to the Director of the Statistique Générale de la France (in a conversation with him in 1935) the 48-hour week was not typical. Unemployment had led to 'short-time' and the typical week in many branches of industry had fallen to 40 to 42 hours.

[3] The average percentage per child rises with the number of children.

[4] Analysis of the *Annuaire* for 1938 shows that at least 143 funds were giving higher allowances than they were obliged to do. Probably a good many more were doing so, but the data given in the *Annuaire* were not up to date in all cases. Further, it should be noted that many funds have given additional increases in their rates of allowance since the summer of 1938. But the minimum rates have also been further raised.

Table 10. *Family Allowances in France: Allowances in Relation to Basic Earnings**

Département in which Fund is located	*Type of Fund*	*Average basic earnings, francs per month*	*Rate of family allowance, francs per month*	*Family allowance as percentage of basic earnings in families with given numbers of dependent children*				
				1 *child*	2 *children*	3 *children*	4 *children*	5 *children*
1. Aisne	I	1,200	35–90–165–275–385+125	2·9	7·5	13·8	22·9	32·1
2. Alpes Maritimes	I	1,400–1,500	40–100–200–320+150[1]	2·9 2·7	7·1 6·7	14·3 13·3	22·9 21·3	33·6 31·3
3. Gard	I	900–1,100	35–90–180–280–400–520+150	3·9 3·2	10·0 8·2	20·0 16·4	31·1 25·5	44·4 36·4
4. Gironde	I	998	30–75–145–245+120[2]	3·0	7·5	14·5	24·5	36·6
5. Isère	P and M[3]	1,100	50–120–210+150[1]	4·5	10·9	19·1	32·7	46·4
6. Lot	I	700	35–75–125–225+100	5·0	10·7	17·9	32·1	46·4
7. Lot-et-Garonne	I	700	30–75–125–200–300–400–500+120	4·3	10·7	17·9	28·6	42·9
8. Mayenne	I	633	25–55–110–170–245+100	3·9	8·7	17·4	26·9	38·7
9. Meuse	M	1,000	30–90–175+125	3·0	9·0	17·5	30·0	42·5
10. Pyrénées, Basses	I	850	30–75–125–200–300–400–500+150	3·5	8·8	14·7	23·5	35·3
11. Rhin, Bas	M	1,000	30–75–127·50–187·50–262·50–350–425–525	3·0	7·5	12·8	18·8	26·3
12. Rhin, Bas	M	800[4]	35–85–150–220+110	4·4	10·6	18·8	27·5	41·3
13. Rhin, Haut	M	1,250	40–100–175–275–400–525–700–900–1,125–1,375	3·2	8·0	14·0	22·0	32·0
14. Rhône	I	1,000	25–70–150–300+150	2·5	7·0	15·0	30·0	45·0
15. Savoie	M	1,000	40–100–180–280–400+120	4·0	10·0	18·0	28·0	40·0
16. Seine Inférieure	M	1,150	40–100–220+150	3·5	8·7	19·1	32·2	45·2
17. Seine Inférieure	M	1,250–1,333	40–105–180–280+120	3·2 3·0	8·4 7·9	14·4 13·5	22·4 21·0	32·0 30·0
18. Seine Inférieure	P	1,050	40–100–180–300+150	3·8	9·5	17·1	28·6	42·9
19. Seine Inférieure	M	1,250	40–100–180–280+120	3·2	8·0	14·4	22·4	32·0
20. Vaucluse	I	780	35–80–160–250–350–450+120	4·5	10·3	20·5	32·1	44·9
21. Seine	Special enterprise	1,000	55–135–300–505–710+205	5·5	13·5	30·0	50·5	71·0
22. Ardenne	Agricultural	35 per day[5]	1·0–2·4–4·4–7·6–10·8+3·2 per day	2·9	6·9	12·6	21·7	30·9
23. Manche	Agricultural	20 per day	0·7–1·6–2·8–4·4+1·6 per day	3·5	8·0	14·0	22·0	30·0
24. Marne	Agricultural	33·33 per day[5]	1·0–2·4–4·4–7·6–10·8+3·2 per day	3·0	7·2	13·2	22·8	32·4

*For Notes on the Table see Note III*h*, p. 438.

remembered that the allowances have been increased largely in response to wage increases, and it does not necessarily follow that there has been any radical change in the relation between family allowances and basic earnings. This is borne out to a considerable extent by Table 10, which shows the relationship between basic earnings and allowances in 1938, for the equalization funds for which the requisite information was available.[1] Analysing, for 1938, the position of families with four dependent children, it will be found that in that year each child received an allowance equal to between 4·7 and 8·2 per cent. of the basic earnings—excluding the special enterprise where, with a very much higher allowance, the grant per child amounted to 12·6 per cent. of the basic earnings. If we compare this with the position in 1935, we may say that according to the available information, the ratio between allowances and basic wages or salary had probably risen by about 30 per cent.[2] This may seem a very marked increase, but the percentages in 1935 were very low, and a large percentage change does not alter the fact that, even in 1938, the family allowances given were very small in proportion to basic earnings. What these allowances mean in terms of the cost of raising a family, and as a possible stimulant of fertility, will be discussed in the next chapter.

It is interesting to compare the outlines given above with the data collected by a semi-official French investigation undertaken in 1938 by Monsieur Partiot, of the Conseil Supérieur de la Natalité.[3] Questionnaires were sent to each

[1] The rapidity of wage changes made it impossible to use, in this Table, the wage data given by the Statistique Générale de la France. Instead, a questionnaire was sent to all the equalization funds listed in the *Annuaire*, in order to obtain the most recent information concerning average earnings and actual family allowance rates. Unfortunately, though many funds replied, few were able to indicate the average earnings of the wage-earners and employees registered with them. The Table given covers all the funds providing data on earnings.

[2] These figures are extremely rough. They are arrived at by comparing the data for 1938 with those which the present writer possesses for 1935. But the wage data for 1935 were probably somewhat too high, so it is likely that the increase in the proportion which family allowances form in relation to basic earnings is smaller than the figures show. It is, however, impossible to make a more accurate comparison as data for average earnings are notoriously unreliable.

[3] Partiot, 'Rapport général sur les résultats pour la famille et la natalité des nouvelles mesures sur les allocations familiales . . .', *XVe Congrès des Commissions Départementales de la Natalité, Limoges*, September 28th, 1938, *Ministère de la Santé Publique*, esp. pp. 1–3.

of the ninety departmental fertility committees, asking for information on the extent to which family allowances had recently been increased, and on the relation the allowances bore to earnings, and replies were received from seventy of the committees. As regards the first point, it was found that almost everywhere the rates of allowance had been raised since June 1936. The increases were frequently substantial, but the level from which the rates were raised was also frequently extremely low. Too often the 1936 rates were at about the same level as in 1924, although the 1926 devaluation and the stimulated business activity of 1928–9 had resulted in a marked rise in the cost of living. As regards the second question, the replies showed a considerable range. For the first child the value of the allowance appeared to vary between 3 and 5 per cent. of the basic earnings, while the range was between 7 and 17 per cent. for the fourth child. In our own inquiry the range for the first child, based on the 24 replies (actually 27 cases) obtained, will be seen to be between 2·5 and 5·5 per cent., with an unweighted average of about 3·6 per cent., while the allowance for the fourth child[1] varies between 6·0 and 20·5 per cent., with an unweighted average of about 10·4 per cent. In the Seine Département, where the allowances were highest, the grant for five children was found, according to Monsieur Partiot's information, to amount to 60 per cent. of the average earnings. In our own inquiry we were not able to obtain wage data for the Seine, but if we take the figure of 14,000 francs per year for a Paris worker, used by the Alliance Nationale in a family budget study,[2] the annual allowances at 720 francs for the first child, 1,200 for the second, 1,800 for the third, and 2,400 for the fourth and for each subsequent child would provide a total grant of 8,520 francs per year for five children, or about 61 per cent. of the basic earnings. For the Départements in which the rates of allowance had not been raised so markedly, the grant for five children was, according to Monsieur Partiot's information, about 30 or 40 per cent. of average earnings. This, again, is very similar to the results of our own inquiry, shown in Table 10.

[1] Obtainable from Table 10 by subtracting the percentage for three children from the percentage for four. [2] *Revue de l'Alliance Nationale*, Jan. 1939, pp. 17–20.

Earlier in this chapter it was said that, in spite of frequent changes in the regulations governing family allowances in France, no fundamental revision of the system had been made. This is true of the position up to the end of 1938, but since then there have been two series of decrees which involve very considerable changes in the system. Attention should first be drawn to the decree-law of 12 November 1938,[1] which came into force on 1 April 1939, making important amendments to the family allowance structure, so far as industry, commerce, and the professions are concerned.[2] In the first place, the population *motif* received much stronger emphasis. This was done in two ways. First, the allowance was to be suppressed when the family contained only one child and when that child had reached the age of 5 years. If, subsequently, another child were born, allowances would then be given for two children, provided, of course, that the first child was still financially dependent upon its parents.[3] Secondly, the propaganda against the employment of married women was given official recognition in this law, which provided that higher rates of allowance should be granted if the mother (or the relative having charge of the children) were not employed in any gainful occupation.[4] Until 15 November 1940 this additional allowance was to amount to 5 per cent. of the average départemental wage, and after that date, to 10 per cent. of the wage. This change may be regarded partly as compensation for the fall in family income, but mainly—judging by the propaganda of recent years—because pro-natalist bodies have united in asserting that 'a mother's place is in the home'.[5] Next, more attention was paid to the use made

[1] The decree-law was published in the *Journal Officiel* of 14–15 Nov. 1938. The present outline is from *Manuel Pratique, mise au courant* Dec. 1938, liii–liv.

[2] The decree-law did not apply to agriculture.

[3] The upper age limit for dependent children was raised to 17 years, provided that the child was studying or was apprenticed, or was, by reason of infirmity or chronic illness, incapable of undertaking any paid employment.

[4] This is referred to as an allowance to the *mère au foyer*. For some of the arguments in favour of such a grant, see *La Mère au Foyer: Ouvrière de Progrès Humain* (extraits du Congrès International de Juin 1937), Paris, n.d., *passim*.

[5] In 1938, 22 funds were giving higher rates of allowance when the mothers were not employed in gainful occupations (Bonvoisin, G., 'La progression des allocations familiales'). But the extra payment cannot be large enough exactly to compensate

of family allowances. A clause in the law stated that allowances might be delayed or suspended for not more than one month if it were found that the children were being brought up in conditions of defective housing, hygiene, and feeding. Further, the basis for establishing minimum rates of allowance was changed. Henceforth, the average wage or salary of an adult male was to be taken as the basis in each Département,[1] and the rates of allowance were to be such that the grant given for the first child should amount to not less than 5 per cent. of the basic earnings, for the second child not less than 10 per cent., and for each subsequent child not less than 15 per cent. With a basic average wage of 1,000 francs per month, the minimum allowances for four dependent children would amount to 450 francs per month, and the allowance per child would represent 11·25 per cent. of the basic earnings. It should be remembered that the use of average earnings as the criterion means that actual allowances, assuming that the legal minima are paid, may represent more or less than 11·25 per cent. of actual earnings per child in the case of a family with four dependent children. They will be more if the actual wage is below, and less if the actual wage is above the average wage. For those workers who receive average wages and have four dependent children, the new law would probably mean an increase of nearly 70 per cent. in the proportion which allowances bear to basic earnings.[2] Finally, a national equalization fund was to be set up, to receive an income from all the individual funds, and to make appropriate grants to funds which have abnormally high charges resulting from the preponderance of married men with dependent children among the employed

for the loss of earnings if a woman gives up her employment. This higher allowance is also to be given to the mother or relative who, although employed, has the exclusive responsibility of the children. The rates of allowance for the *mère au foyer*, cited above, were fixed by a statutory order signed 31 March 1939. This order stipulated, in Article 1, that the additional allowance was reserved for women whose children were of French nationality (*Bulletin Mensuel*, April 1939, p. 64).

[1] The basic wage data were to be adjusted each year.

[2] The actual rates of allowance for the various Départements are given in the note at the end of the present chapter. With these new rates and with the grant to the *mère au foyer* it is probable that family allowances would amount to between 5 and 6 per cent. of the total wages bill, according to Monsieur F. Boverat (in a letter to the present writer, 6 April 1939).

population which these funds cover. The Belgian principle of super-equalization was thus extended to another section of the French system.[1]

The measures promulgated under the decree-law of 12 November 1938 scarcely had time to be applied before even more important changes were introduced by a decree of 29 July 1939, creating the new French Code de la Famille.[2] This Family Code involves an almost complete reconstruction of pro-natalist policy in France and is discussed at some length in the next chapter, but since a considerable part of it concerns family allowances it will be more appropriate to outline the relevant sections at the present stage. Family allowances are dealt with in seven sections, the first of which lays down the general conditions relating to the system in general, while other sections deal with allowances to employees and wage earners, with agriculture, civil servants, and local government employees, and with independent workers and employers in industry, trade, and the liberal professions. Of the general regulations the following are the most important. First, family allowances are to be granted to *all* occupied persons, including independent workers and employers, as well as to the employed population, in agriculture as well as in industry, trade, and the professions. Secondly, the allowances are to be given from the second child onwards—the first child thus not entitling his parents to an allowance[3]—up to the age of 17 years if the child still continues his studies, is serving an apprenticeship, or is, on account of infirmity or chronic illness, unable to work. The allowances are graded, being not less than 10 per cent. of the average adult monthly wage in each Département for the second child, and 20 per cent. for the third and for each subsequent child. A family of four dependent children, in which the father was earning the average wage, would thus receive a total family allowance amounting to 50 per cent.

[1] Note that Article 7 of the decree-law of 12 Nov. 1938 prescribed that when both husband and wife are entitled to receive allowances for their children, the allowance shall be paid only to that one of the two who would benefit from the higher rate of allowance. This presumably will dispose of the anomaly previously mentioned (p. 108).

[2] Published in the *Journal Officiel*, 30 July 1939 (no. 178), pp. 9607–26.

[3] Birth premiums have been substituted instead. See next chapter.

of the basic wage.[1] The allowance, payable for the first year of life of a child, may, if the head of the family desires and can show valid reasons, be capitalized and given as a lump sum calculated on the basis of the life tables. On the other hand, the payment of the family allowance may be suspended—but not longer than a month—if it is found that the children are being brought up in defective conditions of hygiene, feeding, and housing.

As regards employees and wage earners—including domestic servants—attention should be drawn to the grant—equal to 10 per cent. of the average departmental wage—paid when there is at least one dependent child in the family (the children to be of French nationality), provided that there is only one earner in the family, and that the locality is urban in the same sense as that defined in the footnote above. This grant is given, if the family has only one child, until the child reaches 5 years of age. If there is more than one child, it is continued until the youngest reaches 14 years of age, though in certain cases this limit may be extended to 17 years. In agriculture employers, share farmers (*métayers*)[2] and artisans are included, in fact all whose main occupation is, and whose income derives largely from, agriculture as defined by two earlier decrees on the subject. The persons concerned pay a contribution which covers allowances for themselves and for any workers whom they employ, though certain large categories of persons—whose land yields a very small income, or, where the income is higher, if these persons have already brought up a family of at least four children to the age of 14 years—are exempted from the payment of these contributions. In addition to the usual equalization funds, a national super-equalization fund is provided, and the State is to pay two-thirds of the costs incurred by the funds in paying minimum allowances[3] and grants to the *mère au foyer*, and to cover, up to a total of 75 million francs per year,

[1] The average wages are to be calculated separately for the urban areas (localities with a population of over 2,000 grouped together or, if fewer, having an urban character) and the rural areas (with a population of not more than 2,000 or, if more, having a rural character) of the Départements.

[2] *Métayers* pay half the contribution, while the owners of the land farmed on a share basis pay the other half.

[3] And of the cost of the birth premiums described in the next chapter.

the charges due on account of the persons exempted from paying contributions. Comparable provisions are made for employers and independent workers in industry, trade, and the liberal professions, including a national super-equalization fund, an exemption of certain persons with low incomes from the payment of contributions, a State subsidy amounting to two-thirds of the cost of paying minimum allowances to independent workers, not giving more than 20 million francs per year on account of the persons exempted from paying contributions. For civil servants and local government and similar employees, allowances are to be given—as from 1 January 1940—on the same basis as to other employees and wage earners, thus unifying the whole family allowance system, though there still necessarily remain differences in the specific form of application of the general principles. The discussion here has, of course, been only in general terms. It is too early to analyse the regulations in detail, for in practice they may, within the limits of the decree, be modified. In particular, there is no clause in the decree to prevent equalization funds from paying allowances at higher rates than the minima, if employers can be induced to pay the necessary contributions, and we cannot tell at the present stage how this is likely to work out in practice.[1]

Before analysing the family allowance provisions in Belgium it should be emphasized that the equalization funds in France do much more than merely pay out family allowances. Quite early in the post-War history of the family allowance system the funds developed a large number of extra payments and services. At the present time most of the funds provide some form of social service for the families of the employed population covered by the system.[2] Among these extra provisions the most important is that of *infirmières visiteuses*—visiting nurses who look after the health of mothers and children. Holiday camps are a very important

[1] Article 49 states that the clauses relating to family allowances will be codified by decree before 1 April 1940. This may produce the simplification which, it was suggested earlier, appears to be greatly needed.

[2] Bonvoisin, G., 'La progression des allocations familiales', states that 178 out of 228 funds provide some form of service. An analysis of the *Annuaire* shows that 155 out of 230 provide services. But, as has been pointed out before, the information given in the *Annuaire* is often very scanty.

item, too, and in 1937–8 about 22,700 children were sent to such camps. Many of the funds also give birth and suckling premiums. The birth premiums range between 50 and 600 francs, often varying with the order of birth of the child, and sometimes paid in two instalments—the first at the birth of the child, and the second when the child has reached one year of age. The suckling premiums may be as high as 50 francs per month, and may be given for a period of six to ten months after the birth of the child. In addition there are sanatoria, gifts of baby linen, dispensaries, and medical consultations, free milk, and so forth, and free subscriptions to the *Revue de la Famille*. There is no compulsion upon the employers or the funds to provide these additional services, and they are paid for by supplementary contributions by the employers, quite separate from the cost of family allowances themselves.[1]

In Belgium the development of a family allowance system was similar to, though to some extent more rapid than, that in France. The beginnings were later and it is surprising that in so Catholic a country the Papal Encyclical did not have an earlier effect. The initial move appears to have come from the Civil Service between 1907 and 1910, when grants of 36 francs per year to each child under 14 years of age, from the third, were instituted for the employees of the Post Office.[2] The War then intervened, and prevented any significant expansion from taking place. But even during the War there had been some discussion of the idea of allowances, and even some actual schemes,[3] and the post-War inflation gave a new impetus to the movement. As in

[1] An analysis of the *Annuaire* for 1938 shows that 84 of the Funds send children to holiday camps; 78 provide visiting nurses; 71 give birth premiums; 35 give suckling premiums; 32 provide dispensaries; and 22 give collections of baby linen on the birth of children. As regards the combination of these extra-legal provisions, 11 funds give birth and suckling premiums, have visiting nurses, and send children to holiday camps; 13 have birth premiums and visiting nurses, and send children to holiday camps; 8 have birth and suckling premiums; 9 have birth premiums and send children to holiday camps; 23 have birth premiums only; 27 have visiting nurses and send children to holiday camps, but give no premiums; 9 funds give birth premiums in addition to some other service.

[2] Vibart, op. cit., p. 33.

[3] For example, at Tamines, in 1915. See Leener, G. de, *Les Caisses de Compensation des Allocations Familiales en Belgique*, Bruxelles, 1929, p. 13, and Fallon, V., *Les Allocations Familiales en Belgique et en France*, Bruxelles, 1926, p. 25.

France, the development took place during a period of rising prices,[1] and shortly after prices had begun to fall again, after 1929, the State intervened and made the system legally obligatory. In the early post-War years rapidly rising prices caused the workers to demand wage raises to meet the increased cost of living, and resistance on the part of the employers gave rise to many strikes. At the same time the labour shortage in France, and the existence of family allowances in the northern parts of that country, were attracting workers from Belgium. It was as an attempt to solve both these problems that the first equalization fund was created, based upon the French model. This was at Verviers, in 1921, and it was a regional fund. In 1922 this was followed by a national fund for the building trades, and funds for the Tournais region, for the metal founders, for the Renaix Chamber of Commerce, and for the Liége district. Initially, then, the movement was sponsored by employers for reasons which were largely concerned with their own industrial aims.[2] But other motives soon began to play their part. The influence of the Christian trade unions directed public attention to the importance of the family allowances as instruments of social benefit, while the recently formed Ligue des Familles Nombreuses de Belgique was already emphasizing the dangers of a falling birth-rate. As time passed and thc movement grew in strength, the population aspect became increasingly important.[3]

Within the next five years ten additional funds were created, and by the end of 1927, there was a total of nineteen funds.[4] At this point an additional factor entered and helped to stimulate the rate of growth of the movement—State

[1] Prices rose steeply from 1921 to 1929, with the exception of 1924.

[2] Leener, op. cit., p. 23, says that the introduction of allowances was not, especially in Belgium, motivated by reasons foreign to industrial aims. But Goldschmidt, P., in his report to the Comité d'Études in 1923, said that the employers were also anxious to improve the condition of the working class and wished to pursue a policy of social appeasement. See Vulhopp, T., *Une Politique de Familles Nombreuses en Belgique*, Bruxelles–Paris, 1929, p. 264.

[3] It should be noted, however, that the officials co-ordinating the Belgian family allowance system do not place nearly as much emphasis upon the demographic aspect as do the comparable officials in France. Cf. discussion in the next chapter.

[4] Leener, G. de, *Les Transformations du Régime des Allocations Familiales*, Bruxelles, 1934, p. 8.

encouragement. Early in the history of the system public authorities had shown their approval of the principle of family allowances. In 1923 the town council of Liége decided to include a family allowance clause in the contracts given to private firms,[1] and a similar step was taken by the provincial council of Hainaut. The province of Brabant went still further in 1924, by making affiliation to an equalization fund obligatory not only for contractors, but also for their sub-contractors, and by applying similar conditions to all work subsidized by the province, including numerous projects carried out by parishes and Communes. Recognition by the central government was given to these measures in 1926, when a ministerial decree made affiliation to an equalization fund obligatory in all the contracts connected with the Ministry of Public Works. Contractors were obliged to give allowances of at least 10 francs per month for the first child, 12 francs for the second, 14 francs for the third, and 16 francs for each subsequent child, aged under 14 years, to all their salaried and wage-earning employees who earned not more than 12,000 francs per year. This partial application of the principle of family allowances was clearly unsatisfactory, and pressure from various sources—by working-class organizations as well as by pro-natalist bodies—induced the passage of the Act of 14 April 1928, which required the insertion, in the specifications concerning work undertaken or subsidized by the State, the provinces, or the Communes, of a clause making it obligatory for the contractor to affiliate to a recognized equalization fund. The same obligation applied to any industrialist to whom the State, the provinces, or the Communes gave an order amounting to not less than 50,000 francs, and to any sub-contractors undertaking any part of the work referred to above. At the same time a legal minimum rate of allowance was laid down as a condition of recognition of the equalization funds. This rate was 15 francs per month to the first child, 20 for the second, 40 for the third, and 80 francs

[1] Some notoriety appears to be attached to this early measure, because the contractors could successfully evade their obligations by transferring married men with families to work not being done for the town of Liége, and by employing, in the work undertaken for Liége, bachelors or childless married men. See Leener, G. de, *Les Caisses de Compensation*, p. 111.

for each subsequent child under 14 years of age.[1] In September 1928 a royal decree extended the law to many additional public bodies, including the National Bank, the Belgian National Railways, the free and State universities, &c. In many cases the actual allowance was higher than the legal minimum, and the whole system of social and medical services, for which the funds were particularly distinguished, was developed without any legal persuasion.

The Act of 1928 had an immediate effect upon family allowances in other branches of industry and commerce. In the same year another 14 funds were established, and 1929 saw further progress.[2] By the end of 1929 there were 44 funds in private industry, embracing 3,852 firms, and 581,600 employees, and paying 92,630,000 francs in the course of the year to 331,200 dependent children.[3] The funds were co-ordinated by the Comité d'Études des Allocations Familiales, formed at the end of 1922, and comparable in organization and scope to the French Comité Central.

At the same time efforts were being made to generalize the whole system. Bills for this purpose had been drawn up in 1924 and 1926, and it was obvious after the 1928 Act that, since the State had intervened, the intervention needed to be made complete by further legislation, if only to prevent unequal treatment of different sections of the employed population.[4] The Bill, which eventually became the Act of 4 August 1930, was introduced by Monsieur Heyman, Minister of Labour, at the end of 1929. His speech to the Senate is particularly interesting because it contained the following statement: 'Above all, the Bill aims at encouraging births and large families.'[5] Governmental policy was, then, especially concerned with the menace of a declining population. It would, however, be quite incorrect to deduce that the Act was passed largely because of its possible demo-

[1] 'Loi du 14 avril 1928', in Leener, *Les Caisses*, op. cit., pp. 161–87. See especially pp. 161–2.

[2] Leener, G. de, *Les Transformations du Régime des Allocations Familiales*, Bruxelles, 1934, pp. 6–9.

[3] *Le Régime des Allocations Familiales et la Loi du 4 Août 1930* (issued by the Association des Caisses d'Allocations Familiales), Bruxelles, 1933, pp. 3–4.

[4] Industry did not, apparently, desire the establishment of a nationally obligatory system. See Leener, *Les Transformations*, pp. 17–18.

[5] Ibid., p. 12.

graphic results. Much support was given to it for entirely different reasons. Many people simply wanted to remove the inequality created by the 1928 Act, which left over half the employed population out of the scheme. Others were afraid that, unless the State took over the system, it might gradually break up as it had in so many other countries. And certainly the workers' organizations welcomed a measure which removed family allowances from dependence upon the generosity of the employers. The combination of these motives made the passage of the Act an easy matter, and the family allowance system, though of later growth than in France, was made compulsory two years earlier.

The 1930 Act—applied in stages between January 1931 and January 1932—covered the whole field in considerable detail.[1] In the first place, it applied to all workers, whatever their income, and foreigners were to be included if they were employed on the same footing as Belgian nationals.[2] All employers in industry, commerce, agriculture, or other occupations were to affiliate to existing equalization funds, or to form new funds with the approval of the government.[3] Central and local government bodies were, however, permitted to pay allowances directly to their employees, and this permission was also given to a number of other public bodies, such as the Belgian National Railways. The system was to be financed by contributions from employers, plus a State grant of 30 million francs per year, though this latter grant was reserved primarily for paying allowances to third and subsequent children—that is, in the interests of the

[1] See *Allocations Familiales. Loi du 4 Août, 1930* (Extraits du *Moniteur Belge*), Bruxelles, 1930.

[2] The work must be regular. Casual labourers in the strict sense were not included. Nor were the allowances to be cumulative—that is, if a man and his wife were both working, they did not receive a double allowance for their children. No graduation of allowance rates according to the size of the basic income was prescribed, though in fact higher allowances were allotted to civil servants, magistrates, and similar officials.

[3] Equalization funds were to contain at least 7 employers and 1,500 workers. (These numbers might be reduced to 3 and 500 respectively in special cases.) There were special funds for certain defined occupations (such as dock work, inland navigation, shipping, hotels and restaurants, home workers, and commercial travellers. See 1935 report of the Caisse Nationale de Compensation, Table 5.) Employers not belonging to either of the above kinds were compelled to affiliate to the auxiliary fund, which embraced a miscellany of trades.

larger families. The Act, therefore, did more than merely give legal recognition to the existing voluntary institution. Further, the method of levying contributions was quite different from that previously used. Instead of striking a rate, derived by estimating the total liabilities for the year, the employers were obliged to pay 65 centimes per man and 35 centimes per woman for each actual day's work done,[1] and these sums might be raised to 1·10 francs and 60 centimes respectively in the case of the special funds. In addition, each employer was responsible for a proportionate share of the administrative expenses of the fund. Finally, there was a further payment—to be equal to 5 per cent. of the total value of the payments for allowances, birth premiums, &c., made by each affiliated employer to the fund to which he belongs—to be used for creating a reserve balance. This last contribution ceased when the balance accumulated was equal in amount to the value of the other contributions for a period of two months.

The form of administration introduced by the 1930 Act was also rather different from that obtaining previously. The individual funds were still responsible for equalizing employers' expenses in their own locality, but there was in addition a system of super-equalization. Since the amount raised by each fund varied only with the number of workers and days worked, and not with the actual expenditure to be undertaken, it was likely that some funds would show a deficit after paying the allowances which the State had decided were to be the legal minima. On the other hand, in areas or industries where the size of the family was small, or where a large proportion of unmarried men and women was employed, there would be a surplus after paying the legal allowances. Half of this surplus was to be given to a national fund, which would use it to make up the deficits in the other funds.[2] The national fund—governed by a committee of fifteen, including nine representatives of the equalization funds and four workers' delegates—was also

[1] But included as days worked were days when absence from work was caused by illness, involuntary unemployment, or by any other legitimate cause. Note also that contributions did not have to be paid for workers living with their employers, for persons engaged in casual work, or for 'daily women' (servants).

[2] In the case of the auxiliary fund the whole surplus had to be transferred.

charged with the payment of allowances to special categories of workers—e.g. to those 'living in', to adolescent workers who were responsible for younger brothers and sisters, and to workers injured by an industrial accident or illness, after their employment contract had expired.[1]

The Act laid down a minimum rate of allowance applying to the whole kingdom. This was: 15 francs per month for the first child, 20 for the second, 40 for the third, 70 for the fourth, and 100 for each additional child. A family containing four dependent children would, therefore, be entitled to 145 francs per month, while a five-child family would receive 245 francs per month. The amount actually paid depended primarily upon the number of days actually worked, though no deductions were to be made for absence through sickness or involuntary unemployment, or for any other legitimate reason.[2] Secondly, the funds were not, of course, prohibited from paying rates higher than the legal minimum, but they could do so only if they had a surplus. Having given half that surplus to the national fund, the remainder might be used to pay higher allowances, or to provide accessory social or medical services. The allowances themselves were to be payable either monthly or quarterly, and usually through an equalization fund. Where they were paid by employers directly, the allowances were not to be given at the same time as the wage or salary. Payment might be made either to the mother or to the father of the children, but particularly to the mother if there were any doubts as to proper use being made of the money. Payment was due for every dependent child, the age limit being taken at least as far as 14 years, though it was extended to 18 years if the child was a student or apprentice, and indefinitely if he was physically or mentally incapable of following an occupation.[3] Finally, as

[1] The employers paid no contributions for these categories of persons. But they received legal minimum allowances, paid by the national fund.

[2] But the Director of the Caisse Professionnelle Verrière, in a letter to the present writer, dated 27 Feb. 1935, said: 'On the other hand, those workers occupied only part of the time have also had to have partial allowances. That is, instead of 15 francs per month, a family with one child receives only 5 or 10 francs, depending upon the number of days worked.'

[3] Grandchildren, adopted children, illegitimate children if their paternity had been acknowledged, and younger brothers and sisters all came within the meaning of the term 'dependent children'.

in France, a permanent Family Allowances Committee was set up, and the fact that it included two delegates from the Ligue des Familles Nombreuses is indicative of the importance attached to the population question.[1] So, too, is the steep graduation of the allowances in favour of large families.

The application of the 1930 Act has not been entirely harmonious. In the first place, there was, as in France, a considerable amount of evasion by employers of their legal obligations. At the end of 1933 various estimates showed a considerable discrepancy between the number of employers legally obliged to affiliate to equalization funds and the number actually embraced by these funds. One estimate calculated that at least 125,000 employers should have come under the Act, whereas only about 90,000 were actually affiliated by the middle of 1933. Another estimate asserted that 200,000 employers came under the Act, so that there was a gap of some 110,000 employers. This situation naturally made the efficient working of the law impossible. Most of the outstanding employers were probably those who employed relatively few married men with dependent children.[2] Had they actually affiliated to the funds, the financial position would have been a good deal easier, and the funds would have been in a position to give higher allowances or more widespread social and other accessory services. As it was, the super-equalization fund found an annual deficit after paying the sums due for allowances, and this entailed drawing on reserve balances. To solve this problem a Bill was introduced with the object of transferring more than 50 per cent. of the surpluses of individual funds to the national fund, but this was defeated by a united bloc of Socialists and Liberals, who maintained that the only real solution was to enforce the law with greater severity. But to bring in the laggard employers is no easy task, for they are generally the very small manufacturers and distributors, and are difficult to trace and pin down. Moreover, these employers were only following the example set by the State itself, for the annual grant of 30 million francs has not, so far,

[1] The Committee, which was to consist of 17 members, also contained 5 workers' and 5 employers' representatives.

[2] *Le Régime des Allocations Familiales*, pp. 22–3.

been paid. Nevertheless, the system has gradually been extended, so that at the end of 1937 it embraced 131,000 employers and 1,572,000 employees, and was paying about 337 million francs in the course of the year to over a million children.[1]

As regards the monetary value of the allowances, the rates laid down by the 1930 Act have already been mentioned, and these have been the rates applied in practice by most of the funds. Even those funds which in the voluntary period paid much higher rates showed the same tendency. The Verviers Textile Fund, for example, had been paying an allowance of 40, 100, 180, 270, 370, and 470 francs per month for 1 to 6 children, but reduced these rates in 1932 to 15, 35, 75, 145, 245, and 345 francs per month.[2] An inquiry made[3] in 1935 showed that, of 19 funds for which information was obtained, only 2 were paying rates higher than the minimum. But, unfortunately, the sample was too small for any definite conclusions to be drawn. Since 1935 there has also been a number of changes in the legal minimum rate—some made in order to reduce the burden on employers during the depression, and others made in response to changes in the cost of living—and these are summarized in Table 11.

The reduction in 1935, by a decree of 16 January, was made to cut down the costs to employers. But the saving could not have been very great. Father V. Fallon estimated the total economy at 65 million francs, spread among more than 100,000 employers, and causing a reduction in costs amount-to about 50 centimes per 100 francs of the wages bill. Assuming that wages and family allowances together formed 60 per cent. of the cost of production, the reduced allowance would enable an employer to sell at 99 francs 70 centimes an article previously sold for 100 francs.[4] The change in 1936

[1] See Note III*i*, p. 438.

[2] Leener, G. de, *Les Transformations*, p. 90, and a letter to the present writer, dated 15 Dec. 1938, from the Director of the fund.

[3] Made by the present writer. Nine of the 19 funds were giving birth-premiums, 8 provided *infirmières visiteuses*, and 2 gave breast-feeding payments and children's clothing.

[4] Fallon, V., S.J., 'Les allocations familiales dans les entreprises privées', *La Vie Économique et Sociale*, 15 Feb. 1935.

TABLE 11. *Legal Minimum Family Allowance Rates in Belgium*[1]

(*Francs per month*)

	1 Jan. 1931 to 31 Dec. 1934	*1 Jan. 1935 to 30 June 1936*	*1 July 1936 to 30 June 1937**	*1 July 1937 to 1 Jan. 1938**	*From 1 Jan. 1938**
1st child . .	15	9	15	18·75	20·60
2nd child . .	20	12	25	30·00	35·00
3rd child . .	40	32	50	53·00	58·00
4th child . .	70	65	85	86·00	89·00
5th child and each subsequent child .	100	95	120	121·00	124·00

* In these cases the month is reckoned as at least 23 working days.

was made as a result of a recodification of the law relating to family allowances. There had already been decrees on 30 March and 20 May 1936, and the new law was passed to consolidate previous modifications and to introduce fresh changes which practice had shown to be desirable. Many details of administration were affected, but the broad changes which concern us here are first, the creation of a new system of payments by agriculturists employing hired labour; secondly, the establishment of funds (one in each province) for Communes, and public bodies attached to Communes; thirdly, the use of actual working days as a basis for calculating both employers' contributions and allowances payable;[2] fourthly, the creation of a separate basis for computing the contributions due from employers in agriculture;[3]

[1] Report, for 1937, of the *Caisse Nationale*, p. 36, and *Le Guide des Dirigeants*, March 1938. The contributions paid by the employer have, of course, also varied. In 1934 60 centimes per day were due for each man employed and 35 for each woman. In 1935 this was reduced to 50 and 25 centimes respectively. From 1 July 1936 the rates were 90 and 48 centimes per day when less than 23 days per month were worked, and 22·50 and 12 francs per month when the working days were 23 or more. In 1937 (1 July) these rates were again raised to 1·00 franc and 54 centimes per day and 25 and 13·50 francs per month, and from 1 Jan. 1938 to 1·10 francs and 60 centimes per day and 27·50 and 15 francs per month. An additional change was proposed by a decree of 30 March 1936, but the decree was not enforced. The Act of 28 July 1936 was applied instead.

[2] See Note III *j*, p. 439.

[3] The method is complicated. The employer pays, first, the usual contribution for all workers who are permanently and exclusively in his service; secondly, an annual sum proportional to the number of days of work per year normally required on the land or woods which he works or puts to use. Finally, a deduction is made. Three hundred working days are subtracted (*a*) for each worker permanently and exclusively in his employment, and having a labour contract; (*b*) for each relative or

fifthly, the provision of a sliding scale of employers' contributions and of allowance rates, adjustable in accordance with changes in the cost of living.[1] It was because of a rise in the cost of living that the allowance rates were raised as from 1 July 1937, and again from 1 January 1938.

The Belgian family allowance system does not publish an *Annuaire*, comparable to that for France, in which the actual rates of allowance are given. To discover whether the legal minima are customarily paid therefore involves a special inquiry, and for the purpose of the present study questionnaires were sent to each of the Belgian funds. Replies were received from 34 funds including the auxiliary and 4 special funds, and in 28 cases the actual allowance paid was the legal minimum. To understand this situation it should be remembered that the tendency in Belgium has been to use surplus funds for the provision of special services, rather than for giving higher allowances. This in turn is due to the belief that surplus money is used more effectively in that way than by raising allowances. But at the same time the surpluses since 1932 have not been very marked. First, there are classes of persons—domestic servants, 'daily women', victims of industrial accidents or occupational diseases, workers called upon to fulfil military duties, persons who work for several employers none of whom is subject to pay contributions for them under the law relating to family allowances, and so forth—for whom the employers make no specific contributions, but who nevertheless receive allowances. These allowances are paid by the national fund from the income which it derives from the individual funds and from a number of other sources. Finally, and probably

associate employed permanently and exclusively, but not reckoned as having a labour contract; (*c*) for the agriculturist himself, provided that he devotes himself permanently and exclusively to working his land.

[1] The sliding scale is adjustable to four positions of the retail price index—up to 700; between 701 and 750; between 751 and 800; and above 800. The allowances paid from July 1936 to July 1937 were in accordance with the first position, and those in July 1937 were raised to meet a rise in the index to the second position. Since 1 Jan. 1938 the rates have been given for the third position of the index. For the fourth position the rates paid would be 22·50 francs per month for the first child, 40 for the second, 62·50 for the third, 91·50 for the fourth, and 126 for each subsequent child. Presumably if the price index rose much above 800, the rates would be further modified. The change in the index must be for at least 3 months to warrant changed rates.

most important, the present law contains a clause relating to the disposal of the surplus of the individual funds. It will be remembered that originally 50 per cent. of these surpluses —after paying the minimum legal allowances—was to be given to the national fund, and then an attempt was made to raise this proportion. The present law prescribes that after 50 per cent. of the surplus of a fund has been transferred, the remaining portion must not amount to more than 25 per cent. of the total value of the legal minimum family allowances given by the fund. If this amount is exceeded, the excess must also be transferred to the national fund.[1] The reason for introducing this clause was partly to help cover the deficits in super-equalization brought about because many employers were still evading their obligations,[2] and partly because some funds appeared to be spending too much on accessory services in comparison with their expenditure on family allowances.[3] In any case the result is clearly to reduce the money available for raising the rate of allowance above the legal minimum. If any increase is to be given, it must come largely from supplementary, voluntary contributions paid by the employers who are naturally reluctant to incur additional charges.

Our own inquiry was undertaken at the end of 1938. There were also two investigations made by the Belgian Association des Caisses d'Allocations Familiales in 1937 and 1938.[4] The first of these received replies from 32 funds and found that 15 were paying supplementary allowances, a much higher proportion than was found in our own inquiry.

[1] For the legal position at the present time, see *Loi sur les Allocations Familiales*, Bruxelles, 1936 (published by the Comité Central Industriel de Belgique), *passim*. Notice that the clause relating to a State grant of 30 million francs per year has been changed to a statement that the State will pay the national fund an annual grant not less than 5 nor more than 25 million francs.

[2] A. Delattre, Minister of Labour, estimated in 1937 that at least 20,000 employers were still evading their obligations. (In *Senate Report*, No. 213, session of 20 May 1937, p. 71.)

[3] Fallon, V., S.J., in *La Vie Économique*, loc. cit., mentions a case in which a fund spent in 1933, 44,700 francs on family allowances and 112,200 francs on accessory services.

[4] For the 1937 inquiry see 'Allocations familiales. Les œuvres annexes des caisses de compensation' (*Bulletin du Comité Central Industriel de Belgique*, 29 Sept. 1937). The results of the 1938 inquiry, dated 20th April 1938, were received (mimeographed) from Mr. R. Storms.

But included among these 15 were funds which, though not regularly giving family allowances above the legal minimum, provided some occasional grants for special purposes or at special periods. In our own inquiry this was also found. Thus one fund, out of the 34 replying to the questionnaire, stated that whatever the number of days actually worked in a quarter, it pays allowances for the whole quarter. Another fund gives special grants when the husband or wife falls ill, and if the head of the family is ill for a long period it continues to pay allowances beyond the 90 days prescribed by the law. This fund also gives a *prime d'encouragement* to families with 4 or more children, when one of them reaches his or her eleventh year of age, and a grant of 300 francs per year to children over 14 years of age who continue to receive full-time technical or domestic instruction. A third fund gives an additional grant of 50 francs per month and per dependent child when the head of the family is ill for at least 30 days, and a fourth fund pays 100 francs per year for each child between 14 and 18 years of age who continues his or her full-time studies. But these are not what is understood by the payment of rates of allowance higher than the legal minimum. By this description is meant the payment of a family allowance which, for all or for some of the dependent children, is customarily higher than the legal rate. If to this latter category we add the funds which provide occasional or special grants (other than birth or suckling premiums), our inquiry would show 14 out of 34 funds in which extra grants were given. If, however, we restrict the analysis to additional monetary grants regularly given, our inquiry shows only 6 cases, one being doubtful. The 1938 inquiry undertaken by the Belgian family allowance system showed a higher proportion—11 cases out of 32 funds, plus one case which was classed as doubtful since, in replying to our own questionnaire, the fund did not mention any supplementary allowances. In this 1938 inquiry the individual funds are set out and numbered according to their order in the annual report of the Caisse Nationale de Compensation. It is thus possible to combine without duplication these funds with those answering the questionnaire circulated for the purpose of the present study, and the combination shows, out of a total of 49 funds, 11 certain cases of supplementary allowances and three doubtful cases.[1] The supplementary allowances were not very large. The highest amounts to an extra 100 francs per month when there are 3 dependent children, 125 when there are 4, and 150 when there are 5, but this allowance is given only in the winter-time. More generally the addition amounts to 10 to 15 francs per month when there are 2 to 3 children, and 30 to 40 francs per month when there are 4 or more.

As for the relation between family allowances and basic wages or salaries, the available information is even more scanty for Belgium than it is for France. An estimate made for 1929 suggested that in certain cases allowances increased working-class incomes by about 21·5 per cent. in a family with 3 children, by 23 per cent. in a family with 4 children, by 31·5 per cent. in a family with 5 children, and by 57 per cent. in a family with 7 children.[2] This would mean about 6 per cent. per child in families with 5 children and just under 6 per cent. per child in families with 4 children. In 1935 data were available only for Bruxelles, and the figures showed that in families with one earner (the husband), who was receiving a wage of about 1,080 francs per month, the allowance given for 4 children represented 10·9 per cent. of the basic earnings—that is, about 2·7 per cent. per child. But since Bruxelles generally has relatively high wages rates, the percentages would have been larger in many other parts of the country. For 1938 some additional information was given in reply to the questionnaires, and the following Table shows the relationship between the legal minimum rate of allowance—20·6, 55·6, 113·6, 202·6, and 326·6 francs per

[1] In one case our own inquiry indicated some form of additional allowance (amount not stated) while the Belgian inquiry did not mention this for the same fund. In the second case the reverse happened.

[2] These percentages, quoted in *Le Régime des Allocations Familiales*, p. 4, are actually from Goldschmidt, P., 'Rapport moral', *La Journée de Conférences des Allocations Familiales, 1930*, Bruxelles, 1931, p. 38. The figures really relate to a number of workers enrolled in the Verviers Textile Fund, which was notable for paying particularly generous allowances. The basic wages varied between the cases chosen, so that the percentages do not relate to a standard basic wage, but to a few examples which may or may not have been typical. The percentages have, however, been cited because they are the only ones relating to that period known to the present writer.

month for 1 to 5 children[1]—and basic earnings, assuming, as in the case of the comparable table for France, that there is one adult male earner and no female earner in the family. It will be seen that for families with four dependent children the percentages are considerably lower than for France. Yet the Bruxelles figures show a marked rise as compared with

TABLE 12. *Family Allowances in Relation to Basic Earnings in Belgium*

Area for which wage data were available	*Average basic earnings in francs per month*	*Family allowance as percentage of basic earnings in families with given numbers of dependent children*				
		1 child	*2 children*	*3 children*	*4 children*	*5 children*
1. Antwerp[2]	1,650–	1·2	3·4	6·9	12·3	19·8
	1,800	1·1	3·1	6·3	11·3	18·1
2. Antwerp[3]	1,068	1·9	5·2	10·6	19·0	30·6
3. Bruxelles[4]	1,000	2·1	5·6	11·4	20·3	32·7
4. Bruxelles[5]	1,150	1·8	4·8	9·9	17·6	28·4
5. Renaix[6]	880	2·3	6·3	12·9	23·0	37·1
6. Gand[7]	1,500–	1·4	3·7	7·6	13·5	21·8
	2,000	1·0	2·8	5·7	10·1	16·3
7. Tournai	800–	2·6	7·0	14·2	25·3	40·8
	1,125	1·8	4·9	10·1	18·0	29·0

the position in 1935, and it is very probable that, in general, the percentages are higher than they were in 1929. How much higher we cannot tell, for the 1929 figures relate to 'certain cases', the frequency of which is not given.[8]

As in France, the individual funds provide many accessory services and some additional cash grants. Many funds give birth premiums, ranging from 150 to 715 francs for the first-born child, and often rising with the order of birth of the

[1] Obtained by summing the rates for the first, second, third, fourth, and fifth child. The minimum rate was used because, as was stated, only 11 funds out of 49 were found to be paying a higher rate, and for those funds no wage data were available.

[2] Dockworkers.

[3] Ordinary A.B.s in the Belgian mercantile marine.

[4] Workers in the building trades.

[5] Average wages for all kinds of adult male workers—rough estimate from labour exchange lists.

[6] Average wage earned in four weeks at 220 francs per week.

[7] Average salary of adult male employees (*not* wage earners).

[8] See Note III*k*, p. 440.

child. Thus, according to the 1937 inquiry, the regional fund for Flandre Orientale graded its premium from 400 francs for the first child to 1,000 francs for the ninth, though in this case the second child was given only 300 francs.[1] Suckling premiums are also given, and most funds provide visiting nurses, while about half the funds send children to holiday camps. In addition there are certain kinds of supplementary grants, mentioned in an earlier paragraph. Finally, some of the funds provide part of the expenses resulting from the death of the head of the family, some provide part of the initial deposit and of the annual interest charges involved in buying a house, and some give Christmas presents to the children and gifts of baby linen.[2]

To conclude the brief survey of family allowances in Belgium reference should be made to recent legislation which again extends the scope of the obligatory system. The law of 10 June 1937 brings into an obligatory system employers and independent workers—the whole field labelled by the term *non-salariés*. This, again, is a measure for which the Ligue des Familles Nombreuses has long been pressing, and the passage of the new law marks yet another stage in governmental desire to bring about a partial redistribution of income in favour of families with dependent children. But whereas the 1930 Act and its derivatives meant a partial vertical redistribution of income—in so far as this intention has not been nullified by a general depression of wages or a reduction in the ease with which wage raises may be obtained, questions about which no reliable information is obtainable—the new law involves only a horizontal redistribution. That is, the middle classes are to pay for their own allowances. In practice the law covers everyone who is not already brought under the 1930 Act—with the exception of *rentiers*—divided into the two broad categories of employers

[1] The premiums are now much smaller.

[2] Combining our own inquiry with that undertaken by the Belgian family allowance system in 1938, we find that out of 49 funds, 40 gave birth premiums, 23 provided visiting nurses, 19 sent children to holiday camps, and 8 gave suckling premiums. In some funds additional help was given in the form of layettes, monetary assistance in house purchase or construction, free coal, payment of expenses of surgical operations, payment of part of funeral expenses on the death of a child, &c.

and independent workers. The divisions are technical and not natural, for certain kinds of employers—including those in agriculture—are counted in the second category. There is also a third category of assistants (*aidants*), by which is meant those persons who help or deputize for employers or independent workers without the existence of a hiring of services, such as a wife who helps her husband to run his business, or a son who helps his mother in the same way. Finally, employers and independent workers who have retired come into a separate class. The persons in these various groups have to join a special fund or a special section of an existing equalization fund and pay contributions to include payment for the cost of the allowances, for administrative expenses, for building up a reserve fund, and for the provision of extra-legal services or cash grants, and the resultant system is quite separate from that under which allowances are given to employees and wage earners. The basic contribution for the family allowances themselves is 270 francs per year, and the employer-class is generally supposed to pay this full rate, though it may be reduced in certain circumstances. For the independent workers the contribution varies in different categories. In principle it is linked to the value of the property in which they live and practice their profession, but there are special groups paying special rates—such as doctors, surgeons, &c., who pay 89 francs per half year during the first three years of their practice, and other groups, such as the clergy, who generally pay the full rate of 135 francs per half year. It will be noticed that this full rate is equal to the basic amount paid by employers for each person employed by them according to the present codification of the 1930 Act and its derivatives, without taking into account any rise due to subsequent increases in the price level. Employers and independent workers who have retired generally pay in accordance with their relative wealth. In return for the contributions, families with dependent children are given family allowances approximately equal to basic allowances paid to employees under the recodified 1930 Act. These are merely the broad outlines of the system, which is, in reality, rather complicated. But at this stage further details are unnecessary; the 1937

Act has only just been applied in practice.[1] The statutory order (*arrêté royal organique*) necessary appeared in the *Moniteur Belge* of 4 February 1939, and is dated 22 December 1938. It prescribes that the application of the law to employers shall be retroactive, dating from 1 January 1938, while for the other categories the law applies as from 1 January 1939.[2] Originally the Act was supposed to be implemented by 1 January 1938.[3]

It will be seen from the discussion in this chapter, that family allowances now form an integral part of the social structure of France and Belgium, and that they are being extended so as to reach almost every section of the population. In earlier days there was a considerable amount of antagonism against family allowances from working-class organizations, arising not so much from inherent dislike of the principle as from reluctance to accept what might be regarded as patronage by the employers. At the same time there was a fear that family allowances might be used as an excuse for depressing wages, and there was some ground for this fear.[4] But the change from private initiative to a compulsory system has been accompanied by the disappearance of any major cause for antagonism. There are disagreements on details—as to the amount of workers' representation on the funds and Family Allowance Commissions, as to the provision of a State subsidy, and so forth. In general, however, family allowances are now regarded as a necessary part of the system of social services. Certainly, even if they are often small, they provide a very desirable supplement to the earnings of the working- and middle-class population in both France and Belgium.

[1] These outlines are from Fallon, V., S.J., *Les Allocations Familiales pour les Classes Moyennes*, Bruxelles, [1938], and *Les Allocations Familiales pour Non-Salariés*, a mimeographed document issued by the Association des Caisses d'Allocations Familiales in Nov. 1938, and kindly sent to me by Mr. R. Storms. (This has since been published by the Association des Caisses d'Allocations Familiales, under the title of *Les Allocations Familiales aux Non-Salariés*, Bruxelles, 1939.) It is interesting to note that Father Fallon, in his commentary on the law, praises it for, among other reasons, helping to prevent the 'prolétarisation' of the middle classes (p. 13).

[2] See 'Allocations familiales. Rapport au roi et arrêté royal organique . . .', extrait du *Moniteur Belge* of 4 Feb. 1939. The most comprehensive analysis of the new law is given in Gosseries, P., *Les Allocations Familiales aux Non-Salariés en Belgique*, Louvain-Bruxelles, 1939.

[3] See Note III*l*, p. 440.

[4] See Note III*m*, p. 440.

NOTE TO CHAPTER III

THE legal minimum family allowances in industry, commerce, and the professions in France, under the decree of 12 November 1938 in force as from 1 April 1939 are:[1]

Region I: 35 francs per month for 1 child, 105 for 2, 210 for 3, plus 105 per month for each subsequent child. This applies to the Départements of Gers, Landes, Lot, Lozère, Vendée.

Region II: 37·50 francs per month for 1 child, 112·50 for 2, 225 for 3, plus 112·50 per month for each subsequent child. This applies to the Départements of Ariège, Corrèze, Creuse, Dordogne, Haute-Loire, Manche, Mayenne, Tarn-et-Garonne.

Region III: 40 francs per month for 1 child, 120 for 2, 240 for 3, plus 120 per month for each subsequent child. This applies to the Départements of Basses and Hautes-Alpes, Cantal, Corse, Lot-et-Garonne, Orne, Basses and Hautes-Pyrénées, Sarthe.

Region IV: 42·50 francs per month for 1 child, 127·50 for 2, 255 for 3, plus 127·50 per month for each subsequent child. This applies to the Départements of Charente-Inférieure, Côtes-du-Nord, Ille-et-Vilaine, Jura, Morbihan, Deux-Sèvres, Haute-Vienne.

Region V: 45 francs per month for 1 child, 135 for 2, 270 for 3, plus 135 per month for each subsequent child. This applies to the Départements of Ain, Ardèche, Aude, Aveyron, Charente, Côte-d'Or, Eure, Finistère, Gard, Hérault, Indre-et-Loire, Loir-et-Cher, Maine-et-Loire, Nièvre, Pyrénées-Orientales, Bas-Rhin, Haute-Saône, Saône-et-Loire, Tarn, Vienne, Vosges, Yonne.

Region VI: 47·50 francs per month for 1 child, 142·50 for 2, 285 for 3, plus 142·50 per month for each subsequent child. This applies to the Départements of Allier, Calvados, Haute-Garonne, Indre, Haute-Marne, Somme.

Region VII: 50 francs per month for 1 child, 150 for 2, 300 for 3, plus 150 per month for each subsequent child. This applies to the Départements of Aisne, Ardennes, Cher, Doubs, Drôme, Eure-et-Loir, Gironde, Isère, Loire, Loire-Inférieure, Loiret, Marne, Meuse, Oise, Pas-de-Calais, Haut-Rhin, Savoie, Haute-Savoie, Seine-Inférieure, Terr. de Belfort, Vaucluse.

Region VIII: 52·50 francs per month for 1 child, 157·50 for 2, 315 for 3, plus 157·50 per month for each subsequent child. This applies to the Départements of Alpes-Maritimes, Aube, Meurthe-et-Moselle, Moselle, Puy-de-Dôme.

Region IX: 55 francs per month for 1 child, 165 for 2, 330 for 3, plus 165 per month for each subsequent child. This applies to the Départements of Nord, Rhône, Seine-et-Marne, Var.

Region X: 62·50 francs per month for 1 child, 187·50 for 2, 375 for 3, plus

[1] *Bulletin Mensuel des Allocations Familiales*, April 1939, p. 65.

187·50 per month for each subsequent child. This applies to the Département of Bouches-du-Rhône.

Region XI: 75 francs per month for 1 child, 225 for 2, 450 for 3, plus 225 per month for each subsequent child. This applies to the Départements of Seine, and Seine-et-Oise (Zone 1). [60 francs per month for 1 child, 180 for 2, 360 for 3, plus 180 per month for each subsequent child, applies to Zone 2 of Seine-et-Oise.]

IV

FRANCE AND BELGIUM

II. POPULATION POLICIES AND THEIR RESULTS

ALTHOUGH the original reasons for instituting family allowances were not connected with any specific population policy, it is evident that in recent years these allowances have come to be regarded increasingly from the point of view of their possible influence upon the birth-rate. In both France and Belgium the likelihood of declining numbers has aroused a considerable amount of public uneasiness, and a corresponding desire to take effective measures to change the population trend. Family allowances are now part of a large group of measures designed to produce this result.

In France the fear of stationary or declining numbers is by no means new. At most periods in French history concern was expressed on this account.[1] It is true that towards the end of the eighteenth, and in the first part of the nineteenth century, a section of public opinion appeared to be against policies aimed at the stimulation of population growth. In the eighteenth century this was probably rather a result of increasing interest in the individual as an entity—derived from the changing philosophical and political atmosphere of the period—than because of any decided views on the disadvantages of a more rapid rate of population growth. But at the same time it should be emphasized that, even at the height of the French Revolution, concern for the family and the size of the population was expressed in various laws and petitions, and the attitude shown in the legislature seems to have been influenced more by the depopulation fears which had been current in the middle of the eighteenth century than by the belief in individual rights which was so noticeable towards the end of the century. Thus a decree of the 7th Thermidor in the year III (1795) compelled unmarried men and women over 30 years of age to pay an additional 25 per cent. on their personal and

[1] See Note IV*a*, p. 441.

sumptuary taxes, and a law in the year VII (1798–9) ordered the rents paid by bachelors to be raised by a fictitious 50 per cent. in calculating the taxes which they had to pay. In addition to monetary penalties for celibacy, there were also political 'fines'. Article 83 of the constitution, adopted on the 27th Thermidor, in the year III, made marriage obligatory for membership of the Conseil des Anciens and nearly extended this condition to all members of the legislature. The most marked expression of this attitude was probably that shown in a petition to the Convention, made by a local society in the year IV, demanding that the Convention should declare celibacy to be a capital offence and that punishment should be visited upon all those guilty of it.[1] Under Napoleon, too, certain privileges were given to married men. Thus, according to Blet, in 1813 young married men were granted exemption from military service. It is reported that the result was an immediate rise in the marriage rate from 7·68 per thousand in 1812 to 13·28 in 1813, followed by a rise in the birth-rate from 30·72 in 1813 to 33·85 in 1814.[2]

Again, it is true that in the early nineteenth century the influence of Malthus was felt strongly and was partly responsible for the general apathy on the subject of population policies, as well as for a number of instances of public expression of anti-populationist aims. For example, the Prefects of a number of Départements advised the people in their areas to limit the size of their families—this happened in Allier in 1838 and in the Somme in 1842—while in 1852 the Versailles town council founded a 'temperance' prize of 1,000 francs, stipulating that, in awarding this prize to an individual, the moderate number of his children was to be reckoned among the domestic virtues. In the previous year,

[1] Schöne, L., *Histoire de la Population Française*, Paris, 1893, pp. 223 et seq.

[2] Blet, G., *L'Avortement. Est-ce un Crime?*, Macon, 1921, p. 131, n. The marriage and birth-rates are from Bertillon *père*, 'Démographie de la France', in *Dictionnaire Encyclopédique des Sciences Médicales*, 4e série, vol. v, Paris, 1879, p. 416. The *Annuaire Statistique, 1935*, Paris, 1936, p. 11*, gives the number of newly married persons per 1,000 of the population as 15·1 in 1812 and 26·4 in 1813. The number of marriages per 1,000 of the population (the rate given by Bertillon) would thus be 7·55 and 13·2. The birth-rates given are 30·5 in 1813 and 33·9 in 1814. Other Napoleonic measures are mentioned in Levasseur, E., *La Population Française*, vol. iii, Paris, 1892, p. 210.

too (1851), the French Academy had awarded a prize of 3,000 francs to an author who developed the sentiment: 'Happy is the country in which public and private wisdom combine to prevent too rapid a rate of growth of the population.'[1] Yet at the same time, populationist views were also being expressed, even if they were not officially recognized or approved by public opinion. Thus Marbeau, writing in 1845 in favour of *crèches*, said that 'France is far from having to fear an excess of population; our rural areas lack workers (*manquent de bras*); so do the navy and the colonies, especially Algeria'.[2]

Nevertheless, it may be generally agreed that no significant expression of opinion in favour of stimulating population growth was found again until after the middle of the century, especially until after the Austro-Prussian war had brought up the threat of a new and dangerous Germany.[3] According to Schöne, the appeal for a governmental policy to increase population growth was first expressed, in this period, by Legoyt who, writing in the *Journal des Économistes* in 1867, said that it was the government's duty to try to find a means of stimulating marriage frequency.[4] The

[1] Bertillon, J., *La Dépopulation de la France*, Paris, 1911, p. 210 and n. 2. Bertillon notes with satisfaction that in 1907 the Academy awarded prizes to two large families, calling them pious (*sainte*) and heroic. For the general background of legislation relating to the family in France a useful broad survey will be found in Senn, F., et al., *Le Maintien et la Défense de la Famille par le Droit*, Paris, 1930.

[2] Marbeau, J. B. F., *Des Crèches, ou Moyen de Diminuer la Misère en Augmentant la Population*, Paris, 1845, p. 23. (The quotation is from the second edition. The first edition was published in 1844.) Marbeau's view was: 'In the last 200 years the population of France has doubled; but the Frenchman is better housed, better fed, better clothed, because he works more and better. Double again, if you can; work still more and better and you will be still better fed, still better housed, still better clothed' (pp. 22–3). It is interesting that Marbeau should defend the idea of *crèches*—which he believed would reduce infant and child mortality—by pleading that the saving of a number of babies each year would not result in over-population.

[3] There were English references before this; e.g. Marshall, F., *Population and Trade in France in 1861–2*, London, 1862, p. 56: '. . . but if the people refuse to have children, and the births continue to fall at the average rate of the last seventy years, it cannot be expected that the progress of number will last beyond the end of the present century, and it is to be feared that the next generation may see the population of their country going backwards.'

[4] Schöne, L., op. cit., pp. 275 et seq., for details of the rebirth of populationist views; e.g. Frary, R., in *Le Péril National*, Paris, 1881, which was awarded the Montyon Prize (the prize awarded in 1851 to the author who urged public and private wisdom to combine to prevent too rapid a growth of population), recommended a bachelor tax and family allowances, and similar suggestions were made by

Franco-Prussian war, turning the German threat into a reality, gave further encouragement to populationist views, and unloosed an endless flood of population propaganda. Accounting for the decline of fertility by a wide variety of physiological, psychological, and socio-economic explanations—ranging from bicycle riding by women and the coddling of poodles to successoral legislation and 'social capillarity'[1]—French writers made a comparably wide range of counter-proposals. Among the most typical were: the reform of the existing inheritance law (against which there was a continuous drive); the reservation of honours and of civil service and municipal employment for the fathers of large families; electoral reform, to invest the heads of families with additional voting power; special bachelor taxes; the reform of the law relating to abortion; birth premiums and family allowances. The stream of propaganda varied in strength at different periods. It was affected by counter-propaganda from the supporters of birth control and family limitation, especially after 1896;[2] but it gained additional strength from the Great War. It also varied in the methods it used and in the detailed questions on which it concentrated. After the Franco-Prussian war foreign expressions of contempt for France, on account of her low fertility, were customarily quoted.[3] Appeals to patriotism followed the last war, and the Munich agreement of 1938 was succeeded by statements that, without an increase in fertility, France would be useless as an ally, and would therefore lose the friendship of the countries which were still anxious to oppose German domination in Europe, but no longer capable of doing so.[4] At times the propaganda has concentrated mainly

Richet, C., 'L'Accroissement de la population française', *Revue des Deux Mondes*, 15 Apr. 1882, pp. 900–32, and 1 June 1882, pp. 587–616. See also Spengler, J. J., *France faces Depopulation*, chs. vi and x; Legoyt, A., 'Des conditions d'accroissement de la population française', *J. des Économistes*, June 1867, pp. 356–73, and Aug. 1867, pp. 205–28.

[1] See Note IV*b*, p. 441.

[2] 1896 saw the foundation of a militant birth-control movement in France. See subsequent discussion.

[3] See Note IV*c*, p. 441.

[4] Boverat, F., wrote an article 'La dénatalité, c'est la perte de nos alliances', in the Sept. 1938 issue of the *Revue de l'Alliance Nationale*. The October issue contained an open letter to Daladier. Most issues since the *Anschluss* have contained references to the relative strength of the armed forces of France and Germany. See, too, the Oct. 1938 issue of *Familles de France*. See also Loesch, K. C. von, *Die aussenpolitischen Wirkungen des Geburtenrückganges*, Berlin, 1938, which refers specifically to France.

on a single object. This has been particularly the case with abortion, against which the propagandist drives were more than usually strong in 1910 and in 1937. At the same time the means of propaganda have been extended. At the present time most newspapers can be depended upon to take occasional propagandist articles (especially when new birth and death statistics are published), there are periodicals and newspapers devoted exclusively to pro-natalist articles, and the films have provided a new medium.

Large-scale propaganda may be said to date from the beginning of the twentieth century, under the auspices of the Alliance Nationale pour l'accroissement de la population française.[1] This body was founded by Dr. J. Bertillon in 1896 and, although concentrating on publicizing the prospects and dangers of a declining population, has also given considerable attention to demographic research. It was, for example, largely responsible for the establishment of an extra-parliamentary commission on depopulation in 1902,[2] though unfortunately few reports were issued and the scheme soon died of inanition. In recent years it has sponsored the work of A. Sauvy on estimates of the future population of France, and of P. Depoid on reproduction rates of the French Départements. A considerable number of similar bodies—smaller in territorial scope—were set up at about the same time. Thus the Famille Montpelliéraine was begun in 1894, the Union des Familles Nombreuses de Levroux in 1898, the Union des Familles de l'Eure in 1899, the Union des Pères de Famille Méritants (having at least four children) in 1904, and three or four others in the next few

[1] This was its original title. In recent years the phrase *Contre la dépopulation* was added to the *Revue* and in 1937 the title was changed to L'Alliance Nationale Contre la Dépopulation, though its propaganda still implies a growing population as the object of the association. Apart from the *Revue* it produces numerous leaflets and pamphlets.

[2] Actually founded by Waldeck-Rousseau (see *Revue de l'Alliance Nationale*, 15 Apr. 1902). The Commission was reorganized in 1905 and a new Commission was set up in 1912 (see Spengler, op. cit., pp. 126–7, Onslow, H., 'The French Commission on depopulation', *Eugenics Review*, July 1913, pp. 130–52, Auburtin, op. cit., pp. 32–5). The 1902 Commission was set up as a result of a Senate resolution, while that of 1912 was due to M. Klotz, Minister of Finance, and originally consisted of 300 members, added to subsequently. Auburtin (op. cit., p. 33, n. 3) asks—why not 3,000 members? He contrasts it with the Commission of four jurists appointed by Napoleon to draw up the *Code Civil*.

years.[1] Propaganda and discussion were carried on in spite of the War,[2] and in 1919 official recognition was given to the pro-natalist movement[3] by the establishment of the Conseil supérieur de la natalité, attached to the Ministry of Health, and now charged with the task of examining questions bearing on fertility and mortality. The last important move in the creation of a nation-wide propaganda system was made in 1921 with the institution of the Fédération des Associations de Familles Nombreuses de France. This now covers practically all the pro-natalist family associations in the country, of which there are more than a hundred, most of them in turn having numerous local branches. Unlike the Alliance Nationale, of which anybody may be a member, the rules of the Fédération restrict membership to parents with at least three children. On the average, however, the members have approximately five children per family, and since there are now more than 350,000 member families, this association represents a population of considerably more than two millions. Forty-five of the member groups are large enough to produce their own journals and the Fédération itself produces a monthly newspaper as well as a mimeographed bulletin intended for officials of the organization. Since its foundation this body has also held an annual Congrès National de la Natalité for the purpose of discussing and disseminating information about population movements and policies.[4]

[1] Bertillon, J., op. cit., pp. 247–50. There were also organizations dealing with more limited objects, e.g. the Ligue contre la Mortalité Infantile, founded in 1902, and the Ligue contre le Crime d'Avortement, founded in 1909 (this united with the former association in 1910, though retaining its own objects. See Balthazard, Dr., and Prévost, E., *Une Plaie Sociale*, Paris, 1912, introdn., for an account of this association). The work of the Ligue contre la Mortalité Infantile has been continued, in a much wider form, by the Comité National de l'Enfance, founded in 1922. This committee deals with the protection of mothers and infants, and its work has been extended to school children and, most recently, to adolescents. See *Comité National de l'Enfance, 1933*, Paris, n.d. (but apparently 1933), esp. pp. 1–6.

[2] During the war marriage was made easier by allowing soldiers to marry by proxy. Also the position of unmarried *ménages* was made easier by granting, under certain conditions, the same allowances to soldiers' mistresses and their illegitimate children as were given to families where the bread-winner was a soldier (see March, L., 'Some attempts towards race hygiene in France during the War', *Eugenics Review*, Jan. 1919, pp. 195–212).

[3] Pro-natalist groups were formed in the Chambre in 1914 and in the Sénat in 1917.

[4] Information from F. Vieuille, *délégué général* of the federation. The first

In recent years French propaganda has become rather more scientific and at the same time more sensational. That is, in the first place, the factual bases of the propaganda have become more accurate. Before the War, and for a considerable part of the post-War period, the organizations clamouring for more births had no real idea of the annual supply of births necessary to maintain the population or to replace the potentially fertile population. When writers emphasized the need for an annual growth of the population by 0·5 per cent., by 1 per cent., by 300,000–400,000, or simply by a 'proper amount', they showed little sign of understanding the requisite fertilities underlying such demands. The adoption of more refined statistical techniques has now provided a measure of the adequacy of the annual supplies of births for replacing the population, though there is still a considerable range shown in the desires of the various associations—that is, as regards their desires for a stationary or a growing population. In general, however, the implicit aims seem to be largely for a growing population, particularly in the face of post-War political changes in Germany[1] and Italy. Secondly, the nature of the propaganda has been made more sensational because of the use of population estimates. Analyses of populations, by age and sex, for a series of future periods, impress the public by their sheer detail, however valid the assumptions chosen, or however far from prophecy the intention of their authors or sponsors. Thus in recent years the Alliance Nationale has given a great deal of prominence to the computations of A. Sauvy.[2] The first of these appeared

national congress was actually held in 1919 before the federation was formed. Note also that the federation was responsible for founding the Ligue internationale pour la vie et la famille in 1927, as a response to and an attack upon the first international population conference (held in Geneva) which, according to Vieuille, was intended to form 'a striking manifestation in favour of birth control and a strong attempt to spread the doctrines' adhered to by neo-Malthusian organizations. (Vieuille, F., 'Note sur l'activité de la Ligue internationale . . .', *Le VIe Congrès International pour la Vie et la Famille*, Paris-Bruxelles, 1933, pp. 115–21.) Incidentally an English organization—the League of National Life—is a member of this international group.

[1] See Note IV*d*, p. 442.

[2] e.g. in *Prévisions scientifiques sur l'avenir de la population française* (n.d.); Boverat, F., *La Crise de Naissances*, Paris, 1932; Boverat, F., *La Race Blanche en Danger de Mort*, Paris, [1933]; Boverat, F., *L'Effondrement de la Natalité*, Paris, 1935; Boverat, F., *La Dénatalité Mortelle*, Paris, 1937; Boverat, F., *Comment Nous Vaincrons la Dénatalité*, Paris, 1938. Of this last publication Monsieur Boverat said

in 1928–9, and new estimates were published in 1932 and 1937.[1] So far as the total population of the country is concerned, the 1928–9 estimate envisaged a fall from 39·4 millions in 1927 to 38·0 millions in 1956. The second estimate envisaged two possibilities—the more optimistic arriving at a population of 38·9 millions by 1980, and the less optimistic a population of 29·0 millions by that date. The 1937 estimate also gave two sets of computations, the higher result being 35·2 millions by 1980 and the lower 31·7 millions by the same date. The publications of the Alliance Nationale have also emphasized the ageing of the population which would result from a decline in numbers. Most recently (in February 1939) the government set up a Haut Comité de la Population to consider the various aspects of the population question in France.[2]

It is clear from the previous discussion that pro-natalist propaganda is now a basic element in the social pattern of France. This position has been achieved after a campaign extending over the past eighty years, and in opposition to what was, at the end of the nineteenth century, a very militant birth-control movement. In Belgium the period of incubation has been much shorter. This may seem surprising in a country with so overwhelmingly a Catholic population, but it should be remembered that until relatively recently the Belgian birth-rate was very high. At the end of the nineteenth century many French populationists were citing a birth-rate of 25 per thousand as an ideal to be attained by properly planned measures.[3] But in Belgium the birth-rate was above 25 until after 1907, and, apart from the war period, did not fall below 20 until 1924. The rates of population growth in the two countries were also very

(April 1939) that the number issued would soon be 180,000. It should be noted, however, that in each of these publications it is emphasized that 'estimates are not prophecies', and that it is within the power of France to avert the threatened danger. See also the relevant issues of *Pour la Vie*, the monthly organ of the Ligue pour le Relèvement de la Natalité Française, originally founded by Paul Bureau.

[1] The estimates originally appeared in the *Journal de la Société de Statistique de Paris*, Dec. 1928 and Jan. 1929; July–Sept. 1932; June 1937.

[2] See *Revue de l'Alliance Nationale*, Mar. 1939, p. 76.

[3] Not actually attained in France since 1883. Notice also that France had an excess of deaths over births in 1890, 1892, 1895, 1900, 1907, and 1911 (*Statistique du Mouvement de la Population, 1933*, 1ère Partie, Paris, 1936, pp. 4–5).

different. Taking the present territory as the basis for comparison, the population of France was about 36·5 millions in 1851 and 41·5 millions in 1911, showing an increase of about 13·7 per cent. in the period. Comparing the populations of the actual territories belonging to France at the two dates, the rise would be from 35·8 to 39·6 millions, an increase of only 10·6 per cent. But in Belgium, between 1850 and 1911, the population rose from 4·43 to 7·49 millions, an increase of 69·1 per cent. Thus for most of the period the possibility of depopulation in the biological sense was not a question of any political importance. Nevertheless, by the beginning of the twentieth century the falling birth-rate was already causing uneasiness in some circles, and many articles in periodicals attempted to give explanations of the decline and to suggest remedies for it. French influence was a reason sometimes given and one author wrote: 'Since French influence on the French-speaking Belgian population is patent and inevitable, what remains to be desired is a modification of French feeling about legitimate fertility.' But he was not, apparently, very hopeful of such a change, for he believed that only a religious revival in France would enable that country to fight depopulation.[1] Medical circles appear to have been especially concerned with the trend, and in 1910 the Société de Médecine Publique appointed a committee of four—two doctors, a pharmacist, and a lawyer—to examine the situation, report on it, and suggest remedies. Among the suggestions adopted at the general meeting of the society were: State grants to large, needy families; legal reform to place the illegitimate child on the same social and legal footing as the legitimate; legal reform to prohibit the sale of contraceptives or abortifacients

[1] van der Smissen, E., 'La population en Belgique depuis 1875', *La Réforme Sociale*, 1 Oct. 1908, pp. 389–97. See also Jacquart, C., 'Le problème de la natalité en France et sa répercussion en Belgique', *Revue Sociale Catholique*, Mar. 1904, pp. 137–46. An article—'La crise de la natalité en Belgique depuis 1901' (author not stated)—in the Apr. 1913 issue of this latter journal, pp. 161–9, gave a statistical analysis of the decline in fertility in Belgium and emphasized the fact that this became noticeable only after 1865, and developed at a critical rate after 1902. The article suggests that the decline coincided with the spread of birth-control propaganda, was due entirely to 'artificial sterility' (i.e. deliberate birth prevention), and could be changed only by a strong reaction on the part of public opinion. See also the résumé of a report by Dr. Min in the *Journal d'Accouchements*, 11 Dec. 1910.

unless medically prescribed; and the creation of a national association for developing propaganda against the falling birth-rate.[1] The last suggestion was put into force and the Ligue contre l'Infécondité was founded, and issued a bulletin containing discussions of the falling birth-rate.[2]

There was not, however, any large-scale drive until after the War, when, in October 1920, General L. Lemercier founded the Ligue des Familles Nombreuses de Belgique.[3] This association was originally created to improve the conditions of life of the 'large family', understanding by that term families which have, or have had, at least four children. The aim of the Ligue was not, at the beginning, specifically pro-natalist, for the belief in the danger of threatened depopulation was confined to a relatively small section of the population. The large families would have spoiled their chance of gaining public sympathy if, in the early days, they had initiated a pro-natalist campaign. In principle the Ligue still maintains its original attitude, but with the growth of membership and the continued decline of the birth-rate, it has become increasingly a forum for pro-natalist views and has frequently drawn the attention of politicians to the prospects and probable consequences of a declining popula-

[1] See *Le Mouvement Géographique*, 2 Oct. 1910, cols. 491–3; *Journal d'Accouchements*, 4 Sept. and 11 Dec. 1910.

[2] This Ligue was inspired by Cardinal Mercier, and was founded at a meeting of the Médecins Catholiques Belges, held in Bruxelles in Oct. 1910, with Prof. Dr. R. Schockaert as President, publishing a quarterly bulletin called *Bulletin de la Ligue Nationale contre l'Infécondité Intentionnelle*, the first issue being dated 15 Nov. 1910. The name of this periodical was changed to *Bulletin de la Ligue contre la Dépopulation* with the issue of Jan.–Mar. 1912 (this had been the title originally proposed, but dropped at the suggestion of Cardinal Mercier), and to *Bulletin de la Ligue Nationale contre la Dépopulation* with the issue of Oct.–Dec. 1912. The last issue appears to have been that of Apr.–June 1914. At the end of 1911 the Ligue had 544 members—including 92 clergy and 244 doctors (*Bulletin* of 25 Dec. 1911, p. 189).

[3] Vulhopp, T., *Une Politique . . .*, ch. vi. Father Fallon was one of the leaders in the movement which led to the foundation of the Ligue. Father Fallon, in a letter to the present writer (Feb. 1939), states that the Ligue des Familles Nombreuses did not derive from any previous Belgian association. At the time when it was set up the old Ligue contre l'Infécondité, under the presidency of Dr. R. Schockaert, a noted gynaecologist, was also attempting to take up its activities again. But, impressed by the aims of the new Ligue, Dr. Schockaert and his associates abandoned their own attempt and became members of the new body. The Ligue has *membres actifs*, who are the heads of large families, *membres adhérents*, who do not need to be the heads of large families, and *membres protecteurs*, who pay at least 100 francs per year (*Le Guide des Dirigeants*, Feb. 1939).

tion.[1] The growth of the association was rapid. In 1921 it embraced about 3,000 member families, and by 1932 this figure had risen to 161,091. There was a further rise by September 1936 to 166,970 members, covering a total population of about 1,200,000, representing about one-seventh of the total population of Belgium.[2] The last published figures—for September 1938—show a membership of 175,631.[3] The association has pressed for many economic and social changes to the advantage of the family—including family allowances, housing subsidies, cheap fares, and tax rebates—and has been a very powerful factor in bringing about the concessions which are described later. It sends each member a monthly journal—*La Ligue*—devoted to questions concerning the family in the broad sense, including population movements, publishes a special monthly review for its officers, and is responsible for a number of tracts and pamphlets on population.[4] As in France, estimates of the future population have in recent years been used to emphasize the danger of declining numbers. In particular the computations of T. Vulhopp, in 1932,[5] and F. Baudhuin, in 1931,[6] are widely quoted in this connexion. According to the former, Belgian marriages were producing only 2·06 children on the average, and the continuance of current fertility, mortality, and nuptiality would

[1] Additional material on the origins and early intentions of the Ligue was kindly supplied to the writer by Mlle L. van den Plas in a letter dated 25 Feb. 1939.

[2] Information in a letter, dated 20 Dec. 1938, from the Ligue. See also *Almanach des Familles Nombreuses, 1937–8*, Anvers (n.d., but presumably the end of 1936), pp. 120–3.

[3] *La Ligue*, Nov. 1938, p. 151. No figures are given for the total population covered by this membership, but by analogy with the data for 1936 they would presumably amount to about 1·26 millions. The report states that the association now covers about 39·3 per cent. of all the large families of Belgium.

[4] Such as Dembour, E., *La Question de la Population*, Bruxelles, n.d. (apparently 1933 or 1934); Dupréel, E., *Surpeuplement, Eugénisme, Évolution*, Bruxelles, n.d.; [Fallon, V., S.J.] *La Population Belge et son Avenir*, Bruxelles, 1934.

[5] Vulhopp, T., 'La Population belge de demain', *Annales de la Soc. Sc. de Bruxelles, Série D.*, Jan.–Mar. 1932, pp. 28–41, and Vulhopp, T., 'Le développement de la population belge depuis 1830', *Proceedings of the Int. Conf. for Studies on Population, Rome, 1931*, vol. i, Rome, 1933, pp. 149–60.

[6] Baudhuin, F., 'L'avenir de la population belge', *Bulletin d'Information de la Banque Nationale de Belgique*, 10 June 1931; and in *Problems of Population* (ed. G.H.L.-F. Pitt-Rivers), London, 1932; also Baudhuin, F., 'L'Avenir de la population européenne', *Mariage et Natalité* (*Congrès de la Natalité*), Bruxelles-Paris, 1932.

result in a population of about 3·7 millions by the year 2030 (the total population of Belgium being about 8·28 millions at the beginning of 1935). Baudhuin's estimate also assumed the continuance of current fertility and mortality, and arrived at a population of about 6·7 millions by 1980, and 5·8 millions by the year 2000. In 1937 F. de Creeft[1] constructed a third estimate, assuming constant fertility and mortality, and obtaining a population of 7·3 millions by 1980, and 6·53 millions by 1995. These estimates are, however, somewhat crude in technique, and for the purpose of comparison the present writer has constructed a set of two new estimates, beginning from 1 January 1935. The first estimate assumes constant fertility and mortality at the level of 1934–5; and the second, constant mortality at the 1934–5 level and a constant annual supply of births at the absolute level of the average of 1934–5.[2] The total populations derived from these sets of hypotheses are: first estimate, 7·41 millions by 1980, 6·68 by 1995, and 6·45 by 2000, and the second estimate, 8·26 millions by 1980, 8·06 by 1995, 8·02 by 2000, and 7·93 by 2030, thenceforth remaining unchanged.

Having outlined the background of population policies in France and Belgium, the next stage is to discuss the various measures to which these policies have given rise. Broadly speaking the measures may be divided into two groups—repressive and positive. Under the first heading are the various laws aimed at discouraging activities helping to lower the birth-rate, such as birth control and abortion. Under the second are the measures designed to reduce the economic and other difficulties attached to the raising of large families. In some cases it is difficult to decide the precise classification of a measure. For example, a bachelor tax is in itself repressive, but it may be associated with a general system of taxation designed to reduce the burdens upon large families. But, generally speaking, the twofold classification is fairly satisfactory. The measures discussed in this section of the present chapter are those applied before the end of 1938, for,

[1] Creeft, F. de, *Étude sur l'Évolution des Charges Sociales de l'État*, Bruxelles, 1937, p. 28.

[2] *De jure* births were used. See subsequent discussion, p. 200. With the second estimate the population becomes stationary as from 2035, having the age structure of the 1934–5 life table.

clearly, only those measures could have influenced fertility trends up to the present. In France, however, some extremely important changes have been introduced still more recently, especially those specified in the new *Code de la Famille*, promulgated by a decree of 29 July 1939, and applicable as from 1 January 1940.[1] The new measures are far too important to omit from a discussion of French population policy, but since their possible results lie in the future, they are considered separately at the end of the chapter. It may be noted that certain of the new forms of material assistance provided for in the *Code de la Famille* will supersede some of the grants described in the present section. The *encouragement national* grants will cease, and the grants to needy large families will be considerably altered. Similarly, the present system of departmental birth premiums will be replaced by premiums given only for first births, provided that those births occur within the first two years of married life. But the grants and other forms of assistance considered in the present section are the only ones which have any bearing upon the fertility trends analysed in a later section of the chapter.

In France and Belgium purely repressive legislation is concentrated almost exclusively on abortion and birth control. The law relating to abortion is, in both these countries, derived from the *Code Pénal* of 1810, Paragraph 317, according to which penal servitude for five to ten years was prescribed both for the persons procuring the abortion of a pregnant woman and for the woman herself. If the abortion were procured by doctors, surgeons, or other health officials, or by pharmacists, the penalty was raised to hard labour for five to twenty years, entailing transportation to a penal colony.[2] In Belgium the law was repealed in 1867, as part of the general reform of the penal code which it had been

[1] At the time of writing (22 Oct. 1939) no official statement has yet defined the position of the new *Code* in relation to the War. It seems unlikely that many of the measures will be applied by 1 Jan. 1940, though they may be introduced later.

[2] See Garraud, R., *Traité Théorique et Pratique du Droit Pénal Français*, Paris, ed. of 1891, vol. i, p. 605, ed. of 1924 (1937 printing), vol. v, pp. 368–86; Roux, J. A., *Cours de Droit Criminel Français*, Paris, 1927, vol. i, p. 407; Griolet, G., Vergé, C., and Bourdeaux, H., *Code d'Instruction Criminelle et Code Pénal*, Collection Dalloz, Paris, 1912 ed., pp. 424, 413–14, and 308–9; Bourdeaux, H., *Code Pénal*, Collection Dalloz, Paris, 1938 ed., pp. 153–4.

originally intended to carry out in 1830, when the country gained its independence. Under the new law the penalty for procuring an abortion was prescribed as imprisonment for two to five years and a fine of 100 to 500 francs for the abortionist and the pregnant woman herself. If the woman had not given her consent, the penalty was increased to penal servitude for five to ten years, while additional penalties were prescribed for the abortionist if he or she were a doctor, surgeon, accoucheur, midwife, health official, or druggist, or if the woman died as the result of the abortion. This is still the law in Belgium.[1]

In France the unmodified *Code Pénal* persisted for a much longer period, in spite of the numerous attempts to obtain a reform of the law. It should, however, be noted that these attempts to alter the law were not dictated primarily by humanitarian feelings. Naturally, many writers protested against a law which imposed the same penalty upon a poor woman, who, because of poverty, induced an abortion on herself, as upon a professional abortionist. But, in the main, objections to the existing law were based upon a realistic analysis of the ineffectiveness of excessive severity. Between 1881 and 1910, of the cases brought to trial, sentences were given in fewer than 30 cases per year and under 37 per cent. of the persons prosecuted between 1881 and 1905 were actually sentenced. Even when the accused were found guilty, 'extenuating circumstances' were generally admitted by the jury, and this was so in over 80 per cent. of the sentences passed between 1881 and 1905.[2] In practice, therefore, the juries generally refused to implement the law. Regarding the matter from the point of view of married men, they refused to punish persons for an offence of which their own wives were frequently guilty. Hence the reiterated demand that abortion should be made a misdemeanour, to be tried without a jury, instead of a crime. Various Bills were introduced to bring about this change which, however, had to wait until after the War to be carried out. The law of

[1] See Nypels, J. S. G., *Le Code Pénal Belge Interprété*, Bruxelles, 1878, vol. ii, pp. 71–89; *Codes Edmond Picard*, Bruxelles, 1937, vol. ii, pp. 31 and 7.

[2] For earlier figures see Spiral, E.-A., *Essai d'une Étude sur l'Avortement*, Nancy, 1882, p. 59.

1923 then modified Paragraph 317 of the penal code and prescribed the following penalties: imprisonment for six months to two years, and a fine of 100 to 2,000 francs for any woman who induces an abortion on herself or who consents to an abortion procured for her, and imprisonment for one to five years, and a fine of 500 to 10,000 francs for any person procuring or attempting to procure the abortion of a pregnant woman. Guilty persons may also be prohibited from carrying on their normal professions, and temporarily exiled from their place of residence. By reducing the punishment from penal servitude and hard labour to simple imprisonment, abortion cases were henceforth taken out of the hands of the jury. Severity of sentence was sacrificed to certainty of punishment. In Belgium a comparable position obtains, for the *tribunaux correctionnels* (magistrates' courts) are empowered to deal with misdemeanours punishable with imprisonment from eight days to five years. Thus from 1926 to 1935 only five persons involved in abortion cases were tried by jury and 809 came before magistrates' courts.

While attempts have been made in France and Belgium to lessen the frequency of abortion by making the punishment less uncertain, these attempts have not been inspired by any desire to encourage the use of contraceptive appliances as a means of birth prevention. On the contrary, the mainspring of the whole movement has been the general population policy, no less antagonistic to birth control than to abortion. Consequently, both France and Belgium have laws designed to restrict the dissemination of birth-control knowledge. In France the 1920 law[1] prescribes imprisonment for one to six months, and a fine of 100 to 5,000 francs for any one engaging in birth-control propaganda, or who, for this purpose, divulges or offers to divulge, or who facilitates the use of methods for preventing pregnancy. In Belgium the 1923 law, which appears to have imitated the French law, prescribes imprisonment for eight days to six months, and

[1] This law also prescribes imprisonment for six months to three years and a fine of 100 to 3,000 francs for anyone inciting other persons to abortion, even if abortion does not follow, or who engages in the sale or distribution of articles intended for procuring abortion, even if there is no attempt at abortion or if, in fact, these articles could not procure abortion.

a fine of 26 to 500 francs,[1] for any one who displays or distributes articles specially intended for preventing conception; who causes the advertising of such goods in order to encourage their sale; who, for the purpose of profit, displays, sells, or distributes literature which gives birth-control information, advocates birth control or indicates how contraceptives may be obtained or used, or who, with a view to trade or distribution, engages in the making, importing, distributing, or advertising of such literature.

If these laws had been effective, married or unmarried persons wishing to prevent the conception of unwanted children would have been driven to abstention, *coitus interruptus* or *reservatus*, or the 'safe period'. This may have happened,[2] though insufficient evidence is available for any definite conclusion to be reached. But a number of factors weigh against it as a specific consequence of the laws. First, the French law of 1920 and the Belgian law of 1923 are much more effective in theory than they are in practice. In neither country is the condom legally defined as a contraceptive, but as a protection against venereal disease, and one of the most commonly used mechanical contraceptives thus remains outside the provisions drawn up by the law. Moreover, even in France, where interpretation of the law is more rigorous, other devices which may be used for contraception, though not designed for that purpose, are not prohibited. Thus the douche and the sponge may be bought quite openly, and it is not even quite certain if the simple sale of the more specialized contraceptives, unaccompanied by

[1] Increased sevenfold since the devaluation of the Belgian franc. The law provides the same penalties for incitement to abortion, or for engaging in the manufacture, distribution, or publicizing of abortifacients or goods advertised as such. See Garraud, P., and Laborde-Lacoste, M., *La Répression de la Propagande contre la Natalité*, Aix-en-Provence, 1921; Bourdeaux, H., *Code Pénal*, p. 155; *Codes Edmond Picard*, op. cit., p. 34.

[2] An inquiry by Lanval, M. (*L'Amour sous le Masque*, Bruxelles, 2nd ed., 1937, pp. 53–4) throws some light on this. Of 565 women answering a question on contraception, 149 disclaimed any knowledge of birth-control techniques, and of the remaining 416, 337 indicated *coitus interruptus* as the method they knew. But the inquiry dealt with a highly selected population—due to the Press antagonism to it—distributed in France as well as Belgium. Notice also that, as regards the 'safe period', one book describing the method (Marchal, A., and Méro, O. J. de, *La Liberté de la Conception*, Lille, 1935) is reputed to have reached a circulation of over 400,000 by 1937–8.

propaganda, is really illegal. There is in any case a clandestine sale of the reputedly prohibited contraceptives, and soluble pessaries are advertised in at least one French paper. In Belgium the position is even more confused. Scientific works on contraception do not, according to the decision of the Belgian Supreme Court of Appeal on 7 December 1931, come within the scope of the law, and it would appear that only those propagandists who have a profit motive, and only those commercial dealers who engage in propaganda or display, can be penalized.

In both countries, too, there are still birth-control movements demanding the repeal of the relevant laws and pressing for the legalization of abortion, though these movements have little political weight. This absence of political power is indeed a rather striking phenomenon, particularly in relation to legal developments in France. In that country, towards the end of the nineteenth century, the influence of the English birth-control movement was felt very strongly.[1] In 1896 thc Ligue de la Régénération Humaine was founded by Paul Robin, and a journal, *Régénération*, was issued at irregular intervals until 1902, when, with the help of Eugène Humbert, the journal took on a more permanent form. In its beginnings the movement was attacked ferociously by the Press—though the Press subsequently decided that to ignore it completely would be a more effective weapon—and it did not by any means receive whole-hearted support from the working-class political groups, many of which were pro-natalist in doctrine.[2] Nevertheless, the movement grew strongly between 1902 and 1908, and carried on a widespread propaganda. In 1908 internal dissension persuaded Robin to cease publishing his journal, and the movement split. But the separate sections carried on a strong propaganda, spread by new periodicals such as *Génération Consciente*, *Rénovation*, and *Le Malthusien*, and even during the War Gabriel Giroud, another of the leaders in the movement, produced first *Le Néo-malthusien*, and

[1] The English neo-Malthusian movement really inspired the continental birth-control movements in the late nineteenth century, though some of the continental movements were considerably more militant than the English original.

[2] See Note IV*e*, p. 442.

then, after successive suppressions by the censor, *Le Néo-Malthusisme* and *La Grande Question*.[1] The 1920 law brought to an end any hopes of a large-scale birth-control movement, but it did not put an end to publications on the subject. Apart from various novels by Victor Margueritte, Paul Reboux, and others, Eugène Humbert[2] began *La Grande Réforme* as a monthly journal in 1931, and it has continued to appear since that date, helped at times in its propaganda by similar, but less hardy, publications such as *Le Problème Sexuel* and *Pamphlet*. But in spite of fairly widespread and persistent propaganda the birth-control movement has almost completely failed to influence legislation. The proviso 'almost' is inserted because the movement may have possibly postponed the legislation. But in the end the pro-natalist associations have achieved their object. Nevertheless, the birth-control movement has had one effect. It has produced, and, in spite of the 1920 Act, is still producing books and pamphlets in support of family limitation. Marc Lanval, who directs the Belgian birth-control movement, with its membership of about 10,000, says that the result of the Belgian law of 1923 is that 'In practice, the benefit of contraception remains without hindrance for those who "know," i.e. the upper classes, but the poor are not even aware of the subject!'[3] This, however, is certainly much less the case in France, where the residue of the militant birth-control tradition still remains to support the much older tradition of family limitation among the agricultural population.[4]

The second factor to be considered is the importance of abortion as a method of birth prevention. By the end of the nineteenth century, abortion was notoriously common in France. The trade of abortionist was practised fairly openly, the abortionists frequently being midwives, whose legal pro-

[1] See Note IV*f*, p. 443.

[2] A brief biography of Humbert is given in Hardy, G., 'A French propagandist', *Sixth International Neo-Malthusian and Birth Control Conference*, ed. Sanger, M., vol. iv, New York, 1926, pp. 239–40. He was closely connected with the early developments of French neo-Malthusianism.

[3] Lanval, M., 'Birth control in Belgium', *Marriage Hygiene*, May, 1937, pp. 312–13. See also the issues of *Lumière et Liberté*, the journal of the Belgian movement.

[4] See Note IV*g*, p. 443.

fession was to a considerable extent overcrowded, and the charges were often only 50 francs and sometimes as low as 20 or 10 francs.[1] In addition, self-induced abortions formed a very large class, perhaps the largest. The frequency of criminal abortion was variously estimated—at 100,000 per year by Leroy Beaulieu, at 185,000 by Balthazard, at 35 to 40 per cent. of all conceptions by Dr. Doleris, and at 500,000 per year by Dr. Lacassagne, as compared with about 850,000 live births per year. The estimates vary considerably, and none of them can be regarded as more than informed guesses. But the total evidence is sufficient to suggest that at the end of the nineteenth and in the early part of the twentieth century, abortion was very widespread,[2] and that pro-natalist propaganda was quite unable to check it.

Nor do the changes in the French law appear to have had any significant effects. The number of prosecutions is higher than before the War and the percentages of acquittals lower,[3] but recent estimates, even if they show very considerable margins of error, agree in attributing to abortion a significant part in family limitation. Thus the Alliance Nationale asserted, in 1937, that in the large towns there were more abortions than births; that they were spreading into rural districts; and that it would be an understatement to say that there was one abortion for every two births in France.[4] Speaking at the 1937 Medical Conference on fertility, M. Risler, President of the Conseil Supérieur de la Natalité, said: 'It is estimated that the figures [of abortions in France] range between 300,000 and 500,000 per year . . . and I believe that the latter figure is closer to the truth.'[5] Similar estimates of the amount of abortion were quoted by the

[1] See Note IV*h*, p. 444.

[2] See also, for additional estimates, Berthélemy, H., *De la Répression de l'Avortement Criminel*, Paris, 1917, p. 5, n. 2.

[3] In 1931, 1932, 1933, and 1934, the numbers of persons prosecuted were 381, 395, 352, 301, and the numbers acquitted were 77, 57, 61, and 78. (Information from the Ministry of Justice.)

[4] Tract on Abortion (*50.000 naissances de plus par an sans qu'il en coûte rien*), Paris, 1937. For general discussion see Siredy, A., 'La répression de l'avortement', *XIVe Congrès des Commissions Départementales de la Natalité*, Oct. 1937. A view antagonistic to the populationists is given in Pierreville, R., *L'Inégalité Humaine Devant La Mort et La Maladie*, Paris [1936], pp. 136–72.

[5] *La Médecine Générale Française*, Mar. 1937, p. 181.

authors of the 'Clamamus Bill' for modifying the laws of 1920 and 1923,[1] while Dr. Jean Dalsace, who was for many years associated with the sexual reform movement in France, said that 'from very reliable information I can estimate that in Paris there are at least 125 abortions for every 100 births'.[2] Eugène Humbert believes the figure to be about 800,000 abortions per year,[3] and, in a conversation, expressed the view that quite apart from the professional practice of abortion, there are a great many self-induced abortions, intra-uterine injections commonly being used, and also that urethral catheters, sold nominally for the treatment of venereal disease, are employed by women to produce abortion.[4] In Belgium, too, the incidence of abortion is apparently high. Dr. Keiffer estimated that between 1 January 1919 and 31 December 1923 there were between 750,000 and one million abortions. In the same period there were 749,470 confinements, and the courts prosecuted in only 3,323 cases and pronounced only 283 sentences.[5] Marc Lanval considers that 'it is generally accepted that 55 to 60 pregnancies out of a hundred are interrupted artificially',[6] while Mlle Tilla Vulhopp has given a figure of 150,000 to 200,000 abortions per year, as compared with about 150,000 births.[7]

[1] *Proposition de loi tendant à organiser la protection sociale de la maternité et de l'enfance, etc.*, 31 Mar. 1933.

[2] In a letter, dated Oct. 1937, to the present writer.

[3] Supplement to *La Grande Réforme,* May 1938. The issue of Aug. 1937 cites an estimate of 600,000.

[4] Speaking at the Chambre des Députés on 15 Dec. 1938, G. Roulleaux-Dugage drew attention to the enormous increase in abortion, and insisted on the need for a special police brigade, similar to that used for suppressing gambling and the drug traffic. He was supported, next day, by F. de Saint-Just, and the Ministre de l'Intérieur agreed to the proposal. (*Feuille d'Informations, Féd. des Ass. de Fams. Nombs. de France,* 12 Jan. 1939. See also *Revue de l'Alliance Nationale* Mar. 1939, pp. 83–4.) Similar proposals were made in the nineteenth century, and the Mayor of Tourcoing had a special 'flying squad' incite an abortionist to attempt to procure the abortion of a woman who was working with this 'flying squad'. But since the woman was not pregnant this resulted in an 'impossible crime' for which the abortionist could not be prosecuted. (See Roux, M. de, op. cit., p. 81.)

[5] Memorandum of the Belgian Ministry of Health (typescript), n.d. (but probably 1937), and in Terlinden, op. cit., p. 7.

[6] *Marriage Hygiene,* op. cit. In *Lumière et Liberté,* July–Aug. 1936, Lanval estimates miscarriages and abortions at over 200,000 per year.

[7] In *National Life,* May 1931. See also *Une Politique des Familles Nombreuses,* pp. 380–2, and 105. This estimate, too, really derives from Dr. Keiffer, professor of gynaecology at the University of Bruxelles.

Pro-natalists and supporters of birth control agree, therefore, that in both France and Belgium abortion is a customary method of birth prevention.

In these circumstances we must conclude that in neither country does the relevant legislation appear to be effective. Since this is the case—and it is freely admitted even by those who support the existing legislation—and since it is generally agreed by French and Belgian populationists that abortion has harmful consequences in the form of mortality or morbidity, it seems rather surprising not to find legislators, social workers, and doctors prepared, in the main, to accept the development of a birth-control movement. Whatever influence such a movement might have upon fertility trends, the provision of adequate birth control would at least be free from the harmful consequences to health to which abortion is generally assumed to give rise. But French populationists seem irrevocably committed to a policy of suppressing both birth control[1] and abortion, however inconsistent their attitude may be and however unsatisfactory the results of their policy.[2]

Within the sphere of positive encouragements to fertility, the most important form of assistance—family allowances and the services associated with them—has already been treated in some detail. There are, however, many other grants, rebates, and exemptions which need to be discussed

[1] Theoretically, even against the use of the 'safe period', though this appears to be sanctioned by the Catholic Church (cf. R. P. Mayrand, O.P., *Un Problème Moral*, Coublevie, 1934). Some Catholic priests have, however, attacked the use of this method because it provides a possibility of family limitation to persons who were previously prevented, by their religious devotion, from practising any form of restriction other than continence (cf. the remarks of R. P. Dassonville, *XVIIIe Congrès de la Natalité*, report, Laon, 1936, p. 107). An interesting discussion of the question by a supporter of the birth-control movement is given by Bellamy, H., 'D'un néo-malthusianisme catholique et orthodoxe', *Le Problème Sexuel*, Feb. 1935, pp. 19–22.

[2] For further details and bibliographic references see Glass, D. V., op. cit., *Modern Law Review*, Sept. 1938, pp. 97–113. A survey of the pro-natalist writings on abortion makes it clear that there has been a good deal of imitation in the literature. The influence of Tardieu, A., *Étude Médico-Légale sur l'Avortement*, Paris, 1879 (there was a 5th ed. in 1898); Brouardel, P., *L'Avortement*, Paris, 1901; and Du Moriez, S., *L'Avortement*, Paris, 1912, is visible in much of the subsequent literature on the subject. Even certain phrases are found to recur constantly, especially the phrase 'abortion is not regarded as more significant than having a tooth pulled'. For the changes in the abortion law under the new *Code de la Famille*, see present chapter, pp. 216–17.

in order to show the full structure of the population policies of France and Belgium, and before attempting to gauge the probable effects upon population trends in the two countries.[1]

In France a certain amount of help has been given within the framework of relief measures.[2] Under this broad title are included the heads of families whose means (excluding the various benefits which they may be receiving under other laws) are deemed insufficient for bringing up the children dependent upon them. The heads of the families may be the actual parents or, if the children are orphans, any relatives who are taking care of them. The level of 'sufficiency' is fixed by the Conseil Municipal, generally in accordance with a local scale approved by the Préfecture, and is based upon the number of children under 14 years of age, or under 16 years of age if they are ill, apprenticed, or continuing their studies. If both parents are alive, there must be at least four dependent children, the allowance being due from the fourth child onwards. If the mother is dead, the allowance is payable from the third child; from the second, if the father is dead; and to all the children if neither parent is alive. The allowance per dependent child ranges from 270 to 300 francs per year, except in Paris, where, since 1 January 1931, it is 600 francs per year, and is payable in addition to any grants which are due under the Social Insurance Acts. Under this same system of laws[3] pregnant women may receive a total grant of 120 to 420 francs for the four weeks preceding and the four weeks subsequent to their confinement. The women must not be entitled to Social Insurance grants (though their husbands may be), must be in need, must not work during the period, and must not be in receipt of any form of public maternity benefit under the law of 27 June 1904. In general, these grants are given from the birth of the third child, but in cases of necessity they may be given from the first birth. There are also breast-feeding allowances of up to 45 francs per month for the first six months after the birth of the child,

[1] See Dequidt, G., *Le Statut des Familles Nombreuses*, Paris, 1922; Théodore, M., *Le Nouveau Code de la Famille*, Paris, 1937 ed.; *Avantages Réservés aux Familles Nombreuses* (issued by L'Alliance Nationale) ed. of 15 July 1938.

[2] Under the Act of 14 July 1913, modified by subsequent legislation up to and including Art. 5 of the Act of 1 Mar. 1935, and the decree-law of 30 Oct. 1935.

[3] The Acts of 17 June 1913 and 16 Apr. 1930, and the decree-law of 30 Oct. 1935.

and 15 francs per month for the next six months.[1] Women who cannot suckle their children are entitled to allowances for milk for feeding the children. Many towns and Départements provide free clinics for nursing mothers, and the confinement and suckling allowances may be paid through these clinics, which may, in addition, give free milk or extra monetary grants to the mothers if they deem this advisable. Comparable grants are also given under the laws relating to 'national encouragement' to large families,[2] where the family contains at least three dependent children[3] and where the income is not large enough to pay income-tax. As in the case of the previous legislation, there are also allowances for smaller families when the father, or mother, or both are dead or have disappeared or been interned. Where both parents are alive 120 francs per year are paid for the third child, 360 for the fourth, and 540 for the fifth and each subsequent child. Where the mother is dead, the allowance is 360 francs for the third child, and 540 francs for each subsequent child. When the father is dead, 360 francs are given for the second child, and 960 francs for each subsequent child. Finally, where both parents are dead, 360 francs are given for the first child and 960 francs for each subsequent child.[4] These allowances cannot be received at the same time as the monetary relief previously described, nor can they be held while receiving family allowances paid by the State, the Départements, Communes, or public services to their employees, but they may be held together with family allowances under the 1932 Act, and orphans' pensions under the Social Insurance Acts. They are given only where the family is of French nationality, whereas the previously described grants

[1] The Act of 24 Oct. 1919, and later legislation mentioned in n. 3, p. 166.

[2] Acts of 22 July 1923, 13 July 1925, 29 Apr. 1926, 16 Apr. 1930, 13 Aug. 1936; decrees of 27 Feb. 1924, 17 Aug. 1924, 10 Mar. 1928; decree-laws of 4 Apr. 1934, 30 June 1934, and 16 July 1935.

[3] The term 'dependent' having the same meaning as for the assistance to large families.

[4] Under the decrees of 12 Nov. 1938 these sums were increased, as from 1 Apr. 1939, to 240 francs per year for the third child, and 540 for the fourth and for each subsequent child when both parents are alive and living together, with comparable increases for the other cases—a wife living alone (widowed or separated) would receive 360 francs per year for the second child, 960 for the third, and 1,200 for each subsequent child (*Familles de France*, May 1939, p. 3). But this form of *encouragement* has been stopped by the *Code de la Famille*.

are of interest particularly for those aliens with whose countries reciprocal treaties have been concluded in respect of similar forms of assistance—that is, Italians, Poles, Belgians, and citizens of Luxemburg.

Social insurance[1] provisions have also been modified in order to give special advantages to families. Thus a woman who is insured is entitled to an allowance ranging from 3 to 22 francs per day for six weeks before and six weeks after her confinement—in addition to medical attention and the payment of incidental costs—provided that she gives up all paid employment during that period. When the child is born, the woman who is insured is entitled to a suckling allowance, amounting to not more than 850 francs for the whole period, but not less than 175 francs per month for the first four months. If the woman cannot, for medical reasons, suckle her child, but if nevertheless she looks after the child herself, she is entitled to receive coupons for milk up to the value of 510 francs for the first year of the child's life.[2] The same provision may be made if, for medical reasons, the child has to be taken away from the mother. When the insured person has reached 60 years of age, he is entitled to a pension equal to at least 40 per cent. of his annual wage or salary—provided that by that age, or by the age of 65 years he has paid insurance premiums for 30 years—and the pension is increased by 10 per cent. if he has brought up at least three children to the age of 16 years. The allowance paid during illness, or the invalidity pension given to an insured person is also increased for each dependent child, while on the death of the insured person, the capital sum payable—equal to 20 per cent. of the basic annual average wage or salary of the deceased[3]—is increased by 100 francs for each child. At the same time the widows of insured persons are entitled to temporary pensions if they have at least three dependent children, these pensions being payable for the second and

[1] See Note IV*i*, p. 445.

[2] Similar advantages are given to persons who have taken advantage of the optional insurance. But the wives of insured persons—even those unoccupied wives who have taken out a special insurance for themselves—are entitled only to medical attention and maternity benefit, but not to the suckling allowance.

[3] But this capital sum appears to be fixed within the limits of 1,000 and 2,160 francs, excluding the additions in respect of the children.

subsequent children. If both parents are dead, the dependent children are themselves entitled to temporary pensions. Unemployment assistance also varies with the number of children, though in no case may it exceed half the wage or salary (including the family allowances customarily paid for the given occupation and district).

In accordance with the various Acts passed and decrees issued between 1918 and 1935,[1] the State subsidizes Départements and Communes giving premiums of not less than 300 and not more than 1,000 francs on the birth of the third or fourth and subsequent children. Up to November 1935 these premiums could be claimed by all families, whatever their incomes, but since the application of the decree-law of 30 October 1935, the State subsidy is given only when the premiums are restricted to families where the head earns too little to be subject to income-tax.[2] In general, half the grant is payable at the birth of the child, and the remainder when the child is one year of age. In 1937, 85 Départements gave premiums. In 5, the basic premium grant was 100 francs; in 6, 150 francs; in 19, 200 francs; in 4, 250 francs; in 40, 300 francs; in 4, 400 francs; in 2, 500 francs; and in 2, 650 francs; while 3 Départements had no ruling as to the minimum amount, but simply added to the premiums given by the Communes. Most of the Communes share in the premiums, and there are only 5 Départements and less than 1,500 Communes[3] in which birth premiums are not provided. In most cases the basic payment, due for the third or fourth child, is raised at each subsequent birth—often until it reaches 1,000 francs, when it becomes stationary at that figure, or, in some cases, without any prescribed upper limit.

In the field of taxation various rebates are given for families, while additions are made for unmarried and childless.[4] Thus, in the income-tax calculations, an allowance

[1] Acts of 29 June 1918, 30 Apr. 1921, 19 Dec. 1926; decree of 30 Apr. 1920; decree-law of 30 Oct. 1935.

[2] Before the application of the decree-law of 1935, there were four Départements which restricted the premiums to families not subject to income-tax—Indre-et-Loire, Lot-et-Garonne, Sarthe, and Seine-et-Oise.

[3] And more than 11,000 in which they are given.

[4] Acts of 31 July 1917, 25 June 1920, and subsequent Finance Acts; Budget Act of 31 Dec. 1936; Tax Reform Act of 31 Dec. 1936; decree-laws of 4 Apr. and 30 June 1934, 20 July 1934, and 30 Oct. 1935.

of 10,000 francs per year is given for an unmarried man, an additional 5,000 francs if the taxpayer is married or is a widower with dependent children, plus 5,000 francs for each of the first two children, 10,000 francs for the third, and 15,000 francs for each additional child. These provisions apply fully only to incomes below 75,000 francs per year, and the term 'child' is understood to mean any child dependent upon the taxpayer, less than 21 years of age, or with no age limit if the child is incapable of working. By contrast, the income-tax is increased by 30 per cent. if the taxpayer is over 30 years of age, unmarried, widowed or divorced, and childless, and by 15 per cent. if he has been married for more than two years and is still childless.[1] For the different scheduled taxes (*impôts cédulaires*)—on wages and salaries, commercial, industrial, and agricultural profits —there are comparable reductions for children, the rebate on each tax not to exceed 800 francs per dependent child. Inheritance duties are also lowered in proportion to the number of children of the testator and to the number of children of the legatee.[2]

This analysis does not by any means exhaust the list of laws aimed at improving the relative position of the family. In housing, for example, many laws, passed between 1894 and 1938, have been designed to help provide reasonable accommodation at a relatively low price. Thus, under the Ribot Act of 1908, the State gives subsidies to Communes, public institutions, 'cheap housing' societies, savings banks, philanthropic institutions, &c., for the purpose of building cheap houses intended for the use of families having at least four children under 16 years of age. Under the Loucheur Act of 1928 the State gives subsidies to individuals who wish to buy or build their own houses, and to organizations prepared to build cheap houses. For individual borrowers the subsidies amount to 5,000 francs for a family with at least three children under 18 years of age, and are increased by

[1] But apparently adopted children are reckoned on the same footing as natural children for the purpose of avoiding the higher rates of taxation. These higher rates do not apply to women unless they have incomes above 75,000 francs per year.

[2] Note also that under the decree-laws of 29 June 1938 the right to dispose of the family property was modified. (See Canavaggio, D., 'Une grande réforme en faveur de la paysannerie française', *Paris Soir*, 28 July 1938.)

2,500 francs for each additional child, up to a maximum of 15,000 francs. A law of 1922 authorizes *sociétés de crédit immobilier* to lend money to co-operative 'cheap housing' associations in which all the shareholders have more than three children, for buying or building collective houses, in which at least two-thirds of the accommodation must be let to large families. Communes and Départements are authorized to build cheap houses on condition that they shall be intended mainly for large families. Allotments are also provided on easy terms for large families.[1]

Among other advantages given to families the following may be noted. A series of laws reduces the military obligations of members of these families. This applies to military exercises, allowances, reservist classification, and obligation to serve in the colonies. Family allowances are, of course, given to members of the armed forces. As regards secondary and technical education, bursaries are given by preference to children of large families, and school fees are reduced—by as much as 25 per cent. of tuition and boarding costs—when a number of children from the same family are at school at the same time. Reductions in railway fares are given to families with at least three children under 18 years of age—30 per cent. reduction for three children, rising by 10 per cent. for each additional child to a maximum reduction of 70 per cent. for seven or more children. These reductions apply to the parents' fares as well as to those of the children. In addition, a reduction of 30 per cent. is granted to the parents—and to apply throughout their life—if at any time after 10 August 1923 their living children, whatever their age, together with any who were *morts pour la France*, amounted to at least five. Comparable reductions are given by a number of steamship lines and by certain tramway companies. Government employees receive a wide range of

Details of activity under the various headings are usually given in the reports of the annual Congrès de la Natalité. Coutard, J., *Les Habitations à Bon Marché*, Paris, 1938, p. 131, says that the subsidies under article 59 of the Act of 5 Dec. 1922 and article 11 of the Act of 13 July 1928 have been suspended by decree since 1934. See also pp. 51 and 54–5 of the same work. Risler, G., *Rapport du Conseil Supérieur des Habitations à Bon Marché, Année 1937*, (Ministère de la Santé Publique), Paris, 1938, p. 3, also refers to the suppression of the subsidies formerly given to large families. See also *Housing Policy in Europe*, International Labour Office, Geneva, 1930, pp. 205–34, for general discussion of French housing legislation.

special advantages, including relatively valuable family allowances. A State honour—the Médaille de la Famille Française—created in 1920, is reserved for the mothers of large and worthy families with at least five living, legitimate children, and the grades of this medal—bronze, silver, and silver-gilt—rise as the family size increases from five to ten children. Finally, various institutions and individuals have created endowments for awarding annual prizes to large families or their individual members. Judging from the list of prizes, about four million francs are given away each year to about 500 families. Naturally, there is always considerable pressure by pro-natalist associations to obtain further advantages. The family vote is constantly urged, and recently, in imitation of Germany, a strong demand has been made for marriage loans, though one school of thought has recommended that the loans should be on Swedish and not on German principles.[1]

In Belgium there are comparable, though not so numerous advantages, and, as in France, they have been obtained largely through the persistent propaganda of the pro-natalist movement.[2] Birth premiums are given by the State to its employees for legitimate or legitimated children, and amount normally to 250 francs per child.[3] The Provinces follow the same ruling and many Communes also give premiums to their employees and to other persons in their region. Various Friendly Societies provide similar grants and, as has been mentioned, they are also given by a number of equalization funds.

Since the end of the War taxation has also been modified to some extent to reduce the burdens on families. Thus the land tax on a house occupied by the head of a family containing at least three children is reduced by 7 per cent. for each dependent child. Under the general heading of personal taxes there are similar reductions. Certain occupations are, for example, exempt from the professional tax if their taxable

[1] See Note IV*j*, p. 445.

[2] Information obtained from *Almanach des Familles Nombreuses, 1937–8, Le Guide des Dirigeants*, Nov. 1938, and from the material supplied by the secretariat of the Ligue des Familles Nombreuses.

[3] The amount varies with the retail price index—237·5 francs when the index is 648–83, 250 francs when it is 684–717, 262·5 francs when it is 718–52, &c.

incomes are below 7,200 francs per year in Communes with a population of 30,000 or more, 5,600 francs in Communes with 5,000 to 30,000 inhabitants, and so forth, and this exempted minimum is raised by one-fifth for each dependent person.[1] If there are more than two dependent children, the additional exemption is fixed at 2,500 francs for the third and fourth child, 4,000 for the fifth and sixth, and 5,000 francs for each subsequent child, whatever the population of the Commune. Commercial, industrial, and agricultural profits are subject to similar exemptions, except that the exempted income is a third below that in the previous case. For both taxes there are also reductions in the tax itself, amounting to 5 per cent. for each dependent person, this reduction being raised to 7 per cent. for each dependent child from the third onwards. The complementary personal tax is designed in a similar way—with a higher exempted income, increased by one-fifth for each dependent child if the family has at least three children, and the actual tax reduced by 7 per cent. for each dependent child in families with three or more children. The 'crisis tax' (*contribution nationale de crise*) contains comparable provisions, and many of the provincial and communal taxes are designed in the same way. So too are the inheritance duties, which are reduced in proportion to the number of children of the testator and legatee.

Special advantages as regards house accommodation are given in two separate ways. First, there is the system of 'cheap houses' (*habitations à bon marché*) set up under an Act of 1919. The Act aims at slum clearance and the suppression of overcrowding, but is none the less intended to give first preference to large families and grant them rent rebates. Since 1919 the National 'Cheap Housing' Society and its affiliated associations have built 47,000 houses and 13,000 flats, and under the terms of their charter 34 per cent. of the accommodation must be reserved for families of at

[1] By a dependent person is meant any one, child or adult, with an income below a figure varying with the population of the Commune—e.g. 4,500 francs per year in Communes with more than 30,000 inhabitants or when his or her income is included with the taxable income of the head of the family. A family of at least three children may also be a family with two living children and one child killed in the War, or with one living child and two killed in the War.

least 5 persons. The stipulated rent rebates are 20 per cent. for 3 children, 30 per cent. for 4, 40 per cent. for 5, and 50 per cent. when there are 6 or more children. In 1937 these rent rebates appear to have amounted to more than 3 million francs, and the total amount spent on them since 1925 exceeds 21 million francs. For house purchase, too, special concessions are available for families whose annual incomes are not greater than 17,000 to 23,000 francs, according to the population of the Commune in which they live, these amounts being raised by 5 per cent. for 1 child, 10 per cent. for 2 children, and rising to 50 per cent. for 6 or more children, so that the upper limit of income is from 25,500 to 34,500 francs, depending upon the population of the Commune. The State subsidizes the building of these 'cheap houses' and increases the individual subsidies by 10 per cent. for 1 child, 20 per cent. for 2, and an additional 20 per cent. for each further child, no upper limit being stipulated. Similarly, the minimum cost per house authorized by the State is raised by 10 per cent. when there are 4 or more children. In practice, however, the house purchase arrangements do not seem to have worked very satisfactorily. Even with these rebates and subsidies the costs are still too high for the large families, and it is estimated that only 5 per cent. of the families buying 'cheap houses' have 4 or more children.[1] The National 'Cheap Housing' Society was also authorized by the State to lend 35 million francs, at $2\frac{1}{2}$ per cent. interest, to the Ligue des Familles Nombreuses, for the object of setting up a *fonds du logement*. By this means a second system of housing advantages is provided. The *fonds du logement*, created and controlled by the Ligue, consists of three sections. The first obtains its capital from the product of the national lottery, plus a number of grants from the central and local government authorities. The second section receives subscriptions from the *Fonds du Logement* Co-operative Society. These two sections may each lend up to

[1] There are still, according to the director of the Société Nationale de H.B.M., 70,000 overcrowded and 30,000 unimprovable slum houses in Belgium. 20,000 large families live in these dwellings and they contain a total of more than 400,000 persons. (See *Le Guide des Dirigeants*, Nov. 1938.) For general discussion of Belgian housing legislation, see *Housing Policy in Europe*, op. cit., pp. 240–59. See also Gosseries, F., *L'Habitation à Bon Marché*, Louvain-Bruxelles, 1939, especially ch. vi.

5,000 francs at the same time and to the same person, the interest charged being $3\frac{1}{4}$ per cent., and the loan may be given for a period up to 20 years. The third section, which is subsidized by the State through the National 'Cheap Housing' Society, may give individual loans up to 12,000 francs if there are 4 dependent children, plus an additional 2,000 francs for each dependent child beyond the fourth, the loan being extended for as long as 20 years and the rate of interest charged being $3\frac{1}{4}$ per cent.[1] It should be noted that the total loan received from the various sections (a loan cannot simultaneously be held from more than two sections) must not generally exceed 13,500 francs, though in some cases this limit is raised to 17,000 francs, plus an additional 2,000 francs for each dependent child beyond the fourth. The main conditions for obtaining such loans are first, that the family should contain at least four living children sharing the same household, and secondly, that the family should not be 'well-off', but should nevertheless have an income sufficient to allow the regular payment of interest and amortization as well as to cover the normal household expenses.[2]

Educational advantages cover two broad headings. Within the State schools partial or complete remission of fees may be obtained—complete if the annual income of the family does not exceed 15,000 francs, plus 3,000 francs for each dependent child from the second, and partial if the income is between 15,000 and 20,000 francs—together with special reductions in fees for the second and subsequent children of large families. In many schools not exclusively State controlled reductions are also given. Secondly, the Ligue has a *fonds des études*, created largely from subsidies and advances given by the State. From this fund families with at least four children may borrow sums ranging from

[1] The rate of interest is liable to increase when the number of *dependent* children is less than four. The above information is largely from the *Almanach des Familles Nombreuses*, *1937–8*, pp. 53–6, and the *Almanach* for 1939, pp. 56–8. In the interval between the publication of the first and second of these Almanachs the rate of interest was fixed at $3\frac{1}{4}$ per cent. It had formerly been 2 per cent. for the first section, 4 per cent. for the second, and 3 per cent. for the third. The regulations are apparently to be changed again.

[2] Additional information was received, in Dec. 1938, from the Ligue des Familles Nombreuses, and has been incorporated in the summary given above.

750 to 5,000 francs to help in paying the full-time educational expenses of their children. The loans may be spread over 20 years, in which case a payment of 7 per cent. per year on the original loan covers the interest of $2\frac{1}{2}$ per cent. plus amortization and administrative charges. Each loan is made for one school year, but additional loans may, of course, be obtained for further years.

Among the other provisions made for families, the following summary covers the most important examples. As in France, special concessions are given in respect of military service, and are naturally very valuable in countries in which conscription is an integral part of the structure. These concessions in Belgium include exemption from military service—complete or partial—postponement of, or reduction in the length of military service, and certain privileges in time of war. As regards travelling costs, the railways grant 50 per cent. reductions in fares to members of families with at least four children under 21 years of age, and reductions of 75 per cent. for those children who are between 4 and 10 years of age. In association with the railways there are opportunities for specially cheap holidays, accommodation being provided in old railway carriages. Many local tram and bus companies offer special reductions in the price of schoolchildren's season tickets. Provision is also made for widows and orphans. Thus, under the Insurance Act of 1930 and 1937, the widows of insured workers are entitled to a grant of 240 francs per year for each dependent child under 16 years of age, and if both parents die, an annual grant of 420 francs per year is paid to the person or organization taking care of the children. The Ligue itself, moreover, has a number of special funds for helping widows and children.[1] A system of *entr'aide familiale* has been set up by the Ligue, and provides household help—free or paid—in emergencies when, through illness, accident, or unavoidable absence, mothers are unable to look after their children. Many shops in the various Belgian towns give price reductions of 5 to 10 per cent. to the members of the Ligue. The work of the Œuvre Nationale de l'Enfance should not be forgotten. Deriving from the Ligue Nationale, which was

[1] Cf. *La Ligue*, July–Aug. 1937.

founded in 1903, it concerns itself primarily with the health of children and, naturally, with that of expectant mothers. In 1906 it received its first government subsidy and, partly in recognition of the work which it carried on during the War, was transformed into an official but independent body under an Act of 1919, through which it received its present title. By the end of 1937 it was responsible for 144 centres, carrying out home visits to mothers and children in 713 Communes, 8 maternity homes, 63 crèches, and a large number of convalescent homes, as well as for numerous pre- and post-natal medical consultations.[1] Finally, some individual firms give various additional forms of assistance. Thus, four firms give a supplement to the normal wage of each worker who has one or more dependent children and whose wife remains at home to take care of them.[2]

The measures and the propagandist activity briefly described in this and in the previous chapter are directed almost exclusively against the low level of fertility in France and Belgium. There is no doubt that fertility is low in both these countries. In 1935 the gross reproduction rate in France was 1·004, and in Belgium about 0·929 in 1934–5, and the net reproduction rates were 0·866 and about 0·802 respectively. The rates in France were not, it should be emphasized, as low as many propagandists appeared to believe. When the members of the 1936 Congrès de la Natalité began their resolutions on population policy with the statement: 'Seeing that the demographic position in France is more serious than in any other country . . .',[3] they appeared to be unaware of the still lower reproduction rates in England and Wales, Belgium, Norway, and Sweden, though it is true that France was nearer to an actual decline in numbers than these other countries.[4] But it must be

[1] See *Œuvre Nationale de l'Enfance*, Bruxelles, n.d. (but evidently 1938).

[2] These allowances are paid by the employers and are graduated progressively according to the number of dependent children. They are not connected with the grants of the equalization funds which, in Belgium, do not give additional allowances for wives who are not gainfully employed. (See *La Ligue*, Feb. and June 1938.) Two of the firms actually introduced differential allowances in 1929. (See *Familles de France*, April 1938.)

[3] *XVIIIe Congrès de la Natalité* (1936), Laon, 1936, p. 95.

[4] Because France had had net reproduction rates below unity for a much longer period than these other countries. See subsequent discussion.

remembered that opinion in France was, especially in recent years, conditioned by the existence of the large and potentially antagonistic populations of Germany and Italy, and any rate of growth smaller than that shown by these neighbours would, in the view of French pro-natalists, be dangerously low. In Belgium this fear cannot play so important a part since the difference in size of her own population and the populations of her potential opponents is already too great to be influenced materially by natural increase in the near future. Belgium appears to be influenced far more by the possible internal problems resulting from falling numbers. The question of the size of the army is often mentioned, but in recent years far more emphasis has been placed upon the economic disadvantages. At the same time there seems to be some fear—as expressed, for example, by Baudhuin—that attempts to supplement inadequate fertility by immigration could only mean the eventual colonization of the country by Slavs.

But the object of this chapter is not so much to discuss how far present fertility in France and Belgium is inadequate for the maintenance of the population, or to analyse reproductive trends in these countries—though the discussion of both these questions must form an essential part of the chapter[1]—as to examine recent changes in fertility in relation to the attempts to encourage marriage and the raising of families. That is, the question to be answered is: How far have France and Belgium succeeded in checking or changing the downward trend in fertility? We may attempt to answer the question in two ways. First, we may examine the results among the populations receiving most financial encouragement—that is, among the members of the family allowance systems. Secondly, we may attempt to decide, by examining fertility trends in the different parts of France and Belgium, and in the countries as a whole, whether there has been any substantial change in the trends in recent years, and if so, whether this can be attributed to the population policies. But it should be noted in advance that the analysis is necessarily tentative. There are no control groups in the field of social action by which experiments can be tested. At best,

[1] See Note IV*k*, p. 446.

provided that the statistics are adequate, we cannot do more than weigh up the chances that a particular movement in fertility, or a particular fertility differential is due to the various population measures.

Let us begin by examining a specific experiment undertaken in France, the family allowances granted by the firm of Michelin, at Clermont-Ferrand, since 1916. According to a report issued by the firm in 1929,[1] an early investigation undertaken in the firm showed that out of every 100 families of their workers, 62 had no children, 27 had 1 only, 8 had 2, and only 3 had 3 or more children. It occurred to the employers that this situation was not peculiar to their factory, and that if it persisted, France would soon become a desert, or would be colonized by countries more plentifully supplied with children. The Michelin factory would therefore become empty, or else it would have to be filled with foreigners. To remedy the situation in their firm, they decided to give substantial family allowances. By 1926 these apparently amounted to 75 francs per month for 1 child under 16 years of age, 150 for 2 children, 300 for 3, and 100 francs more for each additional child. By 1929 the grants had risen to 100 francs per month for 1 child, 200 for 2 children, 405 for 3, 540 for 4, plus 135 francs per month for each additional child.[2] The results, according to the Michelin Company, may be seen from Table 13, which compares the 1924 birth-rates of Michelin families with those of the population not working in that firm.[3] For the whole Michelin population of Clermont-Ferrand and its suburbs the birth-rate was 25·10 in 1924 and 29·80 in 1928. For the non-Michelin population the corresponding rates were 14·60 and 11·90 per thousand.[4]

These large differences convinced many writers, especially

[1] 'Une expérience de natalité', in *Prospérité*, Jan.–Mar. 1929. This summarizes the position and gives birth data for 1924 and 1928. The original report appears to have been issued in 1926.

[2] See Note IV*l*, p. 446.

[3] These figures are from Dequidt, G., and Forestier, G., 'Une expérience de natalité. L'efficacité des allocations familiales sur la natalité est-elle démontrée?', *Le Mouvement Sanitaire*, 1926, pp. 485–503. This is the article referred to in the subsequent discussion. See also Ichok, G., 'La dénatalité, ses prophètes et ses médecins', *Le Problème Sexuel*, Feb. 1935, pp. 1–7.

[4] *Prospérité*, Jan.–Mar. 1929, p. 8.

journalists, of the success of the experiment. But two doctors, Dequidt and Forestier, believing that the success might not be as unmistakable as the figures appeared to indicate, attempted to make a more rigorous examination of the results. They were unable to obtain full details from Michelin & Co., so they were restricted to one area, Cournon, for which, by way of example, some additional material

TABLE 13. *The Michelin Experiment*

	Births per 1,000 total population in 1924		*Ratios*	
	Non-Michelin families	*Michelin families*	*Non-Michelin families*	*Michelin families*
Clermont-Ferrand .	14·86	21·20	100	143
Riom . . .	14·70	30·60	100	208
Pont-du-Château .	12·94	32·10	100	248
Beaumont . .	8·10	21·50	100	265
Lempdes . .	12·30	40·46	100	329
Aubière . . .	7·34	28·10	100	383
Cournon . . .	10·40	52·06	100	501

had been published. The Michelin families living in Cournon, including the unmarried men and women working for the company, and the servants and grandparents, &c., living with the families—not those living with the unmarried workers—numbered 461 persons and produced 24 births. The non-Michelin population was estimated at 1,249 persons and produced 13 births.[1] But, according to the Michelin company, while the Michelin population contained 277 persons between the ages of 16 and 50 years, the non-Michelin population contained 436 in the same age group. The birth-rates constructed on the basis of these age groups—clearly more reasonable as fertility rates—show an advantage of only three to one in favour of the Michelin families, instead of that of five to one shown by the crude birth-rates. Further, it should be noted that the non-Michelin population includes any servants who were em-

[1] This, according to the 1926 census, was too high a figure for the non-Michelin population, and the resultant birth-rate was therefore too low. But no stress is laid on that fact here, since the position was the reverse for the other districts.

ployed by the unmarried Michelin workers, together with all the young persons who had just left the country to work in the town, and the military conscripts who, for the period of their service, were either infertile or whose fertility would not be imputed to Cournon. The fact that the non-Michelin population consisted of more than 50 per cent. of persons aged 50 years and over is already indicative of abnormality. When the other factors are added it is evident that no comparison would be satisfactory unless full details of age and marital condition were available. This also applies to the other districts where the birth-rate disparities were not so marked.[1] Moreover, since the Michelin families are working class, it would be natural to expect their fertility to be somewhat higher than that of the rest of the population.[2] Nor does the rise in the Michelin birth-rate from 25·1 in 1924 to 26·5 in 1927 and 29·8 in 1928 (per thousand of the Michelin population) give any more conclusive evidence. It is not unlikely that the high allowances attracted workers who in any case wanted to marry and have families, and this was in part admitted by L. Naudeau, though his own view was that in an atmosphere of large families new-comers are more likely to desire large families of their own.[3] But unless a more thorough investigation is made, the Michelin results cannot be accepted as conclusive evidence that family allowances were successful in raising the birth-rate.

A second specific case may be examined—the Haut Rhin equalization fund in France. In October 1927 Professor R. A. Fisher analysed the relationship between the number of employees belonging to the fund and the number of

[1] The present writer asked to be allowed to undertake a more detailed investigation, but was not given permission by the Michelin company (letter to the present writer, dated 1 June 1935). In a letter dated 16 Mar. 1935 the Michelin company stated that owing to significant variations each year in their personnel, no analysis has been made since 1929, it being deemed that the results prior to that year were sufficient evidence of the influence of family allowances.

[2] Dequidt and Forestier, op. cit., p. 501, cite some statistics for 1922 (though they do not give the source) relating to a working-class district of 16,000 persons. Eleven per cent. of the families had 3 or more children, as compared with 10·4 per cent. among the Michelin families in 1924. Dequidt and Forestier also point out, p. 499, that at Cournon 120 heads of Michelin families had a total of 160 children. Considered in relation to the birth-rate this is indicative of a population of young *ménages* but, as they say quite rightly, does not prove a tendency to large families.

[3] *La France Se Regarde*, Paris, 1931, p. 291.

children dependent upon them.[1] A table showing the main points in the analysis is given below. It will be seen that there is a fairly consistent increase in the number of children aged 0–1 per 100 employees. But this by itself does not mean the success of family allowances. In part, at least, it is due to an influx of parents with dependent children. 'Indeed,

TABLE 14. *Haut Rhin Equalization Fund*[2]

(Number of Children of Different Ages per 100 Employees, and Ratios between Children of Different Ages)

Period	*Age 0–1 year (a)*	*Age 1–2 years (b)*	*Age 5–6 years (c)*	*Age 11–12 years (d)*	*Age 12–13 years (e)*	*Age 13–14 years (f)*	*Ratio a/f*	*Ratio b/f*	*Ratio a/e*
1921 . .	3·85	4·22	1·80	3·54	3·70	3·55	1·08	1·19	1·04
1922 . .	3·98	4·08	1·44	3·30	3·50	3·42	1·16	1·19	1·14
1923 . .	3·72	3·85	1·71	3·42	3·30	2·33	1·60	1·65	1·13
1924 . .	3·76	4·13	2·97	3·43	3·56	2·60	1·45	1·59	1·06
1925 . .	3·86	4·07	4·43	3·40	3·37	2·21	1·75	1·84	1·15
1926 . .	3·87	4·29	4·67	2·27	3·56	2·24	1·73	1·92	1·09
1927 . .	3·90	4·11	4·28	2·02	2·18	2·25	1·73	1·83	1·79
1928 . .	4·22	4·45	4·70	1·76	2·02	1·48	2·85	3·01	2·09
1929 . .	4·30	4·68	4·61	1·91	1·72	1·38	3·12	3·39	2·50
1930 . .	4·63	4·67	4·87	3·30	1·93	1·17	3·96	3·99	2·40
1931 . .	4·67	5·03	5·14	5·27	3·55	1·42	3·29	3·54	1·32
1932 . .	4·34	4·94	5·37	5·67	5·52	2·18	1·99	2·27	0·79

it is a natural economic tendency which might be anticipated, that a generous system of allowances will tend to encourage some inward migration of large families and some outward migration of the childless. That this effect has in fact been of importance in increasing the proportion of dependants may be seen by following the same age group in the different years.'[3] Thus, in 1921 the children aged 0 to 1 year amounted to 3·85 per 100 employees. By 1926, when these children would be 5 to 6 years of age, some of them should have died, and the number of children aged 5 to 6 years per 100 employees should have been less than 3·85. But, in fact, in 1926 the rate was 4·67 per 100 employees. And in

[1] 'The effect of family allowances on population', in *Six Aspects of Family Allowances* (lectures given at the London School of Economics), London, 1927.

[2] From Fisher, R. A., op. cit., extended to 1932 with figures kindly supplied by F. Rey, director of the Haut Rhin equalization fund.

[3] Ibid., p. 8.

1932, when these children would be 11 to 12 years of age, their rate per 100 employees had risen to 5·67. Evidently, therefore, there was a marked immigration of relatively large families.

Professor Fisher suggested that there was, however, one test, 'of an extremely precarious nature', which could be applied and which did 'seem to indicate a slight tendency to real increase of fertility within the industry'.

'We might hope that any real increase in fertility, or indeed any tendency for the birth-rate to fall less rapidly, might be reflected in the proportion of these two age groups [0 to 1 and 12 to 13 years] from 1921 to 1926. Any real increase in fertility should be shown by the younger children being relatively more numerous at the later date. In point of fact, they are most numerous in 1925 and least so in 1924, but the general run of the figures does suggest a slight increase of the order of about 2½ per cent. in the five years.'

For the sake of completeness the figures have been extended up to 1932, but the ratios are not comparable after 1926 for the older age groups show the influence of the abnormally low birth-rates of the War period. Professor Fisher believed that for the period 1921–6, it seemed as if there might possibly be a real check to the fall of fertility,[1] yet it should again be emphasized that the material is not really adequate for supporting any definite conclusion. As in the Michelin case, lack of sufficiently detailed material makes it impossible to judge the significance of the visible trends.

In addition to the data already cited, there are, for France, annual demographic surveys relating to the general family allowance system, undertaken by Colonel Guillermin, and published in the reports of the family allowance congresses. It is important to consider these surveys, for considerable weight has been and is still being attached to them by numerous writers, and they have at times been cited in official reports.[2] Each year Colonel Guillermin collects

[1] 'Whether this tendency can be interpreted as an actual effect of the economic situation upon the birth-rate, or whether it should be interpreted as another effect of differential migration, an attraction, this time of the more fertile rather than of the more encumbered parents, it is totally impossible to say' (Fisher, R. A., op. cit., p. 10).

[2] e.g. by F. Saint-Maur, in 1931, in the name of the Senate Commission de Hygiène, de l'Assistance, de l'Assurance, et de la Prévoyance Sociales (see Pinte, J., op. cit., p. 17), and *Circulaire du Ministre du Travail*, 25 June 1932.

TABLE 15. *Birth-rates for the French Equalization Funds (Births per 1,000 employees enrolled in the funds)*

Dates for which birth-rates are given	*Date of Family Allowance Congress*														*Crude birth-rate per 1,000 for France*
	1925	*1926*	*1927*	*1928*	*1929*	*1930*	*1931*	*1932*	*1933*	*1934*	*1935*	*1936*	*1937*	*1938*	
1924	47·3	39·0	36·6	..	..	..	..	..	..	..	..	..	..	..	18·7
1925	..	40·3	40·2	37·00	..	..	..	..	..	..	..	..	..	..	19·0
1926	..	..	42·3	37·99	40·7	..	..	..	..	..	..	..	..	..	18·8
1927	..	..	..	38·90	45·4	..	..	..	..	..	..	..	..	..	18·2
1928	..	..	..	..	44·9	41·4	42·3	..	..	..	..	..	..	..	18·3
1929	..	..	..	..	..	40·2	39·6	38·8	..	..	..	..	..	..	17·7
1930	..	..	..	..	..	..	46·5	72·1	44·4	..	..	..	..	..	18·0
1931	..	..	..	..	..	..	..	91·6	48·8	46·6	..	..	..	..	17·5
1932	..	..	..	..	..	..	..	..	44·2	40·5	34·4	..	..	..	17·3
1933	..	..	..	..	..	..	..	..	..	39·3	26·7	30·4	..	..	16·2
1934	..	..	..	..	..	..	..	..	..	..	29·8	30·8	31·1	..	16·2
1935	..	..	..	..	..	..	..	..	..	..	..	29·8	32·5	..	15·3
1936	..	..	..	..	..	..	..	..	..	..	..	..	33·3	..	15·0
1937	..	..	..	..	..	..	..	..	..	..	..	..	..	28·8	14·7
Number of funds used	20	26	17	N.S.	46	30	N.S.	N.S.	*	28	25	25	36	98	

Sources: (the dates refer to the year in which the congress was held, and the figures following the dates give page reference to the report for that year): 1925, 63; 1926, 83–4; 1927, 45; 1928, 59; 1929, 60; 1930, 122; 1931, 48; 1932, 27; 1933, 50; 1934, 59; 1935, 66; 1936, 59; 1937, 47; 1938, 69. N.S. is printed when the number of funds used in the calculation is not stated. The crude birth rates for France up to and including 1935 are from *Statistique du Mouvement de la Population, 1935*, Part 1, p. 5. The rates for 1936 and 1937, which are provisional, are from *Annuaire Statistique, 1937*, p. 13*.

* p. 47 of the report states that 80 funds gave information for the period 1930–2, but it is not stated whether the same number gave the requisite fertility data.

data from those equalization funds willing and able to supply him with the requisite information, and constructs tables showing the number of employees embraced by the relevant funds and the number of births to those employees or to their wives. The funds change from year to year, and in order to make the comparison more trustworthy, Colonel Guillermin generally gives information for those funds which have been able to supply statistics for a number of consecutive years. Thus in the report for 1929 one table relates to 46 funds which provided the necessary information for the years 1926 to 1928 inclusive, and in the report for 1937 a similar table relates to 36 funds providing data for the years 1934 to 1936 inclusive. It is these statistics, instead of the rates calculated on the basis of all the funds supplying data for one year, which are summarized in Table 15.

A glance at this table will show, first, that for almost any given year there is a range of birth-rates. Thus for the year 1928, the report for 1929 gives a birth-rate of 44·9 per 1,000, the report for 1930 gives a rate of 41·4, and the report for 1931 gives a rate of 42·3. For this year the range is small, but for 1924 it is from 47·3 to 36·6, falling by over 20 per cent. as the funds used change between the 1925 and the 1927 congresses. For the year 1933 the birth-rates calculated on the varying funds range from 39·3 to 26·7, showing a fall of over 30 per cent. between the highest and lowest figures. Unfortunately, averages for each year would not be valid. The information provided is not sufficiently detailed to prevent the same funds from occurring more than once in a given year. Secondly, the table shows striking differences between the birth-rates for the funds and those for France as a whole. Part of these differences must certainly be due to differences in the age limits of the basic populations. That is, the crude birth-rates for France are calculated on the whole population of all ages, while the birth-rates for the funds are calculated on the employed population, which excludes children and persons who have retired, as well as married and unmarried women not gainfully employed. Thus the funds are bound to show higher crude birth-rates than France as a whole. Colonel Guillermin is fully aware of this problem and has attempted to solve it by applying correcting factors. For some years he has adjusted the data for the whole country so as to yield a rate indicating the number of births per thousand persons aged 15 to 60 years, assuming that these are the effective age limits of the employed population embraced by the funds. In the report of the 1926 Congress, for example, he raised the crude birth-rate for France as a whole in 1925—when it was 19·0 per thousand —to 30 in order to relate births to persons aged 15 to 60 years, and compared this adjusted figure with the rate of 40·3 per thousand employees in the 26 funds which gave him the requisite information.[1] In other years he has adjusted the birth-rate of the funds in order to produce a birth-rate per thousand total population, comparable with the crude birth-rate for France as a whole. Thus in the report of the 1936 Congress he lowered the 1935 birth-rate of the funds from 29·8 to 19·0 per thousand, in order to compare the latter figure with the crude birth-rate of 15·2 per thousand for the whole of France.[2] In both these forms of correction adjustment was made only on the basis of age limits assuming that the ratio between persons aged 15 to 60 years and the total population of all ages had remained unchanged since the last census for which data were available. These types of correction have been made in most of the surveys by Colonel Guillermin, and since, even allowing for the corrections, there is always a positive margin in favour of the birth-rates of the funds, Colonel Guillermin concludes that fertility in the funds is higher than outside of them.

But correcting for the age groups 15 to 60 years is not sufficient. In the first place, wives who are not at work will still be excluded, and so will unmarried women who are not gainfully employed, or, at least, not recorded as such. Both these omissions will tend to swell the corrected birth-rates of the funds as compared with those for the whole of France, by reducing the denominator without reducing the numerator used in calculating the birth-rate. Again, the proportion of married persons among all persons embraced by the funds

[1] *VIe Congrès National*, 1926, p. 85.

[2] *XVIe Congrès National*, 1936, p. 59. The birth-rate for France was, according to official statistics, 15·3 per 1,000. Colonel Guillermin's figure was probably provisional.

may be significantly different from that in the general population aged 15 to 60 years. If, for women, gainful employment competes with marriage, and if the funds include a large proportion of women, then the total population of the funds will contain a smaller proportion of married persons than the population aged 15 to 60 years in the whole of France. Further, the employed population, even within the limits of 15 and 60 years, is likely to be younger than the total population in the same age groups in the whole of France.[1] Colonel Guillermin was aware of the difficulties introduced by these factors, and in one report—for the year 1932[2]—he attempted to make further corrections. In that report the crude birth-rates for the funds were amazingly high. Taking all funds which had given the requisite information for 1931, there were 68 funds, 403,070 employees and 25,038 births, or 62·1 per thousand employees. For those funds giving information for the three years 1929 to 1931 (the number is not stated, but it appears to be considerably below 68) the crude birth-rates were 38·8 in 1929, 72·1 in 1930, and 91·6 in 1931. Taking the first figure, 62·1 per thousand, Colonel Guillermin decided that 25 per cent. should be added to the basic population to allow for age differences between the population of the funds and that of France in general. For children this report showed 526 per thousand employees in 1931, so this proportion provided a further correction. Finally, Colonel Guillermin assumed that mothers with two or more children would not be employed, and as families with two or more children formed 49·2 per cent. of all families in 1931, he added 492 per thousand to the denominator for this correction.[3] Thus the birth-rate of 62·1 should really be related to 1,000 + 250 + 526 + 492, or 2,268, and the corrected birth-rate would be

[1] If we take the total population aged 15–59 years in France in 1931 (1931 census, vol. i, pt. 2, p. 36), we find that 38·5 per cent. are 40 years of age and over. If we take the employed population (employees, wage earners, and those 'independent workers' who are classified as employees, see 1931 census, vol. i, pt. 3, p. 65, and pt. 4, Table 1, p. 26, corrected for unstated ages) in the same age groups, we find that only 27·8 per cent. are 40 years of age and over. If we exclude agriculture, forestry, fishing, and public services, we obtain a figure of 29·5 per cent. aged 40 years and over.

[2] *XIIe Congrès National*, 1932, pp. 26–7, and pp. 22–3.

[3] Presumably this correction factor should be smaller, since it should be calculated on the number of families with two or more children per thousand employees.

27·4 per thousand according to Colonel Guillermin, compared with a birth-rate of 17·5[1] for France as a whole. Colonel Guillermin applied this method to the funds which had provided the requisite information for the years 1929 to 1931, this time working directly on the basic figures. The following table shows the corrections made:

TABLE 16. *Corrected Data for Selected Funds**

	1929	*1930*	*1931*
Number of employed persons	215,802	212,799	174,489
Correction for age	53,950	53,199	43,372
Addition for children	108,331	116,129	110,078
Addition for mothers with 2 or more children	28,339	31,002	28,688
Special addition for 1931 to compensate for fall in employed population	..	..	38,310
Corrected total for employed population	406,422	413,129	394,929
Births	8,370	15,335	15,983
Uncorrected birth-rate per 1,000 employed persons	38·8	72·1	91·6
Corrected birth-rate per 1,000 for the equalization funds	20·6	37·1	40·4
Birth-rate for France	17·7	18·0	17·5†

* The figures in this table are taken, without alteration, from Colonel Guillermin's report, *XIIe Congrès National*, 1932, p. 27. The separate items for 1931 do not add exactly to the stated total, but since the difference is insignificant—it is probably due to a typographic error—it has been left uncorrected. The corrected birth-rate for 1931 should be 40·5.

† The birth-rates for France are from *Statistique du Mouvement de la Population*, 1933, pt. i, p. 5.

The differences between the birth-rates for the funds and those for France as a whole are extremely high in 1930 and 1931, and Colonel Guillermin again concludes that this is evidence of higher fertility in the funds. However, it is unlikely that the method of correction really produces rates which are comparable with the crude birth-rates for France. In the first place, two of the elements are quite arbitrary. An addition of 25 per cent. for age differences may be too high or too low, and the assumption that all mothers with two or more children remain at home has no factual foundation. It may be true, but it is not known. Secondly, the addition made for mothers with children apparently refers only to families with at least one dependent child, for other-

[1] Given as 17·4 in the report, and presumably a provisional figure.

wise there would have been no information about them. But there are certainly many mothers who, although their children are no longer dependent, are nevertheless not gainfully employed. The allowance made for married women not enrolled in the funds is, therefore, probably very much too low. Moreover, the fact that the birth-rate of the funds nearly doubled between 1929 and 1931 is probably far more indicative of an abnormal population, or of marked reshuffling of the employed persons in the period, than of a genuine rise in fertility. Colonel Guillermin does, in fact, give some evidence of reshuffling during the period, associated with economic depression. In the Lyon metallurgical fund, in the previous two years, the *effectif allocataire* (those members with at least one dependent child) fell by 16·77 per cent., while the *effectif non allocataire* (those with no dependent children) fell by 37·47 per cent. That is, family men, or at least those with young children, were kept on during the depression, while men with no children or with children who had grown up and were therefore assumed to be self-supporting, were dismissed instead. The rise in the number of *allocataires* per hundred employed persons embraced by the selected funds analysed in the report—from 26·89 in 1929 to 29·35 in 1931—gives additional support to this view, and Colonel Guillermin says that it shows how, once again, French employers were fulfilling their duty by keeping on family men as long as possible.[1] Summing up the position, it does not seem that the methods of adjustment[2] adopted by Colonel Guillermin make it possible to compare the fertility of the equalization funds with that of the whole country. Much more detailed statistics would be necessary in order to discover significant differences, and in particular we should need the fund populations analysed by age, sex, and marital condition (including the ages of wives not themselves enrolled in funds, and of husbands enrolled in funds different from those in which their wives were registered) and the births analysed by the age of the mothers. And, in

[1] *XIIe Congrès National*, 1932, pp. 21–2. See also Vibart, H. H. R., 'The birth-rate in France and the compensation funds', *Family Endowment Chronicle*, Aug. 1932, pp. 17–18.

[2] The method adopted in the 1932 report has not been used again in any subsequent report.

any case, so long as there is differential fertility, and while the family allowance funds apply largely to the working class, we should expect to find some excess of fertility in those funds as compared with the rest of the population.

Nor is it possible to come to any dependable conclusions by ascertaining the time-trends of the birth-rates in the funds. If we look at Table 15 we can see a fairly consistent upward movement in the birth-rates until 1931, and then a fairly consistent downward movement, fluctuating after 1934. But it is difficult to tell exactly what these movements mean. The upward movement relates to the period when the system was expanding, but was still voluntary. Towards the end of the period there was probably some reshuffling of the population on account of economic depression. In the earlier part of the period, too, population movements must have taken place. Thus the report for 1927[1] contains a table which indicates that while the employed population covered by a series of 51 funds rose by 12·28 per cent. between 1924 and 1925, and by 3·40 per cent. between 1925 and 1926, the numbers of *allocataires* rose by 16·46 and 8·97 per cent. during the same years. In 1924, according to Colonel Guillermin, 22·74 per cent. of the persons covered by the funds were men with families, while in 1926 this had risen to 24·85 per cent. And in the period before 1925 this may have been still more marked. P. H. Douglas suggests that the granting of allowances drew large numbers of married employees from other industries, while probably many single men moved away to firms in which allowances were not given, and where the increase in the basic wage rates appears to have been higher. He believes that during the period of post-War unemployment the firms belonging to equalization funds dismissed their unmarried employees first and that a considerable number of these did not return when business conditions improved.[2] Thus the funds contained a large proportion of persons likely to have children. Since the

[1] *VIIe Congrès National*, pp. 43 and 50.

[2] Douglas, P. H., op. cit., pp. 93–4. Note also that Colonel Guillermin, *VIe Congrès National*, p. 89, observations on Table F, says that the marked increase in first births between 1924 and 1925 was doubtless due to the creation of birth and suckling premiums, which attracted young couples (*jeunes ménages*) to the firms giving these grants.

legalization of the system and compulsory extension to further branches of industry and commerce, the likelihood of selection has been smaller, and this has approximately coincided with the fall in the birth-rates of the equalization funds. Yet the numbers of *allocataires* per hundred of the employed population covered by the funds do not seem to have fallen. On the contrary, they were 25·2 in 1926 and 25·5 in 1927 and 1928,[1] but 30 in 1934, 32 in 1935, and 31 in 1936.[2] Presumably, therefore, apart from any changes in age composition which may have been caused by the influx of new members, the extension of the family allowance system has brought in a larger proportion of married men who do not wish to bring up more than one or two children, whereas in the earlier period men who wished to bring up families may have deliberately sought employment in firms which gave allowances. Monsieur G. Bonvoisin, in his report to the 1938 Congress,[3] mentions the fact that the 'corrected' birth-rate of the funds, although still considerably higher than the birth-rate for France, was showing a regular decrease in the margin. Logically, he added, this margin should ultimately fall to practically nothing. He implied that this would take place when every branch of employment (and this would include employers and independent workers) had been brought into the family allowance system. This, of course, is quite true, but it is nevertheless evident that the fall in the margin has taken place through a fall in the birth-rate of the funds, and not through a rise in the birth-rate of the whole country, and this does not lend much support to the view that family allowances have stimulated fertility in France.[4]

[1] *IXe Congrès National*, 1929, p. 59, calculated on a series of 123 funds.

[2] *XVIIe Congrès National*, 1937, p. 44, calculated on a series of 102 funds. Other figures (p. 40), not calculated on the same series of funds, are 30 in 1934 (145 funds), 31 in 1935 (184 funds), and 29 in 1936 (207 funds), not very different from the figures cited above.

[3] *XVIIIe Congrès National*, 1938, pp. 101–2.

[4] In the report for 1938 Bonvoisin uses his own method of 'adjusting' the birth-rate of the funds. He says that in 1937 97 funds, covering 2,877,973 employees, recorded 85,082 births. For France as a whole the total number of employees and wage-earners is 12,168,430, or 29 per cent. of the total population. To compare the fertility of the funds with the birth-rate for France (the provisional figure for 1937 being 15 per 1,000), the 85,082 births recorded by the funds should be related to a population of 2,877,973+71 per cent.=4,921,333, and gives a rate of 17·2 per 1,000. (These are the figures given by Bonvoisin. The 'corrected' birth-rate should be 17·3.) The method is clearly not valid.

TABLE 17. *Infant Mortality Rates for the French Equalization Funds*

(Deaths under 1 year per 1,000 live births in the same year)

Dates for which death-rates are given	*Date of Family Allowance Congress*												*Infant mortality rate for France*
	1927	*1928*	*1929*	*1930*	*1931*	*1932*	*1933*	*1934*	*1935*	*1936*	*1937*	*1938*	
1924 . . .	66·4	..	..	..	..	..	..	..	..	..	..	..	85
1925 . . .	73·4	51·0	..	..	..	..	..	..	..	..	..	..	89
1926 . . .	62·1	62·7	60·0	..	..	..	..	..	..	..	..	..	97
1927 . . .	..	54·3	65·5	..	..	..	..	..	..	..	..	..	83
1928 . . .	..	..	71·4	..	..	..	..	..	..	..	..	..	92
1929 . . .	..	..	..	63·6*	..	63·7	..	..	..	..	..	..	96
1930 . . .	..	..	..	..	51·6	53·8	..	..	..	..	..	..	78
1931 . . .	..	..	..	..	..	46·6	..	..	..	..	..	..	76
1932 . . .	..	..	..	..	..	..	38·0	..	45·2	..	..	..	77
1933 . . .	..	..	..	..	..	..	..	23·3	45·3	..	..	..	75
1934 . . .	..	..	..	..	..	..	..	..	35·7	..	28·0	..	69
1935 . . .	..	..	..	..	..	..	..	..	..	†	28·0	..	69
1936 . . .	..	..	..	..	..	..	..	..	..	..	20·8	..	67
1937 . . .	..	..	..	..	..	..	..	..	..	..	..	33·3‡	65
Number of funds used	6	24	27	N.S.	N.S.	N.S.	N.S.	N.S.	25(?)§	..	36(?)‖	20	

Sources (meaning as in Table 15): 1927, 46; 1928, 61; 1929, 63; 1930, 123; 1931, 50; 1932, 29; 1933, 51; 1934, 59; 1935, 69; 1937, 50; 1938, 70. The infant mortality rates for France are from *Statistique du Mouvement de la Population, 1935*, Part 1, p. 5 (up to and including 1935), and from the *Statistical Year Book of the League of Nations, 1937–8*, p. 44 (for the rates for 1936 and 1937).

* This relates to all the funds providing information for 1929. For a small number of funds which could be followed for several years infant mortality was said to be at an average of 49·3 per 1,000.

† 1936, 61. Colonel Guillermin says that for 'certain funds' in which social services were especially well developed the infant mortality rate in 1935 was 38·1 per 1,000.

‡ For this year, according to the table given by Colonel Guillermin, the deaths under one year of age in 1937 were related to the births occurring in 1936.

§ It is not certain if these rates do really derive from 25 funds. On p. 66, Table III, fertility is definitely stated to refer to 25 funds, but no specific reference is given in later tables in the report.

‖ A qualification similar to that in § applies here.

The annual demographic survey of the equalization funds also contains statistics of infant mortality, and these are summarized in Table 17. Here, again, there are wide ranges of rates for the same year, but the material is not subject to the distortions which apply to fertility calculations. Thus the fairly consistent downward trend of the rates and the fact that they are always well below the rates for the whole country may probably be accepted as real characteristics. How far this is due to family allowances it is impossible to tell with any accuracy, but it seems more probable that it is the result of the whole family allowance system rather than solely of the actual monetary grants. It will be remembered that many of the funds provide medical consultation and care, and this would certainly help to reduce mortality.[1] Also, of course, family allowances, even if too small to stimulate fertility, might nevertheless considerably raise the level of nutrition of infants, and this, too, would probably help to lower mortality.

Apart from the data provided by the family allowance funds, the only way to test the effect of family allowances and other pro-natalist measures upon fertility in France, is by examining the fertility rates for the country and its various regions and attempting to gauge the extent to which declining fertility has been checked or reversed. For Belgium there is no other method at all, as the Belgian family allowance system does not publish fertility statistics. It should be noted, however, that this method is extremely precarious. Pro-natalist measures are not applied in a vacuum. Many other factors are moving at the same time and not necessarily in the same direction. If there is a rise in fertility, it is not easy to be sure that this rise has been produced by specific social measures. Nor, if there has been a fall in fertility, is it easy to be sure that without the pro-natalist measures it might not have been still greater. Bearing this in mind we may examine such fertility rates as it is possible to construct from the available data.

[1] Infant mortality rates for the funds, somewhat different from those given in Table 17, were cited in F. Saint-Maur's report (Pinte, J., op. cit., p. 18). They are 66·9 for 1926, 56·7 for 1927, 60·6 for 1928, 63·6 for 1929, and 51·6 for 1930. With the exception of 1929 and 1930 these figures do not appear in Colonel Guillermin's annual reports, but they may perhaps have been specially prepared for the Senate Commission.

TABLE 18. *Gross Reproduction Rates—France*

Départements	*1910–12*	*1925–7*	*1930–2*	*1936*
1. Ain	1·255	1·188	1·123	0·980
2. Aisne	1·391	1·477	1·450	1·280
3. Allier	1·021	1·000	0·991	0·920
4. Alpes (Basses-)	1·338	1·218	1·125	0·980
5. Alpes (Hautes-)	1·655	1·440	1·301	1·210
6. Alpes-Maritimes	0·990	0·856	0·736	0·650
7. Ardèche	1·471	1·253	1·168	1·100
8. Ardennes	1·357	1·368	1·381	1·240
9. Ariège	1·207	1·036	0·989	0·900
10. Aube	1·165	1·227	1·174	1·120
11. Aude	1·064	1·062	1·089	0·930
12. Aveyron	1·477	1·360	1·245	1·160
13. Belfort (Territoire de)	1·372	1·222	1·242	1·130
14. Bouches-du-Rhône	1·134	0·989	0·836	0·690
15. Calvados	1·348	1·383	1·401	1·290
16. Cantal	1·427	1·405	1·408	1·300
17. Charente	1·195	1·173	1·180	1·130
18. Charente-Inférieure	1·182	1·233	1·241	1·170
19. Cher	1·151	1·068	1·059	1·000
20. Corrèze	1·412	1·187	1·111	0·980
21. Corse	1·533	1·132	0·903	0·840
22. Côte-d'Or	1·086	1·205	1·198	1·120
23. Côtes-du-Nord	1·782	1·532	1·413	1·300
24. Creuse	1·158	1·074	1·015	0·960
25. Dordogne	1·304	1·223	1·186	1·070
26. Doubs	1·476	1·373	1·315	1·180
27. Drôme	1·161	1·058	1·007	0·890
28. Eure	1·363	1·396	1·383	1·270
29. Eure-et-Loir	1·411	1·378	1·384	1·290
30. Finistère	1·905	1·419	1·308	1·190
31. Gard	1·110	0·976	0·953	0·860
32. Garonne (Haute-)	0·990	0·991	0·975	0·910
33. Gers	0·949	1·144	1·077	1·030
34. Gironde	0·895	0·990	0·958	0·870
35. Hérault	1·069	0·941	0·921	0·790
36. Ille-et-Vilaine	1·389	1·318	1·314	1·210
37. Indre	1·185	1·135	1·143	1·100
38. Indre-et-Loire	1·122	1·151	1·184	1·140
39. Isère	1·085	1·103	1·016	0·910
40. Jura	1·342	1·281	1·238	1·090
41. Landes	1·258	1·098	1·051	0·920
42. Loir-et-Cher	1·286	1·222	1·235	1·230
43. Loire	1·119	1·039	1·013	0·920
44. Loire (Haute-)	1·309	1·178	1·147	1·090
45. Loire-Inférieure	1·160	1·166	1·162	1·070
46. Loiret	1·251	1·185	1·181	1·100
47. Lot	1·148	1·151	1·085	1·030
48. Lot-et-Garonne	0·967	1·078	1·096	1·040
49. Lozère	1·752	1·407	1·306	1·190

Départements	*1910–12*	*1925–7*	*1930–2*	*1936*
50. Maine-et-Loire . .	1·102	1·211	1·259	1·200
51. Manche	1·485	1·461	1·482	1·420
52. Marne	1·333	1·352	1·278	1·200
53. Marne (Haute-) . .	1·297	1·401	1·409	1·310
54. Mayenne	1·478	1·404	1·409	1·320
55. Meurthe-et-Moselle . .	1·552	1·448	1·375	1·200
56. Meuse	1·436	1·480	1·453	1·250
57. Morbihan	1·825	1·561	1·496	1·400
58. Moselle	..	1·528	1·364	1·240
59. Nièvre	1·156	1·164	1·147	1·060
60. Nord	1·333	1·191	1·174	1·020
61. Oise	1·335	1·367	1·354	1·240
62. Orne	1·269	1·350	1·341	1·250
63. Pas-de-Calais . . .	1·808	1·615	1·517	1·320
64. Puy-de-Dôme . . .	1·073	1·029	0·983	0·870
65. Pyrénées (Basses-) . .	1·475	1·276	1·157	1·060
66. Pyrénées (Hautes-) . .	1·153	1·199	1·127	1·030
67. Pyrénées-Orientales . .	1·281	0·963	0·870	0·770
68. Rhin (Bas-) . . .	..	1·257	1·151	1·000
69. Rhin (Haut-) . . .	..	1·151	1·107	0·940
70. Rhône	0·847	0·919	0·915	0·790
71. Saône (Haute-) . .	1·363	1·321	1·251	1·200
72. Saône-et-Loire . . .	1·251	1·208	1·158	1·050
73. Sarthe	1·325	1·333	1·369	1·350
74. Savoie	1·462	1·341	1·279	1·190
75. Savoie (Haute-) . .	1·525	1·325	1·182	1·100
76. Seine (Paris et banlieue) .	0·853	0·802	0·766	0·660
77. Seine-Inférieure . .	1·544	1·307	1·294	1·190
78. Seine-et-Marne . .	1·217	1·208	1·226	1·080
79. Seine-et-Oise . . .	1·089	0·946	0·881	0·760
80. Sèvres (Deux-) . .	1·269	1·246	1·309	1·250
81. Somme	1·279	1·315	1·301	1·170
82. Tarn	1·152	1·123	1·065	0·960
83. Tarn-et-Garonne . .	1·069	1·135	1·142	1·100
84. Var	1·057	0·974	0·921	0·870
85. Vaucluse	1·159	1·029	1·034	0·950
86. Vendée	1·413	1·407	1·393	1·340
87. Vienne	1·262	1·220	1·238	1·220
88. Vienne (Haute-) . .	1·281	1·073	1·006	0·870
89. Vosges	1·479	1·263	1·235	1·120
90. Yonne	1·116	1·229	1·218	1·160
Whole country . .	1·221	1·147	1·100	1·000

For 1910–12 and 1925–7 the rates have been computed from the relevant censuses and vital statistics for the Départements. For 1930–2 the series of specific fertility rates given in the *Statistique du Mouvement de la Population* for 1933, Part I, p. lxiii, has been used. The rates for 1936, which are provisional, were calculated by P. Depoid and are from *Revue de l'Alliance Nationale*, Jan. 1939, p. 23. In the Aug. 1938 issue of *Population* comparable rates for 1910–12 and 1930–2 are given in a paper by P. Depoid. There are some differences between the rates for 1910–12 given in the present study and those given by Depoid. Monsieur Depoid was kind enough to look into the reason for these differences and states (in a letter to the present writer) that his rates were calculated from data published in *Statistique du Mouvement de la Population* for 1928, and that, owing to a hitherto unnoticed printer's error, these data were defined as relating to the years 1910–12, whereas they were in fact based upon the years 1911–13.

Table 18 gives a series of gross reproduction rates for France as a whole and for the separate Départements from 1910 to 1912. If we refer back to the rates given in the chapter on England and Wales, we shall see that between 1890–2 and 1930–2 the fall in fertility amounted to 54·5 per cent. For France as a whole the fall was only 24·2 per cent. in the same period—from a gross reproduction rate of 1·451 to one of 1·100. Similarly, the fall in France between 1910–12 and 1930–2 was only 9·9 per cent., while in England and Wales it was 35·7 per cent. But it should be remembered that fertility was falling in France during the greater part of the nineteenth century[1] and that, in consequence, fertility has had a longer period in which to reach a stable, if low, level. Moreover, it was seen that in England and Wales the agricultural districts still tend to have a fertility higher than the average for the country. In periods of high average fertility agricultural regions may well be below the average. But in periods of low fertility the agricultural regions project as islands of relatively high fertility, perhaps because children are less of a disadvantage in the country than in the town. France has remained much more of an agricultural nation than England. The 1931 censuses showed that out of all occupied males 32·9 per cent. were employed in agriculture in France, but only 8·6 per cent. in England and Wales.[2] This, too, may be part of the explanation of the smaller relative decline of fertility in France. Further support of this last thesis may be obtained by analysing the gross reproduction rates for the Départements. The important period, for our purpose, is after the last War. But it is clearly invalid to compare 1920–2 with 1930–2, for at the former date fertility was inflated by the abnormal circumstances of the immediate post-War years. If, however, we compare 1925–7 with 1930–2, we find that the gross reproduction rates rose in twenty-two Départements. We have no data for England and Wales with which to compare these changes, but judging from trends between 1910–12 and 1930–2, it is ex-

[1] The crude birth-rates for France in the nineteenth century were: 1811–20, 31·8 per 1,000; 1821–30, 31·0; 1831–40, 29·0; 1841–50, 27·4; 1851–60, 26·3; 1861–70, 26·3; 1871–80, 25·4; 1881–90, 23·9; 1891–1900, 22·2 (*Annuaire Statistique*, 1935, p. 258*).

[2] Fishermen have been included in the agricultural population of both countries.

tremely unlikely that any counties in 1930–2 had rates higher than in the relatively normal post-War years.[1] But if we look more closely at the French data, we find that of the twenty-two Départements in which fertility rose between 1925–7 and 1930–2, nineteen were areas in which the percentage of occupied males engaged in agriculture was

TABLE 19. *Fertility Changes and Male Occupations*

Départements	*Percentage increase in gross reproduction rates in those Départements showing a rise 1925–7 to 1930–2*	*Percentage of all* occupied males engaged in agriculture (excluding fishing) in 1930–2*
1. Ardennes	0·95	22·8
2. Aude	2·54	61·5
3. Belfort (Territoire de)	1·64	13·8
4. Calvados	1·30	38·6
5. Cantal	0·21	65·9
6. Charente	0·60	56·2
7. Charente-Inférieure	0·65	51·4
8. Eure-et-Loir	0·44	51·3
9. Indre	0·70	61·1
10. Indre-et-Loire	2·87	45·2
11. Loir-et-Cher	1·06	58·1
12. Lot-et-Garonne	1·67	63·3
13. Maine-et-Loire	3·96	50·4
14. Manche	1·44	55·3
15. Marne (Haute-)	0·57	34·7
16. Mayenne	0·36	61·4
17. Sarthe	2·70	51·6
18. Seine-et-Marne	1·49	29·6
19. Sèvres (Deux-)	5·06	63·6
20. Tarn-et-Garonne	0·62	62·4
21. Vaucluse	0·49	46·0
22. Vienne	1·48	61·2

* The percentage for the whole country is 33·4 (which differs from the figure quoted on p. 196, because in the present case men engaged in fishing are excluded from the numerator, while the army is excluded from the denominator), and the average of the percentages of all the Départements is 44·7. The data are from the 1931 census of France, vol. i, pt. 3, pp. 12–13, but the percentages have been recalculated, for some given in the census volume appear to show small errors.

[1] Even if we had data for England and Wales for 1925–7 the comparison would not be quite fair, for the county rates for that period would be abnormally depressed by the fall in births in 1927, following the 1926 general strike. The estimated gross reproduction rate for England and Wales as a whole was 1·062 in 1925, 1·044 in 1926, 0·972 in 1927, and 0·993 in 1928.

above that for the whole country.[1] Since the development of family allowances up to 1932 was almost entirely concentrated upon industry and commerce, it seems prima facie unlikely that the allowances would have had much effect in areas which were predominantly agricultural.[2]

Up to 1930–2 we can at least say that fertility was relatively stable and that in some areas fertility was actually higher—though not very much so—than in 1925–7. But since 1930–2 a new trend of decline seems to have begun. In England and Wales the gross reproduction rate in 1936 was about 0·875, as compared with about 0·929 in 1930–2, a fall of about 6 per cent. in the period. But in France the gross reproduction rate in 1936 was about 1·000,[3] compared with 1·100 in 1930–2, a fall of about 9 per cent. Between 1925–7 and 1930–2 the fall in France was only about 4 per cent. Moreover, with the exception of 1934, the fall in France has been continuous since 1930–2,[4] whereas in England and Wales the gross reproduction rate rose fairly consistently between 1933 and 1937. This latter trend has probably been caused by the increase in nuptiality during the period, a factor which could not have played so important a part in France, where nuptiality was already very high. Nevertheless, it is interesting to find a slight reversal of the fall in fertility in a country with no formulated population policy, contrasted with a new decline in a country in which pro-natalist measures are widespread. Similarly, if we were to examine the provisional gross reproduction rates for the Départements of France for 1936, computed by P. Depoid,[5] we should find that in 89 Départements the 1936 rates are lower than their counterparts for 1930–2, and that in one exceptional case (Loir-et-Cher), it is doubtful if there has been any change at all, since the rate for 1930–2 was 1·235

[1] If we take as our norm the average of the percentages of occupied men engaged in agriculture in each Département (44·7), then seventeen of the areas are above the average.

[2] See Note IV*m*, p. 446.

[3] The 1936 rate, calculated by P. Depoid, of the Statistique Générale de la France, is a provisional figure and is cited from the *Revue de l'Alliance Nationale*, Jan. 1939, p. 23.

[4] The estimated gross reproduction rates for the intervening period are 1·039 in 1933, 1·051 in 1934, and 1·004 in 1935.

[5] Op. cit., p. 23. See Table 18 in the present study, pp. 194–5.

while that for 1936 is estimated at 1·230. This one exception relates to an area in which agriculture is the predominant occupation.[1] A much slower decline is found in net reproduction rates. The rate for France as a whole was 0·924 in 1910–12, 0·930 in 1925–7, 0·927 in 1930–2, and 0·880 in 1936.[2] Comparison with the relevant gross reproduction rates shows the extent to which mortality has fallen in France in recent years. In 1930–2 only 48 of the 90 Départements had rates greater than or equal to unity, and these were mainly in rural areas with a relatively sparse population.[3] Between 1930–2 and 1936, in spite of the further fall in mortality, the net reproduction rate did not rise in a single Département. In 6 rural Départements it remained stationary, and in the remaining 84 it fell. In certain cases the fall has been very marked. Thus for the Seine the fall was from 0·630 to 0·560, in Nord from 0·990 to 0·880, in Puy-de-Dôme from 0·850 to 0·770, in Pyrénées-Orientales from 0·750 to 0·670, in Seine-et-Oise from 0·740 to 0·650, in Haut Rhin from 0·960 to 0·830, and in Landes from 0·930 to 0·830. In 1936 only 39 Départements had net reproduction rates equal to or greater than unity.[4]

For Belgium the statistics are both less comprehensive and poorer in general quality. The last census was in 1930, and there are no published mid-year estimates of the population by age and sex. Moreover, there are no published data relating to the distribution of births by the age of the mothers, and the birth- and death-rates customarily published in the *Annuaire Statistique* are not quite correct because they relate the *de facto* births and deaths to the *de jure* population.[5] However, since the last War the *de jure* births are also stated each year, and on this basis, together with the corresponding census data, estimated gross reproduction rates have been

[1] In 1931, according to the basic data given in the 1931 census, vol. i, pt. 3, p. 12, in Loir-et-Cher 58·1 per cent. of all occupied males were engaged in agriculture.

[2] Life tables for the corresponding years were constructed for calculating the net reproduction rates from 1910–12 to 1930–2. The rate for 1936 was calculated by P. Depoid and is from the *Revue de l'Alliance Nationale*, Oct. 1938, p. 309. This journal (same issue, p. 304) gives the 1937 net reproduction rate as 0·880, as in 1936.

[3] Depoid, P., 'Taux de reproduction et autres indices démographiques . . .', *Population*, Aug. 1938, pp. 57–73.

[4] *Revue de l'Alliance Nationale*, Oct. 1938, pp. 305–9.

[5] See Note IV*n*, p. 447.

computed and are given in Table 20. It will be seen that between 1909–11 and 1929–31 the fall for the whole country was about 27 per cent., nearly three times as great as for France in the same period, and about three-quarters as great as for England and Wales. In 1934–5 the gross reproduction rate for Belgium was about 0·929, showing a fall of about 14 per

TABLE 20. *Belgium—Estimated Gross Reproduction Rates*[1]

Provinces	*1909–11*	*1929–31*
Anvers	1·780	1·186
Brabant	1·219	0·873
Flandre Occidentale	2·035	1·361
Flandre Orientale	1·891	1·184
Hainaut	1·184	0·934
Liége	1·086	0·888
Limbourg	2·424	1·979
Luxembourg	1·549	1·204
Namur	1·219	1·047
Whole country	1·478	1·075

cent. in the ensuing period, greater than in either France or England and Wales.[2] The net reproduction rate in 1934–5 was about 0·802. It is impossible, in view of the available statistics, to make any more thorough analysis of the position in Belgium in relation to the effect of population policies. Table 21 gives the crude birth-rates of France, Belgium, and England and Wales, from 1922, and indicates the comparative rapidity of decline of these rates. But birth-rates are not adequate for conclusive analysis, though they support the argument stated above.

Since much of the data presented in preceding sections is rather confused, it may perhaps be useful to summarize the results which have been obtained. We have seen that in France the birth-rates relating to the Michelin experimen

[1] For 1909–11 the births are *de facto*, since no other data were available for th provinces. For 1929–31 the births are *de jure* (as they are also for 1934–5). Th difference, however, is very slight. For the country as a whole the gross reproductio rate for 1929–31, calculated on the basis of *de facto* births, would be 1·082 instea of the figure of 1·075 given above.

[2] The gross reproduction rate for 1934–5 was calculated on the basis of a estimate of the population (by age and sex) for the end of 1934, kindly supplied b Dr. G. Frumkin of the League of Nations (Financial Section and Econom Intelligence Service).

and to the equalization funds cannot be directly compared with the rates for the country as a whole because of differences in the age and sex composition and marital condition of the population. Nor is it possible to correct for these differences, as adequate basic statistics are not available. For a thorough comparison we should need to have not only

TABLE 21. *Births per 1,000 Total Population*

	France	*Belgium*[1]	*England and Wales*
1922 . . .	19·3	20·5	20·4
1923 . . .	19·1	20·6	19·7
1924 . . .	18·7	20·1	18·8
1925 . . .	19·0	19·8	18·3
1926 . . .	18·8	19·0	17·8
1927 . . .	18·2	18·2	16·6
1928 . . .	18·3	18·3	16·7
1929 . . .	17·7	18·1	16·3
1930 . . .	18·0	18·6	16·3
1931 . . .	17·5	18·2	15·8
1932 . . .	17·3	17·6	15·3
1933 . . .	16·2	16·4	14·4
1934 . . .	16·2	15·9	14·8
1935 . . .	15·3	15·2	14·7
1936 . . .	15·0	15·1	14·8
1937 . . .	14·7	..	14·9

full particulars concerning the population enrolled in the funds, including records of the influx and efflux of labour, but also information for control groups of employees and wage earners not entitled to family allowances, or for the generality of the industrially and commercially employed population. The most detailed attempt to adjust the crude birth-rates for the funds, published by Colonel Guillermin in the report of the 1932 Family Allowance Congress, contained strongly arbitrary elements which rendered it invalid. The corrected birth-rate appeared to double in three years, and that is more indicative of a highly abnormal population than of a genuine rise in fertility.[2] In the same way it is doubtful even if the year-by-year movements of the birth-rates for the funds give any real indication of fertility trends. In the period before the 1932 Act came into force, there was

[1] See Note IV*o*, p. 447. [2] See Note IV*p*, p. 447.

probably some selection, through labour migration, of the population enrolled in the funds, while during periods of economic depression it seems likely that men with families were the last to be discharged from employment. In recent years the crude and 'corrected' birth-rates for the funds have more closely approached the birth-rate for the whole country. But the birth-rate for the country has been falling, and any effect that family allowances may have had on fertility has not been strong enough to prevent a general decline in fertility in France, especially since 1933.

Examination of the gross reproduction rates for France as a whole and for the individual Départements does not bring much evidence to support any contention that French population policy has succeeded in raising fertility. Between 1925–7 and 1930–2 fertility was clearly more stable than in England and Wales, and this may perhaps be attributed to family allowances and other measures. But the generalization of family allowances has not maintained this stability. On the contrary, fertility has fallen more rapidly in the last few years in spite of more widespread and, in terms of money, more significant allowances.[1] In Belgium the data are much more precarious. But an examination of birth-rates or estimated gross reproduction rates shows a significant fall in fertility in recent years. For both France and Belgium it may well be the case that population measures have prevented an even more rapid fall—the available statistics do not allow this hypothesis to be proved or refuted—but it is evident that they have not been influential enough to cause a rise in fertility, or even to stabilize fertility at its already low level of five or ten years ago. On the other hand, it is probably true that the family allowance system in France has helped to reduce infant mortality, and it is likely that this has also been the case in Belgium.[2] But a 10 per cent. fall in infant mortality would have a much smaller effect upon the net reproduction rate than a 10 per cent. rise in fertility. The problem of maintaining the population at a given level is

[1] It should, however, be noted that the increase in the allowances took place largely after 1936. It is possible, therefore, that vital statistics in the subsequent period may show a renewed stability. But the war has intervened and prevents any possible comparison.

[2] See Note IV*q*, p. 448.

now far more dependent upon raising fertility than upon reducing peace-time mortality, and it is from this point of view that the population measures have to be scrutinized.

Taking up this point of view, we may reconsider the various measures which have been applied in France and Belgium and attempt to estimate their significance on general grounds, quite apart from fertility data. First, in preceding sections some account has been given of the propaganda which is being used to promote fertility. This propaganda, which is almost entirely unofficial,[1] has two main forms. It depicts the probability of a declining population in the future and explains the disadvantageous results of such a decline. It also draws attention to the economic and social disadvantages under which large families labour. The first kind of propaganda is thus aimed to stir up feelings of patriotism. Yet part of this stimulation must be cancelled by the clear picture of the economic distress of large families.[2] The Alliance Nationale and kindred organizations in France, as well as the less propagandist Ligue des Familles Nombreuses in Belgium, do not suffer from, nor do they try to spread, any illusions as to the present economic welfare of families with three or more children. On the contrary, they concentrate a large part of their energy on campaigns to raise family allowances, increase tax rebates, and so forth. This is in keeping with the conclusions to which L. Naudeau was impelled after his investigation in France, which led him to say that all pro-natalist propaganda addressed to the individual would generally be useless,[3] and to argue in

[1] It is carried on almost exclusively by voluntary bodies. In France, however, it should be remembered that the Conseil Supérieur de la Natalité is attached to the Ministry of Health. Also, this Ministry organized a series of radio broadcasts, in 1938, on the subject of population, given by members of the Conseil Supérieur (see Duval-Arnould, L., 'Joies et fierté des grandes familles', *Revue de la Plus Grande Famille*, July–Aug. 1938). Note, too, that the Alliance Nationale receives a governmental subsidy, and that two special stamps (*timbres à surtaxe*) were to be issued in March 1939 to raise additional funds for this body. There are also such incidents in France as choosing a mother of ten children to launch a new warship (see *Revue de l'Alliance Nationale*, Feb. 1939, pp. 33 and 34–5).

[2] Bouthoul, G., *La Population dans le Monde*, Paris, 1935, p. 54, emphasizes this. He suggests that pro-natalist propaganda may even draw attention to the fact that procreation can be controlled.

[3] Naudeau, L., 'Conclusions d'une enquête démographique en France', *Proc. Int. Cong. of Studies on Popn. Rome, 1931*, vol. viii, Rome, 1933, pp. 517–21.

favour of economic reforms instead of homilies on virtue, sacrifice, patriotism, social duty, and all those 'sublime abstractions' which would yield no tangible result.[1] But if economic measures are to be applied, they must be widespread and at the same time sufficiently penetrating to make a real difference in the condition of those persons who are to bring up families. How far is this condition fulfilled? We can test this by examining the family allowances and other economic measures which have been discussed in earlier sections.

It has already been mentioned that many writers quote the birth-rates for the French equalization funds as evidence of the positive effect of family allowances. At each Family Allowance Congress Colonel Guillermin and Monsieur Bonvoisin, in their respective reports, maintain that fertility in the funds is higher than in France as a whole.[2] In replying to the questionnaire which was sent out in connexion with the present study, 27 of the French equalization funds expressed themselves on this question, and 15 believed that family allowances had some influence on fertility, while only 8 funds gave a definite 'no' as an answer. In Belgium the funds were less sanguine. Of 28 answering the question 'Do you believe that family allowances have affected fertility?', only 9 funds said 'yes', and one of these meant 'probably', while two others stressed the influence of the allowances in families where there were already three children, since the grants for the fourth and subsequent children are relatively high. On the other hand, only 5 funds definitely gave 'no' as an answer. Most of the answers came within the 'doubtful' or 'do not know' zones.[3] Yet it has been seen that in France and Belgium family allowances have generally been small in relation to basic wages or salaries.[4] A recent article in a lead-

[1] Naudeau, L., *La France se regarde*, Paris, 1931, p. 447.

[2] See also Bonvoisin, G., 'Influence démographique des caisses de compensation et de leurs services sociaux', *Congrès International de la Population*, Paris, 1937, vol. vii, Paris, 1938, pp. 196–9, and same author, 'La politique des allocations exerce-t-elle une influence sur le taux de la natalité?', *Revue Médico-Sociale et de Protection de l'Enfance*, 1938, no. 6, pp. 502–7.

[3] The replies from the Belgian funds are in keeping with the fact that the Belgian family allowance system places much less emphasis than the French on the fertility aspect of allowances. In general there appears to be less pro-natalist propaganda in Belgium than in France.

[4] There appears to be a considerable range of opinion as to the relation, in the

ing French pro-natalist journal stated that very few workers received allowances which amounted to as much as 4 per cent. of their basic earnings for the first child, 8 per cent. for the second, and 12 per cent. for the third and subsequent children.[1] In Belgium, so far as can be judged from the information supplied by a number of funds, the position is no better. Even if we choose the fund which pays the highest supplementary allowance—100 francs per month for 3 children, 125 francs for 4, and 150 for 5 (this additional allowance being paid in the winter only), the total allowance per month received during the peak period would amount to only 213·6 francs for 3 children, 327·6 for 4, and 476·6 for 5. Assuming an average basic wage of 1,000 francs per month, these allowances would constitute 21·4, 32·8, and 47·7 per cent. of the earnings for families of 3, 4, and 5 children.

The important question is—how large an allowance would be necessary to influence fertility? This is a question which cannot be answered directly, because no controlled experiments have been or are likely to be undertaken to discover the effect of increasing income by different proportions. But a rough idea may be obtained by looking at the problem from a more indirect point of view—that is, by estimating the increase in total living costs brought about by an increase in the size of the family. If we base ourselves on English standards, we can make use of R. F. George's new poverty line, which is probably the best of the recent calculations in this field.[2] The minimum weekly cost in 1936, according to this calculation, was (*a*) food, 6*s*. 9*d*. for an adult male (14 to 70 years of age), 5*s*. 9*d*. for an adult

past, between allowances and basic earnings (see previous chapter). For this reason the latest wage data given in the previous chapter were not estimated from published wage-rates, but were obtained by asking each equalization fund for information on average earnings.

[1] *Revue de l'Alliance Nationale*, Dec. 1938, p. 368.

[2] George R. F., 'A new calculation of the poverty line', *J.R.S.S.*, part i, 1937, pp. 74–95. The food requirements are derived from the B.M.A. *Report of Committee on Nutrition*, London, 1933, modified for the new milk needs recommended partly by the Ministry of Health Advisory Committee on Nutrition and partly by the Technical Commission appointed by the Health Committee of the League of Nations. The clothing, fuel, light, and cleaning requirements are George's own estimates.

female, 5*s.* 5*d.* for a child aged 6 to 14 years, and 3*s.* 10*d.* for a child under 6 years of age; (*b*) clothing, 11*d.*, 8*d.*, 7*d.*, and 7*d.* for the individuals specified above; (*c*) cleaning and lighting, 6*d.* for 1 person, 8*d.* for 2, 10*d.* for 3, 1*s.* for 4, and 1*s.* 3*d.* for 5 or more persons; (*d*) fuel, 2*s.* 11*d.* for families of 4 or fewer persons, and 3*s.* 6*d.* for families of 5 or more persons. From these estimates we may set up a series of standards for a number of family types, as in the Table below.

TABLE 22. *Family Types and Minimum Costs per Week*

	Man and wife	*Man, wife, and child aged 10*	*Man, wife, and 2 children aged 7 and 10*	*Man, wife, and 3 children aged 4, 7, and 10*
	s. d.	*s. d.*	*s. d.*	*s. d.*
Food . . .	12 6	17 11	23 4	27 2
Clothing . . .	1 7	2 2	2 9	3 4
Fuel . . .	2 11	2 11	2 11	3 6
Cleaning and lighting	8	10	1 0	1 3
Total . . .	17 8	23 10	30 0	35 3
Rent . . .	8 6	10 6	10 6	10 6
Total . . .	26 2	34 4	40 6	45 9
Other items . .	5 2	5 8	6 2	6 5
Total . . .	31 4	40 0	46 8	52 2
Ratios . . .	100	128	149	166

The remaining items in the family budget are much more difficult to assess. A 'minimum' for rent does not mean very much, for rents vary considerably while families have only a limited ability to move in order to take advantage of the lower rents elsewhere. Similarly, travelling expenses incurred in going to and from work depend upon the location of the household in relation to the place of work. And how should we estimate the cost of sundries—cigarettes, amusements, sickness and burial societies, wireless, newspapers, &c.—on which in even the very low income strata some money is spent? In social surveys the rent, insurance, and travel items are generally subtracted so that the expenditure on food, clothing, fuel, light, and cleaning can be directly compared with the chosen minimum standard. But in the present study it is not possible to follow this method, since it is the total cost with which we are concerned and from which we want to deduce the relative costs of families of different sizes. We have, then, to make rather arbitrary assumptions about the other items of expenditure. For rent, we shall use the figures derived by the Children's Minimum Campaign Committee from the data of the Eastern Survey Area of the *New Survey of London Life and Labour*.[1] For the remaining items we shall assume that compulsory insurance and unavoidable fares amount to 2*s.* 8*d.* per week,[2] unaffected by family size, and that all other items amount to 2*s.* 6*d.* per week for a man and wife (including cigarettes, newspapers, cinemas, &c.) and an additional 6*d.* per week to cover all sundries (including presents, sweets, cinemas, &c.) for each child aged 7 years or more and 3*d.* per week for each child under 7 years of age.

Having obtained approximate cost ratios, and assuming that they apply, if only roughly, to conditions in France and Belgium, the difficulty is to know how to interpret them in relation to basic earnings or to total income. If, from the point of view of cost, we could assume that the average wage was just enough to support a man and his wife, the interpretation would be simple. The ratios would show the approximate minimum increases in income necessary to support children of different ages. But we do not know how far this is the case. The Alliance Nationale, in an analysis of family costs,[3] assumed that for a family of husband and wife in the Paris region, with the husband earning 14,000 francs per year and being the sole earner, there would be exact equilibrium between expenses and receipts. But a Belgian statistician, A. Julin, believed that the earnings of a married

[1] *Memorandum on the Scale of Needs*, &c., London, July 1934, p. 12, and *New Survey of London Life and Labour*, vol. iii, London 1932, p. 53, the assumption being that two rooms are needed for a man and wife and three for the other families specified in the present study. (The figure actually given in the London Survey volume is an average of 3·6 shillings per room for three rooms. But we have chosen, for convenience, the slightly lower figure used by the Children's Minimum Committee.) London rents are relatively high, but Rowntree, B. S., *The Human Needs of Labour*, London, 1937 ed., p. 92, regards 9*s.* 6*d.* per week for a three-bedroom, non-parlour house, as the predominant rent, including rates, 'at the present time'.

[2] These are the figures cited in an example relating to the Bristol Social Survey. See Tout, H., *The Standard of Living in Bristol*, Bristol, 1938, p. 21.

[3] *Revue de l'Alliance Nationale*, Jan. 1939, pp. 17–20.

worker should normally be enough to bring up at least two children.[1] On the other hand, a report presented by Monsieur H. Heyman,[2] at the Belgian Chambre des Représentants, in 1937, disagrees with the view expressed by Julin. Monsieur Heyman, basing his conclusions on what appear to be detailed budget analyses, argued that a working-class family consisting of man and wife, living modestly, would need to spend about 13,595 francs per year. But, in fact, full-time adult unskilled labourers earned between 8,000 and 10,000 francs per year, more specialized labourers (semi-skilled) earned 9,000 to 11,000 francs, and the great majority of skilled workers (*ouvriers qualifiés*) earned between 10,000 and 12,000 francs per year. Thus the majority of workers in Belgium was earning less than the amount required to support a man and wife in a modest but decent fashion, and the result was either that both husband and wife went to work and at least temporarily renounced having children, or else that they lived in cramped quarters, had clothes that were worn out, and spent too little on food. As for children, the minimum satisfactory expenditure per month during the first year of life was estimated at 104 francs 50 centimes, and at about 368 francs during the fourteenth year. A reasonable family allowance would thus be about 110 francs per month per child during the first two years of life, rising by 20 francs at the beginning of each subsequent year, so that each child in his or her fourteenth year would receive 350 francs per month.[3] These were the allowances actually outlined by Monsieur Heyman. He did not, however, propose that these allowances should be granted at the time—he probably felt that the Chambre would not accept them—though he was convinced that one day the country would have to reconsider his suggestions

[1] Julin, A., *Enquête sur les Charges Sociales de l'Industrie*, Bruxelles, 1933, p. 80 says that cost of living inquiries in Belgium show that a married worker, with two or three children, lives in suitable circumstances (*conditions convenables*) on hi earnings.

[2] See Note IV*r*, p. 448.

[3] Notice that allowances at the rate mentioned above would mean a grant o 8,280 francs per year for a family of three children aged 4, 7, and 10 years (17 francs per month for the child aged 4, 230 for that aged 7, and 290 for the chil aged 10 years). Relating this to minimum recommended earnings of 13,595 franc per year, it represents 61 per cent. of these basic earnings, as compared with th increase of 66 per cent. suggested by Table 22 in the present study.

The allowances he proposed that the Chambre should grant at the time were very much smaller, being 25 francs per month for the first child, 50 for the second, 75 for the third, 100 for the fourth, and 150 for the fifth and for each subsequent child. Even these were not accepted by the legislature.

But whatever the position as regards the adequacy of an average wage for supporting a man and wife, one may regard the question from a different but no less pertinent point of view. However high a standard of living the average wage may allow to a man and wife, it is clear that bringing up a family implies a reduction in the standard if wages remain unchanged. So long as earnings bear no relationship to family needs, the economic advantages are all in favour of the childless married couple as contrasted with the large family. Consequently, even if the ratios we have estimated cannot be applied directly to show the increase in the average wage necessary to cover the cost of various numbers of children, they can nevertheless be used to show approximately the increase in the wage needed to maintain the standard of living—apart from unmeasurable social and cultural standards—of families at the same level as that of childless married couples, assuming that the husband is the sole wage earner. Thus with three children of the ages specified, a 66 per cent. increase in income would be needed, or about 22 per cent. per child. It would be absurd to pretend that all parents are affected by economic factors in this way. Many have children in spite of themselves, and many others have children because they believe that the return they receive in non-economic satisfaction balances the fall in the standard of living. But if the economic factor is stressed in propaganda, then it is probable that the allowances given should be at least enough to maintain the standard of living if fertility is to be influenced appreciably. Looked at in this way, it will be seen that actual family allowances are very much below the required level. In the example chosen by the Alliance Nationale the Paris worker earns 14,000 francs per year. Family allowances in the Paris region were particularly high, being 720 francs per year for the first child, 1,200 for the second, 1,800 for the third, and 2,400 for the fourth and for each subsequent child. For a family of three children the total annual allowance would be 3,720 francs, representing only about 27 per cent. of the basic earnings, or 9 per cent. per child, instead of the required 22 per cent. per child.[1] In other regions the rates of allowance are much lower, even in relation to lower earnings. It is therefore not surprising to find that Professor M. Gand, writing of conditions in the industrial and commercial areas of the Nord Département, should conclude that the present family allowances had certainly not produced an increase in births in the families of employees and wage earners, and that, on the contrary, births had fallen, especially in the wage-earning agglomerations.[2] A similar view was obtained from the generality of replies to questionnaires sent to the departmental fertility committees in 1938. Seventy out of the ninety committees replied, the opinion being that family allowances are too small really to stimulate fertility, and that at the most they might act as a brake on the decline.[3] Not even the decree-law of 12 November 1938, raising allowances to the minimum of 5 per cent. of the average earnings of an adult worker in each Département for the first child, 10 per cent. for the second, and 15 per cent. for the third and for each subsequent child, will equalize the standard of life of the childless couple and the large family.

We have seen that in addition to family allowances, there are many other forms of assistance. But how significant are they in terms of actual expenditure? For Belgium this question cannot be answered, but for France an answer was given to the Alliance Nationale in November 1938 by the Minister of Health.[4] Apparently the present annual cost to the State, to the Départements, and to the Communes of

[1] The Alliance Nationale estimate an even higher discrepancy between earnings and needs, assuming that three children would involve an additional expense of 13,000 francs per year to maintain the standard of living. Thus the necessary total income would be 27,000 francs per year, instead of the 17,720 (including allowances) which would be received. See also Boverat, F., *Les Encouragements Matériels à la Natalité*, Paris, n.d., but apparently 1934.

[2] Gand, M., *La Famille Ouvrière et la Famille Paysanne dans le Nord devant les Lois Sociales*, Lille, 1938, p. 13.

[3] Partiot, M., op. cit., pp. 3–4.

[4] *Revue de l'Alliance Nationale*, Jan. 1939, p. 21. No dates are given, but presumably the figures are the latest available. There has been a good deal of criticism of ministerial estimates of amounts specifically spent on 'large families', but that question does not arise here. See, however, the reports of an address by Duval-Arnould, L., in *Revue de la Plus Grande Famille*, Sept.–Oct. and Nov.–Dec. 1938.

the various forms of assistance, tax rebates, family allowances to civil servants and to members of the defence forces, &c., amounts to 3,249·5 million francs. No statistics were available for tax rebates granted by local authorities, or for the family allowances given to the employees of these authorities. Monsieur G. Bonvoisin, in his report to the 1938 Family Allowance Congress, estimated that in 1937 about 950 million francs were spent on allowances to all *fonctionnaires*, and that about 3,300 million francs were spent on all kinds of family allowances.[1] If we omit from Monsieur Bonvoisin's estimate the figure for civil service allowances and add the remainder to the total estimate given by the Minister of Health, we obtain a general total of 5,599·5 million francs. Allowing for all omissions, including about 150 million francs for family allowances in agriculture, it is unlikely that the total cost of French measures directed to help families amounts to much more than 6,000 million francs per year. But if we look at French budgetary expenditure, we find that expenditure actually made under the ordinary budget for the financial year ending 31 May 1938 was 50,076 million francs, while expenditure under the extraordinary budget (*compte des investissements en capital*) is estimated to have been another 15,600 million francs. The 1938 budget as voted amounts to 54,739 millions, plus 14,231 millions under the *compte des investissements*, a total of about 69,000 millions. Of this total, expenditure on defence forces (including capital expenditure) forms almost 22,000 million francs. So expenditure on families is less in size than 10 per cent. of the total budget, and less than a third of the expenditure on defence.[2] Private incomes in France (including government pensions paid to individuals) amounted to about 189,000 million francs in 1936, according to one statistician,[3]

[1] This includes family allowances to retired civil servants.

[2] Anon., 'Le budget, la trésorerie et la dette publique', in *La France Économique en 1937*, Paris, 1938, esp. pp. 55–7 and 74. The addition of the items of the *compte des investissements* is not quite correct in the Table on p. 74. A summary of earlier budget figures is given in Haig, R. M., 'The national budgets of France, 1928–37', *Proc. Acad. Pol. Sci.*, Jan. 1938. Somewhat different figures are given in the *Statistical Year-Book of the League of Nations, 1937–8*, Geneva, 1938, p. 279, for 1937, but the figures for 1938 are practically the same as those cited above.

[3] Dugé de Bernonville, L., 'Les revenus privés', in *La France Économique en 1936*, Paris, 1937, esp. p. 61.

while the average annual national income of France in 1925–34, excluding indirect taxes and interest on war loan, was, according to Colin Clark, about 199,000 million francs.[1] So total annual expenditure on family assistance in France has, up to the present, amounted to only about 3 per cent. of the national income. In Belgium the proportion is probably considerably less. Even this estimate for France may really be too high a figure for the cost specifically to be imputed to the population policy, for some of the expenditure on assistance to families is in directions accepted by most other western countries as necessary for general social reasons, unconnected with any explicit intention to raise fertility. Part of the system of tax rebates and social insurance would certainly come within this category.[2]

In the previous sections we have analysed the pro-natalist measures applied up to the summer of 1939. In Belgium there have been no changes in more recent months (up to September 1939), but for France we must take into account the new *Code de la Famille* promulgated by decree of 29 July 1939, which very considerably alters the range and nature of the measures. It has been pointed out that in France—as in Belgium, too—there has long been a considerable divergence between theory and practice in the field of population policy;[3] that the various organizations mentioned have in the past produced many schemes for increasing the amount of material assistance to the family as well as for heightening the efficiency of the law relating to birth-control propaganda and to abortion;[4] but that governments have been reluctant to bring about any radical change in the distribution of income as between small and large families and high and low income groups, and have therefore not been able to give really substantial monetary incentives for

[1] 7,785 million dollars at 1 franc = 0·03918 dollars. Clark, C., 'Internationaler Vergleich der Volkseinkommen', *Weltwirtschaftliches Archiv*, Jan. 1938, esp. p. 63.

[2] Thus 152 million francs are spent on assistance to women during confinement, and 769 millions on tax rebates by the central government for 'large families'.

[3] For a biting comment on the value of the grants given by central and local authorities in France, see *Manuel Pratique des Allocations Familiales en Agriculture*, 2nd ed., op. cit., p. 2.

[4] See Note IV*s*, p. 448.

raising families. The new *Code de la Famille*[1] is a compromise between the French government and such pro-natalist associations as the Alliance Nationale and the Federation of Large Family Associations, and appears to have gone a fair way to meet the demands of such bodies.

On the positive side, the changes in the family allowance system, briefly described in the previous chapter, mean that a family in which there is only one earner whose wage is equal to the average in his Département, will receive, for four dependent children, an allowance amounting to 50 per cent. of the basic wage. If the family lives in an urban area there will be a further grant—for the *mère au foyer*—equal to 10 per cent. of the basic wage, bringing the total to 60 per cent., or 15 per cent. per child on the average. With three children the total grant, in the same circumstances, would be equivalent to 40 per cent. of the basic wage, or about 13 per cent. per child. These percentages are still below the figures estimated in the earlier analysis of costs, but they are very much higher than any compulsory allowances previously given, and for really large families—with seven or more dependent children—they may more than cover the costs entailed in bringing up the children. This does not, of course, mean that the new allowances will give children all that is required for a desirable standard of living. But it means that, assuming the average Départemental wage is sufficient for husband and wife, persons earning such a wage and having seven or more children will receive allowances probably covering the extra costs entailed by the children. For persons with incomes above the average, assuming that the proportionate cost of children is unchanged, the minimum allowances will not be sufficient to cover the whole additional cost. But in any case, the large majority of families with four or more dependent children will receive allowances very much higher than any paid before.[2]

Two other forms of positive assistance should also be noted. First, each married couple will be entitled to a

[1] See *Journal Officiel*, 30 July 1939, pp. 9607–9626. See also *Revue de l'Alliance Nationale*, Aug. 1939, and *Bulletin Mensuel des Allocations Familiales*, Aug.–Sept. 1939, both of which are almost exclusively devoted to the new *Code*.

[2] Even higher than under the decree of 12 Nov. 1938 for these families.

premium for the birth of the first healthy (*viable*) legitimate child of the marriage, provided that the child is born within two years after the celebration of the marriage and is of French nationality.[1] The premium is to be equal to twice the average monthly wage in the districts with more than 2,000 inhabitants in the Département in which the head of the family is resident, but must not in any case be less than 2,000 francs, and it is payable in two equal parts, the first at birth,[2] and the second at the end of the sixth month following the birth, provided that the child is still alive and is the responsibility of its parents. Generally speaking, the premium is to be paid to the mother, and is to be reduced by half for the beneficiaries of the rural marriage loans discussed subsequently. The costs of the premiums are to be borne by the equalization funds in respect of the persons to whom they give family allowances,[3] by the State and public bodies for their personnel, and by the State for the heads of families not included in the occupied population.

The second form of assistance is loans for helping young country folk to marry and set up households, and to prevent the 'flight from the land' which has been so long one of the most widely discussed questions in France. The loans may be between 5,000 and 20,000 francs, to be used for the purchase of agricultural equipment and stock, for the provision of household equipment and furniture, or for repairs to or the improvement of a dwelling. The loan, which is applied for within two months preceding the marriage, is granted only if certain conditions are fulfilled. The man must be French by birth or naturalized at least five years before and enjoy full citizen rights; have fulfilled his military service or been exempted from it; be over 21 but less than 30 years of age,[4] with an intended wife between 18 and 28 years of age; have worked for at least five years in an institute for agricul-

[1] This strikes at the Italian policy of encouraging Italian women resident in France to return to Italy for their confinements. See Chapter V, p. 224.

[2] Or immediately after application, if application is made after the birth of the child.

[3] But note that in agriculture and for independent workers the State is to pay up to two-thirds of the cost of minimum family allowances and birth premiums.

[4] During the first two years of application of this decree the upper age may be 32 years, and in any case is raised by a period equal to the time spent in active compulsory military service by the person concerned.

tural instruction, in an agricultural enterprise, or with a rural artisan; and make a written declaration agreeing that he and his future wife will spend at least ten consecutive years after the marriage engaged in an agricultural occupation or as rural artisans in France. A medical certificate will have to be supplied for husband and wife, though the grounds for physical disqualification—if any—have still to be determined, and in granting the loan the competent authority will take into consideration the thriftiness and diligence of the applicants and the usefulness of the loan to them. The loan is to be repaid in twenty equal half-year instalments, including interest at $4\frac{1}{4}$ per cent.,[1] and provision is made for partial cancellations on the birth of successive children. At the birth of the first child each subsequent instalment is reduced by an amount equal to 0·5 per cent. of the loan, and the reductions increase until, at the birth of the fifth child, all the remaining instalments are cancelled. The loans are to be granted by the regional agricultural credit funds, derived from money loaned by the central government—at 4 per cent. interest, subject to modification—to the national agricultural credit fund, the cost of cancellations on the birth of children being borne by the central government itself. At the same time a fund will be set up to guarantee the loans.

Other forms of assistance are also provided, and to cover those costs for which the State is to be responsible,[2] as well as to produce a more equitable form of taxation, the income-tax has been changed. We have seen that this tax already contained a graduation to the advantage of the family—rebates for children and a higher rate of tax for unmarried persons and for childless married couples—and this has been increased. Instead of being subject simply to an increase in the rate of tax, every childless unmarried, divorced, or widowed person liable to income-tax has in addition to pay

[1] The rate of interest may be modified by a decree of the Ministers of Agriculture and Finance. The first instalment falls due on the first day of the fifth quarter following the marriage.

[2] In the report which precedes the clauses of the *Code*, the cost to the State is estimated at about 1,450 million francs. This would be lower than previous expenditure. But Boverat, F., *Revue de l'Alliance Nationale*, Aug. 1939, p. 244, says that this is new expenditure. Not until 1941 at the earliest shall we know the actual cost of the measures.

a 'family equalization tax' calculated on the taxable income, and amounting to 3 per cent. of that income for incomes or parts of incomes not exceeding 50,000 francs per year, 6 per cent. between 50,000 and 100,000 francs, 9 per cent. between 100,000 and 200,000 francs, rising until it amounts to 20 per cent. for incomes or parts of incomes above 800,000 francs. Persons married for more than two years, and not having any children, are also subject to this tax, though at lower rates. For incomes or parts of incomes not exceeding 50,000 francs the tax is 2 per cent., rising to 14 per cent. on incomes or parts of incomes above 800,000 francs. At the same time there are changes in death duties, in accordance with the degree of kinship and the number of children which the deceased person had.

On the repressive side, we should note considerable changes in the law relating to abortion. Imprisonment for one to five years and a fine of 500 to 10,000 francs are prescribed for any one who procures or attempts to procure the abortion of a woman who is pregnant or presumed to be so, whether she has agreed to the abortion or not. If the guilty person habitually procures or attempts to procure abortions these penalties are increased to imprisonment for 5 to 10 years and a fine of 5,000 to 20,000 francs. A woman who procures or attempts to procure her own abortion, or agrees to make use of the methods indicated or administered to her, is liable to imprisonment for 6 months to 2 years and a fine of 100 to 2,000 francs. On the other hand, the law is to contain, for the first time, a specific provision allowing abortion to be performed by a doctor, after consultation with two other doctors, one of whom must be inscribed on a special register of experts, if the life of the pregnant woman is in danger. Doctors may also report criminal abortions which they have noticed in the course of carrying on their profession. There are also clauses striking at the sale of abortifacients, and it is forbidden to display, offer, have offered, sell, put on sale or have sold, to distribute or have distributed substances or objects—including intra-uterine catheters—which may be used for procuring abortions (a list of these substances and objects is to be drawn up). These substances and objects may not be sold except on presentation of a medical prescription, and the sale of gynaecological or surgical instruments to the public is also forbidden. The penalty for any infraction of these clauses is imprisonment for 3 months to 2 years and a fine of 500 to 5,000 francs, plus the possibility of a temporary or permanent prohibition, of the individual concerned, to practise his profession.

These are merely the bare outlines of some of the major clauses of the new *Code*. There are many others—there are, altogether, 167 articles—dealing with assistance to needy families, with the legal position and protection of illegitimate children, the conditions of adoption of children, infant mortality, the inspection of maternity homes and clinics, the campaign against alcoholism and offences against public decency, and the wages of rural workers employed by their parents. There is even a clause stipulating that in every school in France the syllabus must include a certain minimum of instruction concerning population problems. But it would not be appropriate to give more detail here, for in many cases special regulations will be necessary for applying the provisions and there will be much legal discussion and interpretation. It is clear that many people will find—and have already found—the *Code* unsatisfactory and/or incomplete. Family allowances of the amounts specified by the *Code* are not legally to be given to unemployed persons. There have been protests at the elimination of the allowance for the first child, and at the fact that under the new system of allowances the financial encouragement is still not really substantial until the family has three or four dependent children. The grant to the *mère au foyer* is, also, far from sufficient to compensate her for giving up a paid occupation. The rural marriage loans are to be repaid with a prohibitive rate of interest, and on the other hand, no encouragement to marry and found a family is given to townsfolk. The assistance to needy families is still ludicrously small, and the problem of cheap and suitable housing has not been dealt with at all. The position of the illegitimate child and the unmarried mother is still unsatisfactory. Moreover, the new *Code* involves a much more determined effort to suppress abortion without in any way relaxing the law relating to birth-control information. That is, in spite of the emphasis upon positive inducements and assistance, the new *Code* is none the less in the customary French pro-natalist tradition, denying to married couples the right to practise family limitation except by those physiological means which fall outside the scope of legal prohibition. But it is also clear that, for the first time in the history of France, a government has actually drawn up a relatively logical and comprehensive plan for checking the decline in fertility. In itself this is an acknowledgement of the failure of past measures to produce appreciable results, and of concern at the facts that immigration has been the chief factor responsible for maintaining the size of the population,[1] and that most of the Départements of France now show an excess of deaths over births.[2]

[1] There were 2·715 million foreigners in the *de facto* population, according to the 1931 census, in addition to 361,000 who were naturalized French citizens (Huber, Bunle, Boverat, op. cit., p. 52).

[2] In 1938, 65 of the 90 Départements had an excess of deaths over births (*Le Matin*, 11 Aug. 1939). In Belgium, because of the much younger age structure of the population, deaths have not yet begun to exceed births, although the net reproduction rate is lower than in France.

V

THE ITALIAN STRUGGLE FOR POPULATION

A HIGHLY developed population policy, embracing many measures for discouraging celibacy and encouraging marriage and the raising of large families, is a very recent feature of Italian governmental initiative. It is specifically a product of the Fascist era, and even during that era it took some time for explicit pro-natalist aims to be expressed and applied. As late as 1924 Mussolini himself drew attention to the very high crude rate of increase of the Italian population. Vital statistics, he asserted, showed that the population was growing by about 446,000 persons per year. Considering the increasing, almost distressing, disproportion between the possibilities of the country and the growing population, the problem was clearly important. Yet he would never favour Malthusian propaganda, nor could one or ought one envisage wars for the conquest of territories for colonization.[1] In 1926 official estimates appeared further to support Mussolini's analysis of population growth. One estimate suggested an increase of about 3 million persons in four years, while a later, corrected, figure estimated the increase at about 1·8 millions. However, these estimates were actually much too high, and Mussolini appeared to hint at this at the opening of the Central Statistical Institute in 1926.[2] But in any case Italian population policy had changed in the intervening period, and November and December 1926 saw two important laws—which will be discussed later—to initiate the new pro-natalist policy.

Italian writers, when they discuss the objects of the new population policy, emphasize the Fascist conception of the relationship between the individual and the State, the abandonment of a hedonistic policy, the importance of checking

[1] See Note V*a*, p. 449.

[2] He spoke of a 'crisi della statistica italiana', and said that Italian statistics 'deve ritrovare la gloria dei suoi primi tempi'. On this, as well as on the estimates mentioned above, see Fischer, A., 'Die Bevölkerungsentwicklung 1925–1928', *Zeitschrift für Geopolitik*, Heft 4, 1928, pp. 335–47.

the decline of fertility, and the desire to rehabilitate the family.[1] But however important these factors may have been in influencing the policy, a still more important factor was mentioned in Mussolini's Ascension Day speech, 26 May 1927, which summarized his views on the question. He asserted that demographic power conditioned the political and thus also the economic and moral power of nations. 'What', he asked, 'are the 40 millions of Italians as opposed to (*di fronte a*) 90 million Germans and 200 million Slavs? Let us turn to the West: What are 40 million Italians as opposed to 40 million French, plus the 90 millions in their colonies, or as opposed to the 46 million English, plus the 450 millions in their colonies? To count for something in the world', he continued, 'Italy must have a population of not less than 60 millions when she arrives at the threshold of the second half of this century'. He pointed out that in spite of the growth of population since 1815 the standard of living had risen enormously. Drawing attention to the reduced rate of population growth, he added: 'For five years we have been saying that the Italian population is like a river overflowing its banks. It is not true!' He went on to insist that every nation and every empire had felt the gnawing of decadence when they had seen their births begin to fall off. 'With a falling population, one does not create an empire but becomes a colony.'[2] It is evident, then, that one of the factors responsible for changing Mussolini's views[3] on the subject of population was the ambition that Italy should have a 'place in the sun'. The desire to achieve this aim has resulted in a considerable series of laws and regulations. Some of these do not appear to be particularly pro-natalist in tendency and similar measures may certainly be found

[1] See Note V*b*, p. 450.

[2] 'Il discorso dell'Ascensione', especially pp. 42–6, in *Scritti e Discorsi dal 1927 al 1928* (*Scritti e Discorsi di Benito Mussolini*, VI), Milan, 1934. Attention should also be drawn to the preface, written by Mussolini, to the Italian translation of R. Korherr's book, *Regresso delle Nascite: Morte dei Popoli*, Rome, 1928. (This had originally appeared, as a special number of the *Süddeutsche Monatshefte*, under the title *Geburtenrückgang*, Munich, 1927.) The preface ends: 'In an Italy completely improved, cultivated, irrigated, and disciplined—that is, a Fascist Italy—there is still room and bread for ten million men. Sixty million Italians will make the weight of their mass and their force felt in the history of the world' (p. 23).

[3] See Note V*c*, p. 450.

in other countries which have no overt population policy. But these regulations are nevertheless included in the discussion because in Italy they are explicitly regarded as part of the campaign for increasing the population of the country.

It has been noted that the Ascension Day speech was delivered after a number of measures had already been introduced. One of these measures shows clearly that the population *motif* was not necessarily always linked to a desire to restore the family to its pristine glory. This measure—or, rather, the first of a series of measures dealing with the same subject—was the suppression in April 1927 of the General Commissariat for Emigration and its replacement by an organization, attached to the Ministry of Foreign Affairs, for the general supervision of all Italians abroad,[1] and introduced a striking change in migration policy. Previous governments had not interfered with emigration. Except during the War period, they had, on the contrary, tried to encourage it, and in the early post-War years, with the economic dislocation depressing industry and employment, emigration was regarded as the easiest means of helping to solve the unemployment problem. Passports for intending emigrants were to be delivered within twenty-four hours of applying for them.[2] There was an emigration fund financed by the State, and specially reduced railway fares were available for Italian workers going abroad[3]—though post-War economic difficulties in the countries to which Italy had formerly sent the major part of her emigrants prevented emigration from continuing to act as an 'automatic safety-valve'.[4]

But with the coming of the Fascist régime, emigration became regarded as an injurious loss of Italian subjects. At first no specific action was taken against it, though in

[1] Royal legislative decree of 28 April 1927, n. 628. See 'L'istituzione di una "direzione generale degli italiani all' estero"', *Bollettino dell' Emigrazione*, May 1927, pp. 623–5.

[2] *Emigration and Immigration: Legislation and Treaties* (International Labour Office), Geneva, 1922, p. 37.

[3] See Woog, C., *La Politique d'Émigration de l'Italie*, Paris, 1930, pp. 115 ff.

[4] See 'La crisi mondiale del lavoro e la valorizzazione degli emigranti', *Bollettino dell' Emigrazione*, Jan. 1922, pp. 1–8.

increasing the general supervision of emigration the government attempted to avoid encouraging it. On 31 March 1927, however, Grandi—then Under-Secretary of State for Foreign Affairs—was much more explicit in his speech to the Italian Chamber of Deputies (Camera dei Deputati). He said that the Italian colonies in foreign countries should really be sections of the mother country. The term 'emigrant' no longer existed—there were only citizens. He recognized emigration as a need, but insisted that it should take place under national sovereignty. Nations now calculated their power in terms of the homogeneity and size of their populations and their demographic vitality. Why should Italy still serve as a kind of human fishpond, to feed countries suffering from demographic impoverishment? And why should Italian mothers continue to bear sons to serve as soldiers for other nations?[1] This speech was followed, in April, by the suppression of the General Commissariat for Emigration,[2] in July 1927 by the suppression of the emigration fund, its revenue being transferred to the general budget,[3] and in October 1927 by the suppression of the Superior Council for Emigration.[4] In March 1928 the issue of the special passport for emigrants ceased,[5] so that nothing remained of the earlier emigration policy save the measures for protecting persons henceforth defined not as emigrants but as Italian citizens living or going abroad.

Instead, new measures made it more difficult for emigration to take place. Thus in October 1927 the specially cheap railway fares for emigrants were abolished, while the reductions in fares for Italian workers abroad who wished to

[1] See *Bollettino dell' Emigrazione*, May 1927, pp. 626–9, 'Spiriti e forme della nuova politica d'emigrazione'. See also Mussolini, Circular no. 77, 20 June 1927, which was sent to Italian embassies and legations in the different countries. 'È negli intendimenti del R. Governo contenere entro ristretti limiti l'emigrazione, che dev' essere considerata come un depauperamento demografico che, in definitiva, non può non indebolire qualitativamente e quantitativamente la compagine della Nazione' (*Boll. dell' Em.*, July 1927, pp. 955–7 at p. 955).

[2] *Boll. dell' Em.*, May 1927, pp. 623–5—Royal legislative decree, 28 April.

[3] Royal decree of 18 June 1927, n. 1636, coming into force 1 July. Ibid., July 1927, pp. 1118–19.

[4] Royal decree of 23 Oct. 1927, n. 2146. Ibid., Nov. 1927, p. 1891.

[5] The new passport which took its place was drawn up by Grandi and approved by Mussolini in Oct. 1927—see ibid., Oct. 1927, pp. 1620–1—but did not come into use until 1 March 1928.

return home were increased from 50 to 75 per cent.[1] In June 1927 three circulars were issued to intensify the control over, and at the same time to restrict, emigration, by stipulating that certain documents had to be produced in order to obtain permission to emigrate to overseas countries. These documents were either a regular labour contract, attested by the competent consul, or a similarly attested document (*atto di chiamata*) from a relative not more distant than the third degree of kinship (husband or wife, parents, children, grandparents, brothers and sisters, maternal and paternal uncles and aunts) asking the individual concerned to go to the country where this relative was already living.[2] Two further circulars, dated 3 November 1927, restricted the number of relatives who could 'claim' an Italian citizen and entitle him to emigrate, to the husband, parents, sons, a brother 'claiming' his unmarried or widowed sister, grandchildren 'claiming' their grandparents. Fiancés were specifically excluded from 'claiming' each other.[3] After July 1928 Italians leaving the country had to promise not to have their families follow them abroad, and after April 1929 foreign employers wanting Italian labour were not allowed to specify by name the workers they wanted, unless they had already employed these workers previously, or if the workers came under certain categories, such as engineers and similar types of workers.[4]

Care was taken to ensure that these numerous restrictions on emigration should not be evaded. Circulars were issued to local authorities, requesting them to intensify their vigilance in preventing clandestine emigration,[5] and other circulars attempted to check indirect overseas migration—

[1] Ibid., Oct. 1927, p. 1620.

[2] 'La nuova disciplina dell' emigrazione', ibid., July 1927, pp. 951–7.

[3] 'La nuova disciplina dell' espatrio', ibid., Nov. 1927, pp. 1737–43. See also Woog, op. cit., pp. 128–9.

[4] Woog, op. cit., pp. 130–1. Woog cites a speech by Mussolini, dated 28 Sept. 1929, implying that in the future only 'good' Italians would be allowed to emigrate —i.e. those Italians believing in the principles of Fascism. Note also a circular dated 3 Jan. 1926, prohibiting the issue of passports to Italians having no definite calling and working as itinerant musicians, because they might cast discredit, in foreign countries, upon Italian workers. See *Migration Laws and Treaties* (International Labour Office), vol. i, Geneva, 1928, p. 70.

[5] See, e.g., *Boll. dell' Em.*, Nov. 1923, pp. 889–90.

especially through Spain to the United States.[1] The punishment for attempts at clandestine emigration was increased by a Legislative Decree of 6 November 1926. If the motives were political, the sentences prescribed were imprisonment for not less than two years and a fine of 20,000 lire. Where political motives were not involved, the sentence was imprisonment for six months and a fine of 2,000 lire. Frontier guards were empowered to fire upon any one attempting to cross the frontier at other than authorized points.[2]

At the same time the Italian government intensified its efforts to prevent the denationalization of Italian subjects working abroad. Where the existing laws increased the likelihood of loss of Italian nationality, the Italian government attempted to procure changes in the law,[3] or, in lieu of this, offered free passage to Italy to pregnant Italian women living abroad, so that their children might be born in Italy,[4] and free passage and holidays to the children of Italians living abroad, so that these children might be duly impressed by the glory of retaining Italian nationality. In the main, these aspects of governmental policy are outside the scope of the present study. But we may note the efforts to procure the right to set up Italian schools for Italian children abroad—this began long before the Fascist era—, to obtain for Italian workers abroad the same social insurance benefits as those due to citizens of the particular countries, and even to obtain direct Italian control over the groups of Italian workers settled in various foreign countries.[5] In addition there was governmental assistance for the production of Italian newspapers for such groups of settlers, and a national finance organization designed not only to give assistance to Italian workers abroad, but also to collect the

[1] See, e.g., *Migration Laws and Treaties*, vol. i, p. 77.

[2] *Migration Laws and Treaties*, vol. i, p. 98. Under the Emigration Act o 19 Nov. 1919 any one inducing an emigrant to 'embark clandestinely' might b imprisoned for up to 6 months and be fined 1,000 lire.

[3] As regards France, for example, see Woog, op. cit., pp. 161–6, and Mauco, G op. cit., pp. 496–9.

[4] See Note V*d*, p. 450.

[5] Attempts to apply these aims in South America led to serious disputes in 192 Mussolini retaliated with a sharp reduction in the number of emigrants. See Harm sen, op. cit., p. 42. On France, see also Harmsen, H., *Bevölkerungsprobleme Frank reichs*, Berlin-Grunewald, 1927, Part 7.

savings of these workers. No doubt, in addition to the desire to retain the nationality of Italian citizens, the Italian government was also concerned to assure, for the mother country, a profit from whatever emigration was allowed.[1] It is not surprising that Fascist emigration policy, together with the various immigration restrictions imposed by the United States and other countries, considerably reduced the flow of emigrants from Italy.[2]

In the preface which he wrote to Korherr's book, *Regresso delle Nascite: Morte dei Popoli*, Mussolini asserted that, with irrigation and reclamation schemes, there would be food and space for many more Italians in Italy. In the background of the population policy there have been efforts to justify this assertion—to make Italy capable of supporting a larger population—and it is advisable briefly to note the major efforts before discussing the more strictly pro-natalist policies. It may be said at once that neither the idea nor the practice of land reclamation is original, in Italy, to the Fascist era. Irrigation and the draining of marshland were undertaken in the Roman Empire. In more recent times, attention may be drawn to the Baccarini Law of 1882, under which land reclamation schemes were divided according to purpose. When the object was primarily improvement in hygiene the government paid half the cost. But where the object was primarily agricultural improvement, only one-tenth of the cost would be covered by the government, the provinces, and the communes.[3] The distinction, according to an official connected with the modern scheme,[4] between

[1] A circular of 6 July 1926 points out that, as a result of recent governmental decisions, it is forbidden to export from Italy, for any purpose and by any person, a sum of more than 10,000 lire. This would affect emigrants who, having a small amount of capital, intend to set up a business in a foreign country.

[2] See Note V*e*, p. 451.

[3] Longobardi, C., *Land-reclamation in Italy*, London, 1936, p. 55 and n.

[4] Serpieri, A. (Under-Secretary of State for *bonifica integrale*), 'Aspects sociaux et politiques de la bonification intégrale en Italie', *Le A. S.*, 6, 1933, pp. 480–91. There were also Acts in 1865 and 1873—Longobardi, op. cit., pp. 52 and 54. As regards the history of land reclamation in Italy, Baravelli, G. C., *Land Reclamation Scheme in Italy*, Florence, 1937, points out (p. 13): 'It has been said that the history of land reclamation constitutes, in a certain measure, the history of the Italian nation. Since the most ancient times the populations of the Peninsula, from one generation to another, have had to snatch the soil, a few feet at a time, from the destructive fury of the floods, from the marshes, from malaria, and from drought.'

Fascist and previous efforts is twofold. First, previous efforts were aimed at specific forms of improvement, while under Fascism the object is *bonifica integrale*—the complete improvement of particular areas, designed primarily for the protection and development of agriculture and rural life. Secondly, far more money has been spent on such reclamation schemes under Fascism than in earlier periods. From the establishment of the kingdom of Italy until 1933 some 5,250 million lire (1933 value) were spent on reclamation, but 3,530 millions were spent during the eleven years of Fascist era, 2,080 millions actually being spent in the four years after 1 July 1929.[1] The Fascist schemes began with the Act of 30 December 1923, under which land reclamation was not restricted solely to the drainage of swamp land, but extended to cover a wide system of measures of improvement. Acts in 1924 and 1925 extended the right of State intervention to all cases where agriculture was in a backward condition and where modernization was possible. Between 1924 and 1928 other Acts dealt with the extension of cereal cultivation, the building of villages, the clearing of land, irrigation, and agricultural credit. As part of the campaign for increasing Italy's capacity to supply herself with food, we should also note the specific 'wheat campaign' (*battaglia del grano*) inaugurated in July 1925 and embracing direct propaganda, the developing of special seed, the scientific use of fertilizers, the provision of agricultural credit, the holding of provincial and national competitions, the imposition of import duties on wheat, and the prescription that a fixed proportion of home-grown wheat should be used in milling. These measures, according to Longobardi,[2] resulted in an increase in the average wheat crop from 4,848,740 metric tons in 1920–1 to 1924–5 to 6,873,740 metric tons in the period 1930–1 to 1934–5, and helped, as was intended, significantly to reduce Italy's adverse balance of trade.[3]

[1] Serpieri, op. cit., p. 480.

[2] Op. cit., pp. 39–40.

[3] Salvemini, G., *Under the Axe of Fascism*, London, 1936, p. 296, n. 3, is not so impressed by the results of combined land reclamation and the wheat campaign. He notes that Senator Ciccotti, speaking in the Senate on 20 May 1931, said that whereas a piece of land in the Roman *Campagna* had formerly produced 46,000 lire p.a. as pasture, it now produced not more than 18,000 lire when put under grain.

The measures noted in the previous paragraph laid the foundations of the Fascist land reclamation movement. The full expression of the movement can be seen in the Act of 24 December 1928 (the Mussolini Act), which came into force on 1 July 1929. This Act classified the various types of reclamation activity upon which the nation was to embark. The major work was to be land drainage and associated irrigation schemes, and additional irrigation schemes in south Italy and the Italian islands. Other sections of the projected work were the construction of rural aqueducts, the building of villages, the construction of irrigation schemes in north and central Italy, and of roads linking up farms, and the provision of drinking-water supplies. The projects were to be completed by 1944—some of them earlier—and it was estimated that over 7,000 million lire would be spent upon them, of which 4,300 million would be provided by the Treasury and the rest would be borne by the landowners.[1] The administration of the Act in local districts—that is, the undertaking of the approved projects—was left largely in the hands of the Consorzi, or Associations of Landowners, and the National Association of Ex-Service Men (Opera Nazionale dei Combattenti). For some of the projects—such as afforestation, and river regulation and alteration in mountainous areas—the State might assume complete monetary responsibility. In other cases, where the benefit was mainly to private individuals, the subsidy was generally one-third of the cost, though in some cases it might be very much higher, up to as much as 75 per cent.[2] In addition to the direct State subsidy, provision was also made for special loans to be granted to landowners through the various financial institutions. The different measures applied for the purpose of land reclamation and improvement were finally consolidated and co-ordinated by a Royal Decree of 13 February 1933. From 1922 to 1936 reclamation and improvement work, under the successive Acts, was applied to about 5·11

[1] Longobardi, op. cit., pp. 63–4, and pp. 197–202. Marcelletti, M., 'Aspects of planned economy in Italy', *International Labour Review*, Sept. 1934, pp. 321–35 at p. 333, gives somewhat different figures—a total expenditure of 7,300 million lire, of which the share of the State would be 3,800 million lire. See also Turnor, C., *Land Reclamation and Drainage in Italy*, London, 1938, pp. 3–5.

[2] Baravelli, op. cit., p. 24.

million hectares of land (12·63 million acres), and on about 2·21 million hectares of this area the work was either complete or nearly so by July 1936. The expenditure actually incurred in the period amounted to about 7,986·5 million lire, including 2,366·7 million lire given as subsidies to private reclamation schemes, the rest being spent by the State directly upon drainage and reclamation, road building in reclaimed areas, and improvement work in mountain districts.[1] By 1 July 1937 these totals had risen to 8,634·2 and 2,556·2 million lire respectively.[2]

This, however, was merely one part of Mussolini's policy of utilizing the 'last square inch of the national territory'.[3] To fulfil the other part there had to be a transference of population to the reclaimed and improved areas, and this was undertaken by the Permanent Committee for Internal Migration and Settlement[4] (Commissariato per la Migrazione e la Colonizzazione interna), set up under a Royal Decree of 4 March 1926 and given the duties, under a Decree of 28 November 1928, of 'regulating internal migration and encouraging movements of the labour supply'.[5] The Committee was reorganized by an Act of 9 April 1931, under which it was authorized to give subsidies to families who were transferred, or who voluntarily moved to the reclaimed areas with the object of permanent settlement (this was retrospective, applying to families which had moved since 28 October 1927). The subsidies were not to exceed 6,000 lire per family, to be paid in four equal annual instalments after the first year of permanent settlement in the new area.[6] The migration supervised by the Committee is thus of two distinct kinds—temporary migration of labour, which

[1] Baravelli, op. cit., pp. 27 and 37.

[2] *Annuario Statistico Italiano, 1938*, p. 73. At the peak of this work—in 1934–5—it employed an average of 72,492 workers daily. The number fell to 43,502 in 1935–6 and to 39,226 in 1936–7—ibid., p. 76. See also 'La bonifica integrale nel primo quinquennio di applicazione della legge Mussolini', *Economia*, Aug. 1935, pp. 165–71.

[3] *Il 1924*, loc. cit., p. 432 (11 Dec. 1924).

[4] For a discussion of the aims of this body, see Razza, L., 'Le commissariat des migrations intérieures et ses devoirs', *Le A. S.*, 5, 1930, pp. 13–20.

[5] Oblath, A., 'The campaign against unemployment in Italy', *International Labour Review*, May 1930, pp. 666–93 at p. 685.

[6] *Le A. S.*, 2, 1931, pp. 91–2. See also ibid., 5, 1933, p. 463; 1, 1935, p. 100; and Longobardi, op. cit., pp. 111–15.

aims at distributing the available labour where, in the Committee's view, it is most needed, and permanent migration of workers and families. The second type of migration is more directly aimed at colonizing the reclaimed zones, and it is also bound up with the anti-urban drive which, in Italy, is part of the general pro-natalist population policy. Mussolini had referred, in his Ascension Day speech, to the sterilizing influence of urbanism and to the need for a return to a more rural condition of life,[1] and he emphasized this view in his preface to Korherr's book,[2] and initiated, in November 1927, a campaign against urbanism, urging that every possible means be used to stem the waves of migration towards the towns.[3] The first official action was a circular, dated 6 December 1928, issued to the Prefects of police by the Ministry of the Interior, calling upon the police to undertake a campaign of persuasion and propaganda to combat the fascination which the great city has for country people, and to show those who had migrated to the towns, especially when they had not found the 'paradise' for which they had hoped, the manifold advantages to be found in the smaller centres. The police authorities already had the power to pay the cost of returning poor persons to the rural areas from which they had come, and also to help them travel to districts where they might be able to find employment. The police were urged to interpret these powers generously with the object of reducing the numbers of urban workers and of sending them to rural districts, though these districts were not suddenly to be flooded with townsfolk. Persons who had migrated to towns, but were unemployed, with no immediate prospect of employment, were to be advised to return to the country. Workers arriving, without means of subsistence or prospects of employment, in a town, were, if the chances of employment seemed remote, to be sent back to the country, compulsorily if necessary. The suggestions made in this circular were confirmed by an Act of 24 December 1928, empowering each Prefect, in consultation with the Provincial Economic Council (Consiglio Provinciale dell' Economia), to issue regulations for checking excessive increase in the town

[1] *Scritti e Discorsi dal 1927 al 1928*, op. cit., pp. 45–6.

[2] Op. cit., pp. 8–10, 18–21.

[3] See Woog, op. cit., p. 148.

population. These regulations were to have the force of law and to be enforced under the administrative powers of the local police.[1]

It is difficult to tell exactly how far these regulations have been applied. A publication of the Central Statistical Institute, issued in 1934,[2] refers to a large number of districts in which specific decrees have been passed in accordance with the 1928 Act. Of the 92 Prefectures 62 had made use of the powers conferred upon them under the Act, while of the 92 Provincial Economic Councils only 5 had adopted measures for attacking urbanism. The measures adopted by the two sets of organizations include not only those for returning town workers to the country, but also schemes for making rural areas more attractive to live in. Thus, especially in the mountainous districts, the local administrations have tried to prevent further depopulation by building new houses, providing electric light and power, and better transport facilities and communal amenities. But it would need a very detailed study to show, even roughly, whether or not the measures have achieved their purpose. It should in any case be remembered that these measures have been and are being applied at the same time as supporting measures in the wider field of internal migration, more directly linked to the policy of *bonifica integrale*. Thus the National Fascist Institute of Social Insurance (Istituto Nazionale Fascista della Previdenza Sociale) reports that, in the six years from 1929 to 1934 inclusive, more than 2·080 million agricultural and industrial workers were moved from areas of dense to areas of more sparse population and settlement, and put to work on the various schemes of land reclamation and other public works.[3] It would certainly be interesting to know how far—

[1] Menna, op. cit., pp. 268–76.

[2] 'L'azione promossa dal Governo Nazionale a favore dell' incremento demografico e contro l'urbanesimo', *Annali di Statistica*, serie vi, vol. xxxii, Rome, 193 (the preface, by F. Savorgnan, attributes the work to E. Strumia and B. Zanon), pp. 53–61. This publication contains a very useful analysis of the various measures adopted, up to 1934, to stimulate population growth.

[3] *Work of the National Fascist Institute of Social Insurance*, Rome, 1935, p. 2 The report says that 'The large number of workers transferred in the years 1929–1934 represents 4,996 families. In 1933 alone 1,963 families, representing 15,93 persons, were settled or simply transferred to settlement zones.' But evidently a large part of the 2·08 million persons must have been temporarily migratory labour.

if at all—the fertility of transferred families has been affected by a change in environment.[1]

Emigration restrictions have been designed to prevent an 'excessive' outward flow of Italian citizens, land reclamation measures to make it possible to support the increased population resulting from this damming back of emigrants, and internal migration and colonization measures have been undertaken partly to distribute that population to the reclaimed and improved areas. But except for the anti-urban regulations, these measures are not specifically intended to stimulate natural increase. There are, however, many other Acts and regulations of a more strictly pro-natalist character. As in the chapter on France and Belgium, these measures may be divided broadly into repressive and positive, though in many cases the distinction is extremely vague. Certain measures relating to birth control and abortion are clearly repressive. But the bachelor tax falls into both categories, and so do many regulations designed to give preference to married men with families as compared with bachelors and with the married but childless couples. For this reason we shall separate only birth-control and abortion legislation as an evident form of repression, and discuss the remaining legislation under one general heading, making a rough chronological division.

It will be remembered that Mussolini, who in 1913 had pledged himself in favour of neo-Malthusian doctrines, stated in 1924 that he would never countenance birth-control propaganda as a means of relieving the pressure of population in Italy. He was, on the contrary, prepared to introduce legislation to suppress neo-Malthusian propaganda,[2] and early in 1926 a Commission was appointed to consider possible measures for protecting the family against this propaganda. The first important result appears to have been the law relating to public safety, sanctioned by Royal Decree of 6 November 1926, prohibiting the display, sale, possession,[3] distribution, manufacture, and importation of literature,

[1] Woog, op. cit., pp. 148–9 gives some population data for the largest cities, but one cannot draw any conclusions from them.

[2] *Il 1924*, op. cit., p. 432. 'Giammai io raccomanderò le propagande più o meno malthusiane: anzi dichiaro che reprimerei con misure di polizia una propaganda di sifatta specie.'

[3] With intent to sell.

engravings, lithographs, drawings, objects, &c., offending public decency, regarding as such anything divulging the means of preventing conception or interrupting pregnancy, while at the same time newspapers and periodicals were forbidden to publish advertisements or communications of any kind referring to such means.[1] These rules were confirmed in the new penal code, approved by Royal Decree of 19 October 1930, and coming into force as from 1 July 1931. Paragraph 553 prescribes a fine of up to 10,000 lire, or penal servitude for not more than one year for any person who publicly incites others to use anti-natalist practices, or who undertakes propaganda on behalf of such practices. When the offence is committed for profit, the penalties shall be applied conjointly.[2] An Act of 18 June 1931 reinforced these clauses by extending the terms of the 1926 Royal Decree. Henceforth it was forbidden to manufacture, import, buy, possess, export, or put into circulation any publications, drawings, illustrations, or other objects which divulged, even indirectly, or under scientific or therapeutic pretexts, means for preventing procreation or procuring abortion, or illustrating the use of such means, or supplying information concerning the way in which these means might be procured or employed. It was forbidden to sell such objects either in the ordinary way of business or privately, as well as to distribute them or publicly to display them, and the local police were authorized to seize any objects coming under these headings.[3] How far these measures

[1] Zingali, G., 'I provvedimenti mussoliniani per lo sviluppo quantitativo e qualitativo della popolazione', *Proc. Int. Conf. for Studies on Population, Rome, 1931*, vol. viii, Rome, 1933, pp. 585–604 at pp. 592–3; 'Regio decreto 6 Novembre 1926', Paragraphs 112, 113, and 115, *Gazzetta Ufficiale*, 8 Nov. 1926, no. 257, pp. 4831–2.

[2] Piromallo, A. J., *Manuale Legislativo per l'Udienza Penale*, 2nd ed., Milan, 1934, p. 536; *Penal Code of the Kingdom of Italy*, London (issued by the Foreign Office, published by H.M.S.O.), 1931, p. 148. Notice also that para. 552 prescribes penal servitude for 6 months to 2 years and a fine of 1,000 to 5,000 lire for any person who renders another person (with his or her consent) incapable of procreation. The consenting person is liable to the same penalty. (The Foreign Office translation reads 'impotent to procreate' and the original text is *impotente alla procreazione*. This would presumably mean sterilization.)

[3] Menna, op. cit., pp. 262–3. The clauses relating to advertisements, &c., in newspapers and periodicals were reaffirmed. See 'Relazione e Regio Decreto 18 Giugno 1931, n. 773', 'Approvazione del testo unico delle leggi di pubblica sicurezza', paragraphs 112 and 114, *Supplemento ordinario alla Gazzetta Ufficiale*, n. 146, 26 June 1931, pp. 14–15.

have prevented the use of modern contraceptive techniques it is impossible to say. So far as all methods of family limitation are concerned, the success in preventing their use is very largely reflected in the trend of fertility and will be discussed subsequently. It may, however, be noted here that Italy never had any really widespread birth-control movement,[1] comparable with that in France or England, though shortly before the last War attempts had been made along those lines. In such circumstances legal action and the general campaign against birth-control propagandists may have had the reverse effect of that desired, and, as Professor Salvemini remarks, may have 'taught many innocent souls that one could enjoy oneself without paying the price'.[2] And for those who learn this lesson, and who can afford to buy contraceptives, condoms are still available, since they are regarded legally as a protection against disease, even though they are still one of the most reliable contraceptives.

The Royal Decree of 6 November 1926 contained some specific references to abortion, and in subsequent years there was a succession of circulars and decrees to intensify the campaign against what was regarded by an Italian gynaecologist, Professor Micheli, as one of the major causes of the fall in fertility.[3] Thus the Act of 23 June 1927 (concerning public health) and the regulations for its application stipulated the notification by doctors of every abortion and miscarriage in regard to which their help had been requested,[4] while a circular to public prosecutors in the Courts of Appeal, issued by the Minister of the Interior, urged them to deal

[1] Harmsen, H , 'Die Bevölkerungspolitik Deutschlands,' &c., op. cit., pp. 51–2, mentions a pamphlet by Professor Cagetano of the University of Naples, published 1924, supporting the Malthusian doctrine. The pamphlet was confiscated and Professor Cagetano dismissed from his employment.

[2] Salvemini, G., op. cit., *Birth Control Review*, March 1933, p. 65. It will be remembered that G. Bouthoul expressed a similar view concerning pro-natalist propaganda in France. (See Ch. IV of present study, p. 203.)

[3] Harmsen, H., 'Die Bevölkerungspolitik Deutschlands,' &c., op. cit., p. 52. Professor Micheli estimated, at the beginning of 1928, that there were 185 abortions for every 1,000 births, as compared with only 48·5 twenty years before.

[4] Information from the Secretary of the Inter-Departmental Committee on Abortion. Note that, according to Article 103 of the Royal Decree of 27 July 1934, no. 1265, doctors must notify provincial medical officers, within two days, and in full detail, of every case of abortion coming to their notice, including any which they may have performed. See also Zingali, op. cit., p. 592.

promptly and rigorously with abortion cases, to ascertain all the facts so as to prevent connivance and attempts to shield guilty persons, and to send detailed reports of each prosecution of this kind to the Minister.[1] The new penal code prescribes heavy penalties for cases of illegal abortion. Penal servitude for 2 to 5 years is the punishment for any one procuring the abortion of a woman, and for the woman herself, in cases where the woman has consented to the abortion. If the abortion is procured without the woman's consent, the penalty shall be penal servitude for 7 to 12 years, and this shall also apply to cases where consent is obtained by violence, threats or suggestions, or by fraud, or where the woman is under 14 years of age, or is incapable of understanding or deciding. If a woman induces her own abortion, the penalty shall be penal servitude for 1 to 4 years, while, apart from accessories to the offence, dealt with under the earlier provisions, any one instigating a pregnant woman to commit abortion, by providing[2] means for that purpose, shall be liable to penal servitude for 6 months to 2 years. Where personal injury follows abortion, the penalty shall be penal servitude for 3 to 8 years if the woman had consented to the abortion, and 10 to 15 years if she had not. If the abortion results in the death of the woman, the respective penalties shall be penal servitude for 5 to 12, and for 12 to 20 years.[3]

Shortly after these provisions had come into force a new circular, issued (13 September 1931) by the Ministry of the Interior to Prefects of police, urged them to keep a register of all cases of abortion,[4] using it for, among other purposes, enforcing the legal penalties prescribed under the 1927 Act, and for supervising the medical profession and the public health authorities. On 10 March 1932 a further circular

1 Menna, op. cit., pp. 254–5. Circular of 28 Nov. 1928.

2 The Foreign Office translation is 'administering'. The original text gives *somministrandole mezzi*, and since a person 'administering' such means would come under the earlier paragraphs, the present writer has used the term 'providing'.

3 See Note V*f*, p. 451.

4 Menna, op. cit., pp. 255–7. Since the term *aborto* covers all kinds of abortions, spontaneous as well as induced, it is often difficult to decide whether or not induced abortions alone are intended. In this circular spontaneous abortions are later specified as being required for inclusion in the monthly reports to be sent to the Ministry of the Interior and are presumably also intended for inclusion in the register.

was issued to the Prefects by the Ministry of the Interior, frankly admitting and deploring the fact that the authorities were not carrying out sufficiently well their duties as regards the prevention of abortion, or of the registration of cases of abortion. The circular contained no specific statement of the facts leading to this conclusion, except a reference to the statistics supplied in accordance with the circular of 13 September 1931 as being evidence of such a situation. The statistics themselves were not cited. Much emphasis was placed upon the pro-natalist motives of the campaign against abortion, and the circular stated that the nation's duty to ensure the maintenance and the integrity of the race was even more important than its duty to combat the offence against morals which abortion also constitutes. Greater care in applying the suggestions of the Ministry was therefore urged, and it was pointed out that a scarcity of notified cases of abortion might often in itself be the clearest evidence that the regulations were not being followed. The circular ended with an expression of confidence that the provincial medical officers of health would carry out their duties in this matter,[1] but in view of the statement made at the beginning of the circular, this expression seems to be one of pious hope rather than of confident anticipation. A circular issued by the Ministry of Justice on 27 December 1933 to the directors of the Courts of Appeal noted that the number of abortion cases was still very high, drew attention to the circulation of literature referring to the means of preventing conception and interrupting pregnancy, and gave directions for a more intensive campaign of repression of these offences,[2] while paragraph 103 of the Royal Decree of 27 July 1934, no. 1265, stipulated that in addition to any other legal provisions which had been made, physicians and surgeons should notify the provincial medical officers of health, in full detail and within two days, of every case of abortion undertaken by them or coming to their knowledge in any way while carrying on their profession.[3] Certainly the problem of abortion is not one that will be solved very easily, even though it may not be as important in Italy as in some other countries.[4]

[1] Menna, op. cit., pp. 258–62.

[2] 'L'azione promossa . . .', p. 71.

[3] See p. 233, n. 4.

[4] See Note Vg, p. 452.

Among other measures adopted early in the demographic campaign, much attention has been drawn to the bachelor tax which was introduced by a Royal Legislative Decree of 19 December 1926, to take effect as from 1 January 1927, and in accordance with regulations laid down by a Royal Legislative Decree of 13 February 1927. Bachelors between the ages of 25 and 65 years were to pay a tax for their celibacy, the tax falling into two distinct parts. The first was graded according to age. Thus for bachelors aged 25 to 35 years the tax was 35 lire per year, while it was 50 lire per year for those aged 35 to 50 years, and 25 lire per year for those aged 50 to 65 years. That is, the first part of the tax was graded so as to induce men to marry at an early age. Once, however, they had shown themselves 'incorrigible bachelors', the penalty was reduced. In any case, it is evident that the penalty for celibacy was, so far as the first part of the tax is concerned, quite small. The second part, however, was more significant and consisted of a tax equal in amount to 25 per cent. of the tax paid on total income, and it applied to all the above bachelors without intermediate age gradations. If the bachelor did not pay a tax on his total income, the second part of the bachelor tax was to be calculated on the basis of the income entered on the tax lists relating to land, buildings, and income from personal property, while if not subject to any of the preceding taxes the bachelor's total income was calculated on a presumptive basis. The only persons exempt from the payment of this double tax were Catholic priests and members of orders who had taken the vow of chastity, seriously injured war invalids, officers, non-commissioned officers, and men in the armed forces of the State for whom marriage was subject to certain conditions and limitations, those forbidden to marry, on account of mental infirmity, by paragraph 61 of the civil code, and foreign subjects, even if permanently resident in Italy. It was hoped that this law would stimulate marriage, and at the same time provide a measure of social justice by taxing those who, from the point of view of family burdens, could best afford to pay. The revenue collected by the tax was given to the work for maternity and child welfare (Opera nazionale per la protezione della maternità e dell' infanzia), to which a more detailed reference will be made in a later section of the present chapter.

In succeeding years the tax was increased a number of times, partly because the influence on the marriage rate was not as great as was hoped, and partly to raise revenue. The Royal Legislative Decree of 24 September 1928 and the Act of 6 December 1928 doubled both parts of the tax as from 1 January 1929, exempting, at the same time, persons permanently incapable of work, or in hospitals or pauper institutes, provided that they had no income of their own which might be taken into account in calculating the second part of the tax. The revenue derived from the bachelor tax rose from 46·234 million lire in 1927 and 53·217 million in 1928 to 106·440 millions in 1929 and 110·940 millions in 1930. But the results, in terms of revenue and marriages, were still apparently insufficient. A Royal Legislative Decree of 14 April 1934 imposed, as from 1 July of that year, an increase of 50 per cent. in both parts of the tax, and this was followed, less than two years later, by another Royal Legislative Decree of 6 February 1936 again raising the tax as from 1 January of the same year. The first part was henceforth to be 115 lire per year for bachelors aged 25 to 30 years, 155 lire per year for those aged 30 to 55 years, and 85 lire per year for those aged 55 to 65 years of age, while the second part of the tax was raised to equal the amount of the complementary tax applied or applicable to the total income of the person concerned. In 1937, by a Royal Legislative Decree of 21 August, the bachelor tax was extended to commissioned and non-commissioned officers in the armed forces, except when expressly forbidden to marry.[1]

Not very long after the introduction of the bachelor tax the Italian government introduced legislation relating to the other extreme of the population—the very large families. The fundamental law in this case was that of 14 June 1928, no. 1312, applying as from 1 July 1928, in accordance with regulations laid down by a Royal Decree of 10 August 1928.

[1] This is bound up with legislation facilitating marriage. See present chapter, p. 256. The preceding account of the bachelor tax is derived from the legal texts given in full in Menna, op. cit., pp. 9–26, together with 'L'azione promossa . . .', pp. 50–2 and 102–5, *Gazzetta Ufficiale*, 15 Sept. 1937, no. 215, pp. 3449 ff., and *Rivista Internazionale di Scienze Sociali* (henceforth cited as *R.I.*), May 1938, p. 608.

It has been pointed out that one of the objects of the bachelor tax was to place the burden of taxation on those persons with the smallest family charges. The 1928 Act, granting certain exemptions and concessions to large families, had the counterbalancing aim of lightening the taxes on those persons with the heaviest family charges, this aim being made possible to achieve by the increase in the bachelor tax in 1928. Large families were divided into two categories. For employees, subordinates, and pensioners of the State, whether civil or military, and of any grade, including also the same groups of persons attached to autonomous and semi-State[1] institutions, an individual was classed as having a large family when he had seven or more dependent children of Italian nationality. Other persons were defined as having large families if they had ten or more dependent children of Italian nationality, or if they had had twelve or more children born alive and viable, at least six of whom were still dependent. These two categories of heads of large families were exempted, for the first 100,000 lire of total income, from income-tax and from the related additional communal tax, as well as from the family tax. They were also entitled to a proportionate reduction in their ascertained income so as to give them exemption, for the first 100,000 lire of total income, from the tax on personal property, from the communal tax on industry and the additional provincial tax, from the tax levied on behalf of the provincial economic councils, from the communal and provincial taxes and supplementary taxes on land and buildings, and from the tax on agricultural income. Further, these persons with large families were given complete exemption, whatever their income, from the communal licence tax, the communal taxes on rentable values, on live stock, and from syndical contributions. Finally, there was a complete exemption from all kinds of school taxes for all persons with the requisite number of live-born and living children of Italian nationality, whether these children were still dependent or not.[2]

[1] The term is *parastatale*, and refers to such organizations as the Fascist confederations.

[2] Menna, op. cit., pp. 76–8 for the legal text, and pp. 78–83 and 85–115 for associated circulars and administrative regulations. See also Bouvier, L., *La Politique Démographique de l'Italie depuis la Guerre*, Lyon, 1938, pp. 203–14.

But these exemptions and rebates are much more important in theory than in practice. In the first place, even in Italy, with its relatively high fertility, families with seven or more children are not very common, and since fertility has been declining, families with seven or more *dependent* children are even less common. Secondly, as there is a social differential in fertility, it is likely that the largest Italian families are also generally the poorest, and thus in any case pay relatively little in direct taxation. In 1928 the Central Statistical Institute undertook an inquiry into the distribution of large families in Italy[1] and found that there were, on 30 June 1928, 1,532,206 families which had, or had had, seven or more children. These families had therefore produced about 13·4 million children altogether, and, including in all the families both father and mother, would represent at the most a total population of about 16·5 millions, or about 41 per cent. of the population of Italy in mid-1928.[2] But this was not the population covered by the 1928 Act. As the Statistical Institute publication pointed out, there were many reductions to be made. First, not all of the families had seven or more children alive at the time of the inquiry. The figures merely indicated the number of families to each of which seven or more children had been born by 1928, and many of these had died before 1928. Secondly, still more of these children were no longer dependent upon their parents. Thirdly, the seven dependent children requirement was for employees and subordinates in State and affiliated employment, and the Statistical Institute estimated that only about 30,000 of the 1,532,206 families to each of which seven or more children had been born were families of persons in such employment. For the remaining families the requirement under the 1928 Act was ten or more dependent children, or else the families must have had twelve or more live-born and living children. But out of the 1,532,206 large families, only 430,451 had, or had had, ten or more children. Even assuming that all these children were alive, that both parents were still alive in each

[1] 'L'azione promossa . . .', pp. 3–5.

[2] *Annuario Statistico Italiano, 1938*, p. 9—mid-year estimate (40·197 millions) derived from arithmetic mean of populations on 31 Dec. 1927 and 1928.

case, and that each of these families received the exemptions under the 1928 Act, the total population covered would still be only about 5·6 millions. But since many of these children had died, and still more were no longer dependent, the actual population covered by the Act was much smaller.

In fact, the figures published by the Central Statistical Institute show an amazingly small number of persons actually exempt.[1] Taking the five main taxes—the direct taxes on land, buildings, personal property, agricultural income, and total income—the number of exemptions in the period 1 July 1928 to 31 December 1931 was only 165,883 and the number of families exempted only 82,757.[2] The Statistical Institute publication says that the Treasury renounced a notable sum in the period. Apparently, however, this amounted to only 23,644,640 lire, plus 16,434,534 lire for exemptions from income-tax and personal property tax of State and kindred employees (19,221 families exempted in the period). The total is only 40,079,174 lire, or an average of about 393 lire per family exempted in the whole period of three and a half years. To this should be added 18,907,012 lire for local and 2,029,860 lire for syndical contributions, the first exempting 114,528 and the second involving 60,640 exemptions. We do not know how far these families include families receiving exemption from direct taxation, but assuming the maximum degree of overlapping, the total exemption under all forms of taxation, distributed among some 115,000 families in a three-and-a-half year period, amounted to only about 530 lire per year. The 115,000 families are not separate families receiving exemptions each year, but the total number of families receiving exemptions in the whole period. Again, assuming the maximum degree of overlapping, 530 lire represents the average annual exemption per family. In 1931, 31,447 families received exemptions from the five main direct taxes (including State and kindred employees), 33,559 from provincial and communal taxes, and there were 18,061 exemptions for syndical dues. The total value of the exemptions was

[1] 'L'azione promossa . . .', pp. 5–32 and 88–98.

[2] That is, 13,840 families exempted in 1928; 17,990 in 1929; 24,534 in 1930; and 26,393 in 1931.

18,020,599 lire, so that assuming the maximum degree of overlapping, the average exemption per family was about 537 lire. This is not large in absolute terms, but if the assumption as regards overlapping is correct, the amount must have formed a significant proportion of earned income, since the average earnings per person in industry could not have been very much higher than 4,000 lire per year in 1928.[1] But it is highly unlikely that the overlapping is complete, and in so far as the same families do not receive exemption from all the taxes, the exemption per family will be smaller. Similarly, in so far as families contain more than one earner, the relative significance of the exemptions will be less.[2]

We should add that, in addition to the reductions and exemptions specified by the 1928 Act, many of the local government areas also gave similar concessions. Many also gave other kinds of material assistance to large families—in the form of free tramway transport and special reductions in the charges for electricity and gas. Assistance of various kinds was also given by the public institutions. We should also note the modifications in the income-tax, under the Royal Legislative Decree of 29 July 1933, according to which 5 per cent. of the income would be subtracted for each dependant before calculating the tax to be paid, the sum subtracted not to exceed 3,000 lire per dependant.[3] And coming within the general field of discrimination against the unmarried and in favour of the married was the Act of 6 June 1929, which explicitly stated that as regards employment by the State, provinces, communes, or by

[1] *The Year-Book of Labour Statistics, 1938*, Geneva, 1938, pp. 87 and 158, gives the number of hours worked per month (calendar month) per worker in industry in 1931 as 171, and the average earnings per hour in June 1931 as 1·99 lire. The annual earnings per worker in 1931 would thus be about 4,083 lire. Note, however, that this average is based on the earnings of males and females. For males separately it would be higher—perhaps considerably so—while in many families both husband and wife would be gainfully occupied. (In 1931 there were, in Italy, 13·359 million gainfully occupied men and 3·904 million gainfully occupied women—ibid. p. 17.)

[2] Nor does the total figure appear very generous in comparison with, say, the value of the tax reductions granted in France. In 1937–8 the total reductions granted by the central government alone (*contributions directes* and *enregistrement*) were valued at 769 million francs—that is, equivalent to about 592 million lire, according to the exchange rates in 1937 (*Revue de l'Alliance Nationale*, Jan. 1939, p. 21).

[3] Menna, op. cit., pp. 83–5.

public assistance or public benefit institutions, preference was not to be given to unmarried men and women. On the contrary, in cases of equal merit, preference was to be given to married persons as against unmarried, and to married persons with children as against those who were childless. This also applied to private employment, while similar rules were to be observed in granting administrative concessions and authorizations, and in the disposal of 'popular' (in the sense of 'people's') or 'cheap' houses, or any others built with the assistance of the central or local government authorities, or of the public assistance or public benefit institutions.[1]

As one of the forms of assistance given partly for pro-natalist reasons, we should mention that concerned with maternity and child welfare. Two broad divisions may be noted—the general protection of maternity and childhood under the Opera nazionale, and the system of maternity insurance under the control of the National Fascist Institute for Social Insurance. The first part derives, in its modern form, from the Act of 10 December 1925,[2] which created the Opera nazionale and endowed it with the tasks of integrating and co-ordinating the work of the various organizations in this field, and surveying and controlling the work of the assistance institutions, and creating propaganda in favour of such work and ensuring that the various laws and regulations were actually applied. The Opera nazionale also had its own sources of income—a State allowance, a percentage of the residence taxes, certain grants from charitable institutions, the surplus obtained by the municipal pawnshops, as well as individual donations and bequests, &c.—and used

[1] Menna, op. cit., pp. 115–17. There were under this Act, and under the modifying Act of 26 May 1930, a few exceptions to the general rule of preference in allocating employment—members of the armed forces of the State, the communes, and the provinces, and women helping to look after mental cases in psychiatric hospitals.

[2] We should also include the regulation of 16 Dec. 1923, no. 2900, concerning foundlings; the Act of 3 Apr. 1926, no. 2247, concerning the moral and physical education of youth; and the Royal Decree of 8 May 1927, no. 798, concerning the system of help for abandoned children. See Fabbri, S., 'L'assistance de la maternité et de l'enfance en Italie', *Le A.S.*, 2, 1932, pp. 37–44. Fabbri points out that, up to the time at which he was writing, there had been many difficulties in practice and that the 1925 Act itself was uncertain on some points. To remedy these difficulties the law of 13 Apr. 1933 was passed, and the whole system was codified and consolidated by the Act of 24 Dec. 1934 (see Menna, op. cit., pp. 122–42).

these to further, in various ways, the health of mothers and children. Thus it gave food coupons to necessitous pregnant women, extended the system of pre-natal and post-natal advice and care, looked after unmarried mothers, sent children to convalescent homes and for summer holidays, and undertook a widespread campaign of propaganda and education directed to eradicate tuberculosis and syphilis and generally to improve the standard of health. It also created a number of marriage and birth premiums, and in order better to inform the public of its aims, as well as to keep the demographic campaign vividly before the public eye, 24 December of each year was ordered by Mussolini to be celebrated in each commune as a 'Mother and Child Day'.[1] On this day money premiums are given by the 92 provincial federations of the Opera nazionale, and by the Committee of Patronage of Rome, for marriages and births and for the hygienic raising of children, and there are also gifts of layettes, food coupons, furniture, and clothing, and so forth. Various other organizations help the Opera nazionale. Thus the National Fascist Institute for Social Insurance, apart from its specific insurance work, has consulting-rooms for maternity advice. The Fascist party itself sends children to holiday and convalescent homes—385,637 children were sent in the year 1932–3—and similar provisions are made by the various civil service associations—19,505 children were sent to these in 1932–3—and a medical service is attached to the Balilla organization for Italian youth. The Fascist party also takes part in helping, financially, Italian women returning temporarily to their own country to bear their children. Taking those returning from France alone, 9,915 were helped in this way during the period 1 September 1928 to 27 October 1932, at a total cost of 1·686 million lire, and in the following year 1,612 were helped, at a cost of 228,900 lire.[2]

So far as statutory maternity protection and insurance is concerned, the system dates from pre-Fascist days. A law of 1902 prohibited women from returning to work until

[1] See Note V*h*, p. 453.

[2] For a general survey of the work of the Opera nazionale and its associated organizations, see the report prepared by the Opera itself, *XIVe Congrès National des Allocations Familiales* (1934), pp. 77–87. For data specifically concerning summer camps, see *Le A.S.*, 3, 1939, pp. 400–4.

a month after their confinements—reducible to three weeks if medical advice allowed this—and compelled employers to allow women to suckle their children either in rooms specially provided by the firms, or by leaving the factory at defined hours for this purpose. An Act of 17 July 1910 extended the protection by instituting maternity insurance—employers and workers contributing 1 to 2 lire per year—entitling women to a confinement benefit of 40 lire, which was raised to 50 lire in 1918, 60 in 1919, and 100 lire in 1920, the latter rate being stabilized—on the basis of a contribution of 4 lire by the employer and 3 lire by the insured woman—under a Legislative Decree of 11 January 1923. Shortly afterwards the insurance system was extended to new categories of workers. Further protection was given by administrative regulations of 13 March 1929, prohibiting the employment of women during the last month of pregnancy or the first month after confinement and obliging employers to keep open the jobs of those women, even when their absence was longer than the prescribed period, provided that this was for duly attested medical reasons. The confinement benefit was raised to 150 lire under an Act of 13 May 1929, and women became entitled, during the whole period of prescribed absence, to a daily allowance equivalent to the normal unemployment benefit, plus another 0·50 lire per day. Subsequent legislation, particularly in 1934 (Royal Decree of 22 March), 1936 (Royal Legislative Decree of 7 August), and 1937 (Royal Legislative Decree of 21 August, Part IV), extended the system of protection and insurance to further branches of female employment, especially to domestic service, agriculture, and governmental service, increased the length of prescribed absence, and fused the confinement benefit and daily allowance into a total grant of 300 lire.[1]

In discussing the various ways in which family life has been encouraged in Italy, it was noted that, under the Act of 6 June 1929, preference was given to married persons with children in providing accommodation in 'cheap' or 'popular' houses. The construction of such houses has been part of the building programme in Italy. Under the Royal

[1] See Note V*i*, p. 453.

Legislative Decree of 10 March 1926, modified by a Royal Decree of 23 January 1928, a credit of 100 million lire was included in the budget of the Ministry of Public Works, this credit to be used to subsidize—up to 20 per cent. of the cost of construction—communes and autonomous institutions prepared to build cheap houses to be sold or to be let with an undertaking that they would be sold in the future—that is, on the hire-purchase system. Between 28 October 1922 and 28 October 1932 building appears to have made fair progress, for in that period 72,676 'cheap' and 'popular' dwellings were constructed,[1] containing 258,429 living-rooms. These dwellings were built by the communes, by special institutions for 'popular' houses, and by co-operative societies and institutions concerned with providing housing accommodation for State employees at a total cost of 4,455·8 million lire,[2] of which the State share was 70·7 millions in annual contributions to the payment of interest charges on loans, and 774·1 millions in the provision of capital. More recently—by an Act of 6 June 1935—it has become possible for each province to set up an autonomous institution for promoting the construction of 'popular' houses for the poorer sections of the population, and pre-existing bodies with similar aims are able to attach themselves—though remaining independent as regards their control and budgets—to these institutions.[3] A national consortium of these institutions has also been created, and they appear already to have provided more than 21,000 dwellings, at a total cost of over 408 million lire.[4] That these dwellings are needed is shown by the results of the housing investigation of 1931, which was confined largely to urban communities. Taking the 422 communes for which the special information was obtained,[5]

[1] It should be noted, however, that of these 72,676 dwellings, 18,384 appear to have been built in zones in which earthquakes had occurred—presumably to replace those destroyed in the earthquakes. See [Simone, D. de, and Bertagnolio, P.], *Rapport sur les Habitations Populaires et Économiques en Italie* (Société des Nations, Organisation d'Hygiène), Geneva, 1935, Table XLIII, p. 140.

[2] This includes the cost of building 706 shops.

[3] Ibid., p. 8.

[4] *Le A.S.*, 6, 1937, pp. 684–5.

[5] The more populous communes were chosen. A still more detailed investigation, conducted at the same time, was confined to 232 communes containing populations of 20,000 and over. See Niceforo, A., 'Le recensement des habitations italiennes', *Le A.S.*, 3, 1936, pp. 129–70, at pp. 129–31.

41 had between 40 and 45 per cent. of their houses occupied by more than two persons per room, 39 had between 45 and 50 per cent., 34 had between 50 and 55 per cent., 23 had between 55 and 60 per cent., 14 had 60 to 65 per cent., 5 had 65 to 70 per cent. and 3 had 70 to 75 per cent. of their houses overcrowded in this way.[1] That is, 79 of the communes had over half of their houses inhabited at the rate of more than two persons per room. Conditions in the rural areas must be much worse,[2] and it will need a very thorough programme appreciably to change the situation.[3]

The object of the preceding pages of this chapter has been briefly to describe the main features of the Italian population policy up to 1936. Some important measures—particularly family allowances—have been omitted because they can be more appropriately discussed in the next section, but allowing for these omissions we can make some general remarks about this stage of Italian policy. First, a large part of the policy was directed towards restricting emigration, in so far as economic conditions made this possible. Secondly, another considerable section concentrated on 'negative' or repressive measures—imposing economic penalties on bachelors and childless married couples, and making it more difficult for women to prevent conception or procure abortion. Of the positive measures, many were not directly pro-natalist, even though they are generally included among the steps taken by the government to encourage marriage and the raising of families. Thus the general system of land reclamation and improvement coming under the head of *bonifica integrale* is not a direct population policy, though it may enable a larger population to be supported at the current or at a higher standard of life. Similar schemes of reclamation have been undertaken in many other countries for reasons quite unconnected with a desire to increase the birth-

[1] Orestano, F., 'Pour une politique de la maison en Italie', *Le A.S.*, 3, 1936, pp. 171–7 at pp. 172–3.

[2] Ibid., p. 174. The 1933 investigation into rural housing—less detailed than the 1931 urban inquiry—found that of 3·646 million dwellings, 160,975 should be pulled down, 523,186 needed major repairs, and 1,007,714 needed slight repairs. Included in the last category were, apparently, 9,630 dwellings made of earth, and 591 cave dwellings.

[3] See Note V*j*, p. 454.

rate. The same applies to the legislation for the protection of maternity and childhood. This is not to deny that such measures are of very great value. On the contrary, it is clear that they are of the utmost importance, and are necessary attributes of every modern community. But it is somewhat inappropriate to invest them with the title of demographic measures, when there is scarcely any modern State which has not been passing similar legislation in the last fifty years. If we subtract these measures from the general group of positive measures introduced in Italy, we are left with very little specifically in the category of encouragements to the raising of families. There are the exemptions and reductions in taxation, but these, by their terms of application, necessarily affected a very small proportion of the population. There are the marriage and birth premiums awarded each year on 'Mother and Child' day, but they were not sufficiently large or widespread significantly to influence reproductive trends. On the whole, therefore, the first stage of Italian population policy did relatively little from a material point of view to make it worth while for people to raise large families. There was, of course, a vast amount of pro-natalist propaganda in the daily press, including enthusiastic reports of the awards of marriage and birth premiums, articles on the duty of the people to increase their reproductive rates, photographs of large families and so forth.[1] Professor Savorgnan wrote, fairly early in the campaign (1931), that a demographic policy which confined itself to urging people to be fruitful and multiply, leaving it to Providence to take heed of the needs of an increase in population, 'would not only be built upon sand, but be of no avail'. Fortunately, he added, the actions of the Duce were inspired by a comprehension of the realities involved.[2] This may well be the case. But, in spite of it, the first stage of Italian policy did not make any fundamental concession to these economic realities.

In more recent years, however, there have been many important changes. As will be shown later, the first stage of Italian policy did not appear to produce any significant

[1] See Note V*k*, p. 454.

[2] Savorgnan, F., 'La politique démographique de l'Italie et ses buts', *Le A.S.*, :, 1931, pp. 50–62 at p. 62.

results. At the same time the German marriage- and birth-rates showed a very marked increase from 1933, and it is not surprising that Italian writers on population questions should turn their attention to the measures adopted in Germany.[1] Nor was the political world unaffected, for the Fascist Grand Council, at its meeting on 3 March 1937,[2] passed a number of resolutions outlining a much more significant population policy than had previously been applied. This policy was to include a broadening of family allowance schemes, preferential employment for the fathers of large families, the foundation of a national association of large families and of a central organization for promoting population policy, and—the German influence being evident here—the institution of marriage or family loans.[3] Many of the resolutions of the Fascist Grand Council have already been implemented by legislation, and it will be reasonably satisfactory to deal with them in the two broad headings of family allowances and encouragements to marriage.

As in most other countries, family allowances in Italy were given to State employees some time before the general population benefited from them. Thus, under an Act of 27 June 1929, permanent State employees not higher than the eighth ministerial grade—excluding schoolmasters—became entitled to a bonus if they were married or widowed and had dependent children. This bonus varied with the grade of employment. In the highest permissible grades it amounted to 150 lire per month, plus 30 lire per month for each dependent child, up to a maximum of three children, while for each child beyond the third, the child allowance was doubled. In the lowest grades the basic bonus was 50 lire per month, plus 10 lire per month for each dependent child up to and including the third, and 20 lire per month for each subsequent child. By a Royal Legislative Decree of 20 November 1930, all these allowances were reduced by 12 per cent., while further reductions were made under a Royal Legislative Decree of 14 April 1934, the latter reductions being graded according to the type of area in which the individual lived. No reduction was made if he lived in

[1] See Note V*l*, p. 454.
[2] *Le A.S.*, 2, 1937, pp. 216–18.
[3] See Note V*m*, p. 454.

a commune containing a population of not less than 500,000. But reductions of 10, 25, 40, and 50 per cent. in the rates paid on 15 April 1934 were made for persons living in communes with populations of 100,000 but less than 500,000; 50,000 but less than 100,000; 20,000 but less than 50,000; and under 20,000 respectively. Elementary schoolmasters[1] came under a special heading and received an allowance composed of a bonus in respect of being married, plus supplementary grants for a wife and for each dependent child under 18 years of age. After the reductions under the 1930 Decree, the bonus amounted to 84 lire per month, plus 16 lire per month for the wife and for each child up to and including the third, and 32 lire per month for each subsequent child. These allowances were then further reduced (as above) under the 1934 Decree. Cost of living bonuses were also given to some branches of the temporary staff of State organizations, and if these are included, about 400,000 employees of State and semi-State organizations were receiving family allowances or other bonuses in 1935.[2]

The extension of a family allowance scheme to workers employed in private enterprises was begun in 1934, under a collective agreement concluded, on 11 October, between the Fascist Confederation of Industry and the Fascist Confederation of Industrial Workers.[3] It should be emphasized, however, that the scheme introduced by this agreement was not primarily concerned with the demographic campaign. Industry was changing over to the 40-hour week in Italy, and it was in order to prevent the consequent wage reductions from falling as heavily on married workers with

1 Women schoolteachers were entitled to this bonus and allowance only when their husbands were permanently unable to work and had no other means of support, or when they were legally declared missing.

2 This information is derived from a memorandum (typescript) kindly supplied, in 1935, by the Commercial Secretary of the British Embassy, Rome.

3 See 'Accordo contenente le norme statutarie, etc.', *Le A.S.* (original edition), 1934, 'Atti ufficiali', pp. 190–6, and Hoffner, C., 'The compulsory payment of family allowances in Belgium, France and Italy', *International Labour Review*, Oct. 1935, pp. 463–91, at pp. 472–5 and 483. Note that, before this collective agreement, an earlier collective agreement, relating to the Biella wool workers, had introduced family allowances financed by employers only. Collective agreements are invested with the force of law in Italy.

dependent children as upon the unmarried, or married but childless, that family allowances were introduced. The scheme was, moreover, a singular one. It was financed by equal contributions from employers and workers, the contributions consisting of two distinct parts. The first was a levy on all industrial workers, amounting to 1 per cent. of the gross earnings of a 40-hour week, a payment of equal amount to be made by the employers. The second was a levy on workers working more than 40 hours a week, amounting to 5 per cent. of the earnings gained in the extra hours, employers again to pay an equal contribution. The employers collected the contributions and paid the family allowances. When the contributions exceeded the allowances, the balance was transferred to the National Fascist Institute for Social Insurance, while this Institute repaid the employers when allowances exceeded contributions. Contributions were first collected in December 1934, and allowances were first granted in January 1935, fixed at 4 lire per week per dependent child under 14 years of age, beginning with the second child, and given to those workers who did not work more than 40 hours per week.

In subsequent months it was found that the contributions were sufficient to enable the allowances to be given for the first child as well, and on 1 July 1935 it was decided to do so. In the first year of operation—1935—family allowances amounting to 163·896 million lire were paid to 650,750 workers in respect of their dependent children, the total contributions under the scheme having been 197·901 million lire.[1] It was soon evident, however, that a system of family allowances linked to the 40-hour week was neither satisfactory nor fair. It was unsatisfactory because as the shorter week became increasingly common in industry, the contributions would decrease while the number of workers entitled to allowances would increase. It was unfair because in industries involving continuous production, or for which there were special provisions regarding hours of work, large classes of

[1] *Le A.S.*, 5, 1934, pp. 444–5; 6, 1934, pp. 559–61; Mikelli, G., 'Composition familiale des ouvriers de l'industrie', *Le A.S.*, 4, 1935, pp. 337–49; Biagi, B., 'Family allowances in Italy', *International Labour Review*, Apr. 1937, pp. 457–87, at pp. 463–9.

workers would be continually debarred from the right to family allowances. Discussion of such questions took place as early as the beginning of 1935, but it was not until the end of May 1936 that the officials in charge of the family allowance system actually began to consider schemes for improving and extending the system, and from that point new measures were introduced in rapid succession.

The first of these measures was the Royal Legislative Decree of 21 August 1936, which related to allowances for industrial workers.[1] Its importance, however, was much greater than is suggested by so brief a description, for it separated these family allowances from their previous link with the 40-hour week, it provided for a State contribution, and it contained the possibilities of extension to other fields of employment. Coming into force on 5 October 1936, it prescribed contributions which, in relation with the gross weekly earnings of the workers, were 1 per cent. paid by the worker and 2·5 per cent. paid by the employer, plus a State grant of 0·50 lira for every allowance paid, while the allowances themselves were to be 4 lire per week for each dependent child under 14 years of age, the whole scheme being administered by a special committee set up within the National Fascist Institute for Social Insurance. About two and a half million industrial workers were covered by this scheme, and about 1·7 million dependent children, while the cost was estimated to be about 344 million lire per year, of which 215 million would be contributed by employers, 86 million by workers and 43 million by the State.[2] Shortly afterwards—on 21 December 1936—an agreement between the two Fascist Confederations in Commerce extended family allowances, as from 1 January 1937, to another 350,000 workers, financed by contributions by workers and employers at the rate of 1 per cent. and 2·5 per cent. respectively of

[1] See *Le A.S.*, original edition, 1936, 'Atti ufficiali', pp. 106–9, 'Disposizioni per la corresponsione obbligatoria di assegni familiari ai prestatori d'opera etc.'; Arena, C., 'L'assurance familiale et le salaire en Italie', *Le A.S.*, 1, 1937, pp. 21–36; Manunta, U., 'Les allocations familiales en Italie', *Le A.S.*, 1, 1937, pp. 64–8; Biagi, op. cit., pp. 473–6; Anselmi, A., 'Les allocations familiales en Italie', in *Première Journée Internationale des Allocations Familiales*, Paris, 1937, pp. 62–70 at pp. 63–6.

[2] Biagi, op. cit., p. 476.

monthly earnings, and amounting, for each dependent child under 15 years of age, to 20 lire per month when the monthly earnings were under 600 lire and 25 lire per month when they were over 600 lire.[1] This, in turn, was followed by a collective agreement—of 29 January 1937—relating to persons employed in credit and insurance firms and in tax-collectors' offices, introducing, as from 1 January 1937, allowances based upon contributions of 60 lire per year from workers,[2] plus a quota from employers calculated on lines similar to those followed in France,[3] plus a possible contribution by the State. The allowances were due not only for each dependent child up to 18 years of age, but also for the wife, and for the worker's parents, if they were dependent upon him. The wife allowance ranged from 12 to 46 lire per month and was between 8 and 50 lire per month for each dependent child and for dependent parents.[4]

The position was again changed by two measures in 1937—a Royal Legislative Decree of 17 June and a Royal Decree of 21 July[5]—which made it obligatory to pay family allowances in respect of dependent children to every family breadwinner,[6] of whatever nationality, employed by other persons,[7]

[1] Biagi, op. cit. pp. 476–9; *Le A.S.*, original edition, 1937, 'Atti ufficiali', pp. 10–14; 'Contratto collettivo per l'estensione degli assegni familiari ai lavoratori del commercio.'

[2] No contribution to be paid by workers whose earnings were not more than 3,000 lire per year. In practice the family allowances are paid for by the employers only, the employees' contributions being used to pay the marriage and birth premiums given to workers in credit, insurance, and kindred employment. See p. 456, n. *o*.

[3] This contribution is calculated by dividing the total allowances by the total number of workers employed and thus obtaining a sum to be paid by each employer for each worker. Each employer had also to pay a non-recurrent contribution of 5 lire per worker to help to cover equalization transactions, administrative costs, and possible failure to pay on the part of some of the employers.

[4] See *Le A.S.*, 1, 1937, pp. 105–7; *Le A.S.*, original edition, 1937, 'Atti ufficiali', pp. 14–19. (The translations should always be compared with the original texts, for in some cases the meaning of these texts is not conveyed quite accurately in the *Supplément*.)

[5] *Le A.S.*, original edition, 1937, 'Atti ufficiali', pp. 175–84 and 207–20; *Le A.S.*, 4, 1937, pp. 431–4; Anselmi, op. cit., pp. 68–70.

[6] Whether a man or a woman.

[7] Excluding domestic servants and persons in family service; wife, parents, and close relatives of employer; home workers; artisans and other workers on own account; certain classes of agricultural workers, including family farm workers; civil and military personnel of the State, of semi-State organizations, and of the Royal Household.

provided only that this head of the family had net earnings not exceeding 2,000 lire per month. For wage-earners, the allowances were payable for dependent children up to 14 years of age, the age limit being extended to 16 years if the child was continuing its education at a secondary or professional school, or if physically or mentally incapable of working. For employees the allowances were to be payable for dependent children up to 18 years of age. As regards contributions and allowances, these were laid down for industry and agriculture by the Decree of 17 June.[1] In industry the contributions were to be 1 per cent. of the gross earnings, paid by the worker, and 3·5 per cent. paid by the employer. This also applied to salaried employees in agriculture, but there were also two other categories in agriculture. For daily workers, journeymen, and so forth, the employer paid 0·35 lira per working day, and the worker paid 0·10 lira, while where there were fixed or customary wages or the workers belonged to collective enterprises, the employer paid 9 lire per month and the worker paid 2·50 lire per month. In addition the State would, if necessary, pay contributions at the rate of not more than 0·60 lira for every weekly allowance given in industry and agriculture, excluding allowances given to employees whose net earnings were more than 1,000 lire per month. The family allowances themselves differed for wage-earners and employees, and were also graded in accordance with the number of dependent children. In industry wage-earners with 1 dependent child received 3·60 lire per week, 4·80 lire per week for each child when they had 2 or 3 dependent children, and 6·00 lire per week per child when they had 4 or more dependent children. For employees the corresponding payments were 4·80, 6·00, and 7·20 lire per child per week. Similar arrangements applied to agriculture. Salaried employees received 4·80, 6·00, and 7·20 lire per week per child, for families with 1, 2 to 3, and 4 or more dependent children, while

[1] *Le A.S.*, original edition, 1937, 'Atti ufficiali', pp. 183–4. For barbers' and hairdressers' assistants, for porters, and for persons employed in bakers' shops, a special collective agreement was signed on 3 Aug. 1937 (see *Le A.S.*, original edition, 1937, 'Atti ufficiali', pp. 311–12). Contributions were fixed at 3·5 per cent. of gross earnings by employers and 1 per cent. by workers, the allowances being the same as in industry (see *Le A.S.*, original edition, 4, 1937, p. 606).

other workers were entitled to corresponding grants of 2·40, 3·60, and 4·80 lire per week per child.[1] Subsequently a Royal Legislative Decree of 17 May 1938[2] issued special regulations for collecting contributions and paying allowances in agriculture, while another Royal Legislative Decree of 27 September 1938[3] raised, as from 1 December 1938, the contributions to be paid by employers in agriculture to 0·40 lira per working day for daily workers, journeymen, &c., and to 10·00 lire per month for workers with fixed wages, &c. The workers' contributions were not changed and salaried employees remained under the earlier regulations. No rates for persons employed in commerce or by professional men or artists were laid down in the 1937 Decrees, so they were arranged by collective agreements between the relevant Fascist Confederations, the agreements for both the additional classes of workers being signed on 3 August 1937.[4] The persons covered were divided into two categories—roughly speaking, salaried or administrative and wage-earning workers. The workers were entitled to monthly allowances of 14·40, 20·40, and 26·40 lire per child for families with 1, 2 to 3, and 4 or more dependent children, while for employees the corresponding grants were 19·20, 24·00, and 28·80 lire per month per child. Contributions were calculated on the gross earnings of the persons employed and amounted to a 3 per cent. payment by the employer and a 1 per cent. payment by the employed person. To conclude this brief survey we should note that the system of allowances to persons employed in credit, insurance, and tax-collecting undertakings was reformed under a collective agreement signed 22 July 1938.[5] Up to the present relatively few statistics appear to have been published, but it is possible to give totals for the main categories. From 2 August 1937—the date when family allowances were really generalized—to 31 August 1938, 473·815 million lire were

[1] A Royal Legislative Decree of 14 July 1937 authorized the National Fascist Institute of Social Insurance to help the speedy implementation of the Royal Legislative Decree of 17 June 1937 by advancing up to 100 million lire for the payment of family allowances. See *Le A.S.*, original edition, 1937, 'Atti ufficiali', p. 185.

[2] *Le A.S.*, original edition, 1938, 'Atti ufficiali', pp. 210–11.

[3] Ibid., 1938, pp. 384–5.

[4] Ibid., 1937, pp. 225–8 and 229–32.

[5] Ibid., 1938, pp. 404–12.

paid in allowances to persons employed in industry, in respect of 2,049,003 dependants. For commerce, in the same period, 47·656 millions were paid on behalf of 243,610 dependants, and in agriculture 93·878 millions on behalf of 774,361 dependants.[1] For the persons employed in credit, insurance, and kindred undertakings, 33·201 million lire were paid in the calendar year 1937–8.[2] It is clear, then, that family allowances have become widespread. But if we relate them to basic average earnings, we find that they are still rather small. Thus in February 1938 the average wage (males and females) in industry appeared to be about 340 lire per month.[3] Even with a family of four dependent children, entitling the wage-earner to the highest rate of allowance, the monthly grant would be only 96 lire, and related to the basic earnings this would mean about 7 per cent. per child. Since, in fact, the typical earnings in industry may have been higher than is suggested by the above figure —because higher wages are paid to men than to women, and because both husband and wife may have been gainfully employed—the percentage cited is more likely to be an exaggeration than an underestimate. Family allowances in Italy are, therefore, still considerably below the cost of maintaining children, though it is likely that they will be increased in the near future.[4]

Marriage or family loans, mentioned earlier as another important feature in the new demographic campaign—which Boldrini describes as a campaign of incentives, in contrast to the earlier campaign of exhortation[5]—were introduced by the Royal Legislative Decree of 21 August 1937.[6] The practice of giving monetary grants to encourage

[1] *Le A.S.*, 5, 1938, p. 514.

[2] See Note V*n*, p. 455.

[3] *Year-Book of Labour Statistics, 1938*, pp. 87 and 158. The estimated monthly wage equals 157 hours at 2·16 lire per hour—or 339·12 lire per month.

[4] See *Le A.S.*, 1, 1939, pp. 103–4.

[5] Boldrini, M., 'Popolazione', *R.I.*, May 1938, p. 286, says that the resolutions passed by the Fascist Grand Council on 6 May 1937 marked the end of the chiefly 'hortatory' phase of Italian population policy.

[6] *Gazzetta Ufficiale*, 15 Sept. 1937, no. 215, pp. 3449–56, and *Le A.S.*, original edition, 1937, 'Atti ufficiale', pp. 283–94. The Decree was converted, with some modifications, into an Act by the Act of 3 Jan. 1939—*Le A.S.*, original edition, 1939, 'Atti ufficiali', pp. 26–9.

marriage was, of course, begun in Italy earlier than this, and some examples have already been mentioned.[1] At the same time there had been many modifications of the regulations relating to the marriage of members of the armed forces of the State—including the reduction of the minimum age at marriage—as well as changes in the law relating to the marriage of civilians.[2] As an additional means of promoting marriage, and to 'encourage the formation of Italian families and assure their development',[3] marriage or family loans were instituted for an experimental period of three years, as from 1 July 1937. These loans, to be granted after the marriage of the couples who applied for them, are to be not less than 1,000 and not more than 3,000 lire, and are to be given only when the husband is of Italian nationality, if neither partner to the marriage is more than 26 years of age when the marriage took place, and if the total income of the couple is not more than 12,000 lire per year. The funds needed for granting the loans—it was estimated that the annual cost, excluding repayments, would be 190 million lire[4]—were to be raised by the individual provinces,[5] and administered by the National Fascist Institute for Social Insurance in conjunction with specially appointed provincial committees. Each loan is given, after the marriage, jointly to the husband and wife, who are also jointly responsible for repayment. Repayment of the loan is at the rate of 1 per cent. per month, free of interest, beginning in the sixth month after the marriage. If, however, there is requisite medical testimony that, in the fifth month after the marriage, the wife is already pregnant, repayment is postponed until eighteen months after the marriage. If, after four years, no children have been born, the rest of the loan

[1] See Note V*o*, p. 455.

[2] Menna, op. cit., pp. 30–75. The Act of 27 May 1929, modifying Section 5 of Book 1 of the civil code, lowered the legal age for marriage to 16 years for males and 14 years for females.

[3] R.D.L. of 21 Aug. 1937, Part I, Para. 1.

[4] Biagi, B., 'Politique démographique de l'Italie', *Le A.S.*, 6, 1937, pp. 597–606, at p. 600.

[5] A Royal Legislative Decree of 22 Nov. 1937 authorized the National Fascist Institute of Social Insurance to give advances to the provincial committees up to a total of 100 million lire, in order to obviate any delays in implementing the scheme (ibid., p. 603).

is to be repaid at the rate of 2 per cent. per month. On the other hand, part of the debt is cancelled at the birth of each live and viable child—10 per cent. for the first, 20 per cent. for the second, 30 per cent. for the third, and the remainder for the fourth child, repayment of the loan being postponed for a year with the occurrence of each birth.[1] The number of loans given amounts to 61,588, at a total of 102·473 million lire, for the period from 1 July 1937 to 31 December 1938. Taking only the period 1 January to 31 December 1938, 54,034 loans were given, amounting to 89·529 million lire—an average of 1,657 lire per loan. For the longer period the average loan amounted to 1,664 lire.[2] The number of loans granted is thus still rather small, though it should be noted that certain categories of persons[3] —those who receive State marriage premiums, and so forth —are not entitled to the loans, and that even in Italy early marriages are not particularly common.[4] It has been pointed out that the marriage loans given under the 1937 decree are for an experimental three-year period only. But, on the other hand, a permanent scheme of marriage and birth premiums has been instituted by a Legislative Decree of 14 April 1939, applying to all workers and employees in all branches of economic activity. This is a system of

[1] See R.D.L., 3 Jan. 1939, modification of para. 9, for cases of spontaneous or therapeutic abortion, and still birth.

[2] *Bollettino Mensile di Statistica*, 21 June 1939, p. 484. Provisional data show that a further 15,753 loans were granted from 1 Jan. to 31 March 1939. As regards the distribution of loans by size, the following data are available: 1937, 3,899 loans of not more than 1,500 and a further 2,486 between 1,501 and 2,000 lire; 1938, 31,427 loans of not more than 1,500, and 15,466 between 1,501 and 2,000 lire; first quarter of 1939, 9,971 loans of not more than 1,500, and 4,025 between 1,501 and 2,000 lire.

[3] R.D.L., 3 Jan. 1939, modification of para. 13, says that these loans are not granted to any person benefiting from marriage premiums given by the State, other public institutions, or by private undertakings. For a general compilation on marriage loans and premiums see Moro, L., *Premi e Prestiti Demografici*, Empoli, 1938.

[4] Data for 1938 marriages are not yet available, but we can use the 1937 statistics (*Movimento della Popolazione, 1937*, p. 19) to give a very rough estimate of the number of marriages entitled to loans. In 1937, of a total of 377,219 marriages, 86,302 occurred between men and women who were each under 25 years of age. It is likely that the number of marriages in which both partners were under 26 years of age was not very far from 100,000. Allowing for couples whose combined incomes were over 12,000 lire per year and for those otherwise excluded, it seems unlikely that less than 80,000 should be able to qualify for the loans.

compulsory social insurance, under which marriage and birth premiums will be paid as from 1 May 1940. As regards marriage premiums, male employees will be entitled to 1,000 lire and female employees to 700 lire, male wage-earners to 700 lire and female wage-earners to 500 lire, while in agriculture—excluded from the previous class—male workers and members of the families of share farmers and colonists will be entitled to 500 and women to 400 lire. As regards birth premiums, employees and wage-earners in occupations other than agriculture will be entitled to 300 lire for the first child, 350 for the second and for the third, and 400 lire for each subsequent child, while in agriculture the classes of persons enumerated in connexion with marriage premiums will be entitled to 150 lire for the first child, 175 for the second and for the third, and 200 lire for each subsequent child.[1]

In addition to instituting marriage loans, the Royal Legislative Decree of 21 August 1937 made a number of other provisions of a pro-natalist character.[2] Some of these have already been mentioned—the extension of maternity insurance to women employed by State organizations, and the application of the bachelor tax to officers and non-commissioned officers in the armed forces. Others include a modification of the rules relating to salary increments for persons in State employment—allowing these to be given from the date of registering the birth of a child instead of at the end of the current period.[3] The maximum age for taking examinations for State appointments is raised by two years for married candidates and by a further year for each living child,[4] while a proportion of the appointments in the lower grades has been reserved for married candidates, including those who have children.[5] At the same time the dowry requirements for the marriages of officers in the armed forces have been repealed.[6] The Decree also provides for a number of extensions in the tax rebates granted to large families. Thus the net income, in calculating income-tax, is reduced by another 5 per cent. for the fifth and each subsequent

[1] From the previously cited paper by Dr. Cau.

[2] See summary in *Le A.S.*, 5, 1937, pp. 575–7.

[3] Para. 22.

[4] Para. 23.

[5] Para. 24.

[6] Para. 25.

dependent child, the reduction not to amount to more than 6,000 lire for any child,[1] and there are further reductions in and exemptions from school taxes and super-taxes, related not to the number of dependent children, but to the number of children born alive and viable. Persons employed by, or pensioners of the State, of semi-State, and of autonomous institutions, obtain total exemption if they have had 7 or more children and 50 per cent. rebate if they have had 5 or 6. Other persons obtain total exemption if they have had 8 or more children, and 50 per cent. rebate if they have had 6 or 7.[2] Further rebates of similar type are included in the Decree.

We should also note a number of other measures with pro-natalist aims, forming part of the new campaign of incentives. Some of them are positive—such as the creation of the Fascist Union of Large Families, by a Royal Decree of 3 June 1937, for the purpose of increasing the prestige of large families (by which term is meant families with 7 or more living children, including as living any sons who fell in war or otherwise for the national cause), undertaking propaganda for the pro-natalist policy, helping large families in any way possible, and surveying the application of existing legislation.[3] Within the category of positive encouragements should be included the provision, by a collective agreement, coming into force on 1 January 1939, between the two Fascist Confederations in industry, that men and women employed in industry are entitled, on marriage, to a holiday lasting eight days, plus a payment equal to wages for 80 hours' work. Under the same agreement, women who give up work for marriage are entitled to a compensatory payment, and there are also provisions relating to absence from work during pregnancy and to compensatory payments to encourage the maintenance of the family as a group when the

[1] Para. 14.

[2] Para. 16.

[3] *Le A.S.*, 6, 1937, pp. 683–4; Boldrini, M., *R.I.*, May 1938, p. 288. Apart from other donations and from membership fees, the State provides an annual grant of 500,000 lire, while the provinces and communes provide the premises and equipment for the local offices of the Union. The Statute of the Fascist Union of Large Families was promulgated by Royal Decree of 22 Nov. 1937, and a National Committee created by Ministerial Decree of 16 Dec. 1937.

head of the household moves to another part of the country.[1] On the negative side there are two important decrees. A Royal Legislative Decree of 28 April 1938 prescribes that bachelors and childless widowers cannot be nominated for the offices of Mayor, Deputy-Mayor, Consultant (*consultore*), President, Vice-President, or Rector (*Rettore*).[2] A Royal Legislative Decree of 21 September 1938 prescribes that promotion to the upper grades of civil service is reserved exclusively for married and widowed persons, and that even for promotion in the lower grades the same condition is indispensable for persons who have attained either 26 or 30 years of age, depending upon their position. These clauses also apply to persons employed by the provinces, communes, and other public institutions.[3] The large number of measures promulgated under the new campaign, and the character of some of the measures, seem to indicate an element of real anxiety on the part of the Italian government.

In considering the results of the Italian struggle for population it is important to remember that Italy differs from almost every other Western nation in still showing a relatively high fertility. In France the net reproduction-rate has long been below unity and in England and Germany replacement fell below the level of adequacy in the early post-War period. But although the Italian birth-rate had been falling since the eighteen-eighties, the net reproduction rate was still well above unity—about 1·334[4] in 1921–2, as compared with about 1·244 in 1881–2, 1·432 in 1900–1, and 1·504 in 1910–12.[5] The Italian campaign was thus not aimed at raising fertility to the level of adequacy, but at checking the decline, and at assuring a growing population. It will be remembered that Mussolini was particularly anxious that Italy should have a population of at least 60 millions by 1950—an aim very far removed from that of simply checking the decline in fertility. Yet even the simpler ambition might not be easy to achieve. Other European countries had experienced a decline which grew more rapid with succeeding decades. It might not take very long before

[1] *Le A.S.*, 1, 1939, pp. 108–9.

[2] *R.I.*, May 1939, pp. 565–6.

[3] Ibid., p. 566.

[4] See Note V*p*, p. 456.

[5] See Note V*q*, p. 456.

Italy followed the same path. In the light of these ambitions how far has the Italian campaign been successful?

Turning, first, to the influence of the various measures upon marriage, it should be noted that it is extremely difficult, unless there are very full data, to trace the year-by-year results. The crude marriage-rate may give a distorted picture, and the absolute number of marriages in any year depends upon the stock of marriageable persons as well as upon the probability of marrying. Nuptiality—or marriage probability—tables can be constructed when there are sufficient data, but although it is possible to give such tables for Italy for the census periods, they cannot be given for the intermediate years,[1] and the analysis of marriage changes in Italy must therefore largely depend upon cruder methods. If, for example, we look at the crude marriage-rate, we find a steady decline from 11·5 per 1,000 of the total population in 1921 to 7·6 in 1925 and to 7·5 in 1926. In the next year the rate rose by one point—or by 6,998 marriages—and it is possible that this increase was produced by the 1926 Act relating to the bachelor tax, which came into force as from 1 January 1927. But in 1928 the marriage-rate fell by five points (see Table 23), or by 17,316 marriages. In September 1928, however, a new Royal Legislative Decree was issued, doubling the tax as from 1 January 1929. This measure may have had some effect, for, perhaps in anticipation of the date when it was to become effective, the number of marriages was 29,082 in November 1928, as compared with 28,733 in November 1927, and 34,563 in December 1928, as compared with 29,443 in the same month of 1927. But the total increase in marriages in 1929 as compared with 1928 was only 2,552, and the crude rate remained unchanged. No further increase in the bachelor tax occurred in the next few years, and after a rise in 1930, unconnected

[1] The present writer knows of only one country—Sweden—for which the published data allow year-by-year marriage probabilities to be computed, and results for recent years are given on p. 263, n. 1. The writer hopes, in the near future, to extend these results and to compare them with other annual fluctuations. For some countries—e.g. England and Wales—rough intercensal marriage probabilities may be calculated (see Chapter I, p. 20), but for Italy the annual marriage data are not given by single years of age, and the migration element is too large to be discounted.

TABLE 23. *Italy—Marriages by Months, 1926–37**

	1926	*1927*	*1928*	*1929*	*1930*	*1931*	*1932*	*1933*	*1934*	*1935*	*1936*	*1937*
January	27,841	26,658	23,991	24,201	26,814	25,588	25,702	21,653	20,639	18,514	15,650	20,622
February	33,171	37,894	33,410	24,708	31,848	32,454	23,808	36,069	29,461	25,471	32,415	24,699
March	14,433	18,583	14,583	12,366	24,021	9,957	11,732	10,281	8,987	21,413	11,722	14,675
April	36,853	33,249	32,921	35,796	30,372	36,036	35,287	31,771	41,296	29,329	32,667	75,191
May	19,858	20,340	17,426	18,115	19,708	15,982	14,370	15,814	15,257	19,877	17,342	30,085
June	18,979	19,526	18,205	20,123	19,850	17,757	16,909	18,436	19,365	21,596	18,646	14,392
July	16,605	17,045	14,468	15,661	14,979	13,246	14,025	15,060	14,727	15,778	14,287	13,229
August	15,693	16,003	14,448	15,129	16,215	15.068	13,183	14,215	15,068	17,786	16,161	15,601
September	23,563	22,929	22,753	23,328	24,488	21,938	20,654	24,451	28,004	26,536	24,483	24,009
October	31,481	32,161	29,398	36,217	35,368	32,951	34,025	37,503	45,039	31,822	46,155	73,064
November	29,174	28,733	29,082	37,115	34,418	31,004	30,237	30,891	33,552	25,507	39,163	33,516
December	27,915	29,443	34,563	25,041	25,133	24,054	27,839	33,771	41,307	34,024	47,823	38,136
Year	295,566	302,564	285,248	287,800	303,214	276,035	267,771	289,915	312,702	287,653	316,514	377,219
Crude marriage rate per 1,000 total population†	7·5	7·6	7·1	7·1	7·4	6·7	6·4	6·9	7·4	6·7	7·4	8·7

* *Movimento della Popolazione*: 1926, p. 95; 1927, p. 67; 1928, p. 71; 1929–30, pt. 2, 1929, p. 33 and 1930, p. 229; 1931, p. 29; 1932, p. 10; 1933, p. 10; 1934, p. 10; 1935, p. 14; 1936, p. 14; 1937, p. 14.

† *Annuario Statistico Italiano, 1938*, p. 25, up to and including 1936, and from *Movimento della Popolazione* for 1937, p. 1*.

with the tax, the crude marriage-rate fell to 6·4 per 1,000 in 1932. Since that year there have been marked fluctuations, which may have been influenced partly by a slight upward movement in economic conditions—in most European countries there was a rise in the marriage rate after 1932[1]—and partly by increases in the bachelor tax in 1934 (from 1 July) and 1936 (1 January). On the other hand, the Abyssinian campaign was partly responsible for the decline in the number of marriages in 1935, while the success of the campaign no doubt influenced the upward swing in 1936 and 1937. Marriage loans were introduced in 1937,[2] while family allowances were considerably extended, and both these factors—particularly the first—may have helped to produce the increase of the crude marriage-rate from 7·4 in 1936 to 8·7 in 1937.[3] Definitive data for 1938 are not yet available, but the provisional data show a fall to 324,843 marriages in 1938[4] as compared with 377,219 in 1937. But here, again, crude data do not show the mechanics of this fall and we do not know whether there has been a real decline in the probability of marriage, or an exhaustion of the stock of marriageable persons. Looking back over the whole post-

[1] Leaving aside Germany, where marriage loans were granted in 1933, the crude marriage-rate rose after 1932 in Belgium, Denmark, Finland, Greece, Hungary, Irish Free State, Latvia, Lithuania, Norway, the Netherlands, England and Wales, Scotland, and Sweden (*Statistical Year-Book of the League of Nations, 1935–6*, p. 47; *Registrar-General's Statistical Review of England and Wales* for 1935, Tables, part ii, p. 6; *Eighty-First Annual Report of the Registrar-General for Scotland: 1935*, p. lviii). In Sweden the probability, for spinsters, of marrying by the fiftieth birthday, rose from 0·769 in 1932 to 0·782 in 1933, and to 0·816 in 1934.

[2] It should be remembered that marriage premiums had already been given for a number of years.

[3] The proportion of all marriages in which both partners were under 25 years of age was 25·56 per cent. in 1935, 22·16 per cent. in 1936, and 22·88 per cent. in 1937 (*Movimento della Popolazione*, 1935, p. 16*; 1936, p. 19*; 1937, p. 24*). The mean age at marriage of bachelors rose up to 1936 (28·06 years) and fell to 27·95 years in 1937, while for spinsters it rose to 24·93 years in 1936 and fell to 24·84 years in 1937 (ibid., 1937, p. 25*).

[4] *Bollettino Mensile di Statistica*, 21 June 1939, p. 475. The provisional data appear to show a slight rise in the first part of 1939—119,064 marriages in the period Jan.–May 1939, as compared with 116,997 for the same period in 1938. The particularly large numbers of marriages in April and Oct. 1937 were due to granting of special bonuses for marriages contracted on certain dates—e.g. a bonus of 500 lire or more was offered to each working-class couple marrying on 28 Oct., the anniversary of the 'March on Rome', and 46,155 marriages took place on that day (*The Times*, 4 Nov. 1937, p. 13; see also *The Times* of 28 April 1937, p. 15).

War period we can, however, say that neither the absolute figures of marriages nor the crude marriage-rate show any significant upward movement until 1936. For 1936 itself a large part of the rise is certainly due to the ending of the Abyssinian campaign, and it is therefore probable that 1937 marks the first really important increase in the probability of marriage. Yet in the period 1935–7 the chances of marriage were still lower than in the pre-War period. Using gross nuptiality tables we find that the probability—for spinsters—of marrying by the fiftieth birthday was 0·882 in 1910–12. In 1930–2 it had fallen to 0·815 and by 1935–7, in spite of very considerable increase in marriages in 1937, it was still only 0·856, about 3 per cent. below the level of 1910–12.[1] This is in contrast to the position in England and Wales, where the probability of marriage, in the years after the 1931 depression, rose to a much higher level than had obtained in 1910–12.

The trend of fertility in Italy is even less suggestive, until 1937, of any result of the demographic campaign. In 1921–2 the gross reproduction rate for the whole country was about 1·861, but from 1922 onwards the annual supply of births decreased every year up to and including 1929—a fall from 1,175,872 live births in 1922 to 1,037,700 in 1929—while the crude birth-rate fell from 30·8 to 25·6 in the same period. In 1930 there was a slight upward movement—the total number of live births was 1,092,678 and the crude birth-rate 26·7—but after that the fall continued, except for very slight upward movements in 1933 and 1935. The increase in the number of live births from 990,995 in 1932 to 995,979 in 1933, and from 992,966 in 1934 to 996,708 in 1935 did certainly not indicate any fundamental improvement in the situation. In 1936 births slumped badly to 962,686,[2] no doubt a result of the Abyssinian campaign, while the rise to 991,867 live births in 1937[3] was certainly due mainly to the ending of that campaign. In terms of gross reproduction rates, we can say that up to and including 1936, there was a practically unbroken fall after 1921–2. The gross reproduc-

[1] See Note V*r*, p. 457.
[2] *Annuario Statistico Italiano*, 1938, p. 25.
[3] *Movimento della Popolazione*, 1937, p. 31*.

tion rate for 1930–2 was 1·587,[1] 14·7 per cent. below that in 1921–2, and it fell in each succeeding year, reaching about 1·437 in 1935.[2] Even for the period 1935–7, including the increase in births in 1937, the gross reproduction rate was only 1·425. That is, there was a fall in fertility of about 10 per cent. between 1930–2 and 1935–7, as compared with a fall of about 6 per cent.[3] in England and Wales in the same period. Mortality also fell considerably during the period—the expectation of life at birth was 56·00 years for females in 1930–2[4] and 57·39 years in 1935–7[5]—but the net reproduction rate, which was 1·224 in 1930–2,[6] was only 1·128 in 1935–7, showing a fall of about 8 per cent. Table 24, which gives estimated gross and net reproduction rates for Italy, tells the same story. It will be seen that in 1881–2 there was little difference in the fertility of the various departments, but that by 1910–12 the regional differences were beginning to become marked. By 1930–2, after the heavy fall in the fertility particularly of the industrial regions, there was a range of more than two to one in the gross reproduction rates, and this was also the case in 1935–7. Moreover, between 1930–2 and 1935–7, not a single department showed a rise in fertility, and only in the agricultural areas was the decline comparatively small. With the progressive industrialization of Italy, fertility continued to fall, in spite of the pro-natalist measures which were applied, and in 1935–7 six of the eighteen departments had net reproduc-

[1] For 1930–2 and subsequent years the gross and net reproduction rates for Italy as a whole are calculated in the customary way. The volumes of the *Movimento della Popolazione*, from 1931 onwards, give the distribution of legitimate births for the whole country by the age of the mother. Dr. G. Frumkin, of the Economic Intelligence Section of the League of Nations, and Professor F. Savorgnan were kind enough to supply the present writer with unpublished material giving the distribution of illegitimate births by the age of the mother.

[2] Mid-year populations of females, by quinquennial age groups, were obtained by interpolation between the 1931 and 1936 censuses, correcting the results in accordance with the mid-year estimates of the total population given in the *Annuario Statistico Italiano, 1938*. On this basis gross reproduction rates were calculated, and they are: 1·493 in 1932, 1·478 in 1933, 1·456 in 1934, and 1·437 in 1935. These results cannot, of course, be regarded as more than rough approximations.

[3] The estimated gross reproduction rate for England and Wales was 0·929 in 1930–2 and 0·874 in 1935–7. The Italian gross reproduction rate rose slightly in 1937 itself to about 1·429.

[4] Galvani, in *Annali di Statistica*, serie vii, vol. i, p. 63.

[5] Computed on the basis of the 1936 census and the births and deaths of 1935–7.

[6] See Note V*s*, p. 457.

TABLE 24. *Estimated Gross and Net Reproduction Rates of the Departments (Compartimenti) of Italy, 1881–2 to 1935–7*

Departments	Gross reproduction rates* 1881–2	1910–12	1930–2	1935–7	Percentage fall 1930–2 to 1935–7	Net reproduction rates 1935–7†
1. Piemonte	2·390	1·620	0·967	0·856	11	0·732
2. Ligùria	2·234	1·608	0·906	0·780	14	0·675
3. Lombardia	2·459	2·226	1·261	1·134	10	0·900
4. Venèzia Tridentina	..	..	1·394	1·290	7	1·058
5. Vèneto	2·445	2·640	1·722	1·517	12	1·277
6. Venèzia Giùla e Zara	..	..	1·235	1·106	10	0·896
7. Emìlia	2·450	2·432	1·365	1·143	16	0·971
8. Toscana	2·486	2·042	1·140	1·027	10	0·891
9. Marche	2·415	2·464	1·692	1·456	14	1·228
10. Ùmbria	2·485	2·382	1·720	1·489	13	1·240
11. Làzio	2·332	2·078	1·626	1·439	12	1·161
12. Abruzzi e Molise	2·568	2·280	2·038	1·880	8	1·434
13. Campània	2·449	2·351	2·169	1·948	10	1·439
14. Pùglie	2·781	2·620	2·332	2·185	6	1·546
15. Lucània	2·707	2·651	2·397	2·322	3	1·635
16. Calàbrie	2·436	2·474	2·240	2·134	5	1·611
17. Sicìlia	2·650	2·306	1·911	1·761	8	1·315
18. Sardegna	2·448	2·221	2·028	1·946	4	1·451

* Estimated—for the separate departments—by applying the specific fertility rates of other countries. For the later years—1930 onwards—maternal ages are available for the country as a whole, but they have not so far been published for the individual regions. The estimated rates might, of course, have been obtained by applying the specific fertility rates for the whole country to the various departments. But the differences involved are extremely small. Thus, if this were done for the period 1935–7, the results for the departments, in the above order, would be (gross reproduction rates): 0·858; 0·779; 1·157; 1·301; 1·522; 1·123; 1·186; 1·042; 1·475; 1·470; 1·420; 1·821; 1·897; 2·077; 2·255; 2·031; 1·723; 1·887. The largest difference, as compared with the rates in the table above, is less than 5 per cent, while in 13 out of the 18 cases the difference is less than 3 per cent.

† Separate life tables were constructed for each department, on the basis of the relevant births, deaths, and census populations.

tion rates below unity, whereas probably not more than five were below unity in 1930–2, and none below in 1910–12.[1]

For the country as a whole it has been shown that this fall in fertility after 1930–2 was not simply a result of the Abyssinian war, and that for every single year between 1931 and 1936 fertility appeared to fall. In 1937 and 1938 births and fertility increased, partly as a result of the ending of the Abyssinian war and partly because of the introduction of marriage loans. How far this rise is likely to be permanent

[1] Using, for 1910–12 and 1930–2, the minimum fertility requirement for the whole country as a rough measure of the fertility requirements of the individual departments.

it is, of course, impossible to say at present. Full data for 1938 are not as yet available, but those for 1937 show, as would be expected, that the increase in births was produced by an increase in first births. In 1936 25·4 per cent. of the legitimate births were first births, whereas in 1937 this proportion was 27·2 per cent.[1] That is, the increase in births in 1937 gave no sign of being due to a fundamental change in fertility, but was rather a result commonly found at the end of a war. Up to 1938, therefore, the less ambitious aim of the Italian struggle for population did not appear to have been successful. The fall in fertility showed no visible check and, in spite of the concurrent fall in mortality, the replacement rate of the Italian people was considerably lower than it had been at the time when pro-natalist measures were first introduced. It is, of course, possible that, but for the measures adopted, the fall in fertility would have been still greater, but that must be poor consolation for a government which has, in various propagandist ways, drawn so much attention to the 'fundamental significance' of the measures applied. It seems probable, to the present writer, that the much more extensive and emphatic policy adopted since 1937 is evidence that the Italian government admits the failure of the earlier campaign and also that it is becoming extremely anxious to reverse the trend in fertility.

If the more modest aim has so far not been attained, it is evident that the more ambitious project—a population of at least 60 millions by 1950—is even less likely to succeed. This should have been clear by 1931, when Gini and de Finetti published their estimates of the future population of Italy.[2] Assuming no emigration or immigration, and a continuance of the fertility and mortality of 1921, the popu-

[1] *Movimento della Popolazione, 1937*, p. 42*. 1936 saw an exceptionally low proportion of first births, largely owing to the Abyssinian campaign. In 1934 the proportion was 25·2 per cent. and in 1935 26·8 per cent. 1936 saw the only interruption, since 1933, in the continuous rise in the proportion of first births.

[2] Op. cit., esp. pp. 24–61. The volume produced by Gini and de Finetti contains a large number of estimates, three only being referred to here. It should be noted that Gini and de Finetti took as their initial population a figure of 38·944 millions in 1921, whereas the *Annuario Statistico Italiano, 1938*, p. 9, gives a figure of 38·023 millions for 31 Dec. 1921. The estimates given above would therefore all be somewhat too high. Up to 1931 the emigration data were obtained from the actual statistics. For subsequent years the assumption of 40,000 per year net emigration was made.

lation of Italy would, according to the computation, amount to 56·154 millions by 1951. Allowing, in this estimate, for a net annual emigration of 40,000 persons, the population of Italy would be only about 54·184 millions by 1951. Finally, assuming both a net annual emigration as stated above, together with a decline of fertility and mortality—fertility falling in accordance with recent experience, and mortality falling towards, though not becoming as low as, that of New Zealand for 1927—the population of Italy would be about 49·633 millions by 1951. Since 1921, of course, both fertility and mortality have fallen appreciably, and the present writer has therefore constructed a number of new estimates of the future population of Italy, taking the census population of 1936[1] as a starting-point. Assuming a continuance of the fertility and mortality[2] of 1935–7, and no emigration or immigration, the population of Italy would be only 48·153 millions by 1951, and even by 1961 it would still be only 51·998 millions. If, with the mortality of 1935–7, there were a constant annual supply of live births at the absolute level of the average for 1935–7—that is, 983,754 per year—the total population would be 47·639 millions by 1951, and if, assuming the same mortality, there were an annual supply of live births at the absolute level of 1937—that is, 991,867 per year—the total population by 1951 would be 47·743 millions.[3] It is clear, then, that however successful the Italian population policy is likely to be in the future, there is very little likelihood that Mussolini will realize his aim of having a population of 60 millions in Italy proper by 1950.

1 The *popolazione presente*. For males a *popolazione speciale* was subsequently estimated by the Central Statistical Institute, including those men who, at the time of the census, were in Abyssinia. Since, however, the mortality data given in *Movimento della Popolazione* are for civil mortality only, the present writer has not used the *popolazione speciale* for males. But in any case the difference is small, the *popolazione presente* giving 20·595 million males and the *popolazione speciale* estimating the number at 21·067 millions. See Savorgnan, F., 'La struttura per età della popolazione italiana e le sue variazioni dal 1931 al 1936', *Atti dell' Istituto Nazionale delle Assicurazioni*, 1938 (reprint, p. 5).

2 The life tables constructed for this estimate show an expectation of life at birth of 54·62 years for males and 57·39 years for females. For 1930–2, Galvani (*Annali di Statistica*, serie vii, vol. i, op. cit., pp. 62 and 63) gives expectations of 53·76 and 56·00 years respectively for males and females.

3 These two latter estimates assume, of course, an ultimately stationary population. Migration is not taken into account in these estimates.

VI

GERMAN POLICY AND THE BIRTH-RATE

ONE of the most striking phenomena of recent years is the change in the trend of marriage- and birth-rates in Germany since 1933. The change has attracted widespread attention not only because Germany is the sole country in which, so far, population policies appear to have had any appreciable results, but also because of the rapidity with which these results followed the coming to power of the National Socialist régime. Many writers have devoted articles and books to an analysis of the causes of this reversal of the trend, some emphasizing the material inducements given under the new régime, some drawing attention to the possible influence of a more rigorous enforcement of the law against abortion and of the suppression of birth-control propaganda, while others—especially German writers—have attributed the change largely to a 'spiritual rebirth' of the nation. The present writer cannot attempt to decide which is the cause or causes. As has been seen in the case of France, it is extremely difficult to measure the influence of material inducements. Large-scale psychological changes—if there have been such—are still less susceptible to measurement, and even qualitative evaluation becomes impossible when, as is only too evident, the Press is subjected to a constant censorship. Nevertheless, any study of population movements and policies would be seriously incomplete if it excluded a discussion of the position in Germany, and this chapter, therefore, will give a broad outline of the demographic background and the measures introduced by the National Socialists, and it will consider some of the factors which may have been responsible for raising fertility by over 30 per cent. since 1933.

Like most other European countries, Germany has experienced a fairly continuous fall in her birth-rate since about the third quarter of the nineteenth century. From a level of 39·2 per 1,000 of the total population in the period 1876–80, a slow but steady fall brought down the rate to 31·6 per

1,000 in 1906–10, and the rapidity of the decline increased in the post-War years, the rate falling to 15·1 in 1932 and 14·7 in 1933.[1] The gross reproduction rate, which was 2·459 in 1881–90, was only 1·116 in 1924–6, 0·862 in 1931, and 0·800 in 1933, and in spite of the fall in mortality during the period—the mean expectation of life at birth for females rose from 40·25 years in 1881–90 to 62·81 years in 1932–4—the net reproduction rate fell from 1·448 in 1881–90 to 0·924 in 1924–6, 0·748 in 1931, and 0·698 in 1933.[2] That is, not very long after the War fertility fell below the level necessary for adequate replacement, and by 1933 was lower than in any other European nation, with the sole exception of Austria.

The declining birth-rate in Germany did not go unnoticed or unregretted. Even in the pre-War period, when fertility was well above the replacement level—in 1901–10 the net reproduction-rate was 1·480[3]—there was a considerable literature on the decline, including many articles and books which lamented the trend and which proposed widespread social and economic reform to combat it. Thus M. von Gruber, in a study[4] which perhaps expressed this lament in its most marked form, recommended measures which markedly anticipated the kind of action taken under the National Socialist régime. The measures urged included the building of houses specially designed for families; the granting of allowances to families with at least three living, healthy children, the allowances to be given until the children

[1] Burgdörfer, F., *Aufbau und Bewegung der Bevölkerung*, Leipzig, 1935, p. 86. For 1932 and 1933 the rates refer to the post-War territory (excluding the Saar, Austria, and Bohemia; the two latter areas are not dealt with at all in the present study). The earlier data refer to the pre-War territory.

[2] The gross and net reproduction rates for 1933 are calculated from the fertility and mortality data for that year. The others are from Kuczynski, R. R., *The Measurement*, &c., pp. 122 and 212. The expectations of life are from *Die Bewegung der Bevölkerung in den Jahren 1932, 1933 und 1934*, Part I (Text), p. I/80. The German Statistical Office gives reproduction rates which appear to take into account the influence of marriage trends, and are therefore slightly different from those cited above—e.g. for 1933 the German official rate is 0·714. See Ibid., Part I, p. I/77, and *Wirtschaft und Statistik*, 1935, Sonderheft 15, 'Neue Beiträge zum deutschen Bevölkerungsproblem', pp. 73–81.

[3] Kuczynski, R. R., *The Measurement*, &c., p. 212.

[4] Gruber, Max von, *Ursachen und Bekämpfung des Geburtenrückgangs im Deutschen Reich* (Bericht erstattet an die 38. Versammlung des Deutschen Vereins für öffentliche Gesundheitspflege, 1913), Munich, 1914.

were at least 14 years of age, and to be continued, at a lower level, until they reached 21 years; the provision of old-age pensions to parents who had brought up at least the required minimum number of children; the granting of special civil distinctions to the parents of large families; special taxes on unmarried, and on childless persons and on one-child families; compulsory insurance entitling married women to additional monetary help during pregnancy and childbirth; the suppression of birth-control and general neo-Malthusian propaganda, and the application of severe ('draconic') penalties for abortion; and an intensive campaign against drunkenness, tuberculosis, and venereal disease.[1] Comparable in attitude, though by no means as intense in tone, A. Grotjahn[2] recognized the individual and social virtues of wise birth control and repudiated any suggestion of legal or police measures against the sale of contraceptives. But he also pointed out the disadvantages of a declining birth-rate and urged the establishment of larger families in contrast to the 'two-child system' which was spreading so rapidly. He believed that economic inducements[3] were the most suitable for encouraging the 'three-child system' and recommended a compulsory 'parenthood insurance' (*Elternschaftsversicherung*)—a proposal to which he very frequently returned in subsequent years—and the maintenance and encouragement of the peasantry. That the declining birth-rate was a widely discussed question in pre-War days is clearly shown by a leading article in the *Deutsche Tageszeitung* of 10 August 1912, which drew attention to the fact that all newspapers were devoting much space to the question, most of them regarding the decline as an evil,

[1] But Gruber recommended, as a method of protection against venereal disease, that the condom should be used in extra-marital sexual intercourse.

[2] Grotjahn, A., *Geburten-Rückgang und Geburten-Regelung, im Lichte der individuellen und der sozialen Hygiene*, Berlin, 1914, pp. 154–63, 267, 328–61. He pointed out that even a 'three-child system' would not be enough to maintain the population. With current mortality the stationary birth-rate would have been 20 per 1,000 of the total (life table) population. But, assuming that it was necessary for the population to grow—as a counterpoise to the rapidly growing populations of the neighbouring peoples, especially in the East—a birth-rate of 25 per 1,000 could be regarded as normal, and below which the country should in no case be allowed to fall, while a rate of about 30 per 1,000 was desirable (ibid., pp. 290–1).

[3] Grotjahn mentions, pp. 336–7, that in pre-War Germany a number of local authorities gave family allowances to their employees—e.g. Charlottenburg, Schöneberg, Frankfurt a./M., Halberstadt, Strassburg.

and urged that really large tax rebates should be given in respect of children, and that there should be a campaign against the practices of birth control and abortion.[1] During the War the same kind of lament at the falling birth-rate was heard—though, unless it can be assumed that war is going to last at least fifteen years, a high fertility is a great economic disadvantage in time of war—and at least two active pro-natalist organizations appear to have been in existence in 1916,[2] while pro-natalist literature was also being published.[3] At the beginning of 1916, Dr. Kruse, chairman of the Düsseldorf region local government authority, instituted gifts of 100 RM. each to about 350 mothers who had brought up more than seven children, and this example was followed in the districts of Solingen and Essen and the towns of Düsseldorf, Mühlheim, and Duisburg. In June 1917 in the Mettmann district (Rheinland) the first German Association of Large Families was founded.[4]

After the War active interest continued to be shown in the question. It should be remembered that the August 1919 constitution of the German Republic contained various references to the family in general and to large families in

[1] But also stressing the spiritual side. See Note VI*a*, p. 457.

[2] These were the *Deutsche Gesellschaft für Bevölkerungspolitik*, and the *Bund zur Erhaltung und Mehrung der deutschen Volkskraft*, both apparently founded during the War. See More, A., *Fecundity versus Civilisation*, 2nd ed., 3rd imp., London, n.d. (*B.M. Catalogue* gives 1916 as date of 1st ed.), pp. 27 and 28. See also Harmsen, H., *Praktische Bevölkerungspolitik*, Berlin, 1931, p. 91. In 1926 the *Deutsche Gesellschaft* became absorbed by the *Arbeitsgemeinschaft für Volksgesundung, E.V.*, which had been founded in 1919.

[3] e.g. Grotjahn, A., *Der Wehrbeitrag der deutschen Frau*, Bonn, 1915 (this was one of the famous *Deutsche Kriegsschriften*, and said that excess of births over deaths meant power, no less than knowledge, money, and a large army, that this excess could only be maintained by the will of German women and that (p. 28) 'den Willen zum Kinde in einem Masse zur Geltung zu bringen, dass der gegenwärtige Bevölkerungsauftrieb unseres Volkes bis in alle Zukunft erhalten bleibt, —das ist der Wehrbeitrag der deutschen Frau'); Stoffers, G., *Kinderreiche Mütter*, Düsseldorf, 1917; Hitze, F., *Geburtenrückgang u. Sozialreform*, M. Gladbach, 1917. Notice also Dr. Kuczynski [R. R.] and Dr. Mansfeld, *Der Pflichtteil des Reiches. Ein Vorschlag zu praktischer Bevölkerungspolitik*, Berlin, 1917, which proposed a modification of the inheritance law. See also p. 313 for a note on Grotjahn.

[4] *Vereinigung kinderreicher Familien und Witwen*. See Engelsmann, R., 'Der "Reichsbund der Kinderreichen Deutschlands zum Schutze der Familie e.V."', *Archiv für Bevölkerungspolitik, Sexualethik und Familienkunde*, 2, 1932, pp. 107–14 at p. 107. (This journal changed its name, with the issue of 1, 1933–4, to *Archiv für Bevölkerungswissenschaft (Volkskunde) und Bevölkerungspolitik*, and is subsequently referred to as *A.f.B.*)

particular. The maintenance and increase of the nation was, Article 119 implied, to be a special care of the constitution, and the central and local government authorities had, as their duty, to protect and encourage the family. The distribution and use of the land was, according to Article 155, 1, to be so watched as to ensure to every German a sound dwelling, and to every German family, particularly to large families, living and working accommodation according to their needs.[1] In October 1919 the 'League of Large Families' (Bund der Kinderreichen)—that is, of families with at least four dependent children—held a meeting in Frankfurt-am-Main, and decided upon a drive for members. Similar groups were formed in Duisburg, Düsseldorf, Bergisch-Gladbach, and Cologne, and in 1921 a general union of these leagues was achieved, following a meeting convened by the Cologne group. In the next two years a definite programme was drawn up and the union, which in 1921 had been entitled the Gesamtverband der Bünde der Kinderreichen Deutschlands zum Schutz der Familie, with head-quarters at Cologne, changed its name to the Reichsbund der Kinderreichen Deutschlands zum Schutz der Familie, and its head-quarters to Berlin. In spite of internal dissension in the early days of this league, the movement spread, organizing annual public gatherings which had something of the nature of mass demonstrations, since, for example, some 5,000 persons took part in the 1927 gathering at Bochum. Each year the gathering discussed some specific topic which was directly concerned with maintenance and encouragement of the family, and the general movement received the support of such prominent statisticians as Burgdörfer and Zahn, as well as Grotjahn, a pioneer of social hygiene, whose earlier writings on the population question have already been mentioned.[2]

[1] Article 119: '. . . Die Reinerhaltung, Gesundung und soziale Förderung der Familie ist Aufgabe des Staats und der Gemeinden. Kinderreiche Familien haben Anspruch auf ausgleichende Fürsorge. . . .' Article 155, 1: 'Die Verteilung und Nutzung des Bodens wird von Staats wegen in einer Weise überwacht, die Missbrauch verhütet und dem Ziele zustrebt, jedem Deutschen eine gesunde Wohnung und allen deutschen Familien, besonders den kinderreichen, eine ihren Bedürfnissen entsprechende Wohn- und Wirtschaftsheimstätte zu sichern . . .' (*A.f.B.*, 1, 1932, p. 1).

[2] Engelsmann, R., op. cit., pp. 107–14.

At the same time both official and unofficial publications drew further attention to the consequences of the declining birth-rate. Thus in 1926 the German Statistical Office published three sets of estimates of the future population of Germany,[1] one estimate—which was in the nature of an extrapolation of current trends—showing a fall in population after about 1950. This estimate assumed that mortality would continue at the level of 1921–3, that marital fertility would fall by 25 per cent. between 1925 and 1955, remaining constant after that date, and that the annual supply of illegitimate births would remain constant at about the level of 1923. Migration was not taken into account. On these assumptions the population, which was 62·313 millions in 1925, would rise to about 67·5 millions by 1950 and would then fall, sinking to 63·676 millions by 1975. But this estimate was relatively optimistic. Fertility declined sharply after 1922, affected particularly by the economic difficulties of the inflation period,[2] and between 1922 and 1930 the crude birth-rate fell from 23·0 to 17·5 per 1,000, about 24 per cent., and the legitimate fertility rate—the number of legitimate live births per 1,000 married women aged 15 to 44 years—fell from 168·3 to 118·3, or about 30 per cent., in the same period.[3] Discussion was aroused by a much publicized pamphlet by R. Korherr, which originally appeared in 1927,[4] and by the issue in 1929 of F. Burgdörfer's study of the declining birth-rate and of the methods of combating it.[5] Professor Grotjahn elaborated his proposals for 'parenthood insurance'[6] and similar measures were dis-

[1] *Die Bewegung der Bevölkerung in den Jahren 1922 und 1923*, Berlin, 1926, pp. 37*–50*. The precise level at which illegitimate births were to remain constant was not specified in the estimate.

[2] See Roesle, E., 'Inflation und Bevölkerungsbewegung. I. Der Geburtenrückgang in den deutschen Städten in den Jahren 1921 bis 1924', *Archiv für Soziale Hygiene und Demographie*, 1925–6, pp. 34–41 (this journal is subsequently referred to as *A.f.S.H.*). In towns with more than 15,000 inhabitants the influence of inflation appears to have been very marked.

[3] Burgdörfer, F., op. cit., pp. 86 and 102.

[4] *Geburtenrückgang* originally appeared as the Dec. 1927 issue of the *Süddeutsche Monatshefte*. The issue consulted by the present writer is the 2nd revised ed., n.d. [1928], containing an introduction by Oswald Spengler.

[5] Burgdörfer, F., *Der Geburtenrückgang und seine Bekämpfung*, Berlin, 1929.

[6] Grotjahn, A., *Der Geburtenrückgang und seine Bekämpfung durch eine Elternschaftsversicherung*, Dresden, n.d. [1929]; ibid., *Die Hygiene der menschlichen*

cussed by other writers.[1] In 1930 the German Statistical Office published another set of estimates of the future population of Germany,[2] based on the mortality of 1924–6. One of these estimates assumed that legitimate and illegitimate fertility would remain at the level of 1927, and on this assumption (not taking migration into account) the population, which was 63·187 millions in 1927, would rise to about 71·5 millions by 1965 and then fall, sinking to about 68 millions by the year 2000. Another estimate, more in keeping with contemporary trends, assumed that legitimate and illegitimate fertility would fall by 25 per cent. by 1955 and would then remain constant (the migration factor was again excluded). This would result in a population which increased to 67·702 millions by 1945, and then fell rapidly, amounting to only 46·891 millions by the year 2000. It is of some interest to note that the actual figures of the population of Germany after 1927 were lower than those computed in the second and lower estimate.[3] Interest in the declining birth-rate was still further stimulated by E. Kahn's book on the international 'birth strike', published in 1930,[4] and by Burgdörfer's very detailed study of the contemporary vital trends and their consequences which first appeared in 1932.[5]

Fortpflanzung, Berlin and Vienna, 1926, ch. 5; ibid., 'Entwurf eines Elternschaftsversicherungsgesetzes nebst Begründung', *A.f.S.H.*, 1925–6, pp. 24–31.

[1] See, e.g., Fetscher, R., 'Familienbeihilfen durch Ausgleichskassen', *A.f.S.H.*, 1925–6, pp. 336–7.

[2] *Statistik des Deutschen Reichs*, vol. 401, II, Berlin, 1930, pp. 641 ff. The estimate assuming constant fertility was not given in tabular form, but only in the graphs in the volume. The remaining estimate assumed constant mortality and a constant annual supply of births at the absolute level of 1927. This therefore implied an ultimately stationary population.

[3] Burgdörfer, F., *Aufbau*, &c., p. 86, gives the mid-year population of Germany (excluding the Saar territory) as 63·603, 63·943, 64·280, 64·616, 64·897, 65.221, and 65·579 millions respectively in the years 1928 to 1934. The populations derived from the estimate assuming a 25 per cent. decline in fertility are 63·779, 64·171, 64·558, 64·933, 65·295, 65·641, and 65·971 millions respectively for the same years (mid-year populations obtained from arithmetic averages of the beginning-of-the-year populations given in *Statistik des Deutschen Reichs*, vol. 401, II, p. 663).

[4] Kahn, E., *Der internationale Geburtenstreik*, Frankfurt a./M., 1930. For an economic discussion see also Nawratzki, C., *Bevölkerungsstillstand als Wirtschaftsproblem unter besonderer Berücksichtigung der Landwirtschaft*, Berlin, 1930, esp. chs. xi ff.

[5] Burgdörfer, F., *Volk ohne Jugend*, Berlin-Grunewald, 1932. There was a second edition in 1934 and a third enlarged edition in 1935. Notice also that the 'large family' association had its own newspapers and periodicals—e.g. *Bundesblatt;*

From the previous outline it is very easy to gain the impression that pro-natalist views were the dominant ones in Germany in the immediate pre-War and in the post-War periods. This impression would, however, be quite false. It is true that, as we have seen in an earlier chapter, Germany has a long tradition of pro-natalist views and measures. Nevertheless, the English neo-Malthusian movement had considerable repercussions in Germany.[1] In 1881 Mrs. Besant's *Law of Population* was published in a German translation in Berlin,[2] in 1889 the Sozial-Harmonischer Verein was formed, and in spite of the antagonism of some doctrinaire Socialists,[3] the early years of the twentieth century saw the creation of definite birth-control organizations, largely due to the activity of Helene Stöcker, who founded the Bund für Mutterschutz und Sexualreform in 1905, and of Dr. F. A. Theilhaber, who founded the Gesellschaft für Sexualreform in 1913.[4] These two organizations were apparently rather middle class and 'intellectual' in outlook, but in the post-War years birth-control information was spread among the working class by numerous handbooks and pamphlets[5] and by the creation of birth-control leagues of a different type. In the immediate post-War years these leagues were often purely commercial, founded by manufacturers of contraceptives and very largely aimed at providing a regular market for specific brands of contraceptives.

Die Familie; Westfälische Blätter für kinderreiche Familien; der Ostdeutsche Kinderreiche; Die Kinderreichen; Bayerisches Familienblatt, &c., as well as a considerable series of pamphlets.

[1] Note Weinhold, C. A., *Von der Uebervölkerung in Mitteleuropa und deren Folgen auf die Staaten und ihre Zivilisation*, Halle, 1827, recommended infibulation as a method of preventing overpopulation (cited by Oestreich, J., *Die Stellung des Nationalsozialismus zur Bevölkerungslehre von Thomas Robert Malthus und seinen Anhängern*, Würzburg, 1936, pp. 16–17. Himes, N., *Medical History*, p. 320, cites Theilhaber as referring to another similar study by Weinhold, published in Leipzig, 1828). Reference has already been made to Wilde, F. A., *Das weibliche Gebär-Unvermögen*, Berlin, 1838, and to Hellmann, R., *Ueber Geschlechtsfreiheit*, Berlin, 1878; see present study, p. 39, n. 3.

[2] *Das Gesetz der Bevölkerung*. See Oestreich, op. cit., p. 14.

[3] See, for example, Ungern-Sternberg, R. von, *The Causes of the Decline in Birth-rate within the European Sphere of Civilization*, Cold Spring Harbor, 1931, pp. 137–8.

[4] Lehfeldt, H., 'Die Laienorganisationen für Geburtenregelung', *A.f.B.*, 2, 1932, pp. 63–87, at p. 63. This article is the basis of most of the present account of the post-War movement.

[5] See report of a paper by H. Harmsen, in *A.f.B.*, 1, 1931, pp. 72–3.

But workers' organizations were soon formed, generally maintaining permanent birth-control clinics in the relatively large towns, and sending ambulatory clinics from place to place in the less densely peopled areas. Some of the clinics were run by lay organizers, but many of them had medical advisors, in spite of the fact that the Prussian Medical Board Committee passed a resolution, in 1928, that 'contraception as a professional practice is to be considered as undesirable . . .'.[1] By 1932 there were fifteen main birth-control organizations[2] in Germany, the most important being the Liga für Mutterschutz und soziale Familienhygiene, with nearly 27,000 members, and the Reichsverband für Geburtenregelung und Sexualhygiene, with a membership of about 20,000. The fifteen organizations probably had a membership of about 113,000, but this does not include members' wives, who appear to have been very active propagandists for the movement, while further publicity was given by three main periodicals—*Liebe und Leben*, with a circulation of about 60,000; *Weckruf*, with a circulation of 30,000, and *Sexualhygiene*, with a circulation of 21,000.[3] Some of the sickness-benefit funds (*Krankenkassen*)—six in Berlin, for example—also took advantage of a clause in the National Insurance regulations to give birth-control advice to their members.[4] If we add to this organized movement the considerable purely commercial activity in the field of birth control, we must conclude that contraception was an accepted part of the general social pattern in post-War and pre-National Socialist Germany[5].

[1] Hodann, M., *History of Modern Morals*, London, 1937, p. 205.

[2] See the tabular analysis given by Lehfeldt, H., op. cit., pp. 84–7.

[3] Other periodicals published by the various organizations included *Die neue Generation; Freies Geschlecht*, with a circulation of 5,000; *Sexualaufklärung zum Schutz der Familie;* and *Die Warte*, the last-named being published by the Düsseldorf Einheitsverband für proletarische Sexualreform und Mutterschutz, the only organization with a specific Communist line. Most of the organizations were unconnected with any political party, though many had a Socialist viewpoint. Lehfeldt, loc. cit.

[4] See Note VI*b*, p. 458.

[5] Though it is, of course, extremely difficult to estimate the precise importance of the trade in birth-control appliances. As early as 1914 Grotjahn (*Geburten-Rückgang und Geburten-Regelung*, pp. 71 ff.) gave a long list of the appliances sold and emphasized the importance of douching by women in the urban population. Hitze, op. cit., p. 19, refers to the widespread publicity carried on by manufacturers. So far as one specific contraceptive is concerned, Wolf, J., *Die neue Sexualmoral und das Geburtenproblem unserer Tage*, Jena, 1928, pp. 71–2, says that 80 to 90 million

We should add that in the view of many writers abortion was a very widespread practice in post-War Germany. Peller suggests that the practice did not become really important as a factor in family limitation until about the beginning of the twentieth century, when the use of mechanical aseptic methods made artificial interruption of pregnancy relatively simple and innocuous, and he presents material which appears to support this thesis.[1] In fact, of course, as has been seen in Chapter I, it is extremely difficult to distinguish between spontaneous and induced abortions, and the numerous records and analyses given for various districts and sickness benefit funds do not attempt to separate the two categories. Peller points out that in German publications on the subject the proportion of criminal, induced, to all abortions ranges from 1·2 to 90–5 per cent.[2] But the publications seen by the present writer appear to attribute most of the abortions to criminal practices, and certainly place the proportion a good deal higher than is generally done in England.[3] Bearing this in mind, we may note various sets of data provided by sickness benefit funds in Germany as to the ratio between abortions and total normal births.[4] Of these data the statistics provided by the Siemens-Werke Fund (Betriebskrankenkasse) are particularly interesting, as they give a continuous record from 1908 to 1932,[5] and show a fairly steady increase in the frequency of abortion during the period, with peaks in 1921–4. In 1908, 1909, and 1910 the normal births were 261, 391, and 450, and the abortions 99, 157, and 177, or in the ratio of 38, 40, and 39 to every 100 normal births. In the period 1929 to 1932 inclusive the

condoms per year were bought in Germany. This constituted less than half of the total output of condoms in Germany, the bulk being exported. See also Gemmer, E., *Das Problem der Geburteneinschränkung und Fehlgeburten vor und nach 1933*, Coburg, 1937, pp. 16–17.

[1] Peller, S., *Fehlgeburt und Bevölkerungsfrage*, Stuttgart-Leipzig, 1930, pp. 124 and 71. Unfortunately the data given are not sufficient to eliminate incomparabilities.

[2] Op. cit., p. 134, citing Hirsch.

[3] See Note VI*c*, p. 458.

[4] The term 'normal birth' is used because in some cases still births are included in the birth statistics, while in other cases there is no clear statement as to whether still births are included or not. As used here the term simply means that the pregnancy terminated naturally, without miscarriage or induced abortion.

[5] Pohlen, P., 'Die Fehlgeburten im Deutschen Reich', *Reichs-Gesundheitsblatt*, 23 Nov. 1933, pp. 895–902, at p. 897. From 1908 to 1927 inclusive the data refer to live births only, no record of still births having apparently been kept in that period.

normal confinements for the separate years amounted to 866, 536, 301, and 211, while the abortions recorded were 733, 456, 329, and 239, giving a ratio of 85, 85, 109, and 113 per 100 normal births. Comparable statistics are available for the Allgemeine Elektrizitäts-Gesellschaft Fund, Berlin, and for the Berlin, Dresden, and Munich municipal funds (Ortskrankenkassen), as well as for the whole of Lübeck, where miscarriages and abortions have been notified continuously since 1927.[1] The results are summarized in Table 25, and although they show a considerable range of variation,[2] even the lowest ratios for the years prior to 1933 still indicate a high abortion frequency. The statistics have been brought up to date as far as is possible, and the trends in the most recent years will be considered later.

So far as the total number of abortions in the whole country is concerned, any estimate is certain to be inaccurate. We may, however, note that in the post-War period common estimates were between 800,000 and one million abortions per year.[3] If this figure is anywhere near the truth, it is evident that abortion must have played an extremely important part in depressing the birth-rate. Moreover, throughout the whole period there was considerable agitation, especially from left-wing political circles,[4] for the further spread of birth control and for the relaxation of the abortion law.

[1] There are data for earlier years, but these are not strictly comparable with the later figures.

[2] For further data see Roesle, E., 'Die Magdeburger Fehlgeburtenstatistik vom Jahre 1924', *A.f.S.H.*, 1925–6, pp. 189–95; Durand-Wever, A-M., op. cit., I, *Die medizinische Welt*, 14 Feb. 1931, pp. 243–5; Pietrusky, F., 'Zur Frage der kriminellen Fruchtabtreibung', *Deutsche Zeitschrift für die gesamte gerichtliche Medizin*, 1930, pp 54–61 (gives methods used in a number of cases); Puppel, E., 'Der kriminelle Abort in Thüringen, 1915–1926', same journal, 1928, pp. 576–84 (gives some data as to prices charged for procuring abortion).

[3] 'About one million' is mentioned by Durand-Wever, op. cit., vol. i, p. 244, as an estimate given by various writers, while Ungern-Sternberg, op. cit., p. 148, says that annual abortion frequency was 'estimated as 800,000 to 1,000,000 . . .'. Wolf, op. cit., p. 72, estimates the frequency at over 600,000 and cites a semi-official estimate of at least 800,000 per year.

[4] e.g. the German Communist party had, among the planks in its programme, the abrogation of those sections of the Penal Code which might be applied against birth-control propaganda or the sale of contraceptives (para. 184), the provision of free contraceptives and birth-control advice, the repeal of the law against abortion, and the provision of free assistance for procuring abortion. This, of course, was before the U.S.S.R. repealed the law which legalized abortion. See 'Richtlinien der KPD. zur Frage der Geburtenregelung', *A.f.B.*, 1, 1931, pp. 57–61.

TABLE 25. *Abortions and Normal Births in Germany, 1926–38*

Years	Siemens-Werke, Berlin*			Allgemeine Elektrizitäts-Gesellschaft, Berlin†‡			Berlin Ortskrankenkasse†§		
	Normal births	*Abortions*	*Abortions per 100 normal births*	*Normal births*	*Abortions*	*Abortions per 100 normal births*	*Normal births*	*Abortions*	*Abortions per 100 normal births*
1926	529	576	109	304	392	129	5,711	5,740	101
1927	438	581	133	226	423	187	5,916	6,289	106
1928	704	777	110	347	388	112	6,521	5,747	88
1929	866	733	85	..	..	..	5,900	6,100	103
1930	536	456	85	248	240	97	..	..	..
1931	301	329	109	178	161	90	..	..	..
1932	211	239	113	108	95	88	..	..	..
1933	..	..	..	81	85	105	..	..	..
1934	..	..	..	217	89	41	..	..	..
1935	..	..	..	..	..	..	21,780	3,654	17
1936	..	..	..	..	..	..	22,405	3,619	16
1937	..	..	..	..	..	..	..	..	..
1938	..	..	..	..	..	..	..	..	..

Munich†			Dresden†‡			Lübeck‖			Munich University clinic for women, and midwifery school ¶			Years
Normal births	*Abortions*	*Abortions per 100 normal births*	*Normal births*	*Abortions*	*Abortions per 100 normal births*	*Normal births*	*Abortions*	*Abortions per 100 normal births*	*Normal births*	*Abortions*	*Abortions per 100 normal births*	
4,372	1,500	34	3,090	1,784	58	..	..	..	..	..	..	1926
3,995	1,583	40	3,074	1,919	62	1,954	947	48	..	..	..	1927
4,419	1,804	41	3,584	2,275	63	2,115	956	45	..	..	..	1928
..	..	..	..	..	..	2,047	915	45	..	..	..	1929
..	..	..	3,685	2,244	61	1,923	899	47	2,411	322	13	1930
..	..	..	2,902	1,694	58	1,728	878	51	2,035	346	17	1931
..	..	..	2,439	1,668	68	1,591	1,036	65	1,726	320	19	1932
..	..	..	2,304	1,329	58	1,606	749	47	1,481	305	21	1933
..	..	..	3,090	1,179	38	2,182	714	33	1,839	250	14	1934
..	..	..	..	..	..	2,352	746	32	1,974	256	13	1935
..	..	..	..	..	..	2,424	587	24	..	..	..	1936
..	..	..	..	..	..	2,604	526	20	..	..	..	1937
..	..	..	..	..	..	2,938	403	14	..	..	..	1938

* Pohlen, K., op. cit., p. 897.

† Riese, H., 'Abortion and suicide in Germany', *International Medical Group for the Investigation of Contraception*, Fourth Issue, London, 1931, p. 17, for data from 1926–8 inclusive.

‡ Unpublished data for 1930–4 inclusive, kindly supplied by Dr. F. Burgdörfer in a letter dated 30 July 1935.

§ 1929 and 1935 from Burgdörfer, F., in Kühn, A., Staemmler, M., and Burgdörfer, F., *Erbkunde, Rassenpflege, Bevölkerungspolitik*, 3rd ed., Leipzig, 1936, p. 277. 1936 from Burgdörfer, F., *Völker am Abgrund*, 2nd ed., Munich–Berlin, 1937, pp. 32–3.

‖ Hillmann, 'Die Fehlgeburten in Lübeck im Jahre 1938', *Reichs-Gesundheitsblatt*, 15 March 1939, pp. 219–22. See also same author, same journal, 17 June 1936, pp. 478–80 and 26 May 1937, pp. 360–3. See also Hartwig, J., 'Die Fehlgeburten in Lübeck (Stadt) in den Jahren 1930 und 1931', *A.f.S.H.*, 1932, pp. 300–2, and same author, same journal, 1933–4, pp. 303–5.

¶ Ploetz, A., 'Zum Zahlenverhältnis von Geburten und Fehlgeburten', *Archiv für Rassen- und Gesellschaftsbiologie*, 2, 1936, pp. 181–2.

The abortion law in force in Germany in the pre-War and immediate post-War years was that contained in paragraphs 218 to 220 of the Penal Code which came into force for the newly established German Empire on 1 January 1872. Penal servitude for up to 5 years was prescribed for a pregnant woman who had an abortion or who had the foetus destroyed in the womb, with a reduction of the penalty to imprisonment for not less than 6 months if there were extenuating circumstances. The same penalties applied to any person helping to procure the abortion or to kill the foetus, the penalties being raised to penal servitude for up to 10 years if the act were performed for money. If the act were performed without the knowledge or consent of the woman, the penalty was penal servitude for not less than 2 years, and if the act resulted in the death of the woman penal servitude for not less than 10 years, or for life, was prescribed.[1] As a result of pressure from the left-wing circles this law was modified in May 1926 and condensed into a single article, the new paragraph 218, under which imprisonment for 1 day to 5 years was prescribed for a woman inducing her own abortion or killing the foetus in the womb, or allowing this to be undertaken by some other person, and also for the person who performed the act upon the woman. If the act were undertaken for money or without the consent of the pregnant woman, the penalty was to be penal servitude for 1 to 15 years, though this might be reduced to imprisonment for not less than 3 months if there were extenuating circumstances.[2] The change in the law was clearly not fundamental, and there was much subsequent discussion and pressure for further amendments. Plays dealing with the subject were written and produced—e.g. Wolff's *Cyankali* and Credé-Hoerder's *Paragraph 218*[3]—a draft of a new Penal Code proposed substantial modifications, an inquiry by the Ham-

[1] Drage, G., *The Criminal Code of the German Empire*, London, 1885, p, 249. Attempts were also punishable. Abortion to save the life of a woman did not constitute a crime. Ibid., p. 146.

[2] *Reichsgesetzblatt* (subsequently cited as *RGB*), 25 May 1926, p. 239, and Liszt, F. von, *Lehrbuch des Deutschen Strafrechts*, 26th ed. (ed. E. Schmidt), Berlin and Leipzig, 1932, vol. i, p. 386. Attempted abortion was also punishable. Penal servitude for 1 to 15 years was also prescribed for any one supplying, for gain, a pregnant woman with the means of procuring an abortion.

[3] Hodann, M., op. cit., pp. 228–9; Ungern-Sternberg, R. von, op. cit., p. 148.

burg Medical Board (Ärztekammer) in 1930 showed that 96 per cent. of the doctors replying regarded some modification of the existing law as desirable,[1] and discussion on the subject was still being actively continued when the National Socialists took over the government and began, almost immediately, to implement a combined race and population policy on lines laid down in *Mein Kampf*.[2] Since the present study is concerned largely with policies for promoting numerical increase, little attention will be paid to the racial or eugenic aspects of the German population policy, except to note that the positive inducements are offered only to 'Aryans' and, in general, only to persons who are free from serious inheritable defects. Detailed information on these points is given in more specialized works,[3] and here we need only note that National Socialist policy is anti-Malthusian in its conception, and aims at what Oestreich describes as 'not unrestricted, but racially qualified growth'.[4]

In June 1933 Dr. Frick, Minister of the Interior, gave the opening address to the group of population and race-policy experts gathered together in Berlin. He outlined the fall in the birth-rate in Germany since the beginning of the twentieth century, pointed out that not only the great cities but also the small towns were no longer capable of maintaining themselves by their own biological increase, and asserted that while healthy German families no longer produced even two children each, on the average, the poor and defective stocks were replacing themselves at twice or even three times that rate. To cure these ills a far-reaching policy was required. 'In the new Germany, the nation, the towns and the communities must judge and, where necessary, reconstruct the whole system of administration from the point of view of population policy.'[5] This speech sets the general tone of the

1 Harmsen, H., in Harmsen *et al.*, § *218. Sinn und Problematik des Abtreibungsparagraphen*, Berlin, [1931], p. 10. But very few believed that the complete medical freedom to procure abortion was desirable.

2 See Harmsen, H., 'Bevölkerungspolitik und Rassenpflege des Nationalsozialismus', *A.f.B.*, 1, 1933, pp. 3–13, and Oestreich, J., op. cit., pp. 20–6.

3 e.g. see Kühn, A., Staemmler, M., and Burgdörfer, F., op. cit., and Magnussen K., *Rassen- und bevölkerungspolitisches Rüstzeug*, Munich, 1936.

4 See Note VI*d*, p. 458.

5 'Ansprache des Herrn Reichsministers des Innern . . .', *Schriftenreihe des Reichsausschusses für Volksgesundheitsdienst*, Heft I, Berlin, 1933, pp. 7–8.

population measures applied by the new régime from 1933 onwards.

Unlike France and Belgium, National Socialist Germany has not, so far, introduced specific measures to prevent the sale of contraceptives[1] or to increase the penalties for procuring abortion. In fact, so far as abortion is concerned, the law, which is basically that introduced in 1926, has been made more liberal by explicitly allowing therapeutic abortion or abortion on eugenic grounds, in accordance with the Act for the 'prevention of hereditarily diseased offspring'.[2] Nevertheless, there has been a very strong drive against birth control and abortion, using methods other than the increasing of penalties. Among these methods should be included the positive inducements to marriage and child-bearing which will be discussed in later paragraphs, but we should also note the repressive and propagandist activity applied to birth control and abortion. In the first place, the police closed the birth-control centres, thus removing organizations which provided low cost contraceptives to a proportion of the working class, and which, by means of their periodicals, carried on birth-control propaganda.[3] At the same time the existing law could be applied to control the advertisement of contraceptives.[4] Under paragraph 184, section 3*a*, of the Penal Code, imprisonment up to one year and/or a fine were prescribed for any one publicly displaying, recommending, or giving information about methods or objects for preventing venereal diseases, if the action were carried on in an offensive manner.[5] The advertising of condoms could thus

[1] Though Schaffstein, F., 'Angriffe auf Rasse und Erbgut', in Gürtner, F., *Das kommende deutsche Strafrecht*, Besonderer Teil, 2nd ed., Berlin, 1936, pp. 115 ff., suggests such a law as a probable result of the Penal Law Commission, which recommended imprisonment, and in some cases penal servitude, for persons publicly urging or inciting others to practise family limitation (apparently with special reference to propaganda for the 'two-child family').

[2] See Note VI*e*, p. 459.

[3] This police action was begun almost as soon as the National Socialists took over the government. The explanation, in some cases, was that the organizations were being used as a cloak for Marxist activity. This reason was also given for closing some branches of the Reichsbund der Kinderreichen—See e.g. *A.f.B.*, 1, 1933–4, p. 55.

[4] See 'Öffentliches Ankündigen von Abtreibungs- und Verhütungsmitteln', *Soziale Praxis*, 1933, no. 27, cols. 830–1.

[5] *Strafgesetzbuch* (Beck publications), 5th ed., Munich and Berlin, 1938, p. 69. Notice that § 184, 3, prescribes the same penalties for the display, recommendation,

be restricted. Further control was given by a notice of 5 May 1936 issued by the Advertising Council for German business, according to which the advertising of methods and objects for curing or alleviating venereal diseases, or for preventing or terminating pregnancy, was allowed only to 'doctors, chemists or persons authorised to trade in such means or apparatus, or in scientific journals which only appeal to such professional circles'. The advertising of means for preventing or terminating pregnancy was allowed only with the permission of the Advertising Council.[1] For suppressing illegal abortion two new legislative measures were introduced. First, under the Act of 26 May 1933, paragraphs 219 and 220 were reintroduced into the Penal Code.[2] The 1933 Act prescribed imprisonment for up to two years, or a fine, for any one publicly advertising or recommending any means for procuring abortion, or displaying such means in a public place.[3] Similar penalties applied to persons offering their own or other people's services for undertaking or furthering abortion.[4] These clauses could be used for suppressing the trade in abortifacients of which so many doctors had previously complained.[5] Secondly, under the fourth order—passed on 18 July 1935—for administering the Act for the 'prevention of hereditarily diseased offspring', it was stipulated that every induced abortion, every miscarriage occurring before the completion of the thirty-second week of pregnancy, and every premature birth must be notified in writing to the competent medical officer within three days.[6] This,

&c., of objects intended for 'lecherous' (*unzüchtig*) purposes, and contraceptives could, if desired, be included in that category.

[1] Document kindly supplied by the Secretary of the Inter-Departmental Committee on Abortion.

[2] These were not the old paragraphs 219 and 220 which were abrogated when, under the 1926 Act, the law relating to abortion was modified and compressed into paragraph 218.

[3] This does not, however, apply if the means which are used for medically prescribed abortion are advertised or recommended to doctors or other persons allowed to trade in such articles, or in professional medical or pharmacological journals.

[4] *Strafgesetzbuch*, pp. 76–7.

[5] See, e.g., Schrader, E., 'Wie könnte durch das Gesetz unerlaubte Schwangerschaftsunterbrechung bekämpft werden?'—*A.f.S.H.*, 1926–7. pp. 165–7, wrote: '. . . Aber in Deutschland hält man die Kurierfreiheit aufrecht und wundert sich über die Zahl der Aborte. Difficile est satiram non scribere!'

[6] The persons responsible for this notification are primarily the doctor or midwife called in to help. But any one else called in to help (except relatives or persons in the

too, might have appreciable results. Women who previously were prepared to undergo illegal abortions, knowing that post-abortive complications could be attended to by a doctor, and that the abortions would not be notified, may now be deterred by the fear of possible legal proceedings from terminating their pregnancies. On the other hand, such action might have the effect of increasing the morbid consequences of illegal abortion by reducing the number of women who, in view of the legal risks involved, are prepared to seek medical treatment for post-abortive complications.

In addition to these legislative measures there has been an increase in the stringency with which the law relating to abortion is applied. A letter from the Ministry of Justice[1] states that since 1933 the law has been applied with special rigour and that, in particular, police drives have led to the discovery of a large number of 'abortion centres' (*Abtreibungsstellen*) which, under the pre-1933 practice of investigating only those cases brought to the attention of the authorities, necessarily remained unknown. This, it is said, accounts for the increase in the number of prosecutions for illegal abortion. A similar explanation is given by Dr. Stolzenburg, of the Ministry of Justice, of the 70 per cent. increase in the number of accused persons in 1937 as compared with 1936, and of the 44 per cent. further increase in the first quarter of 1938 as compared with the average for 1937.[2] It is certainly true that the figures given in Table 25 show a decrease in the ratio between abortions and normal confinements after 1933, but it is difficult to decide how far this trend supports the official argument. We may note that the coming to power of the National Socialists was not immediately followed by any significant increase in the number of persons accused of criminal abortion, and that in 1935 and 1936 the numbers were considerably below the pre-1933 level, except as regards abortion performed with a view to profit. Not until 1937 was the number of accused

same household as the pregnant woman) is also liable to inform the medical officer if no doctor or midwife has been called in, or if the doctor or midwife has been prevented from giving the notification. See *RGB*, 25 July 1935, p. 1037.

[1] To the present writer, dated 6 Oct. 1938.

[2] Dr. Stolzenburg, 'Entwicklung der Kriminalität', *Deutsche Justiz*, 17 June 1938, pp. 933–4.

persons seriously larger than that customary in the days of the Weimar Republic, and since the police drive against abortionists was initiated in 1933, the higher figures for 1937 and 1938 may in fact indicate a real increase in abortion frequency in those years.[1] But whatever the results may have been—and they will be considered in more detail later—there is ample evidence of official desire to suppress or at least very markedly reduce the practice of family limitation, whether that practice is in the form of contraception or of abortion. The medical profession lends its help in urging the fulfilment of motherhood and the various medical committees have issued statements concerning the duties of doctors in the National Socialist State.[2] The government itself has set up a 'Bureau for Explaining Population Policies', and either through this, or through the various women's organizations,[3] has arranged campaigns for the raising of large families. The association protecting the interests of large families—the Reichsbund der Kinderreichen Deutschlands—has been attached to the race-policy department of the National Socialist party and, with a membership of some 300,000 German families[4] of sound heredity, has itself become a powerful organ of propaganda, expressing its opinions in a monthly journal, *Völkische Wacht*.

[1] See Note VI *f*, p. 459.

[2] Hodann, M., in a report on Germany, in *International Medical Group for the Investigation of Contraception*, fifth issue, London, 1934, pp. 22–5, cites the statement issued by the Berlin Medical Council in 1933: '. . . The Berlin Medical Council will not permit weak or malicious practitioners to counter the far-sighted plans of the government for the future of the Nation. . . . The Council warns all practitioners who may seek to save their practice in abortion by alleging that they only get cases in which abortion has already been attempted, that proceedings will be taken against every evil-doer who dares to injure our sacred healthy race.'

[3] Ibid., p. 25 cites the *Opferdienst der Deutschen Frau* of 5 May 1933 as asserting that 'the use of contraceptives means a violation of nature, a degradation of womanhood, motherhood and love'. See also the very interesting study of Kirkpatrick, C., *Woman in Nazi Germany*, London, 1939, especially pp. 149–50, and ch. viii. Kirkpatrick notes, p. 155, that 'one informant told of a small village in which a surprising number of peasant women, approaching middle age, shamefacedly and perhaps a little indignantly produced children at a time when prior children were well grown. The explanation given was that they were no longer able to obtain the usual abortion on which they had come to rely.'

[4] The term 'large family' applies to families with four or more children. If, however, the mother is widowed, the minimum number is lowered to three children. See Ballarin, H.-G., and Rössler, H., *Sonderfürsorge für Kinderreiche*, 2nd ed., Leipzig, n.d. (but not earlier than the end of 1936), p. 70.

On the positive side, the first important measure introduced was the Act of 1 June 1933 designed to reduce unemployment and containing, in section 5, clauses relating to the provision of marriage loans. The Act came into force on 1 August 1933, and was subjected to various modifications both before and after this date.[1] The Act itself was quite short and simple, stating that marriage loans of up to 1,000 marks could be obtained, free of interest, to be repaid in monthly instalments of one per cent., thus refunding the loan in just over eight years. The loans were to be granted in the form of coupons to be used for the purchase of furniture and household equipment, and the primary conditions for granting the loan were that the future wife had been gainfully employed for at least six months during the previous two years, that she gave up this employment upon marriage at the latest, and that she was pledged not subsequently to take up paid employment unless her husband became in need of help.[2] The first modifications[3] of the Act appeared in the regulations issued on 20 June 1933. First, loans might be granted to persons who were already married, provided that the marriage had not taken place before 3 June 1933. Secondly, the applicants had to fulfil certain additional requirements—they had to be German citizens, politically 'right-minded', free from hereditary mental or physical defects which would prevent their marriage from being in the interest of the community, and their character and previous conduct had to be such as to make it reasonable to suppose that they would not evade their obligation to repay the loan. A quarter of the initial loan was to be cancelled on the birth of each child and, in addition, the parents

1 For analysing the changes in the Act the present writer makes use particularly of the collection of legal texts given in Richter, V., and Völker, H., *Das Deutsche Eherecht*, Berlin, n.d. (but probably the beginning of 1936), pp. 169–205.

2 The 1933 Act stated that she should abstain from paid employment so long as her husband had an income of more than 125 marks per month (*RGB*, 1933, i, 2 June, pp. 326–7 at p. 327).

3 Notice that in the original Act, Section V, Para. I, clause 2, a woman was not recognized as having been gainfully employed if she had been engaged in household tasks or in a business belonging to a close relative. But in applying the Act this clause was modified, so that where the future wife had been engaged in household tasks at home the loan was granted if, on her marriage, she was replaced by a domestic servant, a similar condition applying if she had worked in a concern belonging to a close relative.

might, at the birth of a child, be allowed to postpone further repayments for a period of up to twelve months. Further modifications followed, those made before December 1933 generally extending the range of persons to whom loans could be granted. Thus the regulation of 26 July allowed loans to be given where the future wife had worked for at least six months in the period from 1 June 1926 and 31 May 1933. Similarly, the marriage conditions were relaxed. The regulation of 26 July allowed loans to be given to persons who were already married, provided that the marriage had not taken place before 1 June 1932, while the regulation of 22 August allowed the Minister of Finance to make further relaxations in exceptional cases.[1] But by the regulation of 2 December, applying as from 11 December, these transitional relaxations were stopped. Few changes were made in the next three years, and the conditions to be fulfilled for being granted a loan in that period were substantially those enunciated in the ministerial circular issued in February 1935.[2] That is, loans of up to 1,000 marks were to be granted to persons who wished to marry, provided that the future wife had been gainfully employed in Germany for at least nine months in the previous two years, and that she gave up this work before receiving the loan.[3] Applicants had, altogether, to satisfy eleven requirements as regards citizenship, racial stock, political views, freedom from inheritable defects, infectious diseases, &c., and their financial circumstances had to be such that, with the help of the loan, they would be able to set up a fairly secure household. The loans therefore applied to members of the working class and lower middle class.

The funds for granting the loans were raised initially by a tax on all unmarried men and women with incomes of not less than 75 marks per month. Originally it was estimated that this tax would produce about 220 million marks per year, but the actual revenue was much below this figure, while the loans granted up to February 1934 amounted to

[1] See also *Soziale Praxis*, 1933, no. 38, cols. 1112–14.

[2] *Erläuterung zum Gesetz über Förderung der Eheschließungen vom 5. Juli 1933 in der Fassung vom 21. Februar 1935.*

[3] The conditions of replacement of women who had been occupied with household duties at home, &c., were the same as noted previously.

120·5 million marks. This accounts for the tightening of regulations and also for the marked reduction in the size of the average loan. In August and September 1933 the average loan was about 730 marks, but in October it was agreed not to give more than 800 marks save in exceptional cases, and in February 1934 the average loan was only about 560 marks. It was later and more accurately estimated that the annual revenue from the 'bachelor tax' would amount to about 150 million marks, of which 15 million would go to the general national budget, while the remaining 135 millions would be used to provide about 275,000 marriage loans, thus averaging just under 500 marks per loan.[1] With the reform in the income-tax, in October 1934, the levy for marriage loans was incorporated as part of the general structure of income-tax. Up to the end of 1938, 1,121,707 marriage loans had been given, and 980,365 cancellations made on account of births.[2]

It should be remembered that the provision of marriage loans was part of the broader legislation for reducing unemployment. Herr Reinhardt, Secretary of State in the Ministry of Finance—the official to whose initiative the marriage loans were due—reckoned that each marriage under the Act might provide work for two young men. One man would be employed in place of the woman who gave up her paid work, and another might be employed because of the increased demand for furniture and other household goods. In fact, he believed that marriages would be increased by about 200,000 per year, and that unemployment would be reduced by about 400,000 in the first year and by 200,000 in each subsequent year. This would also mean a continuous reduction in the annual cost of unemployment relief, an increase in the revenue derived from taxation, and a general improvement in the German economic situation.[3] The

1 *Erläuterung zum Gesetz*, p. 3, gives an estimated distribution of the 275,000 loans as 5,000 at 1,000 marks each; 15,000 at 800 marks; 30,000 at 700 marks; 100,000 at 600 marks; 60,000 at 500 marks; 40,000 at 400 marks; and 20,000 at 300 marks. This totals 150 million marks, but Burgdörfer, in Kühn, Staemmler, and Burgdörfer, op. cit., p. 286, which is of later date (1936), gives the figure of 135 million marks. See also *Soziale Praxis*, 1934, no. 15, cols. 444–8.

2 *Wirtschaft und Statistik*, 1939, p. 110. This excludes Austria and the Sudetenland.

3 *Erläuterung zum Gesetz*, pp. 1–5.

anxiety to reduce male unemployment must thus be regarded as one of the main reasons—probably the most important one—for the campaign against 'double earnings' (*Doppelverdienertum*) on the part of husband and wife,[1] and for the general attempt to drive women back into the home. The attempt was, of course, accompanied by mass propaganda, carried out especially by women's organizations, which came under the control of the National Socialist government, emphasizing that a woman's place was in the home, that women should confine themselves to work which would not conflict with their maternal functions, and that, in Professor Kirkpatrick's translation of one of the many slogans posted up at the time, 'A job will not bring happiness near, the home alone is your proper sphere'.[2] But the attitude changed as, under the growing needs of public works, armament manufacture, and military service, the unemployment figures were reduced from 4·804 million registered unemployed persons in 1933 to only 912,000 in 1937.[3] In fact, there was an increasing demand for women in industry, and those clauses in the Marriage Loans Act which made the loan conditional upon giving up paid employment were gradually relaxed. By a circular of 30 October 1936 married women who had received marriage loans were allowed to take temporary work for the Christmas trade, or in connexion with stocktaking sales,[4] and subsequent circulars[5] extended this permission to a wider field until, by an Act of 3 November 1937, taking effect as from 1 October of the same year, paid employment in general was thrown open to these women.[6] Henceforth the Marriage Loans Act was purely a measure for encouraging marriage and the raising of children, its possible effect heightened by the fact that the repayments were to be

[1] See, e.g., 'Die Notwendigkeit der Beachtung bevölkerungspolitischer Grundsätze bei der Regelung des Doppelverdienertums', *A.f.B.*, 2, 1933–4, pp. 125–6.

[2] Op. cit., p. 194.

[3] *Year-Book of Labour Statistics, 1938*, p. 53. After 31 July 1933 the statistics of unemployed persons did not include persons working in labour camps.

[4] *Soziale Praxis*, 1936, no. 48, col. 1410.

[5] See ibid., 1937, no. 14, col. 408; no. 43, cols. 1279–80.

[6] Ibid., 1937, no. 48, col. 1429. But if they were employed for more than half the working days in a month, the loan repayments were to be at the rate of 3 per cent. per month instead of 1 per cent.

used for giving special grants to families with dependent children.[1]

These special grants were first introduced by an executive order of 26 September 1935, applying the general order of 15 September of the same year. They were to be given to families which had four or more children (including step-children and adopted children) under 16 years of age, on condition that the parents were German citizens of unobjectionable character and earlier history, that both parents and children were free from inheritable mental or physical defects, and that the financial circumstances of the parents were such that they could not, by their own efforts, provide the goods necessary for the household. For each child under 16 years of age a grant of up to 100 marks could be given, the maximum amount obtainable by a given family not to exceed 1,000 marks. So long as this amount had not been exceeded, further grants for the same purpose could be allocated for children born subsequently. The grants were to be given in the form of coupons which could be used for buying furniture, household utensils, and linen. It was estimated that there were in Germany some 750,000 families with four or more children, and, up to the beginning of June 1936, about 75 million marks had been spent in giving these grants to about 190,000 families.[2] Since the available funds were not sufficient to allow grants to be given to all the families, they were restricted in the first place to families with six or more children, or to those four-child or five-child families whose financial circumstances were exceptionally bad.[3] Various modifications were made by subsequent regulations, and the scheme was codified by the sixth executive order, dated 31 August 1937.[4] Comparing the clauses

[1] This provision is specified in the *Erläuterung zum Gesetz*, p. 5, as taking effect from 1939 onwards. But as will be seen later, such grants (*Kinderbeihilfen*) were introduced before that date, under a regulation of 15 Sept. 1935. See Ballarin, H. G., and Rössler, H., op. cit., pp. 8 ff., from which most of the subsequent analysis of *Kinderbeihilfen* is taken. [2] Burgdörfer, in Kühn, Staemmler, and Burgdörfer, op. cit., p. 291.

[3] See 'Runderlass des Reichsfinanzministers über Kinderbeihilfen an kinderreiche Familien', 10 Oct. 1935—Richter and Völker, op. cit., esp. pp. 214–15.

[4] *Kinderbeihilfen für kinderreiche Familien* (Reichsfinanzministerium), Berlin, 1937, pp. 7–14. In this official publication it is stated, p. 12, that 'linen' (*Wäsche*) definitely includes stockings and underclothing, provided that they are not made mainly of real silk.

of this order with those of the first one, few significant changes are apparent. We should, however, note the inclusion in the scheme of 'settlement grants' (*Siedlungs-Kinderbeihilfen*), which allow the grants given in respect of the children to be used for the acquisition or improvement of a settlement.[1] Still more recently, by decree of 20 December 1938, it was decided that families which did not produce their fourth child until after 1 January 1939 should be given the grants only if these were used in connexion with the acquisition or improvement of settlements. This also applies to families which had received only part of their grants by the specified date.[2]

The grants described in the previous paragraph are categorized as *einmalige Kinderbeihilfen*—that is, they are given once only. But a system of *laufende Kinderbeihilfen* has also been developed—grants given regularly in respect of dependent children, and therefore really coming under the term family allowances. As a prelude to the description of these grants it is useful to outline the history of family allowances in Germany, and to mention some of the allowances given by bodies other than the central government at the present time. Family allowances were first introduced on any scale in Germany in the early post-War period,[3] largely in response to the marked rise in prices in 1920. The movement grew with some rapidity and by 1922 there were eleven important equalization funds, partly based on French models.[4] But the development was not consistent, and in 1923 it was authoritatively stated that there was scarcely an industry in which family allowances had been introduced by all the firms, though, on the other hand, there was scarcely an industry from which allowances were completely absent.[5]

[1] There is no precise translation of this term, which includes the acquisition of a house, as well as of an agricultural holding.

[2] *Soziale Praxis*, 1939, no. 3, cols. 182–4.

[3] Though, according to Vibart, H. H. R., op. cit., p. 42, as many as thirty-one cities were, by 1912, paying family allowances to their municipal employees. There was also some spread of the system to private enterprise during the War, but in 1918–19 most of the schemes appear to have been abandoned.

[4] Hofmann, H., *Familienausgleichskassen in Frankreich und Deutschland*, Dresden, 1936, pp. 69–70.

[5] Fichtel, J., *Der Familienlohn*, Munich, 1934, p. 13, citing the *Reichsarbeitsblatt*, 1923, no. 1. Fichtel, pp. 13–44, gives the early history of family allowances in

At the same time the central government entered the field with the Act of 30 April 1920 (*Besoldungsgesetz*). This was modified by a similar Act of 16 December 1927, under which a grant of 20 marks per month was given to government employees in respect of each legitimate child,[1] primarily until the child was 16 years of age, but continuing up to 21 years if the child was still being educated and did not have a personal income of 30 marks or more per month. The grant was extended indefinitely for children who were physically or mentally incapable of taking employment and who did not have personal incomes of 30 marks or more per month.[2] This Act was in turn modified by a decree of 5 June 1931, under which the allowances were set at 10 marks per month for the first child entitled to the grant, 20 for the second, 25 each for the third and fourth children, and 30 marks per month for each subsequent child.[3] These grants were given to about 80,000 Reich officials and members of the army and navy, costing about 28 million marks per year.[4] But these governmental allowances were almost the only ones that survived the havoc of the inflation period and the opposition of a strong section of the trade-union movement. The only other important scheme in existence in the early nineteen-thirties was that established by the pharmacists. This scheme, which had been initiated in 1919, was itself wrecked by the inflation, but it was established again in 1925 on the basis of contributions from employees only, and broadened in 1927 by an agreement—supported by the German industrial court—that half the contributions should be paid by the employers. The contributions and allowances were modified in 1933 and have subsequently been of the following amounts. The total contribution is 150 marks per quarter for qualified pharmacists and 90

Germany in considerable detail. See also 'The family wage system abroad', *Ministry of Labour Gazette*, March 1923, pp. 86–8.

[1] Also for stepchildren, adopted children, and for illegitimate children if paternity had been established and if the official was responsible for their full support.

[2] *Reichsbesoldungsgesetz vom 16. Dezember 1927*, Textausgabe, Berlin, 1928, pp. 6–7.

[3] Jessen, A., *Was kostet dein Kind?*, Berlin, 1937, p. 45.

[4] Information in a document prepared by the German Ministry of Foreign Affairs, accompanying a letter from the Commercial Counsellor of the British Embassy in Berlin, dated 12 March 1935. See also Kuczynski, R. R., *Post-War Labor Conditions in Germany*, Washington, 1925, pp. 144–5.

marks per quarter for other employees, half these contributions being paid by the employers. The allowances (given to employees only) are complex, grants being made for length of service after being qualified, and for the number of years spent in the same job, as well as in respect of wives and dependent children under 18 years of age, or up to 21 years if they are continuing their education and have no private income. Considering only the family allowances, they have, since the fourth quarter of 1933, been 60 marks per quarter for a wife, and 70 marks per quarter for the first child. The grant for subsequent children increases by 10 marks per quarter up to and including the third child, then by 20, 30, 40, 50, and 60 marks per quarter, so that 290 marks per quarter are paid for the eighth child, while for the ninth and for each subsequent child 360 marks per quarter would be paid. A father of nine dependent children would therefore receive 1,550 marks per quarter, plus a further 60 marks if his wife were still alive.[1]

As might be expected, the National Socialist government encouraged existing family allowance schemes and sponsored new ones. Thus, for example, it sponsored the creation of an equalization fund for German panel doctors, which came into existence as from 1 April 1934 under a decree dated 22 February of the same year, issued by Dr. Wagner, medical leader for the Reich. The provisions were changed by a further decree of 19 September 1934, taking effect as from 1 July of that year, and under the new regulations funds were to be raised by a 2 per cent. levy on the earnings of all panel doctors and sent directly by the separate branches to the central family allowance fund. Doctors who earned at least 1,000 marks per year from their panel practice were entitled to allowances of 50 marks per month for each child from the third onwards, these allowances being paid until the child had completed his twenty-first year of age, though they might be continued to 24 years if the child was still being educated. For daughters payment ceased three months after

[1] Hofmann, H., op. cit., pp. 80–5; Hadrich, J., 'Der Ausgleich der Familienlasten bei den Apothekern', *A.f.B.*, 2, 1933–4, pp. 92–6. See also H. Schlipp, 'Erfahrungen mit der Zuschusskasse (Familienausgleichskasse) der Deutschen Apotheker', *A.f.B.*, 4, 1938, pp. 265–75.

marriage—if, that is, they married before they were 21 or 24 years of age—and the allowance due for the last three months might be paid in a lump sum if so desired.[1] A similar scheme was devised for panel dentists, and has been in operation since 1 January 1935. In return for a levy of 1 per cent. of their earnings, dentists who earn 500 marks or more per year from their panel practice are entitled to allowances of 30 marks per month for each dependent child from the third child onwards.[2] We may also note that in the cigar industry family allowances have been given since 1936, and are now at the rate of 2 marks per week when the family contains up to 2 children under 15 years of age, rising to 5 marks per week when there are 7 or more children under 15 years of age to care for.[3]

The family allowance schemes mentioned above cover relatively small numbers of children, and touched only the fringes of the problem. The grants given by the government —the *laufende Kinderbeihilfen* referred to previously—cover a much larger population. They were begun, as from 1 July 1936, under a decree of 24 March of the same year, and consisted of cash grants—sent by postal orders—of 10 marks per month for the fifth and each subsequent child not having completed his or her sixteenth year of age, in families with five or more children not over 16 years of age, and fulfilling certain other requirements. These were: that the parents were German citizens, of unobjectionable character and previous history, that the head of the household was to be employed in an occupation coming under the health insurance regulations,[4] and that the income available for supporting the children was not more than 185 marks per month where there were only five children.[5] Herr Reinhardt,

[1] Ballarin and Rössler, op. cit., pp. 67–8; Hofmann, op. cit., pp. 85–95; Reichert, ., 'Die Ausgleichskasse der kassenärztlichen Vereinigung Deutschlands', *A.f.B.*, 3, 933–4, pp. 183–8; and *Soziale Praxis*, 1937, no. 16, cols. 465–6.

[2] Hofmann, op. cit., pp. 96–102 and Jessen, op. cit., pp. 172–3.

[3] Ibid., pp. 173–6; Hauffe, R., 'Neue Formen der Lohngestaltung in der Zigarrenerstellung', *Soziale Praxis*, 1936, no. 3, cols. 66–72; Hauffe, R., 'Ermässigung es Umlagesatzes für die Lohnausgleichskasse und Erhöhung der Familienzulage der Zigarrenherstellung', ibid., 1936, no. 13, cols. 387–90.

[4] The term is: 'muss sich in einer invaliden- oder krankenversicherungspflichtigen ätigkeit befinden . . .' (Ballarin and Rössler, op. cit., p. 27).

[5] This clause was specified under the executive order of 20 Aug. 1936. Under the

speaking in May 1937, said that these grants had been given to 240,000 families, in respect of 320,000 children.[1] Since then, the scope and size of the grants have been very appreciably extended, as the result of a decree of 13 March 1938. Four particularly important provisions were made. First, the upper income limit was raised to 8,000 marks per year.[2] (The clause relating to employment in an occupation coming under the health insurance scheme had been removed earlier.) Secondly, the allowances were available for each child up to 21 years of age, provided that they were still continuing their education, or were incapable of taking up employment, and that their personal income was less than 30 marks per month. Thirdly, in addition to the ordinary family allowances due from the fifth child, there were further allowances (*erweiterte laufende Kinderbeihilfen*) available from the third child.[3] These allowances were also 10 marks per month and per child, so that a family conforming to the income requirements, and having seven children under the upper age limit would be entitled to a grant of 80 marks per month. At the upper income limit—8,000 marks per year—this grant would represent 12 per cent. of the basic income. For the bulk of the population the proportionate value of the grant would, of course, be much higher. Finally, the Minister of Finance was empowered to give special or free places,

order of 31 Aug. 1937 it was specified that the income in this case should not be more than 2,100 marks per year. Under this order, too, the condition of employment in an occupation coming under the health insurance scheme was omitted. The order of 31 Aug. 1937 also specified an excess of 120 marks per year as resulting in the withdrawal of the grant due to one child. The provisions of the various decree and regulations are here treated very summarily. For full details see *Kinderbeihilfe für kinderreiche Familien*, op. cit., pp. 14–22, and Ballarin and Rössler, op. cit pp. 27–40.

[1] Jessen, op. cit., pp. 115–16.

[2] As in the order of 31 Aug. 1937, there were also certain property qualification —the total property not to be more than 50,000 marks in the case of a family wit five children, the upper limit rising by 10,000 marks for each subsequent chil Where the child was illegitimate, the property of its father was not taken into ac count.

[3] There were certain income conditions—apart from the size of the total incom which was to be the same as for the ordinary allowances. At least one-third of th income was to be derived from work in the employment of some other person, c from emoluments (*Bezüge*), or from tax free income as defined by a specific sectio of the 1938 income-tax Act. Note that as regards the minimum number of childre necessary for allowances to be obtained, special relaxations were made for widow divorcees, and unmarried women—as in the case of the ordinary allowances.

or educational assistance (*Ausbildungsbeihilfen*) for enabling the children of large families—that is, families with four or more living children, of whatever age—to attend 'middle' or 'upper' schools, technical or secondary schools. The grants in this category, given as from the winter term of 1938–9, may include, in addition to school fees, a payment of 600 marks per year to cover the costs incurred for children who have to live outside of their own homes.[1]

Marriage loans, lump-sum grants, and family allowances have been the chief material encouragements given by the National Socialist government to influence marriage and fertility. There are, however, many less important or less direct inducements given by the State, by the local authorities, and by other public institutions, and it is important, in order to complete the picture, briefly to describe these measures. We may note, for example, the continuance and extension of the programme of rural settlement begun, as Staudinger points out,[2] in 1919, under a régime dissimilar from that of the National Socialists, but particularly emphasized to-day because the creation of a strong peasantry is one of the explicit objects of the present government. The reasons for that desire are both practical—an increase in agricultural production and also, since at present rural families are generally larger than urban, an increase in human fertility—and mystical, the latter being bound up with current 'Nordic' and 'Aryan' mythology. Large estates and national property have been divided into small-holdings, the average size of the new holdings rising since 1933 from 12·3 to just under 19 hectares, and sold on mortgage to applicants who fulfil certain requirements relating to racial stock, heredity, marriage, and agricultural capabilities.[3] Special efforts are made to keep the land in the possession of the family which obtains it and no inheritance tax is levied

[1] For further details concerning the provisions of the 1938 decree, see *Kinderbeihilfen für kinderreiche Familien* (*Sechste KFV. DB. in der ab 1. April 1938 geltenden Fassung der Siebenten KFV. DB.*), (Reichsfinanzministerium), Berlin, 1938.

[2] Staudinger, H., 'Germany's population miracle', *Social Research*, May 1938, pp. 125–48, at p. 142.

[3] A very interesting discussion of the rural settlement scheme is given by Hankins, F. H., 'German policies for increasing births', *American Journal of Sociology*, March 1937, pp. 630–52, at pp. 632–41. The applicants must at least be engaged to be married.

on it. Of such holdings, 20,359 were provided between 1933 and 1938 inclusive, covering a total of 327,430 hectares. It should be noted, however, that 57,457 similar holdings, less rigorously allocated, were set up between 1919 and 1932 inclusive, covering a total of 602,110 hectares, so that neither the intention nor the practice originated with the National Socialists. Provision is also made for increasing the size of existing holdings. Between 1933 and 1938 inclusive 63,912 extra plots of land (*Landzulagen*) were allocated, amounting to a total of 126,075 hectares, as compared with 96,147 plots, totalling 142,098 hectares, in the period 1919 to 1932 inclusive.[1]

As part of this general policy of promoting the development of the rural population, modifications have been made in the regulations concerning marriage loans, affecting loan repayments due after 1 August 1938, and all new loans. Under a decree of 7 July 1938,[2] which applies only to the rural population, a marriage loan can be obtained on special terms if either the future husband or the future wife has been continuously employed in an agricultural or rural occupation for at least five years. If that condition is fulfilled, loan repayments will be postponed for as long as the partner concerned continues to be employed in such an occupation, with a maximum postponement of ten years. If the work has been continuously carried on for ten years after the marriage, all loan repayments are cancelled, and the loan therefore becomes a gift.[3] The regulations do not act as a direct encouragement to the raising of children, since the loan can be cancelled merely by not changing the nature of one's employment. Further provisions for the rural population

1 See Note VIg, p. 459.

2 'Verordnung zur Förderung der Landbevölkerung, vom 7. Juli 1938', *RGB*, 8 July 1938, pp. 835–7.

3 The general nature of the occupation has, therefore, to be the same for fifteen years for either husband or wife—five years before and ten years after the marriage. The other conditions are the same as for ordinary marriage loans, except that if the future wife has worked in some agricultural occupation for her parents, grandparents, or great-grandparents, the granting of a loan is not conditional upon replacing her by paid labour after marriage. The loan is, of course, also cancelled by 25 per cent. on the birth of each child, so that the couple can choose between the two ways of avoiding repayments. The term 'agricultural' includes forestry. See Plischke, A., *Ehestandsdarlehen, Einrichtungsdarlehen und Einrichtungszuschüsse*, Berlin, 1939, pp. 22–7.

are contained in the same decree. These are household loans, applying to persons married after 30 June 1938, and household grants, applying to those married since 31 December 1933. The household loans, which are independent of, and can be obtained in addition to marriage loans, are granted to the rural population on the same terms as marriage loans. But they are paid in cash, instead of in coupons, can be spent on a wider range of goods, including cattle or machinery and tools for use in the particular rural occupation in which the husband or wife is engaged, and amount to 800 marks if both husband and wife have been continuously employed in an agricultural or rural occupation during the last five years preceding their marriage. If only one partner fulfils this condition, the loan is 400 marks. If both husband and wife continue to work in an agricultural or rural occupation for another ten years, 500 marks of the loan will be cancelled, and a further 100 marks for each additional year. The cancellations are halved if only one partner fulfils the condition. But if the continuity is broken, the remainder of the loan must be repaid at the rate of 3 per cent. per month, free of interest. Household grants are direct gifts, paid in cash, and can be repeated every five years. They are obtainable on the same terms as household loans, though they are restricted to agricultural or rural wage earners and employees and amount to 400 marks if both husband and wife have worked continuously in an agricultural or rural occupation for the last five years, and 200 marks if only one partner has fulfilled this condition. In either case the applicant has to declare that he intends to continue the same kind of work, and the provision of further grants is also conditional upon uninterrupted employment in an agricultural or a rural occupation.

Among the more general measures should be included the changes in the income, property, and inheritance taxes, to the advantage of large families. In the income-tax, which, according to Burgdörfer,[1] had formerly been the only tax taking family circumstances into consideration, the deductions for children were raised considerably. Under the earlier tax the exemptions for a family of husband, wife,

[1] In Kühn, Staemmler, and Burgdörfer, op. cit., p. 304.

and four children could not have amounted to more than 1,850 marks, but under the new income-tax law of 16 October 1934 they might amount to 2,900 marks.[1] These sums would be deducted from the income before calculating the tax to be paid. Further rebates were also given on the net taxable income, in respect of dependent children. Under the former law a person liable to assessed income-tax would obtain, for each dependent child, a rebate of 8 per cent. of the income over 720 marks, but not more than 600 marks per child or 8,000 marks for all the children in the family. According to the new law, however, the rebate was to be 15 per cent. for the first child, rising to 100 per cent. for six children, these rebates having certain maximum amounts and applying only within certain income limits.[2] A man with a taxable income—after allowing for the initial deductions—of 10,000 marks per year, would have to pay 1,984 marks in tax if he were unmarried, but only 220 marks if he were married and had five dependent children. The term 'dependent child' has also been extended to include a child up to 25 years of age—provided that he is still continuing his education—instead of 21 years as in earlier provisions.[3] In still more recent years the growing pressure of rearmament has, however, created the need for increasing the national revenue derived from taxation, while solving the unemployment problem, and in 1939 the income-tax law was redesigned to increase the yield initially by 200 million marks, rising to 300 or 320 million marks by 1940. The law of 17 February 1939 therefore omitted the deductions

[1] This latter figure is composed of 500 marks for the insurance of the husband and his family, plus an exemption of 300 marks for the wife, 300 marks for the first child, 400 for the second, 600 for the third, and 800 for the fourth. For each subsequent child an exemption of 1,000 marks was allowed. To encourage the employment of domestic servants—part of the campaign against unemployment—an exemption of 50 marks per month was allowed for each female domestic servant employed. See *Einkommensteuergesetz*, (Reichsfinanzministerium), Berlin, 1934, pp. 10 and 11, and *Reichssteuerblatt*, 8 Jan. 1935, p. 40. On the other hand, the exemptions for childless married couples and for unmarried persons were lower than under the 1925 Act.

[2] The limits and amounts do not, however, appear to be very clearly defined. See, e.g., *Reichssteuerblatt*, 18 Oct. 1934, p. 1197, and 8 Jan. 1935, p. 50.

[3] *Einkommensteuergesetz*, pp. 25 and 40. See also *Reichssteuerblatt*, 8 Jan. 1935, p. 50, and Barth, K., *Das Bevölkerungsproblem und seine Auswirkung in der neuen deutschen Steuerreform*, Leipzig, 1936, pp. 118–24.

allowable for the employment of domestic servants—this would increase the tax paid by about one million couples—and provided a number of separate tax tables. The highest relates to unmarried and widowed persons, and their tax was raised by 12½ per cent. Previously they paid 60 per cent. more than married persons, but as a result of the new Act they would pay 80 per cent. more. At the lowest end of the scale was the table relating to married persons with children, and between this and the first table a new table was inserted, relating to childless married couples, henceforth liable to a tax 40 per cent. above that paid by other married couples.[1] The term 'childless' applies to couples married for five years or more and still without children.[2] Comparable provisions were made under the property tax of 16 October 1934. Previously any one with property valued at over 20,000 marks was liable to the tax on the full value of the property, whereas under the new Act exemptions of 10,000 marks were granted for the taxpayer, his wife, and for each dependent child. A taxpayer owning property worth 35,000 marks and having a wife and three children would thus not be liable to any tax, whereas he would formerly have been taxed on the full 35,000 marks.[3] Under the new inheritance tax, promulgated on the same date, a tax-free inheritance of 30,000 marks was allowed for a child and 10,000 marks for a grandchild. When the inheritance exceeded the stipulated amount, tax was payable on the excess. The earlier law had allowed a tax-free inheritance of only 5,000 marks for a child or a grandchild, and if the inheritance was greater than this, tax was liable on the whole of it, including the first 5,000 marks.[4]

[1] They were not liable to this higher tax if their taxable incomes were not more than 1,800 marks per year, or if either partner was over 65 years of age, or—as a transition measure—if either partner completed 55 years of age in 1938 and if the taxable income in 1937 were not more than 12,000 marks.

[2] See *Soziale Praxis*, 1939, no. 6, cols. 375–6, and *RGB*, 24 Feb. 1939, pp. 283–6. Note that the 1934 income-tax law was also modified by the Act of 1 Feb. 1938. See *A.f.B.*, 3, 1938, pp. 215–17. The outbreak of war saw further increases in taxation.

[3] A further 10,000 marks was exempted, under the new Act, if the owner was incapable of working (or if he were over 60 years of age), and if his income was very small. See *Reichssteuerblatt*, 18 Oct. 1934, p. 1198, and *Reichsbewertungsgesetz (R. Bew. G.) und Vermögensteuergesetz (V.St.G.) vom 16. Oktober 1934*, (Reichsfinanzministerium), Berlin, 1935, pp. 51–4.

[4] *Reichssteuerblatt*, 18 Oct. 1934, p. 1198 and Ballarin and Rössler, op. cit., pp. 54–5.

Other governmental measures range from reductions in railway fares[1] for families with four or more unmarried children not over 18 years of age, to special preferences in the allocation of employment and to various Acts for providing cheap housing accommodation. Under regulations issued in August 1934, for example, attempts were made to balance the age composition of persons employed in various enterprises and public offices, and particularly to replace workers and employees under 25 years of age with the fathers of large families.[2] In the field of housing the government has been concerned not only with the general problem of the housing shortage, but also with the special problems of large families with little means, of suburban building, of communal settlements, of the provision of more extensive and cheaper methods of obtaining mortgages for building, and of the level of rents. Nevertheless, there is still a marked housing shortage. In 1932 about one million families did not have their own dwellings,[3] and in spite of an extensive building programme the number of new households has increased more rapidly than that of houses. In the period 1933 to 1937 inclusive there was an increase of about 1·789 million households, while the net increase in dwellings—including reconstructed and altered dwellings—was only about 1·334 millions, resulting in a total of about 1·5 million families without their own dwellings at the beginning of 1938.[4] To some extent, therefore, the object which found expression in marriage loans has been defeated by lagging building activity. At the other end of the population question—infertility—two recent measures are of considerable interest. In 1936 a special committee of the Reich Insurance Office

[1] Ballarin and Rössler, op. cit., pp. 66–7; and Harmsen, H., 'Die Fahrpreisermässigung für kinderreiche Familien bei der Deutschen Reichsbahngesellschaft' *A.f.B.*, 4, 1933–4, pp. 257–60.

[2] See Note VI*h*, p. 460.

[3] From a statement by Reichsarbeitsminister Seldte, *A.f.B.*, 3, 1935, pp. 199–204

[4] The calculation is derived from data given in Seldte, F., *Sozialpolitik im Dritten Reich 1933–1938*, Munich and Berlin, 1939, p. 172, which should be consulted, pp. 145–212, for details concerning the housing programme. Fey, W., *Der künftige Wohnungs- und Siedlungsbau*, Berlin, 1939, p. 10, also gives an estimate, for the end of 1937, of 1·5 million more households than dwellings. See also Fey, W., *Leistungen und Aufgaben im deutschen Wohnungs- und Siedlungsbau*, Berlin, 1936 *passim*. Notice that the practice, on the part of landlords, of preferring families with no or few children, was still evident in 1937—see statement by Dr. Knorr, *A.f.B.* 5–6, 1937, pp. 425–6.

decided that infertility on the part of a married woman was, from the point of view of social insurance, to be reckoned as an illness if it could be cured by medical treatment and if its cure were in the interest of the community.[1] Secondly, the German marriage law of 6 July 1938 provided that either partner to a marriage can petition for the dissolution of that marriage if the other partner has become prematurely[2] infertile after the marriage, or persistently refuses, without valid reasons, to beget or conceive children, or either uses or causes to be used unjustified[3] means for preventing the occurrence of births. Finally we may note that, in apparent imitation of France, the German government has provided medals for the mothers of large families. The medals are in three grades, the lowest being for mothers who had given birth to four or five live-born children, and the highest to those who had borne eight or more. The first awards were to be made in May 1939.[4]

Provincial governments and municipal authorities have also taken part in the pro-natalist and pro-family campaign. Prussia, Bavaria, and Württemberg, for example, provided for special reductions in school fees when more than one child of the same family was attending school.[5] Among municipal provisions probably the best known are the *Ehrenpatenschaften*—the acceptance of godparenthood by the town. This scheme was first introduced in Berlin in 1934, and applied only to families which already had at least two children and which were prepared to have a third or fourth child. In respect of such a child, provided that it was begotten after an application had been addressed to the Berlin authorities, the city would pay 30 marks per month during the first year of life and 20 marks per month in the

[1] Rott, F., 'Die Unfruchtbarkeit der Frau als Krankheit im Sinne der Reichsversicherungsordnung', *Reichs-Gesundheitsblatt*, 23 Sept. 1936, pp. 738–42.

[2] Premature in the sense of occurring before the end of the normal reproductive period.

[3] The term is *rechtswidrig* and is defined in the commentary as not being justified by such reasons as, e.g., medical advice. See Auert, H., *Das neue grossdeutsche Eherecht*, Berlin, 1938, pp. 14–15, 166–7, and 182–4.

[4] *Wirtschaft und Statistik*, 1939, p. 369. The first awards were to be given to mothers aged 60 years and over and it was estimated that there would be about 2·660 millions of them. But the mothers of inheritably defective and asocial families would be excluded. The net total is not given.

[5] Ballarin and Rössler, op. cit., pp. 58–61.

subsequent years, up to the age of 14.[1] In addition the city would favour the child in allocating employment, housing accommodation, &c. The city was prepared to act as godparent for not more than 2,000 newly born children each year. But in the first year—up to 1 April 1935—of the 2,002 applications received only 311 were granted.[2] Other towns followed the example of Berlin—Frankfurt, Kiel, Mittenwald, and the district of Welzow[3]—or made other provisions for large families.[4] In possibly conscious imitation of the policy of the eighteenth century some towns also attempted to improve the position of the unmarried mother and of the illegitimate child. Perhaps the most striking example is that of Wattenscheid, which in 1939 proposed to give economic assistance for legitimate and illegitimate children alike, provided that the intention to bear a child were communicated to the municipal authorities before conception had actually occurred.[5]

It was pointed out, at the beginning of this chapter, that the coming-to-power of the National Socialist régime was followed by a very striking increase in marriages and births —how striking can be seen from the statistics given on page 305. Absolute figures mean very little and crude marriage- and death-rates are not much more illuminating, but the trend shown by the crude data is borne out by more refined indices for those years for which the necessary calculations are possible. Thus, analysing marriage frequency in terms of nuptiality tables, we find that whereas, in 1932, out of

[1] But the grant ceased if one of the earlier children in the family died, though it was begun again if this death were compensated by a subsequent birth.

[2] See *A.f.B.*, 4, 1933–4, pp. 270–8; Ballarin and Rössler, op. cit., p. 64; Klein, W., 'Ein Jahr Ehrenpatenschaften der Stadt Berlin', *A.f.B.*, 2, 1935, pp. 107–14.

[3] Rössler and Ballarin, op. cit., pp. 64–5; *A.f.B.*, 4, 1933–4, p. 264.

[4] e.g. Stuttgart, Koburg, Wilhelmshaven, Bamberg, and Gera. See ibid. 3, 1936, pp. 193–7 and 5, 1936, pp. 353–4. Note, also, that it is possible to have Adolf Hitler as godfather to one child in a family if the family contains at least nine living legitimate (or legitimized) children or seven living legitimate sons, and fulfils certain other conditions—including sound heredity and 'Aryan' descent. See Richter and Völker, op. cit., pp. 224–5.

[5] *Das Schwarze Korps*, 6 April 1939, Folge 14, p. 6. This, says the article, will mobilize reserves of national strength hitherto unused because 'Dummheit und Unverstand, die Moralriecherei des muffigen Spiessers und das volksfeindliche Gefasel kirchlicher Beichtstuhlwächter ganze Generationen deutscher Frauen zur Unfruchtbarkeit verdammen wollten.'

TABLE 26. *Marriages and Live Births in Germany*[1]

	No. of marriages	Marriages per 1,000 of total population	Index 1932 = 100	No. of live births	Live births per 1,000 of total population	Index 1932 = 100
		A. EXCLUDING THE SAAR TERRITORY				
1929 .	589,611	9·2	116	1,147,458	17·9	119
1930 .	562,648	8·8	111	1,127,450	17·5	116
1931 .	515,403	8·0	101	1,031,770	16·0	106
1932 .	509,597	7·9	100	978,210	15·1	100
1933 .	631,152	9·7	123	956,971	14·7	97
1934 .	732,147	11·2	142	1,182,789	18·0	119
1935 .	643,074	9·7	123	1,246,765	18·9	125
		B. INCLUDING THE SAAR TERRITORY				
1935 .	651,435	9·7	123	1,263,976	18·9	125
1936 .	609,770	9·1	115	1,278,583	19·0	126
1937 .	620,265	9·1	115	1,277,046	18·8	125
1938 .	644,363	9·4	119	1,346,911	19·7	130

1,000 spinsters reaching their sixteenth birthday, 824 could expect to marry by their fiftieth birthday, this probability rose to 889 out of 1,000 in 1933, and 927 in 1934, and then fell slightly to 918 in 1935 and 916 in 1936. These later figures are considerably higher than the probability for 1910–11—889 out of 1,000—which Burgdörfer generally takes as the 'norm' for calculating the excess or deficit of marriages in Germany.[2] Similarly, we find that the gross reproduction-rate was 0·800 in 1933, 0·982 in 1934, 1·037 in 1935, and 1·063 in 1936—a rise of almost 33 per cent. between 1933 and 1936—and the net reproduction-rates for the same years were 0·698, 0·861, 0·906, and 0·934 respectively.[3] In 1938 fertility still appeared to be rising and was probably very close to full replacement level in that year.[4] There is no doubt, then, that the National Socialist

[1] From *Statistik des Deutschen Reichs*, vol. 495, part i, p. I/16, and *Wirtschaft und Statistik*, 1939, p. 336.

[2] See Note VI*i*, p. 460.

[3] Dr. F. Burgdörfer kindly supplied the writer with detailed mid-year estimates of the population, used for calculating the reproduction-rates in the customary way. Some estimation was, however, required, for the 1933 birth distribution data referred to seven States only, and from 1934 onwards no separate divisions for the age-groups of 40–4 and 45–9 years have been given. From 1935 onwards the Saar territory is included in the calculations. The net replacement rates given by official German publications—these rates are not quite the same as net reproduction-rates—are 0·714 in 1933; 0·844 in 1934; 0·89 in 1935; and 0·904 in 1936. (*Statistik des Deutschen Reichs*, vol. 495, part i, p. I/77.)

[4] The official German replacement-rates are 0·904 in 1936 and 1937, and 0·945 in 1938 (*Wirtschaft und Statistik*, 1939, p. 337).

régime did usher in a period of rising marriage probability and fertility. But there still remain two questions. First, to what extent is the change to be imputed to the influence of National Socialism? Secondly, is the change temporary or does it appear to be of a fundamental nature? No precise and unassailable answers can be given to these questions. We can only attempt to weigh up the possibilities and arrive at the most likely result.

If, first of all, we look at the marriage statistics, we find a fairly close coincidence between the granting of marriage loans and the increase in the number of marriages. The coincidence is not complete because loans were not granted until

TABLE 27. *Marriages in Germany (excluding Saar Territory)*[1]

	1932	*1933*	*1934*
First quarter	99,935	94,878	138,111
Second quarter	135,545	158,453	196,781
Third quarter	119,804	157,881	179,070
Fourth quarter	154,313	219,940	218,185

August 1933, while marriages entered upon an upswing in the second quarter of the year. From August 1933 to the end of 1938, 1,121,707 marriage loans were given in Germany, besides the 13,571 loans given in Austria from April 1938.[2] That is, about a third[3] of the marriages occurring during the period were helped by grants valued at not more than 1,000 marks at their maximum. But it is impossible to tell what proportion of these marriages would *not* have occurred if there had been no loans. Burgdörfer himself says that most of the marriages would probably have taken place without the help of loans and adds that many of the births which have resulted from these marriages would have been yielded even if there had been no 25 per cent. cancellation of the initial loan on the birth of a child.[4] It should also

[1] *Statistik des Deutschen Reichs*, vol. 495, part i, p. I/15.

[2] *Wirtschaft und Statistik*, 1939, pp. 110–11.

[3] We cannot say exactly what proportion, because an unknown number of loans was, in 1933, given to couples who were already married.

[4] Burgdörfer, F., *Völker am Abgrund*, 2nd ed., Munich-Berlin, 1937, p. 36. This book deals specifically with the results of the German population policy. So also, though more broadly and with less statistical analysis, does Burgdörfer, F., *Bevölkerungsentwicklung im Dritten Reich*, Heidelberg-Berlin, 1935.

be remembered that in the years immediately preceding the change in the régime Germany went through an extremely severe economic depression, as a result of which many young persons were compelled by unemployment or low wages to postpone intended marriages. But postponement is not indefinite, and when there is both a slight upward movement in business activity and a new government which, however it may be regarded from the point of view of individual liberty, looks as if it might bring a new stability into the economic chaos of Germany, it is only natural that there should have been a sudden increase in the number of marriages. Burgdörfer estimated that, having regard to the numbers of marriageable persons in the population, there should have been about 600,000 marriages per year in Germany in the period 1930–2 if 'normal' conditions had prevailed, but that the existence of an economic crisis had resulted in a deficit of some 330,000 marriages. The 'normal' conditions chosen were those of 1910–11,[1] when, out of 1,000 spinsters at the age of 16, 889 could have expected to marry at least once by their fiftieth birthday. Even without marriage loans, therefore, it is probable that a large proportion of these marriages would have been contracted in 1933 and subsequent years. But it still seems likely that marriage loans were a significant factor. A loan of up to 1,000 marks—but, in practice, generally below 800 marks—for buying furniture and other household goods, would certainly help to remove some of the barriers to an intended marriage, and the fact that the loan had to be repaid would probably not at the time be visible to many people as a marked disadvantage.[2] Compared with the 509,597 marriages in 1932, the period 1933–5 inclusive saw an increase of 477,582 marriages in sum (excluding the Saar Territory), so that the deficit of the depression was more than covered. The preferential allocation of employment to married men, and the inclusion of a

[1] See Note VI*j*, p. 460.

[2] In practice, however, the marriage loan system may prove a disadvantage. A loan of 800 marks would involve repayment at the rate of 8 marks per month, a not inconsiderable sum in relation to an average insured weekly wage of 21·88 marks in 1933 and 22·83 marks in 1934 (*Year-Book of Labour Statistics, 1938*, p. 127), especially as in the early years of the scheme the acceptance of the loan meant that the wife could not take up paid employment.

similar preference in the granting of small-holdings may well have reinforced the influence of the loans, and helped to maintain marriage probability at a high level in 1935 and 1936. Detailed statistics are not yet available for later years, but it seems likely that the position has at least been maintained.

An increase in the number of marriages is generally followed by an increase in births. In England and Wales, where there is no pro-natalist policy, the rise in marriage probability after 1933 was followed by an increase in the gross reproduction-rate from about 0·850 in 1933 to about 0·883 in 1937. It is not surprising, therefore, that in Germany, where marriage probability rose to a much higher level than in England and Wales, the increase in fertility was considerably greater. Here again marriage loans may have been responsible to a marked degree, not only by encouraging marriage but also by offering a 25 per cent. cancellation of the loan on the birth of a child. The force of this argument is strengthened when we remember that part of the pro-natalist campaign has consisted in the suppression of birth-control propaganda—though not the prohibition of the sale of contraceptives—the more rigorous enforcement of the law against abortion, and the initiation of police drives against abortionists. A young married woman thus finds herself confronted with a new situation at the present time. On the one hand, she will not be able to obtain birth-control advice and information as easily as she could have done before 1933, and if she has an unwanted pregnancy it will be both more difficult and more dangerous to procure an abortion than it would have been in earlier years. On the other hand, she will be subjected to intense pro-natalist propaganda and her husband will have part of the repayments due on a marriage loan cancelled if a child is born. Until the end of 1937 women were not generally allowed to take up paid work if their husbands had received marriage loans, so the fear of losing a job on account of pregnancy would not be a factor urging such women to end their pregnancies by abortion. Older married women would also be subjected to the pressure of propaganda and, as Professor Kirkpatrick was told by one informant, would find themselves 'no longer able to obtain the usual abortion on which they had come to rely'.[1] If, moreover, they already had five or more children on an income of less than 185 marks per month, they would be entitled, as from the middle of 1936, to grants of 10 marks per month for each subsequent child.[2] In such circumstances it is likely that a larger proportion of pregnancies would be allowed to go to term, and the estimates given in Table 25 lend some confirmation by showing a considerable fall in the frequency of abortion since 1933.[3] Nor would this explanation conflict with the fact that the increase in births in Germany has been not only in first but also in second, third, and subsequent births.[4]

The explanation given in the preceding paragraph is very rough and not backed by any precise data. It is interesting to compare it with the analysis given by German official statisticians, who go into far greater detail. In a recent number of *Wirtschaft und Statistik*,[5] an article discussing the mechanical factors responsible for the increase in births since 1933 produces the table shown on page 310. The table was constructed with great care, due regard having been given to the influence of age at and duration of marriage upon legitimate fertility, and it shows that while a considerable part of the rise since 1933 is due to the increased number of marriages, a much greater proportion is due to the increase of fertility within marriage. Both the recent marriages[6] and those contracted before 1933 have shown this increase. Two-thirds of the increase in legitimate births,

[1] See present study, p. 286, n. 3.

[2] The grants have since been extended to families with three or more children and raised for the fifth and subsequent children, while higher income limits have been adopted. But the decree responsible was not issued until March 1938, and could not therefore have affected the earlier period. It may, however, have been very important in persuading women to allow their existing pregnancies to go to term and in this way it may have been an important factor in producing the marked further rise in fertility in 1938.

[3] See Note VI*k*, p. 461.

[4] *Wirtschaft und Statistik*, 1938, p. 370, states that in the four years 1934 to 1937 inclusive 1,170,000 more legitimate births have occurred in Germany (including the Saar Territory) than would have been the case if the annual supply had remained at the 1933 level, and that of this excess 461,000 were first births, 381,000 second, 187,000 third, 84,000 fourth, 34,000 fifth, and 23,000 sixth and subsequent births.

[5] Ibid., 1939, pp. 283–6. A very detailed analysis on the same lines is given by Burgdörfer in *Völker am Abgrund*, pp. 39–55. But the data given in Table 28 include more recent years and have therefore been used. They also include the Saar Territory.

[6] See Note VI*l*, p. 461.

TABLE 28. *Official Analysis of the Course of Legitimate Births, 1933–8 (including Still Births)*

Year	Total legitimate births	'Basic number'	Total increase	Extent to which increase is due: (a) to additional marriages	(b) to higher fertility
1933	892,800	873,800	19,000	19,000	..
1934	1,125,500	867,900	257,600	74,700	182,900
1935	1,195,300	862,400	332,900	120,500	212,400
1936	1,210,000	857,700	352,300	127,700	224,600
1937	1,207,500	855,300	352,200	131,300	220,900
1938	1,277,200	849,900	427,300	142,400	284,900

says Burgdörfer, must be attributed to a genuine rise in fertility,[1] and it is evident from the table that 71 per cent. of the extra births were due to this factor in 1934, and 67 per cent. in 1938. Burgdörfer then goes on to say—and he speaks with more authority and less heat than most Germans discussing the question—that this genuine increase in fertility cannot in the main be attributed to direct pro-natalist measures because most of them (he was writing in 1937) were of very recent date and had not yet reached the bulk of the population.[2] An unmeasurable, but probably the major, part of the increase had been the result of the 'psychic population policy',[3] not specifically defined by Burgdörfer, but referred to by other writers as the 'psychic rebirth' of Germany, the new conception of the place of an individual in the State, the new vision of the German future.

But if we look at the successive stages of this analysis, we may perhaps arrive at a less striking conclusion. First, we should note that the 'basic number' of legitimate births, used for calculating the total increase in legitimate births, was obtained by assuming that the number of marriages would remain at the 1932 level, and that marital fertility would remain at the 1933 level. But 1932 was the lowest point for marriages and 1933 was the lowest point for fertility. Burgdörfer himself pointed out that many of the

[1] *Völker am Abgrund*, p. 51. [2] Ibid., p. 51.

[3] Ibid., p. 54. Note that these phrases are very similar to the descriptions given by official writers of the significance of the Fascist revolution in Italy. But Italian fertility did not increase as a result of this 'psychic' population policy.

marriages contracted with the aid of loans would have taken place had there been no loans at all, and any slight improvement in economic conditions would have produced an increase in the number of marriages, which in turn would have affected the supply of births. For this reason the total increase in legitimate births shown in the Table is fictitious and attributes to National Socialism a development which would have occurred, at least in part, if there had been no change in the political structure. Similarly, the economic depression of 1930–2 may have caused married couples to postpone having any or having additional children.[1] An improvement in economic circumstances, under whatever government, might therefore not only have increased the annual number of marriages but also the number of children per marriage. So it may be unrealistic to attribute to the additional marriages contracted after 1933 the same fertility as prevailed in 1933, and to regard the whole excess of births above the numbers which would have been yielded by 1933 rates as indicative of a genuine rise in fertility and a phenomenon peculiar to the National Socialist régime.

If this criticism is valid, then the increase in births attributable to the special measures of National Socialist Germany is considerably less than the total increase. But there has been, nevertheless, *some* real increase, and the question is—has this been caused by a 'psychic rebirth' of the people, or are there more materialistic reasons? It is, of course, quite possible that a change of attitude has been partly responsible. Twenty-two years ago, De Roux, with unconscious cynicism, said that, apart from religious faith, military victory was most likely to influence fertility,[2] and certainly British and French foreign policy prior to 1939 gave Germany military victories which were all the more resounding because they were bloodless. But if 'psychic rebirth' is an important factor in affecting population trends, it should be

[1] Whereas in England and Wales the birth-rate followed a fairly steady curve between 1928 and 1932, the German rate turned downwards very sharply in 1930. But for the particularly marked depression the German birth-rate might perhaps have been about 16 per 1,000 in 1933, instead of the actual rate of 14·7 per 1,000 in that year. In *Statistik des Deutschen Reichs*, vol. 423, p. 31, there is some discussion of the influence of the depression upon the birth-rate.

[2] De Roux, M., *L'État et la Natalité*, Paris, 1918, pp. 280–1.

noted that quite a large section of the population appears as yet untouched by it. Of the 615,630 marriages contracted in 1933 and still in existence on 31 December 1936, 219,334, or 36 per cent., had borne only one child each, and 240,793, or 39 per cent., had borne none. Of the 722,764 marriages contracted in 1934 and still in existence at the end of 1936, 287,888, or 40 per cent., had borne only one child each, and a further 328,295, or 45 per cent., had not borne any children.[1] The present writer believes, however, that the material measures have been more important than the 'psychic' changes, and that, in particular, the suppression of illegal abortion has been a major factor. Table 25 (p. 280) shows some marked decreases in the frequency of abortion, especially in Berlin and Lübeck, and the influence of such a trend would be very considerable. Suppose, for example, that the Lübeck data apply fairly well to the whole of Germany. This would mean that in 1932, when abortion was most frequent, there would have been about 655,000 abortions as compared with 1,007,798 births[2] (including still births). The Lübeck statistics show a fall in the ratio of abortions to normal births from 65 per 100 in 1932 to 14 per 100 in 1938. If we suppose that the total number of pregnancies in Germany had remained at the 1932 level, but that abortion frequency had fallen at the Lübeck rate, there would have been over 1,400,000 live and still births in 1938. Even after allowing for the proportion of still births, this would have meant more live births than were actually produced in Germany in 1938. So if the suppression of illegal abortion has been as successful as it is said to be, that by itself would account for the increase in births in recent years.[3] On the

[1] *Statistisches Jahrbuch für das Deutsche Reich, 1938,* p. 50. The figures cover live and still births, and are not absolutely comprehensive, as children born before marriage and legitimized afterwards have been taken into account only if there has been a child born within the marriage itself. But regarded from the point of view of the fertility within marriage of marriages contracted in 1933 and subsequent years, the statistics do not exaggerate the extent of childlessness. On the other hand, since they include legitimized children in marriages producing a child since 1933, they under-estimate the number of marriages which have borne only one child each since the contraction of the marriage.

[2] Excluding the Saar territory.

[3] For an interesting discussion on this point, see Whelpton, P. K., 'Why the large rise in the German birth-rate?' *American Journal of Sociology,* Nov. 1935, pp. 299–313, at pp. 311–12.

other hand, if the suppression of abortion is the main factor, it is possible that in the course of time women may be able to adjust themselves to the new situation and make more use of contraceptive practices. But what the future course of births will be in Germany the present writer cannot attempt to foretell.[1] Even in peace time it would be difficult enough to take into account the various factors which have been considered. Now war has again changed the situation, and it would be futile to speculate on the attitude that potential parents may have after this war is over.

[1] See Note VI*m*, p. 461.

Addition to footnote, p. 272, n. 3

Grotjahn wrote his war pamphlet on an impulse which, according to Dr. M. Kantorowicz (in some comments sent to the present writer), he afterwards regretted. His later development is best shown in his post-War study, *Die Hygiene der menschlichen Fortpflanzung*, pp. 83 and 132–3, and *Leitsätze zur sozialen und generativen Hygiene*, 4th ed., Karlsruhe, 1927, pp. 29–35. His posthumous work, *Ein Kartothek zu § 218*, Berlin, 1932, analyses the abortion data supplied by a doctor in a small town, and concludes that birth-control knowledge should be disseminated, and that doctors should be empowered to procure abortions on therapeutic, eugenic, and social grounds. (See also the interesting, annotated bibliography by Martin Grotjahn in *A. f. B.*, 1, 1933, pp. 13–20.)

VII

SCANDINAVIA AND THE POPULATION QUESTION[1]

SO far as the continued maintenance of their populations is concerned, Norway, Sweden, and Denmark are in a position similar to that of most other Western countries. In each of the three Scandinavian countries the net reproduction rate is below unity, and in each of these countries

TABLE 29. *Gross and Net Reproduction Rates in the Scandinavian Countries*[2]

Period	*Norway*		*Sweden*		*Denmark*	
	Gross rate	*Net rate*	*Gross rate*	*Net rate*	*Gross rate*	*Net rate*
1906–10 .	..	..*	1·799	..†	1·851	1·486
1926–30 .	..	..	0·992	0·857	1·166	1·012
1931 . .	1·036	0·909‡	0·900	0·785	1·064	0·929
1932 . .	0·989	0·874	0·879	0·775	1·065	0·939
1933 . .	0·899	0·799	0·821	0·733	1·012	0·903
1934 . .	0·883	0·797	0·815	0·727	1·040	0·934
1935 . .	0·869	0·783	0·811	0·729	1·022	0·902
1936 . .	0·874	0·786	0·841	0·756	1·042	0·933

* Kuczynski does not give rates for this period. The gross rate for 1910–11 was 1·853 and the net rate for 1901–10 was 1·556.

† No net rate was available for 1906–10. The net rate for 1901–10 was 1·429.

‡ The rates are for 1930–1, as the appropriate statistics are not available for the separate years. It should be noted that an inaccuracy is introduced into the calculation of net rates for Norway, as the deaths are not given correctly by age groups but, for the bulk of the ages, the age at death is obtained simply by subtracting the year of birth from the year of death. The correct age groups are, however, used—the present writer is informed by Dr. Gunnar Jahn—when the official life tables are constructed.

this is the momentary end-point of a decline in fertility which has been proceeding for some sixty years. Table 29 gives the position up to the most recent years for which the necessary basic statistics are available. The gross reproduction rates show that, with the possible exception of Denmark, no further reduction in mortality would be

[1] This chapter is based largely upon two articles by the present writer: 'Population policies in Scandinavia', *Eugenics Review*, July 1938, and 'The effectiveness of abortion legislation in six countries', *Modern Law Review*, Sept. 1938, together with some additional material which has been obtained in the course of the last year.

[2] See Note VII*a*, p. 461.

sufficient to compensate for the low level of fertility. Even in the case of Denmark it is doubtful if much compensation could be obtained by reducing mortality. In 1934, a year in which mortality was relatively low, the wastage of fertility due to death was about 10·2 per cent., and women could expect to live 31·04 years in the child-bearing period, out of the 35 years which would obtain if there were no deaths occurring to females between birth and the fiftieth birthday. Presumably it will be possible to increase the number of years lived in the child-bearing period, but, with fertility at the 1935 level,[1] women would have to live 33·8 years out of the 35 to raise the net reproduction rate to unity, and the necessary reduction in mortality would not be easy to achieve. This is the case in Denmark, which has the highest fertility of the three countries. In Sweden, with the lowest fertility, the situation is much less favourable. Even in 1930–1 it is doubtful if more than 4 or 5 of the 49 administrative divisions of the country (25 urban and 24 rural) had net reproduction rates equal to or greater than unity,[2] and since then the general level has fallen. The large towns are particularly low on the scale, and in 1935 Stockholm had a net reproduction rate of only about 0·394.[3]

The implications of these rates have not passed unnoticed in Scandinavia. Long before population policies were beginning to take practical shape in any of the three countries estimates of future population had been made, showing the trends in numbers which might be expected if fertility and mortality behaved in accordance with certain sets of assumptions. In 1926 Professor S. D. Wicksell published five such estimates for Sweden, two of which showed a future decline of the population.[4] In 1931 Dr. Adolph Jensen made three estimates of the future population of Denmark, two of which implied a growing and the third an

[1] And assuming the same age-distribution of fertility as in 1935.

[2] From unpublished data kindly provided by Dr. C. E. Quensel, of Lund University.

[3] *Statistisk Årsbok för Stockholms Stad*, 1938, p. 35. This is probably too low, as it is based on the Stockholm life table for 1921–30.

[4] Wicksell, S. D., 'Sveriges framtida befolkning under olika förutsättningar', *Ekonomisk Tidskrift*, Parts 4–5, 1926, pp. 91–123.

eventually stationary population.[1] Subsequent estimates include a series for Norway, published by Professor Wicksell in 1934,[2] and a new series for Sweden given by Professors Myrdal and Wicksell in their report to the Swedish Population Commission.[3] With the possible exception of the last estimates, about which it is too early to judge, the lowest fertilities assumed for the purposes of computation were still higher than have actually been shown in the most recent years. It should be emphasized that these estimates were aimed primarily at elucidating the effects of certain trends, rather than at attempting to forecast the probable populations of the future. Clearly, however, such computations indicate a real interest, among the social scientists at least, in the prospects of the populations of the three countries. But the interest was not translated into concrete proposals until very recently. For one thing, each country had its own immediate problems with which to deal, and for another, it takes a considerable time to change public opinion on the population question, especially when the large majority of progressive writers in the last thirty years have supported neo-Malthusian aims.

Doubtless the attitude of the general public still remains substantially unaltered. But informed public opinion, at least in Sweden, has undergone a considerable change in the last few years. The immediate cause of this change was a book by Alva and Gunnar Myrdal, *Kris i Befolkningsfrågan* (*Crisis in the Population Question*), published at the end of 1934.[4] This book, as a writer in the *Anglo-Swedish*

[1] Jensen, A., 'Horoscope of the population of Denmark', *Bulletin de l'Institut International de Statistique*, vol. xxv, 3me. Livraison, 1931, pp. 41–9. See also Nybølle, H. C., 'Nogle væsentlige Træk af Danmarks nuværende befolkningsmæssige Forhold', *Socialt Tidsskrift*, April 1934, pp. 111–36. For a general discussion of Danish population movements and problems see Jensen, A., *Befolkningsspørgsmaalet i Danmark*, Copenhagen, 1937.

[2] Wicksell, S. D., 'Bidrag till den formella befolkningsteorien. Med tillämpningar på Norges befolkning', *Statsøkonomisk Tidsskrift*, 1934, Parts 1–2, pp. 1–94. An official estimate of the population of Norway—up to 1945—is given in *Folkemengdens Bevegelse, 1921–32*, pp. 194–5.

[3] See Note VII*b*, p. 462.

[4] Myrdal, A., and Myrdal, G., *Kris i Befolkningsfrågan*, Stockholm, 1934. The seventh edition was being sold in 1937, when the present writer bought a copy in Stockholm. A Danish edition was published in 1935 and a Norwegian in 1936.

Review expressed it, dropped a bombshell among the thinking public of Sweden.[1] And apparently the thinking public of Sweden is much larger, proportionately, than that of England, for by the middle of 1937 the book had sold some 16,000 copies, equivalent to a sale of over 100,000 in England and Wales, a figure rarely reached even by popular novels. The book explained the significance of recent trends in fertility, discussed the possible consequences of a fall in population, and examined, in the light of existing knowledge, the reasons for and possible cures of the present low fertility. In particular, it placed the population problem in its social context, and showed that for the bulk of the population the existing alternatives were either poverty or family limitation. *Crisis in the Population Question* was a political and social study expressing the views of two distinguished social democrats, and it provided a factual basis for discussion of the whole question. It met the neo-Malthusian argument with an analysis of probable population trends, and to the Conservative argument that a rise in the standard of living would not increase fertility, it answered that there was nevertheless a case for relieving the pressure to which, in present circumstances, the individual standard was subjected by the raising of children.[2] Discussion of the book was widespread and early in 1935 there were radio broadcasts on the population question.[3] The Riksdag was soon presented with motions by private members for the establishment of a population commission, and a Royal Commission was set up in May 1935. Experts from all the related fields were co-opted—it is a Swedish tradition that experts should play a leading part in the government of the country—and seventeen reports were issued, dealing with various aspects of the subject, including a bulky general introduction to the whole field of Swedish population

[1] 'The depopulation alarm in Sweden', *Anglo-Swedish Review*, January 1935, pp. 14–15.

[2] Mr. R. Sterner, in a letter to the present writer, described the book as a *J'accuse* against prevailing social circumstances—that is, against the circumstances which compelled the bulk of the population to limit their families as the only means of mitigating poverty. Mr. Sterner was one of the Secretaries of the Population Commission and was responsible for some of the special studies.

[3] They were reprinted as *Debatt i Befolkningsfrågan*, Stockholm, 1935.

problems.[1] In the same year a Royal Commission on Population was set up in Denmark, but in Norway there has so far been no attempt to project a coherent and unified policy concerning population problems.[2] Up to the present, Sweden is the only member of the Scandinavian group in which population policies have been implemented on any scale. The remainder of this chapter will therefore be concerned largely with the proposals made and implemented in that country.

The Scandinavian approach to the population problem is distinguished by two special characteristics. First, that the passing of legislation should be preceded by detailed investigations of the various aspects of the population problem. Of no other countries is this true. Even in France, where pro-natalist measures have been applied for many years, and on an ever-increasing scale, no really serious inquiry has been made at any time, either by the Commissions set up early in the twentieth century, or by the Conseil Supérieur de la Natalité, created at the end of the last War. Secondly, in the totalitarian countries—and to a considerable extent in France and Belgium, too—strong elements of repression are evident in the legal structure which has been set up to check declining fertility. In these countries the governments have tried as much to coerce people into having children as to create an environment in which they would be willing to have them. Thus, as we have seen in earlier chapters, there has been a general tightening up of the laws relating to abortion, new laws, or

[1] *Betänkande i Sexualfrågan*, Stockholm, 1936. A popular summary of this report was also published—[Brunskog, M.], *Familj och Moral*, Stockholm, 1937. It should be noted that the entry of the government into the field of population policy was not unreservedly welcomed by political parties. The Conservatives regarded the measures proposed as cloaking the introduction of socialism, while some of the Labour and Social Democrat papers saw 'nationalistic delirium' in the policy. It is also interesting to note that, under the influence of widespread discussion, the name of Myrdal soon became associated with large families and large-scale child breeding.

[2] Though Dr. Jahn (Director of the Norwegian Central Statistical Office) has, with others, urged the setting up of a Royal Commission on population problems. There is a certain amount of public interest in the question in Norway. See, for example, Langeland, O. H., *Det Er Liv Eller Død Det Gjelder*, Oslo, 1937, and Lionæs, A., and Skaug, A., *Dør Vi Ut*, n.d. (this pamphlet is by the two authors responsible for the Norwegian adaptation of the Myrdals' book). A Population Commission has been set up in Finland.

official campaigns to check birth-control propaganda or the use of contraceptives, and attempts to drive women back into the home. But in Scandinavia the initial assumption is that parenthood shall be voluntary. The mandate of the Swedish Commission categorically states that homes which are economically badly off should not be burdened by too many children, while the mandate of the Danish Commission specifies that no repressive measures shall be considered.

In practice this has a very interesting result. It means that along with measures for encouraging fertility, there must also be other measures which make it easier for people to obtain reliable birth-control information. To achieve such an object will involve considerable new activity, for in none of the Scandinavian countries is the knowledge of modern techniques of birth control particularly widespread. In Denmark, for example, there is practically no birth-control movement, though Dr. Leunbach[1] has attempted to create one, and at the end of 1937 there was still only one real birth-control clinic, that set up in 1932 by the World League for Sexual Reform.[2] In addition, the State hospital in Copenhagen had an ante-natal clinic, and the clinic for women's diseases gave birth-control advice in cases where it was regarded as essential. Apart from this, birth-control advice was obtainable only from private doctors.[3] Yet there was considerable pressure from doctors to change this position, and particularly to repeal the law under which birth-control propaganda was deemed a punishable offence.[4]

[1] Dr. J. H. Leunbach was a candidate at the Danish Parliamentary elections of 1935, having a platform of sexual reform—Hodann, M., *History of Modern Morals*, p. 309. See also Leunbach, J. H., 'La réglementation des naissances et de l'avortement en Scandinavie', *Le Problème Sexuel*, July 1934, pp. 31–3.

[2] See Dr. Leunbach's report on Denmark, in *International Medical Group for the Investigation of Contraception*, fifth issue, London, 1934, pp. 20–1. This report also analyses the results of a questionnaire sent in 1932 by the Danish Medical Association to 2,700 doctors. 2,330 answered—though not all of the questions—and were generally in favour of giving contraceptive advice to married and unmarried persons. 1,383 were in favour of birth-control clinics where any one could obtain advice, and only 704 were against this.

[3] e.g. Dr. Leunbach himself fitted Gräfenberg rings to 175 women in the period Sept. 1929 to May 1930—*International Medical Group*, fourth issue, London, 1931, p. 12.

[4] Under Section 235 of the Penal Code of 1913, a fine was prescribed for any one communicating with the public or with an unknown person or persons, either by advertisements, posters, or other means, and offering to sell articles for preventing

In Sweden the position was more advanced, but still very poor at the end of 1937, especially if it is borne in mind that birth-control propaganda in Sweden was begun, partly under English influence, by Professor K. Wicksell, in February 1880,[1] and that a Malthusian League was in existence in Sweden in 1911. But birth control was not a 'respectable' subject for discussion, and only in the post-War period, especially under the influence of the growing workers' educational movement, did the subject make any headway.[2] By the end of 1937 there were four municipal clinics—at Göteborg, Malmö, Lund, and Stockholm (in the Sabbatsberg hospital)—and a private clinic in Stockholm, opened in 1933 by the National Association for Sex Education (Riksförbundet för Sexuell Upplysning), a body supported by over 40,000 members. But the numbers of patients seen by these clinics are very small. In 1935 the Sabbatsberg clinic saw only 116 women patients, the Göteborg clinic 48, the Malmö clinic 48, and that at Lund only 37.[3] The Riksförbund clinic has the largest number of patients, increasing from 747 in 1933–4 to 1,884 in 1936–7, and 2,280 in 1937–8.[4] In addition the association has contracts with doctors in various parts of the country for giving birth-control advice to people who are unable to go to Stockholm, and there is a very considerable postal

the consequences of sexual intercourse. Abortifacients would come under this description. This law did not, however, appear to interfere with the sale of contraceptives. The writer is greatly indebted to the Secretary of the Inter-Departmental Committee on Abortion for many documents dealing with the questions of abortion and birth-control legislation in Scandinavia.

[1] Two addresses given by Wicksell in Feb. 1880. A transcript is given in *The Malthusian*, Aug. 1880, pp. 150–1. See also Myrdal, A. and G., *Kris i Befolkningsfrågan*, p. 39 *n*. The development of neo-Malthusian ideas in Sweden is discussed in some detail in ibid., pp. 35–65.

[2] In 1911 a law was hurriedly passed, intended to be used against the militant birth-control movement which had begun to develop among working-class organizations. But it has rarely been enforced, except against pedlars selling contraceptives at public markets. It was repealed last year—see subsequent discussion.

[3] This data is from Gårdlund, T., 'Bättre polikliniker för födelsekontroll', *Morgonbris*, April 1937, pp. 21–2, and same author, 'Förefintliga rådfrågningsbyråer för sexualupplysning i Sverige', *Betänkande i Sexualfrågan*, pp. 331–49.

[4] These figures were specially obtained from the Riksförbund by the courtesy of Mr. E. von Hofsten of the Stockholm Municipal Statistical Office, and they are very considerably higher than the figures given by Gårdlund for this clinic. The 1937–8 figure is not for the whole year, but from 16 Oct. 1937 to 27 Aug. 1938.

information service, while the President of the Association, Madame Elise Ottesen-Jensen, frequently travels through the country on propaganda tours.[1] Yet, at least until very lately, even this relatively large movement had made little impact upon the total population, and recent investigations carried out in the Stockholm clinics showed that over 60 per cent. of the patients trying to prevent pregnancy had used or were using *coitus interruptus*.[2] And so far as the other clinics are concerned, lack of publicity and official indifference appeared to be chiefly responsible for their poor support.[3]

Norway has a more widely developed system of birth-control clinics, in spite of the existence of paragraph 377 of the Penal Code, which could be used—though it has not been since a test case in 1927—to prohibit the advertising or public display of contraceptives. The Norwegian birth-control movement was effectively begun in 1924 by Madame Katti Anker Møller, who, with the aid of women members of the Labour Party, succeeded in raising 3,000 kroner for the first clinic. Since then the movement has grown considerably, and at the end of 1937 there were twelve clinics, privately and independently run, but all springing from the same initiative and receiving grants from the National Health Insurance Fund and from the local government authorities. Nevertheless, it is unlikely that these clinics touch more than a fraction of the adult population.[4]

It is evident that supporters of the birth-control movement still have a great deal of work to do in the Scandinavian countries. This does not mean that the population is, as a whole, ignorant of the methods of birth prevention. The

[1] In a discussion with Madame Ottesen-Jensen in Sept. 1937. Dr. Alma Sundqvist, another leading figure in the Swedish birth-control movement, told the writer that the Workers' Educational Association frequently asked her and Madame Ottesen-Jensen to tour the country and lecture on birth control.

[2] Gårdlund, T., 'Vissa uppgifter om preventivteknikens utbredning', *Betänkande i Sexualfrågan*, pp. 325–30. A somewhat lower percentage was yielded by a 1930 investigation carried out in connexion with an official inquiry into abortion, but the number of persons covered was very small.

[3] The Sabbatsberg hospital receives each year about 1,000 patients who have had criminal abortions, and 100 of these return the same year with a further abortion (Gårdlund, in *Morgonbris*, loc. cit.).

[4] From discussions with Dr. Gerda Evang and with the superintendent of the Oslo birth-control clinic, in Sept. 1937. See also *Krisen i Befolkningsspørsmålet* (the Norwegian adaptation of the Myrdals' book), pp. 39–50.

decline of fertility gives ample evidence to the contrary. But the methods used are often primitive and modern techniques of contraception—apart from the condom[1]—are not widely known, and the practice of abortion appears to be fairly widespread. In fact the question of abortion has given rise to a good deal of discussion in recent years, both because of the fairly high estimates of its frequency and because the existing laws, while being relatively harsh, are clearly not very effective. In Denmark a Committee was appointed in 1932 by the Ministry of Justice and issued its report in 1936.[2] It had to consider the fact that although, under the Penal Code of 1930,[3] the penalties for abortion had been reduced, Danish juries were still refusing to sentence women for having undergone abortions. Between 1928 and 1932 only 82 women had been accused and only 19 brought to trial. Of these 19, 4 elected to be tried without a jury and were convicted. But of the 15 who were tried by jury, 14 were acquitted, the remaining woman being sentenced because she was found guilty of infanticide. At the same time the Committee estimated that there were between 1,000 and 2,000 criminal abortions per year as compared with about 66,000 births,[4] and one member placed the figure at about 6,000. Another member, Dr. Axel Tofte,

[1] The Danish Population Commission was of the opinion that the knowledge of contraceptive techniques available to men was extremely widespread, and that the chief task of birth-control clinics would be to give advice on the use of pessaries (according to a letter from Mr. H. H. Koch of the *Socialministerium*, 29 Aug. 1938). In fact, of course, the position in Norway and Sweden does not appear to be markedly different from that in England. Denmark is poorer, relatively, in clinics, but birth-control information has nevertheless reached the public. Certainly the methods used by the public appear to be reasonably effective, even if they are crude.

[2] *Betænkning . . . angaaende Lovligheden af Svangerskabsafbrydelse m.V.*, Copenhagen, 1936.

[3] Section 242 of the 1930 Code prescribed detention or imprisonment up to two years for a woman having an abortion, while persons procuring or helping to procure the abortion were to be sentenced to imprisonment for up to four years. (In aggravating circumstances this latter penalty could be increased to eight years, or, if the abortion had been procured without the consent of the woman, for two to twelve years.) Section 243 prescribed a fine, or detention for up to three months, or, in specially aggravating circumstances, imprisonment, for anyone importing, manufacturing, distributing, selling, &c., articles which, though said to be for sexual hygiene, are really intended for terminating pregnancy. This did not apply, of course, to instruments, &c., supplied to doctors or hospitals.

[4] Ibid., p. 24. It was the Medical sub-committee which made these estimates.

subsequently suggested that the figure was probably between 2,000 and 5,000.[1] The Committee felt that it had to strike a balance between an acceptance of the part played by abortion in everyday life, and the need to have some kind of penalty, since complete exemption would be against the conscience of the majority of people. Apart, therefore, from urging social reforms for improving the economic position of married and unmarried mothers, it recommended that abortion should be allowed on ethical,[2] eugenic, and social-humanitarian grounds. At the same time a sub-committee which had been set up by the main Committee urged that access to contraceptives be made as easy as possible, though, in the interests of the public, there should be some supervision of the trade in these articles. The result of this Report was threefold. First, in May 1937, Section 235 of the Penal Code was modified. A fine was still prescribed for the offensive advertising or displaying of contraceptives, as well as for the unsolicited distribution of advertisements to persons not trading in such articles, but chemists shops and other approved stores were explicitly allowed to sell contraceptives.[3] Secondly, a law passed at the same time modified the clauses of the Penal Code relating to abortion,[4] and allowed abortion on eugenic, therapeutic, and ethical grounds. Social grounds have been omitted, but medical grounds are defined more broadly in the Act than in the Report of the Committee, and it will be possible to plead that a further pregnancy would have a serious effect upon the health of a woman who already has a large family and whose income is very small.[5] Thirdly, the Act provided for the establishment by the provincial or municipal authorities of clinics at which persons of both sexes should have access to good and reliable instruction in sexual hygiene and at which pregnant women should be able to receive advice and assistance. This meant the provision of public clinics for

[1] In a discussion with the writer, Sept. 1937.

[2] e.g. in cases of rape, and certain cases of incest.

[3] In Sept. 1937 regulations were issued concerning the authorization of the sale of contraceptives. Apparently condoms and rubber pessaries were the only forms authorized for sale, though other articles might be sold by chemists when a medical prescription was presented.

[4] See Note VII*c*, p. 462.

[5] Information from Mr. H. H. Koch.

birth-control and ante-natal advice, a very great change from the situation current in Denmark at the time. But it should be noted that the Act, which was supposed to come into force on 1 April 1938, was postponed until 1 October 1939. Before that date two new Acts—both of 15 March 1939—have modified the 1937 Act, by omitting the birth-control clinics, and by setting up instead a series of State maternity centres for giving advice and guidance to pregnant women, and for helping them to receive the medical and economic assistance provided for them and for their children both before and after confinement. This Act came into force on 1 April 1939,[1] and the question of birth-control advice has, for the moment at least, been shelved. It appears to be the intention of the government to solve this problem in connexion with the general work of the public hospitals.[2]

In Sweden the problem has been no less serious. A special inquiry undertaken by Dr. Edin[3] showed that in 1930 there had been 10,445 abortions, either in hospitals or institutions or seen by doctors or midwives. Of these, 245 were therapeutic abortions and the remainder consisted of spontaneous and criminal cases, the distribution between these two categories not being known. It is certain, however, that a considerable proportion must have been induced, and Dr. Edin himself considered that the number of criminal abortions was probably over 10,000 per year. This should be compared with 94,220 live births in Sweden in 1930. Dr. Sundqvist regarded 10,000 as a minimum figure,[4] Professor Gunnar Dahlberg thought it probable that a third of all illegitimate pregnancies and a sixth of all legitimate pregnancies are aborted[5]—which would mean over 20,000 abortions per year—while Madame Ottesen-Jensen believed that an estimate of some 50,000 abortions per year would scarcely be an exaggeration.[6] There is, of course, an extremely wide range in these estimates, but they are all large enough to explain why the existing abortion

[1] *Lov om Mødrehjælpsinstitutioner*, 15 March 1939.

[2] Information from Mr. H. H. Koch, 21 June 1939.

[3] Edin, K. A., *Undersökning av Abortförekomsten i Sverige under Senare År*, Lund-Malmö, 1934, pp. 10–11, and 26 ff.

[4] In a conversation, Sept. 1937.

[5] In a conversation, Nov. 1937.

[6] In a conversation, Sept. 1937.

law[1] was regarded as ineffective. Two committees were therefore appointed to consider the question. The first was set up in 1934 and reported in 1935,[2] proposing that abortion should be allowed on ethical, eugenic, and social grounds. Therapeutic abortion was not to come under the proposal, since it was already allowed, though not specifically provided for in the Penal Code. The proposals were then handed, for further consideration, to a special committee of the Population Commission, and a report issued in 1937,[3] proposing that social grounds be excluded and suggesting that it would be better to provide social conditions in which women could bear children without being reduced to destitution, rather than to accept the possibility of destitution and allow women to have their pregnancies interrupted. On this basis the law was drafted and passed on 17 June 1938, coming into force on 1 January 1939. The new law permits abortion on therapeutic, eugenic, and ethical grounds. In other cases the Penal Code still applies. The old clause in the Penal Code relating to birth-control propaganda was also repealed, as from 1 January 1939, by the Riksdag, and the trade in contraceptives has become controlled by the issue of a regulation making it necessary for private distributors to obtain a permit.[4]

Norway, too, had a Committee appointed to consider the question of abortion law reform, and a report was issued in 1935.[5] There had been many demands for revision of the Penal Code, including a resolution of the 1930 Medical Congress and an appeal issued by the Free Churches in

[1] See Note VII*d*, p. 463.

[2] *Betänkande med Förslag till Lagstiftning om Avbrytande av Havandeskap*, Stockholm, 1935.

[3] *Yttrande i Abortfrågan*, Stockholm, 1937. It did, however, recognize medico-social grounds—e.g. where the woman was poor and worn out by child-bearing. This has not been specifically included in the new law though it may possibly be interpreted as coming under 'therapeutic abortion'—where the birth of a child would entail serious danger to the life or health of the woman.

[4] Myrdal, A., 'A programme for family security in Sweden', *International Labour Review*, June 1939, pp. 723–63, at p. 738. This article gives the most thorough and valuable account in English of the objects and measures of Sweden's population policy.

[5] *Instilling nr. 1 . . . angående Forandring i Straffeloven § 245 og angående Utferdigelse av Lov om Avbrytelse av Svangerskap*, Oslo, 1935. The Committee was appointed in June 1934.

1934, and signed by 200,000 persons over 18 years of age. At the same time it was clear that abortion frequency was increasing. In Oslo municipal hospital alone 1,121 women were admitted in 1920 on account of abortion or its immediate sequelae, while in 1933 the number had risen to 2,331. In 1920 115 abortions were performed in hospitals, while in 1933 the number was 1,625. Evidently the interpretation of the term 'therapeutic' had become much broader in the period. The Committee estimated that in 1933 between 1,050 and 2,200 abortions were performed by 'quacks' and that the total number of induced abortions was probably between 3,575 and 5,425, as compared with about 46,000 births. Dr. Gerda Evang, who is closely associated with the Oslo birth-control clinic, considered that this estimate was probably too low.[1] The Committee recommended that abortion should be permissible on therapeutic, ethical, eugenic, humanitarian, and social indications, but stressed the need for an increase in assistance to mothers, of economic assistance to large families, of legislation to prevent women losing their employment on account of pregnancy, and of a definite housing policy. So far the abortion law has not been changed,[2] and as regards the other aspects of the question, very little further progress has been made since 1935.

No doubt many people in Sweden and Denmark have been disappointed by recent legislative changes on the subject of birth control and abortion, and feel in particular that the law has not made sufficient provision for birth-control advice. But at the same time they must acknowledge that the new legislation has at least not been in any way 're-

[1] The reports of this clinic—*Mødrehygienekontoret i Oslo*—show that the women attending in 1935 had had a total of 2,460 births and 693 abortions, or 28·2 abortions per 100 births. In 1936 the proportion among the patients was 34·3 abortions per 100 births. But this includes spontaneous abortions. Dr. Evang—in a letter dated 6 Sept. 1938—considers that Oslo is not typical of Norway as a whole, and that abortion is practised much more in the towns than in the rural districts.

[2] The abortion law—paragraph 245 of the Penal Code of 22 May 1902—prescribes imprisonment for up to three years for a woman who destroys or helps to destroy her foetus. Any one helping the woman shall receive imprisonment for not more than six years (not less than two years if he acted without the consent of the woman; and for life, or for not less than six years, if the woman dies as a result).

pressive' in the sense in which that term applies to France and Belgium, Italy and Germany. The legislators in Sweden and Denmark have genuinely tried to make parenthood more voluntary and less accidental than before.

On the positive side Swedish policy has largely followed the ideas expressed in the Myrdals' book. Briefly these ideas may be summarized as first, to encourage marriage, and secondly, to provide a social and economic environment in which the *extra* costs associated with the bearing and rearing of children are reduced as much as possible. That is, the policy aims at remedying the situation in which all the additional costs fall upon parents, while the unmarried and the childless, to use Mrs. Myrdal's phrase, 'avoid contributing to the necessary investment in the future generation'.[1] An additional principle is that, where possible, assistance shall not be given in money but in goods or services. One reason for this principle is economy. Substantial cash payments for children would be costly, and more 'value for money' could be obtained by central or local government bulk expenditure in such fields as housing, the provision of school meals, and so forth. At the same time the Myrdals consider that by giving specific goods and services there is more likelihood that the benefit will accrue directly to the children. Finally, cash payments for parenthood may encourage the breeding of undesirable elements in the population, a result which it is desired to avoid.[2] But there are, of course, certain spheres in which help may best be given in the form of cash grants.

Under the heading of encouragements to marriage, the most important measure passed is the Act of 30 September 1937,[3] for providing home-furnishing loans. The loans

[1] Myrdal, A., op. cit., p. 740.

[2] See Myrdal, G., 'Population problems and policies', in *Annals Am. Acad. Pol. and Soc. Sc.*, May 1938, pp. 200–15 (this special number of the *Annals*, devoted to 'Social problems and policies in Sweden', contains the most authoritative studies in English of very many aspects of Swedish economic and social life), and *Betänkande angående Barnbeklädnadsbidrag m.m.*, Stockholm, 1938 (report of Population Commission), chs. 2 and 5. Mr. R. Sterner wrote on this point (9 May 1938) 'the most effective way of raising the fertility would be to pay large birth premiums. . . . But this would be very ineffective from a medical and social point of view . . . we have to go another way, even if the quantitative results do not come so soon.'

[3] *Kungl. Maj:ts kungörelse om statliga bosättningslån*, 30 Sept. 1937. See also

have been granted since 1 January 1938, the money being provided by a governmental loan fund administered by the Central Bank and its local branches. Among the regulations in accordance with which the loans are given the most important points are the following: The loans are designed to allow persons who are already married (in which case the application for a loan must be made within six months of the marriage) or who are going to be married (in which case evidence of the intended marriage must be produced) to buy the furniture and other household equipment, the need for which is occasioned by the marriage which has been or is going to be contracted. At their maximum the loans are 1,000 kronor, and they are given only to persons who are Swedish citizens or who will be so as a result of the marriage (in the case of foreign brides); who are in need of the means for buying the necessary household equipment; for whom the grant of the loan is advisable, having regard to the applicants' own conditions and interests; and who are known to be diligent and economically prudent, and have shown the will to save, so far as this has been possible. The loans are to be repaid, with interest not less than that paid by the State for its own obligations, in quarterly instalments of such an amount that the loan shall be completely refunded within not more than five years after it has been granted.[1]

It will be noticed that no racial or physiological demands are made by the regulations. Nor is the loan in any sense a gift—it is not interest-free, and there are no cancellations at the birth of children. In fact the main idea, according to Professor Myrdal, is to enable young couples to escape the dangers of the hire-purchase system, and also, since their current expenses are lowest at the beginning of their married life, to have them repay the loan as quickly as possible.[2]

the Population Commission's report on the subject (*Statens off. utred.*, 1936, 14, pp. 45–7) for the original proposal, which was for loans up to 1,300 kronor repayable in four years. It should be remembered that many of the Commission's proposals have been modified in the course of passing them into laws. Myrdal, A., op. cit., gives an analysis of the original proposals as well as information on the Acts themselves.

[1] Though this rule may be relaxed if circumstances make so rapid a repayment difficult. The present rate of interest is about 3¼ per cent.

[2] In a conversation in Sept. 1937.

Finally, unlike the German marriage loans, there is no attempt to drive women back into the home. On the contrary, the Population Commission is very anxious to safeguard and guarantee the employment of married women, and to establish their right to have children and to take the required absence during pregnancy and childbirth without being subject to the fear of losing their jobs. This has already been laid down under the health insurance system, and has been extended to women employed by the central and local government authorities. A good deal has also been done with the help of the Professional and Business Women's Association by creating public disapproval of certain banks and insurance companies which followed the practice of dismissing women on account of pregnancy or childbirth.

No income limit has been laid down in the regulations for administering the home-furnishing loans, but it is clear that they are intended only for members of the working class.[1] To this extent they leave untouched a problem created by the Swedish educational system. Primary education in Sweden is free, and secondary education is inexpensive, particularly because of the large numbers of bursaries and grants in aid of fees which are available.[2] But little assistance is given to students proceeding to the universities. These students generally borrow from the banks, and the practice has become so well established that students' promissory notes are regarded as safe assets. Thus at the end of a degree course, a student often finds himself with debts of 10,000 kronor, and such an amount must be a serious barrier to early marriage.[3]

[1] Apparently some idea of a lower income limit is involved, since it is unlikely that loans will be given to applicants who are so poor that they could not repay them.

[2] In 1934–5, 371,598 kronor were distributed from the bursary and prize funds, and in 1935 and 1936 there were also grants from a public legacy fund provided by the Government, the amount in 1936 being 60,000 kronor (*Social Work and Legislation in Sweden*, issued by the Royal Social Board, 2nd ed., Stockholm, 1938, p. 328). Mr. Richard Sterner, in a discussion of this question, suggested that the actual cost of secondary education was probably only 120 to 140 kronor per year, but that there were many pupils who paid only half of these fees, and also a considerable number who paid no fees at all.

[3] But the government is proposing to remedy this by providing scholarships and endowments for students at State universities, to cover the basic costs of university life.

It is too early to speak of the effects of the home-furnishing loans, for no detailed marriage statistics are yet available for years subsequent to 1936. So far as the practical application of the Act is concerned, the Riksdag appropriated 2 million kronor for the loans for the fiscal year 1937–8, and 6 millions for 1938–9, and has proposed an appropriation of 5 million kronor for 1939–40. Up to 30 September 1938, 5,759 loans had been granted, amounting to 4,209,565 kronor, and another 1,090 loans had been granted but not yet issued.[1] Theoretically, however, the effect of the loans depends upon whether their net result is merely to speed up marriage without either increasing the total number of marriages or the fertility of each marriage. It is quite true that marriage frequency is low in Sweden. According to the conditions of 1932–4, out of 1,000 spinsters reaching their fifteenth birthday, 790 could expect to be married by their fiftieth birthday, and even in 1934, with the return to relative prosperity, the figure rose only to 816 out of 1,000. But two points should be emphasized. First, even in periods of high fertility, marriage frequency in Sweden has not been high. In 1870–1 the comparable figure was 820, while it was 791 in 1890–1, 790 in 1900–2, and 768 in 1910–12.[2] So the decline in fertility has not been associated with any significant change in marriage frequency. Secondly, there are many common-law marriages in Sweden—known as *stockholmsäktenskap*—and illegitimacy is very high, illegitimate live births amounting to 15·96 per cent. of all live births in 1932, 15·49 per cent. in 1933, and 14·45 per cent. in 1934.[3] It is conceivable, therefore, that if the introduction of marriage loans increases the number of marriages, this may to a considerable extent be due simply to the legalization of these *de facto* marriages. On the other hand, marriage loans may, by lowering the age at marriage and therefore increasing the period of exposure to the 'risk' of child-bearing, increase the number of children per marriage. How the

[1] From a memorandum (in typescript), dated 26 April 1939, supplied by the Social department.

[2] This is gross nuptiality (excluding the influence of mortality). Nor has the mean expectation of unmarried life changed appreciably (also derived from the gross nuptiality tables).

[3] *Befolkningsrörelsen*, 1934, p. 24*.

different factors counterbalance each other will not be known until the detailed statistics are available for a large number of years.[1]

Before dealing with the other steps which have been taken and proposals which have been made, it is important to know some of the facts concerning the economic and social conditions of the Swedish population. Those who have been impressed by journalistic eulogies of Sweden will be surprised to learn that, according to the 1930 census, 76·2 per cent. of the active population earned not more than 2,000 kronor per year, and that 51·9 per cent. earned not more than 1,000 kronor per year. Yet the incomes of 2,000 kronor and more per year formed 66·4 per cent. of the income earned by the employed population as a whole, and the incomes of 10,000 kronor or more per year, earned by only 1·1 per cent. of the employed population, formed 16·4 per cent. of the total income of all employed persons.[2] How this situation affects families of different sizes is shown by the partial census of 1935–6, which made a special investigation of incomes in relation to the family. The main features are given in Table 30.

To a considerable extent this picture is overpainted. First, there is a marked tendency to understate incomes, and, secondly, it is very difficult in the rural districts to estimate the monetary value of income received in kind. The 1936 statistics of wages paid to workers in industry appear to be considerably higher than would be expected from the figures given in Table 30. But it would nevertheless be true to say that there is an inverse relationship between income and the number of dependent children, and this, whether looked at from the point of view of the standard of living or from that of the correlation between income and fertility, still produces the same effect. The larger families are worse off, economically, than the small ones.

Further, housing conditions in Sweden still leave much to be desired, in spite of the fact that slums, in the English sense, are extremely rare. According to the housing census

[1] See Note VII*e*, p. 463.

[2] From Sterner, R., 'Levnadsstandarden i svenska familjer', *Betänkande i Sexualfrågan*, p. 217.

TABLE 30. *Median Incomes (including Husband's and Wife's Combined Incomes) in Marriages with Given Numbers of Children.*[1]

Marriages with the following numbers of children under 16 years of age	*Median incomes per year in kronor*		
	Towns	*Rural districts*	*Kingdom*
0	3,145	1,362	2,148
1	2,967	1,478	2,072
2	3,023	1,459	1,955
3	2,986	1,449	1,751
4	2,790	1,388	1,612
5	2,650	1,349	1,474
6	2,573	1,314	1,425
7	2,500	1,323	1,410
8	..	1,200	1,275
9 or more	..	1,088	1,191
All marriages	3,036	1,421	1,993

of 1933, in which a child under 15 years of age is counted as half an adult unit, and kitchens, halls, and rooms smaller than 9 square metres (about 97 square feet) are reckoned as halves of a room unit, about 13 per cent. of all dwellings were overcrowded in the sense of having more than two adult units per room unit. About 30 per cent. of children under 15 years of age were living in these overcrowded conditions, and so were 47·4 per cent. of the families with three or more children.[2]

These statistics apply only to urban districts—excluding Stockholm, where there had been a housing census in 1930—or to agglomerations in rural districts, excluding therefore most of the agricultural workers.[3] But in rural districts the problem is certainly no less important, since, even if the number of rooms per family is higher, the families are

[1] *Betänkande i Sexualfrågan*, p. 26. The Table refers only to marriages contracted since 1900. In a letter Mr. R. Sterner stated that in 1936 the average annual earnings of full-time or nearly full-time male workers were 2,848 kronor in industry, and between 1,200 and 1,400 kronor in agriculture (including income in kind), with forestry workers at about the same level as, or a little below, agricultural workers.

[2] *Allmänna Bostadsräkningen År 1933*, Stockholm, 1936, pp. 13–14.

[3] Ibid., p. 9. The general inquiry related to 243 areas—196 towns and urban agglomerations, and 47 rural communes, excluding agricultural properties. But the special inquiry from which these percentages are derived related to 45 areas.

larger than in the towns and the quality of accommodation is far worse. According to a special housing inquiry made in connexion with the census of 1935–6, and covering a hundred rural communes, about 15 per cent. of the dwellings were dilapidated and 9 per cent. were damp. About 33 per cent. of all dwellings consisted of not more than one room and a kitchen, as compared with approximately 50 per cent. in the towns, and about 12 per cent. of all dwellings were overcrowded in the sense of having more than two adult units per room unit. In addition, the prevalent 'best room' system further restricted the space used for sleeping, so that of the population in families with three or more children under 15 years of age who were living in small dwellings, about 63 per cent. slept in overcrowded conditions in which there were four or more persons per room.[1] The facts in this and in the preceding paragraph have not been given to try to prove that the Swedish standard of living is low. On the contrary, it is higher than in most other countries. But the facts do show—and the Population Commission recognizes the facts and faces them realistically—that the existing distribution of income in relation to family size and the poor condition of much of the housing are two of the most important problems which have to be solved.

Among the measures taken to relieve the economic burdens incurred in respect of children we may note a number intended to reduce the personal expenses associated with childbirth. Previously a woman could obtain maternity benefit in one of two ways. If she belonged to an approved sickness insurance fund and was entitled to benefit, she would receive a grant of not less than 2 kronor per day for between 30 and 56 days. If she was not entitled to this benefit, and if the taxable income of the family (or her own if she was unmarried) was not over 500 kronor per year, she would be entitled to State relief at the rate of 1 kronor per day for 30 days, minus 2 kronor for registration fee, thus making a total of 28 kronor. A woman who came under the

[1] *Partiella Folkräkningen i Mars 1936: Specialundersökning av Bostadsförhållandena i 100 Landskommuner*, Stockholm, 1938, pp. xii–xvi. Dwellings consisting of not more than two rooms and a kitchen constituted over 58 per cent. of all dwellings in the rural communes. Of these small dwellings over 35 per cent. were dilapidated or/and overcrowded.

Workers' Protection Act, and was prohibited from working for a specified period before and after childbirth, would be entitled to the relief for 56 days. An Act passed in 1937 has now placed the minimum level of maternity insurance benefit at 110 kronor, to be given in a lump sum. In addition, State maternity relief has been increased to a lump sum grant of 75 kronor, while it can be claimed by a woman if the taxable income does not exceed 3,000 kronor per year. Consequently, about 92 per cent. of all mothers are entitled to this relief, whereas formerly only 74 per cent. were so entitled.[1] In addition, another Act passed in 1937 and coming into force as from the beginning of 1938, provides special grants for necessitous mothers. The grants may be given as loans or gifts, and either in money or in goods, and the maximum value is 300 kronor for the birth of each child. During the first stage of application of this Act over 25 per cent. of all mothers received assistance under it.[2]

For the children themselves a number of special provisions has been made. First, under an Act passed in 1938, the income-tax system has been altered, and the exemptions in respect of children have been increased. It was originally intended to introduce a fairly steep graduation of the tax, with a high exemption limit for children, and a special tax on bachelors. But the special Committee on Taxation to which the proposals were handed did not accept the bachelor tax and reduced the exemption level for children. The latter now amounts to about 80 per cent. of the exemption given for a single man and for a wife.[3] Secondly, in 1937 the Riksdag introduced free school meals in districts in which there was unemployment.[4] The scheme is as yet—although widened in 1938—rudimentary, but it is hoped that, eventually, free school meals may be available for all children.

Besides the assistance given to normal families—that is, normal in the sense that both parents are alive, married, and not separated—new provisions have been made for special types of families. Sweden has, for example, taken an im-

[1] Myrdal, A., op. cit., pp. 745–6, and *Social Work and Legislation in Sweden*, pp. 127–8.

[2] Myrdal, A., op. cit., p. 746.

[3] Letter from R. Sterner, and ibid., p. 742.

[4] Ibid., pp. 753–5.

portant step in improving the situation of unmarried mothers and their children. A considerable advance on the position in most other countries was made as long ago as 1917, when the Act relating to children born out of wedlock instituted a system of specially appointed legal guardians to act in the interests of the mothers and their children, generally until the children reached their sixteenth or eighteenth birthdays. But it was found that the maintenance allowance—determined generally by the court, and amounting to 15 to 20 kronor per month in the rural districts, and 20 to 30 kronor in the towns—was often delayed. In 1935 about half the cases liable for this payment showed either complete or partial default.[1] To remedy this the Riksdag decided, in 1937, that a child whose father is liable to support him—and this applies equally to the children of separated or divorced parents—may receive an advance on the payment due to him, such an advance generally being given for a year at a time. The payment is then claimed from the father by the Treasury, and the costs of giving these advances are shared by the Treasury (75 per cent.) and by the particular local district (25 per cent.) from which the advance is received.[2] The same year also saw an Act instituting grants for needy children. Orphans, fatherless children, and the children of certain classes of disabled persons may now receive State allowances. For orphans these amount to 300, 360, or 420 kronor per year, dependent upon the cost of living in the district in which the child is living. The grants are reduced if they are being given to more than one child in the same family, and also if the total family income is above 600, 800, or 1,000 kronor per year, these limits being related to the cost of living in the different localities. At the same time, the grants are increased by 60 kronor per year for children under 2 years of age. For the other classes of children the basic grants are 60 kronor per year less than for orphans. In all cases the allowance ceases at the child's sixteenth birthday.[3]

[1] Sterner, R., 'Levnadsstandarden i svenska familjer', *Betänkande i Sexualfrågan*, p. 230, n. 1.

[2] *Social Work and Legislation in Sweden*, pp. 233–5 and 228–9.

[3] Ibid., pp. 146–7 and information from Mr. R. Sterner.

As regards housing, some improvement has come about in recent years as part of a general public works policy for relieving unemployment. In 1933 the Riksdag appropriated 5 million kronor for granting loans to contractors who wished to build new houses in towns and urban districts, and in 1935 a further grant of 3 million kronor was given, though the latter was also intended to help in the repair of existing dwellings. In 1936 still another grant of 2 million kronor was made, but the fund is now available for repairs only.

Similarly, beginning with 1933, grants were made by the Riksdag for improving and repairing rural dwellings, provided that the applicants were in need of financial aid. The upper limit of the grant is 1,000 kronor per dwelling, and in practice the average amount has been about 700 kronor. At the same time, loans have been made for building new dwellings in the rural districts, at 4 per cent. interest and to be repaid within twenty years, the maximum being 3,000 kronor per dwelling. Since most rural dwellings are built of wood, this sum probably represents the upper limit of about 70 per cent. of the total cost of construction. By the end of 1936 nearly 39 million kronor had been granted for rural housing, of which about 7·5 million kronor were used for putting up new dwellings.[1] Since, however, much of the work was intended immediately to reduce unemployment, control over the quality of the work was not all that could be desired, with the result, according to Professor Myrdal, that in some 2 or 3 per cent. of the repaired houses the repairs were inadequate.[2]

There is also the question of the rent charged for various kinds of accommodation. Since the War the co-operative building societies—of which the two most important examples are the Stockholm Co-operative Housing Society (S.K.B.), founded in 1915, and the Tenants' Savings Fund and Housing Society (H.S.B.), founded in 1923—have helped considerably in reducing rents. It is estimated that in general the rents of co-operative dwellings are 10 to 30 per cent. below those available in the open market, while outside Stockholm they are generally 25 to 30 per cent.

[1] Decree of 30 June 1933. [2] In a conversation in Sept. 1937.

below the prevailing market price; but the co-operative societies have built only a small proportion of the houses in the post-War period. Table 31 shows the rents for small dwellings in the period 1 October 1933 to 30 September 1934.

TABLE 31.[1] *Average Annual Rent in Kronor for Dwellings consisting of:*

	1 room	*1 room + kitchen*	*2 rooms + kitchen*	*3 rooms + kitchen*
Stockholm	611	748	1,124	1,609
70 other towns . . .	277	381	605	898

Reference to Table 30 shows how difficult is the position of families with three or more children. To improve the position of these families the government initiated, and in 1935 the Riksdag agreed to, a project for rehousing 20,000 families with three or more dependent children, who were at present living in overcrowded dwellings in the towns and urban districts. In 1935, 10 million kronor were granted for this purpose, and a further 15 million were given in 1936. From this fund loans for constructing dwellings of not less than two rooms and a kitchen for the accommodation of the large and relatively poor families are granted to the communes, or through the communes to public utility building societies or individual contractors of the same class as the building societies—which would seem to indicate the rapid disappearance of the speculative builder in the near future. Special attention has to be given to the provision of baths, communal laundries, access to parks and playgrounds, and the provision of indoor play centres and crèches if these are thought to be necessary. The dwellings may range from single-family houses to blocks of flats. The loan covers up to 40 per cent. of the value of the dwellings, the rate of interest being that paid by the State for its own borrowing, and the commune concerned must provide the land free of charge and be responsible for the payment of interest and amortization. It must also provide 5 per cent. of the capital required for building. It is estimated that in this way rents will be about 10 to 15 per cent. below those prevailing in the

[1] *Social Work and Legislation in Sweden*, p. 289.

open market. In addition, the State makes grants to the communes for the purpose of further reducing the rents charged to the large families. Thus a family of three dependent children has the rent reduced by 30 per cent., a four-child family has a 40 per cent. reduction, and a family of five or more children is given a 50 per cent. reduction. To cover these rebates 500,000 kronor were allocated by the Riksdag in 1935 and 650,000 kronor in 1936.[1]

As an illustration of the result of this policy on rent charges, a flat in Stockholm built under this scheme, consisting of two rooms, kitchen, and bathroom, and provided with central heating and constant hot water, will be let at 550 kronor per year to a three-child family and 400 kronor per year to a five-child family. The average rent for a dwelling of two rooms and a kitchen in Stockholm in 1933–4 was, as is shown in Table 31, 1,124 kronor per year. In keeping with the general policy, the blocks of flats which Stockholm is setting up for large families are on the outskirts of the town, near to water and the green belt.[2]

In 1938 two important modifications were made in the legislation relating to housing for large families. First, the legislation was applied to owners of homes in rural or urban districts. Secondly, the upper limit of rent rebates was raised, so that the rebate amounts to 60 per cent. when there are six or seven children, and to 70 per cent. when there are eight or more.[3] For the fiscal years 1935–6 to 1939–40 the Riksdag has appropriated 35·5 million kronor for the loan fund for providing accommodation for large families, and by the middle of April 1939 the loans actually granted amounted to 19 million kronor. Up to the present, rent rebates have been granted for some 5,100 dwellings, of which about 4,700 are in blocks of flats.[4]

1 Goodsell, W., 'Housing and the birth rate in Sweden', *American Sociological Review*, Dec. 1937, and *Social Work and Legislation in Sweden*, pp. 296–8.

2 *Social Work in Stockholm* (City of Stockholm Statistical Office), Uppsala, 1937, pp. 71–4. Collective crèches will be provided in the blocks of flats, so that children may be looked after while their mothers work or go out. At one crèche in Stockholm which the present writer visited, a charge of 60 öre per day was made for looking after a child from 7 a.m. to 7 p.m. and giving it three meals in that period. Such crèches are generally found in the H.S.B. blocks of flats.

3 Myrdal, A., op. cit., p. 752.

4 Unpublished report from the Social department.

It has already been noted that few specific measures relating to population policy have been promulgated in either Denmark or Norway. But in both countries a considerable proportion of recent legislation has a direct bearing on the population question and detailed studies of the different aspects of the question are being undertaken both through the Population Commission in Denmark, and by means of *ad hoc* commissions in Norway. As regards Denmark, the question of the establishment of public birth-control clinics has been mentioned in an earlier section of this survey. The Danish Population Commission has also recently issued two reports,[1] one dealing with help to needy mothers, in which it is proposed to follow the Swedish example and give a grant to help cover the costs of bearing a child, the other with the question of providing suitable housing conditions for large families. Here, again, the proposal is along the Swedish lines, consisting essentially of rent rebates of 30 per cent. for three children, 40 per cent. for four, and 50 per cent. for five or more children.

Denmark has, of course, already seen a considerable amount of State help in providing houses and flats. Up till 1 April 1936, by which date the relevant Act fell into abeyance, the State provided loans for up to thirty-six years and covering as much as 95 per cent. of the total cost of construction, including land costs, to public utility building societies, and by 1937 about 20 per cent. of the population of Copenhagen was living in dwellings under public or communal control. Loans for up to 70 per cent. of the costs of construction were also given for private buildings. In both cases the rate of interest charged was $4\frac{1}{2}$ per cent., about 1 per cent. below the market rate.[2] Since 1936, however, such public assistance as is given to housing must come from the communes concerned, unless new provisions

[1] *Betænkning . . . angaaende Moderens Rettigheder i Anledning af Fødsel samt angaaende Seksualoplysning*, Copenhagen, 1938, and *Betænkning . . . angaaende Laan till Boligbyggeri og Huslejefradrag for mindrebemidlede, børnerige Familier*, Copenhagen, 1937.

[2] Boldsen, F. C., 'Der Wohnungs- und Siedlungsbau in Dänemark, Schweden und Norwegen', in *Vom Wirtschaftlichen Bauen*, 18e Folge, ed. R. Stegemann, Dresden, 1937, pp. 53 and 56.

are made under recommendations from the Population Commission.[1]

In Norway less has been done to improve housing, for the task of giving grants to help the provision of new dwellings has fallen entirely to the communes. In Oslo the municipal authorities granted loans covering up to 90 per cent. of the 'normal value', which apparently was equivalent to about 80 per cent. of the actual value. By 1937 about 17 per cent. of the population of Oslo was living in dwellings built under such grants.[2] But the general housing situation in Norway is still very unsatisfactory. According to the reports of the Oslo Birth Control and Maternal Welfare Clinic, 67 per cent. of the patients who attended in 1933 lived in dwellings containing not more than one room and a kitchen, while the percentages were 58·2 in 1934, 58·5 in 1935, and 59·5 in 1936.[3] These figures refer, of course, to a very selected sample of the population. But according to the 1930 census, there was marked overcrowding among the general industrial workers and their families. In Oslo 29·8 per cent. of these workers lived in overcrowded conditions (more than two persons per room), 29·0 per cent. in Bergen, 32·5 per cent. in Trondheim, 27·2 per cent. in Stavanger, and 21·0 per cent. in Drammen.[4] It is possible, however, that the near future will see improvements in housing conditions, since the present government is seriously concerned with the problem.

On the other hand, some important steps have been taken to improve the conditions of mothers and children. Since 1915, for example, mothers who are badly off have been entitled to a subsidy from the communes to help them during pregnancy and childbirth. During the last six weeks of pregnancy they are entitled to the payment of 45 to 110 kronor for the period. For the first month after childbirth they receive between 35 and 110 kronor, and for

[1] For existing social legislation in Denmark, see Steincke, K. K., 'The Danish social reform measures', *International Labour Review*, May 1935, pp. 620–48, and the account given in the *Danish Foreign Office Journal*, June 1939, especially pp. 108–12.

[2] Boldsen, F. C., op. cit., pp. 53 and 58–9.

[3] *Mødrehygienekontoret i Oslo*, Reports for 1924–34, 1934, 1935, and 1936.

[4] *Folketellingen i Norge, 1. desember 1930 ... Boligstatistikk*, Oslo, 1935, pp. 26*–8*.

the next five months their grant is from 30 to 85 kronor per month.[1]

As regards children, there is the now well-known system of 'Oslo breakfasts', which were first instituted under the direction of Professor Carl Schiøtz in Oslo in 1931. These breakfasts, which are generally given half an hour before morning school begins, consist of one-third of a litre of full-cream milk, a 'Kneipp cracker' (made preferably of wholemeal wheat flour) served with margarine and goat's-milk cheese, further wholemeal bread with margarine and cheese *ad lib.*, and, finally, half an apple or orange, or a raw carrot. Margarine was used for economy only, and is probably now being replaced by butter, especially as the government decided to allow public and municipal institutions to buy butter at a reduced price. In March 1938 Professor Schiøtz proposed that half an orange be given in any case (or briar marmalade, which is very rich in vitamin C), as well as a raw carrot or half an apple, and that between September and May a teaspoonful of cod-liver oil should be given to each child at breakfast.

The 'Oslo breakfasts' have been adopted by all the elementary schools in Oslo, Bergen, Trondheim, Tromsö, and many other towns, as well as by a number of schools in rural districts. The breakfasts are given free of charge in the towns, but a charge is made in many of the rural schools, or else the children bring the standard constituents with them to school. In Oslo about 46 per cent. of the school-children receive the breakfasts.[2]

Finally, a Committee set up in 1934 to consider the question of family allowances issued its report in 1938. The Committee was primarily concerned with improving the conditions of children, and not specifically directed to a population policy, and its problem was to decide how far children could be helped by public institutions and how far by direct cash allowances. The majority report concludes

[1] Information given by Dr. Frydenberg of the Social department in Sept. 1937.

[2] From C. Schiøtz, 'Skolefrokosten', *Tidsskrift for den Norske Lægeforening*, 1938, and a special memorandum entitled 'The Oslo Breakfast', both kindly sent to me by Professor Schiøtz. Parents who wish their children to have the breakfasts must state their reasons—poverty or poor health, or both. But Professor Schiøtz said that it was not considered a matter of reproach or shame to get free meals.

that collective effort is best for such needs as housing, and medical attention, but that for the day-to-day needs of life in a country in which the population is scattered and transport slow and expensive, cash family allowances would be the most satisfactory solution, particularly if these allowances were paid to the mothers. It recognizes the need for allowances graded in relation to the cost of living in different parts of the country, but, because of the complexity which such a system would involve, recommends a uniform allowance as between the different districts, graded so that the highest amount is given for the first child, with decreasing amounts for each subsequent child.

The Committee suggests no specific allowance, being willing to leave this question until such time as the government decides to implement the proposal, but in the estimates of costs which were drawn up by Dr. H. Palmstrøm, actuary and member of the Committee, the rates chosen as examples were 100 and 120 kronor per year. If 120 kronor per year were given for each child under 15 years of age, the annual cost would be nearly 82 million kronor. On the other hand, if the allowances were graded so that the first child received 120 kronor, the second child received only 90 kronor, and the third and subsequent children only 60 kronor per year, the cost would amount to nearly 66 million kronor per year. As for raising the necessary funds, the majority report suggests an increase in the turnover tax, a 1 per cent. turnover tax now yielding about 30 million kronor per year.[1] There is as yet no suggestion that the Committee's recommendations will be put into practice in the near future. In fact if anything is done at all, it is more likely to be on the lines laid down in Sweden and not as cash allowances.[2]

It is clear from the account that has been given that in the

[1] *Utkast till Lov om Barnetrygd med Motiver*, Oslo, 1938. Judge G. Wiesener, Chairman of the Committee, kindly sent the writer a copy of the report and a special unpublished summary.

[2] Hertzberg, A., 'Barnetrygd i Norge', *Urd*, 12 March 1938. There was a minority report, drawn up by Mrs. M. Bonnevie, and recommending the establishment of a national equalization fund, financed by the affiliated wage-earners. See also 'The question of family allowances in Norway', *International Labour Review*, July 1939, pp. 56–63, and Skaug, A., and Wold, K. G., 'Barnetrygdkomitéens innstilling', *Socialt Arbeid*, 1938, no. 8, and 1939, no. 4. The writer owes a great deal to Dr. Skaug both for Norwegian publications and for valuable suggestions.

Scandinavian countries there is a real interest in the various problems which arise out of the population question. A great many of the proposals have been modified in the process of application, and very many of them still remain to be applied. But, especially in Sweden, they have been planned carefully, on the basis of a detailed study of the data available. Up to the present the economic assistance actually given to families is still relatively small, and whether the proposals suggested and measures actually introduced will have any significant effect upon the trend of fertility is, of course, impossible to predict. But of the general proposals and measures two things may be said. First, they are in keeping with the thesis of democratic government, for they all emphasize the need for voluntary parenthood. Secondly, whatever their effect upon fertility, they are in any case all socially desirable.

VIII

NATURE AND CONSEQUENCES OF POPULATION TRENDS

IN earlier chapters we have discussed in some detail the extent to which the populations of various countries have been reproducing themselves in recent years. We have seen that in all the countries concerned, fertility fell very markedly from about the third quarter of the nineteenth century, and that, Italy apart, it is now below the level necessary for the permanent maintenance of populations of any given size. This is true of most Western nations to-day. In spite of the rise in fertility since 1933 most of them now have net reproduction rates below unity. Three questions immediately arise from this situation. First, what is going to happen to the populations of the different countries? Secondly, will future trends have 'good' or 'bad' effects upon the economic and social life of the various countries? Thirdly, if the results are mainly 'bad', can we do anything now or in the future either to alter the trends or to minimize the disadvantages that they would otherwise bring in their train? These three questions cover, very broadly, the problems involved in any discussion of the implications of a declining population. Unfortunately, the material at our disposal does not allow us to give definite answers to any of them, and the present chapter will endeavour only to point to some of the more important factors which have to be taken into account.

The first question would appear to be the easiest to answer, for we know that if a country has a net reproduction rate persistently below unity, and if the deficit is not made up by immigration, the population of that country will eventually disappear. The rate of diminution will, of course, depend upon the given conditions of fertility and mortality. We can therefore make various kinds of assumptions, and employ various techniques to compute the rate of decline of a population and the size which will obtain at any given point of time. We can calculate the true rate of natural increase and thus arrive at the ultimate rate of growth of a population and at its stable age composition and birth- and death-rates. These results will apply only from the point at which the effects of given fertility and mortality have permeated the population. For the interim period we can arrive at the size, age composition, and rate of growth either by using highly complex mathematical techniques, or relatively simple—though rather laborious—statistical techniques.

If we are interested only in theoretical considerations, these problems are comparatively straightforward, and the assumptions and techniques chosen will be determined solely by the theoretical questions which the work is designed to illustrate. But in recent years various workers have been concerned not so much with giving the practical proofs of certain theoretical problems as with finding answers to the question—what will be the future trend of a given population? In England the first serious attempt to estimate the future population was made by Professor Cannan in 1895,[1] though this was not so much a prediction as a demonstration that, while many prominent statisticians were still composing laments for the impending overpopulation of the country, there was a strong possibility that the population would decline during the twentieth century. Since the last War the technique of calculation has improved, primarily because more attention has been given to specific fertility and mortality rates as contrasted with the customary pre-War practice of extrapolating birth- and death-rates, crude rates of natural increase, or total populations. Thus in the post-War period we have the estimates of Bowley, and Greenwood, and, rather later, of G. G. Leybourne. It has also become customary to construct estimates on series of hypotheses as regards nuptiality, fertility, and mortality, thus offering a range of possibilities within which the future populations might actually fall. Thus S. D. Wicksell was responsible for such estimates for Norway and Sweden, while W. S. Thompson and P. K. Whelpton have constructed numerous

[1] For detailed references to the various published estimates mentioned in this chapter, see 'Selected list of articles and books containing estimates of future populations or discussions of such estimates', Appendix to present study, pp. 468–72.

estimates for the U.S.A. For England and Wales and for Scotland the most striking examples are those of Enid Charles. Dr. Charles used three separate groups of assumptions for her estimates of the future population of England and Wales. One was rather in the nature of a theoretical demonstration, as it assumed constant fertility and mortality at the 1933 level. Another might be regarded, from Dr. Charles's point of view, as an improbable possibility, in that it assumed some rise in fertility. The third was, from Dr. Charles's point of view, a more probable possibility, for it extrapolated recent trends in fertility and mortality. In none of the assumptions was migration taken into account. Still more recently, F. J. C. Honey constructed an estimate for Great Britain, ending with 1971. At the beginning of his study of the subject he said that, in his opinion, 'in none of the previously published estimates has full account been taken of the available data',[1] and he proceeded to make a detailed analysis of the probable trends of fertility and mortality. His computation probably most nearly approaches an attempted 'horoscope' of the population.

Much publicity has recently been given to various sets of population estimates, and many writers—mainly journalists—have tended to regard them as predictions rather than as statistical exercises. It is, therefore, important to examine the various difficulties which have to be met if a population estimate is to give results which approach closely to the real course of future events. Let us assume that the estimates are constructed by a method which takes into account specific fertility and mortality rates, and which does not obtain its results simply by extrapolation of the birth- and death-rates, or by fitting curves to the total populations. The difficulties which then have to be met consist in making correct assumptions as regards the course of mortality, fertility, and migration, the term 'correct' being used in the sense that these assumptions are borne out exactly by future events.

Assumptions regarding the trend of mortality are generally made on the basis of past experience. That is, some method of extrapolation is used in order to link up past death-rates with future ones in lines or curves which

[1] *J. Inst. Actuaries*, 1937, p. 323.

appear reasonably appropriate. This immediately raises two questions. First, is there any reason to believe that death-rates will show a consistent trend? Secondly, how is the extrapolation to be made? The first question can only be answered in the fields of preventive and curative medicine, subjects of which the present writer, like most people who have in the past constructed population estimates, has very little knowledge. But two suggestions present themselves. First, if populations begin to decline, governments may be spurred to undertaking campaigns of public hygiene and medical research, in order to conserve as far as possible the existing inhabitants and those who will still continue to be born. Secondly, genetic and physiological research are still comparatively new subjects, and even the near future may see striking discoveries. Both possibilities may very markedly extend the number of years which a newly born child can expect to live, and thus retard or postpone the decline of the population, even if effect upon the reproductive ages is small. The retarding influence will be especially noticed if there are considerable reductions in mortality at the later ages, a section of life in which, up to the present, progress has been extremely slow.

The second question is one relating to statistical technique, and has to be answered even if medical and hygienic considerations are taken into account in gauging the future of mortality. The problem is not so much whether to fit straight lines, parabolas, or logistic curves to past mortality data, and continue these into the future—though this is also an important question—as how to look at the death-rates before applying technical methods of curve-fitting. Most extrapolations are made by extending the curves which fit each specific death-rate. But V. P. A. Derrick looks at the problem in a different way.[1] Speaking of the specific death-rates, drawn in the usual way, he says:

'Within a given calendar period the mortality variations at different ages bear little relation to one another; in the period 1866–76 the rates at the younger ages were falling steeply, while at older ages they were stationary or increasing, and between 1906 and 1923 the greatest fall occurred in the middle years of life, accompanied by much

[1] See Note VIII*a*, p. 463.

more gradual decreases both at younger and older ages. Such relation as does exist between the successive age curves must be sought in the common wave form to which they appear to be subject . . . if the series be examined more closely it will be observed that the comparable sections of each wave are separated from one another by an interval of time corresponding very closely to the difference between the ages to which the waves relate . . .'[1]

Drawing the curves on a generation basis—that is, plotting each specific death-rate against the period of birth of the persons to whom the rate applies, instead of the period in which the rate was observed—introduces a remarkable regularity into the graph. Derrick's graphs represented specific death-rates, and the parallelism of the separate age-curves (excluding the ages below 10 years, which seem to follow quite different trends) does suggest that each generation, at least from the age of 10 onwards, tends to carry its own mortality with it. If this is in fact the case, it would explain why there has been so little improvement in mortality at the very late ages, since persons in these ages would have been born at a time when infant and child mortality was extremely high, and thus had their vitality seriously affected by the bad conditions which prevailed during their childhood. We thus have a more reasonable basis for forecasting mortality than by simple extrapolation from the specific age-curves. But even using this new basis, there are very numerous possibilities in extrapolation. We may assume, as Derrick does in his graphs, that the mortality trends in the older ages will parallel those in the younger ones, allowing an appropriate generation lag. But we still do not know how the younger ages will move—whether mortality will continue to fall for a considerable period, or whether the curve will soon parallel the base-line. However, there is a much greater consensus of opinion among vital statisticians and doctors as regards the possibilities of reducing mortality at the younger ages than there is about the older ages. We know that up to the present there has been very little change in the mortality of persons above 60 years of age, and the possibilities as regards the future are not by any means clear. Further, we may use the

[1] *J. Inst. Actuaries*, 1927, pp. 143–4.

idea of generation mortality and extrapolate, not along the age-curves, but along each generation. Cramér and Wold use this method by assuming that the Makeham formula gives a good picture of the relationship between age and mortality for ages over 30 years. Kermack, McKendrick, and McKinlay used a simpler method. They found that diagonals drawn through 10-year age intervals—that is through the age group 10–19 years in 1870, 20–9 years in 1880, 30–9 years in 1890, 40–9 years in 1900, and so forth—exhibited a high consistency, and they used this diagonal method for extrapolation. All these methods give divergent sets of results, even though the divergencies may not, in relative terms, be very great. Three attempts by the present writer to 'forecast' mortality in England and Wales in 1970 have, for example, given female expectations of life of 68·42, 70·15, and 70·46 years, and estimates of the future population based on these expectations would show significant differences in the total population and its age structure.

In extrapolating fertility the difficulties are even greater. Here again, the irregular and apparently incompatible movements of many of the age groups (excepting the group 15 to 19 years, and probably also that of 20 to 24 years) may be made more consistent by treating the question from the generation standpoint. Logarithmic statement of the specific fertility rates plotted against the date of birth of the relevant groups shows considerable regularity in the trends of the separate age rates, and so also does the method—of Barclay and Kermack—of representing the course of each age rate as a percentage of the relevant rate in some base year.[1] The fertility trend shown appears to indicate an initial fall in the older ages, passing successively through each younger age group—that is, the opposite of the trend shown in mortality. The trend described appears plausible, for it would support the *a priori* hypothesis (partly confirmed by questionnaire investigations) that older women were the first to be influenced by birth-control propaganda and to

[1] See Barclay, R. S., and Kermack, W. O., 'The decline of the birth rate: regularities revealed by an analysis of the rates observed in certain European countries', *Proceedings of the Royal Society of Edinburgh*, vol. lviii, part i, 1937–8.

make use of contraceptive techniques. Further, the estimates for England and Wales made by Barclay and Kermack fit in very well with the actual births at the various census years. But the extrapolation problem remains, for all the curves appear to trend towards zero. Logically, there is no reason to jibe at such a trend, but in practice it seems unlikely that there will be a complete birth-strike, even though human fertility is coming increasingly under individual control, and if there is no complete birth-strike, where are the curves to be inflected, and are they to become constant or to turn upwards again? These problems remain, even in countries which have good statistical material covering long periods of time. In Britain, where we have only just begun to provide adequate birth data—adequate, that is, in terms of their scope—the problems are even more complicated.

The fact is that in spite of all our statistical techniques, we have no clear understanding of the *rationale* of changes in fertility. We know—as Dr. D. S. Thomas and others have shown[1]—that there is an association between fertility and economic conditions. But the association is found only in annual fluctuations from the secular trend; the trend itself appears unrelated to measurable economic or social phenomena. We do not even know, for many countries, the mechanism by which the decline is being carried out—whether there is a general low level of size to which all families are tending, or whether there is still a core of high fertility, relatively unaffected by changes among the rest of the population. And until we have information on this aspect of the problem we cannot do more than guess if and when the decline in fertility will eventually check itself. This problem can be seen very clearly in countries containing populations with markedly different fertilities, such as Canada or the Union of South Africa. Canadian fertility is still high because of the French Canadians. If, therefore, we were to extrapolate Canadian fertility into the future, we should have to take two very different population elements into account. Similarly, the white population of the British Empire probably has a net reproduction rate under unity. But if we were to extrapolate the specific fertility rates of the

[1] Thomas, D. S., *Social Aspects of the Business Cycle*, London, 1925.

total female population, we should probably receive an incorrect impression of the future of this population. For it is far more likely that after some initial fluctuations around a stationary population the more fertile elements would assert themselves and the population would begin to grow again, at least for a time.[1] So far we have discussed fertility independently of marriage, although in most Western countries the majority of births are legitimate. Marriage introduces a further set of complications, though from the discussion in the section on nuptial reproduction rates, the influence of marriage on general fertility may be exaggerated—since fertility has fallen within marriage and not significantly because of changes in the amount of marriage. But if there are changes in the sex ratio of the living population, the proportion of involuntary celibacy may be affected, and although this would not necessarily raise legitimate specific fertility rates, it might very well increase the net reproduction rate.

Finally, there is the question of migration, which introduces a further series of problems. In Britain, until very recently, we had an almost continual net balance of outward migration. Consequently, population estimates for this country, even in their most optimistic assumptions, have excluded the possibility of a net balance of inward migration. As with other assumptions, this, too, may be perfectly logical, but it may nevertheless be quite unreasonable. In many countries concern has already been expressed at the prospects of a declining population, and in some countries, as has been seen in earlier chapters, definite policies are being implemented with the aim of changing the prospect. The encouragement of immigration is one of the least difficult of such policies, particularly in view of the number of political refugees who have been and are still anxious to leave the countries of which they were citizens. The encouragement of immigration may influence population trends in at least two ways—it may postpone or retard the

[1] See Kuczynski, R. R., 'The white population of the Empire', *Sociological Review*, July 1937, pp. 221–31 at pp. 230–1. On Canada see Pelletier, A. J., Thompson, F. D., and Rochon, A., *The Canadian Family* (Census Monograph, No. 7), Ottawa, 1938, ch. xi.

decline of the population without influencing the reproduction rate, or it may introduce elements of fertility higher or lower than that commonly prevailing in the country receiving the immigrants. In France, for example, the rate of crude natural increase of the population has for many years largely been maintained by immigration. In the United States immigrants from central and eastern Europe may well have introduced fertility levels which, for a time at least, were considerably higher than those of the native-born population.[1] Moreover, immigration may temporarily raise the *crude* rate of natural increase not simply by a regular supply of fresh persons, but also by bringing into the country people in age groups with a relatively low mortality, who would thus tend to depress the crude death-rates, even if they carried with them higher specific mortality rates than those obtaining in their new country. Ultimately, however, the ability of a population to maintain itself depends upon its reproduction rate, and to make an accurate estimate of the influence of immigration we need to know not only the fertility and mortality rates of the immigrants when they first arrive in the new country, but also the future trend of these rates among the new-comers and among their descendants. Finally, assuming that the British Government, for example, adopts an immigration policy, how many immigrants will come into the country? This depends partly upon the number allowed in by the government, but it also depends upon other factors. In the past immigration has responded to the pull of prosperity from new countries rather than to the push of poverty from their own countries. Once the stock of political refugees has been absorbed, will prosperity in this country be high enough to attract people who are not refugees? And will the governments of other countries allow their citizens to depart freely? Russia does not encourage emigration. Italy tries to prevent her subjects from giving up their nationality, and other countries threatened with falling populations will not be very willing to allow large-scale emigration. Moreover, the pool of emigrants is now almost certainly smaller than it was before

[1] See Spengler, J. J., *The Fecundity of Native and Foreign-Born Women in New England*, Washington, D.C., 1930.

the last War because of the rapid decline in fertility in the past thirty years. So there may be strong competition between countries with low fertility for the surplus inhabitants of countries still having a high fertility.

These are the major technical difficulties which complicate the process of estimating future populations, and it is clear that they make the chances of long-run accuracy almost hopeless. In addition we have to reckon with two quite unpredictable factors—war, and the possibility of an entirely new fertility trend. When war occurs there is not only a sudden loss of a considerable proportion of a given population, but also a fall in fertility during the war. Both of these factors will also influence the future supply of marriages and births.[1] Moreover, if wars occur with devastating regularity and with increasing costliness in terms of human life, they may create, on the part of potential parents, not a blank refusal to produce children, but an increasing repugnance to bear more than the minimum number which will satisfy that blend of selfishness and self-sacrifice which comes under the heading of 'parental instinct'. And that 'instinct' may be satisfied by one child per family, instead of by the larger number necessary for the permanent replacement of the population. On the other hand, as Derrick pointed out in the discussion of F. J. C. Honey's estimate of the future population of Britain, there 'might easily be a reaction from the present preponderance of one-child and no-child families, and in that event, although he could not expect a return to the large families of the Victorian era, there might very well be increases at the smaller end of the scale sufficient to turn the curve of fertility'.[2]

[1] See, for example, Depoid, P., 'Contribution à l'étude théorique des mouvements d'une population', *Bulletin de la Statistique Générale de la France*, April–June 1935, pp. 470–86. Note that deaths among the French armed forces amounted to about 1·345 millions in the period 1914–18 inclusive, and that the crude birth-rate, which was 19·0 in 1913 and 18·1 in 1914, fell to 11·8 in 1915 and to 9·5 in 1916. From 1917 to 1921 inclusive it was 10·4, 12·1, 13·0, 21·4, and 20·7 per 1,000. (*Statistique du Mouvement de la Population* for 1933, Part I, p. 5 and n. (*a*).)

[2] Derrick, V. P. A., in *Journal Inst. Actuaries*, 1937, p. 363. He also said that 'he did not think it was possible to estimate future fertility merely from the curve of the past. He put himself into the position of the statistician of 1876, who then had a birth-rate of 35 per 1,000, with an increasing rather than a declining

But although these difficulties make the chances of long-run accuracy in forecasts almost hopeless, they do not make population estimates useless. On the contrary, such estimates may be extremely valuable if they fulfil certain conditions. First, they may be relatively accurate for short periods—for example, over ten- or twenty-year periods—though not, of course, when there is war. Secondly, the fertility and mortality extrapolations may become more accurate when we have learned more about the causes of fluctuations in these two phenomena. In forecasting fertility, for example, it is possible that we shall be on more solid ground when we have data, for a long period, relating to birth parity—that is, when we know the proportion of first, second, third, and subsequent births in the annual supply of births. From these data we may be able to obtain a more reasonable idea of the likelihood of a self-acting check upon the decline in fertility, and to estimate when such a check would begin to make itself felt upon specific fertility rates. Thirdly—and this seems to be the most pertinent condition at the moment—we may make assumptions which appear to be fairly reasonable at present, and estimate future populations on these assumptions, specifically stating the assumptions used and regarding the results as mere indications of a range of possibilities. This suggestion may appear to be superfluous, but in fact it is extremely necessary that any set of estimates which is published should be categorically defined as a statistical exercise deriving from certain postulates. Such estimates can then be used for considering the economic and social consequences of population movements, and for formulating policies to counterbalance any disadvantageous results, but there will be less likelihood than in the past of hailing them as 'prophecies'.[1]

It is with the third use in mind that the writer includes

tendency. Had that statistician been asked to make a forecast, it would have been utterly impossible for him to foresee that he was on the crest of a wave, from which there would be a cataclysmal descent covering more than half a century. Was the position any better to-day?'

[1] Though it should be noted that most of these computations were regarded by their authors as statistical exercises. Dr. Charles, for example, specifically stated that it was 'beyond the province of social science to predict what the total population of a community will be at some future date'.

in this chapter three new estimates of the 'future population' of England and Wales. These are not intended to supersede earlier estimates by other workers, but were constructed because it might be useful to have computations deriving from assumptions slightly different from those made by Dr. Charles, and taking into account the fact that fertility has risen since 1933, the year chosen by Dr. Charles as the starting-point for her assumptions. The new estimates[1] begin with the data of 1935, and make the following assumptions: Estimate I assumes the continuance of the fertility and mortality of 1935. Life tables constructed for that year show an expectation of life at birth of 60·47 years for males and 64·50 years for females. Not having actual data for computing the specific fertility rates for that year, they were estimated from the rates for Sweden, 1931. The estimated rates—numbers of live births per year per 1,000 females in each age group—are 17·256; 75·661; 93·581; 81·540; 57·742; 27·022; and 3·413 for the seven five-year age groups from 15–19 to 45–9 years inclusive. The estimated net reproduction rate for 1935 is 0·764. Migration is excluded from the computation.

Estimate II assumes the same fertility and mortality as the first estimate. But it also assumes a regular net immigration of 500,000 persons every five years from 1940. (The assumption is stated in these terms in order to simplify the calculation.) The immigrants have been attributed with the same specific fertility and mortality rates as the population of England and Wales in 1935. As regards the age and sex composition of the immigrants, we have very little past experience in England upon which to base assumptions. It has, however, been postulated that the age distribution of male immigrants shall be similar to that shown by male *emigrants* from the United Kingdom in recent years. From the males the estimate of females was obtained by assuming the same sex ratio as was exhibited at the 1931 census for the age groups 0 to 4 and 5 to 9 years; a preponderance of males for the age groups from 10 to 44 years, since there is some reason to believe that there is generally an excess of males among young and middle-aged immigrants; and an

[1] See Note VIII*b*, p. 464.

equality of the sexes from 45 years of age. The assumed age and sex distribution is shown in Table 32.

TABLE 32. *Assumed Age and Sex Distribution of the Immigrants*

	Males	*Females*
0–	21,340	20,915
5–	14,940	14,650
10–	8,540	5,125
15–	13,365	8,015
20–	46,645	27,985
25–	48,035	28,820
30–	37,975	22,785
35–	26,895	16,140
40–	21,220	12,730
45–	16,140	16,140
50–	12,810	12,810
55–	10,675	10,675
60–	7,470	7,470
65–	4,845	4,845
Total	290,895	209,105

Estimate III assumes that fertility and mortality will continue to decline for some years, and excludes the factor of migration. In extrapolating mortality V. P. A. Derrick's suggestions about the generation method were taken into account. From life tables for England and Wales, covering the period from 1851 to 1935, the probabilities of dying between successive birthdays (q_x's) were plotted in logarithmic form and curves fitted to the generations. By extrapolation data were obtained for new life tables, and the assumed expectations of life calculated from these tables are given in Table 33. For the period 1935–40 the 1935 life tables are assumed to apply.

In extrapolating fertility, relatively little guidance could be obtained from past material, for we shall have no reliable data for calculating specific fertility rates for England and Wales until the Population (Statistics) Act has been in force for a long period, and until special questions relating to fertility—similar to, but not the same as those asked in 1911—are included in census schedules. But the trend of the estimated gross reproduction rates was taken into account, together with the separate trends shown by specific

TABLE 33. *Assumed Expectations of Life at Birth (in Years), England and Wales*

	Males	*Females*
1940– . .	61·63	65·24
1945– . .	62·90	66·24
1950– . .	64·04	67·32
1955– . .	65·08	68·14
1960– . .	65·94	68·92
1965– . .	66·92	69·53
1970 and after* .	67·67	70·15

* For 1970 and onwards the mean expectation of life at birth for males and females combined, taking the 1935 sex ratio at birth as constant, would be 68·88 years. This is fairly close to the 69·93 years given in the hypothetical life table constructed by Dublin and Lotka, and entitled 'Hypothetical life table—estimate of longevity attainable under modern medical and sanitary science'. See Dublin, L. I., and Lotka, A. J., *Length of Life*, New York, 1936, p. 194.

fertility rates for Sweden. In view of the recent tendency towards a stabilization of reproduction rates in England and Wales, it was assumed that fertility would become constant at a much higher level than that postulated by Dr. Charles in her second estimate. Dr. Charles assumed that fertility would fall until in 1980–5 the gross reproduction rate would be only 0·259. That is, each 1,000 women passing through the child-bearing period and unaffected by mortality, would bear only about 530 children, as compared with about 1,781 in 1935. The present writer postulates, instead, gross reproduction rates of 0·866 in 1935–40; 0·765 in 1940–5; 0·695 in 1945–50; 0·645 in 1950–5; 0·614 in 1955–60; and 0·600 after 1960. The assumed net reproduction rates are therefore 0·764 in 1935–40; 0·683 in 1940–5; 0·628 in 1945–50; 0·591 in 1950–5; 0·567 in 1955–60; 0·559 in 1960–5; and, since mortality is assumed to fall somewhat longer than fertility, 0·563 in 1965–70, and 0·566 from 1970 onwards. The relation between the ultimate specific fertility rates and those estimated for 1935 is shown in Table 34. It will be seen that the incidence of the decline is assumed to fall most heavily upon the older age groups. This is in keeping with the experience of Sweden and Denmark, and, to a lesser extent, of France, Norway, and Finland.

The main results of these three estimates are given in

TABLE 34. *Estimated and Assumed Specific Fertility Rates, England and Wales (Live Births per Year per 1,000 Women in each Age Group)*

Age (years)	*Estimated for 1935*	*Assumed for 1960 and subsequently*
15–19 .	17·256	17·3
20–4 . .	75·661	58·0
25–9 . .	93·581	62·0
30–4 . .	81·540	53·8
35–9 . .	57·742	37·0
40–4 . .	27·022	17·0
45–9 . .	3·413	1·7

TABLE 35. *Estimates of the 'Future Population' of England and Wales (Mid-Year Populations) in Millions*

	Estimate I			*Estimate II*			*Estimate III*			
Years	*Males*	*Females*	*Total**	*Males*	*Females*	*Total**	*Males*	*Females*	*Total**	*Years*
1935	19·500	21·145	40·645	19·500	21·145	40·645	19·500	21·145	40·645	1935
1940	19·760	21·365	41·125	20·051	21·574	41·625	19·760	21·365	41·125	1940
1945	19·902	21·451	41·353	20·493	21·881	42·374	19·806	21·303	41·109	1945
1950	19·919	21·393	41·312	20·813	22·050	42·863	19·674	21·040	40·714	1950
1955	19·805	21·180	40·985	20·999	22·066	43·065	19·386	20·602	39·988	1955
1960	19·570	20·822	40·392	21·058	21·935	42·993	18·979	20·026	39·005	1960
1965	19·233	20·345	39·578	21·004	21·682	42·687	18·478	19·335	37·814	1965
1970	18·806	19·776	38·582	20·850	21·333	42·182	17·899	18·547	36·445	1970
1975	18·296	19·136	37·432	20·598	20·906	41·505	17·200	17·668	34·868	1975
1980	17·714	18·441	36·156	20·258	20·418	40·676	16·357	16·687	33·044	1980
1985	17·075	17·708	34·782	19·841	19·882	39·723	15·394	15·628	31·022	1985
1990	16·402	16·955	33·357	19·370	19·317	38·687	14·361	14·526	28·887	1990
1995	15·722	16·209	31·931	18·875	18·748	37·623	13·302	13·420	26·722	1995
2000	15·054	15·488	30·543	18·377	18·196	36·574	12·246	12·337	24·583	2000

I. Constant fertility and mortality.
II. Constant fertility and mortality, plus net immigration.
III. Declining fertility and mortality.
* As the totals have been obtained from the full data of the estimates, they are occasionally larger or smaller by one point in the thousands than the results obtained by summing the populations given here for males and females separately.

Tables 35, 36, and 37. All three estimates envisage a declining population, since the net reproduction rate in each case is assumed to remain below unity. The rate of decline varies considerably according to the basic assumptions. Starting from 40·645 millions in mid-1935, the first estimate shows a fall to 30·543 millions by 2,000, the second to 36·574, and the third to only 24·583 millions. That is, there is a range of some 12 millions between the highest and lowest estimates for the year 2000. Nor is it possible appreciably to reduce this 'range of indeterminateness', for no one, at the present time, can say with any certainty which

TABLE 36. *Estimated 'Future Birth- and Death-rates' in England and Wales. (Annual Average Births, Deaths, and Natural Increase per 1,000 of Total Population)*

	Estimate I			*Estimate III*		
Period	*Birth-rate*	*Death-rate*	*Natural increase*	*Birth-rate*	*Death-rate*	*Natural increase*
1935–40 . .	14·54	12·19	+2·35	14·54	12·19	+ 2·35
1940–5 . .	14·15	13·04	+1·11	12·53	12·61	− 0·08
1945–50 . .	13·68	13·88	−0·20	11·08	13·01	− 1·93
1950–5 . .	13·08	14·67	−1·59	9·92	13·52	− 3·60
1955–60 . .	12·50	15·42	−2·92	9·11	14·08	− 4·97
1960–5 . .	12·08	16·15	−4·07	8·58	14·78	− 6·20
1965–70 . .	11·81	16·91	−5·10	8·18	15·55	− 7·37
1970–5 . .	11·67	17·72	−6·05	7·75	16·60	− 8·85
1975–80 . .	11·60	18·54	−6·94	7·35	18·10	−10·75
1980–5 . .	11·53	19·27	−7·74	7·02	19·65	−12·63
1985–90 . .	11·45	19·82	−8·37	6·80	21·05	−14·25
1990–5 . .	11·39	20·12	−8·73	6·67	22·25	−15·58
1995–2000 .	11·36	20·26	−8·90	6·61	23·28	−16·67
Ultimate rates*	11·38	20·30	−8·92	6·48	25·59	−19·11

I. Constant fertility and mortality.
III. Declining fertility and mortality.
* The ultimate rates are calculated by the Lotka system of analysis. See Appendix to present study, section 5.

of the three sets of assumptions is most likely to be borne out in practice. Perhaps fertility will fall as suggested in the third estimate, but this may be accompanied by heavy immigration for a fairly long period. On the other hand, fertility may rise above the present level, and the population may decline much more slowly or—if there is a considerable flow of immigrants—not at all. But it should be remembered that, according to the assumptions of Estimate II, a net immigration of 500,000 persons every five years, beginning with 1940, would not be large enough to prevent an ultimate steady fall in the population. Finally, the present war has not been taken into account. So the data given in the Tables should be used simply as rough indications of possibilities.

The second question—will future trends have 'good' or 'bad' effects?—is complicated not only by the inherent difficulties of the subject, but also by the ambiguity of the

TABLE 37. *Estimates of the 'Future Population' of England and Wales. Percentage Age Distribution, Males and Females Separately, and Ratio of Females to Males in the Total Population*

Years	Estimate I							Estimate III							Years
	Males, percentage age distribution			*Females, percentage age distribution*			*Females per 10,000 males in total population*	*Males, percentage age distribution*			*Females, percentage age distribution*			*Females per 10,000 males in total population*	
	Under 15 years	*15–59*	*60 and over*	*Under 15 years*	*15–59*	*60 and over*		*Under 15 years*	*15–59*	*60 and over*	*Under 15 years*	*15–59*	*60 and over*		
1935	24·029	64·239	11·732	21·665	64·832	13·503	10,844	24·029	64·239	11·732	21·665	64·832	13·503	10,844	1935
1940	21·925	65·206	12·869	19·712	65·191	15·097	10,812	21·925	65·206	12·869	19·712	65·191	15·097	10,812	1940
1945	21·018	65·334	13·648	18·834	64·598	16·568	10,778	20·351	65·816	13·833	18·285	65·105	16·610	10,756	1945
1950	20·552	65·245	14·203	18·431	63·728	17·841	10,740	18·800	66·436	14·764	16·932	65·001	18·067	10,694	1950
1955	20·001	65·356	14·644	18·013	62·968	19·019	10,694	16·871	67·440	15·689	15·274	65·178	19·548	10,627	1955
1960	19·340	65·307	15·353	17·507	62·232	20·261	10,639	15·417	67·570	17·013	14·024	64·719	21·257	10,552	1960
1965	18·674	64·481	16·845	17·003	61·296	21·701	10,578	14·331	66·342	19·326	13·123	63·591	23·286	10,464	1965
1970	18·145	63·524	18·331	16·618	60·170	23·212	10,516	13·574	64·598	21·828	12·530	61·940	25·530	10,362	1970
1975	17·813	62·652	19·534	16·404	59·181	24·416	10,459	13·013	62·877	24·109	12·101	60·295	27·603	10,272	1975
1980	17·651	62·305	20·044	16·329	59·024	24·646	10,411	12·529	61·823	25·649	11·716	59·551	28·733	10,202	1980
1985	17·586	61·274	21·140	16·332	58·114	25·553	10,371	12·067	59·917	28·016	11·334	57·848	30·818	10,152	1985
1990	17·543	61·177	21·281	16·345	58·080	25·575	10,337	11·681	58·976	29·343	11·012	56·970	32·019	10,115	1990
1995	17·480	61·410	21·111	16·330	58·418	25·252	10,309	11·418	58·207	30·375	10·791	56·262	32·947	10,089	1995
2000	17·415	61·516	21·069	16·304	58·649	25·047	10,288	11·282	57·010	31·709	10·679	55·120	34·201	10,074	2000
*Ultimate position	17·370	61·170	21·461	16·308	58·483	25·209	10,258	11·146	56·377	32·477	10·612	54·573	34·815	10,015	*Ultimate position

* The ultimate position is calculated by means of the Lotka system of analysis.

term 'declining population', and by the need to distinguish between short- and long-term effects. As regards the first point, the term 'declining population' may refer to a population which falls for a time and then re-establishes itself—that is, becomes stationary—at a lower level, or to one which persistently has a net reproduction rate below unity and which, in the absence of sufficient immigration, will therefore fall continuously without any sign of cessation. Eventually, if such conditions were maintained, the population referred to in the second interpretation would die out. Clearly the consequences of the two possibilities are very different, and it is understandable that those who regard the white peoples as the highest form of evolution will naturally be repelled by the prospect of their disappearance. Yet though there is nothing illogical in assuming that a population will disappear—and, as was pointed out, this would happen unless the net reproduction rate ultimately rose to unity—there is an element of absurdity in discussing the consequences of the total extinction of a population of 40 millions. Massive changes may occur, and we have, as an example, the growth of the population of England and Wales from 12 millions in 1821 to 41 millions in 1937. But it is also possible that the actual, visible occurrence of a rate of decline of about 2 per cent. per year—that ultimately envisaged in Estimate III of the set given in Tables 35 to 37—or of about 5 per cent. per year—that implied by Dr. Charles's second estimate—would itself produce reactions among the population and help to raise fertility. In the following very brief discussion[1] it will be assumed that the population does stabilize itself eventually.

Making this assumption, we have a number of separate periods to consider. First, the initial transition period during which the fall in numbers is small, while there is at the same time a considerable increase in the proportion of potentially active persons in the population. If we look at Table 35 we notice that, according to Estimate I, the population will have fallen by only 1 million by 1965; by under 3 millions, according to Estimate III; and that it will actually have increased by 2 millions according to Estimate II. Table 37

[1] See Note VIII*c*, p. 464.

shows that in the same period males aged 15–59 years will occupy a larger proportion of the total male population. From 64·2 per cent. in 1935 they will, according to Estimate I, increase to 65·36 per cent. by 1955, and even in 1965 the proportion will still be higher than in 1935. According to Estimate III this increase will persist for a longer period, and even in 1970 the proportion will be above the 1935 level.[1] After this initial transition period the situation would change considerably. First, numbers would fall more rapidly, unless there were counterbalancing immigration. According to the first estimate the population would fall by 7·6 millions between 1965 and 1995, while according to the third estimate the fall in the same period would be more than 11 millions. Secondly, the ageing of the population would become more pronounced, and the proportion of potentially active males would fall. Estimate I shows a decline in the proportion which males aged 15 to 59 years form in the total male population, from 64·48 per cent. in 1965 to 61·41 per cent. in 1995. Estimate III shows a fall from 66·34 to 58·21 per cent. in the same period. On the other hand, Estimate II, with its assumption of a constant flow of immigrants, shows no particularly marked change in 1995 as compared with 1935. After this point there are many possible trends. If fertility continues at a fixed level below that required for permanent replacement, and if there is no net immigration or emigration, the population will soon achieve a fixed age structure. Table 37 shows this ultimate structure for Estimates I and III, and Table 36 shows the fixed birth- and death-rates which would also obtain. But if we assume that at some point fertility will turn upwards and become constant at the level which would secure a stationary population, there will be a further

[1] If we take, instead, the age groups 20–64 years, or 20–69 years as more appropriately representing the potentially active population, the increase will persist for a still longer period. Clark, C., *National Income and Outlay*, London, 1938 issue, pp. 20–2, applying the 1931 age proportions of occupied males to Dr. Charles's estimates, shows a much longer rise in the occupied proportion of the male population, and that according to Dr. Charles's lowest estimate, productivity per head of the population would be increased by this factor, other things being equal, by 10 per cent. between 1935 and 1950 and by an additional 7 per cent. between 1950 and 1975. But, apparently, Clark makes no allowances for possible differences in productivity of men of various ages.

transition period during which the proportion of young persons would increase, while the proportion of old persons would decrease. The total population might either increase or decrease, depending upon the previous course of fertility, but eventually it would become fixed.[1] These subdivisions have been made because although the general *type* of economic problem may be the same whatever the rate of decline of a population, the *specific impact* of the problem will certainly be related to the particular rate of decline.

The general problem itself may be defined as relating to questions of general unemployment, to specific unemployment due to the dislocation of individual industries, and to changes in the burden of taxation consequent upon changes in the size and age structure of the population. Under the first heading we have the prospect suggested by J. M. Keynes. National saving may continue at about the same rate, in relation to income, as before, but the channels into which savings can be directed may become fewer, because a large part of the demand for capital arises from the needs of an increasing population. We may therefore have a tendency to long-term, general unemployment. Under the second heading we have the possibility—taking into account the larger amount of existing capital per head, the likelihood of further improvements in the technique of production, and the temporary increase in the proportion of potentially active males in the population—that income per head will increase and this in turn will probably lead to a larger proportionate expenditure upon goods and services for which the demand is capricious. That is, the regular demand for staple commodities will form a smaller proportion of the total demand for all kinds of commodities, and this in turn may lead to increased likelihood of unemployment in specific industries. Unemployment in specific industries may also occur while the average income rises, because of the small extent to which it is possible to increase the total demand for certain commodities. Thus the demand for agricultural products may decrease more rapidly than the agricultural population can be absorbed by other activities. The decrease in the demand for given commodities may

[1] See Note VIII*d*, p. 465.

also produce an excessive rate of obsolescence of capital equipment, depress enterprise, and increase unemployment. Under the third heading we have the general problem of indebtedness—that is, for example, a debt incurred by a county borough with a population of a million inhabitants would mean an increased burden per ratepayer if the population fell rapidly during the period of repayment. The burden of old-age pensions would also increase as the proportion of old persons rose. At the other end of the scale, a fall in the numbers of children would not mean an exactly corresponding fall in the total cost of education because it would be difficult to redistribute the children and employ a much smaller teaching staff or markedly fewer school buildings. Many other examples might be mentioned, but these few will suffice to show the type of problem involved.[1]

But before deciding, on the basis of the above evidence, whether a fall in population has 'good' or 'bad' results, three points should be considered. First, during the initial period of the decline the difficulties are fewer and less serious. For the first twenty-five or thirty years the fall in total numbers would, according to our estimates, be slight. Moreover, not only would the proportion of potentially active males increase, but also their absolute numbers. According to Estimate I the number of males aged 15 to 59 years, amounting to 12·53 millions in 1935, would reach a peak of 13·00 millions in 1945, but would still be above the 1935 level in 1960, with a figure of 12·78 millions. For Estimate III a similar trend would be visible, with males aged 15 to 59 years amounting to 12·82 millions in 1960, while according to Estimate II males in this age group would still be more numerous in 1980—at 12·79 millions—than in 1935. Other things being equal, the burden of indebtedness or of taxation per taxpayer would therefore fall for a fairly long period. This trend in the adult ages might also lead to an increase in the demand for certain durable goods, such as houses. If, for example, the relationship between the number of private families and the number of adults remains at the level shown by the 1931 census, the total number of families will continue to grow after the total population has begun to fall,

[1] See Note VIII*e*, p. 465.

and may still be above the 1931 level for the next fifty years. Consequently, even without reckoning the existing shortage of houses, there may be an increased demand for houses because of the change in the structure of the population.

The second point is that some of the problems mentioned are not the peculiar product of a declining population and would not automatically be solved if we had either a stationary or a growing population. Admittedly, for some purposes and sections of the community a growing population might, at least temporarily, be the ideal trend. This would particularly be the case for business men, for whom a growing population would provide an atmosphere of considerable optimism, since such a trend would minimize the results of any errors of judgement. But unemployment would not simply cure itself if the population were growing, nor would cyclical fluctuations in economic activity be evaded automatically. Nor, either, would the financial burden of old-age pensions necessarily be reduced. Of course, with given mortality rates a growing population would contain a smaller proportion of old persons than a stationary or a declining one. But even if we raised the net reproduction rate in England to unity (or some margin above), two factors would tend to increase the burden of old age in the future. First, the present age composition is abnormal and does not accurately reflect the high expectation of life at birth which now applies. Secondly, mortality is likely to fall in the future and this will mean a growing proportion of old persons in the community. Table 38 summarizes some information on these questions. It shows that a stationary population at either the mortality of 1935 or the hypothetical mortality of 1970 would contain a considerably higher percentage of persons aged 60 years and over than we have at the present time, and that the stable age structure deriving from the fertility and mortality observed in 1935 or assumed for 1970 would show a still higher percentage of old persons. But it also shows that as between the stationary and stable populations the differences in the proportion of potentially active persons—aged 15 to 59 years—is not very great. Naturally, since only three broad age groups are given, Table 38 tends to minimize the ageing process, but it is

TABLE 38. *Age Distribution (Percentages) in England and Wales*

	Age groups (Years)	*1871*	*1911*	*1931*	*Estimate I* Stationary population according to mortality of 1935	*Estimate I* Stable* population according to fertility and mortality of 1935	*Estimate III* Stationary population according to mortality of 1970	*Estimate III* Stable* population according to fertility and mortality of 1970
Males as a percentage of the total population	Under 15	18·088	15·334	12·037	11·286	8·574	10·777	5·569
	15–59	27·146	29·464	30·721	30·477	30·195	30·212	28·168
	60 and over	3·457	3·567	5·132	7·991	10·594	9·478	16·227
	Total	48·691	48·365	47·890	49·754	49·363	50·467	49·964
Males and females as a percentage of the total population	Under 15	36·113	30·637	23·830	22·156	16·832	21·052	10·879
	15–59	56·413	61·326	64·607	60·311	59·809	59·464	55·474
	60 and over	7·474	8·037	11·563	17·533	23·359	19·484	33·647
	Total	100·000	100·000	100·000	100·000	100·000	100·000	100·000

* These are calculated by means of the Lotka system of analysis.

still true to say that, on the hypotheses chosen, the change in the productive capacity of the population is much less than is often assumed to accompany a declining population.

The third point is that many of the difficulties created or accentuated by a declining population may at least be mitigated by economic and social planning. They may, of course, be avoided entirely for a long time if nations are willing to adopt new immigration policies, and this would probably be the least costly method so long as there is a pool of potential migrants in countries with net reproduction rates above or around unity. Apart from this possibility, we may take advantage of the relative slowness of population movements to forecast trends twenty years ahead—and, war apart, there can be a high degree of accuracy over so short a period—and to make such adjustments in our activity as will minimize the problems mentioned earlier. Thus the tendency to general unemployment may be reduced by lowering the rate of interest, and making it more attractive both for entrepreneurs to make wide use of methods of production which need a great deal of capital equipment, and for consumers to buy goods produced in that way, or the purchase of which has to be spread over a long period of time. Alternatively—and, from the point of view of practical application, this is probably both easier and more effective—the propensity to consume could be increased by altering the distribution of income. A family allowance system subsidized by a levy on the higher incomes and allocating grants for the dependent children of families with incomes below a given limit, would reduce the ratio of national saving to national income. Similarly, there may be at least partial solutions of other problems. Changing habits might increase the demand for durable consumption goods, such as television sets, refrigerators, and motor-cars, while public authorities could, if they desired, very greatly increase the activity of the building industry if they seriously entered the field of housing and town planning. Public enterprise would also be important in another field where difficulties might otherwise occur—that of occupational mobility. No doubt a declining or even a stationary population would make for more immobility than a growing population, for in the latter case adaptation to new demands and new production is met largely by a redirection of young recruits to industry and the professions. But the problem of adaptation and mobility is very closely linked to the educational system, to the type and efficiency of labour exchanges, and to the general nature of the industrial system. Educational improvements would increase the capacity for human adaptation to industrial change, and so would a well-planned system of industrial re-training, while in industry itself the tendency is for the average worker to become a skilled machine-tender, with rather less need for specialized craftsmanship.

All the suggestions made in the last four paragraphs are tentative, subject to many qualifications. But they do at least show that it would be foolish to dogmatize about the effects of a declining population. They will depend upon the rate and length of the decline, the point at which fertility eventually rises to the level required for adequacy—if it ever does so—and the capacity of society to tackle new problems or accentuated forms of old ones. Whatever happens, there will be many problems to solve and many advantages and disadvantages to be weighed against each other. If society decides to implement measures to raise fertility, it may find that the costs involved—in terms of money and dislocations—are greater than it is prepared to pay, at any rate for a long time. On the other hand, it may find that, with judicious planning, considerable advantages can be obtained for a period from the fact that part of society's resources does not have to be used in providing basic equipment for an annual increase in the number of inhabitants. We should also realize that political questions may play a far more important part than economic questions in influencing decisions. Evidence given in the chapters on France, Germany, and Italy shows that in those countries there is far less concern with the economic than with the political implications of a declining population. France has been affected largely by her anxiety over the possibility of invasion and relative military strength of her neighbours, while Italy and Germany have been concerned largely with the desire to justify their statements on the question of 'living-space'. In both Italy and Germany it is possible that, were there a smaller population, the standard of living would be higher, but that is not the point at issue. It would be no exaggeration to say that Italian population policy, when stripped of its fascist mysticism about the individual, the family, and the State, is to a large extent concerned with proving the validity of its claims for more territory.[1] Other political factors may have more justification, and, in the present state of the world, it is certain that differential rates of growth of the populations of the Great Powers give a genuine basis for anxiety. But here, again, it would probably be much cheaper, as well as more satisfactory, to solve the problem by thorough international control of migration and settlement than if each nation were to rush headlong into a demographic armaments race.

There is therefore an urgent need to reformulate the whole question and, in the light of much more research than has so far been undertaken, to see the implications of various kinds of population policy. Presumably, if we have any liking for our own kind, we shall not wish to see the extinction of the population. Nor, if only because of the resultant physical congestion, would many people wish to see a continuously growing population. The choice is then either a stationary population, or one which is allowed to fluctuate within certain defined limits. But how wide a range of fluctuation should be allowed in the second case, or how large a stationary population should be aimed at in the first? Obviously the choice will not be the same for each country, and it may vary considerably over time. Nor are the criteria of choice simple or direct. If a stationary population is considered the most desirable goal, what, for example, will be the factors affecting a decision about the most suitable size? Some statesmen may wish to maximize the income per head of the community by choosing the 'optimum' population. But there is no optimum that holds good for all time,

[1] On the other hand, countries which might perhaps benefit from a considerable increase of population—e.g. Canada and South Africa—are very unwilling to take large supplies of immigrants. For a very able survey of governmental attitudes on the subject of over- and under-population, see Wright, F. C., *Population and Peace* (International Institute of Intellectual Co-operation, L. of N.), Paris, 1939, esp. ch. v. See also Ferenczi, I., *The Synthetic Optimum of Population* (International Institute of Intellectual Co-operation, L. of N.), Paris, 1938, esp. ch. iv.

and the community may in any case decide to forego part of an increase in national income in order to retain a greater physical spaciousness of life. On the other hand, even if a given population were above the optimum at the time, the community might decide to maintain that population because of the difficulties which might be met during the transition period while numbers were falling to the theoretically desirable level, and because, owing to capital accumulation and technical progress, the old excessive size might soon become the new optimal size.

Suppose that, as a result of the 'patient and unambitious research' advocated by Professor Jewkes,[1] we eventually decide what size of the population would best suit us. We should still ultimately have the task of raising the net reproduction rate above its present level, whatever the size of the population at which we might care to stabilize, and we should have to consider the kind of measures most likely to have this result. Unfortunately, we cannot learn much of positive value from past and present experiments, for in one case only—Germany since 1933—does there appear to have been any marked success, and even in that single case the reasons for success are not clear, nor do we know if the results are likely to be of long duration. But we can learn a good deal about the negative side of the question. We can see, for example, that with the exception of Sweden and Denmark, no country has undertaken a really detailed survey of the factors influencing the decline of fertility, or the way in which that decline has been making itself felt. To a large extent, therefore, the pro-natalist measures have been applied blindly. Even the very comprehensive French family code is more the result of intuitive analysis—however shrewd that may be—than of 'patient research'. Secondly, even when certain facts are unmistakably evident, governments deliberately turn a blind eye to them. In most of the countries we have examined—Sweden and Denmark again excepted—pro-natalist measures fall into three broad categories: the use of propaganda to encourage parenthood,

[1] *The Manchester School*, 2, 1939, p. 121. But the present writer disagrees with the term 'unambitious'. Unless research is ambitious enough to look for fundamental causes and results it may miss or misinterpret significant data.

the use of repressive measures to discourage individual control over conception and child-bearing, and the granting of cash and other allowances as a reward for raising families or as a contribution towards the costs incurred in respect of children.[1] But it is clear that the cash-and-kind grants have not, so far, been large enough to cover the additional costs of family life. Even in Sweden, where much time and intelligence has been spent in investigating and analysing—in seventeen reports—the many aspects of the population question, the economic assistance given to families is still very small. At the same time, pro-natalist propaganda has attacked the selfishness of childless married couples and of the parents of one- and two-child families, and has shown that such persons have a substantially higher standard of life, comparing similar income levels, than large families. It is therefore not surprising that the propaganda has largely failed, and that the repressive measures—which, with the apparent exception of Germany, are not in any case wholeheartedly enforced—should not be more conspicuously successful. The record of governmental attempts to stimulate fertility shows one significant and constant fact. However urgently governments may have declared their desire to increase the supply of births, they have nevertheless persistently tried to buy babies at bargain prices. Only the evident failure of such attempts has at last induced some of the governments—France and Italy, for example—to begin to modify their practice.

In a pamphlet by Dr. C. P. Blacker and the present writer, the authors said: 'When we survey the picture of social life in England to-day, we are impressed with the number and the excellence of the reasons why married couples should have few children.'[2] This would apply equally well to most other countries. Leaving aside the possible influence of the threat of war—which may have been a rationalization rather than a genuine cause of the recent decline of fertility—the last seventy years have

[1] In Italy and Germany anti-urbanism is also a feature of pro-natalist legislation.

[2] Glass, D. V., and Blacker, C. P., *Population and Fertility*, London [1939], p. 101.

produced, with cumulative intensity, a social and economic system in which it has become increasingly difficult for parents to bring up large families. Given an initial trend towards smaller families, this trend—however caused—began to alter the economic and cultural pattern of the community. It influenced building design, the type of leisure, the conception of standards of living, and, by so doing, affected in turn the general attitude to the large families of the eighteen-seventies. Few people would urge a return to such large families, and fewer still would deny the advantages—to the community as well as to the individual—which have been gained with the help of the decline in fertility. But once a small family pattern has been established it is very difficult for the average person, if he wishes to keep his standard of living on the same level as that of his friends, to break away from the common pattern.[1] If the large family is to-day often regarded with a mixture of pity and contempt, that may be unfortunate but is scarcely surprising in a society in which self-interest is best served by having few or no children. Whatever pro-natalist propaganda may say on the subject, parenthood is not generally undertaken for altruistic motives.[2] It may therefore be extremely difficult to raise the average family to the level required for the permanent maintenance of the population, even though it would mean a fertility only about half as high as that shown in the eighteen-seventies. The point is, of course, that the population problem is not a single problem, but an aspect of all the social and economic problems by which the individual and the family are affected. To solve the population aspect of such problems may involve either a direct overhaul of the social and

[1] It is not simply a question of poverty, though that is also involved, but of the fact that it is relatively easy for an average married couple to raise a large family in a community consisting of large families, but extremely difficult when the typical family is very small.

[2] Though it may be affected by religious belief. Dr. A. Racine, in Racine, A., and Dupréel, E., *Enquête sur les Conditions de Vie des Familles Nombreuses en Belgique*, Liége, 1933, pp. 43–5, found that of 140 large families at least 80 had been inspired by religious conviction. But here, again, it is very difficult to tell how far rationalization played a part in the answers to the questionnaires, and how far 'religious conviction' simply meant a fear of employing 'forbidden' methods of family limitation.

economic structure,[1] or else the provision of monetary grants which are large enough, when taken in bulk, to allow parents sufficiently to alter the present pattern of social life through the mechanism of effective demand.[2] Nor are these really alternative methods, for both would mean a considerable vertical and horizontal redistribution of income. No doubt many governments will continue to apply the cheaper method of repressive legislation, futile and barbarous though it may be. But we have a considerable period before the actual decline of numbers is likely to be serious. Perhaps in that period society may become convinced that it is worth while to spend almost as much in maintaining the population as in promoting its extinction by unnatural causes.

[1] In a very fascinating essay, Kingsley Davis ('Reproductive institutions and the pressure for population', *Sociological Review*, July 1937, pp. 289–306) suggests that the process of raising fertility to the replacement level may involve a complete change in reproductive institutions. Assuming that 'the family is not indefinitely adaptable to modern society, and that this explains the declining birth-rate', he regards as a possibility the development of a professional childbearing class and the practical disappearance of the family as a biological mechanism. But the professional class, if it were small, would certainly be busily occupied. If only 10 per cent. of women in the reproductive age groups were enrolled in this profession, each of these child-bearers would, at present mortality, have to bear more than 23 children to maintain the total population at any given size, assuming that other women did not bear children.

[2] To deny the utility of such grants on the ground that there is an inverse association between income and fertility is entirely to miss the point.

APPENDIX

THE text of the present study contains little technical information concerning the statistical methods of analysis which have been used in measuring population changes or the factors influencing them. This omission need not prevent the reader from understanding the results derived from the various methods, provided only that the essential idea of a reproduction rate has been grasped. But there is a growing interest in population problems and this will probably result in an increased application of the methods applied in the present study. At the same time, the writer believes that the reader who wishes to study the problems in some detail may find it convenient to have included in the present work a summary of the statistical methods used. It is therefore the object of this Appendix to give, as briefly as is compatible with reasonable completeness, a summary of the most important methods of analysing replacement trends, and a discussion of some of the points which should be borne in mind when interpreting the results obtained. Since the writer has dealt almost exclusively with questions of replacement and reproductivity, this Appendix does not discuss birth-rates, simple fertility rates, or standardized death-rates, but only those indices which are used directly in constructing or explaining reproduction rates. In almost all these rates the life table is a basis, and the summary may therefore appropriately begin with a discussion of life tables.

1. *Life Tables*

The general principle of a life table may be enunciated as follows. Assume that there is, at birth, a cohort of 1,000 female children (this initial cohort is generally called the 'radix' of the table). The problem is then to discover how many survive to various ages, according to the mortality of a given time and place. Let l_{20} be the number who survive to their twentieth birthday, and l_{21} the number who survive to their twenty-first birthday. Then the probability of surviving from the twentieth to the twenty-first birthday is (l_{21}/l_{20}), or p_{20}. But l_{20} itself is likewise compounded of the probabilities of living from birth to 1 year of age, from 1 year of age to 2 years, from 2 years to 3, and so on up to 19 years to 20 years of age, all multiplied together, so that the task of life-table construction becomes that of calculating the separate probabilities of surviving through each of the years up to the last age in which we find any significant number of persons left. The choice of a 'significant number' is largely arbitrary, but it may be said that the full value of a life table will be obtained if the calculation ends at the ages of 102 or 103 years.

Suppose that 50,000 girls aged 20 but less than 21 years are alive at the middle of a year, and that in the year chosen 100 deaths occur to the girls in that age group. We can assume that the deaths are fairly evenly distributed over the year of age, so we can say that the number of girls who would have reached 20 years of age precisely—their twentieth birthday—would be $50{,}000+\frac{1}{2}(100)$, and that the number reaching their twenty-first birthday would be $50{,}000-\frac{1}{2}(100)$. The probability of surviving from the twentieth to the twenty-first birthdays would therefore be $(50{,}000-50)/(50{,}000+50)$, and of every 1,000 girls reaching their twentieth birthday, 1,000 × (49,950/50,050), or 998·00 would reach their twenty-first birthday. Throughout the main body of the life table, the probability of surviving from one birthday to the next may be calculated very simply, in this way, by the formula $\frac{P-\frac{1}{2}d}{P+\frac{1}{2}d}$, where P is the existing population in the age group, say, 20 to 21 years, and d is the number of deaths occurring to people in that age group. The complications introduced by the fact that at practically all ages the numbers of men and women are not equal, together with the importance of ascertaining the differential mortality of the two sexes, make it desirable to calculate separate life tables for males and females. They may be combined quite easily at the end. The formula just given would, for women, thus read $\frac{f_{20-21}-(\frac{1}{2}d_{20-21})}{f_{20-21}+(\frac{1}{2}d_{20-21})}=p_{20}$. For the largest section of the life table the computation may be made still more simple by using five-year age groups, for which the formula would then read $\frac{f_{20-24}-(\frac{1}{2}d_{20-24})}{f_{20-24}+(\frac{1}{2}d_{20-24})}$ for the probability of surviving through any one year in the period between the twentieth and twenty-fifth birthdays, and $\frac{f_{20-24}-(2\frac{1}{2}d_{20-24})}{f_{20-24}+(2\frac{1}{2}d_{20-24})}$ for the probability of surviving through the whole five-year period. Single year computations are advisable for the period up to the fifth birthday, and for that after the seventy-fifth birthday, because in those periods mortality changes fairly rapidly.

For the first year of life births are used as the basic population from which to compute the probability of surviving to the first birthday, because of the inaccuracy of census enumerations of children under 1 year of age. Strictly speaking, the deaths occurring to infants in the first year of life should be related not to the births of the same year, but to the respective calendar years in which the children were born. If, in the year 1939, there are 1,000 deaths of children under 1 year of age, it is clear that some of these children must have been born in 1938, and that they should really be related to the births in that year. To take this problem into account, Dr. R. R. Kuczynski has devised the following formula:

If p_0 = the probability of surviving to the first birthday,
b'' = the children born in the current calendar year,
b' = the children born in the preceding calendar year,
d' = the children born and deceased in the preceding calendar year,
d'' = the children born in the previous calendar year and deceased, at less than one year of age, in the current calendar year,
d''' = the children born and deceased in the current calendar year,

$$p_0=\frac{b'-d'-d''}{b'-d'}\times\frac{b''-d'''}{b''}.$$

But many countries do not give the calendar year of birth of the children who die before reaching their first birthday. In that case it is usual to assume that some proportion of the births of the previous calendar year should be substituted for a like proportion of the births of the current calendar year, and that the deaths in the first year of life should be related to this compound figure. For example, the deaths of children under 1 year old in 1939 might be related to a compound of 70 per cent. of the births of 1939, plus 30 per cent. of the births of 1938. But there is a strongly arbitrary element in all these compounded proportions, and if a life table is being constructed for a period of, say, three years, or for a year in a period in which the numbers of births and deaths in the first year of life have not varied very greatly, accuracy is not significantly impaired by using either the births in the particular year, or the average of the births in the three-year period, and relating the deaths in the first year of life to these births. The formula for p_0 would then read

$$p_0 = \frac{\text{births} - \text{deaths}_{0-1}}{\text{births}}.$$

One final remark concerning life-table construction should be made. It is one of the primary objects of the life table to show the number of years lived between one age and the next. If, out of a 1,000 live born females, 951·33 live until their fourth birthday and 949·34 live until their fifth, then the number of years lived by the 1,000 live born females between the ages of 4 and 5 is $\frac{1}{2}(951{\cdot}33+949{\cdot}34)$, or 950·335, assuming that mortality does not vary very greatly over the different sections of the fifth year of life. Similarly, if 943·70 reach their tenth birthday and 939·46 reach their fifteenth, then the number of years lived between the ages of 10 and 15 by the original 1,000 females is $2\frac{1}{2}(943{\cdot}70+939{\cdot}46)$, or 4,707·900. The years lived in that period by the survivors who had actually reached their tenth birthday would be $\frac{2\frac{1}{2}(943{\cdot}70+939{\cdot}46)\times 1{,}000}{943{\cdot}70}$. The single-year method of calculating the number of years lived, or life-table population, should be used for the ages from 1 to 5, and beyond 75, for in these ages mortality changes fairly rapidly from year to year. But in the central portion of the life table the five-year method may be used without sacrificing much accuracy. For the first year of life, however, much shorter periods should be used, for mortality changes rapidly in the different parts of the year. Taking, as an example, Australia in 1932–4, the computation would proceed on the following lines:

Average annual number of live female births, 1932–4			=	53,898
„	„	„ deaths of females aged 0 to 1 month	=	1,287
„	„	„ deaths of females aged 1 to 3 months	=	183
„	„	„ deaths of females aged 3 to 6 months	=	192
„	„	„ deaths of females aged 6 to 12 months	=	315.

The number of survivors, of 1,000 born, at one month is

$$\frac{53{,}898-1{,}287}{53{,}898} \times 1{,}000 = 976{\cdot}122.$$

Similarly, the survivors at three months are

$$\frac{53{,}898-(1{,}287+183)}{53{,}898-1{,}287} \times 976{\cdot}122 = 972{\cdot}727,$$

and so forth.[1] In this way we find 976·122 survivors at 1 month, 972·727 at 3 months, 969·165 at 6 months, and 963·321 at 1 year of age. (Three decimal places have been used in these calculations so that the survivors at 1 year of age should correspond, to the second decimal place, to the answer obtained from $\frac{53{,}898-1{,}977}{53{,}898}\times 1{,}000 = 963{\cdot}320$, 1,977 being the total number of deaths in the first year of life.) The computation of the number of years lived by the original cohort of 1,000 between birth and the first birthday is then:

Survivors at:		*Years lived by original 1,000 between:*		
0	1,000·000			
		0–1 mth.	(1,000+976·122) × 0·04167	= 82·345[2]
1 mth.	976·122			
		1–3 mths.	(976·122+972·727) × 0·08333	= 162·398
3 mths.	972·727			
		3–6 mths.	(972·727+969·165) × 0·125	= 242·737
6 mths.	969·165			
		6 mths.–1 yr.	(969·165+963·321) × 0·25	= 483·122
1 yr.	963·321			
			Total	970·602

If the rapid change of mortality over the first year of life had not been taken into account, the calculation of the number of years lived would simply have been $\frac{1}{2}$(1,000+963·321), or 981·661, which would have been too high. The result could, of course, be made still more accurate by splitting up the first year into days for the first week, weeks for the first month, and months for the rest of the year, but it is doubtful if the increase in accuracy would be worth the addition in labour.

To show the full results of a life table calculated in the way described, two tables for males and females have been constructed for Australia, 1932–4. The only difference in method used for these tables is that for the ages of 75 and over, the original deaths were smoothed by a simple formula. But this

[1] Alternatively, the l_x columns for the various periods of the first year of life may be obtained directly, and the p_x items calculated from these. Thus the survivors at one month would be $\frac{53{,}898-1{,}287}{53{,}898}\times 1{,}000$, or 976·122, the survivors at 3 months would be $\frac{53{,}898-(1{,}287+183)}{53{,}898}\times 1{,}000$, or 972·726, and so forth. This method being more direct is thus slightly more accurate, though the difference is only in the third decimal place. In the computations given in this section the correction due for a leap-year has not been made, as the error involved in the construction of a life table based on a three-year average is extremely small.

[2] The coefficients used for multiplication are factors for converting the result into years. Thus, for the period of 0 to 1 month, the years lived would in fact be $\frac{\frac{1}{2}(1{,}000+976{\cdot}122)}{12}$ which is 0·04167 × (1,000+976·122); the period of 1 to 3 months would be $\frac{1(976{\cdot}122+972{\cdot}727)}{12}$, which is 0·08333 × (976·122+972·72), and so forth.

smoothing was very slight, as can be seen from the fact that the probability of surviving rises at the age of 100 years, a phenomenon which is not very credible, and which is more probably due to misstatements of age. The p_x and l_x items were computed in the way described above for the first year of life, using the graduated census populations, and are only summarized in Tables 39 and 40.[1] Similarly, single years were used for the ages of 75 and over, and summed into five-year groups for inclusion in the Tables. All items have been multiplied by 1,000. The p_x items for the five-year groups after age 75 were then calculated by dividing the l_x for a given age into the l_x for the age five years later, and multiplying by 1,000—e.g. the probability of surviving from 80 to 85 years equals $1{,}000\left(\frac{l_{85}}{l_{80}}\right)$ which, for females, is $1{,}000\left(\frac{165{\cdot}56}{316{\cdot}31}\right)$ or 523·41. The terms at the head of the life tables have the following meaning:

p_x—the probability of surviving from the age given to the next age below,—e.g. for males, 954·008 represents the number of males surviving to their first birthday, out of 1,000 at birth, and 985·36 the number surviving to 35 out of 1,000 at 30.

l_x—the number of survivors, out of the original cohort of 1,000, at the given age—e.g. for males, 946·32 reached their second birthday and 916·94 their twentieth birthday.

L_x—the number of years lived by the original cohort of 1,000 *between* given ages—e.g. in the life table for males, the original cohort lived 962·463 years between the ages of 0 and 1, and 4,604·925 years between the ages of 15 and 20.

T_x—the number of years lived by the original cohort of 1,000 *after* given ages—e.g. in the life table for males, the total number of years lived by the cohort of 1,000 throughout the whole of the life table was the sum of the items in the L_x column, or 63,400·803 years. The number of years lived after the first birthday was thus (63,400·803 − 962·463) or 62,438·340, and the number of years lived after the fifth birthday was 63,400·803 − (962·463 + 950·164 + 944·510 + 941·335 + 938·955) or 58,663·376.

$\mathring{e}_x$—the expectation of life at a given age. Since the cohort of 1,000 males lived 63,400·803 years through the life table, the average number of years lived by each male was 63·401 years, and this represents the expectation of life of each male at birth. The number of years lived from the first birthday was 62,438·340, but since there were only 954·008 survivors at the first birthday, the expectation of life for each male at his first birthday was $\left(\frac{62{,}438{\cdot}340}{954{\cdot}008}\right)$ or 65·448 years. Similarly, there were 937·94 males surviving at their fifth birthday, and the number of years lived after this date was 58,663·376. The expectation of life at the fifth birthday, or 'mean after-lifetime' as it is sometimes called, was therefore $\left(\frac{58{,}663{\cdot}376}{937{\cdot}94}\right)$, or 62·545 years. Using the same methods we can easily

[1] Strictly speaking, p_x is the probability of surviving from x to $x+1$. But in Tables 39 and 40 the columns relate to five-year periods unless otherwise indicated.

TABLE 39. *Australia—Life Table*, 1932–4, *Males*

Age	p_x (a)	l_x (b)	L_x (c)	T_x (d)	$\mathring{e}_x$ (e)	Official $\mathring{e}_x$ (f)	Ratio (e)/(f) (g)	Age
0	954·008	1,000·000	962·463	63,400·803	63·401	63·478	99·879	0
1	991·94	954·008	950·164	62,438·340	65·448	65·493	99·931	1
2	996·17	946·32	944·510	61,488·176	64·976	65·003	99·958	2
3	997·10	942·70	941·335	60,543,666	64·224	64·247	99·964	3
4	997·84	939·97	938·955	59,602·331	63·409	63·431	99·965	4
5	992·37	937·94	4,671·800	58,663·376	62·545	62·566	99·966	5
10	993·82	930·78	4,639·525	53,991·576	58·007	58·015	99·986	10
15	991·25	925·03	4,604·925	49,352·051	53·352	53·364	99·978	15
20	988·05	916·94	4,557·300	44,747·126	48·800	48·812	99·975	20
25	987·49	905·98	4,501·575	40,189·826	44·361	44·366	99·989	25
30	985·36	894·65	4,440·500	35,688·251	39·891	39·901	99·975	30
35	980·61	881·55	4,365·025	31,247·751	35·446	35·458	99·966	35
40	973·97	864·46	4,266·050	26,882·726	31·098	31·107	99·971	40
45	961·95	841·96	4,129·700	22,616·676	26·862	26·872	99·963	45
50	944·43	809·92	3,937·075	18,486·976	22·826	22·832	99·974	50
55	914·56	764·91	3,661·175	14,549·901	19·022	19·034	99·937	55
60	876·79	699·56	3,282·325	10,888·726	15·565	15·571	99·961	60
65	818·03	613·37	2,787·825	7,606·401	12·401	12·402	99·992	65
70	731·86	501·76	2,172·450	4,818·576	9·603	9·595	100·083	70
75	604·43	367·22	1,474·590	2,646·126	7·206	7·192	100·195	75
80	440·26	221·96	787·560	1,171·536	5·278	5·224	101·034	80
85	296·25	97·72	294·295	383·976	3·929	3·903	100·666	85
90	211·40	28·95	75·475	89·681	3·098	2·985	103·786	90
95	111·76	6·12	12·938	14·206	2·321	2·108	110·104	95
100	169·59	0·684	1·268	1·268	1·854	1·100	168·545	100
103	..	0·116	..	..	..	..	..	103
			63,400·803					

TABLE 40. *Australia—Life Table, 1932–4, Females*

Age	p_x (a)	l_x (b)	L_x (c)	T_x (d)	$\mathring{e}_x$ (e)	Official $\mathring{e}_x$ (f)	Ratio (e)/(f) (g)	Age
0	963·321	1,000·000	970·602	67,104·946	67·105	67·144	99·942	0
1	993·25	963·321	960·071	66,134·344	68·652	68·674	99·968	1
2	996·69	956·82	955·235	65,174·273	68·116	68·118	99·997	2
3	997·57	953·65	952·490	64,219·038	67·340	67·342	99·997	3
4	997·91	951·33	950·335	63·266·548	66·503	66·503	100·000	4
5	994·06	949·34	4,732·600	62,316·213	65·642	65·641	100·002	5
10	995·51	943·70	4,707·900	57,583·613	61·019	61·023	99·993	10
15	993·06	939·46	4,681·000	52,875·713	56·283	56·292	99·984	15
20	989·51	932·94	4,640,225	48,194·713	51·659	51·666	99·986	20
25	987·11	923·15	4,586·000	43,554·488	47·180	47·185	99·989	25
30	985·27	911·25	4,522·700	38,968·488	42·764	42·767	99·993	30
35	981·50	897·83	4,447·625	34,445·788	38·366	38·372	99·984	35
40	978·38	881·22	4,358·475	29,998·163	34·042	34·042	100·000	40
45	970·26	862·17	4,246·750	25,639·688	29·739	29·742	99·990	45
50	958·16	836·53	4,095·150	21,392·938	25·573	25·576	99·988	50
55	942·77	801·53	3,892·975	17,297·788	21·581	21·581	100·000	55
60	915·02	755·66	3,617·750	13,404·813	17·739	17·736	100·017	60
65	863·92	691·44	3,221·975	9,787·063	14·155	14·150	100·035	65
70	790·66	597·35	2,674·125	6,565·088	10·990	10·975	100·137	70
75	669·72	472·30	1,977·185	3,890·963	8·238	8·228	100·122	75
80	523·41	316·31	1,199·415	1,913·778	6·050	6·010	100·666	80
85	350·08	165·56	531·810	714·363	4·315	4·304	100·256	85
90	201·52	57·96	155·100	182·553	3·150	3·047	103·380	90
95	106·85	11·68	25·322	27·453	2·350	1·996	117·735	95
100	197·12	1·248	2·131	2·131	1·708	1·023	166·960	100
103	..	0·246	..	..	..	..	..	103
			67,104·946					

calculate the combined expectations of life of males and females. The expectation of life at birth was 63·401 years for males and 67·105 years for females. But in the period 1932–4, there were 56,661 male and 53,898 female live births per year. The combined expectation of life at birth for males and females was thus:

$$\frac{\left(63{\cdot}401 \times \frac{56{,}661}{53{,}898}\right) + (67{\cdot}105 \times 1)}{\left(1 + \frac{56{,}661}{53{,}898}\right)}$$

or $$\left(63{\cdot}401 \times \frac{56{,}661}{110{,}559}\right) + \left(67{\cdot}105 \times \frac{53{,}898}{110{,}559}\right),$$

both of which equal 65·207 years, thus showing a true death-rate of $\frac{1{,}000}{65{\cdot}207}$, or 15·34 per 1,000, as compared with a crude death-rate of 8·95 per 1,000. If the latter rate were a genuine index of mortality, it would imply an average expectation of life at birth of 111·73 years.

Official $\mathring{e}_x$—these figures represent the expectations of life given in the official life tables for Australia, 1932–4.[1]

The methods used in constructing these official tables are a great deal more complicated and laborious than those indicated here. Yet, as can be seen from column (*g*), the correspondence between the two sets of results is extremely close. In fact, up to and including 85 years of age, they are close enough for any use to which they might be put. From 90 years of age the differences are very marked, but since the number of years lived above 90 is in any case small, the differences have no appreciable effect upon the main body of the life table.

Where fairly approximate figures are sufficient, life tables may be constructed still more easily by proceeding directly from the death-rates which are given in official publications, provided that sufficiently detailed rates have been given. Statistics adequate for this purpose are, for example, published in the German statistical review, *Die Bewegung der Bevölkerung*, for the years 1924–6.[2] The following Table shows the death-rates per 1,000 for females in various age groups:

Age in years	*Death-rate per 1,000 female population in corresponding age group*
Under 1*	94·07
1–4	6·76
5–9	1·75
10–14	1·29
15–19	2·46
&c.	..

* Deaths under one year of age per 1,000 live born females.

[1] *Census of the Commonwealth of Australia, 30th June, 1933.* Australian Life Tables, 1932–4 [1937], pp. 5–6 and 65–6.

[2] *Die Bewegung der Bevölkerung, 1925–7*, p. 47.

For an original cohort of 1,000 at birth the probability of surviving to the first birthday is then

$$\left(\frac{1{,}000-94\cdot07}{1{,}000}\right)\times 1{,}000, \text{ or } 905\cdot93.$$

For the next age group, 1 to 4 years, a special correction has often to be made, since mortality for the period chosen was considerably higher at the beginning of the age group than at the end. Dr. Kuczynski has found that a weight of 1·2 : 2·8 gives a very close approximation to the truth, and the calculation thus becomes $\frac{1{,}000-1\cdot2(6\cdot76)}{1{,}000+2\cdot8(6\cdot76)}\times 1{,}000$, or 973·46.[1] For the remaining ages, the calculation is simply $\frac{1{,}000-2\frac{1}{2}(\text{death-rate})}{1{,}000+2\frac{1}{2}(\text{death-rate})}\times 1{,}000$, and the l_x and L_x computations are carried out in the usual way. The accuracy of this method depends, of course, upon the accuracy with which the official rates are computed. If the basic population has been satisfactorily estimated, as is generally the case, and the rates are given with a sufficient number of decimal places, the resultant life table will be adequate for most purposes, including that of calculating the net reproduction rate. But it will not be possible to obtain the complete expectation of life unless either the death-rates for the various sections of the first year of life are given (and this is often not the case) or unless it is possible to use some correcting factor for estimating the number of years lived from birth to the first birthday. If the death-rates during the first year of life are given in detail, as is the case for England and Wales, the computation is quite simple, as is shown in the following Table based on the statistics of 1936.[2] (l_x's are multiplied by 1,000 as the radix is 1,000.)

	Female deaths per 1,000 female live births	*Cumulative death-rates*	l_x *at:*			*Correct* l_x
			0		1,000·00	1,000·000
Under 4 wks.	25·98	..				
			4 wks.	$=\frac{1{,}000-25\cdot98}{1{,}000}$	974·02	974·023
4 wks.–2 mths.	7·65	33·63				
			3 mths.	$=\frac{1{,}000-33\cdot63}{1{,}000}$	966·37	966·374
3–5 mths.	7·08	40·71				
			6 mths.	$=\frac{1{,}000-40\cdot71}{1{,}000}$	959·29	959·292
6–8 mths.	5·31	46·02				
			9 mths.	$=\frac{1{,}000-46\cdot02}{1{,}000}$	953·98	953·982
9–11 mths.	4·42	50·44				
			1 yr.	$=\frac{1{,}000-50\cdot44}{1{,}000}$	949·56	949·563

[1] As mortality at the early ages is reduced, the correcting factor becomes less necessary. Similarly, declining fertility, by producing an age composition in which the younger children are least numerous, also dispenses with the need for the correcting factor.

[2] Death-rates from the *Registrar General's Statistical Review of England and Wales, 1936*, Tables, Part I, Table 14, p. 53.

It can be seen that an extra decimal place in the death-rates would have given a result as accurate as the customary method. The second procedure may be illustrated from the above Table. According to the l_x items given, the number of years lived by 1,000 females in the first year of life would be 961·653, whereas the average of 1,000 and 949·563 would have given 974·782 years. Suppose that we took as the correcting factor the correction which would be obtained from the Australian Table, which, as we have seen, gave a result implying that $y \times \frac{1}{2}(1{,}000+963{\cdot}321) = 970{\cdot}602$ years. In this case y would equal 0·9887. Applying this factor to the English data would give 963·767 years, which is fairly close. If we used the correcting factor obtained from the 1933 life table for England and Wales, we should have $974{\cdot}782 \times 0{\cdot}9844$, or 959·575 years, which is again fairly close. The conclusion is, then, that if the appropriate death-rates are available, they may be used to construct a fairly satisfactory life table. The difficulty is, of course, that such death-rates are not always available. Moreover, when such rates are available, the original basic data will also generally be given, and in that case it is better to use these data and construct a more accurate table.[1]

2. *Reproduction Rates*

Among the measures of replacement the net reproduction rate is probably most widely used. In essence, it has already been explained in the text as showing the extent to which each girl child, born at the present time, will replace herself in the next generation, or, looked at from a slightly different point of view, the extent to which a woman now passing through the child-bearing period will replace herself by another woman passing through the same period in the next generation. To make this computation, two facts must be known—the number of female children born to each woman passing through the child-bearing period in given conditions of fertility, and the number of these female children who will themselves survive through the child-bearing period in the succeeding generation, in given conditions of mortality. The first fact gives the gross reproduction rate, the best measure of pure fertility. When combined with the second fact, it gives the net reproduction rate, one of the best available measures of net replacement.

To obtain the gross reproduction rate, we need to know, for the particular year or period in which we are interested, the average number of women living at each year of age, or in each five-year age group, within the child-bearing period. This, for most statistical purposes, is generally assumed to be between the fifteenth and the fiftieth years of age, and although there are, absolutely, frequent cases of women who bear children earlier or later than these somewhat arbitrary age limits, these exceptional cases are, for the most part, unimportant. If the gross reproduction rate is being computed for a single year, say 1933, the average number of women is generally represented by the number of women alive in the middle of the year. If a short period is being used, say 1932 to 1934, the average number of women may, in practice, be taken as the number of women alive in the middle of that period, which in this case would again be mid-1933.

[1] See Note App. *a*, p. 465.

We next require to know the number of live births occurring in the year or period in question, and the ages of the women to whom these births occurred. These births are grouped in the same ages as the female population. There are generally some births occurring to women younger or older than the limits of the reproductive period we have chosen, and it is customary to reallocate these. Thus the births to mothers under 15 years of age are generally attributed to the sixteenth year of age (that is, the year beginning at the fifteenth birthday, and ending immediately before the sixteenth), or in the age group 15 to 19 years (that is, the group beginning at the fifteenth birthday and ending immediately before the twentieth), depending upon whether the method of computing the gross reproduction rate makes use of single years or of five-year age groups. Similarly, births to mothers aged 50 years or more are, in practice, included in the fiftieth year of age, or in the age group 45 to 49 years. The births in the particular year, or the annual average of the births in the particular period, are then divided by the corresponding female populations and the result, when multiplied by 1,000, gives specific fertility rates. In the example given here—for Australia, 1932–4—this procedure is shown in Table 41, columns (*b*), (*c*), and (*d*), for single years of age. Column (*d*) shows that, with the fertility of 1932–4, Australian women would bear children at the rate of 2·574 per 1,000 in their sixteenth year, 6·886 per 1,000 in their seventeenth, and so forth. Totalling these items yields the figure of 2,147·347, which shows the total number of children who would be born to 1,000 women living through the child-bearing period, with the fertility of 1932–4. To turn this total fertility rate into a gross reproduction rate simply means multiplying it by the proportion of female live births to all live births in the period—that is, by 53,898/110,559, or 0·4875—and dividing by 1,000. This gives a result of 1·047. Alternatively, if the births to the mothers of various ages are given by sex, the procedure may be that shown in columns (*b*), (*e*), and (*f*), where female births per 1,000 women at each year of age are obtained directly. Totalling the fertility rates of the individual years yields a figure of 1,046·984. Since this represents the total number of female children who would be born to 1,000 women passing through the child-bearing period, the gross reproduction rate for one woman is 1·047, correct to three places of decimals. We can then say that, according to the fertility shown by Australian women in 1932–4, each woman passing through the child-bearing period has 1·047 female children, or, alternatively, that this number of girl children will be born to each newly born girl child, according to the fertility of 1932–4, provided that each newly born girl child lives through the child-bearing period.

But out of every 1,000 newly born girls some will die before reaching the beginning of the child-bearing period, and of the remainder, some will die before reaching the end of that period. We need to know how many, out of the original cohort of 1,000, will be alive in each year of the 35-year period during which women are assumed to be potentially fertile, and we obtain this knowledge from the life table, in the way described in the previous section. Using the official life table for Australia, 1932–4, which gives the survivors by single years of age, we find that out of the original cohort of 1,000 newly born girls, 939·91 will reach their fifteenth, and 938·85 their sixteenth

Table 41. *Fertility Table of Australia, 1932–4*

Years of age (a)	*Females, 30 June 1933** (b)	*Yearly births, 1932–4†* (c)	*Births per 1,000 females (specific fertility rates)* (d)	*Yearly female births, 1932–4* (e)	*Female births per 1,000 females (female specific fertility rates)‡* (f)	*Females in life-table population, 1932–4§* (g)	*Female births per 1,000 life-table survivors* (h)	*Years of age* (i)
15	58,660	151	2·574	74	1·262	939·380	1·185	15
16	59,981	413	6·886	201	3·351	938·265	3·144	16
17	61,302	1,159	18·906	564	9·200	937·035	8·621	17
18	61,983	2,372	38·269	1,155	18·634	935·680	17·435	18
19	61,693	3,580	58·029	1,743	28·253	934·190	26·394	19
20	60,051	4,381	72·955	2,129	35·453	932·555	33·062	20
21	58,469	5,314	90·886	2,582	44·160	930·780	41·103	21
22	57,176	5,964	104·310	2,898	50·686	928·875	47·081	22
23	55,992	6,277	112·105	3,051	54·490	926·850	50·504	23
24	54,924	6,512	118·564	3,166	57·643	924·725	53·304	24
25	53,717	6,512	121·228	3,178	59·162	922·520	54·578	25
26	52,513	6,526	124·274	3,185	60·652	920·240	55.814	26
27	51,268	6,321	123·293	3,085	60·174	917·885	55·233	27
28	50,015	6,065	121·264	2,959	59·162	915·465	54.161	28
29	48,996	5,621	114·724	2,742	55·964	912·990	51·095	29
30	48,194	5,128	106·403	2,503	51·936	910·470	47·286	30
31	47,679	4,649	97·506	2,269	47·589	907·900	43·206	31
32	47,361	4,865	102.722	2,375	50·147	905·265	45,396	32
33	47,211	4,285	90·763	2,092	44·312	902·540	39·993	33
34	47,218	3,939	83·422	1,923	40·726	899·690	36.641	34
35	47,431	3,467	73·096	1,694	35·715	896·700	32·026	35
36	47,591	3,143	66·042	1,536	32·275	893·570	28·840	36
37	47,613	2,849	59·837	1,392	29·236	890·305	26·029	37
38	47,575	2,675	56·227	1,307	27·472	886·935	24·366	38
39	47,288	2,205	46·629	1,078	22·796	883·490	20·140	39
40	46,816	1,856	39·645	906	19·352	879·980	17·029	40
41	46,179	1,334	28·888	651	14·097	876·390	12·354	41
42	45,377	1,192	26·269	582	12·826	872·675	11·193	42
43	44,544	781	17·533	381	8·553	868·785	7·431	43
44	43,557	502	11·525	245	5·625	864·675	4·864	44
45	42,446	282	6·644	137	3·228	860·305	2·777	45
46	41,230	135	3·274	65	1·577	855·645	1·349	46
47	39,943	62	1·552	30	0·751	850.675	0·639	47
48	38,585	27	0·700	13	0·337	845·375	0·285	48
49	37,185	15	0·403	7	0·188	839·720	0·158	49
Totals	1,747,763	110,559 56,661 males 53,898 females	2,147·347 (Total fertility rate)	53,898	1,046·984 (Total female fertility rate)	31,508·525	945·716 (Net total female fertility rate)	

* Graduated population. *Census of the Commonwealth of Australia, 1933*, Part IX, Table 25, p. 721.

† Adjusted to exclude the still births from the cases of multiple births, and for the redistribution of births to mothers of unknown ages. The births in columns (*c*) and (*e*) are average yearly births for the period 1932–4.

‡ The female births have been obtained from the statistics of five-year age groups—the sex of the births not being given by single years of age—and are therefore partly hypothetical. But any error involved would be negligible.

§ The life-table population has been computed from the official life table for Australia, 1932–4. (*Census of the Commonwealth of Australia, 1933*, Australian Life Tables, 1932–4, pp. 65–6).

birthdays. We may therefore assume that ½(939·91 + 938·85), or 939·380, will be the average number living between the fifteenth and sixteenth birthdays. The net replacement of women aged 15 to 16 years will therefore be not 1·262 female births per 1,000 women, but, taking mortality into account, 1·262 × (939·380/1,000), or 1·185 per 1,000. This process of taking mortality into account is applied to all the separate ages in the reproductive period, and the results, when totalled, show the extent to which 1,000 women or 1,000 newly born girls will be replaced in the next generation,[1] taking into account the fertility and mortality obtaining in Australia in 1932–4. This figure is 954·716 per 1,000 women, or 0·955 per woman. If the sex of the births is given only for the total number of births, the figures in column (*d*) would be multiplied by those in column (*g*), and the items, when totalled, multiplied in turn by the proportion of female to all live births.

It is clear that the construction of a table like that for Australia is very laborious. In practice the process is generally simplified by using five-year instead of single-year age groups. The table for Australia in 1932–4 would then be as follows:

TABLE 42. *Fertility Table, Australia, 1932–4—Five-year Age Groups*

Age in years (*a*)	*Females, 30 June 1933* (*b*)	*Yearly births, 1932–4* (*c*)	*Births per 1,000 females* (*d*)	*Females in life-table population 1932–4** (*e*)	*Births per 1,000 females in life-table population* (*f*)
15–19	303,619	7,675	25·3	4,681·00	118·4
20–24	286,612	28,448	99·3	4,640·23	460·8
25–29	256,509	31,045	121·0	4,586·00	554·9
30–34	237,663	22,866	96·2	4,522·70	435·1
35–39	237,498	14,339	60·4	4,447·63	268·6
40–44	226,473	5,665	25·0	4,358·48	109·0
45–49	199,389	521	2·6	4,246·75	11·0
Totals	1,747,763	110,559 53,898 females =0·488 of all live births	429·8 × 5 2,149·0 / 1,000 × 0·488 = G.R.R. = *1·049*	31,482·79	1,957·8 × 0·488 955·0 / 1,000 = N.R.R. = *0·955*

* From the abridged life table given on p. 380.

The only point to be remembered here is that, in the computation of the gross reproduction rate, the total of the separate fertilities of each five-year age group

[1] The emphasis of the mortality factor depends upon the way in which the net reproduction rate is regarded. If it is the replacement of newly born girls, then the mortality data apply to that present generation. If it is the replacement of potentially fertile women, then the mortality data really apply to the new generation of girls which these women bear.

has to be multiplied by five. This is simply because the rate of 99·3 births per 1,000 women aged 20 to 24 years means the rate at which they will bear children in each year between their twentieth and their twenty-fifth birthdays. In the final computation of the net reproduction rate the multiplication has already been done, because each item in the statistics of females in the life-table population represents the average number living through the respective five-year period. It is clear from the above table that the shorter method of constructing gross and net reproduction rates is not significantly less accurate than the full method. The less accurate gross reproduction rate is only 0·2 per cent. higher than the more accurate rate, and the less accurate net reproduction rate is—to three places of decimals—the same as the more accurate one. In practice the short method is always used; the full method is only of use for demonstrating the principles involved in construction.[1]

3. *Substitute Reproduction Rates*

It has been seen that the primary requirements for computing the gross and net reproduction rates are: the female population divided into its several age groups, either by single years or by five-year groups; the distribution of births by the age of the mother; and a life table for females for the period, or, if one has not already been constructed, the deaths by single years or five-year groups so that an appropriate life table may be compiled. In practice the requirement which is least often fulfilled is the distribution of births by the age of the mother. Many countries now give this information, but it may only be available for the country as a whole, and it is often not available for more than a brief section of the period since the introduction of official vital registration in the particular country. In such cases it may be necessary to fall back upon the use of birth-rates and general fertility rates which, as we have seen, are not explicit indices of replacement, and which may also give an inaccurate picture of comparative replacement as between times or places. The purpose of this section is to discover whether there are methods of estimating replacement in cases where the distribution of births by the age of the mother is not given, and to see how accurate these substitute rates may be. It is assumed that there will be available an analysis of the female population in quinquennial age groups, and a reasonably appropriate life table, or the means of constructing one.

(*a*)

The first suggestion is a method which Dr. Kuczynski has himself often used—the process of applying the specific fertility rates of another country or time to the female population in question, calculating the number of births which would have resulted from such rates, obtaining a factor which expresses the ratio between the estimated and actual births, and using this factor for adjusting the total fertility rate derived from the separate rates which were used. Taking the case of Australia in 1932–4, we may apply to the female

[1] For an exhaustive treatment of gross and net reproduction rates, see Kuczynski, R. R., *The Balance of Births and Deaths*, 2 vols., *Fertility and Reproduction*, and *The Measurement of Population Growth*, all previously cited.

population the Swedish confinement rates of 1926–30, with the following result:

	Female population	*Swedish* fertility rates per 1,000*	*Expected births*
15–	303,619	17·8	5,404·4
20–	286,612	83·0	23,788·8
25–	256,509	106·3	27,266·9
30–	237,663	94·9	22,554·2
35–	237,498	70·9	16,838·6
40–	226,473	35·0	7,926·6
45–	199,389	4·3	857·4
		412·2 × 5 = 2,061·0 = Total fertility	104,636·9

* These—and some of the rates used in the following pages—are really confinement rates, but they have been used as specific fertility rates. This does not in any way affect the result.

Since the actual births were 110,559, the correcting factor is 110,559/104,636·9, or 1·0566, and multiplying this by the total fertility rate we have used (2,061·0), we obtain an estimated total fertility of 2,177·7, from which the gross reproduction rate would be computed in the usual way. The true total fertility rate for Australia, 1932–4, calculated on the basis of five-year age groups, was 2,149·0, so that the substitute rate is only 1·34 per cent. higher than the real rate. So close a correspondence between substitute and real rates makes it worth while to examine the question in rather more detail.

Looking at the problem from the theoretical point of view, it is clear that three hypothetical conditions would equate the substitute and the real total fertility rates. First, both rates would be the same if the female population in each five-year age group were equal, no matter what substitute fertility rates were applied to these populations. Secondly, if the fertility at each age were constant, the same total fertility rate would be obtained no matter what variations between ages there might be in the basic female population. Thirdly, if there were considerable variations in the numbers of women at each age, the same total fertility rate would be obtained by applying different sets of specific fertility rates, provided only that these rates showed the same ratios as between the ages, e.g. if each specific fertility rate were twice as high as the corresponding real rate. In practice, unfortunately, none of these three requirements is perfectly fulfilled, and it remains to see how far the actual deviations from the theoretical needs affect the accuracy of the final rate.

If, of course, the numbers of women in each age group varied very greatly, and if at the same time there were marked differences, as between times and places, in the relative fertility at each age, the substitute method would be quite useless. But in practice the range of variation of the factors is very much smaller than might initially be expected. In the first place, there is a marked similarity between the various sets of specific fertility rates relating to the different countries and periods. They all exhibit the same tendency to a maximum near the middle of the reproductive period, and the range of the relative distribution of fertility between the seven quinquennial age groups appears to be fairly narrow. Secondly, although no country has a female population equal in size as between the several age groups, the range of variation of this factor is surprisingly small. An analysis was made of the ratio between the age groups 15 to 19 and 45 to 49 years for a number of countries and for periods from 1851 to the present day. Of the 86 cases analysed, only 20 showed a ratio of 2·0 or more and only one item was above 3·0.

As a check on the range of error introduced into the substitute gross reproduction rate by variations in the separate factors mentioned above, two series of tests are given in tabular form. The first series is designed to show the combined effects of divergent rates, and female populations with varying ratios between the numbers of women in the several age groups. Fictitious populations have been chosen, in which the ratio between the number of women aged 15 to 19 years and the number aged 45 to 49 years ranges from 1·5 : 1 to 4 : 1. The populations are:

Female Populations

	1·5 : 1	*2 : 1*	*2·5 : 1*	*3 : 1*	*4 : 1*
15–	300,000	300,000	300,000	300,000	300,000
20–	290,000	280,000	275,000	275,000	275,000
25–	280,000	260,000	250,000	250,000	245,000
30–	265,000	240,000	225,000	220,000	205,000
35–	250,000	210,000	195,000	180,000	165,000
40–	230,000	180,000	160,000	140,000	125,000
45–	200,000	150,000	120,000	100,000	75,000

To these populations were applied six sets of specific fertility rates, three fictitious, and three real, to show the effects of widely divergent absolute and relative fertilities.

Specific Fertility Rates per 1,000 Females

	A *Equal age rates*	*B* *Descending age rates*	*C* *Ascending age rates*	*D* *Sweden 1926–30*	*E* *Bulgaria 1926–7*	*F* *Sweden 1871–5*
15–	57	89	25	17·8	36·2	9·1
20–	57	84	30	83·0	225·6	105·9
25–	57	79	35	106·3	242·6	207·1
30–	57	57	57	94·9	188·8	233·0
35–	57	35	79	70·9	131·4	203·1
40–	57	30	84	35·0	64·0	121·3
45–	57	25	89	4·3	30·6	18·1
Total fertility	1,995	1,995	1,995	2,061·0	4,596·0	4,488·0

It was assumed that the true fertility rates were those of Australia, 1932–4, and the actual births were calculated from these rates for the various populations.

The substitute total fertility rates were then calculated by the method described at the beginning of this section, and the results are shown in Table 43. It will be seen that where the ratio between the numbers of women in the age groups 15 to 19 and 45 to 49 years is only 1·5: 1, five of the six tests

TABLE 43. *Tests of the Substitute Gross Reproduction Rate [A]*

The Application of Divergent Specific Fertility Rates to Female Populations with varying Differences in the Numbers of Females in the Several Five-year Age Groups

(*a*) *Ratio between number of women aged 15–19 and number aged 45–9*	(*b*) *Substitute fertility rates*	(*c*) *True total fertility rate*	(*d*) *Substitute total fertility rate*	(*e*) *Ratio of (d) to (c) [percentage]*
Ratio 1·5 : 1		2,149		
	A		2,259	105·12
	B		2,145	99·81
	C		2,385	110·98
	D		2,176	101·26
	E		2,171	101·02
	F		2,232	103·86
Ratio 2 : 1		2,149		
	A		2,323	108·10
	B		2,125	98·88
	C		2,561	119·17
	D		2,198	102·28
	E		2,185	101·68
	F		2,305	107·26
Ratio 2·5 : 1		2,149		
	A		2,361	109·87
	B		2,116	98·46
	C		2,671	124·29
	D		2,208	102·75
	E		2,194	102·09
	F		2,341	108·93
Ratio 3 : 1		2,149		
	A		2,412	112·24
	B		2,118	98·56
	C		2,800	130·29
	D		2,220	103·30
	E		2,201	102·42
	F		2,381	110·80
Ratio 4 : 1		2,149		
	A		2,456	114·29
	B		2,110	98·19
	C		2,939	136·76
	D		2,232	103·86
	E		2,208	102·75
	F		2,427	112·94

yield reasonably satisfactory results, and in only one case is the error more than 6 per cent. The range of error increases, however, as the divergences between the numbers of women in each age group become more marked, and when the ratio is 4:1, only three cases out of the six provide satisfactory results.

But it should be remembered that these tests are really in the nature of a *reductio ad absurdum*. In practice neither equal nor ascending specific rates would be applied, while so far as real rates are concerned it is highly unlikely that high rates would be applied to a population the fertility of which is clearly not very high. Moreover, it seems likely that populations with similar total fertility rates would have fairly comparable age distributions of fertility. To test this hypothesis a further series of trials was undertaken on the same series of populations used for the previous tests. It was again assumed that the true fertility rates were those of Australia, 1932–4, but this time five sets of real fertility rates were applied to the divergent populations, and the basis of the choice was that the births yielded by these rates should not differ by more than 10 per cent. from the births calculated according to the fertility rates of Australia, 1932–4. It will be seen from the table below that the five sets of rates chosen refer to countries in which social customs as regards marriage and the family vary considerably, and that there are in fact appreciable variations in the distribution of fertility between the different age groups.

Specific Fertility Rates per 1,000 Females

	G *New Zealand* *1933*	*H* *Latvia* *1929*	*I* *Sweden* *1926–30*	*J* *Germany* *1929*	*K* *France* *1928–31*
15–	16·8	9·7	17·8	18·1	29·0
20–	94·7	82·9	83·0	95·8	127·4
25–	130·6	126·0	106·3	118·1	126·7
30–	100·2	110·7	94·9	88·9	90·9
35–	61·8	77·5	70·9	55·3	53·4
40–	23·4	29·8	35·0	22·0	18·7
45–	2·7	5·9	4·3	2·5	1·8
Total fertility	2,151·0	2,212·5	2,061·0	2,003·5	2,239·5

Yet the tests in Table 44 show that even when there are four times as many women in the age group 15 to 19 years as in that of 45 to 49, the range of error amounts to only 7·26 per cent. Since it has been shown that in the majority of cases the ratio between the numbers of women in the first and last five-year age groups of the reproductive period is less than 3:1, it may be safely assumed that the error involved in using substitute gross reproduction rates in these cases is not more than 6 per cent. This range would be reduced considerably in cases where the specific fertility rates are available for the country as a whole, and where the substitute method is used for estimating the gross reproduction rate for the different parts of the country. This would also be true where it is desired to estimate the gross reproduction rate of a country for a particular year, and where the most recent published rates applied, say, to a period five or ten years previously.

TABLE 44. *Tests of the Substitute Gross Reproduction Rate [B]*

The Application of Sets of Specific Fertility Rates—yielding Expected Births which differ by less than 10 per cent. from Actual Births—to Female Populations with Varying Differences in the Numbers of Females in the Several Five-Year Age Groups

(*a*) Ratio between number of women aged 15–19 and aged 45–49	(*b*) Substitute fertility rates	(*c*) True total fertility rate	(*d*) Substitute total fertility rate	(*e*) Ratio of (*d*) to (*c*) [percentage]	(*f*) Observed maximum range of error [percentage]
Ratio 1·5 : 1		2,149			
	G		2,153	100·19	
	H		2,178	101·35	
	I		2,176	101·26	2·28
	J		2,149	100·00	
	K		2,129	99·07	
Ratio 2·5 : 1		2,149			
	G		2,161	100·56	
	H		2,216	103·12	
	I		2,208	102·75	5·21
	J		2,149	100·00	
	K		2,104	97·91	
Ratio 3·0 : 1		2,149			
	G		2,162	100·60	
	H		2,227	103·63	
	I		2,220	103·30	6·05
	J		2,148	99·95	
	K		2,097	97·58	
Ratio 4·0 : 1		2,149			
	G		2,164	100·70	
	H		2,243	104·37	
	I		2,232	103·86	7·26
	J		2,148	99·95	
	K		2,087	97·11	

By continuing the method, net reproduction rates may be computed from the substitute gross reproduction rates. The process consists simply of multiplying the chosen sets of specific fertility rates by the female life table population in each five-year age group, adding the results and correcting the sum by the factor already obtained when computing the substitute gross reproduction rate. The application of the sex-ratio coefficient completes the procedure. The extra calculations involved in arriving at the substitute net reproduction rate introduce an additional source of error. Not only is an arbitrary age distribution of fertility assumed in computing the gross reproduction rate, but also this age distribution is then applied as a weighting factor to the life-table coefficients. But it is easy to show that the error arising from this source is extremely small.

If we were to calculate directly from the life table the number of children needed to produce a net reproduction rate of unity, the calculation would be $(1+M/F)(S_m/S_a)$, where M/F is the number of male live births per female live births; S_m is the maximum number of years which could be lived in the child-bearing period—that is, 35 years if there were no deaths between birth and the fiftieth birthday; and S_a is the actual number of years lived in the child-bearing period according to the life table for a given time and place. Taking Australia in 1932–4 as an example, the calculation would be 2·051 ×35/31·483, or 2·280 children, and the coefficient of survival would be 2·051/2·280, or 0·900. But fertility is not equally distributed throughout the child-bearing period. It is concentrated largely in the period before the fortieth birthday, so that the wastage due to mortality is less than appears from the direct life-table computation. The real survival coefficient for Australia, 1932–4 (N.R.R./G.R.R.), would be 0·955/1·049, or 0·910, while the minimum number of children necessary to yield a net reproduction rate of unity (T.F./N.R.R.) would be 2·149/0·955, or 2·250. But even in the case of the simple life-table computation the error involved is small, amounting to only 1·3 per cent. In practice, any series of specific fertility rates used for computing the substitute reproduction rates would show a concentration of fertility in the years before the fortieth birthday. Consequently, even if the age distribution of the chosen set of fertility rates were not quite true for the country and period to which they are applied, the additional error involved in the net reproduction rate would be less than 1 per cent. Applying the age distribution of fertility found in Latvia, 1929, for example, would give a survival coefficient of 0·908, which is under a half per cent. less than the true coefficient.

(*b*)

The second set of methods used in computing substitute reproduction rates is based directly upon the principles of a life table, and we must return to the discussion of life-table construction in order to follow these methods.

As a result of constructing a life table for Australia for 1932–4, it was found that, according to the mortality of that period, 1,000 live born males could expect to live 63,400·803 years, and that 1,000 live born females could expect to live 67,104·946 years. Bearing in mind that the ratio of male to female live births was 1,051·3 to 1,000, the number of years lived by a cohort of 205,130 live born children (raising the radix of the life table to 100,000 for the sake of eliminating decimals) would be 13,375,821 years, according to the given sex ratio and mortality. But this also means that, according to the specified sex ratio and mortality, a constant annual supply of 205,130 live births would eventually result in a stationary population of 13,375,821 persons, this population having the age structure of the 1932–4 life-table population. Since Australia had a total population of 6,629,839 persons in 1933, it may be concluded that a stationary population of this size would be attained with a constant annual supply of 101,674 live births. In the period 1932–4 Australia had an annual average of 110,559 live births, so that the reproduction rate should for the period be 1·087. But a stationary population of 6,629,839 persons would have an age composition quite different from that of Australia in 1933. If we calculate the age distribution of the life-table or stationary population—which is done by multiplying the male L_x column by the sex ratio at birth, and then taking each age group of males and females as a proportion of the total life-table population of 13,375,821 persons—we find that there is a considerably larger proportion of old persons in this than in the actual population. The differences are shown in the following table.

TABLE 45. *Number of Males and Females in the Several Age Groups per 100,000 of the Total Population*

	Males		*Females*	
	*1933** *Census*	*1932–4* *Life table*	*1933** *Census*	*1932–4* *Life table*
0–	4,381	3,723	4,201	3,580
5–	4,810	3,672	4,652	3,538
10–	4,788	3,647	4,641	3,520
15–	4,702	3,619	4,580	3,500
20–	4,495	3,582	4,323	3,469
25–	4,185	3,538	3,869	3,429
30–	3,794	3,490	3,585	3,381
35–	3,449	3,431	3,582	3,325
40–	3,467	3,353	3,416	3,258
45–	3,157	3,246	3,007	3,175
50–	2,590	3,094	2,455	3,062
55–	1,996	2,878	1,944	2,910
60–	1,733	2,580	1,716	2,705
65–	1,402	2,191	1,365	2,409
70–	996	1,707	970	1,999
75–	542	1,159	547	1,478
80–	209	619	237	897
85 and over	91	302	123	534
Total males	50,787†	49,831	Total females 49,213	50,169
			Total persons 100,000	100,000

* Graduated Numbers.

† It will be noticed that the actual population contains more males than females. This is due to heavy immigration in the past, the immigrants generally being men.

In particular, it will be seen that whereas women aged 15 to 49 years constituted 26·362 per cent. of the actual population, they amounted to only 23·537 per cent. of the stationary population. These differences are due to past changes in mortality and fertility. High mortality in the past has resulted in a small proportion of old people in the population, while a combination of lower mortality and high fertility in the more recent past has produced a large block of people in the prime of life. In Australia the position is also complicated by past immigration. But the important point here is that whereas there were 1,747,763 women aged 15 to 49 years in 1933, the stationary population having a total size of 6,629,839 would contain only 1,560,465 women in the reproductive age groups. Since the net reproduction rate refers to the replacement of potentially fertile women, it is clear that the life-table substitute will not be comparable unless it applies to a population containing as many women in the reproductive ages as are found in the actual population. For Australia, 1932–4, this would mean a stationary population of 7,425,598 persons, and in order to attain such a population, an annual supply of 113,878 live births would be required. Since the annual average in 1932–4 was only 110,559 live births, the reproduction rate obtained from the life-table computation would be 0·971, as compared with the true net reproduction rate of 0·955.

The calculation just described gives the main outlines of the method used by Dr. F. Burgdörfer.[1] In practice there is a simpler method which is used by Dr. W. S. Thompson. It consists of obtaining the ratio between the general fertility rate of the actual female population (this rate being placed in the numerator) and the general fertility rate of the female life-table population. Various age limits may be chosen for the female population, though 20 to 44 and 15 to 49 years are the most customary. Taking the general fertility rate as the number of live births per 1,000 women aged 15 to 49 years, and using Australia, 1932–4, as an illustration, we have the following calculation. The female life-table population in 1932–4 was 31,482·8,[2] with a radix of 1,000. Bearing in mind the sex ratio at birth, this female population would result from a constant annual supply of 2,051·3 live births, and the life-table fertility rate would be 65·16 per 1,000. But the actual fertility rate in 1932–4 was 63·26 per 1,000, so the substitute reproduction rate is 0·971. If the ages of 20 and 44 had been chosen as the upper and lower limits for calculating the fertility rates, the substitute reproduction rate would be 0·977, and this would also happen if changes were made in the age limits used in Dr. Burgdörfer's method.

These few examples show that the life-table methods yield results which differ from the real net reproduction rate. The questions to be answered are—what factors cause these errors in the life-table substitutes, how far are they consistently in one direction, and how do they compare with the errors in the substitute net reproduction rate calculated by applying to the females of a particular country the specific fertility rates of other countries? Since the methods used by Dr. Burgdörfer and Dr. Thompson are essentially the same, attention will be concentrated on one method only. Dr. A. J. Lotka has written an extremely interesting paper on the latter method,[3] so the subsequent discussion will be confined to that.

In his paper Dr. Lotka makes two statements which bear very closely on the general value of the life-table substitute. First, 'with a purely arbitrary age distribution of the population, there would be no determinate relation at all between the replacement index on the one hand, and the true rate of natural

[1] See Note App. *b*, p. 466.

[2] Using the life table in Table 40 to make the calculation comparable with that given for the Burgdörfer method.

[3] A. J. Lotka, 'The geographic distribution of intrinsic natural increase in the United States, and an examination of the relation between several measures of net reproductivity', *Journal of the American Statistical Association*, June 1936, pp. 273–94.

increase on the other'. This statement applies equally well to the relation between the replacement index and the net reproduction rate. Dr. Lotka then assumes a stable age distribution of the population in order to arrive at a determinate relation, and finds a theoretical curve which fits the data very well. But the value of the life-table substitute still depends upon the extent to which the actual populations of different countries at different times approach, in their age structure, the stable age composition implied by their current fertility and mortality. This can only be determined by experimentation upon actual statistics. Secondly, Dr. Lotka shows that the replacement index will not be exactly equal to the net reproduction rate of a population with a stable age composition unless the net reproduction rate is unity. If the net reproduction rate is unity, 'the replacement index J is also exactly unity for a population with stable age distribution, as it should be, since the stable age distribution in this case reduces simply to the life table age distribution, and the numerator and denominator in the quotient defining J become equal'. For our present purpose it is more useful to invert Dr. Lotka's argument. We can then say that the net reproduction rate and the life-table substitute will be identical if the actual population of females in the reproductive age groups has the same age structure as the corresponding female life-table population used for calculating the substitute rate. This will be true if the net reproduction rate is above, below, or equal to unity. The reason for this may be seen by looking at the example for Australia, 1932–4 (see Table 42, p. 386). If the actual female population were the same as that of the life table, then the annual average number of live births to women aged 15 to 49 years with the specific fertility rates of the given period would be equal to the sum of the net reproduction rate coefficients in column (*f*)—that is, 1,957·8, and the general fertility rate would be 1,957·8/31,482·79. With a sex ratio at birth of 1,051 live-born males to 1,000 live-born females, the life-table fertility rate would be 2,051/31,482·79, and the replacement index would thus be 1,957·8/2,051, which is equal to (1,957·8 × 0·488)/1,000—the final coefficients used in computing the actual net reproduction rate. This identity of the life-table rate and the net reproduction rate will obtain whatever the age limits of the senior age group used—that is, whether the general and life-table fertility rates are calculated on the basis of women aged 15 to 49 or 20 to 44 years.

The existence of a stationary age distribution among the actual population of females in the reproductive ages is the sole condition in which the life-table substitute will be completely accurate. As the actual population deviates from this condition the life-table substitute will show errors. It will become higher than the real net reproduction rate as the actual population becomes increasingly progressive in age structure—that is, as the younger age groups become larger as compared with the older age groups—and lower than the real net reproduction rate as the population becomes increasingly regressive—that is, as the older age groups become larger as compared with the younger ones. In practice, the important question is—how large an error will be introduced into the life-table substitute by deviations of the actual female populations from the age structure of the corresponding female life-table populations? To answer this question, a series of tests were applied, and the results are given in Table 46. Female populations with varying ratios between the size of the several age groups were taken—the same populations as were used in testing the substitute gross reproduction rate—and the life-table substitute was computed, using the specific fertility rates of Australia, 1932–4, to obtain the total number of births, and the life-table population given in Table 40, p. 380. The

TABLE 46. *Tests of Substitute Replacement Rates [A]*

Ratio between number of women aged 15–19 and number aged 45–9 (*a*)	*True* N.R.R.* (*b*)	*Case used* (*c*)	*Substitute replacement rates* (*d*)	*Ratio of* (*d*) *to* (*b*) (*e*)
Ratio 1·5 : 1	0·955			
		G†	0·957	100·21
		H	0·965	101·05
		I	0·964	100·94
		J	0·955	100·00
		K	0·949	99·37
		L.T.(*a*)‡	0·990	103·66
		L.T.(*b*)§	0·979	102·51
Ratio 2·5 : 1	0·955			
		G	0·960	100·52
		H	0·982	102·83
		I	0·978	102·41
		J	0·956	100·10
		K	0·938	98·22
		L.T.(*a*)	1·035	108·38
		L.T.(*b*)	1·024	107·23
Ratio 3·0 : 1	0·955			
		G	0·960	100·52
		H	0·987	103·35
		I	0·984	103·04
		J	0·955	100·00
		K	0·935	97·91
		L.T.(*a*)	1·058	110·79
		L.T.(*b*)	1·042	109·11
Ratio 4·0 : 1	0·955			
		G	0·962	100·73
		H	0·994	104·08
		I	0·989	103·56
		J	0·955	100·00
		K	0·930	97·38
		L.T.(*a*)	1·077	112·77
		L.T.(*b*)	1·057	110·68

* From Table 42, p. 386.

† The letters G to K refer to the set of specific fertility rates used (see p. 391) for calculating the substitute G.R.R.

‡ L.T.(*a*) is the life-table rate computed on the basis of women aged 15 to 49 years.

§ L.T.(*b*) is the life-table rate computed on the basis of women aged 20 to 44 years.

true net reproduction rate for all these calculations was 0·955. At the same time substitute net reproduction rates were computed by applying the series of specific fertility rates on p. 391 (G to K) to the life-table population, adjusting the results by the correction factors obtained in calculating the substitute gross reproduction rates, and then multiplying by the ratio of 488 female to 1,000 total live births.

Two points will be noticed. First, that variations in the age structure of the female populations produce much larger errors in the life-table substitutes than in the net reproduction rate substitutes. In fact, when the age group 15 to 19 years is 2·5 or more times as large as the age group 45 to 49 years, the margin of error in the life-table substitute is too high to allow the rate to be used as anything more than a very rough indication of reproductive trends. Secondly, apart from the theoretical case when the actual population has the same age structure as its corresponding life-table population, the life-table substitute appears to be consistently less accurate than the substitute net reproduction rate. It seemed important to substantiate this conclusion in practice, and for this purpose a further series of tests was made, the results being given in Table 47. A fairly divergent set of thirty-six true net reproduction rates was taken, and for the countries and periods to which they referred three sets of substitute rates were calculated. The first set consists of substitute net reproduction rates, obtained by using specific fertility rates which yielded births differing by less than 10 per cent. from the actual number of births. To ensure that the test should be as searching as possible, in no case was the substitute rate for a country calculated by applying to the female population specific fertility rates relating to the same country, even if they referred to a different period. The second and third sets consist of life-table substitutes calculated on the basis of women aged 15 to 49 years and 20 to 44 years. The table shows that in practice the life-table substitutes appear to be reasonably accurate. Of the rates calculated on the basis of women aged 15 to 49 years, only 5 of the 36 show an error of more than 6 per cent., while for the calculations based on women aged 20 to 44 years, only one showed an error of more than 6 per cent. But it is clear that the substitute reproduction rates are more accurate. In the first place, the largest error among them is less than 5 per cent. Secondly, of the life-table rates based on women aged 20 to 44 years only four cases show an accuracy equal to or greater than that of the net reproduction rate substitutes, while only three cases are found among the life-table rates based on women aged 15 to 49 years. It may thus be concluded that, in practice, substitute net reproduction rates will provide the most accurate estimates of reproductive trends when the distribution of births by the age of the mother is not given. When adequate statistics are available, true net reproduction rates should, of course, be calculated. But failing these statistics, the substitutes may safely be used for most purposes.[1]

[1] Where under-registration of births is suspected, as in many parts of the United States, it is often customary to use a life-table substitute calculated on the ratio of children aged 0 to 4 or 1 to 4 years (obtained from Census data) to women aged 15 to 49 or 20 to 44 years. The errors in this variation are no less than when births are used, and there is also the disadvantage that the substitute rate then refers to a longer period of time than is the case when births are the basis of the calculation.

TABLE 47. *Tests of Substitute Replacement Rates* [*B*]

Country		*Year*	*True N.R.R.*	*Substitute N.R.R.*	*Percentage of true N.R.R.*	*Life table N.R.R.* (*15–19*)	*Percentage of true N.R.R.*	*Life Table N.R.R.* (*20–44*)	*Percentage of true N.R.R.*
Hungary	1	1900–1	1·445	1·461	101·11	1.437	99·45	1·480	102·42
	2	1920–1	1·127	1·158	102·75	1·188	105·41	1·189	105·50
	3	1932–5	1·008	1·016	100·79	1·087	107·84	1·022	101·39
Austria	4	1928	0·782	0·780	99·74	0·808	103·32	0·800	102·30
Saxony	5	1924–6	0·757	0·771	101·85	0·801	105·81	0·797	105·28
France	6	1920–3	0·977	0·977	100·00	0·975	99·80	0·976	99·90
	7	1925–7	0·929	0·932	100·32	0·939	101·08	0·936	100·75
	8	1928–33	0·905	0·900	99·45	0·928	102·54	0·907	100·22
Germany	9	1932–4	0·757	0·764	100·92	0·825	108·98	0·771	101·85
Australia	10	1920–2	1·318	1·323	100·38	1·415	107·36	1·369	103·87
(excluding	11	1932–3	0·976	0·988	101·23	0·988	101·23	0·994	101·84
Aborigines)	12	1935–6	0·956	0·948	99·16	0·979	102·41	0·981	102·62
New Zealand	13	1911–15	1·357	1·358	100·07	1·479	108·99	1·412	104·05
(excluding	14	1921–2	1·291	1·295	100·31	1·332	103·18	1·303	100·93
Maoris)	15	1933	0·978	0·991	101·33	0·995	101·74	1·007	102·97
	16	1935–6	0·949	0·961	101·26	0·982	103·48	0·985	103·79
Norway	17	1930–1	0·909	0·905	99·56	0·941	103·52	0·935	102·86
	18	1932	0·874	0·865	98·97	0·899	102·86	0·893	102·17
	19	1933	0·799	0·788	98·62	0·820	102·63	0·814	101·88
	20	1934	0·797	0·787	98·75	0·820	102·89	0·812	101·88
	21	1935	0·783	0·765	97·70	0·805	102·81	0·798	101·92
Latvia	22	1935–6	0·856	0·863	100·82	0·925	108·06	0·863	100·82
Bulgaria	23	1921–6	1·534	1·586	103·39	1·580	103·00	1·616	105·35
	24	1926–7	1·446	1·516	104·84	1·491	103·11	1·515	104·77
Denmark	25	1931	0·929	0·917	98·71	0·975	104·95	0·966	103·98
	26	1932	0·939	0·927	98·83	0·986	105·12	0·974	103·84
	27	1933	0·903	0·914	101·22	0·950	105·20	0·936	103·65
	28	1934	0·934	0·946	101·28	0·986	105·57	0·968	103·64
	29	1935	0·902	0·914	101·33	0·955	105·88	0·935	103·66
Sweden	30	1931	0·785	0·778	99·11	0·813	103·57	0·804	102·42
	31	1932	0·775	0·768	99·10	0·805	103·87	0·794	102·45
	32	1933	0·733	0·731	99·73	0·762	103·96	0·750	102·32
	33	1934	0·727	0·724	99·59	0·759	104·40	0·743	102·20
Canada	34	1931	1·319	1·330	100·83	1·334	101·14	1·369	103·79
Ukraine	35	1926–7	1·676	1·719	102·57	1·748	104·30	1·801	107·46
Portugal	36	1930–1	1·334	1·330	99·70	1·354	101·50	1·368	102·55

4. *Nuptiality and Nuptial Reproduction Rates*

The use of crude marriage rates for measuring changes in marriage frequency is subject to the same kind of errors as the use of crude birth-rates for measuring changes in fertility. Nor is a marriage rate based on, say, the number of unmarried women aged 15 to 49 years quite satisfactory. For women the likelihood of marriage is generally greatest between the ages of 20 and 35 years, so that even a marriage rate based on the unmarried population aged 15 to 49 years will be influenced by the age composition of that particular population. Moreover, marriage rates are not explicit. To link up marriage with fertility we want to know not merely how many women marry each year, but what, in given conditions, is the probability that a woman will marry at least once by a given age. The age chosen depends upon the use for which the results are wanted. If we are concerned with marital fertility, the fiftieth birthday would be the end point. But if we are interested in changes in marriage habits, we should take as the end point the last age at which a spinster marriage occurs. Since we wish to know the probability of marriage—or, looking at the question from the opposite point of view, the probability of remaining unmarried—it is clear that we must use the technique of the life table.

Taking spinsters as the basis of our calculations,[1] the following argument applies.[2] Since spinsters may disappear by marriage or by death, the numbers of spinsters surviving at the end of a single year of age out of 1,000 who began the year[3] is $\frac{f^s_x - \frac{1}{2}d^s_x - \frac{1}{2}m^s_x}{f^s_x + \frac{1}{2}d^s_x + \frac{1}{2}m^s_x} \times 1{,}000$, where f^s_x is the number of spinsters aged between (x) and $(x+1)$; d^s_x the number of spinster deaths at the same age; and m^s_x the number of spinster marriages at the same age. The numbers of survivors calculated in this way are called the 'net nuptiality' survivors, since they escape both marriage and death. But to estimate the influence of marriage alone, the 'gross nuptiality' survivors are required—those affected by marriage but not by death. At first sight it might seem that these survivors would be given by the formula $\frac{f^s_x - \frac{1}{2}m^s_x}{f^s_x + \frac{1}{2}m^s_x}$, since 'gross nuptiality' is calculated by relating the number of unmarried females at the end of a year of age to the number found at the beginning of that year. But some of the spinsters die before reaching the end of the year of age, and the number at the beginning is therefore $(f^s_x + \frac{1}{2}d^s_x)$. Consequently, the probability of remaining unmarried at the end of the year is $\frac{f^s_x + \frac{1}{2}d^s_x - \frac{1}{2}m^s_x}{f^s_x + \frac{1}{2}d^s_x + \frac{1}{2}m^s_x}$.[4] In accordance with life-table construction, the successive l^s_x items are calculated in the customary way. The number of unmarried survivors at the end of their twenty-fifth year would therefore be $l^s_{25} = l^s_{24} \times \frac{f^s_{24\text{-}5} + \frac{1}{2}d^s_{24\text{-}5} - \frac{1}{2}m^s_{24\text{-}5}}{f^s_{24\text{-}5} + \frac{1}{2}d^s_{24\text{-}5} + \frac{1}{2}m^s_{24\text{-}5}}$. In some cases, however, it is not possible to obtain statistics of female deaths analysed according to marital condition. If in those cases mortality is low in the ages in which most spinsters marry—that is, in general between the ages of 20 and 35 years—a very close approximation to the truth is given by the formula $\frac{f^s_x - \frac{1}{2}m^s_x}{f^s_x + \frac{1}{2}m^s_x}$. Table 48 shows the unmarried survivors of 1,000 spinsters at the age of 15, according to the conditions in

[1] The calculation could, of course, be based on bachelors. Spinsters are used here because the primary interest is in linking the results with the previous fertility analysis.

[2] The technique of analysis is taken entirely from R. R. Kuczynski, 'The analysis of vital statistics: I. Marriage statistics', *Economica*, May 1938.

[3] Assuming, as in the case of short-period life tables, that migration is an unimportant factor in the period for which each table is constructed.

[4] Similarly, the probability of remaining alive, excluding the influence of marriage, would be $\frac{f^s_x + \frac{1}{2}m^s_x - \frac{1}{2}d^s_x}{f^s_x + \frac{1}{2}m^s_x + \frac{1}{2}d^s_x}$.

TABLE 48. *Female Nuptiality in Sweden, 1932–4—First Marriages Only*

Age in years	Gross nuptiality			Net nuptiality	Age in years	Gross nuptiality			Net nuptiality
	p^s_x	l^s_x	L^s_x	l^s_x		p^s_x	l^s_x	L^s	l^s_x
15	999·97	1,000·00	999·985	1,000·00	47	992·18	214·95	214·110	187·10
16	999·76	999·97	999·850	997·98	48	992·66	213·27	212·485	184·46
17	998·76	999·73	999·110	995·60	49	993·92	211·70	211·055	181·46
18	979·59	998·49	988·300	991·77	50	994·25	210·41	209·805	178·84
19	966·03	978·11	961·495	968·74	51	996·11	209·20	208·795	176·24
20	951·81	944·88	922·115	932·92	52	995·84	208·39	207.955	173·98
21	929·59	899·35	867·690	884·97	53	995·97	207·52	207·100	171·60
22	919·28	836·03	802·290	819·70	54	997·36	206·68	206·405	169·34
23	911·31	768·55	734·470	750·84	55	997·85	206·13	205·910	166·98
24	903·38	700·39	666·555	681·76	56	997·95	205·69	205·480	164·61
25	898·49	632·72	600·605	613·50	57	998·11	205·27	205·075	162·13
26	898·95	568·49	539·765	549·02	58	998·09	204·88	204·685	159·60
27	900·03	511·04	485·495	491·57	59	999·05	204·49	204·395	157·08
28	907·23	459·95	438·615	440·48	60	998·64	204·30	204·160	154·50
29	915·19	417·28	399·585	397·94	61	999·18	204·02	203·935	151·43
30	923·26	381·89	367·235	362·60	62	999·24	203·85	203·775	148·72
31	931·66	352·58	340·530	333·50	63	998·93	203·70	203·590	145·73
32	941·69	328·48	318·905	309.54	64	999·44	203·48	203·425	142·51
33	946·83	309·33	301·105	290·23	65	999·69	203·37	203·340	139·08
34	954·09	292·88	286·155	273·44	66	999·66	203·31	203·275	135·29
35	958·83	279·43	273·680	259·72	67	999·70	203·24	203·210	131·62
36	965·84	267·93	263·355	247·70	68	999·78	203·18	203·160	127·42
37	967·25	258·78	254·540	238·04	69	999·54	203·14	203·095	122·75
38	971·76	250·30	246·765	229·32	70	999·76	203·05	203·025	118·22
39	975·44	243·23	240·245	221·75	71	999·58	203·00	202·955	113·74
40	980·39	237·26	234·935	215·25	72	999·89	202·91	202·900	108·66
41	982·82	232·61	230·610	210·03	73	999·89	202·89	202·880	103·61
42	984·76	228·61	226·870	205·33	74	999·88	202·87	202·860	98·11
43	986·38	225·13	223·595	201·04	75	999·86	202·85	202·835	92·21
44	987·71	222·06	220·695	197·15	76	..	202·82	..	86·26
45	989·13	219·33	218·140	193·53					
46	990·79	216·95	215·950	190·12				21,824·910	

Sweden in 1932–4. In constructing this table the full method was used, taking deaths into account, and both 'gross' and 'net' nuptiality survivors are shown.

When discussing life-table construction, it was shown that calculations by quinquennial age groups yield very close approximations to the truth. A similar procedure is possible in constructing nuptiality tables. But the approximation will be less accurate in this case, because the probability of remaining unmarried changes rapidly between the single years of age over a considerable period of the table. This may be seen from the p_x^s column of the table for Sweden, 1932–4. The fact that the probabilities vary a great deal from year to year reduces considerably the accuracy of the ordinary quinquennial method, which depends for its value upon the extent to which one may justifiably assume that within any five-year age group $p_1^s = p_2^s = p_3^s$, &c. If, therefore, nuptiality tables are being used to measure slight changes in marriage habits from year to year, five-year tables cannot be depended upon to give results of sufficient accuracy. But if nuptiality tables are being used to provide a fairly accurate indication of marriage habits in different countries, or for comparing periods some distance apart, five-year tables are extremely useful. Thus for Sweden in 1932–4, the five-year table would show that the probability of marrying by the age of 50 was 0·792, while the single-year table gives 0·790.[1]

Continuing to apply the principles of life-table construction, we may compute the number of years lived by spinsters. If this is done from the 'gross' nuptiality table, the result will not be influenced by mortality, so that for comparing the expectation of unmarried life between periods or countries it is more satisfactory to use 'gross' nuptiality as the basis. Using Sweden in 1932–4 as an illustration, the L_x^s column was obtained simply by the formula $L_x^s = \frac{1}{2}(l_x^s + l_{x+1}^s)$. It will be seen that the number of years lived in the unmarried state by the 1,000 spinsters was 21,824·910 between the ages of 15 and 76 years. Since we are excluding mortality, we must add a further 15,000 years lived between birth and 15 years of age, making a total of 36,824·910 years. But out of the initial cohort of 1,000 women, 202·82 did not marry at all, and these women lived 15,414·320 years between birth and 76 years of age. The number of years lived in the unmarried state by spinsters who eventually

[1] The result of 0·792 was obtained by the formula (*a*) $p_x^s = \dfrac{f_x^s + 2\frac{1}{2}d_x^s - 2\frac{1}{2}m_x^s}{f_x^s + 2\frac{1}{2}d_x^s + 2\frac{1}{2}m_x^s}$, where the subscript x refers to the specific five-year age group. It would also be permissible to use (*b*) $p_x^s = \left(\dfrac{f_x^s + \frac{1}{2}d_x^s - \frac{1}{2}m_x^s}{f_x^s + \frac{1}{2}d_x^s + \frac{1}{2}m_x^s}\right)^5$, where x has the same meaning as in the previous formula. Tests of actual cases show no reason for giving preference to one formula rather than to the other. In considering the difference in accuracy between the quinquennial and the single-year methods, it should be remembered that the accuracy of the basic data may not warrant meticulous methods of calculation. In very few countries are the mid-year estimates of the population according to sex, age, and marital condition really exact, since it is almost impossible completely to account for migration. This is particularly the case for England and Wales, especially as there is at present a considerable influx from Scotland and Ireland of which no accurate analysis is possible. Intercensal estimates of the spinster populations in this country are therefore not very accurate, and tend to become increasingly far from the truth as the census is left behind.

married was, therefore, 21,410·590, and since the number of spinsters who eventually married was 797·18 out of the original 1,000, the expectation of unmarried life of those women who married at least once during their life, according to the conditions of 1932–4, was 21,410·590/797·18, or 26·858 years.[1] This is the best method of measuring changes in the age at marriage. The official figures generally given in the statistical year-books of the different countries are liable to give incorrect indications in the trend of marriage ages, for clearly the average age at marriage, if it is calculated by taking a weighted average of the ages of all spinsters who marry in a given year, is influenced by the age composition of the marriageable population. Thus the increase in marriage frequency in Sweden between 1926 and 1930 was accompanied by a decrease in the expectation of unmarried life, while the official statistics for the same period showed a rise in the average age of spinsters who married. However, it should be remembered that if the differences are slight, they may be due as much to inaccuracies in the basic data as to real changes in marriage habits.

Having calculated the various marriage probabilities, it is now possible to link them with the gross and net reproduction rates. Taking, as an illustration, Sweden in 1932–4, we may arrive at the following computations.[2]

TABLE 49. *Sweden, 1932–4—Nuptial Gross Reproduction Rate*

	Number of females		*Fertility rates*		*Years lived by 1,000 females*		*Live births to 1,000 females*	
Age (*a*)	*Single* (*b*)	*Married, widowed, divorced* (*c*)	*Illegi-timate* (*d*)	*Legi-timate* (*e*)	*Single* (*f*)	*After first marriage* (*g*)	*Illegi-timate* (*h*)	*Legi-timate* (*i*)
15–19	261,551	2,855	11·78	539·61	4,948·740	51·260	58·30	27·66
20–24	221,147	55,145	25·95	265·95	3,993·120	1,006·880	103·62	267·78
25–29	134,114	129,315	18·37	167·01	2,464·065	2,535·935	45·26	423·53
30–34	85,134	160,383	13·00	114·12	1,613·930	3,386·070	20·98	386·42
35–39	60,659	164,156	9·88	71·56	1,278·585	3,721.415	12·63	266·30
40–44	49,839	155,223	4·96	32·12	1,136·705	3,863·295	5·64	124·09
45–49	44,101	146,849	0·58	3·60	1,071·740	3,928·260	0·62	14·14
					16,506.885	18,493·115	247·05	1,509·92

The illegitimate and legitimate fertility rates were obtained by relating the illegitimate births to the population of single females, and the legitimate births to the population of married, widowed, and divorced females. The number of years lived in the single state was obtained by summing the L_x^s column of the gross nuptiality table. Since mortality is not taken into account in this calculation, the number of years lived by 1,000 women after the first marriage was obtained by subtracting each quinquennial L_x^s from 5,000. The fertility rates were then multiplied by these populations and the results totalled. The proportion of female to all live births in the period was 0·485 for illegitimate and

[1] The quinquennial method (*a*) gave a result of 26·876 years, and (*b*) gave a result of 26·916 years.

[2] Computations for Denmark, 1926–30, are given by R. R. Kuczynski in *The Measurement of Population Growth*, pp. 156–9 and 220–1.

0·486 for legitimate births. Thus, according to the fertility and nuptiality of 1932–4, 1,000 women would bear 119·82 illegitimate and 733·82 legitimate girl children, giving a total gross reproduction rate of 0·854.[1] As the probability of marrying at least once by the age of 50 was 0·78959—that is, as only 790 women out of the 1,000 married by this age—the gross reproduction rate of women who married at least once before the end of the child-bearing period was 0·73382/0·78959, or 0·929. This may be called the nuptial gross reproduction rate. A similar computation is used for obtaining the nuptial net reproduction rate, as is shown in the following table.

TABLE 50. *Sweden*, 1932–4—*Nuptial Net Reproduction Rate*

	Fertility rates		*Years lived by 1,000 females*			*Live births to 1,000 females, mortality accounted for*	
Age (*a*)	*Illegi-timate* (*b*)	*Legi-timate* (*c*)	*Total* (*d*)	*Single* (*e*)	*After first marriage* (*f*)	*Illegi-timate* (*g*)	*Legi-timate* (*h*)
15–19	11·78	539·61	4,632·550	4,587·875	44·675	54·05	24·11
20–24	25·95	265·95	4,564·475	3,646·120	918·355	94·62	244·24
25–29	18·37	167·01	4,487·450	2,207·050	2,280·400	40·54	380·85
30–34	13.00	114·12	4,411·300	1,415·230	2,996·070	18·40	341·91
35–39	9·88	71·56	4,331·275	1,094.860	3,236·415	10·82	231·60
40–44	4·96	32·12	4,240·550	949·075	3,291·475	4·71	105·72
45–49	0·58	3·60	4,129·150	866·465	3,262·685	0·50	11·75
			30,796·750	14,766·675	16,030·075	223·64	1,340·18

The number of years lived in the single state was calculated by taking the female probability of surviving to the age of 15 as a starting-point, multiplying through by the net nuptiality probabilities for the consecutive single years of age, and then calculating the L_x^s in the customary way. Summing the results into quinquennial groups, these totals were then subtracted from the corresponding quinquennial groups of the general female life-table population. The separate life-table populations were used as multipliers to produce columns (*g*) and (*h*). Multiplying these columns by the appropriate ratios of female to total live births, we find that, according to the nuptiality, fertility, and mortality of 1932–4, 1,000 women replace themselves by 108 illegitimate and 651 legitimate girl survivors, giving a total net reproduction rate of 0·759.[2] With

[1] Excluding the effect of the nuptiality of 1932–4, the gross reproduction rate would be 0·838. Alternatively, the legitimate and illegitimate fertility rates may be obtained by relating both legitimate and illegitimate births to the *total* female population—in other words, by splitting the ordinary gross reproduction rate into its component parts. This would give 122 illegitimate and 716 legitimate girl children born to 1,000 women passing through the child-bearing period, and the nuptial gross reproduction rate calculated by this method would be 0·907, just over 2 per cent. less than the more accurate result given above, although the numbers of years lived in the single state and after the first marriage are not taken into account.

[2] Excluding the effect of nuptiality the net reproduction rate would be 0·746. Following the method outlined in the previous footnote, this net reproduction rate would be split into 0·110 for illegitimate and 0·635 for legitimate children, giving a nuptial net reproduction rate of 0·804.

a nuptial probability of 0·78959, there would be a nuptial net reproduction rate of 0·824.[1]

5. *The True Rate of Natural Increase and the Stable Population*

Regarded from a purely logical point of view, the net reproduction rate is only the first stage in analysing the relationship between the actual fertility of a given population, and the fertility required, having regard to existing mortality and excluding the influence of migration, perpetually to maintain the number of potentially fertile women in the population and hence also to maintain the size of the total population.[2] The net reproduction rate describes the numerical relationship between the potentially fertile women of one generation and those of the next, assuming the maintenance of the given conditions of fertility and mortality. But if these conditions persist the population will, as was first established by Sharpe and Lotka in 1911,[3] ultimately have a fixed or stable age distribution. It will then also have fixed or stable birth- and death-rates, and a fixed annual rate of increase. There are, therefore, three questions to be answered. First, what will be the ultimate annual rate of growth (r) of a population subject to constant conditions of fertility and mortality? Secondly, what will be the ultimate, stable age-structure of the population, and its birth- and death-rates (b and d)? Thirdly, what will be the numerical course of the chosen population in the period before stability is attained? Consideration of these questions brings us into a more complex field of demographic analysis, in which all the fundamental contributions are those of Dr. A. J. Lotka. His work may be used to answer all three of the questions, but to simplify this section it will be used only to answer the first two. A different method of answering the third has already been referred to in Chapter VIII. In the present discussion the subject will be treated only from the point of view of the actual techniques of analysis. For the mathematical basis and proof of the techniques, the reader should consult the works of Dr. Lotka, especially those noted in the short bibliography at the end of this section.[4]

Given a particular net reproduction rate (R_0), the implied annual rate of growth—or true rate of natural increase—depends upon the mean length of a generation. As a first approximation, we may take as the length of a generation the average age of mothers, at the time they give birth to their daughters, in the life-table population. Referring to Table 41, p. 385, which gives the fertility for Australia, 1932–4, by single years of age, this approximate form of a generation may be calculated from column (h), by multiplying each item by the appropriate average age to which it refers—that is, $15\frac{1}{2} \times 1{\cdot}185$,

[1] See Note App. *c*, p. 466.

[2] Of course, at any moment a net reproduction rate of unity need not imply the maintenance of a total population of precisely the same size as that living at the particular point of time. The stationary population implied may be larger or smaller than the actual population.

[3] Sharpe, F. R., and Lotka, A. J., 'A problem in age-distribution', *Philosophical Magazine*, April 1911.

[4] The writer is greatly indebted to Dr. Lotka not only for providing many very valuable reprints, but also for his detailed suggestions concerning the form of the present summary.

$16\frac{1}{2} \times 3 \cdot 144$, &c. If we sum these items—they may be called R_1 items, the first moment of the fertility-mortality distribution from which the net reproduction rate is derived—and divide the total by the net reproduction rate, we shall obtain the average age of mothers, in the life-table or stationary population, at the time they give birth to their daughters. R_1/R_0 is 27,853·155/954·716, (or 27·853155/0·954716, if the net reproduction rate is interpreted as the replacement per woman instead of per 1,000 women), the answer being 29·17428 years. The approximate form of the true rate of natural increase may then be obtained from the compound interest formula $A = P(1+r)^n$. Calling the approximate generation T_x, r, the annual rate of growth, is $\sqrt[T_x]{R_0}-1$, which is $-0{\cdot}00159$ per head, or a rate of decrease of 0·159 per cent. per year. The above formula assumes that interest is compounded once a year. It would, however, be more correct to assume that interest is compounded continuously, and thus to use the formula $A = Pe^{rn}$, so that r would be $(1/T_x)\log_e R_0$, which in this case is also $(-0{\cdot}0463414/29{\cdot}17428)$, or $-0{\cdot}00159$ per head.

This short method of computing the true rate of natural increase generally gives very accurate results in practice. In principle, however, it is not quite exact, except when the net reproduction rate is unity. When the net reproduction rate is above or below unity the mean length of the stable generation T—that obtaining when, with the persistence of the given conditions of fertility and mortality, the population has reached a stable structure—will differ from that of the stationary generation T_x, and $(1/T)\log_e R_0$ will therefore differ from $(1/T_x)\log_e R_0$.[1] To calculate T and the true r requires a much more complex system of analysis.

Dr. Lotka has shown that the value of r determined by specified conditions of fertility and mortality is given by the real root of the equation

$$1 = \int_0^\infty e^{-rx}\, p(x) f(x)\, dx, \tag{1}$$

where r is the increase per head per year; $p(x)$ is the probability that a newly-born girl will reach a specific age x; and $f(x)$ is the female fertility rate of women of age x, that is the number of live female births[2] per year to each woman of age x. In practice a very close approximation to the real root of equation (1) is given by the quadratic equation

$$\tfrac{1}{2}\beta r^2 + \alpha r - \log_e R_0 = 0, \tag{2}$$

where

$$\alpha = \frac{R_1}{R_0}, \tag{3}$$

$$\beta = \left(\frac{R_1}{R_0}\right)^2 - \frac{R_2}{R_0}, \tag{4}$$

R_1 and R_2 being the first and second moments of the curve representing the age schedule of net reproductivity.

[1] Though only slightly if the net reproduction rate is not far from unity.

[2] As in the computation of the net reproduction rate, the argument here is in terms of females, for whom there is a more definite and shorter reproductive period.

Solving the quadratic equation (2) and retaining only the negative radical—for the positive radical does not correspond to a root of the fundamental integral equation—we have

$$r = \frac{\alpha - \sqrt{(\alpha^2 + 2\beta \log_e R_0)}}{-\beta} \tag{5}$$

or, using the quantities R_0, R_1, and R_2,

$$r = \frac{\dfrac{R_1}{R_0} - \sqrt{\left\{\left(\dfrac{R_1}{R_0}\right)^2 - 2\left[\dfrac{R_2}{R_0} - \left(\dfrac{R_1}{R_0}\right)^2\right] \log_e R_0\right\}}}{\dfrac{R_2}{R_0} - \left(\dfrac{R_1}{R_0}\right)^2}. \tag{6}$$

The method of computation may be seen if we make use of the detailed fertility table for Australia, 1932–4. Since we have used the life-table population in an age group in calculating the net reproduction rate—instead of the probability of surviving to a specific age—we shall follow the same rule here. We thus have the data in Table 51, and dividing the totals by 1,000 in order to obtain the results in terms of 'per female' instead of 'per 1,000 females' we have the items given below.

TABLE 51

(1) *Central age in years*	(2) *Zero moment* R_0 *(Female births per 1,000 female survivors)*	(3) *First moment* R_1 (col. (2) × col. (1))	(4) *Second moment* R_2 (col. (3) × col. (1))
$15\frac{1}{2}$	1·185	18·368	284·704
$16\frac{1}{2}$	3·144	51·876	855·954
$17\frac{1}{2}$	8·621	150·868	2,640·190
$18\frac{1}{2}$	17·435	322·548	5,967·138
..	..	..	..
$46\frac{1}{2}$	1·349	62·729	2,916·899
$47\frac{1}{2}$	0·639	30·353	1,441·768
$48\frac{1}{2}$	0·285	13·823	670·416
$49\frac{1}{2}$	0·158	7·821	387·140
Total	$R_0 = \frac{954{\cdot}716}{1{,}000}$	$R_1 = \frac{27{,}853{\cdot}155}{1{,}000}$	$R_2 = \frac{851{,}825{\cdot}432}{1{,}000}$.

R_1/R_0 is thus 29·17428; $R_2/R_0 = 892{\cdot}22914$; and $(R_1/R_0)^2 = 851{\cdot}13861$. The true rate of natural increase, r, is thus

$$\frac{29{\cdot}17428 - \sqrt{\{851{\cdot}13861 - (82{\cdot}18106 \times -0{\cdot}0463414)\}^{1}}}{41{\cdot}09053}$$

$= -0{\cdot}0015867$ per head, or a decrease of 0·15867 per cent. per year, not appreciably different from the results obtained by the shorter method,

[1] $\log_e x = 2{\cdot}3025851(\log_{10} x)$; $\log_{10} R_0 = \bar{1}{\cdot}9798742 = -0{\cdot}0201258$; $\log_e R_0 = -0{\cdot}0463414$.

since the net reproduction rate is not very far from unity. As with the calculation of the net reproduction rate, the single-year method is too laborious for use in practice, and the quinquennial method is used instead. This introduces certain errors, especially as the ages by which R_0 and R_1 items are multiplied are assumed to be the mid-points of the five-year age groups, and this is inaccurate, especially in the first and the last of the age groups. Thus in the example for Australia, 1932–4, the single-year computation shows the average age in the 15–19-year group to be 18·6 years, and that in the 45–9-year group to be 46·3 years, instead of the 17·5 and 47·5 which would be assumed in a quinquennial computation. But in fact the error introduced has very little effect. The true rate of natural increase for Australia, 1932–4, calculated by five-year age groups, and using the abridged life table given on p. 380, is −0·0015948, not sufficiently different to make it worth while to use the single-year instead of the quinquennial method of computation.

It has been pointed out that the net reproduction rate indicates the extent to which each woman replaces herself in a generation when, after long persistence of the specified conditions of fertility and mortality, the rate of growth of the population has become fixed. From that point onwards, the population grows according to 'the compound interest law', so that

$$R_0 = e^{rT}, \tag{7}$$

where T is the mean length of a generation. That is,

$$T = \frac{1}{r} \log_e R_0; \tag{8}$$

and, in accordance with (2), $T = \alpha + \frac{1}{2}\beta r$ (9)

$$= \frac{1}{2}\left[\frac{R_1}{R_0} + \sqrt{\left\{\left(\frac{R_1}{R_0}\right)^2 - 2\left(\frac{R_2}{R_0} - \left(\frac{R_1}{R_0}\right)^2\right)\log_e R_0\right\}}\right]. \tag{10}$$

Applying this to the data already derived from Table 51, $T = 29{\cdot}2069$ years, slightly different from the first approximation given by R_1/R_0. When the net reproduction rate is near unity, the relation $T = \alpha$ (that is, $T = R_1/R_0$), gives a very close approximation to the mean length of a generation in the stable population.

When the population has settled down to its stable rate of growth, r, the birth-rate per head will be constant or stable and have the value

$$b = \frac{1}{\int_0^\infty e^{-rx} p(x)\, dx}, \tag{11}$$

and a perfectly satisfactory approximation may be obtained from

$$b = \frac{1}{\sum_0^\infty e^{-r(x+\frac{1}{2})} \frac{L_x}{l_0}}, \tag{12}$$

where, as in the section dealing with life tables, L_x is the life-table population in a given year of age, and l_0 is the radix of the life table. With a constant rate of growth r and a constant birth-rate b, the death-rate will be constantly $d = b - r$. With constant birth- and death-rates the age distribution of the population will also be fixed or stable. The proportion of the population in any given year of age (σ_x) may be obtained, with very considerable accuracy, from

$$\sigma_x = be^{-r(x+\frac{1}{2})}\frac{L_x}{l_0}. \qquad (13)$$

Alternatively, as may be seen by comparing (12) and (13), the stable population may be calculated from the life-table population and the stable birth-rate obtained as the reciprocal of the stable population. All these calculations relate primarily to females. But ultimately, given constant conditions of fertility, mortality and the sex ratio at birth, r must be the same for both sexes. Thus the stable birth- and death-rates for males and the age structure of the stable male population may be obtained by using the life table for males, and the comparable rates and age structure for the total population of males and females may be obtained by combining the two separate sexes, taking the sex ratio at birth into account. Alternatively, a life table for the two sexes combined may be used. The relation between the stable populations for the separate sexes will, if the sex ratio at birth is taken into account, give the sex ratio in the stable population.

To show the complete calculation of the true rate of increase, the stable population and the stable birth- and death-rates, an analysis is given for Australia, 1932–4. To simplify the calculations, quinquennial age groups have been used. This means that $e^{-r(x+\frac{1}{2})}$ becomes $e^{-r(x+2\frac{1}{2})}$, and that L_x becomes ${}_5L_x$, the number of years lived in the five-year age group instead of in a single year, according to the life table.

TABLE 52. *Australia, 1932–4—Calculation of r*

Age in years	*Female specific fertility rates*	*Female life-table population*	*Zero moment* R_0	*First moment* R_1	*Second moment* R_2
15–19	12·308	4,681·000	57·614	1,008·245	17,644·288
20–24	48·239	4,640·225	223·840	5,036·400	113,319·000
25–29	59·058	4,586·000	270·840	7,448·100	204,822·750
30–34	46·966	4,522·700	212·413	6,903·423	224,361·248
35–39	29·503	4,447·625	131·218	4,920·675	184,525·313
40–44	12·209	4,358·475	53·213	2,261·553	96,116·003
45–49	1·264	4,246·750	5·368	254·980	12,111·550
			$\frac{954·506}{1,000} = R_0$	$\frac{27,833·376}{1,000} = R_1$	$\frac{852,900·152}{1,000} = R_2$

$$R_1/R_0 = 29·15998;\ (R_1/R_0)^2 = 850·30443;\ R_2/R_0 = 893·55138;$$

$$r = \frac{29·15998 - \sqrt{\{850·30443 - 2(893·55138 - 850·30443)\log_e 0·954506\}}}{893·55138 - 850·30443},$$

$$= \frac{29·15998 - 29·22895}{43·24695} = -0·0015948, \text{ or } 0·15948 \text{ per cent. decrease per year.}$$

$$T = \tfrac{1}{2}(29·15998 + 29·22895) = 29·19447 \text{ years.}$$

The calculation of the stable population[1] is shown in Table 53, while the age distribution per 100,000 is shown in Table 54, which also compares this age distribution with that found in 1933 and with the stationary population according to the life table for 1932–4. It will be seen that the age structure of the stable population does not differ very greatly from that of the stationary population.

TABLE 53. *Stable Population according to the Fertility and Mortality of Australia*, 1932–4

(1) *Age groups*	(2) *Central ages*	(3) $e^{-r(x+2\frac{1}{2})}$	(4) *Years lived by a female in the stationary population*	(5) *Female stable population derivative*	(6) *Years lived by a male in the stationary population* ×1·0513	(7) *Male stable population derivative*
0–4	$2\frac{1}{2}$	1·00399	4·788733	4·807840	4·980457	5·000329
5–9	$7\frac{1}{2}$	1·01203	4·732600	4·789533	4·911463	4·970548
10–14	$12\frac{1}{2}$	1·02013	4·707900	4·802670	4·877533	4·975718
15–19	$17\frac{1}{2}$	1·02830	4·681000	4·813472	4·841158	4·978163
20–24	$22\frac{1}{2}$	1·03653	4·640225	4·809732	4·791089	4·966107
25–29	$27\frac{1}{2}$	1·04483	4·586000	4·791590	4·732506	4·944664
30–34	$32\frac{1}{2}$	1·05320	4.522700	4·763308	4·668298	4·916651
35–39	$37\frac{1}{2}$	1·06163	4.447625	4·721732	4·588951	4·871768
40–44	$42\frac{1}{2}$	1·07013	4·358475	4·664135	4·484898	4·799424
45–49	$47\frac{1}{2}$	1·07870	4·246750	4·580969	4·341554	4·683234
50–54	$52\frac{1}{2}$	1·08733	4·095150	4·452779	4·139047	4·500510
55–59	$57\frac{1}{2}$	1·09604	3·892975	4·266856	3·848993	4·218650
60–64	$62\frac{1}{2}$	1·10481	3·617750	3·996926	3.450708	3·812377
65–69	$67\frac{1}{2}$	1·11366	3·221975	3·588185	2·930840	3·263959
70–74	$72\frac{1}{2}$	1·12257	2·674125	3·001893	2·283897	2·563834
75–79	$77\frac{1}{2}$	1·13156	1·977185	2·237303	1·550236	1·754185
80–84	$82\frac{1}{2}$	1·14062	1·199415	1·368077	0·827962	0·944390
85–89	$87\frac{1}{2}$	1·14975	0·531810	0·611449	0·309392	0·355723
90–94	$92\frac{1}{2}$	1·15895	0·155810	0·179753	0·079347	0·091959
95–99	$97\frac{1}{2}$	1·16823	0·025322	0·029582	0·013602	0·015890
100–102	$101\frac{1}{2}$	1·17571	0·002131	0·002505	0·001333	0·001567
				71·280289		70·629650

Explanation:

Col. (3). If a three-year age group is used, we have $e^{-r(x+1\frac{1}{2})}$.

Col. (4). That is $\frac{{}_5L^f_x}{l^f_0}$ for a five-year age group. See Table 40, p. 380.

Col. (5). That is $e^{-r(x+2\frac{1}{2})}\frac{{}_5L^f_x}{l^f_0}$ for a five-year age group.

Col. (6). Similar to col. (4), for the male life table, but multiplied by the male-female sex ratio of live births in 1932–4.

Col. (7). Derived from col. (6) in the same way as col. (5) is derived from col. (4). That is $e^{-r(x+2\frac{1}{2})}\frac{{}_5L^m_x}{l^m_0}$ for a five-year age group.

[1] Since r is negative (−0·0015948), $e^{-r(x+\frac{1}{2})}$ becomes $e^{+0\cdot0015948(x+\frac{1}{2})}$. This means that the older age groups will form a larger proportion of the stable than of the stationary population. This is the 'ageing process' which occurs when the net reproduction rate falls below unity. The reverse would happen if the net reproduction rate rose above unity.

Table 54. *Australia*, 1932–4

Number of Males and Females in the Several Age Groups per 100,000 of the Total Population

Age	Males: 1933 census	Males: 1932–4 Life table	Males: Stable* population	Females: 1933 census	Females: 1932–4 Life table	Females: Stable* population
0–	4,381	3,723	3,524	4,201	3,580	3,388
5–	4,810	3,672	3,503	4,652	3,538	3,375
10–	4,788	3,647	3,506	4,641	3,520	3,384
15–	4,702	3,619	3,508	4,580	3,500	3,391
20–	4,495	3,582	3,499	4,323	3,469	3,389
25–	4,185	3,538	3,484	3,869	3,429	3,377
30–	3,794	3,490	3,465	3,585	3,381	3,357
35–	3,449	3,431	3,433	3,582	3,325	3,327
40–	3,467	3,353	3,382	3,416	3,258	3,287
45–	3,157	3,246	3,300	3,007	3,175	3,228
50–	2,590	3,094	3,171	2,455	3,062	3,138
55–	1,996	2,878	2,973	1,944	2,910	3,007
60–	1,733	2,580	2,686	1,716	2,705	2,817
65–	1,402	2,191	2,300	1,365	2,409	2,528
70–	996	1,707	1,807	970	1,999	2,115
75–	542	1,159	1,236	547	1,478	1,577
80–	209	619	665	237	897	964
85 and over	91	302	328	123	534	581
Total males	50,787	49,831	49,770			
Total females				49,213	50,169	50,230
Total persons				100,000	100,000	100,000

* The proportion of all persons in each age group of the stable population has been obtained by multiplying the separate entries in cols. (5) and (7) of Table 53 by the stable birth-rate of the total population—i.e. by 2·0513/141·909939, and giving the results in terms of a total population of 100,000.

This is because the net reproduction rate is very close to unity. The female stable birth-rate is $\frac{1}{71{\cdot}280289}$, that is, 0·01403, or 14·03 per thousand of the female population, while the male stable birth-rate is $\frac{1{\cdot}0513}{70{\cdot}629650}$, that is, 0·01488, or 14·88 per thousand of the male population. Since r is a rate of *decrease* in this case, the stable death-rates are 15·62 per thousand for females and 16·47 per thousand for males, thus showing in each case a rate of decrease of 1·59 per thousand per year. The stable birth-rate for the total population is

$\frac{2 \cdot 0513}{141 \cdot 909939}$, or 14·45 per thousand, and the stable death-rate is therefore 16·04 per thousand. The ratio of males to females in the stable population is $\frac{70 \cdot 629650}{71 \cdot 280289}$, or 9,909 males per 10,000 females.

For Australia in 1932–4 it has been shown that the stable age structure does not differ very much from the age structure of the stationary population. But if the net reproduction rate is much above or below unity, the stable population will differ markedly from the stationary population. Two contrasting examples of this difference are given in Tables 55 and 56. In the former case, the stable population has been computed for Sweden, according to the conditions of fertility and mortality in 1933–4. With a net reproduction rate of 0·731, and a true rate of *decrease* of 1·045 per cent. per year, the population would eventually contain a large proportion of old persons. A figure showing the

TABLE 55. *Sweden*, 1933–4

Number of Males and Females in the Several Age Groups per 100,000 of the Total Population

	Males			*Females*		
Age	*31 Dec. 1933 population*	*1933–4 Life table*	*Stable population*	*31 Dec. 1933 population*	*1933–4 Life table*	*Stable population*
0–	3,495	3,741	2,536	3,365	3,572	2,422
5–	3,876	3,689	2,635	3,742	3,532	2,524
10–	4,539	3,661	2,756	4,367	3,510	2,643
15–	4,385	3,627	2,877	4,223	3,478	2,759
20–	4,610	3,575	2,988	4,439	3,429	2,866
25–	4,287	3,515	3,096	4,275	3,373	2,970
30–	3,889	3,456	3,206	3,975	3,318	3,078
35–	3,518	3,391	3,315	3,647	3,260	3,188
40–	3,102	3,315	3,415	3,319	3,195	3,291
45–	2,916	3,219	3,494	3,105	3,113	3,378
50–	2,537	3,091	3,536	2,708	3,003	3,434
55–	2,271	2,916	3,514	2,405	2,853	3,439
60–	1,810	2,677	3,399	1,991	2,648	3,362
65–	1,497	2,341	3,132	1,756	2,355	3,151
70–	1,230	1,890	2,664	1,492	1,948	2,746
75–	805	1,347	2,001	1,005	1,432	2,126
80–	414	768	1,202	540	861	1,347
85 and over	191	406	680	274	495	830
Total males	49,372	50,625	50,446	Total females 50,628	49,375	49,554
				Total persons 100,000	100,000	100,000

TABLE 56. *Australia*, 1920–2

Number of Males and Females in the Several Age Groups per 100,000 of the Total Population

Age	Males: 1921* Census	Males: 1920–22 Life table	Males: Stable population	Females: 1921* Census	Females: 1920–22 Life table	Females: Stable population
0–	5,617	3,862	5,170	5,414	3,715	4,975
5–	5,565	3,778	4,827	5,424	3,645	4,657
10–	4,899	3,745	4,566	4,793	3,618	4,410
15–	4,347	3,710	4,316	4,239	3,590	4,176
20–	4,029	3,660	4,063	4,262	3,548	3,939
25–	4,170	3,598	3,812	4,369	3,492	3,699
30–	4,185	3,528	3,567	4,084	3,426	3,464
35–	3,659	3,445	3,324	3,503	3,350	3,232
40–	3,107	3,341	3,076	2,952	3,265	3,006
45–	2,690	3,205	2,816	2,512	3,166	2,782
50–	2,480	3,028	2,539	2,189	3,042	2,551
55–	2,157	2,798	2,239	1,850	2,880	2,305
60–	1,647	2,487	1,900	1,426	2,663	2,033
65–	1,040	2,087	1,521	905	2,357	1,718
70–	613	1,604	1,115	586	1,927	1,340
75–	360	1,063	705	375	1,379	915
80–	176	543	344	190	789	500
85 and over	86	242	145	100	424	253
Total males	50,827	49,724	50,045	Total females 49,173	50,276	49,955
				Total persons 100,000	100,000	100,000

* Graduated numbers.

stable age structure for this example would be shaped rather like a spinning top, small in the very old ages because of the high mortality in that section of life, but also tapering downwards because of the decreasing annual numbers of births. In the second case, for Australia in 1920–2, the position is reversed. With a net reproduction rate of 1·319 and a true rate of *increase* of 0·936 per cent. per year, there would be a much larger proportion of young persons in the stable population than in the stationary population, and a figure showing this graphically would therefore be like a flattened pyramid.

It is interesting to see the effect of the different levels of fertility on the sex ratio in the stable population. In the actual population this ratio is the product of a complex of factors—past civil and war mortality, changes in migration and in the sex ratio at birth, and the differential between male and female mortality. In the stationary population it is the product of two factors—the sex ratio at birth, and the difference in mortality between males and females. It is found that in most countries at the present time, the excess of male over female births is large enough to counteract the higher mortality among males and produce, in the stationary populations, an excess of males over females at least up to the age group 50 to 54 years. In some countries the excess continues even later. In Sweden, for example, in 1933–4 masculinity at birth was very high (1·0620 to 1·0), and the difference between male and female mortality was relatively small,[1] so that the excess of males in the stationary population would continue up to the age group of 60 to 64 years. Above that age group females would predominate because the expectation of life is higher for females than for males. The sex ratio in the stable population will therefore depend not only upon the excess of male over female births and the difference between the mortality among males and females, but also upon the age structure of the given stable population. If there is a large proportion of young persons—that is, if the population shows an inherent annual increase—the population will tend to be relatively masculine. But if there is low fertility and, consequently, a large proportion of old people, the stable population will tend to be relatively feminine. The stable population for Australia, according to the fertility and mortality of 1932–4, shows a slight increase in femininity as compared with the stationary population—the number of males per 10,000 females falls from 9,933 to 9,909—because the net reproduction rate is only slightly below unity. But even in the case of Sweden for 1933–4, the stable population would still contain 10,180 males per 10,000 females, as compared with 10,253 to 10,000 in the stationary population. The change in the sex ratio is, therefore, generally small. If, for example, we took the mortality of Australia in 1932–4, but assumed that fertility was exactly half of that obtaining in the period—so that the net reproduction rate would be 0·477 and the annual rate of *decrease* 2·491 per cent.—the ratio of males to females in the stable population would still be 9,471 to 10,000 as compared with 9,933 to 10,000 in the stationary population. If, on the other hand, we compute the stable population corresponding to the fertility and mortality of Australia in 1920/2, we find a ratio of 10,018 males to 10,000 females, as compared with 9,890 to 10,000 in the relevant stationary population.

In interpreting the stable population it is important to remember that it has no significance as an absolute figure. It derives not from a given population but from a given life table and given conditions of fertility, and its significance lies entirely in its age distribution. Thus by itself the analysis of the true rate of natural increase gives no precise indication of the size of a population by the time stability has been attained. If, therefore, we are interested in absolute numbers, rather different techniques must be used to cover the transition period during which the population is still in the process of achieving a stable structure, and during which, therefore, the annual rate of growth and the birth- and death-rates will be different from those calculated by the methods described in this section. The techniques for analysing trends during the transition period may be mathematical or statistical. But in either case they

[1] The expectation of life at birth, in 1933–4, was 63·67 years for males and 65·94 years for females, according to life tables computed for the present study.

involve a considerable amount of computation.[1] Once the population has become stable, the derivatives of the true rate of natural increase can, of course, be applied. But stability requires a fairly long period for attainment. Various tests have shown that approximate stability is reached in about two generations. Oscillations about the stable rate of growth are still visible, however, for more than a hundred years after this approximate stability, and though these oscillations are very small, they should be noted as constituting a disturbing factor in the course of population growth.[2]

[1] See Chapter VIII of the present study. A selected bibliography of estimates of future populations, and of discussions of such estimates is given on pp. 468–72. It was originally intended to include in the present study a lengthy analysis of the methods of estimating future populations, including numerous analyses of estimates constructed by various authors. Unfortunately the war has necessitated some economy of tabular material, and the relevant section has therefore been omitted. Perhaps at some later time it may be possible to publish the section separately.

[2] See Note App. *d*, p. 467.

NOTES

(*The figures in parentheses are to the pages of the text.*)

CHAPTER I

(*a*) For the change introduced by the 1874 Act, see the Births and Deaths Registration Act of 1874, 37 & 38 Vict., c. 88 (*Public General Statutes*, London, 1874, pp. 437–60), esp. paras. 1 and 39, and compare with the Registration Act of 1836, 6 & 7 Will. IV, c. 86 (*The Statutes of the United Kingdom of Great Britain and Ireland*, vol. xiv, London, 1838, pp. 272–81), esp. paras. 18 and 19. The 1874 Act placed the onus of registration upon the parents, or in default of them, on the occupier of the house in which to his knowledge the child was born, or on any person present at the birth or having charge of the child, and provided a penalty of not more than forty shillings (for each offence) for a parent failing to give information concerning the birth of such child. The 1836 Act placed the responsibility on the registrar who was authorized and required to inform himself carefully of every birth and death occurring in his district, though parents were bound to give information to the registrar on being requested to do so, and might give notice of a birth within forty-two days after its occurrence. See also *The Story of the General Register Office and Its Origins* (compiled by the Registrar General), London, 1937, p. 25. (1)

(*b*) For Scotland the net outward balance of migration was about 117,000 in 1861–71; 93,000 in 1871–81; 217,000 in 1881–91; 53,000 in 1891–1901; 254,000 in 1901–11; 239,000 in 1911–21; and 392,000 in 1921–31 (*Census of Scotland, 1931*, vol. ii, Tables A and B, pp. vii and viii). For the Northern Ireland area the net outward balance was about 159,000 in 1871–81; 141,000 in 1881–91; 68,000 in 1891–1901; 65,000 in 1901–11; and 58,000 in 1926–37 (Northern Ireland Census of 1937, *Preliminary Report*, Table A, p. 1). For the period 1911–26 a figure of 108,000 is given, but this includes deaths of non-civilians which occurred outside Northern Ireland. For the area of the Irish Free State, the net outward balance was about 502,000 in 1871–81; 597,000 in 1881–91; 396,000 in 1891–1901; 262,000 in 1901–11; 405,000 in 1911–26—war deaths are included in emigration; and 169,000 in 1926–36 (*Census of Population, 1926, Preliminary Report*, p. 6, and *Census of Population, 1936, Preliminary Report*, p. 15). (4)

(*c*) The crude birth-rates have been calculated from the census populations given in Table 1, and the annual averages of live births for the three years centred on each census. For the death-rates the same populations have been used, together with the annual averages of deaths. For the fertility rates the female populations have been taken from the 1931 census, *General Tables*, Tables 20 and 21, pp. 149 and 150. The legitimate fertility rate is calculated on the number of women aged 15–44 years (note that throughout this book the age stated is the age at the last birthday) because the age grouping 15–49 years was not given by marital condition in the censuses of 1881, 1891, and 1901. The legitimate fertility rates for 1920–2 and 1930–2 given above do not agree exactly with the rates given in the *Registrar-General's Statistical Review of England and Wales for 1934*, Text, p. 180 (where they are cited as 178·9 and 122·4 respectively) because the Registrar-General has, for these two periods, obtained the period rates by averaging the fertility rates of the separate years. This also applies to the crude birth-rates. (5)

(*d*) A further point may be mentioned, bearing upon the value of the rate for prognosis. The net reproduction rate is based upon a cross-section of the population in a short period of time, and therefore blends into itself data which derive from many different generations of women. We do not know if the women of 15 to 19 years, observed in, say, 1935, will continue to bear children in their later life at the rates shown by the older women observed in 1935. It is in fact intrinsically unlikely that they will do so. The same applies, of course, to mortality. There is no theoretical reason why generation reproduction rates should not be calculated, and these would give a picture of what has actually happened. But the ordinary net reproduction rate is nevertheless perfectly satisfactory as an index of replacement at a given point of time. (12)

(*e*) For a discussion of the method adopted see pp. 387–93 of the present book. Wherever the term 'estimated reproduction rates' is mentioned, this method has been used. (There are other methods of estimation, described on pp. 393–5, but they appear to give results slightly more inaccurate than the method actually adopted.) The rates given here for England and Wales differ slightly from those given by the present writer in 'Changes in Fertility in England and Wales, 1851 to 1931' (*Political Arithmetic*, ed. Lancelot Hogben, F.R.S., London, 1938). There are two reasons for this. First, an attempt has been made here, by the use of specific fertility rates yielding expected births which differ very little from observed births, to obtain the maximum likelihood of accuracy in estimating fertility. Secondly, in the previous study by the present writer, official life tables were used for the mortality coefficients. But in the years prior to 1910–12 these apply to inappropriate periods of time—1838–54, 1871–80, 1881–90, &c.—and for the present study special life tables have been constructed, applying to the three years about each census—i.e. 1850–2, 1860–2, &c. In constructing these tables, graduated mid-year populations (given in the general report of each census from 1861 onwards) have been used as a basis, and the three-year averages of deaths have been smoothed and, where necessary, interpolated. From 1910–12 to 1930–2 inclusive, the official life tables are appropriate and are from *The Registrar-General's Decennial Supplement, England and Wales, 1921*, Part III, London, 1933, p. 29, and *The Registrar-General's Decennial Supplement, England and Wales, 1931*, Part I, London, 1936, p. 49. Special life tables have also been constructed for each separate year from 1932 onwards. For Scotland special life tables have been constructed in the same way as for England and Wales, except for 1910–12 to 1930–2 inclusive. The table used for 1910–12 is from Dunlop, J. C., and Hunter, R. M., 'The expectation of life in Scotland in the year 1911', *Transactions of the Faculty of Actuaries*, vol. vii, 1915, pp. 365–9; for 1920–2, from Dunlop, J. C., 'Scottish life tables, 1921', ibid., vol. x, 1924–5, pp. 20–1; for 1930–2, from *Supplement to the Seventy-Eighth Annual Report of the Registrar-General for Scotland*, Part I, Edinburgh, 1934, pp. 38–9. Since the reconstructed life tables for the nineteenth century use the quinquennial method upwards from the age of 5 years, all female life table populations (including those derived from official life tables) have also been constructed on the quinquennial method. (12)

(*f*) On the basis of fertility data provided by the 1921 Census, R. R. Kuczynski (*Balance of Births and Deaths*, vol. i, pp. 114–15 and 50) has computed a gross and net reproduction rate for 1921, being 1·312 and 1·087 respectively. The specific fertility rates per 1,000 for the seven quinquennial age groups from 15–19 to 45–9 years calculated by Kuczynski are: 15·36; 107·96; 156·09; 137·53; 96·92; 21·98; and 2·27. Applying these rates we should obtain for 1920–2 a gross reproduction rate of 1·334 and a net rate of 1·105, not differing greatly from the rates cited in the table above. (13)

(*g*) Some official data on legitimate fertility are available for England and Wales (*Registrar-General's Statistical Review for 1932*, Text, p. 136) and Scotland (*Eighty-Third Annual Report of the Registrar General, 1937*, p. liv). The Scottish data were obtained by a 10 per cent. sample of the enumeration books, whereas the English data are based on the general census returns. The Scottish data exclude illegitimate births, and have thus not been used in the present study for comparison with the results given in the above table. Using the English data—the actual method is described subsequently, p. 18—the present writer obtains a gross reproduction rate of 0·927 and a net rate of 0·803 for 1930–2, not significantly different from the rates given above. (13)

(*h*) For 1932 there is also available a sample of 37,370 births for which the ages of the mothers were obtained—total live births in 1932 amounting to 91,000. (See Douglas, C. A., and McKinlay, P. L., *Report on Maternal Morbidity and Mortality in Scotland* (Dept. of Health for Scotland), Edinburgh, 1935, p. 63). This sample gives 5·16 per cent. of the births to mothers under 20 years; 24·87 to those aged 20–4; 28·56 to those aged 25–9; 22·66 to those of 30–4; 13·56 for 35–9; 4·75 for 40–4; and 0·44 per cent. to those aged 45 or more years. Applying these percentages to all births and using the mid-year population of females (unpublished, but kindly supplied by the Registrar-General for Scotland), gives a gross reproduction rate of 1·126, and a net rate of 0·934, not differing greatly from the rates cited above. For a discussion of reproductive trends in Scotland, with particular reference to emigration from the Highlands, see *The Highlands and Islands of Scotland* (Scottish Economic Committee), [Glasgow], 1938, pp. 155–8. The suggestion there made, of including emigration in the measure of reproduction, is somewhat similar to the method used by Jensen, A., in 'Horoscope of the population of Denmark', *Bulletin de l'Institut International de Statistique*, vol. xxv, 3me Livraison, 1931, in constructing a life table. (13)

(*i*) Estimated reproduction rates have also been computed for Ireland. For Ireland as a whole the gross and net rates—in this order—are: 1870–2, 1·907 and 1·392; 1880–2, 1·680 and 1·188; 1890–2, 1·548 and 1·110; 1900–02, 1·417 and 1·028; 1910–12, 1·529 and 1·169; 1925–7, 1·427 and 1·161. For 1925–7 the rates for Northern Ireland are 1·364 and 1·098, and for the Irish Free State they are 1·492 and 1·212. For Northern Ireland, 1925–7, the official life table was used (*The Registrar-General's Review of Vital Statistics of Northern Ireland and Life Tables, 1926*, p. 66). For the other net reproduction rates special life tables were constructed, relating to the relevant years, including a life table for Ireland as a whole, 1925–7. In 1935–7 the gross reproduction rate for the Irish Free State was about 1·386 and the net reproduction rate about 1·162. (The official life table was used in this computation —see Ireland, *Census of Population, 1936*, vol. v, part i, p. 218.) (12)

(*j*) Farr gives expectations of life indicative of the remarkably high mortality in the industrial towns during the period of expansion. Thus, for 1841: Liverpool, 25 years for males and 27 for females; Manchester, 24 years for males. (The Manchester life table appears to be for 1838–44. See *Seventh Annual Report of the Registrar-General*, pp. 329 and 338.) For London the figures were 35 years for males and 38 for females (Whitechapel 31 for males and 34 for females) and for Surrey, 44 years for males and 46 for females (Farr, W., *Vital Statistics*, ed. N. A. Humphreys, London, 1885, pp. 453 et seq.). Some light is thrown on the causes of high mortality in the towns by the Appendix to the *First Report of the Commissioners for Inquiring into the State of Large Towns and Populous Districts*, Parlty. Papers, 1844, vol. 17—see e.g. Duncan, W. H., 'On the physical causes of the high rate of mortality in Liverpool', pp. 12 et seq. (14)

(*k*) See, for example, Titmuss, R. M., *Poverty and Population*, London, 1938, esp. chs. 3, 4, and 5, analysing the geographical distribution of mortality at the present time. Lewis-Faning, E., *A Study of the Trend of Mortality Rates in Urban Communities of England and Wales, with Special Reference to 'Depressed Areas'*, London (H.M.S.O.), 1938, concludes (pp. 65–6) that the higher mortality of the 'depressed areas' is not a new phenomenon, but has been visible for at least twenty years, and was not unfavourably influenced by the economic depression. But his graphs (pp. 43–56) show an increase in the disparity for Merthyr Tydfil and Newport (Mon.), which he recognizes clearly (p. 65). One of the unexplained facts in the distribution of mortality is that in the county boroughs of Northumberland and Durham the male death-rates for all social classes are higher than for England and Wales as a whole. They are also higher in the county boroughs of South Wales (Newport, Cardiff, Merthyr Tydfil, and Swansea), so that it cannot simply be a function of latitude. The most recent official analysis for England and Wales (*Registrar-General's Decennial Supplement for 1931, Part IIa, Occupational Mortality*, London, 1938, esp. pp. 22 and 25 et seq.) shows that class mortality applies to wives as well as to husbands, though wives in the upper social grades do not appear to be as liable to die from 'over-indulgence diseases'—nephritis, diabetes—or from apoplexy as their husbands. The standardized mortality ratios (1930–2) for males aged 20–64 years are 23 per cent. higher for the unskilled than for the professional classes. For women married to the men in these classes the excess is almost 40 per cent. among the unskilled. (16)

(*l*) The legitimate fertility rate for 40–4 years was allocated to the age groups 40–4 and 45–9 years and all rates then adjusted to the annual average of legitimate births for 1930–2. The Registrar-General's legitimate fertility rates are derived from the children under one year of age enumerated at the 1931 census. The Registrar-General's illegitimate rates are based upon those for 1921, which in turn derived from fictitious rates used by the Government Actuary and the Ministry of Health in assessing maternity risk and benefit to unmarried women for the purpose of National Health Insurance. They are almost certainly incorrect, but this would not produce any significant error in calculating the net reproduction rate and they are in any case adequate for our present purpose. (See Kuczynski, R. R., *The Measurement*, &c., pp. 148–9 and 152–3, and *Registrar-General's Statistical Review for 1922*, Text, p. 140.) (18)

(*m*) This may be an exaggeration as it assumes that the fertility of women who otherwise would be unmarried would, once they were married, be the same as that of other married women, whereas it is possible that among the women who never marry the incidence of natural infertility is higher, and that the desire for children is less strong. On the other hand, the figure of 0·938 is somewhat too low because it attributes all illegitimate births to women who never marry. But even the women who do eventually marry spend some years in the single state. The net nuptiality table (nuptiality and mortality combined) shows that out of 1,000 newly-born girls, 136 would survive, unmarried, to their fiftieth birthdays, according to the mortality and marriage frequency of 1930–2, and these will have lived 35 × 136, or 4,760 years in the single state during the child-bearing period (fifteenth to fiftieth birthdays). The total years lived in the single state in the child-bearing period being 12,863·30, women who eventually marry must spend 8,103·30 years in the single state in that period. Assuming that their chances of bearing an illegitimate child when they are in the single state are the same as for women who never marry, the proportion of the illegitimate net reproduction rate to be imputed to women who eventually marry would be approximately (8,103·3/12,863·3)(0·035), or 0·022. It is also likely that part of the illegitimacy occurs to women when they are married, widowed, or divorced. Assuming that the proportion amounts to 5 per cent. of the 0·035, or 0·002, the total net rate of women who marry would be 0·775 + 0·022 + 0·002, and since only 826 out of 1,000 do marry by their fiftieth birthday (mortality has already been taken into account, so the gross probability of marriage is used here), the net rate per woman who married would be 0·799/0·826, or 0·967. Interpretation of this figure as the general net reproduction rate which would obtain if every woman married by her fiftieth birthday is still subject to the assumption that the women who do not now marry are physiologically as fecund as those who do, and that they would in fact bear children at the same rates. (22)

(*n*) To obtain reliable estimates of the frequency distribution of families of different sizes, given the fertility, mortality, and nuptiality levels of a particular period, requires a type of analysis introduced by A. J. Lotka and B. S. Burks and elaborated by P. K. Whelpton and N. E. Jackson. It involves splitting up legitimate specific fertility rates according to birth order and relating them to the female life table population and to the female nuptiality table. See *Population Index*, July 1939, pp. 146–8. Whelpton and Jackson find that in the United States, according to the conditions of the white population in 1929–31, 23·1 per cent. of all wives would be infertile, and 20·0 would have only one child each—that is, of the fertile marriages, about 26 in every 100 would have only one child each. It should be noted that though there will be a close connexion between the net reproduction rate and the frequency distribution of families of different sizes, as calculated by the method mentioned above, the connexion need not be rigid. A low net reproduction may, for example, be found in a community in which childlessness is extremely rare and nuptiality very high. (23)

(*o*) Suppose, for example, we use the same total fertility rate as for 1930–2 (Table 5, last column) but compress the fertility into the age groups of 15–19 and 20–4 years, the number of live births per 1,000 women being 179·9 for the first and 200·0 for the second age group. The gross reproduction rate would be unchanged—0·927—but the net reproduction rate would be 0·828 instead of 0·803. If we then calculate the true rate of annual growth from the equation $\frac{1}{2}\beta r^2 + \alpha r - \log_e R_0 = 0$, we find that for this fictitious case the stable generation would be 20·15 years and the annual rate of growth would be −9·38 per 1,000. But for the actual conditions of 1930–2, with the lower net reproduction rate, the stable generation would be 30·02 years, and r would be −7·29 per 1,000. In practice, of course, the lowering of the marriage age would not have so marked an effect. It should be noted that this conception of the possible results of early marriage may be purely academic. In reality early marriage means a longer exposure to the 'risk' of child-bearing and may therefore in any case result in a higher gross reproduction rate, more than enough to counter-balance the fall in the length of the generation. (24)

(*p*) See Pell, C. E., *The Law of Births and Deaths*, London, 1921, preface and ch. vi; Langdon-Brown, W., 'Some physiological principles', *Medical Press and Circular*, 15 Sept. 1937; Blacker, C. P., 'Medical causes of infertility', ibid., 14 July 1937; Young, J., 'The habitual abortion and stillbirth syndrome and late pregnancy toxaemia', *B.M.J.*, 8 May 1937 (which concludes: 'The evidence reviewed in this communication raises the question as to the part played by diet in racial fertility and more especially as to how far changes in the consumption of essential dietetic elements may have contributed to the declining birth rate'); Gini, C., 'The cyclical rise and fall of population', in *Population* (lectures on the Harris Foundation, 1929), Chicago, 1930, pp. 3–140. Much of the work of Professor R. Pearl suggests that increasing density of population produces a diminished rate of population growth. See esp. Pearl, R., *The Biology of Population Growth*, London, 1926, esp. pp. 146–57. A critique of the significance and validity of the logistic curve used by Pearl and Reed is given by Bowley, A. L., in a discussion of a paper by Stevenson, T. H. C., 'The laws governing population', *J.R.S.S.*, Jan. 1925, and in Hogben, L. T., *Genetic Principles in Medicine and Social Science*, London, 1931, pp. 176–84. An excellent analysis of the possible part played by physiological factors is given by Professor F. H. Hankins, in 'Has the reproductive power of Western peoples declined?', *Problems of Population*, ed. G. H. L. F. Pitt-Rivers, London, 1932, pp. 181–8. (25)

(*q*) Information was available for 90·7 per cent. of all the wives. Kuczynski, R. R., 'Childless marriages', *Sociological Review*, April 1938, pp. 130–7, Oct. 1938, pp. 352–9, gives an analysis of, and commentary on the data collected at the 1911 censuses in England and Wales, Scotland, and Ireland. The Irish statistics are not strictly comparable, for marriages of 35 or more years' duration are excluded. For Scotland women married between their fifteenth and twentieth birthdays and whose marriages had lasted 10 years or longer, showed 2·7 per cent. of childlessness. Those married between their twentieth and twenty-fifth birthdays, and whose marriages had lasted 10 or more years, showed 4·8 per cent. of childlessness. The difference between these percentages and those for England and Wales may perhaps be due to the difference in the extent of contraceptive practice. But on the general question of contraception see subsequent discussion. (26)

(*r*) A certain amount of work has been published for other countries where either more recent official statistics on this subject are available, or where sample or local surveys have been undertaken. Thus Charles, E., 'The changing structure of the family in Australia' (containing some data for the United States), in *Political Arithmetic*, op. cit., esp. pp. 236–7, estimates a considerable increase of childlessness—from 10 to over 20 per cent.—in marriages between 1909–13 and 1929–33. Lorimer, F., and Osborn, F., *Dynamics of Population*, New York, 1934, pp. 255–79, summarize a considerable amount of data including material from an investigation from which they obtained records relating to 308 married women of 'superior social status', aged 40 to 64 years. Sixty of these women were childless, 22 of them stating this to be intentionally so. Although believing that physiological sterility (absolute and relative) play an important part in reducing the reproductivity of some groups, especially where there is late marriage, the authors regard the decline in fertility as largely unrelated to biological factors and due to social causes affecting voluntary limitation. Kiser, C. V., 'Voluntary and involuntary aspects of childlessness', *Milbank Memorial Fund Quarterly*, Jan. 1939, reporting the results of a small sample inquiry in New York City, found that 70 to 80 per cent. of the native white childless women and 80 to 85 per cent. of the foreign white childless women in his sample could perhaps be regarded as involuntarily childless. Pearl, R., *The Natural History of Population*, London, 1939, pp. 165–6, basing himself partly on an inquiry reported by F. W. Notestein in 1931, estimates about 17 per cent. for the native white marriages of the United States, in which the wives were over 45 years old, and for all marriages in existence in 1930 regards 20 per cent. as a conservative estimate of childlessness. It would appear from Pearl and Charles that childlessness has increased considerably in the last twenty years in the United States and Australia, and it is likely that a similar trend has taken place in England and Wales. But we simply do not know at present. Neither Charles's nor Pearl's estimates throw any light on the importance of deliberate limitation as a factor in the childlessness. (27)

(*s*) Himes, *Medical History*, pp. 59–66 for Egypt. See also Ebbell, B., *The Papyrus Ebers*, Copenhagen-London (printed in Denmark), 1937, p. 108: 'To make a woman cease to become pregnant for 1 year, 2 years or 3 years: *ḳꜣꜣ* of acacia, *ḏꜣrt*, dates, are ground fine with a hin of honey, seed-wool is moistened therewith and placed in her vulva.' For Babylon, see Korherr, R., 'Der Untergang der alten Kulturvölker', *Allgemeines Statistisches Archiv*, vol. xxvii, part i, 1937, p. 47, citing Winkler's version of the Code. But in Edwards's version (Edwards, C., *The Hammurabi Code: And the Sinaitic Legislation*, 3rd ed., London, 1921, p. 39) the reference to abortion does not specify that the abortion needed to be intentional. The clauses are: '209. If a man strike the daughter of a Freeman and cause her foetus to fall, he shall pay ten shekels of silver for her foetus. 210. If that woman die, his daughter shall be slain. 211. If he has caused the daughter of a plebeian to let her foetus fall through blows, he shall pay five shekels of silver. 212. If that woman die, he shall pay half a mina of silver. 213. If he has struck the slave of a man and made her foetus fall, he shall pay two shekels of silver. 214. If that slave die, he shall pay a third of a mina of silver.' The abortion may therefore have been quite unintended. In the present study there is no discussion of infanticide since in England and Wales, as in most other Western countries, it is now a comparatively rare method of family limitation. (28)

(*t*) *Coitus interruptus* was mentioned only in the first of the three published handbills, but the sponge in all of them. He was not the first to recommend birth control or the use of the sponge. Bentham, for example, in 1797, recommended the sponge as an aid to reduce poor-rates. See Himes, op. cit., ch. ix (which, with ch. x, are the bases of the subsequent discussion, supplemented by such other sources as are referred to in the notes); Field, op. cit., 'The early propagandist movement in English population theory', pp. 91–129; Himes, N. E., 'The birth control handbills of 1823', *Lancet*, 6 Aug. 1927, pp. 313–16; Place, F., *Illustrations and Proofs of the Principle of Population*, ed. Himes, N. E., London, 1930, introdn. and notes, pp. 7–63, and Appendix A and notes, pp. 283–98; Himes, N. E., 'Jeremy Bentham and the genesis of English neo-Malthusianism' *Economic History* (*E.J.* Supplement), Feb. 1936, pp. 267–76. (31)

(*u*) In the issue of 6 May 1825, pp. 545–69, including a reprint of the handbill *To the Married of Both Sexes of the Working People* (pp. 561–3), Carlile says, pp. 555–6: '*I think this plan for the prevention of conceptions good*, after getting rid of as much prejudice upon the subject as the most fantastical can assume; after three years of consideration; after passing a year with a feeling almost like dread of giving it thought; *I, now, so think it good, and so publicly say it.*' He erroneously attributes to Owen the introduction of the sponge into England from France and says, p. 563: 'I have been informed, that the French women, or some of them, wear these pieces of sponge tied round the waist, so as always to have them at hand.' The article was amazingly frank, particularly in reporting a case of unsuccessful attempts, by a working-class woman, to practice abstinence within marriage, the moral of which would be that abstinence makes the heart grow fonder. The article, in modified form, was published as a book, *Every Woman's Book: or, What is Love?*, the following year. The edition in the Goldsmith's Library is the fourth edition, London, 1826. No first edition has yet been located. (31)

(*v*) e.g. the issue of 1 Nov. 1825, pp. 97–104, 'On the principle of population': 'Early marriages are more conducive to happiness than late ones. . . . If any means could be offered by which families could be limited according to the means and desires of individuals, without requiring any privation, or producing any injury; which shall be voluntary to perform or not to perform by the parties concerned; they would destroy one of the most copious sources of human misery, and prove, by their extent of usefulness, of more value than any other discovery which ever has [been], or is ever likely to be made.—These means have been discovered; they are now in operation; and the more they are extended, the greater will be the benefits felt, not only by individuals, but by the whole community' (p. 101). See also issue of 1 June 1826, 'Owenism, criminals, population, labour, &c.', pp. 433–40, esp. p. 440. (32)

(*w*) Himes, *Medical History*, p. 231, estimates 42,000 in the English editions between 1834 and 1876 and, Himes, 'Charles Knowlton's revolutionary influence on the English birth rate', *New England Journal of Medicine*, 6 Sept. 1928, pp. 461–5, at about 277,000 by 1881 (p. 464). George Standring, a pioneer publisher of neo-Malthusian literature—he published *The Malthusian*—estimates '. . . before the prosecution [the Bradlaugh-Besant trial] the sale of the Knowlton pamphlet averaged about 700 copies a year. Between March and June 1877, no less than 125,000 copies were sold' ('Reminiscent notes on the neo-Malthusian movement', *The Malthusian*, 15 March 1914, pp. 19–20, at p. 19). This latter estimate by Standring was first given in his pamphlet *The Malthusian Handbook* (the present writer's copy is the 4th ed., London, 1898, pp. 25–6). See also Himes's Introdn. in the edition of *Fruits of Philosophy*, ed. Himes, N. E., with medical emendations by Dickinson, R. L., Mount Vernon, New York, 1937. (32)

(*x*) The defendants moved to quash the indictment, or, on technical grounds, to arrest the judgment. They also moved, on various grounds, for a new trial. But the arrest of judgment was refused. The terms of the indictment were that the defendants 'unlawfully and wickedly devising, contriving, and intending, as much as in them lay, to vitiate and corrupt the morals as well of youth as of divers other subjects of the Queen, and to incite and encourage the said subjects to indecent, obscene, unnatural, and immoral practices, and bring them to a state of wickedness, lewdness, and debauchery, unlawfully, &c., did print, publish, sell, and utter a certain indecent, lewd, filthy, and obscene libel, to wit, a certain indecent, lewd, filthy, bawdy, and obscene book called "Fruits of Philosophy", thereby contaminating, . . . &c.'. See 1877, L.R. 2 Q.B. 569. (33)

(*y*) *The Malthusian*, Oct. 1880, p. 162 n. The date of the first publication cited above is from Himes, *Medical History*, p. 437. The article in *The Malthusian* here referred to says: 'Nearly three years have passed away since this little book [*The Law of Population: its Consequences, and its Bearing upon Human Conduct and Morals*] was first issued; . . . . During these three years thirty-five thousand copies of the book have found their way into English homes; across the Atlantic it has found warm welcome, and an American edition of twenty-five thousand copies has been sold, making a sale of sixty thousand to the English-speaking nations. It has been translated into German, Italian, French, and Dutch, and has thus spread over the Continent of Europe, while the English edition has been largely sold in Hindustan' (p. 162). This reference would date the first publication at 1878 at the latest. (34)

(*z*) 'The Malthusian League: its origin and history', ibid., April 1880, pp. 113–14 at 114. Some of the later publications of the League—e.g. membership forms—give the date of foundation as 1878. Some even give both dates—e.g. the *Annual Report for 1908–9*, which gives 1877 on the outside front cover and 1878 on p. 4. But the account in *The Malthusian* cited is so circumstantial that there seems to be no reason for doubting its accuracy. Mrs. Besant, *An Autobiography*, op. cit., p. 229, gives 26 July 1877 as the date of the first meeting of the League, instead of 17 July. Note that there was also a 'Malthusian Society'—unrelated to the League—in existence at the same time—*The Malthusian*, April 1879, p. 20. There had been an earlier Malthusian League, founded by Charles Bradlaugh, but circumstances had not been ripe for its development. It may be of some interest to cite the names of the founding members of the new League. They were Dr. C. R. Drysdale, Mrs. Annie Besant, Mr. Hember, Mr. R. Shearer, Messrs. Bell, Brown, Dray, Page, Mr. and Mrs. T. Parris, Mr. and Mrs. Rennick, Messrs. Rivers, Seyler, Standring, Truelove, Young, and Swaagman. Among the Vice-Presidents elected were Mr. W. J. Birch, Mr. T. Parris, Mr. G. Anderson, and Mr. J. Bryson. For most of these names no biographical material seems to be available. Mr. and Mrs. T. Parris are referred to by Mrs. Besant as helping with the defence fund for the Bradlaugh-Besant and Truelove trials. Dr. Drysdale, b. 1829, d. 1907, son of the Treasurer of the City of Edinburgh, Sir William Drysdale, was originally an engineer and helped in the construction of the *Great Eastern* steamship, later qualified in medicine and was a physician at the Metropolitan Hospital of London. He also took an active part in the Dialectical Society, founded *c.* 1864. Mrs. A. Besant, b. 1847, d. 1933, wife of Rev. Frank Besant, was early associated with Bradlaugh in Freethought propaganda, and wrote pamphlets under the pseudonym 'Ajax', and later became a Theosophist. Edward Truelove, b. 1809, d. 1899, was early drawn into Owenite movement, secretary of John Street institution for nine years, took part in New Harmony venture, opened a bookshop in 1852 and published much Rationalist literature. George Standring, b. 1855, d. 1924, became a Rationalist 1873, honorary secretary of National Secular Society 1875, founded *Republican Chronicle* 1875, and was on the executive of the Fabian Society. His printing works is still being run by his family. George Anderson, b. 1824, d. 1915, was a self-made business man and friend of Bradlaugh, Holyoake, and Watts, and a founder of Rationalist Press Association, which he helped—financially—to publish cheap reprints of Rationalist literature. W. J. Birch, b. 1811, d. 1863, was a barrister, member of Italian Asiatic Society, supporter of the Mazzinians and the Rationalist movement, contributor to the *Reasoner* and the *Investigator*, and author of books on religion and philosophy. See McCabe, J., *A Biographical Dictionary of Modern Rationalists*, London, 1920, cols. 20, 77, 755, and 815; *The Malthusian*, January, 1908, pp. 1–2; McCabe, J., *Life and Letters of George Jacob Holyoake*, vol. ii, London, 1908, pp. 76–84; Besant, A., *An Autobiography*, op. cit., *passim*. (35)

(*aa*) *The Malthusian*, Feb. 1879, p. 2; Mar. 1879, p. 12, p. 15, and p. 16; July 1879, p. 44; Sept. 1879, p. 63; Oct. 1879, p. 68; Nov. 1879, p. 80. The term may have been used earlier, but not much earlier. It appears to have been originated by Dr. S. Van Houten, one-time Prime Minister of Holland and Vice-President of the Malthusian League. Ibid., 15 Mar. 1910, p. 22, and 15 Sept. 1910, p. 76 (statement by Dr. Van Houten himself). Himes obtained confirmation from Dutch sources—Himes, *Medical Journal and Record*, 18 May 1932, op. cit. Attribution of the term really turns on the question—when did Dr. C. R. Drysdale first visit Holland? If it was not until the Amsterdam meeting of 1879, then Dr. Van Houten was not the originator of the term. (See *The Malthusian*, Sept. 1900, p. 69, report by E. Kempe.) Dr. C. V. Drysdale, in a letter dated 9 June 1939 to the present writer, said that he was fairly sure that Dr. S. Van Houten was the originator of the term. (35)

(*bb*) Besant, Mrs. A., in *Lucifer*, July 1891, pp. 394–9 (not to be confused with an American journal of the same name, supporting neo-Malthusianism, issued by Moses Harmon). Mrs. Besant's view was that the sexual instinct was one of the most fruitful sources of human misery, and that it should be controlled rather than indulged by the use of contraceptive techniques. 'Theosophists should sound the note of self restraint within marriage, and the restriction of the marital relation to the perpetuation of the race.' C. R. Drysdale said this was an illustration of Robert Chambers's dictum, 'it seems as if theology never enters the world but for mischief' (*The Malthusian*, Oct. 1891, pp. 73–4 at 74). Hans Ferdy, one of the pioneer neo-Malthusians in Germany, was much harsher, citing the dictum that when the initiation has been accomplished, the initiator either dies or becomes an apostate, adding that Bradlaugh died in January 1891, and that in April of the same year Mrs. Besant deserted the cause. 'Müde sank die muthige Vorkämpferin des freien Gedankens und der socialen Erlösung der Armen in die Netze einer theosophisch-mystischen Buddhisten-Sekte, ein trauriges Opfer geistiger Morphiomanie'. (Ferdy, H., *Die künstliche Beschränkung der Kinderzahl als sittliche Pflicht*, 4th ed., Berlin and Neuwied, 1894, p. 69 n. But on p. 67 he gives a sympathetic account of her struggles.) (41)

(*cc*) It is extraordinarily difficult to obtain an idea of the randomness of the sample of women who attend birth-control clinics for the first time in any year. It seems possible that they are women who contain a more than average proportion of contraceptors, having obtained information from their friends and only going to clinics because they find the method so learned from their friends unsatisfactory or inefficient or both. On the other hand, the fact that between 40 and 50 per cent. of the patients in the inquiry cited used *coitus interruptus* does not make it seem that these women learn a great deal from their friends, and as for the women who do not, on account of religious or moral scruples, practise any form of contraception, the present writer does not see how, by means of an analysis of birth-control clinic patients, it is possible to obtain an idea of their significance in the total female adult population. Until, therefore, one can carry out a reasonably random sample inquiry, our knowledge of the part played by birth control in the modern community will be far from exact. (49)

(*dd*) An investigation into the prevalence of family limitation in England and Wales was undertaken in 1932, in connexion with a series of B.B.C. broadcasts on changes in family life. Listeners and others were invited to apply for a general 'family form' which contained a further invitation to apply for a questionnaire concerning family limitation. 582 completed, usable questionnaires were obtained, the sample showing a marked bias towards higher incomes (e.g. of 313 forms concerning marriages contracted after 1920, only 136 specified a total income of under £260 per year at the date of marriage) as well as in other ways exhibited in the questionnaire used by Dr. Charles. The present writer has analysed the forms and appends the broad results. Of the 582 married couples who completed forms, 539 (92·6 per cent.) definitely practised or had practised some form of limitation (including 26 specifying abstention) and one additional couple admitted contraception when living together before marriage. That leaves only 42 couples definitely stating that no form of family limitation was used, though even here one form stated that the wife needed a slight operation in order to become fertile, and that since she had deliberately *not* undergone the operation, this was really a form of birth control. The forms were analysed by date of marriage—before 1900, 1900–20 inclusive, and 1921 and after. For the first period there were 43 forms of which 39 admitted some form of limitation (including 7 specifying abstention). For the second period there were 226 forms, of which 202 (89·4 per cent.) admitted family limitation (including 6 specifying abstention), while of the 313 forms relating to the third period, family limitation was admitted by 298 (95·2 per cent.), including 13 specifying abstention. It is impossible to give further details, for the questions were framed badly. No details were asked regarding the techniques of family limitation. The main question was simply: 'Have any measures been taken to restrict the number of children born of this marriage?' This further reduces the value of the investigation, but since it has not previously been published—or, in fact, analysed—the writer believes that it may have some interest for persons reading the present study. (49)

(*ee*) Apart from reports by correspondents, there are also articles on the subject cited by Dr. Elderton. Hall, A., and Ransom, W. B., 'Plumbism from the ingestion of diachylon as an abortifacient', *B.M.J.*, 24 Feb. 1906, pp. 428–30, note that the first cases of this kind of abortion were observed at Leicester and reported by Pope in 1893. Cases were observed at Birmingham in 1898, at Nottingham in 1899, at Sheffield in 1901–2 and at Barnsley, Doncaster, Leeds, and Bedford, the practice spreading slowly and apparently being handed on by word of mouth. Inquiries among doctors in the Sheffield area suggested that there had been 100 to 200 cases observed in private practice in 1904–6, in addition to cases seen in hospitals. Inquiries in the Nottingham region suggested a similar frequency. Hall, A. J., 'Diachylon as an abortifacient', *Lancet*, 16 Aug. 1913, p. 492, showed a widening of the practice since 1906, cases having been observed at Leeds, Manchester, London, Bristol, Hull, Newcastle-on-Tyne, Glasgow, Aberdeen, and Cardiff. See also Oliver, T., 'Diachylon or duty: a call to action', *B.M.J.*, 7 June 1913, pp. 1199–1200. (51)

(*ff*) In England the law relating to induced abortion was established by four nineteenth-century Acts, each one repealing the previous legislation. Abortion had been a common-law crime for about 500 years before the 1803 Act (43 Geo. III, c. 58) first made it a statutory offence. Under this Act attempts to procure the abortion of a woman 'quick with child' were punishable by death, with smaller penalties—fine, imprisonment, pillory, whipping, or transportation—if the woman was not, or could not be proved to be, 'quick with child'. Note that whereas in the first part of the Act the death penalty related only to attempts to induce abortion by means of drugs, the second part related to any method. The law was modified by the Acts of 1828 (9 Geo. IV, c. 31) and 1837 (1 Vict., c. 85) and finally by the 1861 Act (24 & 25 Vict., c. 100). The penalties prescribed in the 1861 Act were modified by the Statute Law Revision Act of 1893 and the Penal Servitude Act of 1891, and at present they are: Penal servitude for life or not less than 3 years, or imprisonment with or without hard labour for not more than 2 years for any woman attempting to procure her own abortion or for any one attempting an abortion on a woman; penal servitude for 3 to 5 years or imprisonment with or without hard labour for not more than 2 years for any one unlawfully supplying any commodity, &c., which he knows will be used for attempting to procure abortion. The 1861 Act made it—for the first time—a statutory offence for a woman to attempt to procure her own abortion, but according to this Act the attempt is punishable only if the woman is pregnant. However, it has been decided that if she is not pregnant, the woman can be prosecuted for conspiring to procure abortion. The Infant Life (Preservation) Act, 1929 (19 & 20 Geo. V, c. 34) also contains a clause by which any one who deliberately causes a child to die before it is born (except to preserve the life of the mother) is liable, on conviction, to penal servitude for life. See Parry, L. A., *Criminal Abortion*, London, 1932, pp. 93–4, 101–5; Ellison, J., Goodwin, A., Read, C. D., and Rivett, L. C., *Sex Ethics*, London, 1934, pp. 130–6. On the question of therapeutic abortion, with particular reference to the Bourne Case, see Davies, D. S., 'The law of abortion and necessity', *Modern Law Review*, Sept. 1938, pp. 126–38. See also *Report of the Inter-Departmental Committee on Abortion* (Ministry of Health and Home Office), London, 1939, pp. 26–32. Note that the Ministry of Health *Circular 1622* (May 1937) says, p. 6, 'Many women appear still to be unaware that any interference with the product of conception with intent to procure a miscarriage is a criminal offence.' (52)

(*gg*) *Report of Committee on Medical Aspects of Abortion*, London, 1936, p. 6. Similar views as regards the relation between induced and spontaneous abortion frequencies are given in Ploetz, A., 'Zum Zahlenverhältnis von Geburten und Fehlgeburten', *Archiv für Rassen- und Gesellschafts-Biologie*, July 1936, pp. 181–2. But any estimate of the relative frequency of spontaneous abortion is almost certain to be incorrect. On the one hand, women will tend to hide—if possible—the fact that illegal interference has taken place, and may avoid having medical help after abortion unless it is clearly needed. On the other hand, early spontaneous abortions—within the first month or two of pregnancy—may not even be noticed by the women, who may believe that there has merely been an irregularity in the menstrual cycle. It is impossible to say how far these two errors will tend to cancel each other.

A point of some importance in the abortion question is that some of the women who believe themselves pregnant may not, in fact, be so, and may take drugs or undergo 'quack' treatment quite unnecessarily. (This was emphasized by Madame Ottesen-Jensen, of the Riksförbund för Sexuell Upplysning, in a discussion with the writer in September, 1937. Pregnancy tests showed that many of the women wanting abortions were not pregnant.) This may account for the apparent efficacy of some of the abortifacients marketed to-day, for unless they are markedly toxic in action, and thus dangerous, it is unlikely that they will cause abortion in women who are not already predisposed to it. (54)

(*hh*) The writer has here been influenced by the *Report of the Inter-Departmental Committee on Abortion*, which estimates that about 40 per cent. of the abortions in England and Wales may be due to illegal interference. He is impelled to this conclusion on the basis of the available data, but believes that more accurate investigations—if such were possible—would show a preponderance of criminal abortions, so that the proportions of 40 and 60 per cent. to illegal and spontaneous would probably be reversed. It seems not at all improbable that there are each year about 100,000 illegal abortions in England and Wales. Multiple births have not been taken into account in estimating the number of pregnancies, as there are no official data for England and Wales. (In Scotland in 1937 there were, out of 87,810 births, 1,035 sets of twins and 10 sets of triplets—*Eighty-Third Annual Report of the Registrar-General for Scotland, 1937*, p. lxiii.) But the error is allowed for by assuming the same frequency of multiple conceptions among women having spontaneous and induced abortions as among those whose pregnancies go naturally to term. (54)

(*ii*) *Interim Report of Departmental Committee on Maternal Mortality and Morbidity* (Ministry of Health), London, 1930, pp. 41–2. A special search of the records of the East End Maternity Hospital (Oxley), appears to have been made at the instance of the committee, and showed, for the period 1897–8, 623 abortions out of 3,964 pregnancies during the lives of 898 women—i.e. 15·7 per cent. of the pregnancies ending in abortion. Other data were noted and the present writer has gone back to the original sources and gives them herewith. Whitehead, J., *On the Causes and Treatment of Abortion and Sterility*, London, 1847, pp. 245–6, found that 2,000 pregnant married women admitted for treatment at the Manchester Lying-in Hospital in 1845 and 1846, had had 8,681 previous pregnancies, of which 1,222 had ended in abortions, or 14·1 per cent. On p. 254 the abortions are analysed as: 911 due to 'inward weakness', impaired general health, and acute disease; 222 due to 'accidents, mental perturbation, etc.'; and the rest to 'no assignable' cause. These are divisions made by the patients themselves. Criminal interference is not mentioned. Playfair, W. S., *A Treatise on the Science and Practice of Midwifery*, 6th ed., vol. i, London, 1886, p. 282, suggests that premature expulsion of the foetus (i.e. all types of miscarriage and abortion) is very frequent, and cites Hegar as estimating one abortion to every 8 or 10 deliveries at term. Galabin, A. L., *A Manual of Midwifery*, 3rd ed., London, 1893, p. 385, says 'the proportion of abortions to full-term deliveries has been estimated as being as much as one to five'. Malins, E., *Journal of Obstetrics and Gynaecology of the British Empire*, April 1903, pp. 307–19, at pp. 315–16, found that 4,000 married women in his hospital (Birmingham, according to *Interim Report*) and private practice, prior to 1903, had had 14,430 pregnancies and 2,303 abortions, or 16 per cent. The estimates cited in this note do not distinguish between spontaneous and induced abortions. (55)

(*jj*) As early as 1893, *The Christian World*, one of the influential voices of the nonconformist press, published a leading article which gave considerable support to the principle of family limitation. There had been a correspondence on the burdens borne by wives in families with many children, and the leading article, though noting the decline of the birth-rate in the Western world, and pointing out that some social students found virtue in well-stocked households, stated: 'The conditions are assuredly wrong which bring one member of the married partnership into a bondage so cruel. It is no less evident that the cause of the bondage in such cases lies in the too rapid multiplication of the family. There was a time when any idea of voluntary limitation was regarded by pious people as interfering with Providence. We are beyond that now, and have become capable of recognising that Providence works through the common-sense of individual brains. We limit population just as much by deferring marriage from prudential motives as by any action that may be taken after it.' Referring to the fact that Charles Kingsley, in one of his books, had made a married couple agree to postpone having children because of the 'hardness of the times', the article added: 'It would be obviously impossible for us to enter into the details of such a topic, but this much may, at least, be said, that, apart from certain methods of limitation, the morality of which is gravely questioned by many, there are certain easily understood physiological laws of the subject, the failure to know and to observe which is inexcusable on the part either of men or women in these circumstances.' (*The Christian World*, 15 June 1893, p. 487.)

Nevertheless, Church opinion on the subject is by no means clear. The Catholic view is, of course, defined by Pope Pius XI in his Encyclical, *On Christian Marriage* (issued 31 Dec. 1930), allowing continence when practised by mutual consent (p. 25) and the use of the 'safe period' (p. 28). *Coitus reservatus* is also permitted. (*Coitus interruptus* is not permitted, since it involves a deliberate frustration of the act. But presumably there would be no sin if, although *coitus reservatus* was intended, subsequent withdrawal was followed by emission.) But the Anglican Church is much more vague. It recognizes (see *Lambeth Conference 1930*, London, n.d., pp. 89–92) that there may be justification for family limitation, recommends total abstinence as the 'primary and most obvious way', but also recognizes that there may be 'moral situations which may make it obligatory to use other methods'. The basis for judgement is that if conception 'would clearly be wrong, and if there is good moral reason why the way of abstinence should not be followed, we cannot condemn the use of scientific methods to prevent conception, which are thoughtfully and conscientiously adopted'. The resolution (pp. 43–4) embodying this view was not adopted unanimously, but by 193 votes to 67. According to Ellison, Goodwin, Read, and Rivett, op. cit., pp. 62–3, the Free Church Council, which called a meeting on the subject, shortly after the publication of the Lambeth Conference report, 'very gravely condemned the use of any artificial means of preventing conception, whether mechanical or chemical'. But A. E. Garvie, who had called this meeting, wrote, in *The Christian Ideal for Human Society*, London [1930], pp. 321–2, that if a married couple decide they are justified in using contraceptives on the advice of a doctor, 'condemnation may be unjust to them'. In this case Christian conscience may be acquiescent, 'but cannot be approving'. The most recent statement on the subject is that by the Methodist Church conference on 28 July 1939, which included, among its declarations, the following statement: 'The obligations of parenthood are to be undertaken deliberately, and with forethought. Careless, improvident and undesigned begetting of children is entirely to be deprecated as wrongful to children and injurious to the social order' (*Quarterly Letter* of the Family Planning Association, Aug. 1939). (57)

(*kk*) In 1871 the proportions of women gainfully employed were: 20–4 years, 58·45 per cent.; 25–34 years, 35·48 per cent.; 35–44 years, 28·83 per cent.; 45–54 years, 29·61 per cent. For 1931 the percentage for the same age groups were: 67·46, 36·56, 24·83, and 21·74. Since the 1871 census includes women classed as 'retired', these have also been included in the 1931 percentages, though the difference made is, in any case, very small. For the 1931 census figures the basic data for the age group 20–4 years are not published and the writer is indebted to the Registrar-General for permission to use unpublished material. It should be remembered, of course, that the type of occupation changed very considerably in the period, and there may well have been a significant increase in the proportion of middle-class women engaged in gainful employment. Thus Bowley, A. L., *Wages and Income in the United Kingdom since 1860*, Cambridge, 1937, Appendix E, pp. 127–36, at 129, shows a much more rapid growth of women in middle-class than in working-class occupations—402: 131 in 1931 as compared with 100 for each in 1881. But occupation is often a poor index of the economic or social status of women, and the figures do not show how far there has been a change in the classes of women who work. (59)

(*ll*) Further support is given to this thesis by the way in which fertility has declined. For most of the countries for which the requisite data are available, the decline appears to have begun among the older women—that is, among those who already had borne some children—and has been much more rapid in the later than in the earlier age groups. The deliberate reduction of fertility and the reduction in the average age of mothers would be explained plausibly by the family limitation hypothesis. See Barclay, R. S., and Kermack, W. O., 'The decline of the birth-rate: regularities revealed by an analysis of the rates observed in certain European countries', *Proceedings of the Royal Society of Edinburgh*, 1937–8, vol. lviii, part i, pp. 55–72; same authors, 'The fertility of Scottish married women, with special reference to the period 1926–1935', *Proc. Roy. Soc. Edin.*, 1938–9, vol. lix, part i, pp. 62–80. Support is also given by the widespread and marked fall in fertility in 1933, after the intense economic depression of 1933. Nor can the territorial differentials in fertility in England & Wales really be explained on other than volitional grounds. (61)

(*mm*) See *Seventy-Fourth Annual Report of the Registrar-General of Births, Deaths, and Marriages in England and Wales (1911)*, Table 28 A, pp. 73–87, for details of the occupations included in each social class. In the view of the present writer, the method used by the Registrar-General—and by other workers in the field of demography and general sociology—to construct social classes, begs the whole question of social class and its concomitant associations. A very large arbitrary element is involved in grouping occupations—on *a priori* grounds—into social classes. The result is that if, for example, social mobility, were then measured on the basis of these groups, and found to be high, this might be indicative of genuinely high mobility, but it might just as easily mean that the class divisions obtained by this method were not the real ones. The present writer believes that the problem of social class needs to be tackled afresh and on new lines. More realistic results might be obtained if, instead of constructing arbitrary groups based on occupations, sociologists attempted to discover, by means of empirical investigation, what are the factors which produce, or are at least associated with roughly homogeneous culture groups in modern communities. That is, we need investigations to discover if the possession of common measurable attributes, such as income, education, occupation, &c., does result in the formation of distinctive social classes, measuring the distinctiveness and separateness of such classes by what must, after all, be the fundamental tests—inter-group friendship and marriage. The writer hopes that, in thc not-too-distant future, he will have an opportunity to undertake some research along these lines. (69)

(*nn*) e.g. Fisher, R. A., *The Genetical Theory of Natural Selection*, Oxford, 1930, p. 219; Kuczynski, R. R., *The Measurement*, &c., op. cit., pp. 94–6. Innes, J. W., op. cit., p. 24, supports Stevenson's view largely on the ground that Freeman, B. C., 'Fertility and longevity in married women dying after the end of the reproductive period', *Human Biology*, 1935, pp. 392–418, did not find any significant positive association between fertility and longevity. But a more recent study, Dorn, H. F., and McDowell, A. J., 'The relationship of fertility and longevity', *American Sociological Review*, Apr. 1939, pp. 234–46, presents material which largely supports the hypothesis of a positive association between fertility and longevity. See also Snow, E. C., 'Note on a possible source of fallacy in the interpretation of the census figures relating to the fertility of marriages', *J.R.S.S.*, Feb., 1914, pp. 313–15. See also Gini, C., op. cit., pp. 39–40, for some additional comments on the validity of Stevenson's conclusion. (72)

(*oo*) Webb, S., *The Decline in the Birth-Rate* (Fabian Tract No. 131), London, 1907, pp. 6–8. Incidentally this tract contains the first—so far as the present writer is aware—statistical attempt to evaluate the extent of deliberate family limitation (pp. 8–14). The sub-committee obtained completed, usable forms relating to 316 'middle-class' marriages, and 242 of these stated that deliberate family limitation had been practised. If we exclude the marriages contracted before 1875—6 limited and 17 unlimited—and those contracted after 1902—24 limited and 16 unlimited—this leaves 212 limited and 41 unlimited for the period 1875–1902 inclusive. Further, 13 of the 41 unlimited marriages were sterile, so no occasion for limitation occurred. Of 120 marriages contracted in the decade 1890–99, 107 were limited, and 5 or 6 of the 13 unlimited were still childless at the time the questionnaire was completed. (73)

(*pp*) See, for example, Burks, B. S., 'On the relative contributions of nature and nurture to average group differences in intelligence', *Proceedings of the National Academy of Sciences*, July 1938, pp. 276–82. Penrose, L. S., in a lecture delivered to the conference of Medical Officers of Health, &c., July 1938, discussing his investigation, *A Clinical and Genetic Study of 1,280 Cases of Mental Defect* (Medical Research Council), London, 1938 (see esp. pp. 64–5), drew attention to the fact, noted also by other investigators, that mental defectives have relatively low fertility. He also suggested, in a lecture 'Is our national intelligence declining?', delivered at the International Conference of Mental Hygiene in 1939, that an I.Q. of 90–5 would probably be the level at which any decline in national intelligence would stop, since people with such an I.Q. tend to have the highest fertility, but pointed out that one fact—the increased average weight and height of working-class children—may suggest a possible trend of I.Q. in an upward direction. Dr. Penrose kindly allowed me to see copies of his lectures and also a translation of Visser, F., 'Onderzoek naar gehuwde zwakzinnigen in de gemeente Utrecht', *Mensch en Maatschappij*, xii, 1936, pp. 416–22, which finds a low marriage rate and low marital fertility for mental defectives. See also the pertinent comments in Haldane, J. B. S., *Heredity and Politics*, London, 1938, ch. 4. What is really required is a thorough I.Q. and I.B. analysis of large groups of school children every five years to see what trends are being shown in practice. (75)

(*qq*) Similar trends have been noted for other towns: e.g. Paris (see Hersch, L., 'Situation sociale et natalité d'après les statistiques de la ville de Paris', *Proc. of the Int. Congress for Studies on Population, Rome, 1931*, vol. viii, Rome, 1933, pp. 105–17; Sauvy, A., *Encyclopédie Française*, vol. vii, Paris, 1936, p. 7·84–10) and Stockholm (see Edin, K. A., and Hutchinson, E. P., *Studies of Differential Fertility in Sweden*, London—printed in Stockholm—1935, chs. iii and iv). But reproduction rates are not used in any of these studies and the material for Stockholm is further complicated by the question of illegitimate births. However, Hutchinson, E. P., 'Education and intra-marital fertility in Stockholm', *Milbank Memorial Fund Quarterly*, July 1936, pp. 285–301, argues that this factor does not vitiate the result, which is that there is now a positive instead of a negative correlation between fertility and income (and education) in Stockholm. Tietze, C., 'Differential reproduction in England', *Milbank Memorial Fund Quarterly*, July 1939, using paternal reproduction rates, and comparing the results with those given in his earlier paper, also finds a 'narrowing down of the difference between the least and the most fertile section of the population'. See similar indications for the United States in Kiser, C. V., 'Birth rates and socio-economic attributes in 1935', ibid., Apr. 1939. See also p. 465 (*e*) in the present study. (82)

(*rr*) The article was in *The Times*, 1 May 1901, p. 11, and suggested that a falling birth-rate was not an unmixed blessing, and might produce 'an old man's world', lacking 'variety, sparkle, sunshine, mirth, and the charm of the unexpected and untried'. Robertson wrote, in *The Malthusian*, Oct. 1901, pp. 73–4: 'It makes a writing man wince for his tribe to read such gratuitous ineptitudes. Only in an article mechanically produced, under constraint of all the paralysing conventions of Mrs. Grundy's world, could fairly instructed men so stultify themselves', and, comparing the requirements of medical knowledge with those of 'quack sociology', said: 'But to pronounce on the most far-reaching problems of civilisation and social life, all you need is a pen and a bottle of ink and a faculty for verbiage: with these and the *entrée* to the *Times* you can proceed to instruct the upper and middle classes of England.' (83)

(*ss*) A letter from W. R. Inge (Dean Inge), in the *Eugenics Review*, 1913–14, pp. 261–2, gives what is probably the extreme view on this question. 'Three classes only, it seems to me, are interested in raising the ridiculous cry of "depopulation"—ridiculous, because the births in this country exceed the deaths by about five to three, and even in France the numbers are increasing. These classes are—first, the militarists, who look upon men as food for powder. This is notoriously the motive of the agitation in France. Secondly, the capitalists, who desire an unlimited quantity of cheap labour, with a margin which will give them a favourable position in bidding for it. Thirdly, the advocates of cut-throat competition as the means of producing the maximum of industrial efficiency.' In a review-article in the *Edinburgh Review*, Jan. 1917, pp. 62–83, he recommends, however, the maintenance of an increase of the population for the purpose of populating the Empire. After that had been done, an equilibrium between births and deaths would be best. (83)

(*tt*) *Problems of Population and Parenthood*, London, 1920. See esp. pp. lxxii–vi. The Commission was set up by the National Council of Public Morals. The first Commission was appointed in 1913, consisting largely of religious and medical representatives, and sat for two and a half years, the chairman being first Bishop Boyd Carpenter and later Dean Inge. The first report, *The Declining Birth-Rate: Its Causes and Effects*, London, 1916, did not advocate an unrestricted birth-rate, but (pp. 72–3) considered that 'a stagnation or decline of our population would be injurious to the manifold interests of the nation, and that an increase, consistent with a continually rising standard of health, wealth, education, leisure and happiness for the whole population would in these same interests be desirable . . .'. At the Caxton Hall Conference (Mar. 1918) on 'Marriage and Parenthood', a resolution was passed to reconstitute the Commission. This was done—with the Bishop of Birmingham as President—and the report was issued in 1920, signed by 32 persons, of whom 12 wished to record their dissent from the argument for and their assent to the argument against the use of contraceptives and stated that (p. clxii) 'we hold the opinion that every effort should be made to arrest the decline in the birth-rate'. In addition, one member (Monsignor W. F. Brown) was against any 'anti-physiological' method of preventing conception. (83)

(*uu*) There are some family allowance schemes in England, e.g. at the London School of Economics—members of the Federation of University Teachers receive £30 p.a. per child up to age 13 and £60 p.a. up to 23, if the child is still a student; Wesleyan Methodists—£8. 8*s*. p.a. per child up to 18 years, plus additional £12 p.a. for 6 years for educational costs. Miss M. E. Green, Secretary of the Family Endowment Society, has kindly supplied the writer with information concerning allowances in a number of private firms: e.g. E. S. & A. Robinson, Ltd., Bristol—5*s*. per week per child for third and subsequent children, up to maximum age of 15, or lower if earning, when wage not more than £4 per week; Brittains, Ltd., Leek, Staffs.—1*s*. per week for each child from first up to age 14, no income limit; John Thompson Co., Wolverhampton—1*s*. per week per child to maximum of 4 children, wage limit £2. 10*s*. per week for unskilled and £2.15*s*. per week for semi-skilled workers; Pilkington Bros., St. Helens—5*s*. per week per child for third and later children till 14 (or for whole educational period—at discretion of firm), up to earnings of £400 p.a.; Tootal, Broadhurst, Lee, Co., Ltd., Manchester —4*s*. per week for third and 5*s*. per week for each later child, up to 14 or educational period, earnings limit £6 per week; Cadbury Bros., Ltd., Bournville—5*s*. per week per child for third and later children up to 18 years if continuing education, no earnings limit; Midland Counties Dairy, Ltd., Birmingham—2*s*. 6*d*. per week per child for third and later children up to 14 or longer if continuing education, no earnings limit. There are also schemes at Maclean's, Ltd., Brentford; Bentall's, Kingston-on-Thames; Barlock Co., Nottingham; H. P. Bulmer & Co., Hereford; J. Bibby & Sons, Liverpool; Newton Mill, Ltd., Hyde. (85)

CHAPTER II

(*a*) See Elster, L., 'Bevölkerungslehre und Bevölkerungspolitik', *Handwörterbuch der Staatswissenschaften*, 1924 ed., vol. ii; Rosseeuw St. Hilaire, *Histoire d'Espagne*, vol. x, Paris, 1869, p. 526; Townsend, J., *A Journey Through Spain in the Years 1786 and 1787*, 2nd ed., London, 1792, vol. ii, p. 253. Townsend's account of the Edict is somewhat different from that of Elster. The version used in the text above is taken from Salvá, V., *Novísima Recopilación de las Leyes de España*, Paris, 1854. A copy of the relevant section was kindly sent to me by Mr. R. J. Vile of King's College, Cambridge. See also the works of Hermann Conring, *Operum Tomus IV. Cuius Elenchus Post Praefationem Conspicitur, Continens Varia Scripta Politica Et Historica, Inprimis Descriptiones Potiorum Totius Orbis Rerum Publicarum, . . .*, ed. Johanne Wilhelmo Goebelio, Brunsvigae, 1730, p. 71, from which Elster derives his account. (92)

CHAPTER III

(*a*) At the end of 1920 there were 56 equalization funds, covering 500,000 workers and distributing 64 million francs in allowances. By the end of 1925 the figures had risen to 183 funds, covering 1,220,000 workers and distributing 170 million francs, while by the end of 1930 these figures had again risen to 230 funds, 1,880,000 workers and 380 million francs. These statistics do not include agricultural funds (of which there were 2 in 1920, 22 in 1925, and 36 in 1930), and they exclude workers covered by allowance systems in the public services and in special industrial undertakings (mining, railways, &c.). Including the two latter categories (no details being available for the agricultural funds), in 1930 about 4·3 million workers were enrolled in some form of family allowance scheme, and 1,700 million francs per year were being given in allowances (Pinte, op. cit., pp. 88–90 and 106, and Bonvoisin and Maignan, op. cit., p. 16). In the period 1928–30 the growth of the voluntary system had slowed down, and this partly accounted for the widespread desire, among legislators, to make family allowances legally obligatory. (See *Circulaire du Ministre du Travail*, 25 June 1932.) (103)

(*b*) A law of 30 June 1934, enforced by a decree of 30 July 1937, brought under the specific control of the 1932 Act the employees of all Départements and communes, as well as of the public bodies belonging to these local government units, for whom special family allowance schemes had not already been set up. Under a decree of 24 May 1938 all these bodies must affiliate to a national equalization fund, specially created to bring uniformity into the system of equalization relating to the employees mentioned. (State employees who come under the régime of the 1919 Act, modifying the 1918 Act, are excluded from the above laws and decrees.) This does not, however, mean a single rate of allowance, for a ministerial decree of 17 Aug. 1938, set up, as minimum rates, the minimum legal rates for agricultural occupations in force in each Département (agricultural rates, because most communes are rural in character). *Manuel Pratique*, pp. 5–7. (106)

(*c*) Helleu, op. cit., pp. 155–6 is the authority for this generalization regarding the payment of allowances in practice. He says that in conformity with most of the regulations of the funds, the *allocataire*—the person effectively receiving the allowance—is generally the mother. But Monsieur F. Boverat, in a letter (dated 6 Apr. 1939) to the present writer, says that the allowances are generally paid to the father. The *Annuaire Permanent* gives no information on this point, but the *Manuel Pratique*, p. 16 [8], says that in practice most of the funds have customarily sent the allowance by postal order to the mother. This is recognized by the 1932 Act which allows the funds, if they so determine, to pay the allowance to the mother or other person effectively responsible for bringing up the children. A later statement received from Monsieur Boverat (dated 4 May 1939) says that, according to the most recent information given by the Comité Central des Allocations Familiales, a minority of funds pay the allowance to the mother, but that these funds are the most important ones in France and it is therefore very possible that in reality the system of payment to the mother applies to the majority of beneficiaries. (107)

(*d*) A regional fund must contain at least 100 employers and a minimum number of employees, varying from 40,000 in the Seine Département to 25 per cent. of the total employed population (excluding agricultural workers, public officials, and domestic servants) in Départements having less than 40,000 workers. A professional fund must embrace at least 20 employers (or, if the total number is under 20, all the employers in the industry who are located in the given area) and 50 per cent. of all the workers engaged in the industry, with a minimum of 3,000 (*Manuel Pratique*, p. 18 [1]). Analysing the information given in the 1938 edition of the *Annuaire* (published by the Comité Central at the end of the summer of 1938), there appear to be 230 funds (excluding 2 in Algeria) of which 112 were regional, 93 professional, and 25 multi-professional (i.e. open to many but not to all occupations). Figures relating to the year ending 1 Jan. 1938, received from the Comité Central show a total of 225 funds of which 112 were regional and 113 professional. But the multi-professional funds were included in the latter category, whereas they appear to be more akin to the former. There were also 87 special enterprises affiliated to the Comité Central on 1 Jan. 1938. The *Manuel Pratique*, p. 1, says that there are at present 255 equalization funds, but this number is much higher than figures quoted in other publications. (107)

(*e*) As regards the reasons for the discrepancy between the figures for the employed population and those for the population actually included in the family allowance system, Fernand Rey says: '. . . the application of the law [1932 Act] is inadequate not only because . . . the affiliation decrees do not absorb the various occupations with sufficient regularity and rapidity, but especially because, in the branches already legally affiliated, numbers of employers who have not yet regularized their position *vis-à-vis* the law and the beneficiaries thereof, continue to remain undisturbed'. A letter sent by the Alliance Nationale to the Minister of Labour in March 1936 complained that about 75 per cent. of the employers legally obliged to affiliate to equalization funds were not carrying out their obligations. This applies mainly to establishments employing less than ten workers. (About 25 per cent. of all workers in industry, commerce, and the liberal professions are employed in this type of establishment.) There have been, apparently, very few prosecutions for this disregard of the law—largely because the workers will not lodge a complaint until they have been discharged for other reasons. Keeping their jobs is much more important to them than the additional question of family allowances. (See Rey, F., 'Les épreuves de la loi du 11 mars, 1932', in *XVIe Congrès National des Allocations Familiales*, Strasbourg, 1936.) The statistics of the employed population are from the 1931 Census of France, vol. i, part 3. The progress of the system since the 1932 Act was enforced may be seen from the following Table. The figures exclude public services and special enterprises, and agricultural funds. For agriculture see subsequent discussion.

Year ending	*No. of funds*	*No. of employers*	*Employed population*	*Families receiving allowances*	*Children for whom allowances given*	*Total value of allowances (francs)*
1. 1. 1938	228	390,000	5,315,000	1,617,000	2,869,000	1,340,000,000
1. 1. 1937	225	280,000	4,800,000	1,495,000	2,600,000	872,000,000
1. 1. 1936	222	218,000	4,238,000	1,305,000	2,313,000	780,000,000
1. 1. 1935	208	157,000	3,750,000	(1,183,000)	(2,137,000)	675,000,000

It should be remembered that the figures for 1937 and 1938 reflect the results of raising the school-leaving age, and that, in addition, there were considerable increases in the rates of family allowances during 1937. The figures have been obtained from the various *comptes-rendus* of the Congrès des Allocations Familiales, and are only approximate. Since the current figures given at each Congress are provisional, the practice followed in the above table is to give for a specific year the relevant figures quoted at the Congress in the next year (except for 1938)—i.e. the figures for 1937 are those quoted for comparison at the 1938 Congress, not those given at the Congress of 1937. In the last three years the number of employers evading their legal obligations appears to have diminished considerably. The figures in brackets do not relate exactly to the calendar year, but were obtained by inquiries made just before the 1935 congress (see *XVe Congrès National*, p. 91). (109)

(*f*) Information in a letter (dated 7 Apr. 1939) from the Comité Central des Allocations Familiales. This letter confirms the previous statement that the statistics given each year by Monsieur Bonvoisin exclude family allowances in agriculture. The number of funds in 1930, cited above, does not agree exactly with the figure cited previously (p. 435, III *a*) from Pinte, op. cit., p. 106, or with the figure given in Bonvoisin and Maignan, op. cit., p. 278 (given as 37 at the beginning of 1930). But differences of this kind are very common in the field of family allowances. The total population engaged in agriculture, forestry, and fishing in 1931 was 7·704 millions (1931 Census, vol. i, part 3, p. 94), including 24,893 unemployed persons. Wage earners and employees (excluding the unemployed) amounted to 2·147 millions, and there were also about 371,000 of the *isolés* who were classed as being in irregular employment. (112)

(*g*) For the Département of the Seine and 9 Communes of Seine-et-Oise the new rate was 30 francs per month for the first child, 80 for 2 children, 200 for 3, and 200 for each subsequent child. For the rest of Seine-et-Oise, for Seine-et-Marne, and for the Canton of Creil, the new rate was 30, 70, 160 francs per month for families with 1 to 3 children, and 160 francs per month for each subsequent child (*Bulletin Mensuel*, Oct. 1936, p. 165). At the beginning of 1938 the rate for the Seine was 60 francs per month for the first child, 160 for 2 children, 310 for 3, plus a further 200 francs per month for each additional child (see *Revue de l'Alliance Nationale*, Jan. 1939, p. 19), raised by a Ministerial decree of 18 Dec. 1937. By 1 Jan. 1938, the minimum rate for Seine-et-Marne was 55, 135, and 250 francs per month for 1 to 3 children, plus 160 francs for each additional child, while that for Seine-et-Oise was 60, 160, and 310 francs, plus 200 francs for each additional child. (115)

(*h*) The rates of allowance are those given at the end of 1938. Some funds mentioned that there would be further increases in 1939, but these have been omitted because the situation in 1939 was changed by a recent decree (see discussion in the text). I = Interprofessional; P = Professional; M = Multi-professional.

(1) These rates of allowance are given when the wife remains at home. If both husband and wife work, lower rates are paid.

(2) This is the 'normal' rate. Special sections of the Fund pay higher rates, the highest being 60–160–210+200 francs per month.

(3) The fund has five sections, of which four are professional and one multi-professional.

(4) The average earnings are derived from the total wages-bill, and are almost certainly too low.

(5) The average earnings quoted are from the official figures used as a basis in calculating compensation due for industrial accidents. The actual earnings are slightly below these figures.

General explanation of the family allowance rates. The rates are given for families of various sizes, with the additional grant for each subsequent child if the allowance has become stable by that point. Thus in the case for Aisne, the allowance is 35 francs per month for 1 child, 90 francs per month for 2 children, &c., while 125 francs per month are given for the sixth and for each subsequent child. If the rate has not become stable by the last figure cited, no plus sign is printed. (117)

(*i*) The following data are given in the Report for 1937 of the *Caisse Nationale de Compensation*, Bruxelles, 1938, pp. 30–4 (mimeographed):

Last quarter of	*No. of employers*	*Employed population*	*No. of families receiving allowances*	*No. of children for whom allowances paid*	*Total value of allowances (francs) paid during the year*
1937	130,780	1,571,667	566,722	1,049,067	336,631,410
1936	120,855	1,483,027	549,514	990,126	231,879,732
1935	109,091	1,353,374	502,036	905,655	170,005,331
1934	101,887	1,234,484	473,428	857,970	236,436,716
1933	96,222	1,277,674	488,416	881,133	246,857,379
1932	83,931	1,309,312	493,234	888,959	229,262,431
1931	28,620	1,257,891	459,458	802,567	168,241,920

The steady progression in the number of employers may lend support to the estimate of 200,000 who should be embraced by the family allowance system. At the end of 1937 there were 78 primary funds, 7 special funds, the auxiliary fund and the national fund—a total of 87. The auxiliary fund and 38 of the primary funds are regional (i.e. multi-professional). The special funds and the remaining primary funds are professional. The figures given above exclude allowances paid directly by public institutions, and by the central and local government bodies. There are apparently no regular data for these excluded sections, but according to information given by the Minister of Labour, and kindly communicated to the present writer by Mr. R. Storms, in the year ending 31 Dec. 1935, allowances were paid in respect of 91,236 children of State employees (central government only), including the army and the police, but excluding employees in State educational institutions.

It is impossible accurately to compare the figures of the employed population embraced by the funds with the data given in the 1930 Census, because under *professions libérales* and *service de la maison, des biens et des personnes* no analysis is given of how many of these persons are employees, wage earners, &c. There seems, however, to be a considerable discrepancy between the total employed population and that section covered by allowance funds. If we take only the employees and wage earners enumerated at the 1930 Census (*Annuaire Statistique de la Belgique et du Congo Belge, 1938*, pp. 38–9) in commerce, industry, and agriculture (including forestry and fishing) we find a total of 2,102,415. This excludes *aidants*. But the 'employed population' given in the Belgian family allowance statistics does not offer a fair comparison. To it should be added the unemployed workers entitled to a family allowance as part of their unemployment benefit, and the central and local government employees and magistrates and judges who are also entitled to family allowances. In November 1937, for example, 225,740 unemployed were enumerated among the workers affiliated to the unemployment bureaux on the last working day of the month, while it is likely (according to information received from Mr. Storms) that the number of civil servants and other central and local government employees (salaried and wage-earning), including the judicature and the armed forces, added about another 200,000 individuals to the personnel entitled to allowances. That would raise the total active population entitled to allowances to practically two million persons. (133)

(*j*) The number of days actually worked is the new basis—including absences due to accidents or illness, compensatory rest days under the 8-hour-day Act, and absences to fulfil military duties, but excluding days of involuntary unemployment and apparently also excluding holidays. This was introduced by the decree of 30 Mar. 1936, but was foreshadowed by a decree of 27 Feb. 1935, which contained the following clause: 'As regards the branches of industry, commerce and agriculture which are affected by the (economic) crisis, the right to allowances for days of unemployment and for Sundays and other days of rest, is suspended. . . .' So far as strikes are concerned, no specific provision is made in the law. But, according to information received from a number of funds, it is apparently customary to suspend allowances during a strike, but to pay them for this suspended period if the strike ends in favour of the workers. (134)

(*k*) Different rates of allowances are given for public servants. Magistrates and the personnel of the Cour des Comptes do not receive any allowances for the first or second children, but are given 130 francs per month for the third, 260 per month for the fourth, and 410 per month for each subsequent child. Other servants of the State or of the provincial authorities receive 10 francs per month for the first child, 15 for the second (attempts are being made to increase these to the level of the general system; at present the legal minimum rates for the first and second child are given only if the family has not more than 2 children; in larger families the lower rates are given for the first 2 children), 100 for the third, 150 for the fourth, and 200 francs per month for each subsequent child. These are the basic rates; they are adjusted in accordance with changes in the retail price index (*Almanach des Familles Nombreuses, 1937–8*, Antwerp, pp. 38–9). (139)

(*l*) Estimates of the number of persons coming under the new scheme are given in the report cited in n. 2, p. 142, and in Fallon, V., 'Les allocations familiales pour les classes moyennes. Loi du 10 Juin 1937 et arrêté royal organique du 22 Décembre 1938' (special supplement of *Le Guide des Dirigeants*, Apr. 1939). According to these estimates, about 1·256 million persons will be liable to contribute towards the cost of the scheme, allowances will be given in respect of about 661,000 children (the scheme includes a number of persons—estimated at about 45,000—who will not pay any contributions but will nevertheless be entitled to allowances if they have dependent children) and will cost about 194 million francs per year with the retail price index at 700, while total receipts (including a State subsidy of 5 million francs) will amount to about 203 million francs. The minimum rate of allowance stipulated when the price index is between 651 and 700 is 15, 25, 50, and 85 francs per month for the first, second, third, and fourth children, and 120 per month for each subsequent child. If we take the total number of persons covered by the scheme (some of whom are retired from gainful employment) at 1·301 millions, and add the 1·572 millions of employees and wage earners covered by allowance funds at the end of 1937, the total number of persons who will be entitled to family allowances, if they have dependent children (excluding central and local government employees and the personnel of public institutions) will be 2·873 millions, and if we add the unemployed previously mentioned, the total will be 3·099 millions. But even omitting the excluded category receiving grants directly, the gainfully employed population enumerated at the 1930 Census was about 3·582 millions (3·553 millions if we also exclude *professions non déterminées*). (142)

(*m*) Vibart, op. cit., p. 159, quotes the following statement made by G. Bonvoisin in 1922: 'We could cite examples where family allowances have made it possible to carry out without damage reductions in wages (which had become essential)', and also mentions the Paris regional fund as reporting, in Dec. 1922, that allowances had never up till then been the cause of a fall in wages, but had several times prevented a rise in them. Note that in France, Paragraph 74 K of the Code de travail, added as a result of the Act of 9 Dec. 1934, stipulates that the introduction of compulsory family allowances may not be used as a reason for reducing wages or salaries. But it is difficult to see how evasion of this law could be prevented, though at least in one case damages on this count have been awarded against an employer (see *Family Endowment Chronicle*, Apr. 1935, p. 28). (142)

CHAPTER IV

(*a*) Undoubtedly the best survey of the whole background of French views on population and population policies is given by Spengler, J. J., in his superb book *France faces Depopulation* 1938, Durham, North Carolina. A more detailed study of the views in a specific period is also given by Professor Spengler in 'French population theory since 1800' (*Journal of Political Economy*, Oct. and Dec. 1936). The existence of these two studies allows the present writer to omit any detailed references to the background of present French policy, since such references can be obtained from Spengler's work. This chapter therefore concentrates upon a more detailed analysis of present policy than is given by Spengler, and upon a statistical attempt to check up the effect of present policy upon the birth-rate. As regards Belgium the survey has to be somewhat broader since, so far as the present writer is aware, there has been no general study of the situation subsequent to Vulhopp, T., *Une Politique des Familles Nombreuses en Belgique*, Bruxelles-Paris, 1929. As regards repressive aspects of population policies in their relation to birth-control and abortion see Spengler, J. J., 'Birth prevention in France' (*Marriage Hygiene*, May and Aug. 1936) and Glass, D. V., 'The effectiveness of abortion legislation in six countries' (*Modern Law Review*, Sept. 1938) and the detailed references given in each of these papers. (145)

(*b*) See Spengler, op. cit., ch. vii; Bouthoul, G., *Étude Sociologique des Variations de la Natalité*, Paris, 1922, pp. 14 et seq.; Dumont, A., *Dépopulation et Civilisation*, Paris, 1890; Auburtin, F., *La Natalité*, Paris, 3rd ed., 1921. In addition there is a vast literature explaining specific forms of depopulation, e.g. the rural exodus (cf. Dumas, L., *La Dépopulation des Campagnes*, Paris, 1900; Guillau, J., *L'Émigration des Campagnes*, Paris, 1905; Mauco, G., *Les Étrangers en France*, Paris, 1932, ch. ii; Richard, G., 'L'exode rural en France au dix-neuvième siècle', in *Proc. Int. Cong. for Studies on Popn., Rome, 1931*, vol. ix, Rome, 1933), and the depopulation of particular regions (cf. for some recent studies, Callon, G., in *Revue Générale du Centre-Ouest de la France*, Sept. 1928; Roux, P. (ed.), *Les Populations Rurales du Puy-de-Dôme*, Clermont-Ferrand, 1933; Canal, S., *Un Département Exsangue* [Tarn-et-Garonne], Paris, 1934; Letinois, Dr., *Étude Démographique sur Corvol-L'Orgueilleux (Nièvre)*, Paris, 1935; Callon, G., in *Bulletin de la Société Archéologique du Finistère*, 1935, i; most of the reports of the annual *Congrès de la Natalité* also contain special studies of individual regions). (148)

(*c*) e.g. Rommel, *Au Pays de la Revanche*, Geneva, 1886, was frequently quoted as saying that France could not possibly win a war against Germany, and that Germany, with her growing population, would soon need French territory (e.g. in Roux, M. de, *L'État et la Natalité*, Paris, 1918, p. 6). Rommel is still being quoted to-day (e.g. in Bonvoisin, G., *La Dénatalité*, Paris, n.d.—but evidently 1937—p. 15) as evidence of one of the disadvantageous consequences of an inadequate fertility. Auburtin, op. cit., p. 21 n., says that 'Rommel' was the pseudonym of a Frenchman, who adopted the German name and high-handed style in order better to convince his fellow countrymen of the imminence of the danger. Quotations from Japanese newspapers were also common. Thus, the *Taiyô* is reported to have said in 1909 that the population of France was falling from day to day, that France would soon cease to be a power, and that all her colonizing efforts in Asia would be stopped because of her low fertility (e.g. in Du Moriez, S., *L'Avortement*, Paris, 1912). Von Moltke's statement that because of her infertility, France was losing a battle every day, was also very widely quoted. (148)

(*d*) Germany was still being used as a threat in the early post-war period; e.g. Vieuille, F., 'Le mouvement nataliste en Allemagne' (*Septième Congrès National de la Natalité*, [1925], Clermont-Ferrand, 1926, pp. 153–6) in speaking of a meeting of the German association of large families in 1924 reminded his audience that the orators were more concerned with revenge than with fertility in itself, and said: 'While we French fathers are concerned above all with the desire for a greater social justice and a greater human solidarity, German fathers aim specially at giving back to Germany the forces with which she will be able to slake her thirst for vengeance and domination.' Le Vicomte Terlinden, a Belgian, also stressed, quoting from an article in the *Deutsche Zeitung* of 12 June 1924, German pleasure that France was undergoing serious difficulties, and quoted '. . . we shall see that a nation which is decadent and lazy, and which suffers from continuous depopulation, does not possess the force to direct a peace gained without victory' (*Bulletin des Arrêts de la Cour de Cassation*, Oct. 1924, p. 2). (151)

(*e*) Thus Vargas, R., *Que Devons-Nous Penser du Néo-Malthusianisme?* Montpellier, 1909, believed (p. 17) that neo-Malthusianism was logically contradictory to revolutionary ideas, and was thus really (p. 18) counter-revolutionary. One of the birth-control propagandists, Kolney, F., *La Grève des Ventres*, Paris, 5th thousand, 1908, insisted, however (p. 10), that communism and collectivism could not enter the period of practical realization until they had been given Malthusianism as their *point de départ*. Apart from the references to periodical literature given in the subsequent discussion, the following may be noted as a few examples of the birth-control propagandist literature of the period. Dates of publication are given wherever possible. Robin, P., *Libre Amour, Libre Maternité*, Paris, 1900; same author, *Pain, Loisir, Amour*, Paris, 1907; same author, *Population et Prudence Procréatice*, Paris, 4th ed., 10th thousand, 1907; same author, *Contre la Nature*, Paris, [1902]; same author, *Malthus et les Néo-Malthusiens*, Paris, 1905 ed.; same author, *Vers Régénérateurs*, Paris, 1906 (some of these verses appeared in English translation in issues of *The Malthusian*); Naquet, A., et al., *Le Néo-Malthusisme Est-il Moral?*, Paris, [1910]; Naquet, A., and Hardy, G., *Néo-Malthusisme et Socialisme*, Paris, [1910]; Faure, S., et al., *Défendons-Nous! Pour le Néo-Malthusisme Contre l'Immoralité des Moralistes*, Paris, 1910; Kolney, F., *Le Crime d'Engendrer*, Paris, 5th thousand, 1909; Kolney, F., *La Société Mourante et le Neo-Malthusisme*, Paris, n.d. (but not earlier than 1912); Devaldès, M., *La Chair à Canon*, Paris, new ed., 15th thousand, 1913; Devaldès, M., *La Brute Prolifique*, Paris, 1914; Devaldès, M., *La Famille*

Néo-Malthusienne, Paris, 1914; Devaldès, M., *L'Individualité Féminine*, Paris, 1914; Lip Tay (really Alberto Liptay), Dr., *La Préservation Sexuelle*, 3rd ed., 11th to 20th thousand, Paris, 1907; Lip Tay, Dr., *Pour et Contre Malthus*, Paris, 1911; Hardy (really Giroud), G., *Moyens d'Éviter la Grossesse*, Paris, 1908; Hardy, G., *La Loi de Malthus*, Paris, [1909]; Méric, V., *Le Problème Sexuel*, Paris, n.d. (but not earlier than 1908); Pelletier, M., *L'Émancipation Sexuelle de la Femme*, Paris, 1912 (title-page gives 1911, cover gives 1912 as date). There were also many novels with birth control or abortion as the theme. (161)

(*f*) See Giroud, G., *Paul Robin*, Paris, [1937], especially chs. x and xi, for an account by a protagonist of the movement. An antagonistic account is given by Bertillon, J., op. cit., pp. 210–46. In mentioning that *La Régénération* reappeared in 1900, having received two important donations, he adds, in a footnote: 'People have thought that they (the donations) came from a country which is an enemy of France. Nothing is more logical than this supposition, but it has not been proved' (p. 217 n.). See also Félice, R. de, *Les Naissances en France*, Paris, 1910. Giroud himself, under the pseudonym of G. Hardy, wrote a book containing a description of various methods of procuring abortion (*La Question de Population*, originally published in 1914 under the title of *L'Avortement, sa Nécessité, ses Procédés, ses Dangers*) which is reputed to have had an extremely wide circulation. See also Leroy-Beaulieu, P., *La Question de la Population*, Paris, 1913, pp. 320–38. (162)

(*g*) It is extremely difficult to obtain information regarding the history of the birth-control movement in Belgium. Monsieur Lanval, in a letter (dated 14 Mar. 1939) to the present writer, suggested that there is a conspiracy of silence on the subject, especially because many of the men in political and other circles who were in favour of birth control before the last War are now pro-natalists. Monsieur Lanval mentioned the following facts: In Nov. 1891 Paul Robin lectured on neo-Malthusianism at the *Maison du Peuple*, in Bruxelles; and he lectured in Gand in Oct. 1895. In Dec. 1896 General Brialmont read a paper to a section of the Académie Royale de Belgique, *De l'Accroissement de la Population et de ses Effets dans l'Avenir* (General Brialmont was President of the Belgian Royal Academy and this lecture was afterwards published as a pamphlet: the copy seen by the present writer was published in Paris in 1903), concluding that overpopulation leads to war, but he refused to join an association for spreading neo-Malthusian propaganda. In Jan. 1903 Emile Vandervelde, socialist politician, received a letter from Robin, asking his help in spreading propaganda by means of the socialist press, but did not reply (Vandervelde was one of the few socialist members of parliament who, according to Lanval, voted in favour of the 1923 Belgian law for suppressing birth-control propaganda). The present writer has also collected some additional information, detailed herewith: About 1899 a translation of Knowlton's work was published in Belgium—Knowlton, C., *Plus d'Avortements! Moyens Scientifiques, Licites et Pratiques de Limiter la Fécondite de la Femme*, trans. Lennox, G., Notes du Dr. Z., Namur, *c.* 1899. *The Malthusian*, Apr. 1905, p. 31, refers to the existence of a Malthusian League in Belgium, though in the issue of Oct. 1908, p. 79, the date of the Belgian Ligue Néo-Malthusienne is given as 1906. (This may, however, refer to the year in which the Belgian league joined the Fédération Universelle de la Régénération Humaine—(Federation of Neo-Malthusian Leagues, with Dr. C. R. Drysdale as the first president and Paul Robin as vice-president.) The issue of April 1907, p. 30, refers to *Procréation Consciente* as the organ of the Belgian league, and in the issue of Aug. 1907, p. 59, it is stated 'Dr. Fernand Mascaux writes to say that the railway authorities in Belgium, incited by the Catholic priests, have refused to carry his journal *Procréation Consciente*, and therefore that the title of his paper has been changed to that of *La Vie Heureuse*'. (Notice that the issue of Oct. 1908, p. 79, refers to the Belgian journal as being *Génération Consciente*, published in Paris.) In 1909 Émile Vinck published *Procréation Consciente. Réponse à la Lettre Pastorale de Monseigneur Mercier*, Gand, 1909, a critique of the whole attitude of the populationists. He regarded marriage not merely as a means, but also as an end in itself (p. 6) and contrasted this view with populationist attitudes (p. 5, 'Pour Napoléon il fallait des soldats. Pour le capitaliste il faut des ouvriers. Pour l'Église il faut des chrétiens'). A report by E. Leemans, given at the International Neo-Malthusian Conference at the Hague (*The Malthusian*, 15 Sept. 1910, pp. 79–80), outlined the situation in the Flemish provinces of Belgium, and dates the effective growth of the movement in this area from a lecture by Dr. J. Rutgers (Dutch) at Malines in 1905. Some time after this a society was formed and affiliated to the Dutch League. Leemans said 'since then the propaganda has continued incessantly and everywhere—in the factory, the café, meetings, periodicals, and pamphlets. We have distributed thousands of pamphlets in the villages throughout the country.' In 1910 there were 'societies in Malines, Antwerp and Louvain, and correspondents in several towns and villages.' The movement was attacked by the Catholic opposition led by Archbishop Mercier of Malines. In *The Malthusian* of 15 July 1912 (inside front cover) reference is made to the Flemish Neo-Malthusian League (National Verbond ter Regeling van het Kindertal) as belonging to the Fédération Universelle (the date is given as 1912). An account of the famous prosecution of Dr. Mascaux is given in Hanssens, E., *Le Néo-Malthusisme en Belgique*, Bruxelles, 1910. The title of this book is not really indicative of its contents. It is simply a report of the pleading of Hanssens, a well-known barrister, before the Court of Appeal. The appeal was unsuccessful. The present writer is indebted to Dr. A. Racine for enabling him to obtain a typescript copy of sections of Hanssen's book. The present writer has also seen a copy of Chapelier, E., *Ayons Peu d'Enfants! Pourquoi? Comment?* (partly written by J. Rahier), St. Gilles-Bruxelles, n.d. (but evidently before 1914), 37th thousand. The inside front cover refers to additional works by Chapelier, and to neo-Malthusian literature by other authors, including Mascaux, F., and Rutgers, J., *Moyens d'Éviter les Grandes Familles* (presumably a translation from the Dutch). The outside back cover consists of the advertisement of a Bruxelles firm dealing in contraceptives. (162)

(*h*) See, e.g. Pelletier, M., *Le Droit à l'Avortement*, 2nd ed., Paris, 1913, p. 9. An article summarized in the Belgian *Journal d'Accouchements*, 28 Aug. 1910, gives a statement by midwives on the question. According to them, self-induced abortion was the main factor. There were many books explaining how to induce abortion and any woman could buy, for 60 centimes, a uterine syringe and use this to induce an abortion. But the 18 Dec. issue of the same journal shows that midwives advertised their services for procuring abortion, and quotes the following advertisement as an example: 'Accoucheuse aux Dames, Retards. Seule méthode spéciale et inoffensive, rue . . . n°. . . . *Maison de confiance*.' This kind of advertisement was also widespread in French newspapers and could still be seen in 1939 in many publications. For further opinions on the large part played by midwives in procuring criminal abortions in Belgium, see Dr. Dejace and Dr. O. Dauwe in *Bulletin de la Ligue contre l'Infécondité Intentionnelle*, 15 Nov. 1910, and Dr. O. Dauwe, ibid., 31 Jan. 1911, p. 37. Some account of the methods used in procuring criminal abortion is given by Jurborskis, M. L., *Procédés Actuels de l'Avortement Criminel*, Strasbourg, 1933, and Mondor, H., *Les Avortements Mortels*, Paris, 1936. (163)

(*i*) Acts of 5 Aug. 1928, 5 Aug. 1929, and 1 May 1930; decrees of 19 May and 25 June 1930; decree-law of 31 Oct. 1935, Act of 26 Aug. 1936; Statutory order of 8 Oct. 1936. Membership of the social insurance system is now obligatory for all employed persons whose income, excluding family allowances, is not more than 21,000 francs per year or, if having at least one dependent child, not more than 25,000 francs per year. It is optional for a number of other categories, e.g. farmers, *métayers*, small employers, &c., and specially available for the unoccupied wives of insured persons (without the consent of their husbands—this is one of the few cases in which French women enjoy full juridical capacity). So far as medical attention and costs are concerned, the wife of an insured worker is automatically entitled to them without any special insurance on her part. So too, are the insured person's dependent children. Note also that under the 1909 Act and its derivatives, every pregnant woman is entitled to at least 12 consecutive weeks of absence from work without the employer being able to dismiss her for this reason. (168)

(*j*) Marriage loans were introduced for *orphelins de guerre* and *pupilles de la nation* as from 1 April 1938, and amount to a maximum of 5,000 francs, to be repaid in 10 years (the first payment not being required until the end of the fourth year following the marriage), with interest at 1 per cent. A cancellation of 1,000 francs of the debt is granted at the birth of the first child, another 500 when the child reaches one year of age, another 1,500 at the birth of a second child, and the rest when a third child is born. The candidates must pass a medical examination. The Bank of France gives marriage loans to its staff, provided that the salary earned is not more than 25,000 francs per year (the total of both partners not to exceed 40,000 per year if both are employed by the Bank). The loans are up to a maximum of 10,000 francs, interest free, generally for persons between 18 and 27 years of age, to be repaid within 5 years if no birth occurs in that period. The loans are to be used for the purchase of furniture and household linens and utensils, and, in certain cases, for covering the first rent payments. Each birth postpones repayment by two years, and there are cancellations of part of the loan on the birth of each child. The birth of a fourth child results in the cancellation of the remainder of the loan. (See *Revue de l'Alliance Nationale*, Mar. 1939, pp. 88–9.) For a discussion of French marriage-loan proposals see Boverat, F., 'Prêts au mariage', *Revue Médico-Sociale et de Protection de l'Enfance*, 1938, no. 5, and *Familles de*

France, Jan. 1938. See also the report (mimeographed) of Monsieur P. Pailhiez to the 'Journées Familiales des Jeunes', Montpellier, 2 and 3 Oct. 1937. (172)

(*k*) Apart from Spengler's survey of the material, population movements in France are discussed in Levasseur, E., *La Population Française*, 3 vols., Paris, 1889–92; Huber, M., Bunle, H., and Boverat, F., *La Population de la France*, Paris, n.d. but 1937; Landry, A., *La Révolution Démographique*, Paris, 1934 (containing an historical survey of the decline in fertility). There are also many useful studies to be found in the volumes of the *Bulletin de la Statistique Générale de la France* and of the *Journal de la Société de Statistique de Paris*, and some interesting information in the previously mentioned article by Bertillon *père*. A number of foreign studies contain useful accounts, e.g. Goldstein, J., *Bevölkerungsprobleme und Berufsgliederung in Frankreich*, Berlin, 1900; Harmsen, H., *Bevölkerungsprobleme Frankreichs*, Berlin-Grunewald, 1927; Ungern-Sternberg, R. von, *Die Bevölkerungsverhältnisse in Frankreich*, Berlin, 1938; Posadowsky-Wehner, H. von, *Das Bevölkerungsproblem in Frankreich*, Leipzig, 1939; Lasorsa, G., *Lo Spopolamento della Francia*, Milano, 1934. For Belgium fewer studies are available. Some (by Vulhopp, Jacquart, &c.) have already been cited. Others are Horn, J. E., *Bevölkerungswissenschaftliche Studien aus Belgien*, Leipzig, 1854; Fallon, V., 'La structure de la population belge', *Annales de la Soc. Sc. de Bruxelles*, Série D, 1933; Fallon, V., 'Les Communes belges le plus gravement atteintes par la denatalité', same journal, 1934; Fallon, V., 'Tableau du mouvement de la population belge de 1876 à 1935', same journal, 1938; Demeyère, J., *Le Mouvement de la Population Belge et l'Avenir Économique du Pays*, Bruxelles, n.d., but probably 1937. An analysis in graphs is given by Jacquart, J., *Démographie de la Belgique*, Bruxelles, 1937. See also Selleslags, W., *La Mortalité en Belgique*, Bruxelles, 1938. (178)

(*l*) Theoretically these high allowances were generally abandoned when the 1932 Act came into force. But in fact they were still payable to workers who, having been taken on before 15 April 1933, already had families, or to whom a child was born before 15 April 1934. For workers taken on after April 1933 they were payable in a modified form, after the workers had been in the firm for 6 months—up to 2 completed years of age if one child; up to the end of the second year of age of the second child, if there were two children under 14 years old; and up to 14 completed years if there were three or more children, the children over 14 years of age not being taken into account in calculating the allowances. The regional equalization fund rate for Clermont-Ferrand was 20 francs per month for one child, 50 for two children, 90 for three, 140 for four, plus 60 for each additional child. (See Société Michelin et Cie., *Règlement du Service d'Allocations Familiales*, Clermont-Ferrand, 1933.) (179)

(*m*) A correlation analysis was undertaken to test this more closely. From the *Annuaire* for 1930–1 of the Comité Central des Allocations Familiales, the numbers of employees enrolled in family allowance funds were calculated for each Département. (These excluded allowances paid in the public services. The total amounted to 1,708,000 as compared with the figure of 1,820,000 on 1 Jan. 1930, cited by Bonvoisin and Maignan, op. cit., p. 16, the difference being due to the fact that for some of the funds the present writer could not obtain accurate information.) Agriculture was then excluded, and the other workers enrolled in the funds were related to the numbers of employees and wage-earners occupied in industry and commerce (groups 3, 4, 5, and 6 in Table VII relating to each Département, 1931 Census, vols. ii and iii) in those Départements in which the percentage of males engaged in industry (see 1931 Census, vol. i, pt. 3, p. 12, and vols. ii and iii, Tables VI and VII, groups 3, 4, 5, and 9*b*) was above the average for all the Départements. These proportions (of workers enrolled in the family allowance funds to all workers in industry and commerce) were compared with the gross reproduction rates of the selected Départements and no significant correlation was found. (198)

(*n*) See Vulhopp, T., 'Le développement de la population belge depuis 1830', *Proc. Int. Cong. for Studies on Popn. 1931*, vol. i, Rome, 1933, pp. 149–60, which says that since 1866 the Belgian census data relate to the *de jure* population. The statement regarding the birth- and death-rates is confirmed by a letter to the present writer from Professor E. Lesoir, dated 23 Feb. 1939. This is not very important as regards the birth-rates, but is significant as regards the death-rates. According to Greenwood, M., and Granville Edge, P., *The Official Vital Statistics of the Kingdom of Belgium*, Geneva, 1924, p. 25, the *Acte de naissance* of a legitimate child contains the ages of the child's parents. Thus specific fertility rates could be calculated. But the data do not appear to be tabulated in Belgium. In estimating gross reproduction rates the sex ratio of *de jure* births has been assumed to be the same as for the *de facto*, for the *de jure* births are not given by sex. (199)

(*o*) For Belgium *de jure* births (from *Annuaire Statistique de la Belgique, 1934*, p. 6*, and *1938*, p. 6*) are used. The basic populations are mid-year estimates, being the arithmetic means of the 31 Dec. *de jure* populations given in the *Annuaire Statistique, 1938*, p. 41. The birth-rates given in the *Annuaire Statistique, 1938*, p. 41, are arrived at by relating the *de facto* births to the *de jure* population at the end of each year. The differences are, however, small. Shortly after these rates for Belgium were computed, Professor E. Lesoir, formerly Director of the Belgian Statistical Office and now Secretary of the Institut International des Sciences Administratives, kindly sent the present writer a specially compiled unpublished table of *de jure* populations (for the end of each year) and births. For 1922 the *de jure* births in this table differ from those given in the *Annuaire Statistique*, and so do the populations for the years 1921, 1923, 1924, 1928, and 1930. Using Professor Lesoir's data, the *de jure* birth-rates calculated on estimated mid-year populations would be 20·3 per 1,000 in 1922, 20·5 in 1923, 19·9 in 1924, 19·7 in 1925, and 18·1 in 1931. The remaining birth-rates would be unchanged. The birth-rates for England and Wales are from the *Registrar General's Statistical Review* for 1937, Tables, Part II, Civil, p. 6. The birth-rates for France are from *Annuaire Statistique, 1937*, p. 13*. (201)

(*p*) One of the methods cited in the 1932 report would yield opposed results if applied in later years. For example, the report for 1937 (p. 47) gives a crude birth-rate for the 36 selected funds of 32·5 per 1,000 employees in 1935. Following the method described on p. 187, we should add to the denominator 250 for age correction, 570 for dependent children (102 funds show 57 dependent children per 100 employed persons enrolled in the funds —p. 44) and 514 for mothers with 2 or more children (59 funds show 48·6 per cent. of families having one child only—p. 46. This is the method followed by Colonel Guillermin described in the report for 1932, p. 26). The birth-rate of 32·5 should thus be related to a denominator of 1,000+250+570+514 = 2,334, and the corrected birth-rate would be 13·9 per 1,000, as compared with a rate of 15·3 for France as a whole. But it seems unlikely that the fertility of the funds was really lower than that of the whole of France in 1935, and the method is, in fact, unsatisfactory. (201)

(*q*) Leener, G. de, *Les Caisses de Compensation*, pp. 86–8, cites data, of which the following are examples. For the Brabant equalization fund infant mortality was 58 per 1,000 in 1925 and 51 in 1926, while the rate for the whole region was 85·8 in 1923 (for Brabant it was 94·1 in 1921–5 and 91·7 in 1926–30—*La Mortalité Infantile en Belgique de 1926 à 1935*, Œuvre Nationale de l'Enfance, Bruxelles, n.d., p. 6); the fund for the Liége region had rates of 108·0 in 1925 and 46·3 in 1926 (Liége province had 86·0 in 1921–5 and 84·3 in 1926–30); the Verviers textile fund had a rate of 58·9 in 1925 (Verviers *arrondissement* had 77·9 in 1926–30); the fund for the Anvers region had a rate of 92·5 in 1926 (Anvers province had 103·9 in 1921–5 and 97·6 in 1926–30). For data on infant mortality in France, see, in addition to the volumes of the *Statistique du Mouvement de la Population*, Lesage, A., and Moine, M., 'La mortalité infantile pendant un siècle (1831–1935)', *Bulletin de l'Académie de Médécine*, 1937, no. 28; Lesage, A., *Rapport Annuel de la Commission Permanente de l'Hygiène de l'Enfance, 1935*, Paris, 1937; Lesage, A., and Moine, M., *Étude Générale de la Mortalité de l'Enfant de Première Année* (Office National d'Hygiène Sociale et Comité National de l'Enfance), Melun, 1929–38 (10 volumes up to date). The latter work was awarded the Prix Montyon in 1937. (202)

(*r*) *Proposition de Loi Pour le Relèvement du Taux des Allocations Familiales. Développements, Chambre des Représentants*, no. 373, 8 June 1937. The costs analysis presented in the report had been undertaken with the help of the Service des Études of the Confédération des Syndicats Chrétiens. This organization subsequently published in its monthly bulletin *C.S.C.*, Mar. 1938, pp. 316–25, the results of a family budget inquiry undertaken in 1938. According to prices in Jan. 1938, a working-class family living in comfortable (*convenable*) circumstances in a large urban agglomeration would spend about 16,150 francs per year for husband and wife, 1,586 francs for a child in its second year of life, and 4,903 francs for a child in its thirteenth year. On the other hand the expenditure of a poor family would be 9,715, 940, and 2,969 francs per year for the members specified above. The figures cited by Heyman are nearer the expenditure of the 'comfortable' family. (208)

(*s*) It should be noted, however, that, in recent months, at the same time as the promulgation of the new French 'family code', there has been a bitter and comparatively strong campaign against pro-natalist policy in France. This campaign has come from left-wing pacifist circles and to some extent from the feminist movement. As regards the former group, evidence may be seen in articles in the weekly paper *Sia* (*Solidarité internationale antifasciste*), which, the present writer has been told, has a circulation of about 45,000. In the issues of 1, 8, 15, and 29 June and 6 and 20 July 1939, there are articles attacking French *lapinisme* in general and Fernand Boverat in particular. On more than one occasion writers of anti-natalist articles in this periodical have been imprisoned under the 1920 law (including authors of articles in the issues cited). One article (in the issue of 6 July 1939) is particularly interesting, offering satirical praise to Fernand Boverat, whose campaign against abortionists would make women more careful in preventing conception from taking place. See also *La Patrie Humaine* (a pacifist weekly, said to have a circulation of about 30,000) of 16 June 1939. For the feminist attack see *Le Journal de la Femme* (said to have a circulation of about 200,000) of 19 May 1939. But it should be remembered that among the nationally known daily papers, pro-natalist articles are the rule and appear very frequently. *Paris-Soir*, for example, recently conducted a series of investigations into the reasons for the falling population in many départements. See also, on this point, an article by Bied-Charreton, R., in a Belgian periodical, *Les Dossiers de l'Action Sociale Catholique*, June 1939, pp. 533–48. So far as the general attitude of the French population is concerned, the only investigation available is that undertaken by the French Institute of Public Opinion in the summer of 1939, a typescript of which has been seen by the present writer. Of the persons questioned (the number is not stated) 85 per cent. agreed that the e is a 'crisis' in fertility and that it presents dangers for the future of France, and only 15 per cent. denied this. Among the reasons given for present low fertility, the most typical (given as the main reason by 65 per cent. of the informants) was the 'high cost of life' or 'lack of sufficient material resources'. 'Economic insecurity' and 'fear of war' came next, each with 40 per cent., and then the 'weakening of the idea of the family', the 'rural exodus', and the 'housing crisis' were the remaining important reasons given. Various other reasons were also mentioned by the informants. As regards remedies, most emphasis was placed upon family allowances, grants to the *mère au foyer*, and the suppression of abortion. Comparing the results of the investigation with the level of fertility in France it would appear that, however strongly individuals may regard a higher fertility as desirable for the nation, each has, from his own point of view, good and proper reasons for limiting the size of his own family. (212)

CHAPTER V

(*a*) *Il 1924* (*Scritti e Discorsi di Benito Mussolini*, IV), Milan, 1934, pp. 431–2. The statements were made in an address to the Senate, 11 Dec. 1924. As regards a war of conquest, he was not quite so certain in the interview he gave to the correspondent of the Turkish newspaper *Aksciam* in 1926. Mussolini specified a 5-point programme for solving the population problem (in the context of the interview it was the 'overpopulation problem' he was proposing to solve), the first four of which covered internal and external colonization and migration and agreements on materials of vital necessity. Asked whether his fifth point—which he had not stated—referred to a new colony, he said:

'Quì metto un punto interrogativo: è ancora in dominio dell' avvenire. Tengo d'altronde a fare osservare che l'insieme di questi cinque punti forma un programma a lungo respiro, la cui effettuazione richiederà un certo numero di anni' (*Boll. dell' Em.*, July 1926, pp. 836–7). See also Michels, R., *Italien von heute*, Zürich-Leipzig, 1930, p. 332. (219)

(*b*) See, for example, Somogyi, S., 'La concezione fascista della politica demografica', *Economia*, Feb. 1934, pp. 119–34; Lojacono, L., 'Il numero è potenza', *L'Economia Italiana*, 1934 (special number), pp. 3–15; Gini, C., 'The Italian demographic problem and the fascist policy on population', *Journal of Political Economy*, Dec. 1930, pp. 682–97, esp. pp. 688–90; Grossi, G., *Legge e Potenza del Numero*, Bologna, 1935, pp. 3–14. See also Colin, A., *La Famille dans la Législation Italienne*, Paris, 1931, esp. pp. 49–62; Savorgnan, F., 'La politique démographique de l'Italie et ses buts', *Le Assicurazioni Sociali*, Part 1, 1931, pp. 50–62 (the *Supplément* version of *Le A.S.* has been used for the purpose of the present chapter, except where legal texts and decisions and collective agreements are cited. The *Supplément* gives foreign articles in their original languages and Italian articles in French translations. References to it are henceforth noted as *Le A.S.* The original edition —in Italian—also contains legal texts, &c., relating to various social measures. It is subsequently noted as *Le A.S.*, original edition); Camanni, V., 'La famille italienne dans l'assurance sociale', ibid., Part 3, 1931, pp. 1–27. (220)

(*c*) Although, in his 1924 speech, Mussolini said that he would never approve of Malthusian propaganda, he was, not very much earlier, an ardent supporter of birth control. In 1913 Dr. Luigi Berta founded an Italian neo-Malthusian association, having as its journal *L'Educazione Sessuale*. A questionnaire was sent to various relatively well-known persons, asking their views on birth control and eugenics. In his reply Mussolini said that he considered prudence in the begetting of children was an act of wisdom, responsibility, and honesty, that he did not believe the courts should have the power to judge theories and doctrines—else there would be a return to the medieval inquisition—and that he pledged his complete and active adherence to an association which aimed at the spreading, especially among the working class, of the theory and practice of neo-Malthusianism. See Giroud, G., *Paul Robin*, Paris, [1937], pp. 259–60, and Harmsen, H., 'Die Bevölkerungspolitik Deutschlands, Frankreichs und des italienischen Faschismus', in Harmsen, H., et al., *Die deutsche Bevölkerungsfrage im europäischen Raum*, Berlin-Grunewald, 1929, p. 51. (220)

(*d*) Salvemini, G., 'Do Italian women obey Mussolini?', *Birth Control Review*, Mar. 1933, pp. 64–6, suggests that in 1929 five or six thousand Italian women were sent to Italy to have their confinements. Between the end of Oct. 1931 and about the beginning of Mar. 1932, the Italian fascist party helped 6,512 mothers temporarily repatriated from abroad—see *Le A.S.*, 1, 1932, p. 85. Notice the circular issued 12 July 1928 by the National Director of the National Fascist Party to the Provincial Delegates of the Fasci Femminili, urging that the return of these temporarily repatriated Italian women should be celebrated (in each area) by a ceremony of 'homage to the mother and almost symbolic adoption of the newly born child'. Each mother would be sent a small gift (not defined) by the National Director, to be presented at that ceremony. Every delegate, the circular continued, would realize the 'profound beauty and the deep religious and patriotic significance of this movement for repatriation', and would therefore ensure that each mother returning to her country would find 'constant and loving material and moral help awaiting her' and would realize the 'holy sisterhood of fascist women'. Menna, E., *Le Provvidenze del Regime Fascista per la Battaglia Demografica in Italia*, Como, 1936, pp. 295–7. (This book consists of a very useful compilation of laws, regulations, and circulars relating to the Italian population policy.) (224)

(*e*) It is, of course, impossible to estimate the relative importance of the two separate factors. One can only point to the reduction in the annual outward balance of migration. Two sets of statistics are available. The first—*Annuario Statistico Italiano, 1937*, p. 38—is based on direct passport statistics, and shows an excess of *espatriati* over *rimpatriati* amounting to 77,292 in 1921; 170,484 in 1922; 270,219 in 1923; 191,559 in 1924; 90,360 in 1925; 84,779 in 1926; 78,506 in 1927; 51,215 in 1928; 33,913 in 1929; and, rising again with economic depression, the Italian government falling back upon emigration as a partial solution of unemployment, to 151,074 in 1930. From 1931 to 1936 inclusive, the outward balance in the separate years was 58,130; 10,173; 17,228; 18,634; 17,938; and 8,950. The second set of statistics—see, e.g. *Bollettino Mensile di Statistica*, 21 Dec. 1929, p. 1164—is based on records of departures and arrivals, and shows an outward balance of migration of 126,000 in 1921; 143,000 in 1922; 240,000 in 1923; 177,000 in 1924; 81,000 in 1925; 72,000 in 1926; 76,000 in 1927; and 44,000 in 1928. In both sets of statistics, the data prior to 1928 are not comparable with those for later years, for in 1928 the criteria used for classifying emigrants were changed. The last important measure concerning emigration was in the creation in 1938 of a Permanent Commission for the repatriation of Italians living abroad. A Royal Decree Law of 28 Nov. 1938 sets aside 10 million lire to cover contingencies which might arise in connexion with the repatriation of Italians (*Le A.S.*, 6, 1938, p. 656). Note that in the most recent years an increase in temporary migration has been encouraged by Italo-German agreements. Justifying this new policy, U. Manunta ('Les accords italo-allemands pour l'émigration italienne en Allemagne', *Le A.S.*, 5, 1938, pp. 436–43) says that so long as there is work of reclamation and improvement to be done in the world, emigration is an instrument of civilization and thus a requirement of modern life. (But, of course, as this emigration is between the two partners of the Axis, it has a special dignity and justification which would not apply in other cases.) (225)

(*f*) *Penal Code*, paras. 545–9 inclusive, pp. 146–7. Under para. 550 penalties ranging from penal servitude for 3 months to 3 years, to penal servitude for 10 to 18 years (paras. 582–4, pp. 156–7) are prescribed if means administered to, or acts committed upon a woman believed to be pregnant, with the object of procuring her abortion, result in personal injury or death. The penalties are reduced if the consent of the woman had been given, and all penalties under paras. 545–50 inclusive are reduced (under para. 551) by a half to two-thirds if the offence is committed to save one's own honour or that of a near relative. See Piromallo, op. cit., pp. 529–35. Notice that under the penal code of 1889 (*Nuovo Codice Penale per il Regno d'Italia*, Naples, 1889, p. 85), remaining in force until the new code was applied (cf., for example, with Franchi, L., *Cinque Codici*, Milan, 1929, *Codice Penale*, pp. 66–7), paras. 381–5 inclusive provided the following penalties: Imprisonment (*detenzione*) for 1 to 4 years for a woman whose abortion is procured by whatever means either by herself, or, with her consent, by some other person. The person procuring her abortion, with her consent, was liable to penal servitude (*reclusione*) for 30 months to 5 years, and if the abortion resulted in death, to penal servitude for 4 to 7 years (5 to 10 years if death resulted from the use of means more dangerous than those to which the woman had given her consent). Where the means for procuring abortion were administered without the consent of the woman, or against her will, the penalty was penal servitude for 30 months to 6 years, for 7 to 12 years if abortion actually took place, and for 15 to 20 years if it resulted in the death of the woman, the penalties being increased by one-sixth if the guilty person was the husband. In cases where a question of honour was involved, the penalties were reduced by one to two-thirds, and imprisonment substituted for penal servitude. But where the guilty person carried on a *professione sanitaria* or any other profession or craft of a kind subject to supervision in the interests of the public health, the penalties were increased by one-sixth, and the punishment always had as a result the suspension of the person from his profession for a period equal to the length of the sentence. (Under the old code the sentences of imprisonment were: *ergastolo*—penal servitude for life; *reclusione*—penal servitude for 3 days to 24 years; *detenzione*—imprisonment for 3 days to 24 years. Under the new code they are: *ergastolo*—as above; *reclusione*—penal servitude for 15 days to 24 years; and *arresto*—imprisonment for 5 days to 3 years.) The new penal code did not make any fundamental changes in the penalties for abortion, but Piromallo, op. cit., pp. 529–30, says that it aims at greater simplicity and a greater opportunity for repression of abortion. (234)

(*g*) 'L'azione promossa . . .', p. 42, gives the number of cases reported from 1 Jan. 1929 to 30 June 1931, as 1,863, involving 3,755 persons, while p. 68 states that, in 1932, 754 cases of induced abortion were reported to the judicial authorities, and 465 in 1933. As regards the total frequency of abortion, Allaria, G. B., *Il Problema Demografico Italiano Osservato da un Pediatra*, 2nd ed., Turin, 1935, p. 122, says that a figure of 1 to 10 as the ratio between abortions and live births (which would mean 99,671 abortions in 1935) would underestimate the real frequency. But these include spontaneous as well as induced abortions. Professor Allaria reports an inquiry made by the Istituto Pediatrico of the University of Turin in 1915–19 (the most recent dates given by him) showing 12 per cent. of pregnancies ending in abortions. Of these abortions 3·5 per cent. were admitted to have been procured by the woman, while in 51·6 per cent. of the cases the causes were said not to be known. Professor Allaria believes that part of these 'unknowns' must certainly be attributed to criminal induction. But Dr. S. Alberti, working on the records of the Milan Clinica Pediatrica for 1923–9, finds a very low rate of criminal abortion—the highest being 1·04 abortions per 100 conceptions. Livi, commenting on these figures, says that they have a certain illustrative value (Dr. Alberti gives rates for broad occupational groups and for women who were either unmarried or who did not state the occupation of their husbands), though the large majority of criminal abortions are not notified (Livi, L., 'Rassegna di demografia e statistica, *Economia*, Apr.-May 1934, pp. 382–4). That the abortion problem is still causing concern may be seen from a study by P. Pagani, 'L'aborto nel quadro della denatalità: divagazioni statistiche', *Economia*, July 1938, pp. 11–29, which points out how little is really known of the facts. He says (pp. 14–15): 'Si parla di numeri impressionanti, si grida al pericolo, si reclamano provvidenze; sta bene. . . . Ma è in me la convinzione che in questa materia, non controllata dalla ricerca metodica statistica, molto si lavori di fantasia, e si repeta un frasario fatto, si operi sul sentito dire.' (235)

(*h*) *Le A.S.*, 2, 1933, p. 176; 1, 1934, pp. 100–1; 6, 1934, pp. 565–6; 6, 1935, p. 534; 6, 1936, p. 411; 6, 1938, pp. 650–1. The following money premiums were given away at the Mother and Child Days of the various years: 1933, 10,522 marriage premiums totalling 4,162,306 lire, 12,839 birth premiums totalling 2,934,519 lire, 6,108 child-rearing premiums totalling 476,065 lire; 1934, 9,076 marriage premiums at 3,209,670 lire, 15,450 birth premiums at 3,439,876 lire, 15,131 child-rearing premiums at about 1,245,510 lire; 1935, 25,000 marriage premiums at about 9 million lire, 22,000 birth premiums at about 4 million lire, 27,000 child-rearing premiums at about 1·5 million lire, 7,500 large family premiums at 700,000 lire; 1936, 20,000 marriage premiums at about 7 million lire, 23,074 birth premiums at about 4 million lire, 27,000 child-rearing premiums at about 1·6 million lire, and about 6,000 premiums for large families at 520,000 lire; 1937 (*Le A.S.*, original edition, 6, 1937, p. 1036), about 80,000 marriage and birth premiums and 25,000 premiums for child rearing; 1938 (*Le A.S.*, original edition, 6, 1938, pp. 1103–4), about 110,000 premiums. (243)

(*i*) A grant was—as under previous Acts—also given when a miscarriage or therapeutic abortion terminated the pregnancy after the third month. The grant was 100 lire. The system in agriculture was not quite the same as in industry. The contributions were different and the confinement benefit only 100 lire (75 lire for miscarriage or therapeutic abortion) plus medical and surgical assistance. For accounts of the various laws and of the development of the system, see 'L.C.' (Luigi Clerici?), 'L'Activité de la caisse nationale des assurances sociales pendant les dix premières années du régime fasciste', *Le A.S.*, 6, 1932, pp. 80–92; Manunta, U., 'Les nouvelles dispositions légales pour la protection de la maternité des travailleuses en Italie', *Le A.S.*, 2, 1934, pp. 180–6; Buffa, A., 'Développement démographique et défense de la maternité dans l'agriculture en Italie', *Le A.S.*, 4, 1936, pp. 222–7; Biagi, B., 'La prévoyance sociale, dix ans après la proclamation de la charte du travail', ibid., 2, 1937, pp. 125–55; *Le A.S.*, 4, 1936, pp. 265–6; *Le A.S.*, 5, 1937, pp. 576–7; *Gazzetta Ufficiale*, 15 Sept. 1937, no. 215, pp. 3453–55; *Le A.S.* (original edition), 1, 1939, pp. 89–91; Menna, op. cit., pp. 122–42. The law relating to social insurance was codified and extended by the Royal Legislative Decree of 4 Oct. 1935, no. 1827 (see *Le A.S.*, original edition, 'Atti ufficiali', 1935, pp. 136–79). The law has again been completely overhauled —see *Le A.S.*, 1, 1939, pp. 99–104, and Giudice, R. del, 'La réforme fasciste de la prévoyance sociale', ibid., 3, 1939, pp. 309–21. (244)

(*j*) On housing see also Orestano, F., 'Retour à la "domus"', *Le A.S.*, 1, 1937, pp. 8–20; Crollalanza, A. di, 'Le problème social de l'habitation en Italie', *Le A.S.*, 4, 1931, pp. 1–4. As regards the effect of the housing legislation on rents, it is very difficult to come to any definite conclusion. The *Rapport sur Habitations Populaires, etc.*, Table XXXIII, p. 74, shows an increasing proportion of the family budget spent on house accommodation over the period 1927–34 (1933 appears to be the peak year in most cases) in the 11 largest towns—e.g. Turin, 17·5 per cent. in 1927, 20·6 per cent. in 1934; Milan, 14·7 and 20·2 per cent.; Venice, 14·1 and 18·4 per cent.; Trieste, 15·5 and 22·4 per cent.; Naples, 19·7 and 25·8 per cent. This may indicate that money wages fell more rapidly than rents during the period. Money wages for men and women in industry as a whole were 1·80 lire per hour in 1934, having fallen consistently since 1928, and there had also been a fall in the number of hours worked per month. See *Year-Book of Labour Statistics, 1938* (I.L.O.), pp. 132 and 100. (246)

(*k*) A few of the articles appearing between Nov. 1934 and Jan. 1935 are: 'La tutela della razza in Regime Fascista', *Giornale d'Italia*, 7.11.1934; 'Nuove provvidenze per le famiglie numerose', *Corriere della Sera*, 12.12.1934; 'Feconda attività assistenziale dell' Opera per la protezione della Maternità e dell' Infanzia', *Brennero*, 19.12.1934; 'La "Giornata della Madre"', *Resto del Carlino*, 21.12.1934; 'I diplomi e le medaglie dell' O.N.M.I. consegnati alle prolifiche madri italiane', *La Nazione*, 21.12.1934; 'Madri italiane', *Avvenire d'Italia*, 22.12.1934; 'Il saluto del Duce alle madri italiane', *Messaggero*, 23.12.1934; 'La giornata della madre e del fanciullo', *Corriere della Sera*, 24.12.1934; 'Per la madre e il fanciullo', *Gazzetta del Popolo*, 24.11.1934; 'La tutela della maternità e del fanciullo', *Piccolo di Trieste*, 25.11.1934; 'I premi della Provincia alle madri nubili', *Giornale d'Italia*, 11.1.1935. Salvemini, G. (*Birth Control Review*, March 1933, op. cit., p. 66), says that in 1932, when the demographic campaign was seen to have failed, it was 'discovered' that slender women generally had fewer children than fat women, and that, in consequence, a campaign in favour of fat women was initiated. (247)

(*l*) See, for example, Livi, L., 'I primi risultati della politica demografica nazista', *Economia*, May 1935, pp. 498–501; Somogyi, S., *La Politica Demografica del Governo Nazional-Socialista*, Rome, 1936; Livi, L., 'Considerazioni sui risultati della politica demografica nazional-socialista, e sull' andamento della natalità in Italia', *Economia*, Feb. 1937, pp. 112–23; Livi, L., 'Un' inchiesta sugli effetti della politica demografica nazional-socialista' (contains statements by F. Zahn, A. Hesse, M. L. Meyer, E. Wagemann, U. Giusti, R. Bachi, S. Golzio), *Economia*, July–Aug. 1937, pp. 20–36. Notice also that on the invitation of the German Office for Racial Policy, some of the Fascist leaders interested in population questions and policy—Count di Marsanich, Professor Laurinsich, Professor Bruguier, &c.—visited Germany, 28 May to 7 June 1937, in order to study the German measures and meet the officials directing them (see *Archiv für Bevölkerungswissenschaft*, 3, 1937, pp. 220–2). (248)

(*m*) *Le A.S.*, 2, 1937, pp. 214–18. The proposals also related to further taxation rebates and exemptions and to maternity insurance. There was also a proposal to reconsider the provincial and communal areas in the light of the

1941 census, suppressing those in which 'a scanty and effete population no longer requires the services of public institutions' (p. 215). Still more recently the régime has adopted some of the racial ideas of Germany (see the declaration approved by the Fascist Grand Council on 6 Oct. 1938, *Le A.S.*, 5, 1938, pp. 518–20). Boldrini, M., 'Popolazione', *Rivista Internazionale di Scienze Sociali*, May, 1938, p. 290, cites the *Informazione Diplomatica* of 17 Feb. 1938, as saying that although vigorous measures were to be taken against elements hostile to the Fascist régime, the Fascist government did not 'contemplate, nor has it ever contemplated adopting any political, economic or moral measures against the Jews as such'. This scarcely agrees with the Fascist Council's declaration. Nor does this latter declaration agree with Mussolini's previous statements on the subject of racialism. See, for example, the citations in Cohen, I., 'Jews in Italy', *Political Quarterly*, July–Sept. 1939, pp. 405–18. But it is scarcely unusual to find sudden changes in the Duce's attitude on various questions. To some people—depending upon their political opinions—these volte-face are signs of the Duce's capacity for intellectual growth. To others they are evidence of opportunism. It seems fairly evident that axis politics, together with the desire to gain Moslem support in attacking British interests in the Mediterranean, were responsible for the Duce's conversion to the new racial policy. (248)

(*n*) Data kindly supplied by Professor F. Savorgnan, President of the Central Statistical Institute. Subsequent to completing this chapter, the writer was fortunate enough to obtain the typescript of a paper communicated by Dr. Cau, of the Ministry of Corporations, to the *Deuxième Journée Internationale des Allocations Familiales*, held at Liége in July 1939. This paper contained a considerable number of statistical data concerning family allowances in Italy, of which the following are a selection. In industry, in 1937, 358·062 million lire were given in allowances for 1·702 million dependants, while for 1938 the comparable figures were 566·547 million lire for 2·144 million dependants. In agriculture the 1937 figures were 16·340 million lire for 514,000 dependants, with 120·908 million lire for 810,000 dependants in 1938. For commerce the figures are: 1937, 36·986 million lire for 221,000 dependants; 1938, 48·965 million lire for 215,000 dependants. Finally the figures for credit and insurance employments are: 1937, 35 million lire for 44,000 dependants; and the same figures for 1938. (255)

(*o*) As additional examples we may note: (*a*) in 1935, marriage bonuses, ranging from 1,500 to 4,000 lire, were introduced for employees in State and semi-State organizations, while they were 5,000 lire for officers in the armed forces. The marriages had to take place within certain age limits—under 30 years for some categories and under 32 years for others. Birth premiums were also given—400 lire for the first child, 600 for the second, 1,000 for the third, &c. These grants were later extended to militia officers (see Menna, op. cit., pp. 299–302, and *Le A.S.*, 3, 1935, p. 332 and 4, 1935, p. 410). From May 1935 to the end of 1938 the following premiums were given—33,176 marriage premiums, at a total cost of 79·376 million lire; 144,376 birth premiums, at a total cost of 180·652 million lire; 18,396 premiums for multiple births, at a total cost of 12·169 million lire (statistics from Professor Savorgnan). A Royal Legislative Decree of 12 Aug. 1937 assured an annual State grant of 42 million lire for the payment of marriage and birth premiums to members of the armed forces and State employees, including grants of 600–800 lire for the birth of twins and 800–1,000 lire for the birth of triplets (*Le A.S.*, 5, 1937, p. 578). (*b*) Marriage and birth premiums were provided, as well as family allowances, under the collective agreements relating to persons employed in credit, insurance, and kindred enterprises. Up to the end of 1937 there were 1,636 marriage premiums at a total cost of 1·636 million lire, and 2,828 birth premiums at a total cost of 1·148 million lire (*Le A.S.*, 1, 1938, p. 45). By the end of Sept. 1938 these totals had risen to 2,884 marriage premiums, costing 2·884 million lire, and 5,701 birth premiums, costing 2·327 million lire (*Le A.S.*, 5, 1938, p. 515). (256)

(*p*) Kuczynski, R. R., *The Balance of Births and Deaths*, vol. ii, p. 59, gives a net reproduction rate of 'about 1·4' for 1921–2, basing his calculations on an estimated fertility distribution (ibid., p. 149) published by Gini, C., and de Finetti, B., in 'Calcoli sullo sviluppo futuro della popolazione italiana', *Annali di Statistica*, serie vi, vol. x, Rome, 1931, p. 31. The present writer derives his estimated rates from the specific fertility rates of other countries. The life table used was constructed according to the method described in the Appendix to the present study. Note, however, that it is difficult to know what corrections to make to the 1921 census data. The census enumerated a population (*popolazione presente*—used whenever this was separately specified at the census) of 38·711 millions on 1 Dec. 1921, but the *Annuario Statistico Italiano, 1938*, p. 9, gives the *popolazione presente* on 31 Dec. 1921 as 38·023 millions, and Gini and de Finetti, op. cit., p. 61, begin their estimates with a population of 38·944 millions for the end of 1921. For the construction of the estimated reproduction rate for 1921–2 the census population was used without any correction (*Censimento della Popolazione del Regno d'Italia al 1° Dicembre 1921*, vol. xix, p. 101*). (260)

(*q*) Mortality changed a good deal during the period—the expectation of life at birth for females was 35·65 years in 1881–2, 47·33 years in 1910–12, and 50·75 years in 1921–2 (Gini, C., and Galvani, L., 'Tavole di mortalità della popolazione italiana', *Annali di Statistica*, serie vi, vol. viii, Rome, 1931, pp. 394, 382, and 326)—but the gross reproduction rate was fairly steady, the estimated rates being: 1881–2, 2·476; 1900–1, 2·368; 1910–12, 2·273; 1921–2, 1·861. The period used for the calculation is two years when the census was taken at or near the beginning or end of the year, and three years when it was taken near the middle of the year (1881, 31 Dec.; 1911, 10 June; 1921, 1 Dec.; 1931, 21 Apr.; 1936, 21 Apr. For 1901 the population for 1 Jan. was used—taken from Gini and Galvani). Abridged life tables were constructed for each period in order to achieve consistency in the method of computation and to obtain data relating to the actual territory to which each specific census applied. But the results they give differ very little from those obtained by using published life tables for Italy—e.g. Gini and Galvani, op. cit. (life tables from 1881–2 to 1921–2); Galvani, L., 'Tavole di mortalità della popolazione italiana 1930–32', in *VII Censimento Generale della Popolazione, 21 Aprile 1931–IX*, vol. iv, part i, pp. 185*–99*; Galvani, L., 'Tavole di mortalità della popolazione italiana 1930–32', *Annali di Statistica*, serie vii, vol. i, Rome, 1937, pp. 1–156. (260)

(r) The nuptiality tables have been constructed from the formula $(P_x + 2\frac{1}{2}d_x - 2\frac{1}{2}m_x)/(P_x + 2\frac{1}{2}d_x + 2\frac{1}{2}m_x)$—the subscript x referring to the specific five-year group—for five-year age groups, with appropriate modifications for 1930–2 and 1935–7 when the younger ages were treated in the groups of 15–20 and 21–4 years, as given in the published returns of marriages. For 1910–12 interpolation was necessary for distributing spinster deaths in the same age groups as those for which marriage data were given. These nuptiality tables were computed because the published Italian tables either indicate net nuptiality or completely exclude deaths from gross nuptiality computations. But the gross nuptiality table for 1930–2 computed by Somogyi (excluding deaths from the computation) gives a probability of marriage for spinsters by their fiftieth birthday of 0·810, not significantly different from the result given above. Somogyi also gives a probability of 0·892 for 1899–1902. See Somogyi, S., 'Tavole di nuzialità e di vedovanza per la popolazione italiana 1930–1932', *Annali di Statistica*, serie vii, vol. i, pp. 195–292, at p. 268. (The volume also contains Medani, P., 'Tavole di nuzialità italiane per celibi e nubili 1930–1932', pp. 293–316.) For other recent studies relating to Italy see the following articles in the *Giornale degli Economisti e Rivista di Statistica*: Medani, P., 'Tavole di nuzialità per la popolazione italiana', Oct. 1936, pp. 695–701; Hirschmann, O. A., 'Nota su due recenti tavole di nuzialità della popolazione italiana', Jan. 1938, pp. 40–7; Parenti, G., 'Ancora su due recenti tavole di nuzialità della popolazione italiana', July 1938, pp. 570–8. (264)

(s) Lenti, L., 'Osservazioni sulle tavole di fecondità', *Giornale degli Economisti e Annali di Economia* Jan.-Feb. 1939, pp. 28–50, uses rather more detail and obtains, p. 42, a net reproduction rate of 1·22373 for 1930–2, and, p. 50, an r of +6·605 per 1,000. This is the only Italian study known to the present writer, which specifically analyses the fertility of Italy in terms of the net reproduction rate and the true rate of natural increase. (See also same author, 'Considerazione sulle tavole di fecondità femminile', in *Atti della III Riunione della Società Italiana di Demografia e Statistica*, Florence, 1939, pp. 136–54.) Mortara, G., has an analysis of replacement trends—though not by means of net reproduction rates—in 'La capacità di riproduzione della popolazione italiana', *Giornale degli Economisti e Rivista di Statistica*, Apr. 1935, pp. 338–40. This journal contains a considerable number of studies of Italian demographic trends, by Mortara, Baffi, P., Bachi, R., Marchiori, A., and others. See also Vergottini, M. de, 'Die Bevölkerungspolitik des Faschismus und ihre Grundlagen', *Archiv für Bevölkerungswissenschaft und Bevölkerungspolitik*, 1938, part v, pp. 289–315, and same author, 'Développement de la population italienne de 1931 à 1936', *Journal de la Société Hongroise de Statistique*, 1938, nos. 2–3, pp. 193–212. (265)

CHAPTER VI

(a) The article noted that, as evidence of the current interest in the question, even *Simplizissimus* had devoted a special number to it—though adding that *Simplizissimus* 'sich nicht scheute, seinen schalen Witz auch hier zu versuchen'. .. For further pre-War discussions see Roesle, E., *Der Geburtenrückgang: seine Literatur und die Methodik seiner Ausmaßbestimmung*, Leipzig,

1914; Brentano, L., *Die Malthussche Lehre und die Bevölkerungsbewegung der letzten Dezennien*, Munich, 1909; Bornträger, J., *Der Geburtenrückgang in Deutschland*, Würzburg, 1913; Wolf, J., *Der Geburtenrückgang*, Jena, 1912; Theilhaber, F. A., *Das sterile Berlin*, Berlin, 1913. For an analysis of the influence of birth control and abortion, by a supporter of birth control, see Hirsch, M., *Fruchtabtreibung und Präventivverkehr in Zusammenhang mit dem Geburtenrückgang*, Würzburg, 1914. Hirsch was not in favour of abortion as a method of family limitation, but believed that repressive action would not prevent abortion from being practised, but that it would merely drive women into the arms of quacks. (272)

(*b*) Para. 363 of the *RVO*. The point of view of the funds was that during the economic crisis many women resorted to abortion to prevent births from taking place, so that the funds became overburdened with post-abortive medical attention. Also, infant mortality was apparently very high in the large families and thus meant a good deal of unproductive expenditure. See Durand-Wever, A.-M., 'Umfang und Ursachen der Geburtenbeschränkung', Part II, *Die medizinische Welt*, 28 Feb. 1931, pp. 315–17. Dr. Durand-Wever said that on the basis of her personal experience she believed that in Berlin at least 80 per cent. of the upper-class persons practised some form of birth control, and that an unwanted child was rarely conceived and rarely born. In her private practice she had come across only five families not practising birth control and these—with one exception—were cases in which children were wanted. In the one exception occasional abstinence was practised. (277)

(*c*) e.g. Hitze, op. cit., p. 20, cites Olshausen as saying that 80 per cent., and Lindemann-Halle as saying that 96 per cent., of all miscarriages are induced. Liepmann, W., 'Arzt und § 218', *Medizinische Klinik*, 17 Jan. 1930, pp. 77–9, places the proportion at 99 per cent. as compared with the 89 per cent. estimated by Schäfer and with Olshausen's 80 per cent. Ploetz, A., 'Zum Zahlenverhältnis von Geburten und Fehlgeburten', *Archiv für Rassen- und Gesellschaftsbiologie*, 2, 1936, pp. 181–2, cites Professor Eymer, of the Munich University Clinic for Women, as saying that at least 90 per cent. of all abortions are likely to be criminally induced. Dr. Rambke (Landgerichtsdirektor in Berlin), 'Der Kampf des Staates gegen die bevölkerungspolitische Gefahr der Abtreibung', *Monatsblätter für Gerichtshilfe, Gefangenen- und Entlassenenfürsorge*, Apr.-May 1936, pp. 133–7, says that according to general expert medical opinion about 75 to 90 per cent. of all abortions are induced. (278)

(*d*) It is much more difficult to obtain for Germany than it was for Italy official statements concerning the specific objects of the population policy. *Mein Kampf* is by no means clear on the subject—except as regards racial policy—and Hitler himself wrote of the 'terrific (*rasend*) rate of growth of the German population in the pre-War period', and of the consequent importance of the question of supplying daily needs (*Mein Kampf*, 129–130th ed., Munich, 1935, p. 255). Among official writers some, like Burgdörfer, seem to be concerned mainly with guaranteeing the adequate replacement of the population. Others, however, appear to aim at a very much larger population than that currently living in Germany—e.g. Dr. Braschwitz, 'Die Abtreibung und ihre Bekämpfung', *Fortschritte der Medizin*, 11 Feb. 1935, speaks of the need for an annual supply of 2 million births to secure the position of the German people. This would mean—assuming the mortality of 1932–4—an ultimate stationary population of about 122·6 millions. Other writers go still further—e.g. Danzer, P., *Geburtenkrieg*, 2nd ed., Munich-Berlin, 1937, pp. 24–5, says, in discussing the objects of a population policy, that this can only be a return to 'natural fertility' ('das Ziel kann nur die Rückkehr zur naturgegebenen Fruchtbarkeit sein, ohne Einschränkungen und Vorbehalte'). and refers (p. 34) to birth control as an utter fraud existing only in overwrought brains ('. . . "Geburtenregelung" ist ein plumper Schwindel, den es nur in überspannten Gehirnen gibt'). That military considerations play a part in conditioning the attitude can be seen from a study by Burgdörfer, F., *Volks- und Wehrkraft, Krieg und Rasse*, Berlin, 1936, which estimates the future man-power of various countries, but nevertheless emphasizes the fact that war and racial hygiene are completely inimical, that racial hygiene can only be carried out if there is peace. A brief but very illuminating comment on the *Lebensraum* argument in relation to population policy is given in Kuczynski, R. R., '*Living-Space' and Population Problems* (Oxford Pamphlet, No. 8), Oxford, 1939. (282)

(*e*) Under the *Gesetz zur Verhütung erbkranken Nachwuchses*, of 14 July 1933, as amended by the Act of 26 June 1935 (*RGB*, 1, 1935, p. 773), if the court decides to sterilize a woman who is pregnant when the operation is to be performed, the pregnancy may be interrupted with the consent of the woman, unless the foetus is already capable of living, or if the abortion would seriously endanger the life or health of the woman. Sterilization or abortion not performed in accordance with this law is legally permissible only when undertaken by a doctor for the purpose of saving the life or health of the woman, and with her consent. The law therefore not only provides for abortion on eugenic grounds but also explicitly recognizes therapeutic abortion. But the earlier law also allowed abortion for saving the life of the mother, though this was not stated explicitly. Drage, G., op. cit., p. 146, says of the abortion clause of the Imperial Code, that for the crime of abortion to have been committed, there must have been unlawful and intentional abortion—that is, not to save the mother's life. (283)

(*f*) The figures of prosecutions for criminal abortion are given under three headings: (*a*) simple abortion or killing of the foetus; (*b*) abortion or killing of the foetus or assistance therein, with a view to profit; (*c*) abortion, &c., without the consent of the pregnant woman. For (*a*) the numbers of persons accused in the years 1932 to 1937 inclusive are 4,510, 4,104, 4,669, 2,541, 3,517 and 5,741, and the numbers of persons receiving sentences are 4,023, 3,615, 4,146, 2,280, 3,109, and 5,118. Under (*b*) the two sets of figures are first, 201, 192, 396, 488, 442, 618, and, secondly, 190, 184, 344, 437, 387, and 555. There are very few cases under (*c*) and they show no consistent trend. (From information received from the Ministry of Justice. According to these figures the increase between 1936 and 1937 in the number of persons accused is not as much as 70 per cent.) (286)

(*g*) 'Die Bauernsiedlung im Jahre 1938', *Wirtschaft und Statistik*, 1939, pp. 414–17. See also Schottky, I., 'Die neuen bevölkerungspolitisch wichtigen Bestimmungen für das Bauerntum', *A.f.B.*, 1, 1936, pp. 47–51; and *Soziale*

Praxis, 1938, no. 12, cols. 757–60, and no. 16, cols. 978–9. Typical official expressions of the present German attitude towards the peasantry can be found in Rechenbach, H., 'Die bevölkerungspolitische Bedeutung und Aufgabe des Bauerntums im deutschen Volke'; and Schultz, B. K., 'Rassenhygienische Gesichtspunkte bei der Neubildung deutschen Bauerntums'; both in Harmsen, H., and Lohse, F., *Bevölkerungsfragen*, Munich, 1936, pp. 814–19 and pp. 822–7. But neither under the Weimar Republic nor—so far—under the National Socialist régime were governments prepared to antagonize the large landowners by making really extensive systems of peasant holdings. (298)

(*h*) See 'Anordnung über die Verteilung von Arbeitskräften, vom 28. August 1934', *A.f.B.*, 5, 1933–4, pp. 333–8. (Notice that certain classes of persons under 25 years of age were exempt from this regulation—including those who had spent at least a year in voluntary labour service, as well as a large number of members of various sections of the National Socialist party.) Comparable aims were the basis of the measures introduced 'voluntarily' by various firms—e.g. the Reemtsma cigarette company gave 600 marks to every woman who had been employed by them for at least one year and who married by the end of 1933. Men were to be substituted for these women. The firm of Brinkmann gave 500 marks and allowed the women to be replaced by their husbands if the latter were unemployed. Note, however, that this was followed, in Sept. 1933, by a 2 per cent. reduction in wages. See Harmsen, H., 'Bevölkerungspolitische Maßnahmen in der Zigarettenindustrie', *A.f.B.*, 1, 1933–4, pp. 45–7. (302)

(*i*) These probabilities have been calculated directly from the age-specific marriage-rates for spinsters, given in *Statistisches Jahrbuch für das Deutsche Reich, 1935*, p. 40, and *1938*, p. 45. The formula used is $(1{,}000-\frac{1}{2}m)/(1{,}000+\frac{1}{2}m)$ where m is the marriage-rate, the appropriate adjustment being made for the five-year computation necessary for the age groups 40–4 and 45–9 years. Since the original marriage-rates had only one decimal, and since it was not possible to take spinster deaths into account in estimating the basic populations, the resultant marriage probabilities cannot be fully accurate. But a more accurate calculation, based on the 1933 census, taking deaths into account and worked throughout by single years of age gave the probability as 885 for 1933. So the approximate versions cannot be significantly far from the truth. Similar calculations give a marriage probability of 860 out of 1,000 in 1930 and 831 in 1931. (305)

(*j*) Burgdörfer, F., *Bevölkerungsentwicklung im Dritten Reich*, pp. 26–7, and *Wirtschaft und Statistik*, 1934, p. 766. There were actually 1,587,648 marriages in 1930–2 and, assuming a normal 600,000 per year, this would show a deficit of about 212,000 marriages only. Presumably, however, the normal number was nearer 640,000. The full explanation is given in *Statistik des Deutschen Reichs*, vol. 495, part i, pp. 1–27. The 1910–11 marriage probabilities were used only in relation to men aged 24 to under 33 years, and showed a deficit of about 198,000 marriages. But bearing in mind the general trend in post-War years, there were also too few marriages of men in the age groups below and above the central group of 24 to 32 years. The explanation concludes that in fact the marriage deficiency up to the beginning of 1933 was not 200,000 but much more probably about 300,000. (307)

(*k*) The influence of loans and of stricter enforcement of the abortion law may persuade unmarried women to marry when they become pregnant, rather than to resort to abortion. It may be noticed that in the first eight months after the introduction of the loans—from August 1933 to the end of March 1934—43,108 cancellations were given on the birth of children (*Statistisches Jahrbuch für das Deutsche Reich, 1938*, p. 48) and many of these births might have been aborted if the loans and cancellations had not been available. Some of them were probably conceived before marriage, but we cannot state the proportion, for there are no published statistics relating to the number of couples already married when they applied for loans in 1933. It may also be noticed that there was a slight fall in the number of illegitimate births in Germany after 1933, and that whereas illegitimate births (including still-births) formed 10·7 per cent. of all births (including still-births) in 1933 the proportion had fallen to 7·8 per cent. by 1936 (ibid., p. 39). (309)

(*l*) Some writers have drawn attention to the fact that marriages contracted with the aid of loans have been more fertile than those not so aided. Thus Burgdörfer, *Völker am Abgrund*, pp. 37–8, notes that in 1933–5 inclusive there were 520,455 marriages helped by loans and 1,485,334 which did not receive loans, and that while the former yielded 159,370 births (including still births) in 1935, or 306 births per 1,000 marriages, the latter yielded only 327,195 births, or 220 per 1,000 marriages. (Similar analyses for various parts of Germany are given in *Aus Hamburgs Verwaltung und Wirtschaft*, 1936, no. 1, pp. 5–6; *Soziale Praxis*, 1937, no. 14, cols. 405–8 and 1939, no. 9, cols. 565–6). This is, however, to be expected since, as Burgdörfer admits, the persons receiving marriage loans are not a random sample of the marrying population, are drawn mainly from the working and lower-middle classes, and would naturally exhibit a somewhat higher fertility than the rest. Their age composition may also be different and many of the women may already be pregnant when application is made for a marriage loan. (309)

(*m*) The German Statistical Office recently produced two new sets of estimates of the future population. The second is of theoretical interest only. The first assumes the mortality of 1932–4, except for infant mortality, where a fall to 40 per 1,000 is postulated. The fertility assumption is based upon the data of 1936, but it is postulated that the probability of marriage will rise to such an extent that the birth deficit, stated to be 9·6 per cent. in 1936, will eventually be only 7·5 per cent. These hypotheses apply to Germany proper, but it is also assumed that in Austria there will be the same fertility development as in Germany, and that the German life table will soon apply to Austria too. Migration is excluded. On these assumptions the total population of Germany and Austria will continue to grow, reaching 80·535 millions by 1970, and then fall, sinking to 77·031 millions by 2000. See *Wirtschaft und Statistik*, 1938, pp. 971–6. (313)

CHAPTER VII

(*a*) The rates for 1906–10 and 1926–30 are from Kuczynski, R. R., *The Measurement*, &c., pp. 122–3 and 212–13. The rest have been calculated from the basic data provided in the Norwegian *Folkemengdens Bevegelse*, the Swedish

Befolkningsrörelsen, and the Danish *Befolkningens Bevægelser* for the relevant years. There are occasionally differences, in the third place of decimals, between the gross reproduction rates given here and those given in the official publications cited. This is presumably due to differences in the number of decimals used in the computations. The differences in the net reproduction rates are, however, due to the fact that official publications often use inappropriate life tables—e.g. a life table for 1921–30 used for calculating the net reproduction rate for 1934. For the rates above, separate life tables were constructed for each year. The writer is indebted to Dr. Einar Cohn, of the Danish Statistical Office, for a number of unpublished mid-year estimates of the population by age and sex. (314)

(*b*) Myrdal, G., and Wicksell, S. D., 'Utsikterna i fråga om den framtida befolkningsutvecklingen i Sverige och de ekonomiska verkningarna av olika alternativt möjliga befolkningsutvecklingar', *Betänkande i Sexualfrågan*, Stockholm, 1936, pp. 252–95. A more thorough discussion of the bases of these estimates will be found in Wicksell, S. D., and Quensel, C. E., 'Prognoser över Sveriges folkmängd under de närmaste årtiondena', *Betänkande med vissa Demografiska Utredningar*, Stockholm, 1938, pp. 133–65, which gives the results of four sets of assumptions. The first extrapolates the decline of fertility in recent years, though at a decreasing rate. The second assumes the same marital and illegitimate fertility as in 1933 with nuptiality at the level of 1901–10. The third assumes the same conditions of fertility as in the second estimate, but with nuptiality 25 per cent. higher than in 1901–10. The fourth assumes a nuptiality 50 per cent. higher than in 1901–10, the marital fertility of 1933, and a regular decline in illegitimate fertility until, from 1956 onwards, it is 50 per cent. below the level of 1933. Migration is excluded, and all the estimates assume the mortality of 1933. The results all show a continued increase in population for a time, and then a fall. From 6·249 millions at the end of 1935, it falls to 4·398 millions by the end of 1985 according to the first estimate; to 5·413 according to the second; to 5·812 according to the third; and to 5·929 millions according to the fourth (op. cit., (pp. 146–51). (316)

(*c*) *Lov om Foranstaltninger i Anledning af Svangerskab m.m.*, 18 May 1937. A complete translation is given in the *Eugenics Review*, Apr. 1938, pp. 43–6. For infractions of the law the following penalties were prescribed: (*a*) A woman who has an abortion, performed by herself or by someone else who is not an authorized doctor, to be sentenced—even if there are legitimate grounds for the abortion—to not more than 3 months' imprisonment though this may be dispensed with in particularly extenuating circumstances. (*b*) In cases of illegal abortions or attempted abortions, the man responsible for the pregnancy may be sentenced to not more than 1 year's imprisonment if it is proved that he refused to grant the woman reasonable personal or economic assistance, in spite of her request for it, and that this refusal was a decisive reason for the abortion or attempted abortion. (*c*) An authorized doctor who procures or helps to procure an illegal abortion shall be sentenced to not more than 2 years' imprisonment or, in aggravating circumstances, to not more than 4 years' imprisonment (minor infractions of the law receive much lighter penalties). (*d*) An unauthorized person may, in the cases falling under (*c*) be imprisoned for 4 or 8 years as maximum sentences. Repeated offences shall be punished by imprisonment for 2 to 12 years. (*e*) If abortion is procured without the woman's consent, the penalty is imprisonment for 2 to 12 years. (*f*) Anyone illegally coercing or using threats or promises of reward to induce a woman to have an abortion, shall be punished, even if the abortion is performed under the prescribed conditions, to imprisonment for not more than 2 years, or for not more than 4 years if the abortion is performed by someone who is not an authorized doctor. Infractions of the law will be tried without jury. (323)

(*d*) The Penal Code, modified by the Act of 30 June 1921, prescribed the following penalties: (*a*) Imprisonment for a woman having an abortion or killing the foetus; if the attempt is unsuccessful, imprisonment for not more than 6 months, or a fine. (*b*) Anyone helping to procure the abortion shall receive imprisonment for not less than 6 months, or hard labour for 6 months to 2 years. The maximum term of imprisonment is reduced to 1 year if the attempt is unsuccessful, and is increased, if abortion is procured for gain or habitually, to hard labour for 1 to 6 years (not more than 1 year if the attempt fails). (*c*) If the woman has not given her consent, the penalty shall be hard labour for 6 months to 2 years if the attempt fails; for 6 months to 10 years if abortion results; for 10 years or life if the woman is severely injured by the abortion, and for life if she dies. Therapeutic abortion was allowed, as in Denmark, though not expressly provided for. (325)

(*e*) In 1932–4 the combined ex-nuptial and nuptial net reproduction rate for Sweden was 0·759 and the net reproduction rate of women who had married at least once by their fiftieth birthday was 0·824. Assuming that during their unmarried life these women bore illegitimate children at the same rate as the women who did not marry by their fiftieth birthday and that 5 per cent. of the illegitimate births are borne by married women, the nuptial net reproduction rate would be 0·914. This would be the highest resultant net reproduction rate with universal marriage, assuming that, apart from the increase in marriage, other things remained unchanged. But there might be a considerable fall in the age at marriage and an increase in marital fertility. On the other hand, there may be more involuntary sterility among the unmarried than among the married. There will certainly be more physical infirmity among the unmarried and life tables for unmarried persons show a lower expectation of life than for the married. This is probably due largely to the selective character of marriage. Extremely interesting studies of marital fertility in Sweden are given by Wicksell, S. D., 'Fruktsamhet och förökning', *Hygienisk Revy*, 1936, and Wicksell, S. D., and Quensel, C. E., 'Den äktenskapliga fruktsamheten i Sverige efter hustruns ålder och äktenskapets varaktighetstid', *Betänkande med vissa Demografiska Utredningar*, pp. 9–47. (331)

CHAPTER VIII

(*a*) Derrick, V. P. A., 'Observations on (1) errors of age in the population statistics of England and Wales, and (2) the changes in mortality indicated by the national records' (*Journal of the Institute of Actuaries*, July 1927). See also Kermack, W. O., McKendrick, A. G., and McKinlay, P. L., 'Death rates in Great Britain and Sweden. Some general regularities and their significance' (*Lancet*, 31 March 1934); Kermack, W. O., McKendrick, A. G., and McKinlay, P. L., 'Death rates in Great Britain and Sweden: Expression of specific mortality rates as products of two factors, and some consequences thereof' (*Journal of Hygiene*, Dec. 1934); Cramér, H., and Wold, H., 'Mortality variations in Sweden. A study in graduation and forecasting' (*Skandinavisk Aktuarietidskrift*, 1935); and Greenwood, Major, 'English death rates, past, present and future' (*Journal of the Royal Statistical Society*, Part IV, 1936).

(347)

(*b*) These estimates were constructed by five-year age groups, the life-table method being used. That is, the population aged 10–14 years in 1940 bears the same ratio to the population aged 5–9 years in 1935 as the life-table population in the 10–14 years age group bears to that in the age group 5–9 years. Births were calculated by applying the chosen specific fertility rates to the average numbers of women in each of the seven five-year age groups of the reproductive period in each quinquennium. They were then allocated by sex, assuming the sex-ratio of 1935 to apply constantly, and the population aged 0–4 years was obtained by multiplying the births by the ratio of the life-table population under 5 years to the radix of the life table. These calculations therefore assume that the age structure within each five-year group is the same as in the life table, and this is incorrect. But the error involved is extremely small—see, for example, the tests made by Dr. Charles in *London and Cambridge Economic Service*, Special Memorandum No. 40, Aug. 1935, p. 5.

(355)

(*c*) The possible consequences of a declining population are given an extremely brief treatment in the present study, and readers are advised to refer to: Adams, W., *A Financial Officer's Concern in the Probable Decline of the Population*, London, 1939 (Institute of Municipal Treasurers and Accountants); Baker, O. E., 'Significance of population trends to American agriculture', *Milbank Memorial Fund Quarterly*, April 1937, pp. 121–34; Creeft, F. de, op. cit.; Glass, D. V., 'The falling birth-rate and its effects on secondary schools', *Review of Headmasters' Association*, April 1938; Harrod, R. F., 'Modern population trends', *The Manchester School*, i, 1939, pp. 1–20; Jewkes, J., 'The population scare', same journal, ii, 1939, pp. 101–21; Keynes, J. M., 'Some economic consequences of a declining population', *Eugenics Review*, April 1937, pp. 13–17; Kuczynski, R. R., 'Economic causes and consequences of population movements', *Index*, Nov. 1936, pp. 223–33; Lorimer, F., 'The significance of imminent population changes in the United States', *Milbank M. F. Quart.*, July 1937, pp. 207–18; Reddaway, W. B., *The Economics of a Declining Population*, London, 1939 (the most thorough analysis so far published); Robbins, L., 'Notes on some probable consequences of the advent of a stationary population in Great Britain', *Economica*, April 1929, pp. 71–82; Spengler, J. J., *France Faces Depopulation*, ch. xi; idem, 'Population movements, employment, and income', *Southern Economic Journal*, Oct. 1938, pp. 129–57; Wilson, N., *Expected Population Changes and Their Effect Upon Social Services*, London, 1935. See also Lösch, A., *Bevölkerungswellen und Wechsellagen*, Jena, 1936, for a theory of the relation between population waves and economic waves. These references cover a considerable variety of opinions and methods of approach to the problem. (361)

(*d*) Note that, in fact, these analyses assume that ultimately mortality also becomes stationary. Fluctuations in mortality, once fertility had become constant, would naturally produce variations—however slight—in the net reproduction rate and/or in the size of the stationary population deriving from a given annual supply of births. It should be remembered that, with a given mortality schedule and a given age distribution of fertility, maintaining a net reproduction rate of unity ultimately equates—though not necessarily at the same total population—with maintaining a constant annual supply of births. The precise size of the stationary population depends upon the size of that constant supply, while the existence of the stationary population depends upon maintaining the requisite number of births per woman passing through the child-bearing age groups. (363)

(*e*) The eugenic problem—the influence of differential decline of groups within a population—has not been considered since the same problem might exist in a growing population. There is also the question of the closing up of the differential. A recent study of differential fertility (Karpinos, B. D., and Kiser, C. V., 'The differential fertility and potential rates of growth of various income and educational classes of urban populations in the United States', *Milbank Mem. Fnd. Quart.*, Oct. 1939, pp. 367–91) which is distinguished because, among other reasons, it makes use of gross and net reproduction rates for various income and educational classes, emphasizes the existing disparity in reproductive levels between such classes. In the urban populations investigation found a range in gross reproduction rates from 0·42 where the annual family income was $3,000 and over to 1·15 for the population on relief, having annual family incomes below $1,000. But that disparity does not contradict the view that differentials are narrowing, since the investigation related only to 1935–6. The present writer also found a marked disparity between the London boroughs in 1930–2—see Chapter I, Table 8—but also some evidence that the differentials had been significantly greater in 1911–12—see Table 9. It is also interesting to note three Italian studies which are far less pessimistic on the subject of the relation between fertility and intelligence than many British studies. See Gini, C., 'Di alcune recenti ricerche sulle variazioni che presenterebbero taluni caratteri secondo il numero dei figli della famiglia', *Genus*, May 1938, pp. 1–30; Boldrini, M., 'La fertilità degli individui deficienti e difettosi', and Uggè, A., 'Effetti sulla popolazione di un paese del diverso accrescimento delle sue classi', both in *Contributi del Laboratorio di Statistica* (Pubblicazioni dell' Università Cattolica del S. Cuore), Milan, 1939. (364)

APPENDIX

(*a*) For an analysis of the construction and application of life tables, see among others: Kuczynski, R. R., *The Measurement of Population Growth*; idem, 'The analysis of vital statistics: II. Birth and death statistics', *Economica*, Aug. 1938; Dublin, L. I., and Lotka, A. J., *Length of Life* (New York, 1936);

Wolfenden, H. H., et al., *Population Statistics and their Compilation* (New York, 1925); and Elston, J. S., et al., *Sources and Characteristics of the Principal Mortality Tables* (2nd ed., New York, 1932). An interesting account of life-table construction has also been given by Hayward, T. E., in 'On life tables: their construction and practical application' (*Journal of the Royal Statistical Society*, Sept. 1899). A brief but extremely able survey of the more complex questions of life-table construction is given in Linder, A., *Methoden zur Berechnung von Volkssterbetafeln*, Berne, 1934. Finally, almost every official life table has an introduction outlining the methods used in constructing the particular table. (383)

(*b*) See Burgdörfer, F., *Der Geburtenrückgang und seine Bekämpfung* (Berlin, 1929), and *Aufbau und Bewegung der Bevölkerung* (Leipzig, 1935), pp. 134–43. References to this method will also be found in 'Bewegung der Bevölkerung in den Jahren 1925 bis 1927' (*Statistik des Deutschen Reichs*, vol. 360, Berlin, 1930), pp. 48–57. Dr. Burgdörfer occasionally makes an allowance for the excess of females over males in the reproductive age groups, in order to eliminate the effects of the Great War. This allowance results in a higher substitute reproduction rate. In practice Dr. Burgdörfer uses a more indirect method. He begins with the true death-rate derived from the life table, and then calculates the birth-rate on the basis of the existing general fertility rate related to the stationary population. Subtracting the true death-rate from the adjusted birth-rate gives him a 'refined' rate of natural increase. Using Australia, 1932–4, as an illustration, the calculation would take the following form: There was an annual average of 110,559 live births in the period, and since there were 1,747,763 women aged 15 to 49 years in 1933, the general fertility rate was 63·26 per 1,000 potentially fertile women. Since the stationary population of the same total size as that of Australia in 1933 would contain only 1,560,465 women aged 15 to 49 years, these women would have 98,715 live births according to the general fertility rate of 1932–4, which would mean a birth-rate of 14·89 per 1,000 total population, instead of the crude birth-rate of 16·68 per 1,000 in 1932–4. But the true death rate according to the life table was 15·34 per 1,000, so the 'refined' rate of natural increase would be −0·45 per 1,000. The crude birth- and-death rates were 16·68 and 8·95 respectively, so the crude rate of natural increase would be +7·73 per 1,000. Unfortunately this more indirect method has no precise meaning. The true rate of natural increase is obtained only by using the methods of analysis described in section 5 of the present Appendix. (395)

(*c*) This should perhaps be somewhat higher. Taking mortality (from birth) and nuptiality together, there were 166·75 unmarried survivors at age 50, and these lived 5,836·25 years in the child-bearing period. Since the total number of years lived in the unmarried state was 14,766·675, women who eventually married must have lived 8,930·425 years in the single state. If we assume that the fertility of these women when in the single state was as high as that of the women who did not marry by the age of 50, we may estimate that the women who afterwards married bore 60·48 per cent. of the illegitimate children, or 65 of them. In this case the nuptial net reproduction rate would be approximately $\frac{0{\cdot}651+0{\cdot}065}{0{\cdot}78959}$, or 0·907. If we assume that 5 per cent. of the illegitimate children were actually born to married women, the nuptial net reproduction rate would be raised to 0·914. This would represent the maximum general net reproduction rate which could obtain if, with the fertility of 1932–4, there were universal marriage, and is almost certainly an over-estimate, since there is no reason to suppose that women who do not marry are physiologically as fertile as those who do. (405)

(*d*) For a detailed discussion of the true rate of natural increase and its derivatives, the reader should consult the following papers by Dr. A. J. Lotka: 'Relation between birth rates and death rates', *Science*, 5 July 1907; 'A natural population norm', *Journal of the Washington Academy of Sciences*, 4 May and 19 May 1913; 'The stability of the normal age distribution', *Proceedings of the National Academy of Sciences*, Nov. 1922; 'The progressive adjustment of age distribution to fecundity', *Journal of the Washington Academy of Sciences*, 18 Nov. 1926; 'The spread of generations', *Human Biology*, 1929, vol. i; 'Modern trends in the birth rate', *Annals of the Am. Acad. Pol. and Soc. Sc.*, Nov. 1936; (with Sharpe, F. R.), 'A problem in age-distribution', *Philosophical Magazine*, April 1911; (with Dublin, L. I.), 'On the true rate of natural increase as exemplified by the population of the United States, 1920', *Journal of the American Statistical Association*, Sept. 1925; (with Dublin, L. I.), 'The true rate of natural increase of the population of the United States', *Metron*, June 1930. See also Wicksell, S. D., 'Nuptiality, fertility and reproductivity', *Skandinavisk Aktuarietidskrift*, 1931; Rich, C. D., 'The measurement of the rate of population growth', *Journal of the Institute of Actuaries*, 1924, Part I; Fisher, R. A., *The Genetical Theory of Natural Selection*, Oxford, 1930, pp. 22–30; von Bortkiewicz, L., 'Die Sterbeziffer und der Frauenüberschuß in der stationären und in der progressiven Bevölkerung', *Bulletin de l'Institut International de Statistique*, vol. xix, 1911, 1ère livraison; Karpinos, B. D., 'A stationary population (a study of Iowa population)', *Human Biology*, Dec. 1935; Linder, A., 'Die Vermehrungsrate der stabilen Bevölkerung', *Archiv für mathematische Wirtschafts- und Sozialforschung*, 1938, Part 2; Kuczynski, R. R., *Fertility and Reproduction*, already cited. A very thorough account of the mathematical analysis of population trends will be given in a forthcoming study by Dr. E. C. Rhodes, appearing in the *Journal of the Royal Statistical Society*. (415)

SELECTED LIST OF ARTICLES AND BOOKS

CONTAINING ESTIMATES OF FUTURE POPULATIONS OR DISCUSSIONS OF SUCH ESTIMATES

1. AUSTRALIA. 'The Australian Population: Growth or Decline?' *Circular of the Bank of New South Wales*, 10 Feb. 1936, pp. 1–9.
2. BAUDHUIN, F. 'L'avenir de la population belge.' *Bulletin d'Information de la Banque Nationale de Belgique*, 10 June 1931, pp. 361–7.
3. —— 'L'avenir de la population belge.' *Problems of Population*, London, 1932, pp. 240–55.
4. BONZ and HILBURG. 'Die voraussichtliche Bevölkerungsentwicklung in Deutschland.' *Zeitschrift für angewandte Mathematik und Mechanik*, 1931.
5. BOWLEY, A. L. 'Births and population in Great Britain.' *Economic Journal*, June 1924, pp. 188–92.
6. —— *Estimates of the Working Population of Certain Countries in 1931 and 1941*. (League of Nations, Economic and Financial Section, Geneva, 1926.) [The countries are Great Britain, Sweden, Denmark, Belgium, Germany, France, Switzerland, Italy, United States of America, Australia, and Japan.]
7. BUNLE, H. 'Les prévisions démographiques.' *Journal de la Société de Statistique de Paris*, Nov. 1932, pp. 423–4.
8. BURGDÖRFER, F. 'Die Dynamik der künftigen Bevölkerungsentwicklung im Deutschen Reich.' *Allgemeines statistisches Archiv*, 1932, pp. 161–79.
9. —— 'Zur Frage der bereinigten Lebensbilanz und der Vorausberechnungen über die Bevölkerungsentwicklung.' *Allgemeines statistisches Archiv*, 1935, pp. 155–66.
10. —— *Volk ohne Jugend*. 1st ed. Berlin-Grunewald, 1932, and subsequent editions.
11. CANNAN, E. 'The probability of a cessation of the growth of population in England and Wales during the next century.' *Economic Journal*, Dec. 1895, pp. 505–15.
12. CHARLES, E. 'The effect of present trends in fertility and mortality upon the future population of England and Wales and upon its age composition.' *London and Cambridge Economic Service*. Special Memorandum no. 40, 1935.
13. —— 'The effect of present trends in fertility and mortality upon the future population of Scotland and upon its age composition.' *Proceedings of the Royal Society of Edinburgh*, vol. lvi, part i, 1935–6, pp. 6–12.
14. CRAMÉR, H. Estimates for Sweden in *Besparingskommittén och pensionsförsäkringen*, Stockholm, 1925.
15. —— 'Über die Vorausberechnung der Bevölkerungsentwicklung in Schweden.' *Skandinavisk Aktuarietidskrift*, 1935, Häft 1–2, pp. 35–54.
16. CREEFT, F. DE. *Étude sur l'Évolution des Charges Sociales de l'État*, Bruxelles, 1937.

17. DENEFFE, P. J. *Die Berechnungen über die künftige deutsche Bevölkerungsentwicklung*, Leipzig, 1938.
18. DENMARK. See notes on *Statistik des Deutschen Reichs*, vol. 401.
19. DUBLIN, L. I. 'The outlook for the American birth-rate.' *Problems of Population*, London, 1932, pp. 115–25.
20. FRANCE. See notes on *Statistik des Deutschen Reichs*, vol. 401.
21. GEARY, R. C. 'The future population of Saorstát Éireann and some observations on population statistics.' *Journal of the Statistical and Social Inquiry Society of Ireland*, 1935–6, pp. 15–32.
22. GINI, C. 'Calcolo di previsione della popolazione Italiana dal 1921 al 1961.' *Bulletin de l'Institut International de Statistique*, 1931, 3ème livraison, pp. 35–9.
23. GINI, C., and FINETTI, B. DE. 'Calcoli sullo sviluppo futuro della popolazione italiana.' *Annali di Statistica*, serie vi, vol. x, Rome, 1931.
24. GLASS, D. V. 'European population movements in the Union of South Africa.' *South African Journal of Economics*, March 1939, pp. 41–65.
25. GREAT BRITAIN. See notes on *Statistik des Deutschen Reichs*, vol. 401.
26. GREENWOOD, MAJOR. 'The growth of population in England and Wales.' *Metron*, 1 Sept. 1925, pp. 66–85.
27. GÜNTHER, E. 'Wert oder Unwert der Vorausberechnung der künftigen Bevölkerung.' *Allgemeines statistisches Archiv*, 1935, pp. 404–15.
28. HAGE, F. 'Vorausberechnungen über Bevölkerungsentwicklung.' *Deutsches Statistisches Zentralblatt*, 1931.
29. HONEY, F. J. C. 'The estimated population of Great Britain, 1941–71.' *Journal of the Institute of Actuaries*, 1937, pp. 323–47.
30. ISHII, R. *Population Pressure and Economic Life in Japan*, London, 1937.
31. ITALY. See notes on *Statistik des Deutschen Reichs*, vol. 401.
32. JENSEN, A. 'Nogle Træk of Danmarks Befolkning i Belysning af Fødsels- og Dodstallene.' *Meddelelser om Danmarks Antropologi*, 1927.
33. —— 'Horoscope of the population of Denmark.' *Bulletin de l'Institut International de Statistique*, vol. xxv, 3ème livraison, 1931, pp. 41–9.
34. KAHN, E. *Der internationale Geburtenstreik*, Frankfurt am Main, 1930.
35. KARPINOS, B. D. 'A stationary population (A study of Iowa population).' *Human Biology*, Dec. 1935, pp. 514–38.
36. KNIBBS, G. H. 'The laws of growth of a population.' *Journal of the American Statistical Association*, Dec. 1926.
37. —— *The Shadow of the World's Future*, London, 1928.
38. LEYBOURNE, G. G. 'An estimate of the future population of Great Britain.' *Sociological Review*, April 1934, pp. 130–8.
39. —— 'An estimate of the number of private families in England and Wales.' *Sociological Review*, Oct. 1934, pp. 407–11.
40. LÖSCH, A. *Was ist vom Geburtenrückgang zu halten?* Parts 1 and 2, Heidenheim (Württemberg), 1932.
41. MOELLENDORFF, W. VON. *Volkswirtschaftlicher Elementarvergleich zwischen Ver. Staaten von Amerika, Deutschland, Großbritannien, Frankreich, Italien*, Part I, Berlin, 1930.
42. MYRDAL, G., and WICKSELL, S. D. 'Utsikterna i fråga om den framtida befolkningsutvecklingen i Sverige och de ekonomiska verkningarna av olika

alternativt möjliga befolkningsutvecklingar.' (In *Betänkande i Sexualfrågan*, Stockholm, 1936, pp. 252–95.)

43. NETHERLANDS. See notes on *Statistik des Deutschen Reichs*, vol. 401.

44. NORWAY. See notes on *Statistik des Deutschen Reichs*, vol. 401.

45. —— *Folkemengdens Bevegelse, 1921–1932, utgitt av det Statistiske Centralbyrå*, Oslo, 1935, pp. 194–5.

46. NYBØLLE, H. C. 'Nogle væsentlige Træk af Danmarks nuværende befolkningsmæssige Forhold.' *Socialt Tidsskrift*, April 1934, pp. 111–36.

47. PAULINUS, G. *Prolegomena zu einer Bevölkerungsprognose*, Leipzig, 1934.

48. —— 'Der innere Zusammenhang der wichtigsten bevölkerungsstatistischen Größen und die Grenzen der Vorausberechenbarkeit der Bevölkerungsgröße.' *Allgemeines statistisches Archiv*, 1935, pp. 143–55.

49. POLAND. See notes on *Statistik des Deutschen Reichs*, vol. 401.

50. PRITCHETT, H. S. 'A formula for predicting the population of the United States.' *Publications of the American Statistical Association*, 1891 (June), pp. 278–86. (Originally appeared in *Transactions of the Academy of Science*, St. Louis, 1891.)

51. PTOUKHA, M. 'La population de l'Ukraïne jusqu'en 1960.' *Bulletin de l'Institut International de Statistique*, 1931, 3ème livraison, pp. 59–88.

52. RASTOIN, E. 'Analyse et prévision démographiques.' *Journal de la Société de Statistique de Paris*, Oct. 1932, pp. 367–79.

53. REED, L. J. 'Time changes in the number of gainfully employed men and women in the United States in relation to population growth.' *Problems of Population*, London, 1932, pp. 65–74.

54. —— 'Population growth and forecasts.' (In *The American People, The Annals of the American Academy of Political and Social Science*, Nov. 1936, pp. 159–66.)

55. SAUVY, A. 'La population française jusqu'en 1956.' *Journal de la Société de Statistique de Paris*, Dec. 1928, pp. 321–7, and Jan. 1929, pp. 8–13.

56. —— 'Calculs démographiques sur la population française jusqu'en 1980.' *Journal de la Société de Statistique de Paris*, 1932, July–Sept., pp. 319–37.

57. —— 'Perspectives statistiques sur la population, l'enseignement et le chômage.' *Journal de la Société de Statistique de Paris*, June 1937, pp. 227–41.

58. SHEINFIELD, A. [An estimate of the future population of South Wales.] (In Chapter I of *The Second Industrial Survey of South Wales*, vol. i, Cardiff, 1937.)

59. SMITHIES, A. 'The future of the Australian population.' (In *Australian Population*, report prepared for the British Commonwealth Relations Conference, 1938.) Australian Institute of International Affairs, Sydney, 1938. (Mimeographed.)

60. SPAGNOLLI, G. (Estimates of the Italian population) Tesi di Laurea, Università Cattolica del Sacro Cuore, 1929–30.

61. SPENGLER, J. J. 'Population prediction in nineteenth-century America.' *American Sociological Review*, Dec. 1936, pp. 905–21.

62. *Statistik des Deutschen Reichs*, Band 316, Berlin, 1926, pp. 37*–50*. Appendix. Richtlinien zur Beurteilung des Bevölkerungsproblems Deutschlands für die nächsten 50 Jahre.

63. *Statistik des Deutschen Reichs*, Band 401, Teil II. Berlin, 1930, pp. 641–83. Appendix. Ausblick auf die zukünftige Bevölkerungsentwicklung im Deutschen Reich. (Also contains estimates for a number of other countries.)

64. *Statistik des Deutschen Reichs*, Band 407, Berlin, 1930, p. 43. Appendix. Die voraussichtliche Entwicklung der Haushaltungszahl.

65. *Statistik des Deutschen Reichs*, Band 408, Berlin, 1931, pp. 312–33. Appendix. Die voraussichtliche Entwicklung der Zahl der Erwerbstätigen und der Arbeitnehmer im Deutschen Reich bis zum Jahre 1940.

66. Swaroop, S., and Lal, R. B. 'Logistic law of growth and structure of Indian population.' *Population*, Aug. 1938, pp. 100–21.

67. Sweden. See notes on *Statistik des Deutschen Reichs*, vol. 401.

68. Thompson, W. S. 'Probable future growth of population in the United States.' *Bulletin de l'Institut International de Statistique*, 3ème livraison, 1931, pp. 88–97.

69. Thompson, W. S., and Whelpton, P. K. *Population Trends in the United States*, New York, 1933.

70. —— —— *Estimates of Future Population by States* (National Resources Board), Washington, D.C., 1934.

71. —— —— *Estimates of Future Population of States, by Urban, Rural-Nonfarm, and Rural-Farm Areas and by Five-Year Age Periods and Time Intervals, 1935 to 1960* (Scripps Foundation for Research in Population Problems, Mimeographed), Oct. 1935.

72. —— —— 'Estimates of the future population of the United States, 1940–80.' *Population Statistics, I. National Data* (National Resources Committee), Washington, D.C., 1937, pp. 1–25.

73. Ukraine. See notes on *Statistik des Deutschen Reichs*, vol. 401.

74. Uyeda, T. 'Future of the Japanese population.' (Prepared for *Fifth Biennial Conference of the Institute of Pacific Relations*, Aug. 1933, pp. 1–25.)

75. —— 'Bevölkerungsfrage und Wirtschaft im heutigen Japan.' *Weltwirtschaftliches Archiv*, July 1937, pp. 93–117.

76. Vulhopp, T. 'La population belge de demain.' *Annales de la Société Scientifique de Bruxelles*, series D, Jan.–March 1932, pp. 28–41.

77. Whelpton, P. K. 'Population of the United States, 1925–1975.' *American Journal of Sociology*, Sept. 1928, pp. 253–70.

78. —— 'The future growth of the population of the United States.' *Problems of Population*, London, 1932, pp. 77–86.

79. —— 'The population prospect.' (In *Proceedings of the Third International Conference of Agricultural Economists*, Bad Eilsen, Aug.-Sept. 1934, pp. 250–63.)

80. —— 'An empirical method of calculating future population.' *Journal of the American Statistical Association*, Sept. 1936, pp. 457–73.

81. Wicksell, S. D. 'Sveriges framtida befolkning under olika förutsättningar.' *Ekonomisk Tidskrift*, parts 4–5, 1926, pp. 91–123.

82. Wicksell, S. D. '1928 års pensionsförsäkringskommitté', *Statistiska undersökningar och kostnadsberäkningar*. Stat. off. utr. 1930: 15, Stockholm.

83. —— 'Bidrag till den formella befolkningsteorien. Med tillämpningar på Norges befolkning.' *Statsøkonomisk Tidsskrift*, 1934, parts 1–2, pp. 1–94.

84. Wicksell, S. D., and Quensel, C. E. 'Prognoser över Sveriges folkmängd under de närmaste årtiondena.' *Betänkande med vissa Demografiska Utredningar*, Stockholm, 1938, pp. 133–65.

85. Wilkinson, H. L. *The World's Population Problems and a White Australia*, London, 1930.

86. Willcox, W. F. 'Methods of estimating the population of the United States.' *Metron*, 1 June 1925, pp. 27–37.

87. Wilson, N. *Expected Population Changes and Their Effect upon Social Services*, Institute of Public Administration, London, 1935.

88. *Wirtschaft und Statistik* (Germany). In *Sonderheft*, no. 15, 'Die biologische Methode der Bevölkerungsvorausberechnung', 1935, pp. 83–96.

89. *Wirtschaft und Statistik* (Germany). 'Die voraussichtliche Bevölkerungsentwicklung im Deutschen Reich', 1 Dec. 1938, pp. 971–6, and 2 March 1939, pp. 247–50.

90. Wolstenholme, S. H. 'The future of the Australian population.' *Economic Record*, Dec. 1936, pp. 195–213.

91. Yule, G. Udny. 'The growth of population and the factors which control it.' *Journal of the Royal Statistical Society*, Jan. 1925, pp. 1–58.

INDEX OF SUBJECTS

Abortion:
- Babylonian laws, 28, 422 (*s*).
- by using diachylon, 51, 427 (*ee*).
- early practice of, 28–9, 422 (*s*).
- literature on abortion in France, 443 (*f*).
- suppression of abortion in Germany:
  - by controlling advertisements, 284.
  - by police measures, 283, 285.
  - effect on fertility trend, 312–13.
- suppression of abortion in Italy: by police measures, 234–5.

Abortion frequency:
- Belgium, 164–5, 444 (*h*).
- Denmark, 322–3.
- England and Wales, 50–5, 428 (*gg*), 428 (*hh*), 429 (*ii*).
- France, 162–4.
- Germany:
  - abortions to normal births in some Sickness Funds, 278–80.
  - effect of police measures under National Socialism, 285–6.
  - effect on birth-rate, 279.
  - estimates of induced abortions, 278, 428 (*gg*), 458 (*c*).
  - influence of marriage loans on abortion frequency, 461 (*k*).
- Italy, 452 (*g*)
- Norway, 326.
- Sweden, 324.

Abortion Law Reform, reports of Committees:
- Denmark, 322–3.
- Norway, 325–6.
- Sweden, 325.

Abortion Legislation:
- Belgium, 157–8, 159, 165.
- Denmark, 322, 323–4, 462 (*c*).
- England and Wales, 427 (*ff*).
- France, 157–9, 165; under the *Code de la Famille*, 216–17.
- Germany:
  - agitation for relaxing abortion law, 279, 281–2.
  - pre-National Socialism, 281.
  - under National Socialism, 283–6, 459 (*e*).
- Italy, 231–2, 233–5, 451 (*f*).
- Norway, 325–6.
- Sweden, 324–5, 463 (*d*).

Abortion Prosecutions:
- Belgium, 159.
- Denmark, 322.
- France, 158, 163.
- Germany, 285–6, 459 (*f*).

Adultery, Augustinian laws on, 86–7.

Bachelor tax:
- Germany, to finance marriage loans, 288–9.
- Italy, 236–7.
- Sweden, proposal for, 334.

Birth control:
- attitude of the churches, 429 (*jj*).
- changes in contraceptive technique, 29–30, 423 (*t*), 423 (*u*).
- difficulties in determining extent of, 48–9, 426 (*cc*).
- earliest record of the condom, 30.
- early practice of birth control, 28–9.
- effectiveness and reliability of contraception, 30.
- extent of birth control:
  - Belgium, 162.
  - England and Wales, 46–50, 426 (*dd*), 432 (*oo*).
  - Germany, 277, 458 (*b*).
  - U.S.A., 47, 49–50.
- origin of term, 28.
- suppression of birth control:
  - France, Catholic opinion, 165.
  - Germany, by controlling advertisements, 284; by police measures, 283.

Birth-control associations:
- England and Wales, 44–6.
- Germany, pre-National Socialism, 276–7.

Birth-control clinics:
- Denmark, 319, 322, 323–4.
- England and Wales, 44–6.
- Norway, 321.
- Sweden, 320–1.

Birth-control law reform, report of Committee: Denmark, 323.

Birth-control legislation:
Belgium, 159–60; in practice, 160–1.
Denmark, 319, 323–4.
France, 159; in practice, 160–1.
Germany, under National Socialism, 283–4.
Italy, 231–3.
Norway, 321.
Sweden, 320, 325.
Birth-control movement:
Belgium, 161–2, 443 (*g*).
Denmark, 319, 322.
England and Wales:
aims of, 43–4.
influence on fertility trend, 46–50, 55–61, 431 (*ll*).
literature, 30–5, 40–3, 44.
origin, 30 ff.
post-War movement, 44–6.
prosecutions, 32–5.
social and economic background, 57–60, 82–4.
see also Malthusian League, The.
France, 161–2, 443 (*f*); literature, 161–2, 442 (*e*).
Germany, 276–7.
Italy, 233.
Norway, 321–2.
Sweden, 320–2.
Birth premiums:
Belgium, 172.
France, 169; under the *Code de la Famille*, 213–14.
Italy, 243, 257–8, 453 (*h*), 455 (*o*).
Birth-rates:
crude birth-rates:
Belgium, 152, 200–1.
England and Wales, 5–6, 200–1.
France, 146, 152, 200–1.
Germany, 269–70, 305.
general fertility rates, England and Wales, 5–6, 7–8.
general legitimate fertility rates, England and Wales, 5.
specific fertility rates, 384; England and Wales, 8–9, 18.
specific illegitimate fertility rates, England and Wales, 18.
specific legitimate fertility rates, England and Wales, 18.
Births registration: England and Wales, 1, 416 (*a*).
Bradlaugh-Besant Trial, The, 14, 32–4, 35, 40, 41, 56, 424 (*x*), 425 (*z*).
Childlessness:
estimates of childlessness in England and Wales, 25–7, 421 (*q*).
inquiries into extent of childlessness, 422 (*r*).
views on the causes of childlessness, 25, 27–8, 421 (*p*), 422 (*r*).
Class fertility:
England and Wales, 68–71.
see also Differential fertility.
Crèches: in Stockholm flats, 338.
Death-rates:
crude death-rates, England and Wales, 5–7.
standardized death-rates, England and Wales, 6–8.
Deaths registration, England and Wales, 1, 416 (*a*).
Declining population:
ambiguity of term, 359–61.
effects of a declining population, 363–9.
futility of repressive legislation, 371, 373.
general analysis of measures to raise net reproduction rate, 370–3.
political implications of a declining population, 368–9.
problems minimized by economic and social planning, 367–8.
result of present social and economic system, 372–3.
studies on the consequences of a declining population, 464 (*c*).
types of declining populations, 361–3.
Differential fertility:
between social classes, 465 (*e*).
changes in differential fertility in England and Wales, 71–82.
dysgenic aspects, 74–5, 432 (*pp*).
employment of women and marriage factors in England and Wales, 66–8.
rates to use in measuring differential fertility, 75.
socio-economic differential fertility, 75–82, 433 (*qq*).
see also Class fertility, Regional fertility.
Economic and social conditions, Sweden, 331–8.

Employment of women:
changes in employment of women in England and Wales, 59, 430 (*kk*).
changing attitude in Germany, 289–90.
effect on differential fertility in England and Wales, 66–8.
encouragement of employment of married women in Sweden, 329.
propaganda against employment of married women in France, 120.
Employment preference:
to fathers of large families in Germany, 302.
to married persons in Italy, 241–2, 258, 260.
Expectation of life, 378–81.
Australia, 16.
Denmark, 315.
England and Wales, 7, 14–16; estimates of Farr, W., 419 (*j*).
Germany, 270.
New Zealand, 16.

Family allowances:
definition of a family allowance, 99.
effect in a declining population, 367.
essential minimum increase in income per child, 209.
past attempts at family allowances: Austria, 95; France, 92–3; Roman Empire, 89.
Belgium:
administration of, 129–32, 134–6.
calculation of, 130–1, 134–5, 439 (*j*).
development of, 125–9.
early history of, 125–6.
equalization funds, 126, 129; extra services of funds, 139–40.
extent of family allowance system, 132–3, 438 (*i*), 440 (*l*).
financing, 129–31, 134–6, 140–1.
in unemployment and strikes, 439 (*j*).
legislation, 127 ff., 133–5, 140–2.
motives for family allowances, 99, 126, 128–9, 132, 142, 145.
occupations covered, 129, 135, 140–1.
payment of, 131.
rates of, 131, 133–8, 141.
relation to wages, 138–9, 204–5.
State encouragement, 126–9.
super-equalization, 130–1.
to agricultural workers, 134.
to civil servants and employees of public bodies, 125, 129, 440 (*k*).
to domestic workers, 135.
to employers, 140–1.
to foreigners, 129.
voluntary family allowances, 125–6.
England and Wales, 85, 434 (*uu*).
France:
administration of, 107–8.
see also equalization funds, super-equalization.
calculation of, 110–13, 121, 122–4.
development of, 101–6.
early history of, 92–3, 99–100.
equalization funds, 102–3, 106, 107, 112, 436 (*d*); extra services of funds, 124–5.
extent of family allowance system, 108–9, 112, 435 III (*a*), 436 (*e*), 437 (*f*).
extra allowances for the *mère au foyer*, 120, 123, 213.
legislation, 101, 105 ff., 120, 122.
motives for family allowances, 99, 103–5, 120, 142, 145.
occupations covered, 100–3, 106, 108–9, 120, 122, 123, 124.
payment of, 107–8, 436 (*c*).
rates of, 113–16, 118–19, 120–1, 122–4, 143–4, 437 (*g*).
reduction of wages, 440 (*m*).
relation to wages, 115–19, 120–1, 122–3, 204–5, 209–10; under the *Code de la Famille*, 213.
significance of, 203–12.
State encouragement, 100–1, 105–6.
super-equalization, 110, 121–2, 123–4.
to agricultural workers, 109–12, 113, 114, 116, 123.
to civil servants and employees of public bodies, 100–1, 105, 124, 435 (*b*).
to domestic workers, 123.
to employers, 122–4.
to foreigners, 106.
voluntary family allowances, 100–5.
Germany: 292–6.
extent of family allowance system, 295.

Family allowances: Germany (*cont.*)
government allowances: laufende Kinderbeihilfen, 295–6; erweiterte laufende Kinderbeihilfen, 296.
history of, 292–5.
in cigar industry, 295.
motives for family allowances, 292.
to panel dentists, 295.
to panel doctors, 294–5.
to pharmacists, 293–4.
to State employees, 293.
Italy: 248–55.
contributions for financing, 250, 251–2, 253–4.
development of, 248–51.
extent and cost of, 251, 254–5, 455 (*n*).
generalization of, 252–5.
motives for, 249–50, 250–1.
rates of, 250, 251–2, 253–4.
relation to wages, 255.
to agricultural workers, 253–4, 255.
to commercial workers, 251–5.
to credit and insurance workers, 252, 254, 255.
to industrial workers, 249–55.
to State and semi-State employees, 248–9.
Norway, report of Committee on, 341–2.
Family size, to estimate frequency distribution of family size, 420 (*n*).
Fertility, effect of war on fertility, 353.
Fertility trend:
Belgium, 152–3, 199–200, 202.
Denmark, 314–15.
England and Wales, 12–16.
effect of changes in employment of women, 66–8.
influence of birth-control movement, 61, 431 (*ll*).
influence of marriage, 17–24.
influence of mortality, 14–16.
number of children per woman necessary for unit replacement, 13.
number of children per married woman necessary for unit replacement, 23–4.
France, 193–9.
fertility of population in family allowance system, 178–91, 200–2, 204, 446 (*m*).
influence of population measures, 202–3.
occupational fertility, 197–8.
Germany, 269–70, 304–6, 308–13.
effect of abortion, 279.
effect of inflation period, 274.
effect of suppressing abortion, 308-9, 312–13.
factors influencing fertility trend, 308–13.
influence of economic depression, 311.
influence of foreign policy, 311.
influence of marriage loans, 308, 461 (*l*).
influence of pro-natalist propaganda and measures, 308–9.
influence of 'psychic rebirth' and psychic population policy, 310–12.
literature on declining birth-rate, 270–5, 457 (*a*).
official explanation of fertility trend, 309–11.
public concern at declining birth-rate, 270–5, 457 (*a*).
Italy, 264–7.
effect of Abyssinian war, 264, 266.
effect of marriage loans, 266.
Norway, 314–15.
Scotland, migration influence, 418 (*h*).
Sweden, 314–15.

Gross reproduction rates, 8–9, 383–7.
Belgium, 177; provinces, 199–200.
Denmark, 314.
England and Wales, 13; Registration Counties, 62–3.
France, 177; departments, 194–9.
Germany, 270, 305.
Ireland, 418 (*i*).
Italy, 264–5; departments, 265–6.
London, 63, 78.
Norway, 314.
Scotland, 13.
Sweden, 314.

Home-furnishing loans: Sweden, 327–31; effect on marriage and fertility, 330–1; extent of, 330.

Housing conditions:
  Germany, 302.
  Italy, 245–6, 454 (*j*).
  Norway, 340.
  Sweden, 331–3.
Housing legislation:
  Belgium, 173–5.
  France, 170–1.
  Italy, 244–6.
Housing loans:
  Denmark, 339–40.
  Norway, 340.
Housing policy: Sweden, 336–8; average rents of urban dwellings, 336–7; rehousing of large families, 337–8.

Illegitimacy:
  past attempts to reduce disgrace attaching to, 95–6.
  Germany, improvement in position of mother and child, 304.
  Sweden, effect of home-furnishing loans, 330; legislation for illegitimate children, 335.
Immigration policy, to avoid a declining population, 367.
Income, in relation to family size in Sweden, 331–2.
Infant mortality: effect of family allowances in Belgium, 202, 448 (*q*); in France, 192–3, 202–3, 448 (*q*).
Infanticide, 29, 423 (*s*).
Infertility:
  as grounds for marriage dissolution in Germany, 303.
  considered as an illness if curable in Germany, 302–3.
  views on physiological infertility, 25, 421 (*p*).
Inheritance:
  Augustinian laws, 87–8.
  duties in favour of families in Belgium, 173; in France, 170; under the *Code de la Famille*, 216; in Germany, 301.

Land reclamation schemes: Italy, origin, 225; under Fascism, 225–8.
Life-table population, 376–7, 378–80.
Life tables, 374–83, 465 (*a*).
Living costs, minimum:
  estimates for France and Belgium, 207–8.
  relative to size of family, 205–7.
Longevity and fertility, 71–2, 432 (*nn*).

Malthusian League, The:
  lectures given by, 36–7.
  origin of, 35, 424 (*z*).
  propaganda of, 35–8.
  publications of, 37, 42–3.
Marital reproductivity, England and Wales, 17–24; Sweden, 403–5, 463 (*e*).
Marriage, encouragement of:
  early laws in:
    Austria, 95.
    England, 95.
    France, 92–3, 97–8.
    Prussia, 95.
    Roman Empire, 87–8.
    Spain, 91.
  Germany: 460 (*h*).
    see also Marriage loans.
  Italy:
    compensation to women leaving work, 259.
    holiday given on marriage, 259.
    in armed forces, 258, 455 (*o*).
    to State and semi-State employees, 455 (*o*).
    see also Marriage loans, Marriage premiums.
  Sweden, *see* Home-furnishing loans.
Marriage age, effects of lowering the marriage age, 24, 421 (*o*).
Marriage frequency:
  England and Wales, 17–24.
  Italy, effect of Abyssinian war, 263, 264.
    influence of population policy, 261–4.
  Germany, 304–8; influence of economic depression, 307; influence of marriage loans, 306–8.
  Sweden, and fertility, 330, 463 (*e*).
Marriage loans:
  France, 445 (*j*); under the *Code de la Famille*, 214–15.
  Germany, 287–91.
    average loan, 289.
    effect in reducing unemployment, 289–90.
    extent of, 289.
    financing of funds for, 288.
    influence on abortion, 461 (*k*).
    influence on fertility, 308, 461 (*l*).

Marriage loans: Germany (*cont.*)
influence on marriage frequency, 306–8.
legislation, 287–8.
see also Rural marriage loans.
Italy, 255–7; extent of, 257.
Marriage premiums: Italy, 243, 257–8, 453 (*h*), 455 (*o*).
Maternity grants: Norway, 340–1.
Migration:
early laws on migration in:
France, 94–5, 97.
Other States, 96, 97.
Spain, 91.
England and Wales:
data, 1–4; Irish immigrants, 4; refugees, 3–4.
Ireland: 416 (*b*).
Italy:
efforts to retain nationality of Italian emigrants, 224–5, 450 (*d*).
encouragement of emigration, 221.
internal migration policy, 228–31; anti-urban drive, 229–30; colonization of reclaimed land, 228–30.
legislation, 221–5.
outward balance of migration, 451 (*e*).
Permanent Commission for repatriation of Italians living abroad, 451 (*e*).
restrictions on emigration, 221–5.
Scotland: 416 (*b*).
Mortality in England and Wales:
geographical distribution, 419 (*k*).
some causes of high mortality in towns, 419 (*j*).
Mortality trend:
England and Wales, 5, 6–7, 14–16.
Italy, 265, 456 (*q*).
Mussolini:
on demographic power, 220.
on increase of Italian population, 219.
on Malthusian propaganda, 219, 231, 450 (*c*).
on overpopulation, 449 (*a*).
on urbanism, 229.

Natural increase, true rate of, 10–11, 405–15, 467 (*d*).
Neo-Malthusian, origin of term, 35, 425 (*aa*).
Neo-Malthusian movement:
England and Wales:
aims of movement, 43–4.
extent of neo-Malthusian publications, 40–3.
influence of, 55–61, 82–3.
influence on the Continent; 161, 276.
origin on the Continent, 38–40.
see also Birth-control movement, Malthusian League, The.
Neo-Malthusianism and Socialism, 442 (*e*).
Neo-Malthusians, on decline in mortality, 15.
Net reproduction rates, 383–7; definition and validity, 9–12, 417 (*d*); problem of raising net reproduction rate, 370–3.
Belgium, 177, 200.
Denmark, 314.
England and Wales, 13; Registration Counties, 62–3.
France, 177, 199.
Germany, 270, 305.
Ireland, 418 (*i*).
Italy, 260, 265; departments, 265–6.
London, 63.
Norway, 314.
Scotland, 13.
Stockholm, 315.
Sweden, 314, 315.
Nuptiality, 399–405.
England and Wales: gross, 19–20; net, 20–2.
Germany, 304–5.
Italy, 264, 457 (*r*).
Sweden, 403–5.
Nuptial reproduction rates, 399–405.
nuptial gross reproduction rate, Sweden, 403–4.
nuptial net reproduction rate, England and Wales, 22, 420 (*m*); Sweden, 404–5.

Optimum population, choice of an optimum population, 369–70.
Oslo breakfasts: Norway, 341.

Population commission:
Denmark, 317–18; report, 339.
Sweden, 317; report, 325.
Population estimates, 468–72.
fertility assumptions, 349–51.
migration assumptions, 351–3.
mortality assumptions, 346–9.

validity and implications, 344–60.
value of, 354.
Belgium, 155–6.
Denmark, 315–16.
England and Wales, 84, 354–9.
France, 151–2.
Germany, 274–5, 461 (*m*).
Italy, 219, 267–8.
Norway, 316.
Sweden, 315–16, 462 (*b*).
Population growth:
Belgium, 153.
England and Wales, measurement by:
annual rate of growth, 10–11.
generation rate of growth, 8–12.
intercensal increase, 2–3.
natural increase, 2, 4–8.
France, 153.
Population measures:
general analysis of, 370–3.
Belgium:
effect on fertility, 193, 199–200, 202–3.
positive measures, 172–7; advantages given to families, 175–7; social insurance provisions for widows and orphans, 176; *see* Birth premiums, Family allowances, Housing legislation, Inheritance duties, Taxation.
significance of population measures, 203 ff.
Denmark: 339–40.
France:
effect on fertility, 193–9, 200–3.
expenditure on, 210–12.
positive measures, 165–72; advantages given to families, 171–2; national encouragement of large families, 167–8; social insurance provisions for large families, 168–9; unemployment assistance to families, 169; *see* Birth premiums, Family allowances, Housing legislation, Inheritance duties, Relief measures, Taxation.
recent measures, 212–18.
significance of population measures, 203 ff.
Germany:
positive measures:
advantages given to families: 296–7, 302–4.
godparenthood by Adolf Hitler, 304.
godparenthood by towns, 303–4.
grants to large families: pre-National Socialism, 272; under National Socialism, 291–2.
large family associations: pre-National Socialism, 273, 275–6; under National Socialism, 286.
See Employment preference, Family allowances, Inheritance duties, Marriage loans, Rural household grants, Rural household loans, Rural marriage loans, Taxation.
Italy:
positive measures: advantages given to families, 241–2, 258–9; encouragement of family as a group, 259–60; maternity and childhood protection, 242–3, 453 (*i*); maternity insurance, 243–4; premiums for child-rearing, 453 (*h*); premiums to large families, 453 (*h*); *see* Birth premiums, Employment preference, Family allowances, Housing legislation, Marriage, encouragement of, Marriage loans, Marriage premiums, Taxation.
recent legislation, 258–60.
Norway: 340–2.
Sweden:
positive measures: free school meals to children, 334; grants to needy children, 335; maternity grants for necessitous mothers, 334; maternity insurance benefit, 333–4; State assistance to special types of families, 334–5; State maternity relief, 333–4; *see* Employment of women, Home-furnishing loans, Housing policy.
principles and aims of population measures, 327.
Population policies:
early population policies:
Babylonia, 86.
France, 92–5, 97–8.
Japan, 96–7.
Other countries, 95–6, 97–8.
Roman Empire, 86–90.
Spain, 91–2.

influence of Christianity on early policies, 89–90.
influence of Mercantilism on early policies, 90–1.
Belgium: background to, 152–6; motives for, 177–8.
France: background to, 145–52; motives for, 177–8; public attitude towards, 449 (*s*).
Germany:
aims of National Socialist policy, 282–3, 458 (*d*).
pre-National Socialism, 270–3.
psychic population policy, 310–12.
Italy:
general analysis of, 246–8.
German influence on, 454 (*l*), 454 (*m*).
origin, 219–21.
Scandinavia:
background and development, 315–18.
method of approach to, 318–19.
Population problem:
England and Wales:
development of public interest, 82–5, 434 (*tt*).
Eugenists' attitude, 83, 433 (*ss*).
Socialists' attitude, 83.
Population studies:
for Belgium, 441 (*a*), 446 (*k*).
France, 441 (*a*), 441 (*b*), 446 (*k*).
Italy, 450 (*b*), 451 (*d*), 457 (*s*).
Pro-natalist organizations:
Belgium, 153–5.
France, 149–50, 152.
Germany, pre-National Socialism, 272, 273; under National Socialism, 286.
Pro-natalist propaganda:
Belgium, 154–6, 203–4.
France, 147–52, 203–4, 441 (*c*), 442 (*d*).
Germany, under National Socialism, 286.
Italy, 247, 454 (*k*).

Refugees, immigration of refugees into England and Wales, 3–4.
Regional fertility:
Belgium, 199–200.
England and Wales, 61–8.
France, 193–9.
Italy, 265–6.
Relief measures:
France: 166–8.
allowances to dependent children, 166, 167–8.
confinement allowances, 166–7.
suckling allowances, 166–7.
Reproduction rates, 383–7.
Rural household grants: Germany, 299.
Rural household loans; Germany, 299.
Rural marriage loans: Germany, 298.
Rural settlement policy: Germany, 297–8.

Social classes:
problem how to construct, 431 (*mm*).
see Class fertility.
Stable population, 405–15.
Stationary population:
England and Wales, 11–12.
problems of a stationary population, 365–7.
Substitute reproduction rates, 387–99.
using life-table principle, 393–9.
using specific fertility rates, 387–93.

Taxation in favour of families:
early laws in France, 92; Spain, 91.
Belgium, 172–3.
England, 73.
France, 169–70; under the *Code de la Famille*, 215–16.
Germany, 299–301.
Italy, 237–8, 241, 258–9; significance of, 239–41.
Sweden, 334.
Therapeutic abortion:
Denmark and Sweden, 463 (*d*).
Germany, 459 (*e*).

Unemployment, general and specific unemployment in a declining population, 363.

INDEX OF AUTHORS, PERSONS, AND ORGANIZATIONS

Adams, W., 464 (*c*).
Advertising Council for German business, 284.
Alberti, S., 452 (*g*).
Alexander, Tsar, 96.
Allaria, G. B., 452 (*g*).
Allbutt, H. A., 34–5, 38, 41.
Alliance Nationale pour l'Accroissement de la Population Française (now Alliance Nationale contre la Dépopulation), 100–1, 104, 115, 149, 150, 151, 152, 163, 166, 203, 207, 209–10, 436 (*e*).
Anderson, G., 425 (*z*).
Ansell, C., 70.
Anselmi, A., 251, 252.
Aptekar, H., 29.
Arena, C., 251.
Association des Caisses d'Allocations Familiales (Belgium), 128, 136, 142.
Auburtin, F., 149, 441 (*b*), 442 (*c*).
Auert, H., 303.
Augustus, Emperor, 86–8, 89.

Bachi, R., 454 (*l*), 457 (*s*).
Baffi, P., 457 (*s*).
Baker, O. E., 464 (*c*).
Balilla (organization for Italian youth), 243.
Ballarin, H.-G., and Rössler, H., 286, 291, 295, 296, 301, 302, 303, 304.
Balthazard, Dr., and Prévost, E., 150, 163.
Baravelli, G. C., 225, 227, 228.
Barclay, R. S., and Kermack, W. O., 349, 350, 431 (*ll*).
Barth, K., 300.
'Battaglia del grano' (Italy), 226.
Baudhuin, F., 155–6, 178, 468.
Begbie, E., 59.
Bellamy, H., 165.
Bentham, J., 423 (*t*).
Berta, L., 450 (*c*).
Berthélemy, H., 163.
Bertillon, J., 94, 147, 149, 150, 443 (*f*).
Bertillon (père), 146, 446 (*k*).
Besant, A., 32–4, 36, 37, 41, 52, 56, 276, 424 (*y*), 424–5 (*z*), 426 (*bb*).
Beveridge, W. H., 83.
Biagi, B., 250, 251, 252, 256, 453 (*i*).
Bied-Charreton, R., 449 (*s*).
Birch, W. J., 425 (*z*).
Birchall, E. V., 70.
Birth Control International Information Centre, 45.
Birth Control Investigation Committee, 45, 49.
Blacker, C. P., 49, 371, 421 (*p*).
Blavatsky, Mme, 41.
Blet, G., 146.
Boeckh, R., 9.
Bokanowski, Monsieur, 105.
Boldrini, M., 255, 259, 455 (*m*), 465 (*e*).
Boldsen, F. C., 339, 340.
'Bonifica integrale' (Italy), 225, 226, 228.
Bonnevie, M., 342.
Bonser, T. O., 37.
Bonvoisin, G., 108, 110, 111, 113, 115, 116, 120, 124, 191, 204, 211, 440 (*m*), 441 (*c*).
Bonvoisin, G., and Maignan, G., 100, 104, 114, 116, 435 III (*a*), 437 (*f*), 446 (*m*).
Bonz and Hilburg, 468.
Booker, H. S., 71.
Bornträger, J. 458 (*a*).
Bortkiewicz, L. von, 467 (*d*).
Bourdeaux, H., 157, 160.
Bouthoul, G., 203, 233, 441 (*b*).
Bouvier, L., 238.
Boverat, F., 100, 113, 121, 148, 151–2, 210, 215, 436 (*c*), 445 (*j*), 449 (*s*).
Bowley, A. L., 84, 345, 421 (*p*), 431 (*kk*), 468.
Bradlaugh, C., 32–4, 41, 52, 425 (*z*), 426 (*bb*).
Bramwell, *L. J.*, 33.
Braschwitz, Dr., 458 (*d*).
Brentano, L., 457 (*a*).
Brett, *L. J.*, 33.
Brialmont, General, 443 (*g*).
British Medical Association, reports, 54, 205.
Brouardel, P., 165.

Brown, J. W., Greenwood, M., and Wood, F., 56.
Brown, Monsignor W. F., 434 (*tt*).
Bruguier, Professor, 454 (*l*).
Brunskog, M., 318.
Bryson, J. 425 (*z*).
Buer, M. C., 12.
Buffa, A., 453 (*i*).
Bund der Kinderreichen (Germany), 273.
Bund für Mutterschutz und Sexualreform (Germany), 276.
Bund zur Erhaltung und Mehrung der deutschen Volkskraft, 272.
Bunle, H., 468.
Bureau for Explaining Population Policies (Germany), 286.
Bureau, P., 152.
Burgdörfer, F., 270, 273, 274, 275, 280, 289, 291, 299, 305, 306, 309–11, 395, 458 (*d*), 459 (*d*), 460 (*j*), 461 (*l*), 466 (*b*), 468.
Burks, B. S., 420 (*n*), 432 (*pp*).

Cagetano, Professor, 233.
Caisse Nationale de Compensation (Belgium), 129, 134, 137.
Callon, G., 441 (*b*).
Camanni, V., 450 (*b*).
Cambridge Women's Welfare Association, 47.
Campion, R., 31.
Canal, S., 441 (*b*).
Canavaggio, D., 170.
Cannan, E., 84, 345, 468.
Caracalla, 89.
Carlile, R., 31, 423 (*u*).
Carpenter, Bishop Boyd, 434 (*tt*).
Carrothers, W. A., 3.
Carr-Saunders, A. M., 4, 29.
Carr-Saunders, A. M., and Jones, D. C., 70, 71.
Casanova, E., 96.
Cassius, Dion, 88.
Catherine of Russia, 96.
Cattell, R. B., 74.
Cau, Dr., 258, 455 (*n*).
Chapelier, E., 444 (*g*)
Charles, E., 27, 49, 64, 74, 84, 346, 354, 355, 357, 361, 362, 422 (*r*), 426 (*dd*), 464 (*b*), 468.
Charles, E., and Moshinsky, P., 64, 66, 67, 77.
Children's Minimum Campaign Committee, 207.
Ciccotti, E., 88.
Ciccotti, Senator, 226.
Clapham, J. H., 57.
Clark, C., 212, 362.
Clerici, L., 453 (*i*).
Cobb, J. A., 74.
Cobbett, W., 31.
Cockburn, *C. J.*, 33.
Code de la Famille (France), 157, 212–18.
Codes Edmond Picard, 158, 160.
Cohen, I., 455 (*m*).
Cohn, E., 462 (*a*).
Colbert, J.-B., 92–5, 98.
Colin, A., 450 (*b*).
Comité Central des Allocations Familiales (France), 104, 108, 109, 114, 115, 436 (*d*), 437 (*f*).
Comité Central Industriel de Belgique, 136.
Comité d'Études des Allocations Familiales (Belgium), 128.
Comité National de l'Enfance (France), 150.
Congrès National (France), reports of Family Allowance Congresses, 183–93.
Conring, H., 435 II (*a*).
Conseil Supérieur de la Natalité, 118, 150, 163, 203.
Constantine, Emperor, 90.
Cook, H., 32.
Cooke, R. G., 53.
Coutard, J., 171.
Cramér, H., 468.
Cramér, H., and Wold, H., 349, 464 (*a*).
Credé-Hoerder, 281.
Creeft, F. de, 156, 464 (*c*), 468.
Crew, F. A. E., 60.
Crollalanza, A. di., 454 (*j*).
Cross, R. H., 4.

Dahlberg, G., 324.
Daladier, Monsieur, 148.
Dalsace, J., 164.
Dalton, H., 83.
Danzer, P., 459 (*d*).
Dassonville, R. P., 165.
Dauwe, O., 445 (*h*).
Davies, D. S., 428 (*ff*).
Davis, K., 373.

Dejace, Dr., 445 (*h*).
Delattre, A., 136.
Dembour, E., 155.
Demeyère, J., 446 (*k*).
Deneffe, P. J., 469.
Depoid, P., 149, 195, 198, 199, 353.
Dequidt, G., 166.
Dequidt, G., and Forestier, G., 179, 180–1.
Derrick, V. P. A., 347–8, 353, 356, 463 (*a*).
Deutsche Gesellschaft für Bevölkerungspolitik, 272.
Devaldés, M., 442 (*e*).
Doleris, Dr., 163.
Dorn, H. F., and McDowell, A. J., 432 (*nn*).
Douglas, C. A., and McKinlay, P. L., 418 (*h*).
Douglas, P. H., 100, 104, 190.
Drage, G., 281, 459 (*e*).
Drysdale, B., 39, 43, 45.
Drysdale, C. R., 35, 36, 38, 39, 425 (*z*), 425 (*aa*), 426 (*bb*), 444 (g).
Drysdale, C. V., 15, 40, 43, 44, 425 (*aa*).
Drysdale, G., 32, 40.
Dublin, L. I., 469.
Dublin, L. I., and Lotka, A. J., 15, 357, 465 (*a*), 467 (*d*).
Dugé de Bernonville, L., 211.
Dumas, L., 441 (*b*).
Dumont, A., 441 (*b*).
Du Moriez, S., 165, 442 (*c*).
Duncan, J. M., 25–6.
Duncan, W. H., 419 (*j*).
Dunlop, B., 39, 44, 83.
Dunlop, J. C., 417 (*e*).
Dunlop, J. C., and Hunter, R. M., 417 (*e*).
Dupréel, E., 155.
Durand-Wever, A.-M., 279, 458 (*b*).
Düsseldorf Einheitsverband für proletarische Sexualreform und Mutterschutz, 277.
Duval-Arnould, L., 203, 210.

Ebbell, B., 422 (*s*).
Edin, K. A., 324.
Edin, K. A., and Hutchinson, E. P., 433 (*qq*).
Edwards, C., 422 (*s*).
Elderton, E. M., 51–2, 55, 57, 427 (*ee*).
Elderton, E. M., Barrington, A., Jones, H. G., Lamotte, E. M. M. de G., Laski, H. J., and Pearson, K., 74.
Elizabeth, Queen of England, 95.
Ellison, J., Goodwin, A., Read, C. D., and Rivett, L. C., 428 (*ff*), 430 (*jj*).
Elster, L., 91, 435 II (*a*).
Elston, J. S., 466 (*a*).
Engelsmann, R., 272, 273.
Ensor, R. C. K., 57.
Evang, G., 321, 326.
Eymer, Professor, 458 (*c*).

Fabbri, S., 242.
Fabian Society, The, 73.
Fallon, V., 125, 133, 136, 142, 154, 155, 440 (*l*), 446 (*k*).
Fallopius, G., 30.
Famille Montpelliéraine, 149.
Family Planning Association (formerly National Birth Control Association), 45, 46.
Farr, W., 5, 419 (*j*).
Fascist Confederations in Commerce (Italy), 251, 254.
Fascist Confederation of Industrial Workers (Italy), 249.
Fascist Confederation of Industry (Italy), 249, 259.
Fascist Grand Council (Italy), 248, 255, 455 (*m*).
Fascist Union of Large Families (Italy), 259.
Faure, S., 442 (*e*).
Fédération des Associations de Familles Nombreuses de France, 150.
Fédération Universelle de la Régénération Humaine, 39, 40, 444 (*g*).
Félice, R. de, 443 (*f*).
Ferdy, H., 426 (*bb*).
Ferenczi, I., 369.
Ferté, J., 109.
Fetscher, R., 275.
Fey, W., 302.
Fichtel, J., 292–3.
Field, J. A., 31.
Filangieri, G., 86, 98.
Fischer, A., 219.
Fisher, R. A., 74, 181–3, 432 (*nn*), 467 (*d*).
Florence, L. S., 47.
Foote, E. B., 28.
Franchi, L., 452 (*f*).
Frary, R., 147.

Fraser Roberts, J. A., Norman, R. M., and Griffiths, R., 74.
Frederick the Great, 95, 96.
Frederick William I, 95.
Freeman, B. C., 432 (*nn*).
Freethought Publishing Company (Bradlaugh and Besant), 41.
Frick, Dr., 282.
Frumkin, G., 200, 265.
Frydenberg, Dr., 341.

Galabin, A. L., 429 (*ii*).
Galton, F., 74.
Galvani, L., 265, 268, 456 (*q*).
Gand, M., 210.
Gårdlund, T., 320, 321.
Garraud, P., and Laborde-Lacoste, M., 160.
Garraud, R., 157.
Garvie, A. E., 430 (*jj*).
Gaskell, G. A., 37.
Geary, R. C., 469.
Gemmer, E., 278.
General Commissariat for Emigration (Italy), 221, 222.
George, R. F., 205–6.
Gesamtverband der Bünde der Kinderreichen Deutschlands, 273.
Gesellschaft für Sexualreform (Germany), 276.
Gini, C., 421 (*p*), 432 (*nn*), 450 (*b*), 465 (*e*), 469.
Gini, C., and Finetti, B. de, 267–8, 456 (*p*), 469.
Gini, C., and Galvani, L., 456 (*q*).
Giroud, G., 39, 161–2, 443 (*e*), 443 (*f*), 450 (*c*).
Giudice, R. del, 453 (*i*).
Giusti, U., 454 (*l*).
Glass, D. V., 67, 76, 80, 82, 165, 314, 417 (*e*), 441 (*a*), 464 (*c*), 469.
Glass, D. V., and Blacker, C. P., 371.
Godwin, W., 31.
Goebelio, J. W., 435 II (*a*).
Goldschmidt, P., 126, 138.
Goldstein, J., 446 (*k*).
Gollan, J., 58.
Golzio, S., 454 (*l*).
Gomont, de, 92.
Goodsell, W., 59, 338.
Gosseries, F., 174.
Gosseries, P., 142.
Grandi, Signor, 222.
Green, M. E., 116, 434 (*uu*).
Greenwood, M., 15, 84, 345, 464 (*a*), 469.
Greenwood, M., and Granville Edge, P., 447 (*n*).
Greven, Professor, 39.
Griffith, G. T., 12.
Griolet, G., Vergé, C., and Bourdeaux, H., 157.
Grossi, G., 450 (*b*).
Grotjahn, A., 271, 272, 273, 274–5, 277, 313.
Grotjahn, M., 313.
Gruber, M. von, 270–1.
Guillau, J., 441 (*b*).
Guillermin, Colonel, 183–93, 201, 204, 448 (*p*).
Günther, E., 469.
Gürtner, F., 283.

Hadrich, J., 294.
Hage, F., 469.
Haig, R. M., 211.
Haldane, J. B. S., 433 (*pp*).
Hall, A. J., 427 (*ee*).
Hall, A., and Ransom, W. B., 427 (*ee*).
Hallsworth, J., 58.
Hammurabi, 28, 86, 422 (*s*).
Hankins, F. H., 297, 421 (*p*).
Hanssens, E., 444 (*g*).
Hardy, G., 162, 443 (*e*), 443 (*f*).
Harmel, L., 100.
Harmsen, H., 224, 233, 272, 276, 282, 302, 446 (*k*), 450 (*c*), 460 (*h*).
Harmsen, H., and Lohse, F., 460 (*g*).
Harrod, R. F., 464 (*c*).
Hartranft, C. D., 90.
Hartwig, J., 280.
Hassell, R., 31.
Haufe, R., 295.
Haut Comité de la Population (France), 152.
Hayward, T. E., 466 (*a*).
Hazlitt, W., 31.
Headlam, S., 36.
Hecht, G. H., 94.
Helleu, Y., 100, 106, 108, 436 (*c*).
Hellmann, R., 39, 276.
Heron, D., 72–3, 77.
Hersch, L., 433 (*qq*).
Hertzberg, A., 342.
Hesse, A., 454 (*l*).

Heyman, H., 128, 208, 448 (*r*).
Hillmann, Dr., 280.
Himes, N. E., 28, 29, 30, 31, 39, 40, 41, 43, 47, 276, 422 (*s*), 423 (*t*), 424 (*w*), 424 (*y*), 425 (*aa*).
Himes, N. E., and Dickinson, R. L. 424 (*w*).
Hirsch, M., 278, 458 (*a*).
Hirschmann, O. A., 457 (*r*).
Hitler, A., 304, 458 (*d*).
Hitze, F., 272, 277, 458 (*c*).
Hoare, Sir S., 4.
Hodann, M., 277, 281, 286, 319.
Hoffner, C., 249.
Hofmann, H., 292, 294, 295.
Hofsten, E. von, 320.
Hogben, L. T., 27, 421 (*p*).
Hohman, H. F., 31.
Holyoake, G. J., 425 (*z*).
Homo, L., 89.
Honey, F. J. C., 346, 353, 469.
Honorius, 90.
Horn, J. E., 446 (*k*).
Houten, S. van, 39, 425 (*aa*).
How-Martyn, E., and Breed, M., 39, 45.
Huber, M., Bunle, H., and Boverat, F., 218, 446 (*k*).
Humbert, E., 161, 162, 164.
Humphreys, N. A., 419 (*j*).
Hutchins, B. L., and Harrison, A., 57.
Hutchinson, E. P., 433 (*qq*).

Ichok, G., 179.
Inge, W. R., 433 (*ss*), 434 (*tt*).
Innes, J. W., 14, 69, 75–6, 432 (*nn*).
Inter-Departmental Committee on Abortion (Ministry of Health), 46–7, 53, 54, 55, 233, 428 (*ff*), 428 (*hh*).
International Labour Office, studies of, 171, 174, 221, 223, 224.
International Neo-Malthusian Conferences, 39–40, 444 (*g*).
Isambert, Decrusy, and Taillandier, 93.
Ishii, R., 97, 469.

Jacobs, A., 39.
Jacquart, C., 153.
Jacquart, J., 446 (*k*).
Jahn, G., 314, 318.
Jaubert, P., 94.
Jenkins, A., 46.
Jensen, A., 315–16, 418 (*h*), 469.
Jessen, A., 293, 295, 296.
Jewkes, J., 370, 464 (*c*).
Johnson, S. C., 3.
Jones, D. C., 71.
Julin, A., 207–8.
Jurborskis, M. L., 445 (*h*).
Justinian, 90.
Juvenile Employment, London Regional Advisory Council for, 58.

Kahn, E., 275, 469.
Kantorowicz, M., 313.
Karpinos, B. D., 467 (*d*), 469.
Karpinos, B. D., and Kiser, C. V., 465 (*e*).
Keiffer, Dr., 164.
Kempe, E., 425 (*aa*).
Kendall, W., 86.
Kermack, W. O., McKendrick, A. G., and McKinlay, P. L., 349, 464 (*a*).
Keynes, J. M., 83, 363, 464 (*c*).
Kirkpatrick, C., 286, 290, 308.
Kiser, C. V., 422 (*r*), 433 (*qq*).
Klein, W., 304.
Klotz, Monsieur, 149.
Klotz-Forest, Dr., 29.
Knibbs, G. H., 469.
Knorr, Dr., 302.
Knowlton, C., 32, 34, 41, 424 (*w*), 424 (*x*), 443 (*g*).
Koch, H. H., 322, 323, 324.
Kolney, F., 442 (*e*).
Korherr, R., 86, 220, 225, 229, 274, 422 (*s*).
Kruse, Dr., 272.
Kuczynski, R. R., 5, 6, 9, 19, 76, 270, 314, 351, 375, 382, 387, 400, 403, 418 (*f*), 420 (*l*), 421 (*q*), 432 (*nn*), 456 (*p*), 459 (*d*), 461 (*a*), 464 (*c*), 465 (*a*), 467 (*d*).
Kuczynski, R. R., and Dr. Mansfield, 272.
Kühn, A., Staemmler, M., and Burgdörfer, F., 280, 282, 289, 291, 299.

Lacassagne, Dr., 163.
Landry, A., 446 (*k*).
Langdon-Brown, W., 421 (*p*).
Langeland, O. H., 318.
Lanval, M., 160, 162, 164, 443 (*g*).
Lasorsa, G., 446 (*k*).
Last, H., 86.
Laurinsich, Professor, 454 (*l*).

League of National Life, The, 84, 151.
Leemans, E., 444 (*g*).
Leener, G. de, 125, 126, 127, 128, 133, 448 (*q*).
Legoyt, A., 147, 148.
Lehfeldt, H., 276, 277.
Lemercier, General L., 154.
Lennox, G., 443 (*g*).
Lenti, L., 457 (*s*).
Leo XII, Pope, 100.
Le Play, F., 100.
Leroy-Beaulieu, P., 163, 443 (*f*).
Lesage, A., 448 (*q*).
Lesage, A., and Moine, M., 448 (*q*).
Lesoir, E., 447 (*n*), 447 (*o*).
Letinois, Dr., 441 (*b*).
Leunbach, J. H., 319.
Levasseur, E., 94, 146, 446 (*k*).
Lewis-Faning, E., 419 (*k*).
Leybourne, G. G., 58, 84, 345, 469.
Liepmann, W., 458 (*c*).
Liga für Mutterschutz und soziale Familienhygiene (Germany), 277.
Ligue de la Régénération Humaine (France), 39, 161.
Ligue des Familles Nombreuses de Belgique, 126, 132, 140, 154, 172, 174, 175, 176, 203.
Ligue Nationale contre l'Infécondité Intentionelle (the name later changed to Ligue Nationale contre la Dépopulation) (Belgium), 154–5.
Ligue Néo-Malthusienne (Belgium), 443 (*g*).
Ligue pour la Vie (France), 104.
Ligue pour le Relèvement de la Natalité française, 152.
Linder, A., 466 (*a*), 467 (*d*).
Lionæs, A., and Skaug, A., 318.
Lip Tay, Dr., 443 (*e*).
Liszt, F. von, 281.
Livi, L., 453 (*g*), 454 (*l*).
Loader, H., 34.
Loesch, K. C. von, 148.
Lojacono, L., 450 (*b*).
London County Council, annual reports of, [abortion references], 52–3.
Longobardi, C., 225, 226, 227, 228.
Lorimer, F., 464 (*c*).
Lorimer, F., and Osborn, F., 72, 422 (*r*).
Lösch, A., 464 (*c*), 469.
Lotka, A. J., 10, 15, 395–6, 405, 420 (*n*), 467 (*d*).
Louis XI, 90.
Lowndes, G. A. N., 58.

Macdonald, M., 4.
Magnussen, R., 282.
Malins, E., 429 (*ii*).
Malthus, T. R., 30–1, 146.
Malthusian League, The, 34, 35–40, 42–4, 45–6, 56, 424 (*z*).
Malthusian Society, The, 424 (*z*).
Manunta, U., 251, 451 (*e*), 453 (*i*).
Marbeau, J. B. F., 147.
Marcelletti, M., 227.
March, L., 150.
Marchal, A., and Méro, O. J. de, 160.
Marchant, J., 84.
Marchiori, A., 457 (*s*).
Margueritte, V., 162.
Maria Theresa, Empress, 95.
Marsanich, Count di, 454 (*l*).
Marshall, F., 147.
Marshall, T. H., 12.
Martin, W. J., 67, 72.
Mascaux, F., 444 (*g*).
Mathorez, J., 94.
Mauco, G., 224, 441 (*b*).
Mayrand, O.P., R. P., 165.
McCabe, J., 39, 425 (*z*).
Medani, P., 457 (*r*).
Menna, E., 230, 232, 234, 235, 237, 238, 241, 242, 256, 451 (*d*), 453 (*i*), 455 (*o*).
Mercier, Cardinal (Archbishop), 154, 444 (*g*).
Méric, V., 443 (*e*).
Meyer, M. L., 454 (*l*).
Micheli, Professor, 233.
Michelin Company, 179–81, 200–1, 446 (*l*).
Michels, R., 450 (*a*).
Midwifery, Joint Council of, 53.
Mikelli, G., 250.
Mill, J. S., 31.
Min, Dr., 153.
Ministry of Health, circulars of, [on the provision of birth-control clinics], 46.
Ministry of Health, reports of:
on abortion, 46–7, 53, 54, 55, 428 (*ff*), 428 (*hh*).
on maternal mortality, 55, 429 (*ii*).
Mitra, K., 72.
Moellendorff, W. von, 469.
Møller, K. A., 321.

Mondor, H., 445 (*h*).
Monpin, R., 29.
More, A., 272.
Moro, L., 257.
Mortara, G., 457 (*s*).
Moshinsky, P., 74.
Mussolini, B., 219, 220, 222, 223, 225, 228, 229, 231, 243, 260, 449 (*a*), 450 (*c*), 455 (*m*).
Myrdal, A., 325, 327, 328, 334, 338.
Myrdal, A. and G., 316, 318, 320, 321, 327.
Myrdal, G., 327, 328, 336.
Myrdal, G., and Wicksell, S. D., 316, 462 (*b*), 469.

Napoleon, 146, 149.
Naquet, A., 442 (*e*).
Naquet, A., and Hardy, G., 442 (*e*).
National Birth Control Association (now called Family Planning Association), 45, 46.
National Birth Rate Commission, The, 83–4, 434 (*tt*).
National Council of Public Morals, The, 434 (*tt*).
National Council of Social Service, 59.
National Fascist Institute of Social Insurance (Istituto nazionale fascista della previdenza sociale) (Italy), 230, 242, 243, 250, 251, 254, 256.
National Secular Society, The, 34.
National Verbond ter Regeling van het Kindertal (Flemish Neo-Malthusian League), 444 (*g*).
Naudeau, L., 181, 203–4.
Nawratzki, C., 275.
Nerva, 88–9.
New Survey of London Life and Labour, 207.
Newsholme, A., 84.
Niceforo, A., 245.
Nieuw-Malthusiaansche Bond (Holland), 39.
Notestein, F. W., 30, 422 (*r*).
Nybølle, H. C., 316, 470.
Nypels, J. S. G., 158.

Oblath, A., 228.
Oestreich, J., 276, 282.
Œuvre Nationale de l'Enfance, 176–7.
Oliver, T., 427 (*ee*).
Onslow, H., 149.
'Opera nazionale dei combattenti' (Italy), 227.
Opera nazionale per la protezione della maternità e dell' infanza (Italy), 236, 242–3.
Orestano, F., 89, 246, 454 (*j*).
Ottesen-Jensen, E., 321, 324, 428 (*gg*).
Owen, R., 423 (*u*).
Owen, R. D., 32, 34, 41.

Pagani, P., 453 (*g*).
Pailhiez, P., 446 (*j*).
Palmer, J. H., 34.
Palmstrøm, H., 342.
Parenti, G., 457 (*r*).
Parish, T. N., 53.
Parris, T., 32, 36, 37, 425 (*z*).
Parry, L. A., 55, 428 (*ff*).
Partiot, Monsieur, 118, 119, 210.
Paulinus, G., 470.
Pearl, R., 30, 47, 49–50 421 (*p*), 422 (*r*).
Pearson, K., 74, 83.
Pell, C. E., 421 (*p*).
Peller, S., 278.
Pelletier, A. J., Thompson, F. D., and Rochon, A., 351.
Pelletier, M., 443 (*e*), 444 (*h*).
Penrose, L. S., 432 (*pp*).
P.E.P. Reports, 59.
Permanent Committee for Internal Migration and Settlement (Commissariato per la Migrazione e la Colonizzazione interna) (Italy), 228.
Peter the Great, 96.
Philip IV, 91.
Pierpoint, R., 40.
Pierreville, R., 163.
Pietrusky, F., 279.
Pindar, D., 53.
Pinte, J., 100, 104, 106, 109, 115, 183, 193, 435 III (*a*), 437 (*f*).
Pipkin, C. W., 59.
Piromallo, A. J., 232, 451 (*f*).
Pitt-Rivers, G. H. L. F., 155, 421 (*p*).
Pius XI, Pope, 430 (*jj*).
Place, F., 31, 423 (*t*).
Playfair, W. S., 429 (*ii*).
Plischke, A., 298.
Ploetz, A., 280, 428 (*gg*), 458 (*c*).
Pohlen, P., 278, 280.
Population (Statistics) Act, 12, 85.
Posadowsky-Wehner, H. von, 446 (*k*).

Pritchett, H. S., 470.
Ptoukha, M., 470.
Puppel, E., 279.

Quensel, C. E., 315.

Racine, A., 444 (*g*).
Racine, A., and Dupréel, E., 372.
Rahier, J., 444 (*g*)
Rambke, Dr., 458 (*c*).
Rastoin, E., 470.
Razza, L., 228.
Reboux, P., 162.
Rechenbach, H., 460 (*g*).
Reddaway, W. B., 464 (*c*).
Reed, L. J., 470.
Reichert, F., 295.
Reichsbund der Kinderreichen Deutschlands zum Schutz der Familie, 273, 283, 286.
Reichsverband für Geburtenregelung und Sexualhygiene (Germany), 277.
Reinhardt, Staatsekretär, 289, 295–6.
Rey, F., 182, 436–7 (*e*).
Rhein, R., 106.
Rhodes, E. C., 467 (*d*).
Ricardo, D., 31.
Rich, C. D., 467 (*d*).
Richard, G., 441 (*b*).
Richet, C., 148.
Richter, V., and Völker, H., 287, 291, 304.
Riese, H., 280.
Riksförbundet för Sexuell Upplysning (Sweden), 320.
Risler, G., 163, 171.
Robbins, L., 464 (*c*).
Robertson, J. M., 83, 433 (*rr*).
Robin, P., 38, 39, 161, 442 (*e*), 443 (*g*), 444 (*g*).
Robinson, C. H., 47.
Roesle, E., 274, 279, 457 (*a*).
Romanet, E., 101, 102.
Rommel, Dr., 441 (*c*).
Roscher, W., 94, 98.
Rott, F., 303.
Roulleaux-Dugage, G., 164.
Roux, J. A., 157.
Roux, M. de, 164, 311, 441 (*c*).
Roux, P., 441 (*b*).
Rowntree, B. S., 207.
Rutgers, J., 444 (*g*).
Rutgers-Hoitsema, Mme, 39.
St. Hilaire, Rosseeuw, 435 II (*a*).
Saint-Just, F. de, 164.
Saint-Maur, F., 183, 193.
Salvá, V., 435 II (*a*).
Salvemini, G., 226, 233, 450 (*d*), 454 (*k*).
Sanger, M., 28, 40, 162.
Sauvy, A., 90, 149, 151–2, 433 (*qq*), 470.
Savorgnan, F., 230, 247, 265, 268, 450 (*b*), 455 (*n*), 455 (*o*).
Schaffstein, F., 283.
Schiøtz, C., 341.
Schlipp, H., 294.
Schmidt, E., 281.
Schockaert, R., 154.
Schöne, L., 91, 92, 94, 146, 147.
Schottky, I., 459 (*g*).
Schrader, E., 284.
Schultz, B. K., 460 (*g*).
Schünemann, K., 96.
Scottish Economic Committee, 418 (*h*).
Seldte, F., 302.
Selleslags, W., 446 (*k*).
Senn, F., 147.
Serpieri, A., 225, 226.
Severus, Septimius, 89.
Sharpe, F. R., and Lotka, A. J., 405, 467 (*d*).
Sheffield Women's Welfare Clinic, 47.
Sheinfeld, A., 470.
Shelley, P. B., 31.
Simone, D. de, and Bertagnolio, P., 245.
Siredy, A., 163.
Skaug, A., 4.
Skaug, A., and Wold, K. G., 342.
Skene Smith, N., 97.
Smithies, A., 470.
Snow, E. C., 432 (*nn*).
Société de Médecine Publique (Belgium), 153–4.
Société Nationale de Habitations à Bon Marché (Belgian National 'Cheap Housing' Society), 173–5.
Society for Constructive Birth Control, The, 46.
Society for the Provision of Birth Control Clinics, The, 45, 53.
Somogyi, S., 450 (*b*), 454 (*l*), 457 (*r*).
Soranos, 28.
Sozial-Harmonische Verein, 39, 276.
Sozomenus, 89–90.

Spagnolli, G., 470.
Spengler, J. J., 148, 149, 352, 441 (*a*), 441 (*b*), 464 (*c*), 470.
Spengler, O., 274.
Spiral, E.-A., 158.
Stadelmann, R., 95.
Staffers, G., 272.
Standring, G., 34, 35, 37, 44, 424 (*w*), 425 (*z*).
Stangeland, C. E., 31, 86.
Staudinger, H., 297.
Steincke, K. K., 340.
Sterner, R., 317, 327, 329, 331, 332, 334, 335.
Stevenson, T. H. C., 69, 71, 72, 75, 421 (*p*), 432 (*nn*).
Stix, R. K., and Notestein, F. W., 30.
Stöcker, H., 276.
Stolzenburg, Dr., 285.
Stopes, M. C., 39, 42, 44–5, 47.
Storms, R., 136, 439 (*i*).
Strumia, E., and Zanon, B., 230, 235, 237, 239, 240, 452 (*g*).
Sundqvist, A., 321, 324.
Superior Council for Emigration (Italy), 222.
Sutherland, H. E. G., 74.
Swaroop, S., and Lal, R. B., 471.

Tacitus, 88.
Tardieu, A., 165.
Taussig, F. J., 28.
Tawney, R. H., 58.
Terlinden, le Vicomte, 164, 442 (*d*).
Theilhaber, F. A., 276, 458 (*a*).
Théodore, M., 166.
Theodosius, 90.
Thomas, D. S., 350.
Thompson, W. S., 395, 471.
Thompson, W. S., and Whelpton, P. K., 345, 471.
Tietze, C., 76, 433 (*qq*).
Titmuss, R., 419 (*k*).
Toësca, L., 51.
Tofte, A., 322.
Tout, H., 71, 207.
Townsend, J., 91–2, 435 II (*a*).
Trajan, 88–9.
Trall, R. T., 42.
Truelove, E., 34, 35, 41, 56, 425 (*z*).
Turnor, C., 227.

Uggé, A., 465 (*e*).
Ungern-Sternberg, R. von, 276, 279, 281, 446 (*k*).
Union des Familles de l'Eure (France), 149.
Union des Familles Nombreuses de Levroux (France), 149.
Union des Pères de Famille Méritants (France), 149.
Uyeda, T., 471.

Van den Plas, L., 155.
Van der Smissen, E., 153.
Vandervelde, E., 443 (*g*).
Vargas, R., 442 (*e*)
Vaughan, B., 84.
Vereinigung kinderreicher Familien und Witwen (Germany), 272.
Vergottini, M. de, 457 (*s*).
Vibart, H. H. R., 100, 103, 125, 189, 292, 440 (*m*).
Vickery, A., 39.
Vieuille, F., 150–1, 442 (*d*).
Vile, R. J., 435 II (*a*).
Vinck, E., 444 (*g*).
Visser, F., 433 (*pp*).
Vulhopp, T., 126, 154, 155, 164, 441 (*a*), 447 (*n*), 471.

Wagemann, E., 454 (*l*).
Wagner, Dr. (Reich medical leader), 294.
Waldeck-Rousseau, Monsieur, 149.
Ward, H., 58.
Watts, C., 32, 41, 425 (*z*).
Webb, S., 83, 432 (*oo*).
Weinhold, C. A., 276.
Whelpton, P. K., 312, 471.
Whelpton, P. K., and Jackson, N. E., 420 (*n*).
Whetham, W. C. D., 73.
Whetham, W. C. D., and C. D., 73.
Whitehead, J., 429 (*ii*).
Whitehouse, B., 52, 55.
Wicksell, K., 320.
Wicksell, S. D., 315, 316, 345, 463 (*e*), 467 (*d*), 471–2.
Wicksell, S. D., and Quensel, C. E., 462 (*b*), 463 (*e*), 472.
Wiesener, Judge, 342.
Wilde, F. A., 39, 276.
Wilkinson, H. L., 472.
Willcox, W. F., 472.
Wilson, N., 464 (*c*), 472.
Wolf, J., 277, 279, 458 (*a*).

Wolfenden, H. H., 466 (*a*).
Wolff, F., 281.
Wolstenholme, S. H., 472.
Woodward, E. L., 57.
Woog, C., 221, 223, 224, 229, 231.
Wooler, T. J., 31.
Workers' Birth Control Group, The, 45.
World League for Sexual Reform, 319.
Wright, F. C., 369.

Young, H. S., 34.
Young, J., 55, 421 (*p*).
Yule, G. Udny, 472.

Zahn, F., 273, 454 (*l*).
Zingali, G., 232.

PRINTED IN
GREAT BRITAIN
AT THE
UNIVERSITY PRESS
OXFORD
BY
JOHN JOHNSON
PRINTER
TO THE
UNIVERSITY